The
New
Humanities

Culture,
Crisis,
Change

The
New
Humanities

Culture,
Crisis,
Change

RALPH L. CARNES
VALERIE CARNES
Roosevelt University

Holt, Rinehart and Winston, Inc.
New York   Chicago   San Francisco
Atlanta   Dallas   Montreal   Toronto

Library of Congress Catalog Card Number: 72–174549
ISBN: 0–03–085611–6
Printed in the United States of America
2345 090 9 8 7 6 5 4 3 2 1

93835

This book is dedicated to:

Our Parents,
  Out of Filial Piety

The Wolsungs,
  Out of Love

And to Papa: Doctor Harry M. Dobson,
  Whose admonition is the key to this book:

"No theme must be invented
For mere invention's sake,
All worked out
Merely for the sake
Of working out;
But must spring
From some arousing human vision,
Some undying human need,
And answer in all its changes
To the life and mood it created."

Ralph and Valerie Carnes

Preface

Books are slices of time: they provide us with cross-sections of the process of history, interpretations of the structure of human experience. This book is an attempt to establish a new genre: an anthology about contemporary culture that is interdisciplinary in subject matter, informal in approach, but which also provides an over-view of the divergent perspectives it contains.

The authors whose essays are presented here constitute a new species of humanist. They have commented on and in some cases helped to create the foundations of mass culture in the United States. They have devoted their considerable talents to a meticulous analysis of the myriad popular social, political, economic, ethnic, literary, and philosophical problems which either have produced our current cultural milieu or are a product of it. They are, in a word, the humanists of mass culture, communicating their observations through the mass media.

The important thing about such works, aside from their historical and aesthetic value, lies precisely in what made them timely in the first place: they are commentaries on the values, the problems, the ills, the anxieties, the fads, and the assumptions of the age they represent. And they are not merely commentaries: they symbolize the age itself, thus becoming a part of the history which they attempt to record. Hence, this book is not merely another collection of essays on contemporary culture, but, because of its approach and the manner of its execution, is itself a part of the coverage, a commentary in its own right, which embodies both the style and the substance of the world it describes.

A comprehensive Reader's Guide has been written as a companion to the text, consisting of a series of informal "conversations" between the authors and our readers. We have been told by our editor that the Guide reflects much of our enthusiasm for the text. We hope that the enthusiasm is contagious, for, as Gore Vidal tells us in his essay, "The wheel of man's history is once again beginning to turn." We all have an investment in its direction.

Chicago   Ralph and Valerie Carnes
August 1971

Acknowledgments

We wish to thank, first of all, Otto Wirth, George Watson, Paul Olscamp, Elmer Klemke, Jack Foster, and Carol Stern, all of whom helped to make available to us the time needed to write and edit this book and thus contributed materially to its completion. Also we wish to thank Mary Facko for her unending patience and good humor and her excellent typing on the four original essays in the book. Special thanks are also due to Miss Lynn Burton to whom we have tried unsuccessfully to write many times; we have taken the liberty of quoting some ten lines from her poem "Anarchy: A Personal Statement" in the Introduction to Part Three.

And to the following people we extend our heartfelt thanks for their contributions to the book: Edwin Olmstead, Alan Karabus, Richard Fritz, Thaddeus Jochim, William West, Douglas Rankin, Kathy Blecha, Warren Solomon, Carol and Dick Kessler, Benjamin Lee Whorf, Randall Julian Carnes, Leslie Hornsby, Charles Heckman, Joris-Karl Huysmans, Ben Collins, John Milton, Jimmy Cleveland, Richard J. Daley, George, Paul, John and Ringo, Kristin Lauer, Paul Simon, J. William Fullbright, Richard Wagner, Igor Stravinsky, Mary Shelley, Charles Hartshorne, Federico Fellini, Abbie Hoffman, Jerome Lonnes, David Susskind, James Jordan, Lawrence Durrell, and Arthur Jacobson.

And finally special thanks are due to our long-suffering sales representative and editor, respectively—William Thompson and Jane Ross.

Ralph and Valerie Carnes

Contents

And there, lying upon the table in the yellow lamplight, lay the great interlinear . . . cross-hatched, crabbed, starred with questions and answers in different-coloured inks, in typescript. It seemed to me then to be somehow symbolic of the very reality we had shared—a palimpsest upon which each of us had left his or her individual traces, layer by layer.

—Lawrence Durrell

Human beings constitute the evidence as to human experience of the nature of things. Every belief is to be approached with respectful enquiry. The final chapter of philosophy consists in the search for the unexpressed presuppositions which underlie the beliefs of every finite human intellect. In this way philosophy makes its slow advance by the introduction of new ideas, vision and adjusting clashes.

—Alfred North Whitehead

That Was
the Scene
That Was

If Rory Storme hadn't come along and then the Beatles, I'd have continued running around in the Teddy-boy gangs. Today, well, I'd probably just be a laborer. I'm glad I'm not, of course. It'll be nice to be part of history, some sort of history anyway. What I'd like to be is in school history books and be read by kids.

Ringo Starr

Before the victory's won maybe some more will have to get scarred up, lose jobs, face the problem of being called bad names. Before the victory's won, maybe some more will have to face the tragedy of physical death.

Martin Luther King, Jr.

But don't you give me that you love me and make me do the same thinking when there's nothing in our backgrounds nor anything around us which in any way gives either of us reason to love each other. Let's be real!

Malcolm X

I do not believe that a beautiful relationship has to always end in carnage.

Eldridge Cleaver

Either write books or blow up bridges.

William Borden

Did I say that? That's not bad.

William Borden

The first duty of a revolutionist is not to get caught.

Abbie Hoffman

Introduction to Part One

We
Like
To think
Of history
As broken down
Into easily rec-
koned segments: 5th
Century Athens, Middle
Ages, Renaissance, the Age
Of Reason, Enlightenment, the
Various Victorians, Industrial
Revolution. But by the time we
Arrive fresh in the twentieth century,
With the advent of modern mass communica-
tion, and with the richness of personal re-
collection, we break time into smaller pieces.
Hence, there were the 20s, when youth flamed
Brightly, the 30s, when the flame went out on that
Black Friday, 40s, early, when we were at war, 40s
Late, when a catclysm ended one war, started another, cold.
The Eisenhower Years, divided into Witch Hunts, Cold War, Arms
Race, Brinkmanship, golf on the White House lawn, the 50s when
We made the grade, bought a split-level, built a barbecue pit and
Pasted Green Stamps into books for shiny junk; and Zing! Zap! Pow!
The New Frontier drove up in a gold Cadillac, Beatniks faded into
A background haze behind the light of Jackie, JFK, Bobby, Hyannis-
port. All that ended. Camelot was gone by 1963. Malcolm, Kennedy,
Three boys under a dam in Mississippi, Mrs. Liuzzo killed, Coq au
Vin gave way to barbecue in the White House, we saved lightbulbs and
Went deeper into Vietnam as if to forget the Bay of Pigs. Medgar
Evers, Oswald, Ruby, assassination nightly fare on color TV, and
Oh Wow! Ken Kesey, Leary, turned the switch and blew the minds on
Perry Lane———Guerilla Theater———body paint———holy stoned———Bill
Graham made a mint on Fillmore East with the Acid Test———freaky, man
———The Berkeley Free Speech Movement———Ginsberg got turned on by
Leary———The Beatles exported Pop———Mary Quant cut hems and
splashed color———The Great Gathering of the Tribes for the Human Be-in,
Haight-Ashbury 1967——grass, speed, smack, psilocybin——the Doors, the
Grape, the Dead, Big Brother, the Airplane, Beatles, Stones——
REVOLUTION, SDS, NSA——riots at Columbia, everywhere——Panthers,
Blackstone Rangers——Huntley-Brinkley——King shot, another Kennedy
shot—Chicago Riots, 1968—Alice's Restaurant—Blow-Up, Vixen—The Great
Marijuana Border Patrol Massacree—Easy Rider—Zabriskie Point—Free
Huey, Huey Freed—the Chicago Grant Park Riot of 1970—nerve gas
dumped at sea—ecology—communes—Back to the Garden—Dennis Hopper,
the Conspiracy Show—Abbie, Jerry, Mark, Witch, Weathermen and
women and by now history has become unpunctuated just a list
of names and events real and unreal all the names of all the pictures
that flash and flash and which we will never in a thousand years begin
to get together into any kind of coherentpatternunlessweSTOP
for a minute. And try to see where we were before this pyramid
Sat down on top of us. So that we can at least see where in the Hell
We are now.
And maybe then where we are going.

We compress time into shorter and shorter segments in proportion to the apparently direct relevance of significant events within those segments. Most of us are no longer interested in the Middle Ages because we do not think that Medieval events will effect or affect to any significant degree what happens tomorrow. On the other hand, it seems essential to know the outline of today's headlined happenings, because today's events seem to be the efficient cause of tomorrow. The market will be bullish or bearish, the troops will charge or pull out, we will trip or not trip, the university will stand or fall, all according to the multiplicity of events that occur, appear to have occurred, are interpreted, misinterpreted, invented, or merely reported each day. Each event, however small, enters its mass-communication-media-journalistic phase every night on the 7:00 news, complete with appropriate tags: "significant," informed," "disturbing," "far-reaching," "seemingly impossible." Both "Spiro" and "Apocalypse" have become household words.

Daniel Boorstin *(The Image: A Guide to Pseudo-events in America)* outlines a theory of the "pseudo-event": the nonnatural, contrived, manufactured happening, a self-fulfilling prophecy invented in order to create news. Orrin Klapp *(Heroes, Villains, and Fools)* shows us the images Americans look to for leadership, wickedness, or simply for laughs: "heroes of the surface" (precisely why Gore Vidal was right when he had Myra Breckinridge say that there were no unimportant movies in America during the thirties and forties). We have, as Ken Kesey tried consciously, become our movies. In the classroom today's professor competes not only with his colleagues: he also competes for his students' attention with all the pop-heroes of the times. During spring semester of 1970, the Abbie and Jerry show was a hard act to follow.

The manufacture of pseudo-events has now reached the level of second-order abstractions: pseudo-events give rise to pseudo-pseudo-events. The false and the true, the spontaneous and the contrived, have, as Boorstin warned us they would, become so inextricably intermixed that it is impossible to separate them. With Kent State, we see that pseudo-events can become horribly real. A clue to the amount of theater implicit in the Kent demonstrations before the actual shootings can be found in the statement made by a student who was there: "I thought they were shooting blanks, man. I couldn't believe that they were shooting real bullets." The black students must have given a grim chuckle at that, as they waited for what they all knew would happen at Jackson. And although there is nothing in any of this that has not been reported over and over in literature, poetry, history, and philosophy, classrooms are boring and books seem stale. Why? Because the history, poetry, literature, and philosophy of Now have the force of existential reality, reinforced by dramatic mass communication, whatever the medium. Paul Simon and Art Garfunkel saw all too clearly that the future was inscribed on the walls of subway stations.

The ascendancy of pop-culture in the late 1960s in the United States has seen the institutionalization of an autonomous youth culture. One of pop's own gurus, Roger Vadim, said in 1952 that youth had become a class.

If economically dependent, in America youth has become ideologically self-sustaining. Like the news brought by Nietzsche's madman, the event has already happened, we did it with our own hands, and we seem unaware of it. The Movement, as the culture has come to be called, had its roots in the development of a youth consumer market after World War II, the emergence of the Beatnik and Hipster subculture in the late fifties, the growth of TV and the record industry during the Eisenhower years, the introduction and subsequent mystical interpretation of the marijuana and LSD experience as the American young middle class began to emulate the Underground in 1967, the viability of the Merry Prankster world-view, guerilla theater, the saturation of political involvement during the post-Kennedy years, the threat of death from the Vietnam war, the riots in Chicago in 1968, and the seeming attraction of the Back-to-the-Garden movement. The number of elements in the institutionalization of Youth-culture in America is as large as the number of pop-events that have called attention to and emphasized the importance of youth.

"What happened during the sixties?" is a popular question among members of straight society. The answer is neither simple nor easily stated. The process of institutionalization is complex, and not usually recognizable until the institution has already come into existence. There is no simple answer, satisfying to all, however badly we may wish that there were. The myth of the Simple Answer is itself an important element in the process.

Academic people tend either to emulate their students with a slavishness that betrays advancing years, or to dismiss mass-culture and pop culture out of hand as trivial, ephemeral, or simply superfluous. However, at a time when educational institutions are no longer free from armed attack (from both sides!), when textbook choices are often dictated by the current interests of students, when culture-heroes offer a more exciting curriculum than the Academy, when Joyce is replaced by Vonnegut, Proust by Heinlein, Yeats by McKuen, Dylan by Dylan, Bach by Buddy Miles, to dismiss the convulsions of mass-culture is to turn one's back on most of the forces operant in today's classroom. It is an ancient struggle, accelerated and amplified by electronic media. With the advent of course evaluations by students, the classroom sometimes follows the paradigm of the political arena. As Humpty Dumpty put it to Alice when disputing the meaning of "glory": ". . . the question is . . . which is to be master, that's all."

The movement of American pop-culture during the last few years has been toward the affirmation of the values and obligations of the present moment (remember in 1968 when everybody said that Janis and Jimi and Jim Morrison knew that they would die from speed, but "it was the only way" that they could sing in their sincere, funky way? It was supposed to be a self-sacrifice for hippies everywhere. The myth of the heroic sacrifice of the young for the young is a perennial ingredient of romanticism, whatever the age. The Scene moves on the knife edge of the present. It is romantic, post-logical, post-literate, tribal, Edenic, and therapy-oriented. It is nourished by establishment money and sustained by the hip media and the hip sell. Its cultural-tribal autonomy is strengthened by ritual music (rock), ritual performance by tribal heroes (the rock concert), totems (LSD, grass, speed and other drugs), and similar apparel (currently in Chicago: (a) lots of leather, (b) pioneer clothes, with fake cotton print patchwork, boots, bonnets, and expensive leather fringed handbags, (c) no-bra post-mod, (d) blankets, moccasins, Indian headbands, hunting knives, and in some cases, warpaint, (e) various combinations of clothing, centered around tie-dyed pre-frayed flared denims, (f) slick mod and/or Edwardian, (g) old army clothes with paratrooper's boots, (h) Hyde Park Aggressively Grubby: dirty clothes, dirty hair, bib-overalls, no shoes).

Ritual thinking goes with ritual dress. The importance of the individual is absorbed into the transcendent importance of the group (reinforced by sensitivity sessions and I Ching castings). There is a ritual affirmation of certain views on freedom, sex, politics, cops, school, ecology, involvement, drugs, and feeling. Contradictions appear numerous, depending on the orientation of the particular subculture. It is a mistake to think that the Movement is all of a piece. There are individuals and groups that do not hassle tomorrow; and there are other people who work continuously and constructively for better schools, cleaner air, peace and understanding. Rugged Individualism and anti-establishmentarianism are old stories in America. They are part of a counter-culture that has always existed. However, the institutionalization of the counter-culture during the 60s specifically as a youth culture has splintered a movement that cuts across all ages, hence reducing the overall effectiveness of constructive dissent.

Differences aside, the single most powerfully unifying factor in the counter-culture as a whole is the rejection on all levels of the acquisitiveness and exploitativeness of the generations that have controlled the destiny of America for the past fifty years. Often accompanying this rejection is an affirmation of the values of more distant times: the (apparent) purity of the life of the American Indian and of the African, the vision of freedom as interpreted by Jefferson, the Medieval fascination with magic, satanism, witchcraft and the occult, and a desire to get back to the land. We have, then, come 'round to that stage when Americans look back to a Golden Age, when life was (apparently) more authentic, people were (apparently) happier, and when there was (apparently) hope for the future.

Add to this heady mixture the crescendo of racial strife in America: the assassination of Malcolm X, of Medgar Evers, of Martin Luther King; the deaths of Fred Hampton, of the two white Chicago policemen who had made friends with the black children at Cabrini Green. Also add the limited success of the peaceful civil rights movement in the South, and the inevitable growth of the Black Power Movement. Add to all of this the gigantic hustle for black money through white-owned Dashiki manufacturers, white-owned black media, white-owned soul food shops, white-owned wig manufacturers, and white-owned advertising companies complete with the Corporation Tom, legislating what it is "natural" for the black man to wear, think, say, do, and believe. Jive.

It is a cliché and it is an oversimplification to say that the Movement was created by the media. But the media have provided a methodology as well as a means of communication. Every slick magazine had its hippie article during 1967. Every major network was at the Chicago convention in 1968. "I hope you all watch TV," said Abbie Hoffman at an address to the Northwestern University Law School in 1969 (when he cited the seven-year-olds as the vanguard of the revolution). And who has not seen the seemingly endless panels on dope, sex, communes, hair, and riots? This book itself is a part of the coverage, but with different ends in mind. Consequently, the movement has the immediacy of tomorrow's news: it is electric, it shimmers, it explodes in chain reactions. Most important of all, the values implicit in the counter-culture affect the entire range of experience for Americans, whether they are revolutionary, straight, freak or grease. There are no places where the effects do not reach; there is no classroom where the problems of the counter-culture are not ever-present. The age of the security of specialization is over. The age of amateurism is ascendant, by popular demand, both from behind and in front of the lectern. It is no longer possible for classes to embody the cool, uninvolved intellectual detachment of the best of the fifties. The need for Renaissance men has never been more obvious. The dangers of dilettantism have never been more acute.

Within the scope of the articles included in this section, we see the development of a new American Mythos ("myth" used in its widest religio-anthropological sense): a mythos that gathers force with each increase in population, each new unpopular war, each new instance of governmental indifference, each new method of polluting the environment, each new killing, at home and abroad. But, unfortunately, it is the mythology of a culture, large segments of which are presently trapped in a consumerism that is a linear outgrowth of the middle-class culture that it condemns. There is widespread dependence on the facilities, values, attractions and comforts of modern "pig" America (free clinics, free medicine, free food, the family credit cards, free rock concerts, free education). There is also a sense of aimlessness and impotence that finally manifests itself in violent rhetoric from avowedly peaceful people: the futility of people trying to communicate with institutions. The level of naïveté evident in the attempt to enlist workers in the revolution, the disastrous ineptitude of bomb-makers, the shrill desperation of Women's Lib; all serve oftentimes only more solidly to entrench establishment opinion against the plethora of bona-fide complaints against Middle America's apparent indifference toward racial inequality, bad government, war, repression of dissent, loss of civil rights, and the refusal to grant to women the rights of full citizenship.

We are all, for good or ill, children of John Dewey at his worst: we have accepted for too many years an epistemology which bases the test of truth on the satisfaction we derive from affirming a particular proposition (see Bertrand Russell's *A History of Western Philosophy* for an analysis of some of the elementary difficulties in Dewey's theory of knowledge). As

Richard Hofstadter indicates *(Anti-Intellectualism in America),* we have traded the education of the intellect for life-adjustment and education for commodity-producing skills. In view of our present ecological crisis, perhaps we have been (as Russell feared the children of Dewey would be, without the chastening notion that truth is independent of human desire) guilty of a cosmic impiety. We have certainly reached a stage where there are evident disturbing similarities to the state as described in Book 8 of Plato's *Republic:* the refinements of civilization are trampled underfoot, demagogues appeal to the baser elements in our nature, and teachers have to flatter their students in order to keep their jobs. Lines have been drawn, walls have been put up, the war is on. There will be no winners.

But in the midst of it all, there are some of us who, like my wife and me, feel the necessity of friendship and brotherhood, of informality and a sharing of our world, who acknowledge that we are indeed all "strangers in a strange land," should "share water" with the members of our culture; but who also love the subtle beauties of Milton and Donne, of Russell and Wittgenstein, Yeats and Dylan Thomas, Mozart and Wagner. We love the privacy of our thoughts and the lonely joy that comes from writing. We are no more capable of desiring or embracing fully a culture that is tribal, totemic, mystical, post-logical and post-literate than we are of pushing the Red Button. Both would kill us equally dead.

The other world is lethal to us too: the world that worships Soames Forsyte as a "solid citizen;" the world of well-meaning Babbitts who think of *us* as freaks; the MLA mentality, the Academic Plainstyle, aggressively dowdy collectors of gourds and unknown artists, the ones who grow yogurt in their basement instead of writing in their field. In short, all the people who serve to corroborate the cliché notions about the nature of the scholar: the Old Maid School Teacher and the Absent Minded Professor. These are the only archetypes for the American professor. Both are comic. Both are a product of pop culture. And worse, the pedants, the lovers of form for form's sake, the priests of the academy who are interested only in the academy as an institution, and not in the academy's responsibility to its students and to the growth of knowledge and understanding. These people serve only to complement the anarchistic nihilism of the speed freak. The output of either is irrelevant, redundant and boring.

To see behind the lifestyles to the causes, to go beyond the pseudo-events to the realities, to go in an old-fashioned way (a book) toward a reunion of worlds in the classroom: that is part of the purpose of this text. The first part is what we consider to be a necessary bit of history (titled in the past tense for obvious reasons), probably as instructive to the teacher as to the student. The rest of it is an attempt to get it all together. That's what the knowledge business is about anyway (some people on both sides seem to have forgotten that). Some of the articles will reflect your own views. Some of them will infuriate you (it's called "a balanced text"). Good. The myth of consensus is perhaps even more insidious than the myth of the Simple Answer. The important thing is to see and to understand, to examine ideas and to chew on ideologies, and not to allow yourself to be hustled by easy solutions.

Our planet has produced a fascinating species, as Commander Spock would say. The species merits close study if we are to discover its Prime Directive.

Good luck to us all.

Ralph L. Carnes

If you were going to San Francisco...

The Know-Nothing Bohemians

NORMAN PODHORETZ

Allen Ginsberg's little volume of poems, *Howl,* which got the San Francisco renaissance off to a screaming start a year or so ago, was dedicated to Jack Kerouac ("new Buddha of American prose, who spit forth intelligence into eleven books written in half the number of years . . . creating a spontaneous bop prosody and original classic literature"), William Seward Burroughs ("author of *Naked Lunch,* an endless novel which will drive everybody mad"), and Neal Cassady ("author of *The First Third,* an autobiography . . . which enlightened Buddha"). So far, everybody's sanity has been spared by the inability of *Naked Lunch* to find a publisher, and we may never get the chance to discover what Buddha learned from Neal Cassady's autobiography, but thanks to the Viking and Grove Presses, two of Kerouac's original classics, *On the Road* and *The Subterraneans,* have now been revealed to the world. When *On the Road* appeared last year, Gilbert Milstein commemorated the event in the New York *Times* by declaring it to be "a historic occasion" comparable to the publication of *The Sun Also Rises* in the 1920's. But even before the novel was actually published, the word got around that Kerouac was the spokesman of a new group of rebels and Bohemians who called themselves the Beat Generation, and soon his photogenic countenance (unshaven, of course, and topped by an unruly crop of rich black hair falling over his forehead) was showing up in various mass-circulation magazines, he was being interviewed earnestly on television, and he was being featured in a Greenwich Village nightclub where, in San Francisco fashion, he read specimens of his spontaneous bop prosody against a background of jazz music.

Reprinted with the permission of Farrar, Straus & Giroux, Inc. from *Doings and Undoings* by Norman Podhoretz, copyright © 1958, 1964 by Norman Podhoretz.

Though the nightclub act reportedly flopped, *On the Road* sold well enough to hit the best-seller lists for several weeks, and it isn't hard to understand why. Americans love nothing so much as representative documents, and what could be more interesting in this Age of Sociology than a novel that speaks for the "young generation?" (The fact that Kerouac is thirty-five or thereabouts was generously not held against him.) Beyond that, however, I think that the unveiling of the Beat Generation was greeted with a certain relief by many people who had been disturbed by the notorious respectability and "maturity" of post-war writing. This was more like it—restless, rebellious, confused youth living it up, instead of thin, balding, buttoned-down instructors of English composing ironic verses with one hand while changing the baby's diapers with the other. Bohemianism is not particularly fashionable nowadays, but the image of Bohemia still exerts a powerful fascination—nowhere more so than in the suburbs, which are filled to overflowing with men and women who uneasily think of themselves as conformists and of Bohemianism as the heroic road. The whole point of *Marjorie Morningstar* was to assure the young marrieds of Mamaroneck that they were better off than the apparently glamorous *luftmenschen* of Greenwich Village, and the fact that Wouk had to work so hard at making this idea seem convincing is a good indication of the strength of prevailing doubt on the matter.

On the surface, at least, the Bohemianism of *On the Road* is very attractive. Here is a group of high-spirited young men running back and forth across the country (mostly hitch-hiking, sometimes in their own second-hand cars), going to "wild" parties in New York and Denver and San Francisco, living on a shoe-string (GI educational benefits, an occasional fifty bucks from a kindly aunt, an odd job as a typist, a fruit-picker, a parking-lot attendant), talking intensely about love and God and salvation, getting high on marijuana (but never heroin or cocaine), listening feverishly to jazz in crowded little joints, and sleeping freely with beautiful girls. Now and again there is a reference to gloom and melancholy, but the characteristic note struck by Kerouac is exuberance:

We stopped along the road for a bite to eat. The cowboy went off to have a spare tire patched, and Eddie and I sat down in a kind of homemade diner. I heard a great laugh, the greatest laugh in the world, and here came this rawhide oldtimes Nebraska farmer with a bunch of other boys into the diner; you could hear his raspy cries clear across the plains, across the whole gray world of them that day. Everybody else laughed with him. He didn't have a care in the world and had the hugest regard for everybody. I said to myself, Wham, listen to that man laugh. That's the West, here I am in the West. He came booming into the diner, calling Maw's name, and she made the sweetest cherry pie in Nebraska, and I had some with a mountainous scoop of ice cream on top. "Maw, rustle me up some grub afore I have to start eatin myself or some damn silly idee like that." And he threw himself on a stool and went hyaw hyaw hyaw hyaw. "And throw some beans in it." It was the spirit of the West sitting right next to me. I wished I knew his whole raw life and what the hell he'd been doing all these years besides laughing and yelling like that. Whooee, I told my soul, and the cowboy came back and off we went to Grand Island.

Kerouac's enthusiasm for the Nebraska farmer is part of his general readiness to find the source of all vitality and virtue in simple rural types and in the dispossessed urban groups (Negroes, bums, whores). His idea of life in New York is "millions and millions hustling forever for a buck among themselves . . . grabbing, taking, giving, sighing, dying, just so they could be buried in those awful cemetery cities beyond Long Island City," whereas the rest of America is populated almost exclusively by the true of heart. There are intimations here of a kind of know-nothing populist sentiment, but in other ways this attitude resembles Nelson Algren's belief that bums and whores and junkies are more interesting than white-collar workers or civil servants. The difference is that Algren hates middle-class respectability for moral and political reasons—the middle class exploits and persecutes—while Kerouac, who is thoroughly unpolitical, seems to feel that respectability is a sign not of moral corruption but of spiritual death. "The only people for me," says Sal Paradise, the narrator of *On the Road,* "are the mad ones, the ones who are mad to live, mad to talk, mad to be saved, desirous of everything at the same time, the ones who never yawn or say a commonplace thing, but burn, burn, burn like fabulous yellow roman candles exploding like spiders across the stars . . ." This tremendous emphasis on emotional intensity, this notion that to be hopped-up is the most desirable of all human conditions, lies at the heart of the Beat Generation ethos and distinguishes it radically from the Bohemianism of the past.

The Bohemianism of the 1920's represented a repudiation of the provinciality, philistinism, and moral hypocrisy of American life—a life, incidentally, which was still essentially small-town and rural in tone. Bohemia, in other words, was a movement created in the name of civilization: its ideals were intelligence, cultivation, spiritual refinement. The typical literary figure of the 1920's was a midwesterner (Hemingway, Fitzgerald, Sinclair Lewis, Eliot, Pound) who had fled from his home town to New York or Paris in search of a freer, more expansive, more enlightened way of life than was possible in Ohio or Minnesota or Michigan. The political radicalism that supplied the characteristic coloring of Bohemianism in the 1930's did nothing to alter the urban, cosmopolitan bias of the 1920's. At its best, the radicalism of the 1930's was marked by deep intellectual seriousness and aimed at a state of society in which the fruits of civilization would be more widely available—and ultimately available to all.

The Bohemianism of the 1950's is another kettle of fish altogether. It is hostile to civilization; it worships primitivism, instinct, energy, "blood." To the extent that it has intellectual interests at all, they run to mystical doctrines, irrationalist philosophies, and left-wing Reichianism. The only art the new Bohemians have any use for is jazz, mainly of the cool variety. Their predilection for bop language is a way of demonstrating solidarity with the primitive vitality and spontaneity they find in jazz and of expressing contempt for coherent, rational discourse which, being a product of the mind, is in their view a form of death. To be articulate is to admit that you have no feelings (for how can real feelings be expressed in syntactical language?), that you can't respond to anything (Kerouac responds to everything by saying "Wow!"), and that you are probably impotent.

At the one end of the spectrum, this ethos shades off into violence and criminality, main-line drug addiction and madness. Allen Ginsberg's poetry, with its lurid apocalyptic celebration of "angel-headed hipsters," speaks for the darker side of the new Bohemianism. Kerouac is milder. He shows little taste for violence, and the criminality he admires is the harmless kind. The hero of *On the Road*, Dean Moriarty, has a record: "From the age of eleven to seventeen he was usually in reform school. His specialty was stealing cars, gunning for girls coming out of high school in the afternoon, driving them out to the mountains, making them, and coming back to sleep in any available hotel bathtub in town." But Dean's criminality, we are told, "was not something that sulked and sneered; it was a wild yea-saying overburst of American joy; it was Western, the west wind, an ode from the Plains, something new, long prophesied, long a-coming (he only stole cars for joy rides)." And, in fact, the species of Bohemian that Kerouac writes about is on the whole rather law-abiding. In *The Subterraneans,* a bunch of drunken boys steal a pushcart in the middle of the night, and when they leave it in front of a friend's apartment building, he denounces them angrily for "screwing up the security of my pad." When Sal Paradise (in *On the Road*) steals some groceries from the canteen of an itinerant workers' camp in which he has taken a temporary job as a barracks guard, he comments, "I suddenly began to realize that everybody in America is a natural-born thief"—which, of course, is a way of turning his own stealing into a bit of boyish prankishness. Nevertheless, Kerouac is attracted to criminality, and that in itself is more significant than the fact that he personally feels constrained to put the brakes on his own destructive impulses.

Sex has always played a very important role in Bohemianism: sleeping around was the Bohemian's most dramatic demonstration of his freedom from conventional moral standards, and a defiant denial of the idea that sex was permissible only in marriage and then only for the sake of a family. At the same time, to be "promiscuous" was to assert the validity of sexual experience in and for itself. The "meaning" of Bohemian sex, then, was at once social and personal, a crucial element in the Bohemian's ideal of civilization. Here again the contrast with Beat Generation Bohemianism is sharp. On the one hand, there is a fair amount of sexual activity in *On the Road* and *The Subterraneans*. Dean Moriarty is a "new kind of American saint" at least partly because of his amazing sexual power: he can keep three women satisfied simultaneously and he can make love any time, anywhere (once he mounts a girl in the back seat of a car while poor Sal Paradise is trying to sleep in front). Sal, too, is always on the make, and though he isn't as successful as the great Dean, he does pretty well: offhand I can remember a girl in Denver, one on a bus, and another in New York, but a little research would certainly unearth a few more. The heroine of *The Subterraneans,* a Negro girl named Mardou Fox, seems to have switched from one to another member of the same gang and back again ("This has been an incestuous group in its time"), and we are given to understand that there is nothing unusual about such an arrangement. But the point of all this hustle and bustle is not freedom from ordinary social restrictions or defiance of convention (except in relation to homosexuality, which is Ginsberg's preserve: among "the best minds" of Ginsberg's generation who were destroyed by America are those "who let themselves be ———— in the —— by saintly motorcyclists, and screamed with joy,/who blew and were blown by those human seraphim, the sailors, caresses of Atlantic and Caribbean love"). The sex in Kerouac's books goes hand in hand with a great deal of talk about forming permanent relationships ("although I have a hot feeling sexually and all that for her," says the poet Adam Moorad in *The Subterraneans,* "I really don't want to get any further into her not only for these reasons but finally, the big one, if I'm going to get involved with a girl now I want to be permanent like permanent and serious and long termed and I can't do that with her"), and a habit of getting married and then duly divorced and re-married when another girl comes along. In fact, there are as many marriages and divorces in *On the Road* as in the Hollywood movie colony (must be that California climate): "All those years I was looking for the woman I wanted to marry," Sal Paradise tells us. "I couldn't meet a girl without saying to myself, What kind of wife would she make?" Even more revealing is Kerouac's refusal to admit that any of his characters ever make love wantonly or lecherously—no matter how casual the encounter it must always entail sweet feelings toward the girl. Sal, for example, is fixed up with Rita Bettencourt in Denver, whom he has never met before. "I got her in my bedroom after a long talk in the dark of the front room. She was a nice little girl, simple and true [naturally], and tremendously frightened of sex. I told her it was beautiful. I wanted to prove this to her. She let me prove it, but I was too impatient and proved nothing. She sighed in the dark. 'What do you want out of life?' I asked, and I used to ask that all the time of girls." This is rather touching, but only because the narrator is really just as frightened of sex as that nice little girl was. He is frightened of failure and he worries about his performance. For *performance* is the point—performance and "good orgasms," which are the first duty of man and the only duty of woman. What seems to be involved here, in short, is sexual anxiety of enormous proportions—an anxiety that comes out very clearly in *The Subterraneans,* which is about a love affair between the young writer, Leo Percepied, and the Negro girl, Mardou Fox. Despite its protestations, the book is one long agony of fear and trembling over sex:

I spend long nights and many hours making her, finally I have her, I pray for it to come, I can hear her breathing harder, I hope against hope it's time, a noise in the hall (or whoop of drunkards next door) takes her mind off and she can't make it and laughs—but when she does make it I hear her crying, whimpering, the shuddering electrical female orgasm makes her sound like a little girl crying, moaning in the night, it lasts a good twenty seconds and when it's over she moans, "O why can't it last longer," and "O when will I when you do?"—"Soon now I bet," I say, "you're getting closer and closer"—

Very primitive, very spontaneous, very elemental, very beat.

For the new Bohemians interracial friendships and love affairs apparently play the same role of social defiance that sex used to play in older Bohemian circles. Negroes and whites associate freely on a basis of complete equality and without a trace of racial hostility. But putting it that way understates the case, for not only is there no racial hostility, there is positive adulation for the "happy, true-hearted, ecstatic Negroes of America."

At lilac evening I walked with every muscle aching among the lights of 27th and Welton in the Denver colored section, wishing I were a Negro, feeling that the best the white world had offered was not enough ecstasy for me, not enough life, joy, kicks, darkness, music, not enough night. . . . I wished I were a Denver Mexican, or even a poor overworked Jap, anything but what I was so drearily, a "white man" disillusioned. All my life I'd had white ambitions. . . . I passed the dark porches of Mexican and Negro homes; soft voices were there, occasionally the dusky knee of some mysterious sensuous gal; and dark faces of the men behind rose arbors. Little children sat like sages in ancient rocking chairs.

It will be news to the Negroes to learn that they are so happy and ecstatic; I doubt if a more idyllic picture of Negro life has been painted since certain Southern ideologues tried to convince the world that things were just as fine as fine could be for the slaves on the old plantations. Be that as it may, Kerouac's love for Negroes and other dark-skinned groups is tied up with his worship of primitivism, not with any radical social attitudes. Ironically enough, in fact, to see the Negro as more elemental than the white man, as Ned Polsky has acutely remarked, is "an inverted form of keeping the nigger in his place." But even if it were true that American Negroes, by virtue of their position in our culture, have been able to retain a degree of primitive spontaneity, the last place you would expect to find evidence of this is among Bohemian Negroes. Bohemianism, after all, is for the Negro a means of entry into the world of the whites, and no Negro Bohemian is going to cooperate in the attempt to identify him with Harlem or Dixieland. The only major Negro character in either of Kerouac's two novels is Mardou Fox, and she is about as primitive as Wilhelm Reich himself.

The plain truth is that the primitivism of the Beat Generation serves first of all as a cover for an anti-intellectualism so bitter that it makes the ordinary American's hatred of eggheads seem positively benign. Kerouac and his friends like to think of themselves as intellectuals ("they are intellectual as hell and know all about Pound without being pretentious or talking too much about it"), but this is only a form of newspeak. Here is an example of what Kerouac considers intelligent discourse—"formal and shining and complete, without the tedious intellectualness":

> We passed a little kid who was throwing stones at the cars in the road. "Think of it," said Dean. "One day he'll put a stone through a man's windshield and the man will crash and die—all on account of that little kid. You see what I mean? God exists without qualms. As we roll along this way I am positive beyond doubt that everything will be taken care of for us—that even you, as you drive, fearful of the wheel . . . the thing will go along of itself and you won't go off the road and I can sleep. Furthermore we know America, we're at home; I can go anywhere in America and get what I want because it's the same in every corner, I know the people, I know what they do. We give and take and go in the incredibly complicated sweetness zigzagging every side."

You see what he means? Formal and shining and complete. No tedious intellectualness. Completely unpretentious. "There was nothing clear about the things he said but what he meant to say was somehow made pure and clear." *Somehow.* Of course. If what he wanted to say had been carefully thought out and precisely articulated, that would have been tedious and pretentious and, no doubt, *somehow* unclear and clearly impure. But so long as he utters these banalities with his tongue tied and with no comprehension of their meaning, so long as he makes noises that come out of his soul (since they couldn't possibly have come out of his mind), he passes the test of true intellectuality.

Which brings us to Kerouac's spontaneous bop prosody. This "prosody" is not to be confused with bop language itself, which has such a limited vocabulary (Basic English is a verbal treasure-house by comparison) that you couldn't write a note to the milkman in it, much less a novel. Kerouac, however, manages to remain true to the spirit of hipster slang while making forays into enemy territory (i.e., the English language) by his simple inability to express anything in words. The only method he has of describing an object is to summon up the same half-dozen adjectives over and over again: "greatest," "tremendous," "crazy," "mad," "wild," and perhaps one or two others. When it's more than just mad or crazy or wild, it becomes "really mad" or "really crazy" or "really wild." (All quantities in excess of three, incidentally, are subsumed under the rubric "innumerable," a word used innumerable times in *On the Road* but not so innumerably in *The Subterraneans*.) The same poverty of resources is apparent in those passages where Kerouac tries to handle a situation involving even slightly complicated feelings. His usual tactic is to run for cover behind cliché and vague signals to the reader. For instance: "I looked at him; my eyes were watering with embarrassment and tears. Still he stared at me. Now his eyes were blank and looking through me. . . . Something clicked in both of us. In me it was suddenly concern for a man who was years younger than I, five years, and whose fate was wound with mine across the passage of the recent years; in him it was a matter that I can ascertain only from what he did afterward." If you can ascertain what this is all about, either beforehand, during, or afterward, you are surely no square.

In keeping with its populistic bias, the style of *On the Road* is folksy and lyrical. The prose of *The Subterraneans,* on the other hand, sounds like an inept parody of Faulkner at his worst, the main difference being that Faulkner usually produces bad writing out of an impluse to inflate the commonplace while Kerouac gets into trouble by pursuing "spontaneity." Strictly speaking, spontaneity is a quality of feeling, not of writing: when we call a piece of writing spontaneous, we are registering our impression that the author hit upon the right words without sweating, that no "art" and no calculation entered into the picture, that his feelings seem to have spoken themselves, seem to have sprouted a tongue at the moment of composition. Kerouac apparently thinks that spontaneity is a matter of saying whatever comes into your head, in any order you happen to feel like saying it. It isn't the *right* words he wants (even if he knows what they might be), but the first words, or at any rate the words that most obviously announce themselves as deriving from emotion rather than cerebration, as coming from "life" rather than "literature," from the guts rather than the brain. (The brain, remember, is the angel of death.) But writing that springs easily and "spontaneously" out of strong feelings is *never* vague; it always has a quality of sharpness and precision because it is in the nature of strong feelings to be aroused by specific objects. The notion that a diffuse, generalized, and unrelenting enthusiasm is the mark of great sensitivity and responsiveness is utterly fantastic, an idea that comes from taking drunkenness or drug-addiction as the state of perfect emotional vigor. The effect of such enthusiasm is actually to wipe out the world altogether, for if a filling station will serve as well as the Rocky Mountains to arouse a sense of awe and wonder, then both the filling station and the mountains are robbed of their reality. Kerouac's conception of feeling is one that only a solipsist could believe in—and a solipsist, be it noted, is a man who does not relate to anything outside himself.

Solipsism is precisely what characterizes Kerouac's fiction. *On the Road* and *The Subterraneans* are so patently autobiographical in content that they become almost impossible to discuss as novels; if spontaneity were indeed a matter of destroying the distinction between life and literature, these books would unquestionably be It. "As we were going out to the car Babe slipped and fell flat on her face. Poor girl was overwrought. Her brother Tim and I helped her up. We got in the car; Major and Betty joined us. The sad ride back to Denver began." Babe is a girl who is mentioned a few times in the course of *On the Road;* we don't know why she is overwrought on this occasion, and even if we did it wouldn't matter, since there is no reason for her presence in the book at all. But Kerouac tells us that she fell flat on her face while walking toward a car. It is impossible to believe that Kerouac made this detail up, that his imagination was creating a world real enough to include wholly gratuitous elements; if that were the case, Babe would have come alive as a human being. But she is only a name; Kerouac never even describes her. She is in the book because the sister of one of Kerouac's friends was there when he took a trip to Central City, Colorado, and she slips in *On the Road* because she slipped that day on the way to the car. What is true of Babe who fell flat on her face is true of virtually every incident in *On the Road* and *The Subterraneans*. Nothing that happens has any dramatic reason for happening. Sal Paradise meets such-and-such people on the road whom he likes or (rarely) dislikes; they exchange a few words, they have a few beers together, they part. It is all very unremarkable and commonplace, but for Kerouac it is always the greatest, the wildest, the most. What you get in these two books is a man proclaiming that he is *alive* and offering every trivial experience he has ever had in evidence. Once I did this, once I did that (he is saying) and by God, it *meant* something! Because I *responded!* But if it meant something, and you responded so powerfully, why can't you explain what it meant, and why do you have to insist so?

I think it is legitimate to say, then, that the Beat Generation's worship of primitivism and spontaneity is more than a cover for hostility to intelligence; it arises from a pathetic poverty of feeling as well. The hipsters and hipster-lovers of the Beat Generation are rebels, all right, but not against anything so sociological and historical as the middle class or capitalism or even respectability. This is the revolt of the spiritually underprivileged and the crippled of soul—young men who can't think straight and so hate anyone who can; young men who can't get outside the morass of self and so construct definitions of feeling that exclude all human beings who manage to live, even miserably, in a world of objects; young men who are burdened unto death with the specially poignant sexual anxiety that America—in its eternal promise of erotic glory and its spiteful withholding of actual erotic possibility—seems bent on breeding, and who therefore dream of the unattainable perfect orgasm, which excuses all sexual failures in the real world. Not long ago, Norman Mailer suggested that the rise of the hipster may represent "the first wind of a second revolution in this century, moving not forward toward action and more rational equitable distribution, but backward toward being and the secrets of human energy." To tell the truth, whenever I hear anyone talking about instinct and being and the secrets of human energy, I get nervous; next thing you know he'll be saying that violence is just fine, and then I begin wondering whether he really thinks that kicking someone in the teeth or sticking a knife between his ribs are deeds to be admired. History, after all—and especially the history of modern times—teaches that there is a close connection between ideologies of primitivistic vitalism and a willingness to look upon cruelty and blood-letting with complacency, if not downright enthusiasm. The reason I bring this up is that the spirit of hipsterism and the Beat Generation strikes me as the same spirit which animates the young savages in leather jackets who have been running amuck in the last few years with their switch-blades and zip guns. What does Mailer think of those wretched kids, I wonder? What does he think of the gang that stoned a nine-year-old boy to death in Central Park in broad daylight a few months ago, or the one that set fire to an old man drowsing on a bench near the Brooklyn waterfront one summer's day, or the one that pounced on a crippled child and orgiastically stabbed him over and over and over again even after he was good and dead? Is that what he means by the liberation of instinct and the mysteries of being? Maybe so. At least he says somewhere in his article that two eighteen-year-old hoodlums who bash in the brains of a candy-store keeper are murdering an institution, committing an act that "violates private property" —which is one of the most morally gruesome ideas I have ever come across, and which indicates where the ideology of hipsterism can lead. I happen to believe that there is a direct connection between the flabbiness of American middle-class life and the spread of juvenile crime in the 1950's, but I also believe that juvenile crime can be explained partly in terms of the same resentment against normal feeling and the attempt to cope with the world through intelligence that lies behind Kerouac and Ginsberg. Even the relatively mild ethos of Kerouac's books can spill over easily into brutality, for there is a suppressed cry in those books: Kill the intellectuals who can talk coherently, kill the people who can sit still for five minutes at a time, kill those incomprehensible characters who are capable of getting seriously involved with a woman, a job, a cause. How can anyone in his right mind pretend that this has anything to do with private property or the middle class? No. Being for or against what the Beat Generation stands for has to do with denying that incoherence is superior to precision; that ignorance is superior to knowledge; that the exercise of mind and discrimination is a form of death. It has to do with fighting the notion that sordid acts of violence are justifiable so long as they are committed in the name of "instinct." It even has to do with fighting the poisonous glorification of the adolescent in American popular culture. It has to do, in other words, with being for or against intelligence itself.

The Flowering
of the Hippies

MARK HARRIS

The hippie "scene" on Haight Street in San Francisco was so very visual that photographers came from everywhere to shoot it, reporters came from everywhere to write it up with speed, and opportunists came from everywhere to exploit its drug addiction, its sexual possibility, and its political or social ferment. Prospective hippies came from everywhere for one "summer of love" or maybe longer, some older folk to indulge their latent hippie tendencies, and the police to contain, survey, or arrest. "Haight"—old Quaker name—rhymed with "hate," but hippies held that the theme of the street was love, and the best of hippies, like the best of visitors and the best of the police, hoped to reclaim and distill the best promise of a movement which might yet invigorate American movement everywhere. It might, by resurrecting the word "love," and giving it a refreshened definition, open the national mind, as if by the chemical LSD, to the hypocrisy of violence and prejudice in a nation dedicated to peace and accord.

It was easier to see than understand: the visual came first, and the visual was so discordant that tourists drove with their cars locked and an alarmed citizenry beseeched the police to clean it out.

It was easy to see that the young men who were hippies on Haight Street wore beards and long hair and sometimes earrings and weird-o granny eyeglasses, that they were barefoot or in sandals, and that they were generally dirty. A great many of the young men, by design or by accident, resembled Jesus Christ, whose name came up on campaign pins or lavatory walls or posters or bumper stickers. *Are You Bombing With Me, Baby Jesus. Jesus Is God's Atom Bomb.*

The script was "psychedelic." That is to say, it was characterized by flourishes, spirals, and curlicues in camouflaged tones—blues against purples, pinks against reds—as if the hippie behind the message weren't really sure he wanted to say what he was saying. It was an item of hippie thought that speech was irrelevant. *You Don't Say Love You Do It. Those Who Speak Don't Know Those Who Know Don't Speak.* But it was also my suspicion that hippies would speak when they could; meanwhile, their muteness suggested doubt. In one shop the wall was dominated by an old movie advertisement—Ronald Reagan and June Travis in *Love Is in the Air* (Warner Brothers), their faces paper-white, blank, drained. I asked the hippie at the counter why it was there, but she didn't trust herself to try. "It's what you make of it," she said.

It was easy to see that the young women who were hippies were draped, not dressed; that they, too, were dirty from toe to head; that they looked unwell, pale, sallow, hair hung down in strings unwashed. Or they wore jeans, men's T-shirts over brassieres. When shoes were shoes the laces were missing or trailing, gowns were sacks, and sacks were gowns. *If You Can't Eat It Wear It.*

A fashion model was quoted in a newspaper as saying, "They don't really exist," who meant to say, of course, "I *wish* they didn't." The young ladies were experimenting in drugs, in sexual license, living in communal quarters furnished with mattresses. *Praise The Pill. Bless Our Pad.* Girls who might have been in fashion were panhandling. "Sorry, I've got to go panhandle," I heard a hippie lady say, which was not only against the law but against the American creed, which holds that work is virtue, no matter what work you do. Hippie girls gave flowers to strangers, and they encouraged their dirty young men to avoid the war in Vietnam. *Thou Shalt Not Kill This Means You. Caution: Military Service May Be Hazardous To Your Health.*

The shops of the "hip" merchants were colorful and cordial. The "straight" merchants of Haight Street sold necessities, but the hip shops smelled of incense, the walls were hung with posters and paintings, and the counters were laden with thousands of items of nonutilitarian non-sense—metal jewelry, glass beads, dirty pictures, "underground" maga-zines, photographs of old-time movie stars, colored chalk, dirty combs, kazoos, Halloween masks, fancy matchboxes, odd bits of stained glass, and single shoes. Every vacant wall was a bulletin board for communica-tion among people not yet quite settled ("Jack and Frank from Iowa leave a message here").

The music everywhere was rock 'n' roll out of Beatles, folk, African drums, American pop, jazz, swing, and martial.

Anybody who was anybody among hippies had been arrested for some-thing, or so he said—for "possession" (of drugs), for "contributing" (to the delinquency of a minor), for panhandling, for obstructing the sidewalk, and if for nothing else, for "resisting" (arrest). The principal cause of their conflict with the police was their smoking marijuana, probably harmless but definitely illegal. Such clear proof of the failure of the law to meet the knowledge of the age presented itself to the querulous minds of hippies as sufficient grounds to condemn the law complete.

Hippies thought they saw on Haight Street that everyone's eyes were filled with loving joy and giving, but the eyes of the hippies were often in fact sorrowful and frightened, for they had plunged themselves into an experiment they were uncertain they could carry through. Fortified by LSD (*Better Living Through Chemistry*), they had come far enough to see distance behind them, but no clear course ahead. One branch of their philosophy was Oriental concentration and meditation; now it often focused upon the question "How to kick" (drugs).

The ennobling idea of the hippies, forgotten or lost in the visual scene, diverted by chemistry, was their plan for *community*. For *community* they had come. What kind of community, upon what model? Hippies wore brilliant Mexican *chalecos,* Oriental robes, and red-Indian headdress. They dressed as cowboys. They dressed as frontiersmen. They dressed as

Puritans. Doubtful who they were, trying on new clothes, how could they know where they were going until they saw what fit? They wore military insignia. Among bracelets and bells they wore Nazi swastikas and the German Iron Cross, knowing, without knowing much more, that the swastika offended the Establishment, and no enemy of the Establishment could be all bad. They had been born, give or take a year or two, in the year of Hiroshima.

Once the visual scene was ignored, almost the first point of interest about the hippies was that they were middle-class American children to the bone. To citizens inclined to alarm this was the thing most maddening, that these were not Negroes disaffected by color or immigrants by strangeness but boys and girls with white skins from the right side of the economy in all-American cities and towns from Honolulu to Baltimore. After regular educations, if only they'd want them, they could commute to fine jobs from the suburbs, and own nice houses with bathrooms, where they could shave and wash up.

Many hippies lived with the help of remittances from home, whose parents, so straight, so square, so seeming compliant, rejected, in fact, a great portion of that official American program rejected by the hippies in psychedelic script. *The 19th Century Was A Mistake The 20th Century Is A Disaster.* Even in arrest they found approval from their parents, who had taught them in years of civil rights and resistance to the war in Vietnam that authority was often questionable, sometimes despicable. George F. Babbitt, forty years before in Zenith, U.S.A., declared his hope, at the end of a famous book, that his son might go farther than Babbitt had dared along lines of break and rebellion.

When hippies first came to San Francisco they were an isolated minority, mistrustful, turned inward by drugs, lacking acquaintance beyond themselves. But they were spirited enough, after all, to have fled from home, to have endured the discomforts of a cramped existence along Haight Street, proud enough to have endured the insults of the police, and alert enough to have identified the major calamities of their age.

In part a hoax of American journalism, known even to themselves only as they saw themselves in the media, they began at last, and especially with the approach of the "summer of love," to assess their community, their quest, and themselves.

They slowly became, in the word that seemed to cover it, polarized, distinct in division among themselves between, on one hand, weekend or summertime hippies, and on the other, hippies for whom the visual scene was an insubstantial substitute for genuine community. The most perceptive or advanced among the hippies then began to undertake the labor of community which could be accomplished only behind the scene, out of the eye of the camera, beyond the will of the quick reporter.

The visual scene was four blocks long on Haight Street. Haight Street itself was nineteen, extending east two miles from Golden Gate Park, through the visual scene, through a portion of the Negro district known as the Fillmore, past the former campus of San Francisco State College, and flowing at its terminus into Market Street, into the straight city, across the Bay Bridge, and into that wider United States whose values the hippies were testing, whose traditions were their own propulsion in spite of their denials, and whose future the hippies might yet affect in singular ways unimagined by either those States or those hippies. From the corner of Haight and Ashbury Streets it was three miles to Broadway and Columbus, heart of North Beach, where the Beats had gathered ten years before.

The Haight-Ashbury district is a hundred square blocks of homes and parks. One of the parks is the Panhandle of Golden Gate, thrusting itself into the district, preserving, eight blocks long, a green and lovely relief unimpaired by prohibitions against free play by children or the free promenade of adults along its mall. Planted in pine, maple, redwood, and eucalyptus, its only serious resistance to natural things is a statue honoring William McKinley, but consigned to the farthest extremity, for which, in 1903, Theodore Roosevelt broke the ground.

The Panhandle is the symbolic and spiritual center of the district, its stay against confusion. On March 28, 1966, after a struggle of several years —and by a single vote of the San Francisco Supervisors—the residents of the Haight-Ashbury district were able to rescue the Panhandle from the bulldozer, which would have replaced it with a freeway assisting commuters to save six minutes between downtown and the Golden Gate Bridge.

In one of the few triumphs of neighborhood over redevelopment the power of the district lay in the spiritual and intellectual composition of its population, which tended toward firm views of the necessity to save six minutes and toward a skeptical view of the promise of "developers" to "plant it over" afterward. Apart from the Panhandle controversy, the people of the district had firm views clustering about the conviction that three-story Tudor and Victorian dwellings are preferable to skyscrapers, that streets should serve people before automobiles, that a neighborhood was meant for living as well as sleeping, that habitation implies some human dirt, that small shops foster human acquaintance as department stores don't, and that schools which are integrated are more educational than schools which are segregated.

One of the effects of the victory of the bulldozer would have been the obliteration of low-cost housing adjacent to the Panhandle, and therefore the disappearance of poorer people from the district. But the people of the Haight-Ashbury failed of enthusiasm. "Fair streets are better than silver," wrote Vachel Lindsay, leading hippie of Springfield, Illinois, half a century ago, and considered that part of his message central enough to carry it in psychedelic banners on the end pages of his *Collected Poems*.

The Haight-Ashbury—to give it its San Francisco sound—had long been a favorite residential area for persons of liberal disposition in many occupations, in business, labor, the arts, the professions, and academic life. It had been equally hospitable to avant-garde expression, to racial diversity, and to the Okies and Arkies who came after World War II. Its polyglot population, estimated at 30,000, was predominantly white, but it included Negroes and Orientals in sizable numbers and general distribution, and immigrants of many nations. Here William Saroyan and Erskine Caldwell had lived.

During the decade of the sixties it was a positive attraction to many San Franciscans who could easily have lived at "better addresses" but who chose the Haight-Ashbury for its congeniality and cultural range. Here they could prove to anyone who cared, and especially to their children, the possibilities of racial integration. The Haight-Ashbury was the only neighborhood in the nation, as far as I know, to send its own delegation—one white man, one Negro woman—to the civil rights March on Washington in 1963.

Wealth and comfort ascended with the hills in the southern portion of the district. In the low, flat streets near the Panhandle, where the hippies lived, the residents were poorer, darker, and more likely to be of foreign extraction. There, too, students and young artists lived, and numbers of white families who had chosen the perils of integration above the loss of their proximity to the Panhandle. With the threat of the freeway many families had moved away and many stores had become vacant, and when the threat had passed, a vacuum remained.

The hippies came, lured by availability, low rents, low prices, and the spirit of historic openness. The prevailing weather was good in a city where weather varied with the contours of hills. Here a hippie might live barefoot most of the months of the year, lounge in sunswept doorways slightly out of the wind, and be fairly certain that political liberals, bedeviled Negroes, and propertyless whites were more likely than neighbors elsewhere to admit him to community.

The mood of the Haight-Ashbury ranged from occasional opposition to the hippies to serene indifference, to tolerance, to interest, and to delight. As trouble increased between hippies and police, and as alarm increased elsewhere in the city, the Haight-Ashbury kept its head. It valued the passions of the young, especially when the young were, as hippies were, nonviolent. No doubt, at least among liberals, it saw something of its own earlier life in the lives of hippies.

Last March the Haight-Ashbury Neighborhood Council, formed in 1957 to meet a crisis similar to the Panhandle controversy, committed itself to a policy of extended patience. It declared that "we particularly resent the official position of law-enforcement agencies, as announced by [Police] Chief Cahill, that hippies are not an asset to the community. The chief has not distinguished among the many kinds of citizens who comprise the hippie culture. . . . War against a class of citizens, regardless of how they dress or choose to live, within the latitude of the law, is intolerable in a free society. We remember the regrettable history of officially condoned crusades against the Chinese population of San Francisco whose life style did not meet with the approval of the established community and whose lives and property were objects of terrorism and persecution."

If any neighborhood in America was prepared to accommodate the hippies, it was the Haight-Ashbury. On the heights and on the level rich and poor were by and large secure, open, liberal, pro-civil-rights, and in high proportion anti-war. Its U.S. congressman was Philip Burton, a firm and forthright liberal, and its California assemblyman was Willie Brown, a Negro of unquestioned intellect and integrity. Here the hippies might gain time to shape their message and translate to coherence the confusion of the visual scene. If the hippies were unable to make, of all scenes, the Haight-Ashbury scene, then there was something wrong with *them*.

LYSERGIC ACID DIETHYLAMIDE

The principal distinction between the hippies and every other endeavor in utopian community was LSD, which concentrated upon the liver, produced chemical change in the body, and thereby affected the brain. Whether LSD produced physical harm remained an argument, but its most ardent advocates and users (not always the same persons) never denied its potentially dangerous emotional effects. Those effects depended a great deal on the user's predisposition. Among the hippies of San Francisco, LSD precipitated suicide and other forms of self-destructive or antisocial behavior. For some hippies it produced little or nothing, and was therefore a disappointment. For many, it precipitated gorgeous hallucinations, a wide variety of sensual perceptions never before available to the user, and breathtaking panoramic visions of human and social perfection accompanied by profound insights into the user's own past.

It could be manufactured in large quantities by simple processes, like gin in a bathtub, easily carried about, and easily retained without detection. In liquid it was odorless and colorless; in powder it was minute. Its administration required no needles or other paraphernalia, and since it was taken orally, it left no "tracks" upon the body.

Technically it was nonaddictive, but it conspicuously induced in the user—the younger he was, the more so—a strong desire for another "trip": the pleasures of life under LSD exceeded the realities of sober perception. More far-reaching than liquor, quicker for insights than college or psychiatry, the pure and instant magic of LSD appeared for an interesting moment to capture the mind of the hippies. Everybody loved a panacea.

Their text was *The Psychedelic Experience,* by Leary, Metzner, and Alpert, "a manual based on the Tibetan Book of the Dead," whose jacket assured the reader that the book had been completed free of academic auspices. It was likely that the hippies' interest in the book lay, in any case, rather in its use as "manual" than in its historical reference.

Bob Dylan, favorite of many hippies, told in a line of song, "To live outside the law you must be honest." But hippies were Puritan Americans, gorged with moral purpose, and loath to confess that their captivation was basically the pursuit of pleasure. They therefore attached to the mystique of LSD the conviction that by opening their minds to chemical visions they were gaining insights from which society soon should profit.

Hippies themselves might have profited, as anyone might, from LSD

in a clinical environment, but the direction of their confidence lay elsewhere, and they placed themselves beneath the supervision mainly of
other hippies. Dialogue was confined among themselves, no light was
shed upon the meaning of their visions, and their preoccupation became
LSD itself—what it did to them last time, and what it might do next. Tool
had become symbol, and symbol principle. If the hippie ideal of community failed, it would fail upon lines of a dull, familiar scheme: the means
had become the end.

Far from achieving an exemplary community of their own, with connections to existing community, the hippies had achieved only, in the language of one of their vanguard, "a community of acid-heads." If LSD was
all the hippies talked about, the outlying community could hardly be
blamed for thinking this was all they were. Visions of community seen
under LSD had not been imparted to anyone, remaining visible only to
hippies, or entering the visual scene only in the form of commentary upon
LSD itself, jokes and claims for its efficacy growing shriller with the increase of dependence. But the argument had been that LSD inspired
transcendence, that it was, as one hippie phrased it, "a stepping-stone to
get out of your environment and look at it."

Under the influence of LSD hippies had written things down, or drawn
pictures, but upon examination the writings or the pictures proved less
perfect than they had appeared while the trip was on. Great utterances
delivered under LSD were somehow unutterable otherwise. Great thoughts
the hippies had thought under LSD they could never soberly convey, nor
reproduce the startling new designs for happier social arrangements.

Two years after the clear beginnings of the hippies in San Francisco, a
date established by the opening of the Psychedelic Shop, hippies and
others had begun to recognize that LSD, if it had not failed, had surely
not fully succeeded. ("We have serious doubts," said a Quaker report,
"whether drugs offer the spiritual illumination which bears fruit in Christ-
like lives.") Perhaps, as some hippies claimed, their perceptions had
quickened, carrying them forward to a point of social readiness. It had
turned them on, then off.

Whatever the explanation, by the time of the "summer of love" their
relationship with the surrounding community had badly deteriorated. The
most obvious failure of perception was the hippies' failure to discriminate
among elements of the Establishment, whether in the Haight-Ashbury or
in San Francisco in general. Their paranoia was the paranoia of all youthful heretics. *Even Paranoids Have Real Enemies.* True. But they saw all the
world as straight but them; all cops were brutes, and everyone else was
an arm of the cops. Disaffiliating with all persons and all institutions but
themselves, they disaffiliated with all possible foundations of community.

It was only partly true, as hippies complained, that "the Establishment
isn't listening to us." The Establishment never listened to anyone until it
was forced to. That segment of the Establishment known as the Haight-
Ashbury, having welcomed the hippies with friendliness and hope, had
listened with more courtesy to hippies than hippies had listened to the
Haight-Ashbury.

Hippies had theories of community, theories of work, theories of child care, theories of creativity. Creative hippies were extremely creative about things the city and the district could do for them. For example, the city could cease harassing hippies who picked flowers in Golden Gate Park to give them away on Haight Street. The city replied that the flowers of Golden Gate Park were for all people—were *community* flowers—and suggested that hippies plant flowers of their own. Hippies imagined an all-powerful city presided over by an all-powerful mayor who, said a hippie, "wants to stop human growth." They imagined an all-powerful Board of Supervisors which with inexhaustible funds could solve all problems simultaneously if only it wanted to.

Their illusions, their unreason, their devil theories, their inexperience of life, and their failures of perception had begun to persuade even the more sympathetic elements of the Haight-Ashbury that the hippies perhaps failed of perception in general. The failure of the hippies to communicate reasonably cast doubt upon their reliability as observers, especially with respect to the most abrasive of all issues, their relationship with the police.

Was it merely proof of its basic old rigidity that the Haight-Ashbury believed that community implied social relief, that visions implied translation to social action? *Squares Love, Too: Haight-Ashbury For All People.* So read an answering campaign pin as friction increased. But the hippies, declining self-regulation, aloof, self-absorbed, dumped mountains of garbage on the Panhandle. The venereal rate of the Haight-Ashbury multiplied by six. (The hippies accused Dr. Ellis Sox of the health department of sexual repression.) The danger grew alarmingly of rats, food poisoning, hepatitis, pulmonary tuberculosis, and of meningitis caused by overcrowded housing. "If hippies don't want to observe city and state laws," said Dr. Sox, "let them at least observe a few natural laws."

Hippies behaved so much like visitors to the community that their neighbors, who intended to live in the district forever, questioned whether proclamations of community did not require *acts* of community. Hippies had theories of love, which might have meant, at the simplest level, muting music for the benefit of neighbors who must rise in the morning for work. Would the Haight-Ashbury once again, if the emergency arose, expend years of its life to retain a Panhandle for hippies to dump their garbage on? Or would it abandon the hippies to the most primitive interpretations of law, permit their dispersion, and see their experiment end without beginning?

At no point was the hippies' failure to seek community so apparent as with relation to the Negroes of the district. With the passage of the civil rights movement from demonstrations to legal implementation excellent opportunities existed for the show of love. What grand new design in black and white had hippies seen under LSD? If Negroes were expected to share with hippies the gestures of love, then hippies ought to have shared with Negroes visions of equal rights.

The burdens of the Negroes of the district were real. Negro tenants *desired* the attention of the health department, *desired* the attention of agencies whom hippies monopolized with appeals for food and housing for the "summer of love." The needs of the Negroes, especially for jobs, appeared to Negroes a great deal more urgent than the needs of white middle-class hippies who had dropped out of affluence to play games of poverty in San Francisco. "Things should be given away free," said a Negro man in a public debate, "to people that *really* need them."

One afternoon, on Masonic Street, a hundred feet off Haight, I saw a Negro boy, perhaps twelve years old, repairing an old bicycle that had been repaired before. His tools lay on the sidewalk beside him, arranged in a systematic way, as if according to an order he had learned from his father. His face was intent, the work was complicated. Nearby, the hippies masqueraded. I mentioned to a lady the small boy at work, the big boys at play. "Yes," she said, "the hippies have usurped the prerogatives of children—to dress up and be irresponsible."

THE POLARIZATION
OF THE HIPPIES

A hippie record is entitled *Notes From Underground.* The hippie behind the counter told me that "underground" was a hippie word. He had not yet heard of Dostoevsky, whose title the record borrowed, or of the anti-slavery underground in America, or of the World War II underground in France. A movement which thought itself the world's first underground was bound to make mistakes it could have avoided by consultation with the past, and there was evidence that the hippies had begun to know it.

Nobody asked the hippies to accept or acknowledge the texts of the past. Their reading revealed their search for self-help, not conducted among the traditional books of the Western world but of the Orient—in *I Ching* and *The Prophet,* and in the novels of the German Hermann Hesse, especially the "Oriental" *Siddhartha.* Betrayed by science and reason, hippies indulged earnestly in the occult, the astrological, the mystical, the horoscopic, and the Ouija. Did hippies know that Ouija boards were a popular fad not long ago?

Or did they know that *The Prophet* of Kahlil Gibran, reprinted seventy-seven times since 1923, lies well within the tradition of American self-help subliterature? No sillier book exists, whose "prose poetry," faintly biblical, offers homiletic advice covering one by one all the departments of life (On Love, On Marriage, On Children, On Giving, On Eating and Drinking, On Work—on and on) in a manner so ambiguous as to permit the reader to interpret all tendencies as acceptable and to end by doing as he pleases, as if with the sanction of the prophet.

Hesse was a German, born in 1877, who turned consciously to romantic expression after age forty, but the wide interest of the hippies in *Siddhartha* is less conscious than Hesse's. To the hero's search for unity between self and nature they respond as German youth responded to Hesse, or as an earlier generation of Americans responded to the spacious, ambiguous outcry of Thomas Wolfe.

Inevitably, they were going through all these things twice, unaware of things gone through before. Inherent in everything printed or hanging in the visual scene on Haight Street was satirical rejection of cultural platitudes, but in the very form and style of the platitudes themselves. Children of television, they parodied it, spoofing Batman, as if Batman mattered. The satire in which they rejoiced was television's own artistic outpost. The walls of Haight Street bore, at a better level, the stamp of *Mad* magazine or collages satirizing the chaos of advertising: but anyone could see the same who turned the pages of *Reader's Digest* fast.

Of all the ways in which hippies began to polarize toward work their withdrawal from the visual scene was most astute. They had begun to learn, after flight, rebellion, and the pleasures of satirizing things they hoped they could reject, that work requires solitude and privacy, and that to work well means to resist the shaping influence of the media, abandoning the visual scene to those whom it gratifies.

The ideal of work—not simply jobs, but meaningful work, work as service—had been a hippie ideal from the outset. The apprehension of quiet, positive acts as meaningful, requiring time and *liaison,* was a more difficult act than parading the streets in costume. The act of extending community beyond oneself, beyond other hippies, beyond the comfort of drugs to the wider community of diverse color and class was nearer than hippies had thought to the unity of self and nature.

At the start, it was frightening to undertake. Finally, it was instructive and exalting. To share *community,* to arrive finally at the meaning of one's own world, was to feel life from a point of view formerly hidden from oneself, and only partly revealed by mystical reading. Self-regulation was more satisfying than regulation by the police, and conformity to enduring objectives more liberating finally than chemical visions.

The hippies patrolled their garbage—the "sweep-in"—and modulated their music. If such acts were this side millennium, they were nevertheless gestures of community reflecting an emergence of the hippies from the isolation of their first two years in San Francisco. Acquaintance with the straight community increased as work and work projects proliferated. Acquaintance produced degrees of trust and accurate identity. Generalizations failed. Not all straights were pure straight, even as hippies differed one from another.

The life of the hippie community began to reveal a history of its own. It had evolved through flight, drugs, and conflict, and back into the straight world, which it now knew in a manner different from before. To direct the Hip Job Co-op, the Free Store, public feedings in the Panhandle, to produce even one memorable edition of the *Oracle* (Volume I, Number 7, preserving the essence of hippie theory in debate among Ginsberg, Leary, Snyder, and Watts) required a pooling of skills, resources, and confrontation with the straight community. It meant, even, coming face to face with the telephone company, and it meant, as well, the ironic recognition that necessary work invited imitation of the very processes hippies had formerly despised. To purchase houses to shelter hippies, food to feed them, required compromise with the community, a show of dependable intentions. In the language of Leonard Wolf, San Francisco State College professor who organized formal instruction among hippies, it required "coming to terms with the ethical quandary of money." Projects with long-range implications, such as the purchase of rural sites for hippie communities, required leadership, planning, authority, discipline, and more or less continuous sobriety.

At some moments the process of learning was almost visible. "The American passion is murder," said a hippie spokesman, challenging a straight audience of physicians, lawyers, teachers, and others, including police officers, to rise and shout him down. None of his listeners betrayed alarm—some feared that his words were too true. "I would like to see the American Establishment give more examples of love, and fewer pronouncements." He appeared suddenly to be aware that he had heard these sentiments before, and indeed it was a complaint some members of the Establishment had made forever and ever. Hippies were scarcely the first to discover hypocrisy.

A hippie said, at the same meeting, "The American empire is driving our sons and daughters to Haight Street. All America knows is profit and property. We all know . . ."—that is, we all just this minute realized; that was to say, *he* just this minute realized—"we all know all we need to know to act, but we don't act. Everyone knows what's wrong . . ." perceiving in that moment a straight community which shared with him, among other things, its powerlessness. It, too, had fought its battles with authority, and he saw it now in its diversity, rather than as monolith.

At such moments of meeting hippies knew sensations of reconciliation and escape from their own isolation. They learned, as American minorities before them had learned, that nothing was more instructive about human life than to have been a minority group, and to have emerged. Acquaintance clarified: straights had not so much opposed drugs or dirt as their inefficiency; runaway children broke real hearts; plagues of rats, by the agreement of mankind, were unaesthetic; straights, too, resisted work, yearned for varieties of love, and found the balance. Frank Kavanaugh, teacher at a Catholic high school, resident of the Haight-Ashbury for fourteen years, summarized the positive aspects of polarization in a public statement widely applauded. He wrote in part:

> I would estimate that even though there have been many unwelcome incidents occasioned by both the old and new community, there has still arisen an area of understanding and mutual appreciation. I would describe it in this fashion. The new community by its rejection of certain middle-class attitudes of comfort, security, position, and property has pointed out to us our exaggerated concern for these material distractions. In their effort to create new life styles based on personalism and simple awareness of the basic joys of sensible creation, they make us more aware of the overlooked pleasures of colors, sounds, trees, children, smiles. Yet I think that they have learned much from us too. They have learned that the neighborhood in which they have chosen to demonstrate their rejection of middle-class conformity is not such

a bad neighborhood after all. If they have been the victims of generalized attitudes by authority, they have also been the perpetrators of generalized attitudes themselves. Not all middle-class people are squares. Generally speaking, upon the close, personal examination of any square by any hippie, the sharp corners soften considerably and the image of a human being appears. . . . Given more time and the absence of undue friction, the dialogue could bear rich fruit. The old and new could form one community, unique and rich in human resources, a community that could demonstrate that such a neighborhood could flourish despite the system; indeed, one that could bear the seed for a joyous revolution of attitudes in the entire city and produce a large urban community based on the real needs of its inhabitants.

The hippies had come for help. The freedom of cities had always attracted a significant segment of every generation seeking to resolve American dilemmas unrestrained by commitments to family obligations in home communities. New York and Chicago had always known waves of hippies fleeing Winesburg, Ohio. In San Francisco, as hippies engaged in public dialogue, they forced the city to examine and modify standing practices. Laws governing marijuana became exposed for their paradoxes. Accurate information on drugs became an objective. Police methods were reviewed. Perhaps the most useful debate involved new and imaginative uses of public facilities: a city which could entertain and amuse immense conventions, sporting crowds, providing for visitors luxurious frivolities of every kind, could, for example, release Kezar Stadium, site of professional football during certain seasons, to the tents of hippies for their "summer of love." Haight-Ashbury Assemblyman Willie Brown, in a letter to the Supervisors, placed in perspective the nature of the conflicting forces: "It appears to me that you are in danger of making a very fundamental mistake concerning both your own identity and that of the young people who are coming to us. *They* are not some horde of invading foreigners. They are our children, yours and mine, exercising their right to move freely about a country which will soon be very much their own. You for your part are not some select group of medieval chieftains who can, at will, close up your town and withdraw behind the walls of your own closed society. The City of St. Francis deserves better from you. Whether we like or dislike, agree or disagree with the 'Hip' community is not the issue here. The issue *is* whether you can by fiat declare a minority unwelcome in our community. If you declare against these young people today, what minority is going to bear the brunt of your discrimination tomorrow?"

THE COP'S DIRECTIVE

Somewhat forgotten among general fears was the hippies' unwavering adherence to the ideal of nonviolence. Miraculously, they retained it in a community and in a world whose easiest tendency was guns. For that virtue, if for no other, they valuably challenged American life. If they did not oppose the war in Vietnam in the way of organized groups, they opposed it by the argument of example, avoiding violence under all circumstances. They owned no guns. By contrast, the manner in which the major Establishment of San Francisco approached the hippies chillingly suggested the basis of American failure abroad: never questioning its own values, lacking the instinct for difficult dialogue, it sought to suppress by exclusion; exclusion failing, it was prepared to call the police.

The trouble on the visual scene was drugs, and drugs brought cops; the trouble was runaway children (some as young as ten years old) lost among hippies, and runaway children brought cops; dirty books brought cops. The trouble was hazardous housing, which brought the health department, and in the wake of the health department, cops.

The trouble with the police, from the point of view of the hippies, was false arrest, illegal arrest, incitement to arrest, cops with swinging clubs, obscene cops diseased by racial hatred, and the tendency of any appearance by police to stimulate excitement where none had been. They accused cops of accepting bribes from drug peddlers and then arresting users, and they singled out a few officers whose zeal for the enforcement of standard morality exceeded reason. The cop was the enemy-visible in a marked car, whom hippies viewed as the living symbol of all the vice and hypocrisy of the Establishment.

The San Francisco cop had never lived in Haight-Ashbury. Now, by and large, he lived in the Richmond, the Sunset, or within the thirty-mile suburban radius established by law, in a house with a patch of grass and a garage with an oil-proof floor he might live long enough to pay for. He earned $9000 for a forty-nine-week year, and he would receive a pension at age sixty-five, or after thirty years of service. He read his Hearst newspaper and watched television and went to church and Candlestick Park. He hated the sound of sirens: his occupational hazard was heart failure at an early age from too many surges of adrenalin.

For the San Francisco cop the sixties had been, said one, "the age of riots," not food riots, not labor strikes, for objectives or upon principles he understood, but disorders emanating from obscure causes and upheld for their justice by those elements of the community the cop had always associated with normal process and quietude. Said the same cop: "I am caught in the bind of history."

The first significant confrontation of the decade between police and the new antagonist occurred on Friday, May 13, 1960, in the rotunda of city hall, where several hundred persons had gathered to attend, in a spirit of protest, a hearing of a House Committee on Un-American Activities. Denied admission to the hearing room, the crowd sang, chanted, and appeared to represent potential violence. Four hundred policemen, a contingent larger than the gathering itself, dispersed the crowd with clubs and fire hoses, jailed more than fifty persons, brought one to trial (a Berkeley student)—and failed to convict him.

But to the astonishment of the cop, in so clear a case, instead of commendation from a grateful public for having quelled a disorder, he was abused for his "brutality." The next day thousands of persons gathered at various points of the city to protest not only the continued presence of the subcommittee, but also the cop, the two causes becoming one. In the years which followed, all issues were to be repeatedly merged with the issue of police action: the cop himself became an issue.

The San Francisco Police Department, between 1960 and 1967, undertook liberal reforms never dramatic enough to please its critics. Its leadership had always been proud of the department's flexibility, its openness to innovation. It was the *servant* of the city. Now, in a new climate, it intended to acquaint itself with new problems, especially the problems of racial or temperamental minorities.

The creation in 1962 of a Community Relations Unit, which grew from two members to thirteen, was an experiment of remarkable promise and frequent achievement. Its goal was to anticipate commotion rather than to react in panic, to understand the aims of dissident groups, and to survey rather than to arrest. The role of the unit was to provide "feedback" between police and public, often by sponsoring or attending public meetings where dialogue might ensue between citizen and cop, who had never before met.

The unit wore no uniform, made no arrests, and identified itself wherever it went. Honorably, it never carried back hard information to the department. It had somewhat the aspect of the intellectual wing of the police, asking *why,* never *who,* though the position was relative, and in the short run it was a long way down the line from the new, informed, even theoretical cop to the rank-and-file cop in the car, riding scared, feeling himself surrounded by alien and sinister forces, feeling eyes of contempt and hatred upon him, anxious for his own safety, and moved finally to rely upon the same old weapons he still treasured above all sociology, all theory, and all goodwill.

He was a better-informed, more feeling cop than he had been eight years before, but he could never quite remain abreast of history. He had learned to accept the aspirations of Negroes, but he was now confronted by hippies, who were patently and undeniably breaking laws for reasons beyond the cop's comprehension. The Beats, who were the forerunners of the hippies, had obstructed the sidewalks of North Beach and offended cops by their strange untidiness, but they had gathered in a traditional bohemian quarter, and they were *beat,* they admitted it, prepared to flee.

The instinct of the cop was ancient: break the law, be punished. Typical of the citizenry of San Francisco, his heart the repository of all populist values, the cop would uphold the law at every stage of its interpretation. In the main, he transcended his emotions. He waited to see whether the hippies would triumph over their visual scene, whether their shift from street to community would occur before the Haight-Ashbury or the city beyond arrived at last at disenchantment. If the Haight-Ashbury abandoned the hippies the mood of the city at large would be released in the direction of his own gut responses. Then the anxiety of the cop would be shared by all powers, the nervous system of the cop, the city, and the Haight-Ashbury would vibrate upon one note. Then the directive of the cop would be clear. Then the cop *would* move in.

The Social History of the Hippies

WARREN HINCKLE

An elderly school bus, painted like a fluorescent Easter egg in orange, chartreuse, cerise, white, green, blue and, yes, black, was parked outside the solitary mountain cabin, which made it an easy guess that Ken Kesey, the novelist turned psychedelic Hotspur, was inside. So, of course, was Neal Cassady, the Tristram Shandy of the Beat Generation, prototype hero of Jack Kerouac's *On The Road,* who had sworn off allegiance to Kerouac when the beat scene became menopausal and signed up as the driver of Kesey's fun and games bus, which is rumored to run on LSD. Except for these notorious luminaries, the Summit Meeting of the leaders of the new hippie subculture, convened in the lowlands of California's High Sierras during an early spring weekend last month, seemed a little like an Apalachin Mafia gathering without Joe Bananas.

Where was Allen Ginsberg, father goddam to two generations of the underground? In New York, reading his poetry to freshmen. And where was Timothy Leary, self-styled guru to tens or is it hundreds of thousands of turned-on people? Off to some nowhere place like Stockton, to preach the gospel of Lysergic Acid Diethylamide to nice ladies in drip dry dresses.

The absence of the elder statesmen of America's synthetic gypsy movement meant something. It meant that the leaders of the booming psychedelic bohemia in the seminal city of San Francisco were their own men—and strangely serious men, indeed, for hippies. Ginsberg and Leary may be Pied Pipers, but they are largely playing old tunes. The young men who make the new scene accept Ginsberg as a revered observer from the elder generation; Leary they abide as an Elmer Gantry on their side, to be used for proselytizing squares, only.

The mountain symposium had been called for the extraordinary purpose of discussing the political future of the hippies. Hippies are many things, but most prominently the bearded and beaded inhabitants of the

Haight-Ashbury, a little psychedelic city-state edging Golden Gate Park. There, in a daily street-fair atmosphere, upwards of 15,000 unbonded girls and boys interact in a tribal, love-seeking, free-swinging, acid-based type of society where, if you are a hippie and you have a dime, you can put it in a parking meter and lie down in the street for an hour's suntan (30 minutes for a nickel) and most drivers will be careful not to run you over.

Speaking, sometimes all at once, inside the Sierra cabin were many voices of conscience and vision of the Haight-Ashbury—belonging to men who, except for their Raggedy Andy hair, paisley shirts and pre-mod western levi jackets, sounded for all the world like Young Republicans.

They talked about reducing governmental controls, the sanctity of the individual, the need for equality among men. They talked, very seriously, about the kind of society they wanted to live in, and the fact that if they wanted an ideal world they would have to go out and make it for themselves, because nobody, least of all the government, was going to do it for them.

The utopian sentiments of these hippies were not to be put down lightly. Hippies have a clear vision of the ideal community—a psychedelic community, to be sure—where everyone is turned on and beautiful and loving and happy and floating free. But it is a vision that, despite the Alice in Wonderland phraseology hippies usually breathlessly employ to describe it, necessarily embodies a radical political philosophy: communal life, drastic restriction of private property, rejection of violence, creativity before consumption, freedom before authority, de-emphasis of government and traditional forms of leadership.

Despite a disturbing tendency to quietism, all hippies *ipso facto* have a political posture—one of unremitting opposition to the Establishment which insists on branding them criminals because they take LSD and marijuana, and hating them, anyway, because they enjoy sleeping nine in a room and three to a bed, seem to have free sex and guiltless minds, and can raise healthy children in dirty clothes.

The hippie choice of weapons is to love the Establishment to death rather than protest it or blow it up (hippies possess a confounding disconcern about traditional political methods or issues). But they are decidedly and forever outside the Consensus on which this society places such a premium, and since the hippie scene is so much the scene of those people under 25 that Time magazine warns will soon constitute half our population, this is a significant political fact.

This is all very solemn talk about people who like to skip rope and wear bright colors, but after spending some time with these fun and fey individuals you realize that, in a very unexpected way, they are as serious about what they're doing as the John Birch Society or the Junior League. It is not improbable, after a few more mountain seminars by those purposeful young men wearing beads, that the Haight-Ashbury may spawn the first utopian collectivist community since Brook Farm.

That this society finds it so difficult to take such rascally looking types seriously is no doubt the indication of a deep-rooted hang-up. But to comprehend the psychosis of America in the computer age, you have to know what's with the hippies.

[KEN KESEY—I]
Games people play,
Merry Prankster Division

Let us go, then, on a trip.

You can't miss the Tripmaster: the thick-necked lad in the blue and white striped pants with the red belt and the golden eagle buckle, a watershed of wasted promise in his pale blue eyes, one front tooth capped in patriotic red, white and blue, his hair downy, flaxen, straddling the incredibly wide divide of his high forehead like two small toupees pasted on sideways. Ken Kesey, Heir Apparent Number One to the grand American tradition of blowing one's artistic talent to do some other thing, was sitting in a surprisingly comfortable chair inside the bus with the psychedelic crust, puffing absentmindedly on a harmonica.

The bus itself was ambulatory at about 50 miles an hour, jogging along a back road in sylvan Marin County, four loudspeakers turned all the way up, broadcasting both inside and outside Carl Orff's Carmina Burana and filled with two dozen people simultaneously smoking marijuana and looking for an open ice cream store. It was the Thursday night before the Summit Meeting weekend and Kesey, along with some 15 members of the turned-on yes men and women who call him "Chief" and whom he calls the "Merry Pranksters" in return, was demonstrating a "game" to a delegation of visiting hippie firemen.

Crossing north over the Golden Gate Bridge from San Francisco to Marin County to pay Kesey a state visit were seven members of The Diggers, a radical organization even by Haight-Ashbury standards, which exists to give things away, free. The Diggers started out giving out free food, free clothes, free lodging and free legal advice, and hope eventually to create a totally free cooperative community. They had come to ask Kesey to get serious and attend the weekend meeting on the state of the nation of the hippies.

The dialogue had hardly begun, however, before Kesey loaded all comers into the bus and pushed off into the dark to search for a nocturnal ice cream store. The bus, which may be the closest modern man has yet come to aping the self-sufficiency of Captain Nemo's submarine, has its own power supply and is equipped with instruments for a full rock band, microphones, loudspeakers, spotlights and comfortable seats all around. The Pranksters are presently installing microphones every three feet on the bus walls so everybody can broadcast to everybody else all at once.

At the helm was the Intrepid Traveler, Ken Babbs, who is auxiliary chief of the Merry Pranksters when Kesey is out of town or incommunicado or in jail, all three of which he has recently been. Babbs, who is said to be the model for the heroes of both Kesey novels, *One Flew Over the Cuckoo's Nest* and *Sometimes A Great Notion,* picked up a microphone to address the guests in the rear of the bus, like the driver of a Grayline tour: "We are being followed by a police car. Will someone watch and tell me when he turns on his red light."

The law was not unexpected, of course, because any cop who sees Kesey's bus just about *has* to follow it, would probably end up with some form of professional D.T.'s if he didn't. It is part of the game: the cop was now playing on their terms, and Kesey and his Pranksters were delighted. In fact, a discernible wave of disappointment swept across the bus when the cop finally gave up chasing this particular U.F.O. and turned onto another road.

The games he plays are very important to Kesey. In many ways his intellectual rebellion has come full circle; he has long ago rejected the structured nature of society—the foolscap rings of success, conformity and acceptance "normal" people must regularly jump through. To the liberated intellect, no doubt, these requirements constitute the most sordid type of game. But, once rejecting all the norms of society, the artist is free to create his own structures—and along with any new set of rules, however personal, there is necessarily, the shell to the tortoise, a new set of games. In Kesey's case, at least, the games are usually fun. Running around the outside of an insane society, the healthiest thing you can do is laugh.

It helps to look at this sort of complicated if not confused intellectual proposition in bas relief, as if you were looking at the simple pictures on Wedgewood china. Stand Successful Author Ken Kesey off against, say, Successful Author Truman Capote. Capote, as long as his game is accepted by the system, is free to be as mad as he can. So he tosses the biggest, most vulgar ball in a long history of vulgar balls, and achieves the perfect idiot synthesis of the upper middle and lower royal classes. Kesey, who cares as much about the system as he does about the Eddie Cantor Memorial Forest, invents his own game. He purchases a pre-40s International Harvester school bus, paints it psychedelic, fills it with undistinguished though lovable individuals in varying stages of eccentricity, and drives brazenly down the nation's highways, high on LSD, watching and waiting for the cops to blow their minds.

At the least, Kesey's posture has the advantage of being intellectually consistent with the point of view of his novels. In *One Flew Over the Cuckoo's Nest,* he uses the setting of an insane asylum as a metaphor for what he considers to be the basic insanity, or at least the fundamentally bizarre illogic, of American society. Since the world forces you into a game that is both mad and unfair, you are better off inventing your own game. Then, at least, you have a chance of winning. At least that's what Kesey thinks.

[KEN KESEY—II]
The Curry Is Very Hot;
Merry Pranksters Are Having Pot

There wasn't much doing on late afternoon television, and the Merry Pranksters were a little restless. A few were turning on; one Prankster amused himself squirting his friends with a yellow plastic watergun; another staggered into the living room, exhausted from peddling a bicycle in ever-diminishing circles in the middle of the street. They were all waiting, quite patiently, for dinner, which the Chief was whipping up himself. It was a curry, the recipe of no doubt cabalistic origin. Kesey evidently took his cooking seriously, because he stood guard by the pot for an hour and a half, stirring, concentrating on the little clock on the stove that didn't work.

There you have a slice of domestic life, February 1967, from the swish Marin County home of Attorney Brian Rohan. As might be surmised, Rohan is Kesey's attorney, and the novelist and his *aides de camp* had parked their bus outside for the duration. The duration might last a long time, because Kesey has dropped out of the hippie scene. Some might say that he was pushed, because he fell, very hard, from favor among the hippies last year when he announced that he, Kesey, personally, was going to help reform the psychedelic scene. This sudden social conscience may have had something to do with beating a jail sentence on a compounded marijuana charge, but when Kesey obtained his freedom with instructions from the judge "to preach an anti-LSD warning to teenagers" it was a little too much for the Haight-Ashbury set. Kesey, after all, was the man who had turned on the Hell's Angels.

That was when the novelist was living in La Honda, a small community in the Skyline mountain range overgrown with trees and, after Kesey invited the Hell's Angels to several house parties, overgrown with sheriff's deputies. It was in this Sherwood Forest setting, after he had finished his second novel with LSD as his co-pilot, that Kesey inaugurated his band of Merry Pranksters (they have an official seal from the State of California incorporating them as "Intrepid Trips, Inc."), painted the school bus in glow sock colors, announced he would write no more ("Rather than write, I will ride buses, study the insides of jails, and see what goes on"), and set up fun-time housekeeping on a full-time basis with the Pranksters, his wife and their three small children (one confounding thing about Kesey is the amorphous quality of the personal relationships in his entourage—the several attractive women don't seem, from the outside, to belong to any particular man; children are loved enough, but seem to be held in common).

When the Hell's Angels rumbled by, Kesey welcomed them with LSD. "We're in the same business. You break people's bones, I break people's heads," he told them. The Angels seem to like the whole acid thing, because today they are a fairly constant act in the Haight-Ashbury show, while Kesey had abdicated his role as Scoutmaster to fledgling acid heads and exiled himself across the Bay. This self-imposed Elba came about when Kesey sensed that the hippie community had soured on him. He had committed the one mortal sin in the hippie ethic: *telling* people what to do. "Get into a responsibility bag," he urged some 400 friends attending a private Halloween party. Kesey hasn't been seen much in the Haight-Ashbury since that night, and though the Diggers did succeed in getting him to attend the weekend discussion, it is doubtful they will succeed in getting the novelist involved in any serious effort to shape the Haight-Ashbury future. At 31, Ken Kesey is a hippie has-been.

[KEN KESEY—III]
The Acid Tests—
From Unitarians to Watts

Kesey is now a self-sufficient but lonely figure—if you can be lonely with dozens of Merry Pranksters running around your house all day. If he ever gets maudlin, which is doubtful, he can look back fondly on his hippie memories, which are definitely in the wow! category, because Ken Kesey did for acid roughly what Johnny Appleseed did for trees, and probably more.

He did it through a unique and short-lived American institution called the Acid Test. A lot of things happened at an Acid Test, but the main thing was that, in the Haight-Ashbury vernacular, everyone in the audience got zonked out of their minds on LSD. LSD in Pepsi. LSD in coffee. LSD in cake. LSD in the community punch. Most people were generally surprised, because they didn't know they were getting any LSD until it was too late. Later, when word got around that this sort of mad thing was happening at Acid Tests, Kesey sometimes didn't give out LSD on purpose, just so people wouldn't know whether they did or did not have LSD. Another game.

The Acid Tests began calmly enough. In the early versions Kesey merely gave a heart-to-heart psychedelic talk and handed LSD around like the Eucharist, which first happened at a Unitarian conference in Big Sur in August of 1965. He repeated this ritual several times, at private gatherings in his home in La Honda, on college campuses, and once at a Vietnam Day Committee rally at Berkeley. Then Kesey added the Grateful Dead, a pioneer San Francisco rock group, to his Acid Tests and, the cherry on the matzos, the light show atmospheric technique of projecting slides and wild colors on the walls during rock dances. This combination he called "trips." Trip is the word for an LSD experience, but in Kesey's lexicon it also meant kicks, which were achieved by rapidly changing the audience's sensory environment what seemed like approximately ten million times during an evening by manipulating bright colored lights, tape recorders, slide projectors, weird sound machines, and whatever else may be found in the electronic sink, while the participants danced under stroboscopic lights to a wild rock band or just played around on the floor.

It was a fulgurous, electronically orgiastic thing (the most advanced Tests had closed circuit television sets on the dance floor so you could see what you were doing), which made psychedelics very "fun" indeed, and the hippies came in droves. Almost every hippie in the Bay Area went to at least one Acid Test, and it is not exceeding the bounds of reasonable speculation to say that Kesey may have turned on at least 10,000 people to LSD during the 24 presentations of the Acid Test. (During these Tests the Merry Pranksters painted everything including themselves in fluorescent tones, and bright colors became the permanent in-thing in psychedelic dress.)

Turning so many unsuspecting people on to LSD at once could be dangerous, as the Pranksters discovered on a 1965 psychedelic road show when they staged the ill-fated Watts Acid Test. Many of the leading citizens of Watts came to the show, which was all very fine except that whoever put the LSD in the free punch that was passed around put in too much by a factor of about four. This served to make for a very wild Acid Test, and one or two participants "freaked out" and had a very hard time of it for the next few days.

After the California legislature played Prohibition and outlawed LSD on October 6, 1966, Kesey wound up the Acid Test syndrome with what was billed as a huge "Trips Festival" in San Francisco. People who regularly turn on say the Trips Festival was a bore: it embodied all the Acid Test elements except acid and, happily for the coffers of Interpid Trips, Inc., attracted a huge crowd of newspapermen, narcotics agents and other squares, but very few hippies. The Merry Pranksters slyly passed out plain sugar cubes for the benefit of the undercover agents.

Suddenly San Francisco, which for a grown-up city gets excited very easily, was talking about almost nothing but "trips" and LSD. Hippies, like overnight, had become fashionable.

If you are inclined to give thanks for this sort of thing, they go to the bad boy wonder of Psychedelphia, disappearing there over the horizon in his wayward bus.

[HISTORIAN CHESTER ANDERSON—I]
The Ghosts of Scenes Past, or
How We Got Here from There
Like Frederick J. Turner and Arnold Toynbee, Chester Anderson has a theory of history. His theory is psychedelic, but that is perfectly natural since he is a veteran acid head. Anderson, a 35-year-old professional bohemian who looks 45, considers himself the unofficial historian of the psychedelic movement and has amassed enough footnotes to argue somewhat convincingly that the past 15 years of social change in the United States—all the underground movements, and a significant part of the cultural changes—have been intimately connected with drugs.

If he is going to press his argument all the way, he may have to punch it out with Marshal McLuhan, who no doubt would assert that such phenomena as hippie colonies are nothing but a return to "tribal" culture, an inevitable reaction to our electronic age. And any social historian worth his salt will put it that every society has found some way to allow the sons and daughters of its middle class to drop out and cut up (most hippies by the way, are from middle class stock, so what's the difference from, say, the Teddy Boys?) Maybe lots, maybe none. But there is no disputing the cultural and artistic flip-flops this country has gone through in the last decade. The jazz musicians' vogue meant something. So did the Beat

Generation. So, we suppose, did Pop Art, and Rock and Roll, and so, of course, the hippies. If, in briefly tracing the derivation of the hippies from their seminal reasons in the intellectual uneasiness of the early 1950's, we chance to favor the testimony of Chester Anderson, it is only because he was there.

That was some bad year, 1953. There was a war on in Korea, a confusing, undefined war, the first big American war that wasn't the one to end all wars, because the aftermath of World War II had blown that phobia. And now the Bomb was with us, and with it the staccato series of disturbing headline events that stood for the Cold War; college was the only escape from the draft, but eggheads were becoming unpopular; Stevenson had lost the election and the Rosenbergs had been executed. It was all gloom, gloom, and dullsville, and if you were young and intellectual you were hard-pressed to find a hero or even a beautiful person. The only really alive, free thing, it seemed, was jazz—and the arrival of the long playing record had sparked a jazz renaissance, and with it the first drug heroes: most kids sympathized with Gene Krupa's marijuana busts, the agony of Lady Day's junk hangup was universal, and Charlie Parker had his own drugstore.

Lady Day's way wasn't the way of the new generation, Chester Anderson will be quick to tell you, because she was on "body" drugs. Whatever else body drugs—heroin, opium, barbiturates, alcohol, tranquilizers—may do, they eventually turn you off, and contemporary heads like to be turned on—i.e., senses intensified, stimulated rather than depressed. "Head" drugs, which do the latter, are both cheaper and easier to get than body drugs, and come in approximately 18 varieties in three different classifications—natural drugs like marijuana, hashish, peyote, morning glory seeds, Hawaiian wood rose seeds, and certain types of Mexican mushrooms; artificial psychedelics like mescaline, LSD, psilocybin and psilocin, and whatever the ingredient is that makes Romilar cough syrup so popular with young heads; and synthetic stimulants which, used in large doses by heads, are known as "speed"—dexedrine, benzedrine and methedrine.

But in the early 1950's there wasn't such a complete psychedelic medicine shelf to choose from, and the culturally disenchanted pioneers who began to settle new colonies in New York's Village and San Francisco's North Beach had to make do with pot. In a climate dominated by Dwight Eisenhower in the newspapers and Ed Sullivan on television, they also began to turn on to the pacifist, humanist philosophies of Asia— particularly Buddhism, most especially Zen—while Christianity as a workable concept became more meaningless, despite the exemplary efforts of such men as Brother Antoninus and Thomas Merton. American churchmen seemed to have neither the patience nor the fortitude to deal with people who were, well, *unsettled*. Folk music, which had been slowly dying, perked up a little, and there was a new interest in fresh, tuned-in poetry. As the '50s approached middle age and McCarthy went on the rampage, the few signs of life in a stagnant society centered around the disoriented peace movement, the fledgling civil rights movement, the young political left, jazz and folk music, poetry and Zen. Most of these followers were, of course, taking pot, while the rest of the country remained on booze and sleeping pills.

(If, in memory of the 85th anniversary of Anthony Trollope's death, we may be permitted an aside to the reader, it would be to say that one of the things that is considered original, but is in fact not, about the hippies is the concept of "dropping out" of society. Without adopting the histrionics of Hogarth crusading against the masses drinking gin, it is true that alcohol is an opiate which serves to help tens of millions of busy businessmen and lethargic housewives to "drop out" of any essential involvement in life and remain political and artistic boors. But alcohol is legal so nobody cares. If pot and LSD were ever legalized, it would be a mortal blow to this bohemia. Hippies have a political posture essentially because of the enforced criminality of their daily dose, and if taking LSD meant no more in society than the commuter slugging down his seventh martini, the conspiratorial magic would go out of the movement.)

Meanwhile, in San Francisco, Allen Ginsberg remembers an evening in 1955 which could stand as well as any for the starting point of what was to become the most thorough repudiation of America's middlebrow culture since the expatriates walked out on the country in the 1930's. The vanguard of what was to be the Beat Generation had gathered at the 6 Gallery on Fillmore Street for a poetry reading moderated by Kenneth Rexroth, a respectable leftish intellectual who was later to become the Public Defender of the Beats. Lawrence Ferlinghetti was in the audience, and so were Kerouac and his then sidekick, Neal Cassady, listening to Michael McClure, Phil Lamantia, Gary Snyder and Philip Whalen read their poetry. Ginsberg was there too, and delighted everyone with a section of the still unfinished "Howl," better known to Beats as the Declaration of Independence.

Two distinct strains in the underground movement of the '50s were represented at this salient gathering. One was a distinctly fascist trend, embodied in Kerouac, which can be recognized by a totalitarian insistence on action and nihilism, and usually accompanied by a Superman concept. This strain runs, deeper and less silent, through the hippie scene today. It is into this fascist bag that you can put Kesey and his friends, the Hell's Angels, and, in a more subtle way, Dr. Timothy Leary.

The other, majority, side of the Beats was a cultural reaction to the existential brinkmanship forced on them by the Cold War, and a lively attack on the concurrent rhetoric of complacency and self-satisfaction that pervaded the literary establishment all the way from the Atlantic Monthly to Lionel Trilling. Led by men like Ginsberg and Ferlinghetti, the early Beats weighed America by its words and deeds, and found it pennyweight. They took upon themselves the role of conscience for the machine. They rejected all values and when, in attempting to carve a new creative force, they told America to "go fuck itself," America reacted, predictably, with an obscenity trial.

The early distant warnings of the drug-based culture that would dominate the Haight-Ashbury a decade later were there in the early days of North Beach. Marijuana was as popular as Coke at a Baptist wedding, and the available hallucinogens—peyote and mescaline—were part of the Beat rebellion. Gary Snyder, poet, mountain climber, formal Yamabushi Buddhist, and a highly respected leader of the hippie scene today, first experimented with peyote while living with the Indian tribe of the same name in 1948; Ginsberg first took it in New York in 1951; Lamantia, Kerouac and Cassady were turned on by Beat impresario Hymie D'Angolo at his Big Sur retreat in 1952. And Beat parties, whether they served peyote, marijuana or near beer, were rituals, community sacraments, setting the format for contemporary hippie rituals.

But the psychedelic community didn't really begin to flourish until late 1957 and 1958 in New York, and for that story we take you to Chester Anderson in the Village.

[HISTORIAN CHESTER ANDERSON—II]
Was the Kingston Trio Really Red Guards?
On Thanksgiving Day, 1957, Chester Anderson was turned on to grass by a bongo-playing superhippie who went by the code name of Mr. Sulks. Grass, if you don't know and don't have an underground glossary handy, is translated marijuana, and from that day forward, Anderson, who once studied music at the University of Miami so he could write string quartets like Brahms, became a professional Turn-On and migrated with bohemia, east to west to east to west, from the Village to North Beach back to the Village to the Haight-Ashbury, where he can be found today—a prototype of the older psychedelic type who mixes with the drifting, turning on kids to form the central nervous system of any body of hippies.

The first psychedelic drug to reach the Village in any quantity was peyote, an obscure hallucinatory cactus bud used by Indians in religious ceremonies. Peyote was cheap and plentiful (it can still be ordered by mail from Laredo at $10 for 100 "buttons") and became highly touted—Havelock Ellis and Aldous Huxley recommended it. The only problem with peyote was that it tasted absolutely terrible, and, as peyote cults sprang up, peyote cookbooks came out with recipes for preparing the awful stuff in ways that would kill the taste. "Man," Chester recalls a head telling him at the time, "if I thought it'd get me high, I'd eat shit." As with most new head drugs, the taking of peyote was treated as a quasi-religious event. The first time Chester took it, he did so with great ritual before a statue of the Buddha.

Peyote was the thing in late 1957, and by the summer of 1958 mescaline, the first synthetic psychedelic, was widely distributed. The heads reacted like unwed mothers being handed birth control pills—they were no longer dependent on nature. Turn-ons could be *manufactured!*

According to Chester's files, LSD didn't arrive in any large, consumer-intended supply in the Village until the winter of 1961–62, and not in the Bay Area until the summer of 1964, but by that time something unusual had happened to America's psychedelic gypsies: they had become formal enemies of the State. Massive harassment by the cops in San Francisco, by the coffeehouse license inspectors in New York, had led the heads and the young middle class types who came in caravan proportions, to test the no-more-teachers, no-more-books way of bohemian life, to view the Establishment as the bad guy who would crush their individuality and spirituality in any way he could. This is the derivation of whatever political posture the hippies have today. It will be significant, of course, only if the Haight-Ashbury scene doesn't go the way of the Beat Generation—assimilated by a kick-hungry society. For the serious, literary Beats, it was all over but the shouting when the Co-existence Bagel Shop became a stop on sightseeing tours.

In 1962, the Village was pulsating with psychedelic evangelism. LSD was so cheap and so plentiful that it became a big thing among heads to turn on new people as fast as they could give LSD away.

Pot, also, was being used more widely than ever by middle class adults, and spread from the urban bohemias to the hinterlands by small folk music circles that were to be found everywhere from Jacksonville, Florida, to Wausau, Wisconsin. At the same time, almost the entire Village was treating LSD like it was a selection on a free lunch counter, and a scruffy folknik called Bobby Dylan was beginning to play charitable guest sets in the Washington Square coffeehouses. "Things," Chester said, "were happening more rapidly than we knew."

What was happening, Mr. Jones, was that folk music, under the influence of early acid culture, was giving way to rock and roll. Rock spread the hippie way of life like a psychedelic plague, and it metamorphosed in such rapid fashion from the popularity of folk music, that a very suspicious person might ask if seemingly safe groups like the Kingston Trio were not, in fact, the Red Guards of the hippie cultural revolution.

There was a rock and roll before, of course, but it was all bad seed. The likes of Frankie Avalon, Fabian and Elvis Presley sent good rock and roll musicians running to folk music. Then absolutely the world's greatest musical blitz fell and the Beatles landed, everywhere, all at once. The impact of their popular music was analogous to the Industrial Revolution on the 19th century. They brought music out of the juke box and into the street. The Beatles' ecstatic, alive, electric sound had a total sensory impact, and was inescapably participational. It was "psychedelic music." "The Beatles are a trip," Chester said. Whether the Beatles or Dylan or the Rolling Stones actually came to their style through psychedelic involvement (Kenneth Tynan says a recent Beatles song "Tomorrow Never Knows" is "the best musical evocation of LSD I've ever heard") is not as important as the fact that their songs reflect LSD values—love, life, getting along with other people, and that this type of involving, turn-on music galvanized the entire hippie underground into overt, brassy existence—particularly in San Francisco.

Drug song lyrics may, in fact, be the entire literary output of the hippie generation. The hippies' general disregard for anything as static as a book is a fact over which Chester Anderson and Marshall McLuhan can shake hands. For acid heads are, in McLuhan's phrase, "post-literate." Hippies do not share our written, linear society—they like textures better than surfaces, prefer the electronic to the mechanical, like group, tribal activities. Theirs is an ecstatic, do-it-now culture, and rock and roll is their art form.

[THE MERCHANT PRINCES—I]
Dr. Leary—
Pretender to the Hippie Throne

The suit was Brooks Brothers '59, and the paisley tie J. Press contemporary, but the bone-carved Egyptian mandala hanging around his neck, unless it was made in occupied Japan, had to be at least 2000 years old. Dr. Timothy Leary, B.A. University of Alabama, PhD University of California, LSD Cuernavaca and 86'd Harvard College, was dressed up for a night on the town, but as his devotees say of this tireless proselytizer of the psychedelic cause, it was work, work, work. Tonight Leary was scouting somebody else's act, a Swami's at that, who was turning on the hippies at the Avalon Ballroom by leading them in an hour-long Hindu chant without stopping much for breath. The Avalon is one of the great, drafty ballrooms where San Francisco hippies, hippie-hangers-on and young hippies-to-be congregate each weekend to participate in the psychedelic rock and light shows that are now as much a part of San Francisco as cable cars and a lot noisier.

This dance was a benefit for the new Swami, recently installed in a Haight-Ashbury storefront, with a fair passage sign from Allen Ginsberg whom he had bumped into in India. The hippies were turning out to see just what the Swami's *schtick* was, but Dr. Leary had a different purpose. He has a vested, professional interest in turning people on, and here was this Swami, trying to do it with just a chant, like it was natural childbirth or something.

The word professional is not used lightly. There is a large group of professionals making it by servicing and stimulating the hippie world—in the spirit of the Haight-Ashbury we should refer to these men as merchant princes—and Timothy Leary is the pretender to the throne.

Dr. Leary claims to have launched the first indigenous religion in America. That may very well be, though as a religious leader he is Aimee Semple McPherson in drag. Dr. Leary, who identifies himself as a "prophet," recently played the Bay Area in his LSD road show, where he sold $4 seats to lots of squares but few hippies (Dr. Leary's pitch is to the straight world), showed a technicolor movie billed as simulating an LSD experience (it was big on close-ups of enlarged blood vessels), burned incense, dressed like a holy man in white cotton pajamas, and told everybody to "turn on, tune in, and drop out."

In case you are inclined to make light of this philosophic advice you should not laugh out loud. Because Dr. Leary is serious about his work, he cannot be dismissed as a cross between a white Father Divine and Nietzsche, no matter how tempting the analogy. He has made a substantial historical contribution to the psychedelic scene, although his arrest records may figure more prominently than his philosophy in future hippie histories.

Since, something like Eve, he first bit into the sacred psychedelic mushroom while lounging beside a swimming pool in Cuernavaca, he has been hounded by the consequences of his act. Since Dr. Leary discovered LSD, he has been booted out of Harvard for experimenting a little too widely with it among the undergraduate population, asked to leave several foreign countries for roughly the same reasons, and is now comfortably if temporarily ensconced in a turned-on billionaire friend's estate near Poughkeepsie, New York, while awaiting judicial determination of a 30-year prison sentence for transporting a half-ounce of marijuana across the Rio Grande without paying the Texas marijuana tax, which has not been enforced since the time of the Lone Ranger.

If he were asked to contribute to the "L" volume of the World Book Encyclopedia, Dr. Leary would no doubt sum up his work as "having turned on American culture," though his actual accomplishments are somewhat more prosaic. Together with Richard Alpert, who was to Dr. Leary what Bill Moyers was to President Johnson, Leary wrote an article in May 1962 in, surprise, The Bulletin of the Atomic Scientists. The article warned that in event of war, the Russians were likely to douse all our reservoirs with LSD in order to make people so complacent that they wouldn't particularly care about being invaded, and as a civil defense precaution we ought to do it ourselves first—you know, douse our own reservoirs—so that when the reds got *their* chance the country would know just what was coming off. It was back to the old drawing board after that article, but Alpert and Dr. Leary made their main contribution to the incredibly swift spread of LSD through the nation in 1964 by the simple act of publishing a formula for LSD, all that was needed by any enterprising housewife with a B-plus in high school chemistry and an inclination for black market activity. Dr. Leary's religious crusade has been a bust, convert-wise, and not so salutary financially, either, so he announced recently that he was dropping out, himself, to contemplate his navel under the influence. It would be easier to take Dr. Leary seriously if he could overcome his penchant for treating LSD as a patent snake-bite medicine.

An enlightening example of this panacea philosophy is found back among the truss ads in the September 1966 issue of Playboy. In the midst of a lengthy interview when, as happens in Playboy, the subject got around to sex, Dr. Leary was all answers, "An LSD session that does not involve an ultimate merging with a person of the opposite sex isn't really complete," he said, a facet of the drug he neglected to mention to the Methodist ladies he was attempting to turn on in Stockton, California. But this time, Dr. Leary was out to turn on the Playboy audience.

The following selection from the interview is reprinted in its entirety. Italics are Playboy's.

Playboy: We've heard that some women who ordinarily have difficulty achieving orgasm find themselves capable of multiple orgasms under LSD. Is that true?

Leary: In a carefully prepared, loving LSD session, a woman will inevitably have several hundred orgasms.

Playboy: Several *hundred?*

Leary: Yes. Several hundred.

After recovering from that intelligence, the Playboy interviewer, phrasing the question as diplomatically as possible, asked Dr. Leary if he got much, being such a handsome LSD turn-on figure. Dr. Leary allowed that women were always falling over him, but responded with the decorum of Pope Paul being translated from the Latin: "Any charismatic person who is conscious of his own mythic potency awakens this basic hunger in women and pays reverence to it at the level that is harmonious and appropriate at the time."

Dr. Leary also said that LSD is a "specific *cure* for homosexuality."

The final measurement of the tilt of Dr. Leary's windmill, his no doubt earnest claim to be the prophet of this generation, must be made by weighing such recorded conversations against his frequent and urgent pleas to young people to "drop out of politics, protest, petitions and pickets" and join his "new religion" where, as he said recently:

"You have to be out of your mind to pray."

Perhaps, and quite probably so.

[THE MERCHANT PRINCES—II]
Where Dun & Bradstreet
Fears to Tread

Allen Ginsberg asked 10,000 people to turn towards the sea and chant with him. They all did just that, and then picked up the papers and miscellaneous droppings on the turf of Golden Gate Park's Polo Field and went contentedly home. This was the end of the first Human Be-In, a gargantuan hippie happening held only for the joy of it in mid-January. The hippie tribes gathered under clear skies with rock bands, incense, chimes, flutes, feathers, candles, banners and drums. Even the Hell's Angels were on their good behavior—announcing that they would guard the sound truck against unspecified evil forces. It was all so successful that the organizers are talking about another be-in this summer to be held at the bottom of the Grand Canyon with maybe 200,000 hippies being-in.

The local papers didn't quite know how to treat this one, except for the San Francisco Chronicle's ace society editor Frances Moffat, who ran through the crowd picking out local socialites and taking notes on the fashions.

Mrs. Moffat's intense interest reflects the very in, very marketable character of San Francisco Hippiedom. Relatively high-priced mod clothing and trinket stores are as common in the Haight-Ashbury as pissoirs used to be in Paris. They are run by hippie merchants mostly for square customers, but that doesn't mean that the hippies themselves aren't brand name conscious. Professing a distaste for competitive society, hippies are, contradictorily, frantic consumers. Unlike the Beats, they do not disdain money. Indeed, when they have it, which with many is often, they use it to buy something pretty or pleasureful. You will find only the best hi-fi sets in hippie flats.

In this commercial sense, the hippies have not only accepted assimilation (the Beats fought it, and lost), they have swallowed it whole. The hippie culture is in many ways a prototype of the most ephemeral aspects of the larger American society: if the people looking in from the suburbs want change, clothes, fun, and some lightheadedness from the new gypsies, the hippies are delivering—and some of them are becoming rich hippies because of it.

The biggest Robber Baron is dance promoter Bill Graham, a Jewish boy from New York who made it big in San Francisco by cornering the hippie bread and circuses concession. His weekend combination rock and roll dances and light shows at the cavernous, creaky old Fillmore Auditorium on the main street of San Francisco's Negro ghetto are jammed every night. Even Andy Warhol played the Fillmore. Although Graham is happy providing these weekend spiritual experiences, he's not trying to be a leader. "I don't want to make cadres, just money," he said. Graham's cross-town competitor is Chet Helms, a rimless-glasses variety hippie from Texas who has turned the pioneer, non-profit San Francisco rock group called The Family Dog, into a very profit-making enterprise at the Avalon Ballroom.

A side-product of the light show dances, and probably the only other permanent manifestation of hippie culture to date, is the revival in a gangbusters way of Art Nouveau poster art. Wes Wilson, who letters his posters in 18, 24 and 36 point Illegible . . . originated the basic style in posters for the Fillmore dances. Graham found he could make as much money selling posters as dance tickets, so he is now in the poster business, too.

The posters, at $1 apiece, as common as window shades in the Haight-Ashbury, demand total involvement from the reader, and are thus considered psychedelic manifestations of the existential, non-verbal character of hippie culture. What's it all about? A shy, bush-bearded and very nice little postermaker named Mouse!, when asked his definition of hippie art, replied:

Haight Street, the Fifth Avenue of Hippiedom, is geographically parallel to Golden Gate Park but several blocks uphill, where rows of half vacant store fronts only indicated the gradual decline of a middle class neighborhood. But all that changed, dramatically, during the past 18 months. Haight Street now looks like the Metropolitan Opera Company backstage on the opening night of Aida. The stores are all occupied, but with mercantile ventures that might give Dun & Bradstreet cause to wonder. Threaded among the older meat markets, discount furniture stores, laundromats and proletarian bars are a variety of leather goods shops, art galleries, mod clothing stores and boutiques specializing in psychedelic paraphernalia like beads, prisms and marijuana pipes, and of course there is the Psychedelic Shop itself.

The Psychedelic Shop is treated as a hippie landmark of sorts, but the Haight-Ashbury scene was percolating long before the Thelin brothers, Ron and Jay, stuffed a disconcertingly modern glass and steel store front full of amulets, psychedelic books, a large stock of the underground press, and some effete gadgetry for acid heads. The hippie phenomena began to metamorphose from a personal to a social happening around the fall of 1965 after the kids at Berkeley turned on to LSD, Ken Kesey started holding Acid Tests, and The Family Dog staged its first dance.

Instrumental in spreading the word was the Chronicle's highly regarded jazz critic, Ralph J. Gleason. Gleason is read religiously by hippies. Besides explaining to the square readers what is happening, he is also the unofficial arbitrator of good taste in the Haight-Ashbury community. Gleason was quick to tell Ken Kesey, in print, when he was out of line, and did the same for Dr. Leary. Gleason's writings tuned in other members of the Chronicle staff and the extensive, often headline publicity the newspaper gave to the hippie scene (Kesey's return from a self-imposed Mexican exile was treated with the seriousness of a reasonably large earthquake) helped escalate the Haight-Ashbury population explosion.

So there is plenty of business for the hippie merchants, but some of them, like the Thelin brothers, are beginning to wonder where it will all lead. At the prodding of the Diggers, the Thelins are considering making the store a non-profit cooperative that will help "the kids get high and stay high" at low cost. They may also take the same steps with The Oracle, the Haight-Ashbury monthly tabloid. The majority of the hip merchants, however, are very comfortable with the ascending publicity and sales, and have as little vision of what they are helping create than did Alexander Bell when he spilled acid on himself.

· · ·

[EMMETT GROGAN—I]
Will the Real Frodo
Baggins Please Stand Up?

Except for the obvious fact that he wasn't covered with fur, you would have said to yourself that for sure there was old Frodo Baggins, crossing Haight Street. Frodo Baggins is the hero of the English antiquarian J.R.R. Tolkien's classic trilogy, *Lord of the Rings,* absolutely the favorite book of every hippie, about a race of little people called Hobbits who live somewhere in pre-history in a place called Middle Earth. Hobbits are hedonistic, happy little fellows who love beauty and pretty colors. Hobbits have their own scene and resent intrusion, pass the time eating three or four meals a day and smoke burning leaves of herb in pipes of clay. You can see why hippies would like Hobbits.

The hustling, heroic-looking fellow with the mistaken identity was Emmett Grogan, kingpin of The Diggers and the closest thing the hippies in the Haight-Ashbury have to a real live hero. Grogan, 23, with blond, unruly hair and a fair, freckled Irish face, has the aquiline nose of a leader, but he would prefer to say that he "just presents alternatives." He is in and out of jail 17 times a week, sometimes busted for smashing a cop in the nose (Grogan has a very intolerant attitude toward policemen), sometimes bailing out a friend, and sometimes, like Monopoly, just visiting. The alternatives he presents are rather disturbing to the hippie bourgeoisie, since he thinks they have no business charging hippies money for their daily needs and should have the decency to give things away free, like The Diggers do, or at least charge the squares and help out the hippies.

Grogan has a very clear view of what freedom means in society ("Why can't I stand on the corner and wait for nobody? Why can't everyone?") and an even clearer view of the social position of the hippie merchants ("They just want to expand their sales, they don't care what happens to people here; they're nothing but goddamn shopkeepers with beards.")

Everyone is a little afraid of Grogan in the Haight-Ashbury, including the cops. A one-man crusade for purity of purpose, he is the conscience of the hippie community. He is also a bit of a daredevil and a madman, and could easily pass for McMurphy, the roguish hero in Kesey's novel set in an insane asylum. There is a bit of J. P. Donleavy's *Ginger Man* in him, too.

A few weeks ago, out collecting supplies for The Diggers' daily free feed, Grogan went into a San Francisco wholesale butcher and asked for soup bones and meat scraps. "No free food here, we work for what we eat," said the head butcher, a tattooed Bulgar named Louie, who was in the icebox flanked by his seven assistant butchers. "You're a fascist pig and a coward," replied Grogan, whom Louie immediately smashed in the skull with the blunt side of a carving knife. That turned out to be a mistake, because the seven assistant butchers didn't like Louie much, and all jumped him. While all those white coats were grunting and rolling in the sawdust, a bleeding Grogan crawled out with four cardboard boxes full of meat.

This was a typical day in Dogpatch for Grogan, who has had his share of knocks. A Brooklyn boy, he ran away from home at 15 and spent the next six years in Europe, working as a busboy in the Alps, and, later, studying film making in Italy under Antonioni. Grogan had naturally forgotten to register for the draft, so when he returned to the United States he was in the Army four days later. That didn't last long, however, because the first thing Grogan had to do was clean the barracks. His idea of cleaning barracks was to throw all the guns out the window, plus a few of the rusty beds, and artistically displeasing foot lockers. Then he began painting the remaining bed frames yellow. "I threw out everything that was not esthetically pleasing," he told the sergeant.

Two days later Grogan was in the psychiatric ward of Letterman Hospital in San Francisco where he stayed for six months before the authorities decided they couldn't quite afford to keep him. That was shortly after an Army doctor, learning of his film training, ordered Grogan to the photo lab for "work therapy." It was a "beautiful, tremendously equipped lab," Grogan recalls, and since it wasn't used very much, he took a picture of his own big blond face and proceeded to make 5000 prints. When the doctors caught up with him, he had some 4700 nine by twelve glossies of Emmett Grogan neatly stacked on the floor, and all lab machines: driers, enlargers, developers were going like mad, and the water was running over on the floor. "What did you do *that* for?" a doctor screamed.

Grogan shrugged. "I'm crazy," he said.

He was released a little later, and acted for a while with the San Francisco Mime Troupe, the city's original and brilliant radical theatre ensemble. Then last fall, when the Negro riots broke out in San Francisco and the National Guard put a curfew on the Haight-Ashbury, the Diggers happened. "Everybody was trying to figure how to react to the curfew. The SDS came down and said ignore it, go to jail. The merchants put up chicken posters saying 'for your own safety, get off the street.' Somehow, none of those ideas seemed right. If you had something to do on the streets, you should do it and tell the cops to go screw off. If you didn't, you might as well be inside."

Something to do, to Grogan, was to eat if you were hungry, so at 8 p.m., at the curfew witching hour, he and an actor friend named Billy Landau set up a delicious free dinner in the park, right under the cops' noses, and the hippies came and ate and have been chowing down, free, every night since. The Haight-Ashbury has never been quite the same.

[EMMETT GROGAN—II]
A Psychedelic
"Grapes of Wrath"

Every bohemian community has its inevitable coterie of visionaries who claim to know what it is all about. But The Diggers are, somehow, different. They are bent on creating a wholly cooperative subculture and, so far, they are not just hallucinating, they are doing it.

Free clothes (used) are there for whomever wants them. Free meals are served every day. Next, Grogan plans to open a smart mod clothing store on Haight Street and give the clothes away free, too (the hippie merchants accused him of "trying to undercut our prices"). He wants to start Digger farms where participants will raise their own produce. He wants to give away free acid, to eliminate junky stuff and end profiteering. He wants cooperative living to forestall inevitable rent exploitation when the Haight-Ashbury becomes chic.

Not since Brook Farm, not since the Catholic Workers, has any group in this dreadfully co-optive, consumer society been so serious about a utopian community.

If Grogan succeeds or fails in the Haight-Ashbury it will not be as important as the fact that he has tried. For he is, at least, providing the real possibility of what he calls "alternatives" in the down-the-rabbit-hole-culture of the hippies.

Grogan is very hung up on freedom. "Do your thing, be what you are, and nothing will ever bother you," he says. His heroes are the Mad Bomber of New York who blissfully blew up all kinds of things around Manhattan over 30 years because he just liked to blow things up, and poet Gary Snyder, whom he considers the "most important person in the Haight-Ashbury" because instead of sitting around sniffing incense and talking about it, he went off to Japan and became a Zen master. "He did it, man."

This is an interesting activist ethic, but it remains doubtful just what the hippies will do. Not that many, certainly, will join Grogan's utopia, because utopias, after all, have a size limit.

The New Left has been flirting with the hippies lately, even to the extent of singing "The Yellow Submarine" at a Berkeley protest rally, but it looks from here like a largely unrequited love.

The hip merchants will, of course, go on making money.

And the youngsters will continue to come to the Haight-Ashbury and do—what?

That was the question put to the hippie leaders at their Summit Meeting. They resolved their goals, but not the means, and the loud noise you heard from outside was probably Emmett Grogan pounding the table with his shoe.

The crisis of the happy hippie ethic is precisely this: it is all right to turn on, but it is not enough to drop out. Grogan sees the issue in the gap "between the radical political philosophy of Jerry Rubin and Mario Savio and psychedelic love philosophy." He, himself, is not interested in the war in Vietnam, but on the other hand he does not want to spend his days like Ferdinand sniffing pretty flowers.

This is why he is so furious at the hip merchants. "They created the myth of this utopia; now they aren't going to do anything about it." Grogan takes the evils of society very personally, and he gets very angry, almost physically sick, when a pregnant 15-year-old hippie's baby starves in her stomach, a disaster which is not untypical in the Haight-Ashbury, and which Grogan sees being repeated ten-fold this summer when upwards of 200,000 migrant teenagers and college kids come, as a psychedelic "Grapes of Wrath," to utopia in search of the heralded turn-on.

The danger in the hippie movement is more than overcrowded streets and possible hunger riots this summer. If more and more youngsters begin to share the hippie political posture of unrelenting quietism, the future of activist, serious politics is bound to be affected. The hippies have shown that it can be pleasant to drop out of the arduous task of attempting to steer a difficult, unrewarding society. But when that is done, you leave the driving to the Hell's Angels.

Black Is Beautiful, Baby

A Library of Negro History

C. VANN WOODWARD

Of the current need for Negro history—the writing, the teaching, and the learning of it—there can be no reasonable doubt. The old history, what there was of it, and whether it was written by whites or blacks, needs revising in the light of new knowledge. There is reasonable excuse for the lack of African history, so much of which is buried in the preliterate tribal past. But large numbers of people of African blood now live in the New World with an experience developed in the full light of modern history. The denial of their rightful place in American history and the neglect and distortion of their own history are largely due to their former slave status and to the fact that the "Negro history" that white men read was written by other whites.

The demand for Negro history is therefore legitimate. But the fulfillment of the need will not be instant, the learning of the history painless, or the content of it exclusively or predominantly glorious. The meaning of such history—its "lessons"—will not always be clear. Its pages are likely to be tortured with ambiguities and doubts and enigmas as ironic and inglorious as the Poor Peoples Crusade of 1968, and there will be chapters crowded with charlatans, knaves, and rakehells. The Father Divines and Daddy Graces will outnumber the Martin Luther Kings. Even the most glorious heroes—a Nat Turner, perhaps—may turn out to have moments of hesitation and dubious encounters that the more pious biographer would prefer to skip. Which is only to say that it will be human history.

The most important response so far to the demand for Negro history

Originally appeared as "The Hidden Sources of Negro History," January 18, 1969, *Saturday Review*. It was written as a review of the Arno Press Negro History series. Copyright 1969 by Saturday Review, Inc. Reprinted by permission of C. Vann Woodward and Saturday Review, Inc.

is the forty-four-volume series entitled, "The American Negro: His History and Literature" published by the Arno Press and *The New York Times.* The character of the books chosen and the prices charged for them, if nothing else, put this particular enterprise beyond suspicion of vulgar commercialism. It is a serious effort to meet a legitimate need. It is not popular history. It belongs in the scholar's library rather than the activist's. Those who raise the loudest demand for "black studies" will rarely bury themselves in these volumes, and they are not likely to burden the shelves of the average Muslim temple or organizer's pad.

It is not easy to characterize a series that includes so many varieties and categories of literature. Given the prevalence of autobiography and reminiscence, the historian would classify the series broadly under "source materials," but that would not take care of several works of scholarship, journalism, and polemics that are included. In spite of the promise implied by the subtitle "History and Literature," only one volume, *The New Negro,* edited by Alain Locke in 1925, includes any poetry, fiction, or drama. (We are assured that the second series has a more literary emphasis.) All the volumes are reprints, apparently done by a photo-offset process that reproduces illustrations fairly well.

The problem is that reprinting a book, especially one long-forgotten, inevitably implies a sort of endorsement. Without scholarly guidance, the uninformed reader is likely to be unintentionally misled. Too many volumes in this series run that risk. In all but five volumes, the only contribution made by the editors is a brief one-to-two-page introduction to each volume that can do little more than identify the author.

Roughly three-quarters of the books reprinted deal with slavery and its aftermath, which means they are concerned with the middle third of the nineteenth century. Given the importance of the period and the subject, this is a natural emphasis. The selection of books, however, and the period of their origin reflect some of the present-day motivation and interest in Negro history. Much of it is history with a purpose—polemical, philopietistic, and uncritical. It is valuable to the historian, but often misleading as history.

Unfortunately, there are no slave reminiscences that go back to Africa, such as those recently reprinted by the Wisconsin University Press. The only African experience is found in *Captain Canot, or Twenty Years of an African Slaver* (1854). The Captain's memoirs illustrate the intractability of historical documents, for he was as genial and impenitent a pirate as ever sailed the Spanish Main, blithely persuaded that he was doing the Africans a jolly good turn with a free ride to the New World.

One large and important category of Negro writings, the fugitive slave narrative, is represented by nine autobiographical works. Five of the shorter ones, including some of the better accounts, such as those of Lunsford Lane and William W. Brown, are bound in one volume. The classic of the genre and one of the classics of American autobiography is Frederick Douglass's *My Bondage and My Freedom.* Some scholars prefer the first and smallest of his three autobiographies, but I think this,

his second, published in 1855, is the wiser choice. If I were forced to recommend one volume above all others in the series, *My Bondage* would
be the choice. It contains more insights into the nature of slavery and
slave society than any other book I know of that is written from the slave's
point of view. Douglass does not stop at recording his sufferings and his
protest, as most of the slave authors do. He analyzes perceptively what
slavery did to children, mothers, and fathers of slave families, and what it
did to drivers, overseers, masters, and their families. Along with the work
of his white Southern contemporary George Fitzhugh (not represented
here, of course), Douglass's book marks the beginnings of a sociology of
slave society.

The only class of literature in which white authors in any number are
represented in the series is the one dealing with the anti-slavery movement. Garrison's *Thoughts on African Colonization* (1832) marks the break
of young radicals from the conservative colonization movement. Lydia
Maria Child in *An Appeal in Favor of That Class of Americans Called
Africans* (1836) makes a comparative study of slavery to indict her country and explores anthropology to defend black Americans from racial
bigots. One of the most striking defenses of the enslaved race made during the slavery period was *The Condition . . . of the Colored People*
(1852) written by Martin R. Delany, "this most extraordinary and intelligent
black man," as Lincoln described him. It was an excellent idea to revive
his book. From the white side and the inside of the abolitionist movement,
Samuel J. May's *Recollections* (1869) provides an informal history of the
crusade against slavery.

In addition to anti-slavery polemics, ideology, and history, there is a
great mass of anti-slavery propaganda. It could not be better represented
than by the most famous and influential example, *American Slavery As It Is*
(1839), the work of two South Carolina aristocrats, the Grimke sisters,
and Angelina Grimke's husband, Theodore Dwight Weld. They faithfully
followed the advice of a friend who urged that atrocities "which are
merely *horrid* must give place to those which are absolutely diabolical."
The book was intended to make people fighting mad about the horrors
of slavery. It did. It still can. It was superb propaganda, and no historian
can ignore it. But there is a difference nonetheless between history and
propaganda.

No aspect of the anti-slavery crusade has stirred the American imagination more deeply than the romantic and fabled Underground Railroad.
That story is the subject of three massive volumes of this series. Two of
them are written by participants and may be considered "documentary."
William Still, son of ex-slave parents, kept full records of the Philadelphia
Vigilance Committee for helping fugitive slaves in the 1850s and published
them in his 800-page book, *The Underground Railroad* (1872). The stories
he preserved of hundreds of fugitives are personal, detailed, and circumstantial, and with due allowance for the human proclivity for making a
good story better, they can be read with profit. Almost as bulky are the
Reminiscences (1876) of Levi Coffin, a North Carolina Quaker who moved

to Illinois, and, according to the subtitle of his book, became "The Reputed President of the Underground Railroad." His stories are fascinating, and considering the memory handicaps of their eighty-seven-year-old author, they are also worthwhile reading.

The third contribution on this subject is by a professor of history with all the claims to authority his profession lends. Professor Wilbur H. Siebert, who published his *Underground Railroad* in 1898, formulated the remarkable theory that age improves rather than impairs a man's memory. He interviewed hundreds of aging abolitionists in the 1890s and made their reminiscences the substance of his history. The passage of half a century had not dimmed the heroism, the glamour, and the conspiratorial daring and mystery of their youthful exploits. It did seem to enhance the role of noble white benefactors at the expense of the daring fugitives and their black friends in the North, who incurred the main risks and did most of the work. A recent monograph has pointed out that Siebert contributed more to myth and legend than history.

The most legendary and controversial figure in abolitionist annals is John Brown of Harpers Ferry fame. Of the two score or more biographies of Brown, the series reprints the one by Richard J. Hinton published in 1894. Hinton was an associate of Brown during the latter's Kansas exploits, and the biography is a eulogy and a defense. The present editor admits that "it was not intended as purely disinterested history." James C. Malin, the only professional historian who has tackled the subject, goes further to issue "a warning to those uninitiated in the propaganda of the John Brown legend" that Hinton manipulated evidence irresponsibly and played fast and loose with the truth. *Caveat emptor.*

Neglect of the important part played by black Americans in the Civil War has been partly remedied by modern historians. They owe much to the work of early Negro writers whose books are known only to a few specialists. An impressive example is *The Black Phalanx* (1888) by Joseph T. Wilson, a veteran of the Union Army who writes of the Negro soldiers and their war. Two volumes by Negro women enrich the story. Susie King Taylor's charming *Reminiscences* (1902) includes an account of her service as an army nurse and teacher. Of greater historical significance is *Behind the Scenes* (1868), the memoirs of Elizabeth Keckley, seamstress for the wives of Jefferson Davis and Abraham Lincoln. She admired both men. Her candid and intimate stories of four years in the White House and her association with Mary Lincoln make excellent reading.

Long known to specialists and deserving a much wider public is *The Facts of Reconstruction* (1913) by the distinguished mulatto Congressman from Mississippi, John R. Lynch. Part memoir and part history, it demolishes battalions of popular and scholarly myths concerning the politics of Reconstruction and the nature of race relations in Mississippi. It is especially recommended to prematurely aging freedom riders and civil rights crusaders. As an exemplary prototype of the latter from the 1860s, Elizabeth Hyde Botume should have special appeal and sober instruction for white crusaders of the 1960s. Her *First Days Among the Contrabands*

(1893) recounts her missionary and teaching experiences among the ex-slaves of the Port Royal Experiment in the South Carolina sea islands. Another crusader, with a larger ego, Thomas Wentworth Higginson has left his account in *Cheerful Yesterdays* (1899).

A rather welcome contrast to the melancholy memoirs encountered so far is *The Life and Adventures of Nat Love* (1907). An unabashed rogue and tall-tale teller, Nat Love, self-styled "Deadwood Dick," was the black cowboy who integrated the Wild West in the 1870s and 1880s. A dead shot—by his own account he "never missed anything" and "defeated all comers in riding, roping, and shooting"—he enjoyed watching "painted savages" and "dirty Mexicans" bite the dust as much as any white marksman and consorted with the murderous Billy the Kid in integrated drinking and shooting situations. As an anticlimax to his Wild West career, he settled down as a prosperous Pullman porter.

Missing from this library of Negro authors are any books of the two most notable figures of the black elite, Booker T. Washington and W. E. B. DuBois, both of whom were prolific writers. Both are readily available in existing editions, which accounts for their absence here. On the other hand, their followers and opponents are well represented. Booker Washington wrote an introduction to the autobiography of Mifflin Wister Gibbs, *Shadow and Light* (1902). Gibbs operated on many fronts: in the Far West as a businessman, in Arkansas as a judge and politician, in the Orient as a U.S. consul. His motto was: "Labor to make yourself as indispensable as possible in all your relations with the dominant race," but he did speak out against injustice and discrimination.

Born in slavery, T. Thomas Fortune became a peppery and extraordinarily adaptable journalist intellectual. As editor of the leading Negro paper of the 1880s and 1890s, he shifted from DuBois radicalism—anticipated in his *Black and White* (1884)—to Washingtonian conservatism after 1895, and wound up as editor of Marcus Garvey's black nationalist *Negro World*. Garvey's black separatism, the doctrine that inspired by far the greatest upheaval of black nationalism in our history, is embodied in the Jamaican's *Philosophy and Opinions* (1923), edited by his second wife. In this strange book Garvey acknowledged his affinity with Booker Washington as well as his differences. DuBois, of course, rejected Garveyism.

Washington enjoyed the support of a brilliant defender, Kelly Miller, who was the author of two volumes bound as one in this series, *Race Adjustment* (1908) and *The Everlasting Stain* (1924). It is incredible that he could have written so eloquently on lynching and still have declared in 1908: "We are in the midst of an era of good feeling." Kelly considered the Negro "a great storehouse of conservatism," but admitted in the 1920s that had Washington lived, "he would not be able to hold the Negro to his avowed doctrine of prudential silence on the issue of manhood rights."

The Harlem Renaissance of the 1920s is treated by three able Negro writers. James Weldon Johnson, with a distinguished writing career already behind him, began his *Black Manhattan* (1930) with a running history of Negroes in New York City, beginning in 1626, when the black population numbered eleven. He is concerned throughout this informative volume with the Negro in the arts, especially the theater, and more than half the book is devoted to the 1920s. Back in the days when Harlem was an enthusiasm instead of a fighting word, Johnson reminds us that for Negroes it had "better, cleaner, more modern, more airy, more sunny houses than they had ever lived in before." In its heyday, Harlem was "known in Europe and the Orient, . . . talked about by natives in the interior of Africa," and celebrated as "exotic, colorful, and sensuous; a place of laughing, singing, and dancing; a place where life wakes up at night." He knew the seamier side, but the side he exhibits with love and warmth is not that of Malcolm X. "Gaity is characteristic of Harlem," he wrote.

One is grateful for the samplings of poetry, fiction, drama, music, painting, design, and criticism that Alain Locke rounded up in *The New Negro: An Interpretation* (1925) as the fruit of Harlem at its peak. Time has been kinder to the poetry than to the fiction and drama, but it all breathes the excitement of the moment. "Cultural adolescence and the approach to maturity," Locke called it. The mood was naïve and nostalgic. It was still a time when James Weldon Johnson could apostrophize: "O Southland, dear Southland," and Locke could boast that "a leaven of humor, sentiment, imagination and tropic nonchalance" attributed to the South was the gift of the Negro. Cynicism and hate were kept at bay, he thought, by "a truly characteristic gentleness of spirit." It all seems long ago.

Roi Ottley's book, *New World A-Coming* (1943), brings us closer to the dreadful present, but stops short of it in spirit. Ottley's Harlem, pictured in a jaunty but not imperceptive journalism, was that of the Depression, the abode of Father Divine and Daddy Grace, of Madame C. J. Walker, the hair-straightening millionaire, of Joe Louis and Langston Hughes. But Adam Clayton Powell was already on the scene, and the riot of 1935 had already taken place. No later period is covered by books of the series. Again, the reason is to be found in their general availability.

Negro scholarship in history and sociology is represented by several volumes. The weightiest by far, and in many ways the most impressive, is really twelve monographs bound together. These studies of the Negro's social problems, published between 1896 and 1914, were done at Atlanta University by students and staff of W. E. B. DuBois. All but two were edited by him. Covering such subjects as urban life, church, family, crime, and morals, they avoided politics, civil rights, and sexual race relations as "too controversial." Crude by modern standards, they were probably unsurpassed in their own period, for they were pioneering new ground and setting the pace for a new field of study. This was a "first" for Negro scholarship that deserves acknowledgement. A more advanced piece of work was *The Negro in Chicago* (1922), done by a commission nearly half of whom were Negroes. A forerunner of the recent Kerner Report, it was a comprehensive study of the anti-Negro riot of 1919 and its background.

Three important and expensive volumes of this library are entirely for the scholar—for reference and research rather than for reading. Indispensible for any historian, is the huge *Negro Population, 1790–1915,* originally published by the Bureau of the Census in 1918. Since 90 per cent or more of the Negroes lived in the South during most of this period, the volume is concerned mainly with this area. Its statistical essays, tables, and maps are the starting point for Negro history. Until more competent dictionaries of Negro biography replace it, William J. Simmons's 1,100-page *Men of Mark* (1887) remains, for all its shortcomings, a standard reference. Of more limited interest but more permanent significance is the *Proceedings of the Constitutional Convention of South Carolina* (1868). With its Negro majority, the Reconstruction convention wrote the first democratic constitution of the state, a constitution unchanged until 1895, and then only to deny its benefits to a majority of the state's citizens, the blacks.

One of the most admirable decisions the editors made was to reprint George W. Williams's huge two-volume *History of the Negro Race in America.* Williams was the father of Negro history and his book, published in 1883, is a monument in American historiography. The rhetoric will sometimes jar modern readers, for he has leaders "consumed with the sacred fires of patriotism," and God giving "all the races of mankind civilization to start with." But those are the shortcomings of the times rather than the man. George Bancroft could write such things in the same period.

What is impressive about Williams is his sense of the high seriousness of his calling. "Not as the blind panegyrist of my race," he wrote, "nor as the partisan apologist, but from a love for *'the truth of history,'* I have striven to record the truth. . . ." The true correction of bias and prejudice and distortion in Negro history is not eulogy and apology and panegyrics, but rather the spirit that informed the work of George Williams.

The Case
for a
New Federalism

W. H. FERRY

Earlier this spring the National Advisory Commission on Civil Disorders shook the nation briefly with its findings on the turmoils in the Negro areas of American cities—blacktown. The Commission's report sternly and definitely pins the donkey's tail on white racism, where it belongs. Its accounting of deprivation, despair, and frustration is unsparing. Its castigation of anachronisms like the welfare system and harsh police practices is overdue. Its recommendations take note of the fateful paradox of so much want and suffering in an unimaginably rich society. It has a deeply felt sense of urgency. Yet the report misses the point, and misses it quite badly. The Commission ascribed the riots to neglect, poor education, lack of jobs, advertising-stimulated expectations, and many other familiar results of white racism and white-directed culture. All these factors doubtless played their part. But a far more important force was the explosive renascence of the idea of black manhood, of black dignity and worth, of the black's desire finally to run his own affairs.

I regard this welling-up within the black psyche as a permanent force in our national life and a matter for great rejoicing. There is little explicit discussion of such issues in the report, and unhappily the Commission takes a foreboding view of these first flickerings of what is surely an American enough impulse to be independent, to play the part of citizen not serf, to be responsible for one's own actions and institutions. Thus the Commission's findings in this regard emerge as warnings against "two societies, separate and unequal."

The Commission took too limited a view of the consequences of white racism, seeing its corrosive force mainly at work in school systems, job markets, and the like. But the real corrosion is of the spirit, and psychic reparation is far harder to effect than physical renovation. In short, I fear the Commission here betrayed, first, its inexpungible whiteness and, second, its lack of political vision. It was unable to imagine a new and mutually beneficial relationship between black and white which would not be either integration or apartheid.

In his assignment to the Commission, President Johnson asked what could be done to prevent it from happening again. By "it" the President meant racial rebellions, and he rightly hopes that such bloody and ignominious displays can be averted or diminished in fury. But to me "it" means essentially the black assertion of self and the black's desire not to see himself as an imitation white, or a psychological cripple, or an invisible man. My hope is that this "it" will not be prevented but encouraged.

Finally, there are the Commission's expensive, numerous, and occasionally unorthodox recommendations. I have no objection to the costs involved, nor to novelties, such as the guaranteed income, which is among the more sensational proposals. I object to the *spirit* of the recommendations, for, by and large, it is the old spirit of what "we" must do for "them" written in boxcar figures.

This misdirected spirit derives, naturally enough, from the Commission's failure to make the proper assessment of the causes of the riots. With a few inconspicuous exceptions—such as more federal money for small loans in the ghetto and the creation of "community service officers" to help police black streets—the recommendations amount to *more* administration of blacks by whites, to more benevolence ministering to helplessness, thereby missing the core of the issue. As I see it, the issue is the creation of a new kind of coexistence between blacktown and whitetown.

It is widely surmised that for various reasons few of the Commission's recommendations will be adopted. I agree. I also think it is possible that a miracle of social regeneration could be achieved, probably at less cost than that envisioned by the Commission, if whitetown and its public authorities would take intelligent heed of the message that the blacks are semaphoring, and with political inventiveness help them toward independence of person and institution. But this, clearly, is not to be, in the discernible future at any rate. So we must look forward to more and greater national shame.

What whitetown evidently believes *will* work is austerity, counsels of patience, and guns. Congressmen, doubtless with the approval of their constituents, commented variously that there isn't enough money to do what the Commission advised, and that the pre-eminent need anyway is law and order. At best, we can hope for far too little far too late, and that little administered in the wrong way. This looks to me like a certain prescription for more blood and carnage, and perhaps even civil war.

Blacktown, to be sure, wants more of everything this nation offers: more education, health care, decent housing, economic opportunity, mobility. These can be supplied by whitetown, though not on the terms conceived by whitetown's leaders. But what blacktown *most* wants, whitetown cannot confer. Blacktown wants independence and the authority to run its own affairs. It wants to recover its manhood, its self-love, and to develop its ability to conduct a self-reliant community. In the best of times it no longer wants whitetown's patronizing customs and benign guidance; nor in the worst of times will it suffer whitetown's neglect and humiliations. It wants the experience of self-reliance, that highest of whitetown's virtues, with all its satisfactions and pains. Blacktown does not want to withdraw from the American way, but to enter it for the first time. It does not care to be victimized by whitetown's magnanimity any more than by its machine guns. It wants to develop its own culture—a "culture that is more moral in terms of human relationships than that of the rest of society," in the words of Oscar Brown, Jr. In short, blacktown is expressing aspirations for its own community.

These are not un-American ideas. They are the mirror image of the drive that lies behind whitetown's multitude of villages, school districts, sewer authorities, and other local organizations—the drive to self-rule and self-development. Yet somehow blacktown's claim to its share of self-government is regarded on the white side of the tracks as something foreign and threatening. Even the white liberals, of whom better might be expected, show an almost universal misapprehension about the cries going up from blacktown.

I do not have much hope that whitetown will soon get the reasonableness of the message that is being flashed at it so imperatively by blacktown. But perhaps, given much more time than I think we in fact have, some modest experiments in coexistence may bring whitetown away from its fears and dependence on anti-riot laws and rifles.

Coexistence primarily calls for maximum feasible participation by blacktown, minimum participation by whitetown. Let blacks do it themselves. Let them choose their own leaders. Don't try to run things. Stay away until you are invited, and go away when you have provided whatever it is that you can offer blacktown. Don't offer advice unless you are asked for it. You may know a lot—but you do not know about blacktown and its way of doing things. Throw away the requirements and conditions, the police records, the credit ratings, the performance charts, and efficiency tests that whitetown depends on. They have nothing to do with the case in blacktown. Push neither strings nor friendship at blacktown: it is suspicious of both. Trust young people, for the rising generation is blacktown's saving remnant.

It is no easy thing to organize a polity, and the emerging polity of blacktown faces formidable complications. As I have indicated, one of the principal complications will be whitetown's insistence on "keeping a hand on things," whether this hand appears in the form of traditional conditions imposed on the use of funds or as the paternal direction and overseeing of black enterprises. A more subtle complication will be whitetown's obsession with efficiency. A good deal of inefficiency must be expected and tolerated. So will many mistakes and failures. Blacktown will fall off its new bike many times before it learns to ride; but it will never learn to ride with someone always holding on. The fierce desire to forge its own successes and to be allowed to cope with its own mistakes is, I believe, the principal thing that whitetown must learn to understand and encourage.

The most comprehensive possibilities lie in adapting the corporation to the political structures of blacktown. If authority is to be transferred formally from whitetown, there must be a live institution to receive it. The neighborhood corporation is already in action—in Bedford-Stuyvesant, New York, in Columbus, Ohio, and a few other places. As our industrial and financial history shows, the corporation is capable of limitless forms and variations. The same versatility can, given the will, find expression in neighborhood corporations. They can be organized to exercise political authority, to channel funds, to undertake a great many of the tasks that confront a reconstituting blacktown.

Theories and models of neighborhood corporations have been worked out, notably by Milton Kotler, of the Institute of Policy Studies in Washington, D.C. These adaptations can in some places be put into action forthwith. In some states and municipalities, enabling legislation is needed. The greatest value of the neighborhood corporation is as an instrument for accepting political obligations on one hand and for enhancing political participation on the other. For, in simplest terms, the residents of the neighborhood are the stockholders. There is little novelty in this scheme except in the name; all cities and most towns are also corporations, chartered by the state.

The major difference between the ghetto and the rest of America is that its residents are effectually outside the economic machine. New means of moving private and public capital into blacktown must be devised. The economic apparatus of whitetown, as it now operates, cannot meet the needs—it simply is not geared to the tasks.

The aim of those blacks espousing social and economic independence is peoplehood, dignity, and participation in the American system on new terms. They see they cannot take part on equal terms: apart from social inequalities, it is a simple fact of ghetto life that little capital is available for home purchase or setting up small businesses or cooperatives. Chattel loans available to blacktown's residents are by convention usurious and harmful. Not much attention has been given to this aspect of the ghetto dilemma. World Bank machinery is an analogue to the kind of very large public financial institution that may be needed to deal with the numerous billion-dollar renovations that are due in blacktown. Such a new institution is also the likeliest way to get "risk capital" to the growing number of blacks wishing to establish their own enterprises.

This kind of capital is of prime importance as blacks move toward some kind of self-sufficiency. "One's own business" is a major demonstration of the American economic system. Blacks want this demonstration in their own community. The unavailability of capital to aspiring blacks is a matter of bitter record: exorbitant interest; giving up the big "piece of the action" —a 51 per cent or greater share in the enterprise being established— meeting whitetown standards of loan qualifications at banks or savings and loan associations, which, by definition, few ghetto residents are able to do.

There seem to be many possibilities in tax-exempt foundations, set afloat and financed by white businessmen (contributions deductible), which would make low-interest, long-term loans to potential young businessmen and organizers of blacktown cooperatives, without requiring either security or a "piece of the action," only a showing of competence and earnestness on the part of the applicant. Their central contribution would be a revolving loan fund for ghetto businesses and cooperatives, periodically replenished by deductible contributions from the white business community, providing funds that will be *made available but not supervised* by the donor.

A coalition of Protestant, Roman Catholic, and Jewish leaders has announced its intention to raise $10,000,000 "to help black Americans develop political and economic power." The plan was accepted tentatively by blacks in Detroit, on condition that it be "made available to the black community to use as it sees fit." This is coexistence being worked out in a nontheoretical and pragmatic way, though no one can guess how it will turn out, for only $90,000 of the $10,000,000 is yet in hand.

There are doubtless many such schemes to be canvassed, as there are variants of the World Bank idea. All ought to be examined, for a great many connecting links between the white and black communities are going to be needed in the economic field. Executives of the large corporations that are now operating uneasily in the ghettos should be encouraged to reassess their policies with a view to enabling far more participation by blacktown in their work at all levels. This means fresh attitudes not only toward all-black staffing but toward ultimate sharing in the business itself.

A very few undaunted corporations have already stepped into this chancy new world with undertakings that aim finally at ghetto ownership and in the meantime at black management. These include ingenious corporate schemes by E.G. & G., Inc., in Roxbury, Massachusetts; Aerojet General and its Watts Manufacturing Company; AVCO, also in Roxbury. All have discarded precedent; all are coping steadily with the novel challenges of industrial coexistence.

A few things must be said about those forms of corporate intervention in blacktown that are workable and desirable and those forms that are not. The problem is not jobs at all costs and under any conditions. Blacktown is going to be more and more canny and farsighted and self-interested about the source of its jobs than ever before. Benevolent whites were startled when the residents of Watts said recently that they wanted no part of an industrial park in their city. To the benevolent white an industrial park looked like a humming job market. To residents of Watts it looked like another generation of dirty, low-paying, and uncertain jobs. The ownership of the factories would be light-miles away and likely to close up shop for bad reasons and good. Watts had experienced this before, had called it exploitation, and decided it wanted no more of it.

The terms of corporate participation in blacktown are still being worked out by the pioneers. They are unlike contracts that corporations usually agree to. The management of the corporation settling down in blacktown must be black from top to bottom. From the outset the aim must be ultimate black ownership. The financial terms must be long and easy. The jobs must be of a kind that the average resident of blacktown can perform; and if he cannot at first perform them, the corporation must be willing to train him. The corporation must plan on years in the red, and many failures and frustrations, on much seeming ingratitude on blacktown's part, on many difficulties with its stockholders. It is important to view these tentative expeditions into blacktown as something really new in corporate operation, not a mere variation. Widespread adoption of this approach by large corporations—black management, black jobs, ultimate black ownership—could turn out to be the private sector's single greatest contribution to peaceful coexistence. But there are so many things against it that one should not expect much more than a few experiments of the kind already described.

Turning to the political area, I think that there will certainly be transfers of authority to blacktown. The terms of these transfers are important political questions. The authority that is transferred has to operate. Welfare and police and public works departments will have to function. Educational systems will have to be maintained. So I suggest the need for teams of experts, most of them white, who will be on call as the black community struggles to organize its own private and public operations. The questions are manifold. What is the best way to mobilize the experience and expertness that the white community has in abundance but which is in very short supply in the ghetto? What is the proper attitude of such visiting experts? Is providing teams of experts an appropriate function for a chamber of commerce, a foundation, a university, a municipality?

The old go-betweens between blacktown and whitetown have lost much of their usefulness. The new relations between black and white require a new style of diplomacy which is still very much in the making. The hearty, liberal "we are all brothers" approach is outmoded, especially with the younger blacks. Hostility and distance are showing up everywhere, even on Ivy League campuses. Needless friction might be avoided by creating schools for diplomats, for the training of those who will work in this highly charged area of constant negotiation between the two communities. Whites will have trouble treating blacks as equals, and vice versa. As Hazel Stewart observes, "Every black person in this society lives in an alien world."

I see nothing wrong, finally, in the idea of turning over control of blacktown's education to its residents. This is too big and complicated a proposition to argue here. But blacktown seems to have more concern about the education of its children than about any other issue. This feeling must be respected. Coexistence between school systems in blacktown and whitetown is perfectly feasible, even if difficult to arrange at first. It is also very long overdue. White efforts to come to terms with the dead ends of blacktown education have been energetic failures. Even respectable white scholars show themselves congenitally incapable of understanding or even seeing black participation in the history of this country.

I bring this list of desiderata to an end with a category that might be called extravagances and improbabilities. Land reform in blacktown is as logical as it is in Colombia and Vietnam and perhaps just as urgent. This would mean the acquisition of large amounts of property by the federal government, by purchase or condemnation if need be, and getting it into the hands of ghetto inhabitants by lease, gift, or loan. The unlikelihood of such a program does not need to be pointed out. Here, as at all other places, white racism stands squarely across the path. Yet I see no other way, within a reasonable time, to enable blacks to share in the wholesome satisfaction of owning a bit of property of one's own.

It is clear that the agenda for development of workable black polities will be challenging, requiring the minds and hands of hundreds of thousands and calling forth inventiveness at every level. Most of what I have said has to do with a plan for coexistence from whitetown's side of the fence. But such a large effort would perforce have to be accompanied by constructive activity of an even more intense kind in blacktown. It is no secret that the ghetto at this point is scarcely ready to take up its share of the complicated burdens of building a community. What is more needed than anything else is an all-black think tank devoted wholly to the problems and possibilities of the emerging black communities—a center for the study of black institutions. There is already a considerable stir. CORE has announced a novel multimillion-dollar development scheme in Cleveland. Variations of this idea are in motion elsewhere, with the initiative often arising in blacktown. Self-reliance and independence are moving through the ghetto's damaged arteries like a fever.

When the Reverend Albert Cleage turned down $100,000 from well-meaning Detroiters because there were white strings on the grant, he provided millions of dollars worth of pride and self-confidence to blacktowns everywhere. It *is* possible to reject the white man's benevolence!

It is clear, I think, that few of my suggestions are new. A year ago Arthur Waskow proposed several of the measures I have listed. Foundations and corporations and cultural centers and self-help plans in generous variety are afoot. We hear little about them, thanks to the inclination of the mass media to see blacktown only as a source of trouble and danger. But many things are happening there which lack only the appropriate machinery and resources from whitetown. It seems to me that whitetown's worries about rebellions and civil disorder would evaporate once blacktown's residents become engrossed in the problems of building their community on a fresh and exciting base. What would there be to riot about?

A successful plan for coexistence will not bring utopia into being in blacktown. Autonomous, interdependent blacktown will be no better and no worse than other parts of the urban scene. Blacks can be expected to exploit blacks, even as whites exploit whites. There will be bankruptcies aplenty, as there are along Main Street. There will be quarrels and walk-outs and demonstrations and the inevitable ambiguities about leaders and leadership. There will be personal scandals and misuse of money and authority. Whitetown will be accused of parsimony and trying to control things even if it enters into the scheme of coexistence with the best possible intent. There will even be times, I imagine, when blacktown will wish that it had never opted for the adventure of self-rule.

So the vision of coexistence is not that of the New Jerusalem, nor is it that of a national community struggling with the untenable doctrines of integration. It is a vision of a new federalism that will give 10 per cent of our citizens the chance they are seeking to make whatever they want to make of themselves, their culture, and their community.

The New
Black Myths

PETER SCHRAG

The rush is on. Come and get it: Afro-Americanism, black studies, the Negro heritage. From Harvard to Ocean Hill, from Duke to Madison Avenue, they are trying, as they say, to restore the Negro to his rightful place in American history and culture; black (and white) intellectuals, scholars, teachers, politicians, hustlers busy with black restoration. The spirit is upon them, the writers and publishers, the polemicists and pushers, and the implications are enormous. But the richest soil is education, the schools and colleges, and the processes of growing up in which they're involved.

The academy is an obvious mark because it is an accessible purveyor of culture, because it tends to be guilt-ridden anyway, and because it has apparently failed black children not only in its practice but in its mythology. The school was supposed to offer—had claimed it could offer—equality, democracy, and opportunity. Instead what it provided was selectivity; it selected people in, and selected them out. By and large, black people were selected out, not because the school was independently discriminatory, but because it offered and gave what the society asked. When finally we looked inside the little black box—the mystique of education and advancement, the mystique of academic standards and professionalism—it turned out to be empty. If teachers and schools knew anything about teaching anybody (which is an open question) they plainly knew little about teaching people who did not already belong to the middle class or who refused to conform to its culture.

Black restoration was not invented inside the schools, but the intellectuals have taken it up, the students are promoting it, and the academics are debating it. Moreover, it is—for better or worse—accessible to every amateur. The line between history and mythology is indefinite, but where the first is at least theoretically subject to disciplinary standards, the latter is not. Any number can play.

Black studies can have just as much legitimacy as anything else; if Harvard has a program on East Asia or Latin America, why not Africa? If American Negro experience has been left out of American history courses —as it has—then surely it should be restored. But the significance of black restoration—even aside from its separatist extremities (the establishment of an independent black state in America, for example)—has greater and more ambiguous implications. Is the American Negro, by whatever name, an American or an African, the heir of a separate culture, or the most indigenous of citizens? Is fiction or music produced by American Negroes uniquely a product of black experience or of an "African heritage," or is it, like all art, dependent on styles and materials from every conceivable source and tradition? Is there white art and black art in America, or just art? Is the Negro experience on this continent more significant for its uniqueness or for its human universality? "I am proud to be black," writes the sixth-grade kid in Harlem. "Say it loud: 'I am proud.'" Here it is, a response to a pile of clichés and labels, a response that may mean something, or that may be just another cliché, this one more vicious because it promised more.

For three hundred years one of the black man's problems in America has been growing up—to be a man but not a white man, to be a woman but not a chattel, to be black and visible as a complete human being. The hackneyed descriptions of self-hate and childishness may be partly the fantasy of intellectuals who are shocked that Negroes don't behave like college professors, yet clearly the price of admission to the white world has been self-denial and the willingness to play one of the stock parts by which the white world justified its own discrimination. Little Black Sambo, Uncle Tom, Uppity Nigger, House Nigger, Bourgeois Black, the urban poor. And in school, the culturally deprived, the disruptive child, "black but *bright*." Clearly all Americans have had similar problems—to grow up, to establish an adult identity on one's own terms. But it is, nonetheless, a special problem for anyone born black, and it has, in recent years, been magnified—even glorified—by the growing consciousness of the subtleties of polite discrimination.

"Each generation," wrote the Negro psychiatrists William H. Grier and Price M. Cobbs, "grows up alone." The past, it is said, exists, but it has been erased from memory, devalued, lost, and denied—denied often by the most well-meaning and liberal of Americans. Is a black man anything but a white man incomplete? Other ethnic groups seem to have the armament of a unique history and tradition—or simply the tradition of the "West"—to carry them into the mainstream. In a sense the Negro has always been in that mainstream—as a slave and servant who knew the master better than the master knew himself—but always as a Negro who could never quite aspire to full citizenship as a valid social protagonist. He was often the carrier of the culture, or even its creator: in music, in patterns of speech, in the cadences of a whole region that resented his blood but talked more of his language than it ever cared to admit. Here was the waiter who determined the appropriate status of the guests and placed them at tables according to *his* assessment of *their* merits; here was the maid who knew the secrets of the household, its triumphs and scandals; there the musician who gave his art and style to generations of white performers but never, until recently, shared in the recognition. Here was a whole race that had walked through all the rooms of the white culture but had never been allowed through the front door. The problem for the Negro was that his culture and his life became too much mainstream, that it was hard to distinguish what he had done and what he had absorbed, but that it was always easy to distinguish *him* by the color of his skin.

James Baldwin once referred to himself as a "bastard of the West." There was no full citizenship—and no recognized tradition—for the black man in America, yet there was no other place to go either.

> When I followed the line of my past [Baldwin wrote] I did not find myself in Europe but in Africa. And this meant that in some subtle way, in a really profound way, I brought to Shakespeare, Bach, Rembrandt, to the stones of Paris, to the cathedral of Chartres, and to the Empire State Building, a special attitude. These were not really my creations, they did not contain my history; I might search in them in vain forever for any reflection of myself. I was an interloper; this was not my heritage. At the same time I had no other heritage which I could possibly hope to use—I had certainly been unfitted for the jungle or the tribe. I would have to appropriate these white centuries, I would have to make them mine—I would have to accept my special attitude, my special place in this scheme—otherwise I would have no place in any scheme. . . .

Baldwin's problem was, and still is, the problem of every black person in America—and certainly of every black child in school. Was there a way to succeed in America without denying one's own blackness, to make it *regardless* of (not in spite of) one's negritude? Was there a black identity beyond the limited roles that the official world allowed? One could always hustle the world, could con it, or adopt some form of Tomism, but was there a way of really making it without pretending that one was white?

Almost every black writer in America has been preoccupied with this question, yet until recently it remained in the realm of literature. It was something that came from the imagination, and therefore wasn't quite real. Perhaps such a problem doesn't in fact exist until someone can invent a language—an imaginative form—to describe it. In this sense, then, it always remains a literary problem and the response, whether it is a child's poem or a professional's novel, is a rhetorical response. Nonetheless, the literature, and the vast amount of derivative material coming from the mimeograph machines, are expressing a new set of attitudes, giving shape to a new style of personal and political behavior, and shaping the content and practices of education. There are reasons for what that child in Harlem wrote, for the fact that there are public schools teaching

Swahili, and that Malcolm X is an appropriate figure for public school commemoration.

In the past decade, perception of the Negro problem has moved in two directions: on the one hand, it has become pop sociology; on the other, it has been incorporated into a new mythology. The first is the rhetoric of the matriarchal family, the lack of father figures, the passion for a "relevant curriculum"; the second, the growth of a world of African culture, black pride, and black power. Preston Wilcox, who has been an intellectual spokesman for the black school movement (and is now chairman of the Association of Afro-American Educators), recently declared:

> The surge to restore the Black community in intellectual, psychological, physical, social, economic, and political terms is taking place in the form of a cultural revolution at the doorstep of the traditional Little Red Schoolhouse from which Black Americans have been planfully excluded. This culturally radical effort forces one to view the Black Restoration Movement as a nation-building activity—a process designed to build into the instinct and habit systems of Black people a need to view the many pieces of the struggle as a single conceptual response to white America's design to turn Black people away from their African heritage—and their historic charge to *figuratively* return to Africa to join in the liberation struggle of Black people around the world.

Examine the language: Black Restoration, nation-building activity, the figurative return to Africa. With the exception of Marcus Garvey and his African nationalists, no American has ever talked this way before. Black Americans are not to invent an identity, or to regard themselves as complete Americans and fight for a place within the prevailing culture, they are to restore, to return, to reclaim the things that America has taken away.

The compelling central figure in this drama is not the bourgeois manager negotiating with the Establishment for more jobs or for a civil-rights law, nor even a Christian martyr, but a street fighter, a hustler, a high-style liver who masters the adversities on his own terms, the man who synthesizes new meaning from familiar experience. Martin Luther King still wins the polls as "a great Negro leader," but it is the gut fighters who command the imagination. King was the ultimate Southern preacher, the man who used traditional materials—the cadences of the prayer meeting, the imperatives of the Christian witness, the moral confrontation—and improvised a new style. Suffering promised salvation even to the oppressor. His style was Baptist, Southern, and rural. The new figures are urban. They begin as compromised individuals, men who have not simply been victimized as Negroes, but who have, often joyously, participated in the underworld of the ghetto. Men like Eldridge Cleaver, Claude Brown, and Malcolm X may never become mythic heroes, but their experiences on the city streets, however untypical, are now closer to home than those of the Southern plantation. (For certain intellectuals, black and white, they may also be a way of identifying with—and romanticizing—the poor.)

The prophetic hero is Malcolm X, the man who solved the riddle of blackness, and—apparently—grew up. Other Americans had come from the depths of the common black experience, had been corrupted by the white culture, and had risen above it. Malcolm did not invent the new cosmology—black power, black is beautiful, think black—or the mystique of Africanism. As he tells it in the *Autobiography,* it was all revealed to him, first in prison, and later on a visit to Mecca. But it was Malcolm who delivered it to the world, who spread the gospel:

> "You don't even know who you are," Reginald [his brother] had said. "You don't even know, the white devil has hidden it from you, that you are of a race of people of ancient civilizations, and riches in gold and kings. You don't even know your true family name, you wouldn't recognize your true language if you heard it. You have been cut off by the devil white man from all true knowledge of your own kind. You have been a victim of the evil of the devil white man ever since he murdered and raped and stole from your native land in the seeds of your forefathers. . . ."

All these revelations amounted to a religious experience, a transformation that he likened to the experience of St. Paul hearing the voice of Christ on the road to Damascus. What Malcolm heard was a coherent legend—a myth of plunder and conspiracy—that matched any classic tale of creation. The story came from Elijah Muhammad, the patriarch of the Muslims, whose servant Malcolm later became. According to the story, which runs for three pages in Malcolm's *Autobiography,* the first humans were black, among them the tribe of Shabazz from "which America's Negroes, so-called, descend." Among them was born a mad scientist named Mr. Yacub who was exiled with his followers. In his hatred toward Allah, Mr. Yacub created a white devil race which enslaved black men and turned what "had been a peaceful heaven on earth into a hell by quarreling and fighting." The story prophesied that this race would rule the earth for six thousand years and would then destroy itself. At that time the non-white people would rise again. That time was now at hand.

Malcolm eventually broke with Muhammad, and he repudiated the devil theory, but the story symbolizes the senses of racial theft that enrages the black teachers and intellectuals who are articulating the objectives of black schools and black culture. If Ben Franklin and Horatio Alger symbolized the mythology of the traditional American school—the school of hard work crowned by worldly success—Malcolm is coming to share with them a rhetorical and symbolic role in the ghetto school run by blacks. The significance of the mythology is not in its blackness, and certainly not in its disdain for hard work—Malcolm was as much of a Puritan as any Yankee schoolmarm—but in its apparent capacity to organize ghetto experience against the bankrupt claims of the official system. As a symbolic representation—a fantasy and a projection—it provides a rationale for the pursuit of African history and culture, for African dress and hair styles, and for the passionate search for history and tradition. If much of that history has to be created or magnified, if petty chiefs are being elevated into great kings, if obscure tinkerers are growing into great scientists, that does not fully obviate the validity of the myth or the needs it fulfills. Rather it enhances them. Every travesty of scholarship conducted in the name of African culture reflects a corresponding travesty in the name of American history and civilization.

At the heart of that mythology, however, lies a naïve faith in some sort of collective identity, and in the magical transformation that will produce it. That faith grows partly out of intimidation—intimidation, that is, by the self-congratulatory declarations of groups which have made it—and partly out of the bewilderment of a misunderstood and largely illusory failure. It assumes, for example, that the Negro is not an American, is, indeed, not much of anything, a sort of cultural savage who was stripped of his inheritance and given little in return. In its most primitive form—in its blackest versions—the myth depicts the white man as a thief who stole everything he has, whose economic and political power was achieved at the expense of the Negro. The Negro, in other words, was not merely a slave in America, he was the prime source of the white man's wealth. But in seeking to emulate other ethnic groups, even the sophisticated black nationalist who knows economic history better than to ascribe all American wealth to slavery—even he remains the victim of the white man's sociology. The Jews made it—according to the current notion—because they came to America with cultural traditions and an ethnic cohesiveness that provided identity and a basis for collective action. The Negro in this vision is still an immigrant; he, too, will make it by reclaiming his immigrant's baggage and starting the process of acculturation all over again. By going back, back, back into some sort of primordial past, into the African kingdoms, to ancient Egypt, even to the beginnings of human life (which, we are now told, can be placed in Africa), the Negro will find himself and achieve the power to be personally and socially effective.

This is confusion confounded. Malcolm never shed his innocent's belief that in some Eastern or African state, in some distant land, men had achieved the ability to live together in harmony without friction or exploitation. His narrative of the royal treatment he received from Arabian sheiks and African politicians is the story of a hustler pushing the golden elixir, a hipster's version of the promised land. In his exotic descriptions of his pilgrimage to the East, there is never a suggestion that Arabia is still a feudal state which exploits its underclass as ruthlessly as any society on earth and whose record of slavery is unmatched in human history. For Malcolm, the Middle East was a blessed society of mutual respect, racial brotherhood, and personal dignity, and American civilization was feudal and corrupt.

The American myth has, in effect, been turned inside out, but it is still the American myth. Malcolm, in his last years, shed his Muslim preoccupations and his mystical racism. But he never resolved his ambiguities about American values. Nor did he fully come to understand either his own Americanism or what it means to be an American Negro. Every black Peace Corps volunteer in Senegal or Tanzania has discovered that in every respect that matters he is not an African come home, but an American abroad. The nationalist still imagines that he can will himself into an African, and that by so doing, he can become what in nineteenth-century romantic thought was described as the American Adam, the new man, free from the corruptions of the old world (then Europe, now America), who, in a new Eden (then America, now a country still to be imagined) could build a world untainted by sin. The African mythology, rather than affirming the Negro's American identity, rather than glorifying it, wants to strip him of it.

The black drive for recognition and the pressure for the institution of black forms—African and American—is riven with inconsistencies and ambiguities. It wants to send the American Negro on two symbolic trans-atlantic voyages when he probably has no need to make even one. At the same time it is divided between the urge to foster an indigenous Afro-American culture and its passion to give Negroes the power and possibilities to control Western institutions, technology, and culture. To deny anyone the opportunity to learn Swahili may well be parochial or even racist; but to demand—in the name of black power—that Swahili be taught is to ask a luxury that few people—white or black— can afford. This is not to say that the search for the black past and for the legitimate recognition of the black present is worthless. It means only that it is misdirected and still too much subject to the implications of white supremacy.

What the nationalists want to do with the schools is simply to replace white boredom with black. They have, of course, every right to ask for it. It is no more damaging to fall asleep over Benjamin Banneker, Crispus Attucks, and the kingdoms of the Nile than it is over Thomas Edison, Sam Adams, and the tariff of 1820. But in doing it the nationalists are confusing symbol and substance and aping those forms and styles that constitute the weakest elements of the existing system. In one breath they have declared the prevailing American myth a sham; in the next they have adopted it, colored it black, and labeled it good. Scratch African national-ism just a little bit, and it comes out American: puritanical, messianic, and bourgeois. Deep inside him, Malcolm was a cross between the Ben Franklin of hard work and thrift, the George F. Babbitt who knew that it paid to advertise, and the Calvinistic moralist decrying the decline in values. Without knowing it, Malcolm, too, was a bastard of the West. A school run largely on his ultimate premises—and there are not likely to be many—would make any Yankee schoolmaster proud.

Which is not to denigrate the idea of black power, only to redefine and liberate it from the pursuit of a false ethnic model. A disproportionate number of Negro intellectuals—and black militants—are bemused by Jews. Because the entire mythology of urban education and ethnic cohesiveness is saturated with Jewish examples, and because in New York the schools are predominantly Jewish, that bemusement is understandable. The Jews used the schools, why shouldn't the Negro? The Jews have Israel, why shouldn't the Negroes have Africa? If the Jews relied on their old-world culture to propel them into the mainstream of America, why not the Negroes? The American Negro, in other words, is supposed to turn himself into an African so that he can become a Jew and thereby transform himself into a WASP.

It may well be true that the Jews were more successful than most ethnic groups in using the schools to gain advancement. Yet clearly that success—of whatever degree—was based on the character of the cultural content of Jewish tradition and not simply the existence of a culture. To the extent that they succeeded in the public schools, the Jews—and especially the European Jews—were superbly matched to the demands and style of their teachers and curriculum. The tradition of education, and the respect for teachers and learning was, in most instances, reinforced by the sense of mercantile values. Both coincided with the values and aspirations of the schools. The Jews were qualified bourgeois clients for bourgeois education. That those schools also happened to be Protestant—with "nondenominational" prayers and hymns and Protestant teachers—merely reinforced ethnic and religious cohesiveness and provided enough discrimination to motivate the recruits.

Most other immigrant groups did not use the schools for advancement into the mainstream. Irish or Italian power was exercised through the Church, the political ward, and a vast array of semi- or non-skilled political or commercial occupations, some of them of doubtful legality. Neither the Italians nor the Irish brought any great passion for intellectual attainment. Most of the Italians were southern villagers among whom there was no ideology of change. "Intellectual curiosity and originality were ridiculed or suppressed," wrote Nathan Glazer in *Beyond the Melting Pot*. " 'Do not make your child better than you are,' runs a south Italian proverb." And while the Irish dutifully sent their children to school (often to parochial school), they rarely expected the school to do much more than enforce standards of discipline, order, and morality.

The historical precedents for black power are, therefore, not educational but political; ethnic pride and cohesiveness manifested themselves in political activity or in social and commercial associations, but they were antithetical to the educational practices and mythology of the schools. Even when the schools recognized ethnic distinctions, they usually did so in terms of condescending clichés: Italian grocers, Chinese laundries, Jewish tailors, and all the rest. In many instances, the best the schools ever did for any real display of cultural individuality was to treat it as quaint, and the frequent result was that children of immigrant parents were embarrassed by the customs and manners of their elders.

Black power, despite its mythological overtones, is more like Irish or Italian power than Jewish power. Though its prime objective in the cities includes the schools, the most immediate results are likely to be political and not educational. What it contains in educational or cultural theory—leaving aside its African mystique—is not very far from the mainstream.

At the same time, restoration of some form of political ward system (which, after all, is what local control resembles) may be the most effective route of entry into the mainstream. The schools and social services generally (welfare, social work, poverty programs) are the major growth areas in the social economy today.

The claims of black or community power for school control are, needless to say, perfectly legitimate, not because they necessarily promise educational superiority, but because in the American political tradition public institutions are presumably controlled by the people they serve. When a black community leader declares that a particular public school is "our school," he is speaking as an American, not as an educational theorist. To oppose colonialism, after all, is not necessarily to be an African. "We are," said a Negro who was demonstrating for local control, "like Boston Tea Party Indians."

What the black experience can bring to the classroom and to the educational process (in black schools as well as white) is its own passion, its own humanity, its own techniques for survival in a society that threatens increasingly to make every individual invisible. There is no necessity to make a virtue of suffering, or to romanticize the glories of Negro survival under brutalizing conditions. The image of the ubiquitous plantation revolutionary—every man a Nat Turner—is as sentimental as the mythology of the happy slave. Stereotypes, it seems, always tend to breed counter-types. Nonetheless, there is hardly any argument against the assertion—the fact—that the Negro's life in America and his accumulated experience and passions represent something that demands recognition, something that this society and especially its schools desperately needs.

The trouble with the conventional school is not its failure to credit the achievements of "great Negroes"—one sees their pictures pinned to every wallboard of every black school in America: King, Thurgood Marshall, Dr. Charles Drew, William H. Hastie, Baldwin—but its failure to recognize the cultural and social importance of the Negro experience. The pictures on the wall (or the names in the book) affirm that a bunch of black guys, given a chance, can do as well as whites in the white man's game. And surely this is important. But perhaps it is equally important—more important—to indicate that some whites, if they work hard at it, are almost as good as blacks as jazz musicians, dancers, athletes, and human beings; that, indeed, there are whites who believe as fervently in justice as blacks. Which is to say that the schools might begin to consider the question of whether the many things to which they now pay only lip service may not be of greater value than the things they actually practice and reward. Where is the school that regards the arts, music, literature on a par with formalized and routinized operations of the three R's, and that upholds the graces of civilized life—good food, good stories, personal and moral courage, and political and legal justice—with the rhetoric of petty bourgeois life: thrift, punctuality, conformity? In this respect, it is not the bourgeois character of the schools that can and should be altered, but their pettiness. What they lack is the sense of high purpose. They suffer, in short, from an historic innocence. Yes, they are out of place, but they are also out of time and out of mind. They exist in a middle world like prisons, police stations, and penal colonies—are, in a sense, part of a world that is neither black nor white, neither modern and technological, nor traditional and humane. If they are irrelevant to the Negro, it is not simply because they are missing the peculiar idiom of the ghetto, because they deal in white picket fences and green lawns while their pupils know only tenements and asphalt. It is because they don't deal in the fundamentals of life at all: birth, death, love, violence, passion; because they don't recognize the morality or the brevity of human existence; because, in their passion for fundamentals they miss the elemental: the tragic, the heroic, the beautiful, the ugly. And it is in these things that the Negro and his experience may have far more to ask, far more to contribute.

> That man [wrote Baldwin] who is forced each day to snatch his manhood, his dignity, out of the fire of human cruelty that rages to destroy it, knows if he survives his effort, and even if he does not survive it, something about himself and human life that no school on earth—and indeed, no church—can teach.

And indeed, these cannot be taught, they can only be learned, yet clearly they can be part of the ethos in which schools and teachers operate. The schools can recognize that singing the blues is not an aberration, but a universal condition.

Dialogue Concerning the Two Chief World Systems

Student Power: The Rhetoric and the Possibilities

CHARLES FRANKEL

It has finally come to be accepted that American colleges and universities are in trouble. The questions about them mount in number: Who is to blame for the disruptions and ugly incidents that have left American campuses disturbed? Is it the students? The administrations? The police? Why are the young so angry, and what do they want anyway? Why are the old so dim-witted, and why do they resist change and progress? But the answers to these questions will not tell us what is wrong with American higher education, or what principles should be employed in setting about to improve it.

No reforms can be discussed intelligently unless we take the phrases that are now dominating discussion—"student rights," "student power," "participation," "democracy," "a relevant education," and all the rest—and ask seriously what they mean, and what assumptions are behind them. For it is astonishing how little genuine public discussion there has been of such matters and how little of what has been said has gone beneath the surface of slogan and generality. People have used words to show on which side of the barricades their loyalties lie. But little has been said that suggests that possibly the answers do not all fall neatly on one side of the fence or the other. It is remarkable how many learned men there are, men who enjoy the ambiguities of John Donne's poetry or who spend their lives refining the refinements of Wittgenstein's philosophy, who nevertheless sail into the middle of social controversies with all their answers ready and all their powers of qualified judgment put aside.

Designing a university is not, after all, a form of action-painting. Nor is it a matter of setting forth broad general principles and reasoning deductively from them, so that one is invariably in favor of "student power" or opposed to it, on the side of "university democracy" or against it. General principles are relevant to what one thinks about such matters, but specific problems differ, and the application of these general principles, in consequence, cannot always be the same.

The obvious place to begin is with the concept of "student power." What does the phrase mean? Before we talk about the reforms for which the phrase stands, we should recognize that it also gives a good description of a fact that has long existed. This fact is that students are not only the objects of education, but its principal instruments. An institution and its faculty can provide facilities, stimulation, some guidance and orientation, a sense of standards and of models to emulate. But the primary environment for the student is other students. They set the pace for one another; they have more to do than any other group in the university with what the student pays attention to from day to day; they do much of the teaching that counts.

Moreover, students also have great influence on the evolution of educational theory and practice. They have not, in the past, voted on curricula or met with the faculty in formal sessions. Just the same, they have had an effect—like the effect of the climate—on curriculum, the character of the teaching staff, the rules of campus life, and the composition of future student bodies. General education was for a long time, for example, an exciting and viable part of the curricula of many undergraduate institutions. Increasingly, over the past decade or so, there have been countercurrents. And the largest reason has been that students have changed. They come to college differently and better prepared than their predecessors, or with more highly developed interests in specializing, or with greater impatience to get on to vocationally useful subjects. The colleges have responded to these new attitudes because inattention or resistance in the classroom requires a response.

The power that students have should not, of course, be exaggerated. It works slowly. It is small comfort to a young man or woman to know that, four or five years after he or she has left the university, the dear, slow thing with catch on and mend its ways. And not only is the power that students have slow in achieving an effect, but it is limited. Other sources of power and influence work on a university, as they should, and students do not get everything they want, even slowly. Yet the influence of students, limited though it may be, is nevertheless real and significant. If one has a long enough time-span in mind, students exercise an influence as large as any other group's in bringing about alterations in higher education.

Thus, the question raised by present demands for student power is not really whether students should finally be given the right to say something about what happens to them. It is whether it would be educationally desirable to create arrangements permitting students to participate more visibly and formally in the making of educational decisions. Considered as a general proposition, there can be little doubt, I think, that this is the direction in which change should proceed.

The most important reasons are drawn from educational and democratic theory. If people have some power over the way in which they live and work, they have more interest in their experience, and they learn more from it. If they have some power, they tend to become more responsible. They are more likely to make the connections between ideas and action, rhetoric and reality, that are at once the tests and the pleasures of the moral life. These propositions have been tried in other fields and found to have a substantial amount of truth in them. They have not been tried to the extent that they could be in higher education.

But these are generalities. They tell us about a desirable direction of change. They do not tell us how far the change should go, or if there are any areas in which it should not take place at all. When we get down to brass tacks, what can "student power" mean?

Should students, for example, participate in the selection and promotion of members of the faculty? When they think a good teacher has been fired, they certainly have a right to complain. When faculty members treat them as odd and anonymous objects, to be avoided whenever possible, they have a right to demand the services for which they or the community are paying. Students do not have, in most American universities, the ways and means to assert these rights in an effective and orderly fashion. That situation requires repair.

But students nevertheless cannot have a formal role in the selection of faculty. The most important reason is that this would be incompatible with academic freedom. It exposes the teacher to intimidation. Academic freedom is the product of a long and difficult struggle. It has been achieved by excluding all groups but professors from any formal power over what goes on in the classroom. The exclusion applies to administrators, trustees, legislators, parents, alumni, and the public. There are questions that can be asked about academic freedom—about its range and extent, about misinterpretations of it, about departures from it that have been defended in its name—but there are no reasons for reconsidering the role of students in relation to it. There is nothing about students to justify giving them power no other group has.

Students have no common professional perspective or shared occupational interest in academic freedom. Judging from the record, numbers of them are subject to the same bouts of intolerance in the face of upsetting ideas that affect bankers or legislators. A wise faculty and administration will do well to try to find out what student opinions about teachers are. But they had better conduct the canvass informally and discreetly. Teaching is a professional relationship, not a popularity contest. To invite students to participate in the selection or promotion of their teachers is to create a relationship in the classroom inappropriate to teaching.

Should students have the right to demand the introduction of certain courses? Again, there are limits. The fact that students want a course is a reason to consider giving it. But it is not, by itself, a sufficient reason. There may be nobody competent to teach the course. It may be a non-course—an excuse for bull sessions on company time, with no literature worth studying and no tradition of discourse and inquiry to hold things in bounds. Besides, since university budgets have been known to be limited, there is always the disagreeable possibility that the introduction of a new course requires the dropping of an old one. A judgment of comparative worth therefore has to be made. Students are not the right jury to make such a judgment.

Yet these arguments merely define the limits of student power. They do not argue against it. Students have things to teach their teachers. And there are invaluable things they can learn about their education, about universities, about themselves, from taking part in the examination, with their teachers, of the design of their education. The entire spirit within an institution of learning is likely to be better if there is a sense within it that its members are constantly cooperating in the appraisal of what it is doing. There ought to be regular, established procedures for consultation between faculties and student bodies. They should provide for the genuine, serious, and continuing examination of curriculum—a process incompatible with mass meetings, demonstrations, and sloganeering. It should not be expected that all student recommendations be accepted, but it should be expected that the consideration of students' points of view will not be merely *pro forma*.

Such arrangements would have a number of merits, not least among them the possibility that a myth generally accepted by students would finally be exploded. Students might discover that on many issues, particularly those directly related to courses and curriculum, it is not professors but deans and presidents who are their natural allies. By and large, judging from my own experience, it is members of the faculty, and not administrators, who are the opponents of educational reforms. This is not because deans and presidents are naturally more liberal. It is simply because most men's recognition of the need for reform grows in direct proportion to the distance of the proposed reform from their own territory. If students are talking about the reform of the curriculum, they will probably find more sympathy among deans, who don't work in classrooms. If students have complaints about the food served in dining halls, they will probably find the most sympathetic listeners, on the other hand, among members of the faculty. Professors don't have to balance the budget or hire the cooks.

But what about the largest single demand implicit in slogans such as "student power" and "university democracy"? This is the claim that faculty and students ought to share with trustees and administrators, or take over altogether, the powers which these latter groups have hitherto exercised alone. The claim is a political one. Its justification, if it has any, is the general one that democratic principles call for the establishment of student power in higher education. Is this what "democratic principles" do entail? Indeed, do they apply to institutions of learning? Are colleges and universities sufficiently like cities or national governments, or unions or factories, to justify the use of the same political arguments in relation to them?

There is a fundamental respect in which the administrators of a university are in a different position from the managers of a company. The university administrators cannot create a total plan of work, define jobs within it, and then assign individual workers to them. Of course, now that labor unions have the power they have, managers cannot do this as easily as they once could either. But the difference between their position and that of university administrators is still very great. The product of a factory is a corporate product to which individuals contribute. The product of a university is many separate, individual products, for which the corporate arrangements provide protection and support, but for which the individuals have basic responsibility.

Most of the odd, novel, or shocking things that are being said about the condition of students in the United States today, and many of the discussions taking place about the reallocation of powers within universities, come from the application of loose and unexamined analogies, drawn from other types of social organization, to the structure of institutions of learning. A university is at once a highly individualistic and unavoidably hierarchical human organization. It is based on the premise that some people know more than other people, and that it cannot perform its tasks effectively unless these gradations in knowledge are recognized in its form of government.

This is not an abuse of "democracy." The right of a citizen of the larger society to vote just as the next man can, without regard to hierarchy, is based on the premise that, where the major policies of the state are concerned, where the nature of what is good for society is at issue, only extreme inadequacies, like illiteracy or a criminal record, are disqualifying. The basic reason for this view is that there are no reasonably defensible general procedures by which the citizenry can be divided into the class of those who know enough to have an opinion worth counting or an interest worth expressing, and the class of those who don't.

In contrast, while universities are democratic organizations in the sense that individuals have a broad array of personal rights within them, and that there is a play of opinion inside them which has a massive effect on their evolution, they are not democratic organizations in the sense that majority rule applies to them. For within a university there are acceptable procedures by which people can be graded in accordance with their competence, and grading people in this way is essential to the conduct of the university's special business. The egalitarian ideal does not apply across the board in universities any more than it does in any other field where *skill* is the essence of the issue. To suggest that it should apply is to make hash of the idea of learning. If there is a case to be made for student participation in the higher reaches of university government, therefore, it is a case that is not based upon *rights,* but upon considerations of good educational and administrative practice.

Does this imply that the government of colleges and universities by trustees is a good system? No; but it helps to put this system in perspective. The case which is generally presented against trustee control of universities mixes truths with exaggerations. It is true that most trustees tend to be preoccupied with other matters than education, that they are inaccessible to teachers and students, and that a dispiriting number of them have reached an age and station in life calculated to protect them against fresh ideas. It is not surprising, therefore, that professors and students are sparing in the confidence they lavish on trustees. The government of American universities by boards of trustees is not an example of government by the consent of the governed.

However, neither is it an example of tyranny. The powers of trustees are severely limited by custom and law, and by the realities of a university. In any well established university, trustees normally leave educational decisions to the faculty. One of their primary educational functions, indeed, is simply to provide the educational community of the university—its students and faculty—with protective insulation. The trustees throw their mantle of influence and respectability around it, deflecting and absorbing criticisms and denunciations, and thus guarding the community's freedom. Indeed, it is doubtful that faculties and student bodies could by themselves, in many parts of the country, and without the help of trustees, successfully defend their autonomy, even assuming that their economic problems could be solved. It is odd that trustees should be attacked as though their presence was in contravention of academic freedom. Their presence is usually a condition for it.

Still, it can be asked whether this form of government is the best form for a college or university. Trustees (or regents) do make educational decisions, even if most of these are only indirect. They allocate resources, do more for one field of learning than for another, and make arrangements affecting the relation of the university to the larger society which affect the daily lives of teachers and students. Would it not be better if trustees continued to do their work of finding the money, but surrendered the other powers they exercise to the people who really constitute the university—namely, its students and teachers? Obviously, it is doubtful that many trustees would accept this proposal that they should supply the money but keep quiet about the way it is used. Just to see where the argument goes, however, let us imagine that trustees have a capacity for self-immolation not conspicuous in most human beings. Would it be a good thing for them to retire from the scene?

Not entirely. They are the buffers of the university against external pressures. As we have seen, an educational institution requires such protection. Most organizations, furthermore, benefit from having a lay group of critics with deep commitments to them, who are nevertheless not part of their daily operations. In addition, since universities must maintain relations with the surrounding society, they require people on their board of governors who have interests and experience in that society. And it is always well to remember that though education, like the law, is in part a professional business, it is also everybody's business. If students have a stake in what happens to them, by the same token, so do their parents and so do lay members of the community. In courts of law, juries are not composed of professional lawyers. On the university scene, the outsider, though he should not have as decisive a place as a juror has, also deserves to be represented.

Yet these same considerations call for change in the composition of most boards of trustees. They call, equally clearly, for changes in the manner in which they communicate with the communities they govern. Boards of trustees ought to have more younger people on them, and poorer people. They ought to have recent graduates, not only older ones. They ought to have people who have not yet arrived, not only those swollen with success. The surrounding neighborhood should, if possible, be represented. That is not always easy to arrange because there are so often disagreements about who is "representative" of whom. But if it can be done without creating quarrels that did not exist before, then it should be done. And students and faculty members either should be represented on the board or assured of regular consultation with it.

The participation of students in the supreme governing bodies of a university undoubtedly raises equally subtle issues. Students are inexperienced. They are present on a campus for only a short period, and could serve on committees and boards for only a shorter period. It takes time, on most boards and committees, before new members learn enough to become genuinely useful. Furthermore, student generations change in their styles and opinions and sometimes very quickly. Students, therefore, bring an element of discontinuity, a shortened perspective, and sometimes a short fuse, into the consideration of matters of policy. In educational institutions particularly, continuity of perspective and some sense of the time-dimension are essential.

Nevertheless, the idea is worth experimentation, even though the number of students who belong to a board, or who sit with it when certain issues are discussed, should probably be small. There is little question, apart from the formalities of representation on a board of trustees, that machinery for regular face-to-face meetings between students and trustees is desirable. Discontinuity in policy is dangerous, but so is automatic, thoughtless continuity. The long view is estimable, but impatience is useful too. And if inexperience is a handicap, so is experience: it dulls one to novelty. Trustees could learn things from students that they will never learn from administrators or other trustees.

In the end, we are discussing not matters of right and justice, but matters of political wisdom. Trustees will not know what they should know unless they mix with the people who can tell them. The community they govern will not understand why the trustees have made the decisions they have, and will not have confidence in these decisions, unless it has its own trusted emissaries to keep it in touch with the board. Faulty communication is the heart of the political problem in the American universities that are having trouble today. Demands for "student power" and "faculty power," so interpreted, are more than justifiable.

The Cops and the Kids

JAMES RIDGEWAY

Chicago

The clashes between police and demonstrators began as calculated maneuvers by The National Mobilization Committee to End the War in Vietnam, and the Youth International Party. The strategy was to confront the Chicago police, and thereby demonstrate that America was a police state. It ended as a full-blown insurrection of middle-class people against that state.

For the people who took part in this, the Democratic Convention was irrelevant; for them, politics is in the street. They either will be in the streets in increasing numbers from now on, or they will be returning to live the underground existence of the 1950's over again, leaving politics to the police.

The Chicago police department, not Mayor Daley, was the clear winner in the street fights. And the officers knew it. After they beat up the demonstrators Wednesday night, they were exultant. Where the youngsters had once made fun of the police, the officers now took to openly taunting the citizens—any citizen. Out of the debacle in Chicago, the police have emerged as an important political force. No candidate in America can run from now on without coming to terms with the police.

The city refused to give either the mobilization (mobs) or the yippies (yips) permits for their gathering. Instead they tried to run them out of town.

Plainclothesmen were assigned to tail both Rennie Davis and Tom Hayden, the two mobs leaders. Others followed Paul Krassner and Jerry Rubin of the yips. This was good humored for a time; Krassner had a tail advise him where the best food was. Then on Sunday evening in Lincoln Park, near the lake in northern Chicago, where the yips were headquartered, Hayden and Davis tried to slip the dicks by running off into the

Reprinted by permission of *The New Republic,* © 1968, Harrison-Blaine of New Jersey, Inc.

darkness. By mistake, Hayden ran across the two officers, who threw him up against the side of a police car. Hayden yelled for help and a small crowd gathered. "We're going to get you, you son-of-a-bitch," the dicks told Hayden, then they freed him.

Monday afternoon, the yips again gathered in Lincoln Park and Hayden and Krassner discussed plans for the Miss Yippie contest and the Yippie Olympics which Krassner was especially keen to begin. Hayden was talking to a group of people when he noticed the two dicks who had nabbed him the evening before approaching with a small convoy of paddy wagons and officers on motorcycles. They came right up, collared him and threw him into the paddy wagon and drove off before anybody could make a move.

On the way to the stationhouse, one of the officers turned to Hayden and pleasantly said to him, "We're going to get rid of you, you son-of-a-bitch." At the police station he was taken to a room, and while awaiting processing with others, was told to sit on the floor. As he waited a number of officers stopped off to pass the time of day. "If you guys want to kick the shit out of the cops," one of them said, "we'll kill every one of you."

"We'll spray you fuckers with submachine guns," said another.

"Phew," said a third, holding his nose. "God, do you stink."

(The police were especially angered by the radicals' slovenly dress and body odors. "Animals," they said in disgust.

"Pigs," replied the yips. "Oink, oink.")

Shortly after Hayden was taken, the yips gathered, and after hoisting Red and Viet Cong flags, marched downtown to the police station. They were led by a sporty looking fellow with a plaid jacket and a peace-dove button pinned on it. He walked along with a black man dressed in green pants and sporting a McCarthy button. Both these characters were dicks.

At first the police were badly outnumbered and flustered as they ran along to catch up with the march. But they soon recovered their verve and dashed into the marchers and hauled out a lad. Pinning his arms behind his back, they threw him into a paddy wagon. A mild-looking man wearing glasses rushed up to protest. A policeman knocked off his glasses and sprayed some mace in his face. As they marched into the city, an air of insurgency swept through the crowd. Gail Carter of Berkeley, wearing a black beret, was hoisted onto a boy's shoulders, where she chanted, "Ho, Ho, Ho Chi Minh," and "Dump the Hump."

The marchers finally reached the police station, which was guarded by what looked to be several hundred officers; then they went over to Grant Park, which is opposite the Hilton Hotel, the convention headquarters. There they clustered around the statue of General Logan, a Civil War hero. A couple of boys climbed up on the statue and decked it with the Viet Cong flag. This angered the police, and several hundred of them formed a skirmish line. The officers charged at the statue, laying their billies to any youngster in the way. The youngsters rushed off from the statue in another direction, yelling, "Here come de pig. Oink. Oink. Pig. Pig. Oink. Oink."

Meanwhile, Miss Carter approached the line of police, and going up to each man in the manner of an inspecting officer she paused, looked him hard in the eye, and said, "And you. What about you? I care for you. You know what I am saying. What do you feel in your heart? Or are you afraid to say what's in your heart?" A group of plainclothesmen took her picture with a polaroid camera. But the films wouldn't develop properly and they fell to quarreling among themselves on that score and quite lost track of Miss Carter, who wandered off elsewhere.

Later that evening, the police charged into Lincoln Park, spraying tear gas into the yippies and others who had barricaded themselves in. The officers beat up the reporters and anyone else they could lay their hands on. Meanwhile, Hayden was charged with disorderly conduct for sitting on the grass and was bailed out. About midnight, he was about to enter the Hilton Hotel when a house dick recognized him and ordered him away. Coming away from the hotel, Hayden spotted two tails coming down the street. Seeking to avoid them, he walked across the intersection. At that moment, another plainclothesman, standing up the block, recognized Hayden and yelled out to the officer directing traffic, "Get him. Stop him." A dick grabbed Hayden from behind and threw him to the pavement. More police converged. Hayden yelled, "What have I done? I haven't done anything." But he was hustled off to the police station. An attorney who managed to see him there said the police wanted to charge Hayden with aggravated assault, but this was later dropped and he was charged with simple assault for spitting on a police officer. Bail was set at $1,000.

Hayden was released from custody about 3:30 that morning. On leaving the stationhouse with a handful of reporters and friends, he quickly ran into another car carrying plainclothesmen. At an intersection both dicks jumped out and said, "Hello, we're police officers, can we help you fellows?" After examining a White House press pass, they retreated. About an hour later, Hayden decided to go underground.

Tuesday evening, the yips, mobs, McCarthy youths and a lot of other people gathered to celebrate LBJ's birthday at the Colosseum which is a few blocks down Lake Michigan from the Hilton. There they listened to Jean Genet and William Burroughs berate the police. Draft cards were burned. Rock bands played. David Dellinger gave out the usual stuff about the movement. Paul Krassner gave LBJ the finger. Then the crowd joined in singing Happy Birthday LBJ, and "Fuck you, Lyndon Johnson."

At the end of the evening's entertainment, Rennie Davis said the plan was to disperse in small groups, then gather in full view of the television cameras at Grant Park. There they could greet the returning delegates.

It was midnight. The police were lined up on both sides of the street in front of the Hilton. A small band of people from Lincoln Park had already arrived and were waiting for the others from the Colosseum to march up. Scattered among them were the usual lot of plainclothesmen, doing their best to look like hippies but, as usual, chattering about the unwashed smell of the slobs they were sent to observe. Standing among them was a man with a porkpie hat and with a neat mustache. He chatted amiably with another fellow who appeared to be listening to the convention on a small transistor radio. Both looked rather like the artificially got-up detectives. But they weren't. The man in the hat was Hayden and his companion wasn't listening to the convention; he was tuned to the police radio bands, following the cops' movements. Here among the police was the mobs' field communications headquarters.

As the throng from the Colosseum flitted into the dark of the park, an air of expectancy grew. The police brought in buses full of fresh men and lined them up two deep. People began to chant, "Peace now, peace now," and then to burn draft cards before the television cameras. They yelled "Fuck you, LBJ," "Fuck you, Daley." More police were marched up. Helicopters circled overhead. Now word was coming over the transistor radios that the police had once more cleared Lincoln Park, using tear gas, which in addition to forcing the yips from the park, had gotten into drivers' eyes and stalled traffic on the highway. The crowds were moving through the streets stoning cars, and a group began to march towards Grant Park. More police were lined up before the Hilton. They were five deep in some places. They quietly moved in behind the park and on both sides of it. A police officer walked among the apprehensive reporters, suggesting they might better watch the scene from across the street. The convention adjourned. Buses carrying delegates were returning and the crowd, now numbering about 3,500, yelled at them, "Peace now"; "Join us, join us." First a few, then more, opened the bus windows and made the "V" sign at the crowd. There were cheers. "Join us, join us," went the chant. Fires were lit in the park. Now across the street in the hotel room lights were flashed on and off, giving the SOS signal. McCarthy youths began appearing at the windows, waving and calling out support. First one, then another came out on the street. "I didn't feel comfortable in that hotel with the pigs protecting us from you people," an Alabama challenge delegate said. "The real convention is in the streets," another said.

Although the gathering was pretty placid, with only a brief scuffle now and then, the police seemed increasingly edgy. At about 3 a.m. the first units of the Illinois National Guard were brought in. They got off their jeeps with rifles at the ready, and the police were marched off. The Guard commander, Brigadier-General Richard Dunn, tried to speak on his own microphone. But the crowd leaders suggested he come over and speak on theirs, instead. Dunn tried to do so, but was drowned out as Peter, Paul and Mary began singing, "If I Had a Hammer." Finally, Dunn was able to say that the National Guard didn't want to bother anyone. He retired to his jeep, which looked a little like a rabbit hutch, covered over with mesh wire for the commander's protection.

The insurrection was full-blown by Wednesday afternoon. Ten thousand people gathered at a band shell in the park, some distance from the hotel. When a youngster ran down the American flag, the police charged in swinging. One group of people wanted to go to the amphitheater, another to the Hilton. Both were blocked by troop movements which closed the bridges out of the park. To get out of the park, people walked north past the barricaded bridges. They milled around for a while, then seized upon one bridge which was still open to traffic, and blocked it. The police moved in, firing tear-gas barrages to break up the crowd. The gas spread back into the city, choking people in the streets and hotels. The demonstrators now split up and moved back through the different streets toward the Hilton, grouping finally on Michigan Avenue and marching on the hotel. Medics moved through the crowds, dampening handkerchiefs with water to fend off tear gas. Waving their hands in the "V" sign, chanting "Peace now, peace now," an enormous crowd marched on the hotel. The crowd came up against the police lines in front of the Hilton, milled around the edge of the hotel, held from below by the police and on the side by the military. It was about 8 p.m. Then the police charged, moving in skirmish line, columns and two and three man groups. They hit the lines of marchers, clubbing down a man and then pulling him out for the arrest. A group to the south of the hotel fell back through stalled traffic before the police attack. The automobiles confused the officers and reduced the force of the attack. But suddenly 50 other officers burst out of a side street, hitting the march flank and driving the youngsters across the street against a wall. There they charged them, beating them indiscriminately.

A group gathered across from the hotel in the park. The police charged into it, beating people at will. They would pull them out into the street, fight them and then throw them into the paddy wagon. Others watching this from the Hilton grabbed anything they could find and threw it out the windows at the police.

The hotel was filled with nearly hysterical people, older women in faints, youngsters with blood streaming down their faces, girls crying.

At McCarthy's headquarters, on the Hilton's fifteenth floor, frenzied youths ripped up the sheets for bandages. The hotel manager was furious that his sheets were being torn and twice he sent the police up to raid the McCarthy headquarters. The hotel management refused use of the hotel elevators to some people. The police sealed off the hotel and wouldn't let injured people enter.

Outside, the police continued forays into the crowd, beating and clubbing the people to make them disperse. The streets in front of the hotel were completely cut off. There was a no man's land around the side entrances where people darted in and out.

Vicious as this attack was, the demonstrators came back to Grant Park by midnight in large numbers. Thousands of people continued to gather there under the rifles of the troops, into the small hours of the morning. The lights flicked on and off in the hotel in support, but efforts to get the major candidates to come down and speak to the people ended in failure; Senator McCarthy wanted to go, but the Secret Service men dissuaded him.

That night there was a new group of people there from the South Side of Chicago—white youths—and they stood behind the police lines to support their boys. "Fruit," they yelled at a reporter wearing a checked coat. "Ya fuckin' coppa. Fruit." Long into the night, these two groups of Americans faced each other.

Following out their scheme to promote a continuing confrontation between growing numbers of people and the police—they figured that the Chicago officials would respond by bringing in more police and troops, and so make clear to all those looking on that Chicago was an armed camp and America was a police state—the radicals talked enthusiastically about little acts of violence, like a stink bomb in the hotel, or dirty words on some walls, to provoke the police and manipulate the liberal McCarthy youths into their own ranks. In effect, the idea was to simulate a little guerrilla war. By Wednesday night, it was clear that everyone—McCarthy youngsters, reporters, radicals, yips, well-to-do people walking their dogs, delegates to the convention, even some blacks—all sorts of people who had never heard of Tom Hayden or David Dellinger, were caught up in an insurrection in the streets. There were no real leaders. They came and went, sometimes carried out bleeding, sometimes arrested, sometimes off in a corner plotting. It made no real difference; to the crowds in the streets, it didn't matter who was at the microphone. Nobody manipulated these people. On Tuesday night they waved the Viet Cong flag and yelled, "Fuck you, LBJ." By Wednesday night, after they had been beaten by the Chicago police, held off by armed troops, gassed, they still came back to Grant Park in great numbers. At last they confronted the armed forces occupying the city, not with the Viet Cong flag, but with the American flag. Chicago smelled of revolution.

Why Cops
Hate Liberals
—and Vice Versa

SEYMOUR MARTIN LIPSET

I

There is an increasing body of evidence which suggests an affinity between police work and support for radical-right politics, particularly when linked to racial unrest. During the presidential campaign, George

Wallace was unmistakably a hero to many policemen. John Harrington, the president of the Fraternal Order of Police, the largest police organization in America, with over 90,000 members and affiliates in more than 900 communities, publicly endorsed him. And Wallace has reciprocated this affection for some time. While governor of Alabama, he placed the slogan, popularized by the Birch Society, "Support Your Local Police" on the automobile license plates of the state of Alabama. During the 1964 and 1968 presidential campaigns, he frequently referred to the heroic activities of the police, and denounced the Supreme Court, and bleeding-heart liberals and intellectuals, for undermining the police efforts to maintain law and order. The police were pictured as the victims of an Establishment conspiracy to foster confrontationist forms of protest and law violation, particularly on the part of Negroes and student activists.

Similar reports concerning police support for right-wing or conservative candidates who have campaigned against civil rights and integration proposals have appeared frequently in the press. Thus in 1967, Boston journalists commented on the general support for Louise Day Hicks among the police of that city. Mrs. Hicks had won her political spurs in the fight which she waged as chairman of the Boston School Committee against school integration. And when she ran for mayor, the police were seemingly among her most enthusiastic backers. In New York City, police have stood out among the constituency of the Conservative Party, an organization which also has opposed public efforts to enforce school integration. The New York Conservative Party was the one partisan group in the city to fight a civilian review board of the police department, an issue which has come up in many other communities.

Jerome Skolnick of the University of Chicago made a study of the Oakland, California, police in 1964 based on interviews with many of them. He concluded that "a Goldwater type of conservatism was the dominant political and emotional persuasion of the police." During the 1964 campaign, a broadcaster on the New York City police radio suddenly made an emotional appeal for support of Senator Goldwater. Many police called in to endorse this talk. Almost no one out in police cars that night phoned in to back Lyndon Johnson, or to complain about the use of the police radio for partisan purposes. In Los Angeles, an official order had to be issued in 1964 telling the police that they could not have bumper stickers or other campaign materials on their police cars, because of the large number who had publicly so supported Goldwater. The late chief of police of the city, William H. Parker, stated his belief that the majority of the nation's peace officers were "conservative, ultraconservative, and very right wing," a description which fit his own orientation.

There is also evidence of strong support and sympathy among the police for the John Birch Society. In 1964, John Rousselot, then national director of the Society, claimed that "substantial numbers" of its members were policemen, and a study of the national membership of the Society by Fred Grupp, a political scientist at Louisiana State, confirms this contention. Mr. Grupp sent out a questionnaire to a random sample of the

Birch membership with the help of the Society and found that over 3 percent of those who reported their occupations were policemen, a figure which is over four times the proportion of police in the national labor force. In New York City in July, 1965, a reporter judged that the majority of the audience at a large rally in Town Hall sponsored by the Birch Society's Speakers Bureau wore "Patrolmen's Benevolent Association badges." The Society itself "estimates that it has five hundred members in the New York City Police Department." In Philadelphia, the mayor placed a number of police on limited duty because of their membership in the Society. In a recent interview, Richard MacEachern, head of the Boston Police Patrolmen's Association, frequently referred to Birch Society material as the source of his information concerning "The Plan" of black militants to destroy the police through use of deliberate violence.

That peace officers in high places are sympathetic with the Society may be seen in the fact that former Sheriff James Clark of Selma, Alabama, who not only played a major role in suppressing civil rights demonstrations in his city but also has been a frequent speaker for the Birch Society, was elected president of the national organization of sheriffs. While serving as chief of the Los Angeles Police Department, William H. Parker took part in the Manion Forum, a right-wing radio discussion program run by Clarence Manion, a leader of the Birch Society. According to William Turner, in his book *The Police Establishment,* Louis Neese, the police chief of Trenton, New Jersey, "incorporated sections of a Birch 'Support Your Local Police' circular into a declaration of departmental policy."

All this is no new development. The identification between the police and right-wing extremism is not simply a reflection of recent tensions. During the 1930s, investigations of the Black Legion, a neofascist organization in the industrial Midwest, which engaged in terror and vigilante activities, indicated that it appealed to police. Not only did it include many patrolmen in Michigan and elsewhere, but a grand jury in Oakland County, Michigan, reported that the chief of police in Pontiac was an active member. The Legion, it should be noted, engaged in kidnapping, flogging, and even murder of suspected Communists. Father Coughlin, who was probably the most important profascist leader of the 1930s, also found heavy backing within police ranks. An investigation of his organization, the Christian Front, revealed that 407 of New York's finest belonged to it.

Gunnar Myrdal, in his classic study of the race problem in America, *An American Dilemma,* conducted in the late thirties and early forties, asserted that one of the principal sources of Ku Klux Klan activity in the South at that time came from law enforcement officers. This finding jibed with reports of the membership of the Klan during the early 1920s when it was at the height of its power, controlling politics in many Northern as well as Southern states. Klan leaders according to one account "took particular pride in emphasizing the large number of law enforcement officers . . . that had joined their order." Typical of Klan propaganda which attracted police support was the plank in the program of the Chicago Klan which called for "Supporting Officials in all Phases of Law

Enforcement," a slogan close to the "Support Your Local Police" campaign waged by the Birch Society and George Wallace four decades
later. According to Charles Jackson, membership lists seized in different
parts of California indicated that "roughly 10 percent of the . . . policemen in practically every California city," including the chiefs of police in
Los Angeles and Bakersfield and the sheriff of Los Angeles County,
belonged to the Klan. In Atlanta, the home base of the organization, a
study reports that "a very high percentage" of the police were members.
Considerable police backing for the Klan was also reported in analyses of
its operation in cities as diverse as Portland (Oregon), Tulsa, Madison,
and Memphis.

Looking back through the history of religious bigotry in this country,
we find that the anti-Catholic nativist American Protective Association
(APA), which flourished in the early 1890s, also appears to have been
supported by the police. My own researches on this movement and its
membership indicate that the police were considerably overrepresented
among APA members. In Minneapolis 6.5 percent were policemen, in
Sacramento 8 percent, and in San Jose 7 percent.

II

Although there is a general understanding that the police should be
politically neutral, their role as public employees has inevitably involved
them in local politics. Prior to the emergence of civil service examina-
tions, appointment to the force was a political plum in most cities. And
once a man was hired, chances for promotion often depended on access
to local officeholders. In many communities, the police were part of the
machine organization. The widespread pattern of toleration of corruption
and the rackets which characterized urban political life until the 1940s
usually depended on the cooperation, if not direct participation, of the
police. Those who controlled the rackets paid special attention to
municipal politics, to those who dominated city hall, in order to make
sure that they would not be interfered with by the authorities.

Although machine and racketeer domination of local government is
largely a thing of the past in most cities, the police are of necessity still
deeply interested in local politics. High-level appointments are almost
invariably made by elected officials, and those who control city politics
determine police pay and working conditions. Hence, the police as individuals and as a body must be actively concerned with access to the
political power structure. They must be prepared to adjust their law
enforcement policies in ways which are acceptable to the political leaders.

Such assumptions would lead us to believe that police would avoid any
contact with radical groups, with those who seek to change the existing
structures of political power or community leadership. Thus the evidence
that significant minorities of police have been moved to join or openly
back right-wing and bigoted movements is particularly impressive. For
every policeman who has taken part in such activities, we may assume
that there were many others who sympathized, but refrained from such
behavior so as to avoid endangering their job prospects. (This comment,

of course, does not apply to those communities which were actually dominated by extremist movements.)

The propensity of policemen to support rightist activities derives from a number of elements in their occupational role and social background. Many of the police are not much different in their social outlook from others in the lower middle class or working class. Twenty-five years ago, Gunnar Myrdal noted that police in the South were prone to express deep-seated anti-Negro feelings in brutal actions against Negroes and thus undo "much of what Northern philanthropy and Southern state governments are trying to accomplish through education and other means." He accounted for the phenomenon as resulting from the fact that the police generally had the prejudices of the poor whites. "The average Southern policeman is a promoted poor white with a legal sanction to use a weapon. His social heritage has taught him to despise the Negroes, and he has had little education which could have changed him." A recent study of the New York City police by Arthur Niederhoffer, a former member of the Department, reports that "for the past fifteen years, during a cycle of prosperity, the bulk of police candidates has been upper lower class with a sprinkling of lower middle class; about ninety-five per cent has had no college training." In a survey of the occupations of the fathers of 12,000 recruits who graduated from the New York Police Academy, he found that more than three-quarters of them were manual or service workers.

The Birch Society apart, movements of ethnic intolerance and right-wing radicalism have tended to recruit from the more conservative segments of the lower and less-educated strata. On the whole, the less education people have, the more likely they are to be intolerant of those who differ from themselves. whether in opinions, modes of culturally and morally relevant behavior, religion, ethnic background, or race. The police, who are recruited from the conservative, less-educated groups, reflect the background from which they come. John H. McNamara recently found that when he separated the New York police recruits into two status groups on the basis of their fathers' occupations, those "with fathers in the higher skill classification were less likely to feel that the leniency of courts and laws account for assaults on the police" than those who came from lower socioeconomic origins.

Once they are employed as policemen, their job experiences enhance the possibility that whatever authoritarian traits they bring from their social background will increase rather than decrease. McNamara found a sizable increase in the proportion of police recruits who resented legal restrictions on their authority or propensity to use force. At the beginning of recruit training, only 6 percent agreed with the statement "The present system of state and local laws has undermined the patrolman's authority to a dangerous extent," while 46 percent disagreed. After one year in field assignments, 25 percent of the same group of men agreed with the statement, and only 19 percent disagreed. Similar changes in attitudes occurred with respect to the proposition "If patrolmen working in tough neighborhoods had more leeway and fewer restrictions on the use of force many of the serious police problems in these neighborhoods would be greatly reduced." Fourteen percent agreed with the statement at the beginning of their career, as compared with 30 percent after one year in the field, and 39 percent among a different group of policemen who had been employed for two years.

In general, the policeman's job requires him to be suspicious of people, to prefer conventional behavior, to value toughness. A policeman must be suspicious and cynical about human behavior. As Niederhoffer points out, "He needs the intuitive ability to sense plots and conspiracies on the basis of embryonic evidence." The political counterpart of such an outlook is a monistic theory which simplifies political conflict into a black-and-white fight, and which is ready to accept a conspiratorial view of the sources of evil, terms which basically describe the outlook of extremist groups, whether of the left or right.

The propensity of police to support a radical political posture is also related to their sense of being a low-status out-group in American society. The Oakland study revealed that when police were asked to rank the most serious problems they have, the category most frequently selected was "lack of respect for the police. . . . Of the two hundred and eighty-two . . . policemen who rated the prestige police work receives from others, 70 per cent ranked it as only fair or poor." The New York City study also indicated that the majority of the police did not feel that they enjoyed the respect of the public. James Q. Wilson found that a majority of Chicago police sergeants who completed questionnaires in 1960 and 1965 felt that the public did not cooperate with or respect the police. Many articles in police journals comment on the alleged antagonism to the police voiced by the mass media. Studies of police opinion have indicated that some police conceal their occupation from their neighbors because many people do not like to associate with policemen.

If policemen judge their social worth by their incomes, they are right in rating it low. A recent article in *Fortune* reports that "the patrolman's pay in major cities now averages about $7,500 per year—33 percent less than is needed to sustain a family of four in moderate circumstances in a large city, according to the U.S. Bureau of Labor Statistics." As a result, many are forced to moonlight to earn a living. Fletcher Knebel cites an expert estimate that from a third to half of all the patrolmen in the country have a second job. The relative socioeconomic status of the police has worsened over time. Richard Wade, an urban historian at the University of Chicago, points out that the situation has changed considerably from that of fifty years ago when "policemen had an income higher than other trades and there were more applicants than there were jobs." John H. McNamara, who has studied the New York Department, concludes:

During the Depression the department was able to recruit from a population which included many unemployed or low-paid college graduates. . . . As general economic conditions have improved, however, the job of police officer has become less attractive to college graduates.

In his surveys of police opinion in Chicago, Boston, and Washington, D.C., Albert J. Reiss reports that 59 percent believe that the prestige of police work is lower than it was twenty years ago. Lower police morale is not simply a function of a relative decline in income or in perceived status. The police believe their conditions of work have also worsened. Eighty percent state that "police work [is] more hazardous today than five years ago." Sixty percent believe that the way the public behaves toward the police has changed for the worse since they joined the force.

The policeman's role is particularly subject to fostering feelings of resentment against society, which flow from a typical source of radical politics, "status discrepancies." This term refers to a sociological concept which is used to describe the positions of individuals or groups who are ranked relatively high on one status attribute and low on another.

Presumably the fact of having a claim to some deference makes people indignantly resent as morally improper any evidence that they are held in low regard because of some other factor in their background or activities. In the case of the police, they are given considerable authority by society to enforce its laws and are expected to risk their lives if necessary; on the other hand, they feel they receive little prestige; and they get a relatively low salary as compared with that of other occupational groups which have much less authority.

Many police have consciously come to look upon themselves as an oppressed minority, subject to the same kind of prejudice as other minorities. Thus Chief Parker explained some of the bitterness of the police as stemming from the "shell of minorityism" within which they lived. This view was given eloquent voice in 1965 by the then New York City Police Commissioner, Michael J. Murphy: "The police officer, too, belongs to a minority group—a highly visible minority group, and is also subject to stereotyping and mass attack. Yet he, like every member of every minority, is entitled to be judged as an individual and on the basis of his individual acts, not as a group." Clearly, the police appear to be a deprived group, one which feels deep resentment about the public's lack of appreciation for the risks it takes for the community's safety. These risks are not negligible in the United States. In 1967, for example, one out of every eight policemen was assaulted. This rate is considerably higher than in any other developed democratic country.

The belief that police are rejected by the public results, as Wilson argues, in a "sense of alienation from society" which presses the police to develop their own "sub-culture" with norms which can provide them with "a basis for self-respect independent to some degree of civilian attitudes." Given the assumption of the police that they are unappreciated even by the honest middle-class citizenry, they are prone to accept a cynical view of society and its institutions, and social isolation and alienation can lead to political alienation.

The police have faced overt hostility and even contempt from spokesmen for liberal and leftist groups, racial minorities, and intellectuals generally. The only ones who appreciate their contribution to society and the risks they take are the conservatives, and particularly the extreme right. The radical left has almost invariably been hostile, the radical right friendly. It is not surprising therefore that police are more likely to be found in the ranks of the right.

In the larger context, American politics tends to press the police to support conservative or rightist politics. Liberals and leftists have been more concerned than conservatives with the legal rights of the less power-ful and the underprivileged. They have tried to limit the power of the police to deal with suspects and have sought to enlarge the scope of due process. Efforts to enhance the rights of defendants, to guarantee them legal representation, to prevent the authorities from unduly pressuring those taken into police custody, have largely concerned liberals. The American Civil Liberties Union and other comparable groups have fought hard to weaken the discretionary power of the police. To many policemen, the liberals' constant struggle is to make their job more difficult, to increase the physical danger to which they are subject. Many are con-vinced that dangerous criminals or revolutionists are freely walking the streets because of the efforts of softhearted liberals. To police, who are constantly exposed to the seamy side of life, who view many deviants and lawbreakers as outside the protection of the law, the constant concern for the civil rights of such people makes little sense, unless it reflects moral weakness on the part of the liberals, or more dangerously, is an aspect of a plot to undermine legitimate authority. And the fact that the Supreme Court has sided with the civil-libertarian interpretations of in-dividual rights in recent years on issues concerning police tactics in securing confessions—the use of wiretaps, and the like—constitutes evi-dence as to how far moral corruption has reached into high places. Reiss's survey of police opinion found that 90 percent of the police inter-viewed felt that the Supreme Court "has gone too far in making rules favoring and protecting criminal offenders." The liberal world, then, is perceived as an enemy, an enemy which may attack directly in demonstra-tions or riots, or indirectly through its pressure on the courts.

III

The fights over the establishment of civilian police review boards which have occurred in many cities have largely taken the form of a struggle between the liberal political forces which favor creating such checks over the power of police departments to discipline their own members and the conservatives who oppose these. In the best-publicized case, the referendum in New York City of November, 1966, to repeal the law creating such a board, the ideological lineup was clear-cut. The Patrolmen's Benevolent Association was supported in its successful efforts by the Conservative Party of New York and the John Birch Society. It was opposed by New York's liberal Republican mayor, John Lindsay, as well as by Robert Kennedy, the reform Democrats, the Liberal Party, the New York *Times,* and the New York *Post.* There can be little doubt that this struggle has helped to strengthen the police backing for the Conservative Party.

The greater willingness of police to join or back groups which have been antagonistic to religious (Catholics in the nineteenth century, Jews in the twentieth) and racial minorities also may be a function of concrete job experience, as well as of the degree of prejudice present in their social milieu. Ethnic slums characteristically have been centers of crime, violence, and vice. Most immigrant groups living in urban America in the past, as well as more recent Negro migrants, have contributed disproportionately to the ranks of criminals and racketeers. Hence, the police have often found that their experience confirmed the negative cultural stereotypes which have existed about such groups while they lived in the crowded, dirty, slum conditions. The ethnic minorities have, in fact, often appeared as sympathetic to criminals, as supporters of violence directed against the police. The ethnic slum historically has been an enemy stronghold, a place of considerable insecurity. Right-wing political groupings which define minorities or leftist radicals as conspiratorial corrupters of American morality have strongly appealed to the morally outraged police.

In evaluating the disposition of the police to participate in the radical right, it is important to note that only a minority of the police are involved in most communities. Most police, though relatively conservative and conventional, are normally more concerned with the politics of collective bargaining, with getting more for themselves, than with the politics of right-wing extremism. The Patrolmen's Benevolent Association is basically a trade union which seeks alliances with other labor unions, particularly those within the civil service, and with the powerful within the dominant political parties. Police have struck for higher wages, much as other groups have done. There have been occasions when they have shown sympathy for striking workers on the picket line, particularly when the workers and the police have belonged to the same ethnic groups. One of the main attractions of police work is the lifelong economic security and early pensions which it gives. In this sense, the policeman, like others from low-income backgrounds, is concerned for the expansion of the welfare state.

Like all others, the police are interested in upgrading the public image of their job. They do not like being attacked as thugs, as authoritarians, as lusting for power. Some cities have successfully sought to increase the educational level of new recruits and to have a continuing education program for those on the force. The academic quality of the courses given at police academies and colleges in various communities has been improving, and there is much that is hopeful going on.

Yet the fact remains that recent events have sorely strained the tempers of many police. Almost two-thirds of the police interviewed in Reiss's study feel that "demonstrations are a main cause of violence these days." The reactions of police organizations around the country suggest that Ortega y Gasset was correct when he suggested in his book *The Revolt of the Masses,* published in 1930, that free societies would come to fear their police. He predicted that those who rely on the police to maintain order are foolish if they imagine that the police "are always going to be content to preserve . . . order [as defined by government]. . . . Inevitably they [the police] will end by themselves defining and deciding on the order they are going to impose—which, naturally, will be that which suits them best." In some cities, leaders of police organizations have openly threatened that the police will disobey orders to be permissive when dealing with black or student demonstrators. The Boston Police Patrolmen's Association has stated that the police there will enforce the law, no matter what politicians say. The president of the New York Patrolmen's Benevolent Association has announced that his members "will enforce the law 100 per cent," even when ordered not to do so.

This "rebellion of the police" is a response to their being faced with "confrontation tactics" by student and black radical militants. New Left radicals and black nationalists openly advocate confrontation tactics. They seeks deliberately to inflame the police so as to enrage them into engaging in various forms of brutality. Stokely Carmichael has declared that a demonstration which does not result in police action against the participants is a failure. The events at Chicago during the Democratic Convention constitute the best recent example of the way in which a major police force can completely lose its head when faced by a confrontationist demonstration.[1] Some black and white New Radicals openly declare that the killing of police in the ghetto area is not murder, that it is an inherent form of self-defense. But police have been shot at and occasionally killed in ambush.

The current tensions between the police and New Left student and black nationalist radicals probably involve the most extreme example of deliberate provocation which the police have ever faced. The tactics of the campus-based opposition rouse the most deep-seated feelings of class

[1] Ironically, the Chicago police force has been one of the few major ones which had made real efforts to adjust to changing conditions. William Turner's recent book, *The Police Establishment*, states that close to 25 percent of the force is Negro, a proportion far above that of New York and Los Angeles. It also deliberately lowered the height requirements "to make more Puerto Ricans eligible." Although, as Turner documents, there has been considerable tension between the Chicago police and the black community, a study of the attitudes of Negroes in four cities by Gary Marx in his *Protest and Prejudice* reported that the percentage of adult Negroes answering "very well" or "fairly well" to the question of how they thought the police treated Negroes in their city was 64 percent in Chicago, 56 percent in New York, 53 percent in Atlanta, and 31 percent in Birmingham. In spite of the fact that the Chicago Police Department has been in the lead in adapting its recruitment policies to the new climate of race relations, in a study of three cities Reiss found that police in the Windy City were much less likely than those in Boston or Washington, D.C., to blame "civil rights groups" for arousing the public against the police. These comparative data also indicate that the morale of the Chicago police was higher than that of those in Boston and Washington. Over half of the Chicago police interviewed believe that the public rate the prestige of police higher than twenty years ago, while only a fifth of those in the Eastern cities have this opinion. "Chicago police officers are considerably more likely to advise both their sons and other young men to consider a career as a police officer" than are those in the other communities. George O'Connor, the director of professional standards for the International Association of Chiefs of Police, has rated the Chicago department "the best equipped, best-administered police force in the United States." Given such data, it is likely that Tom Hayden, one of the leaders of the Chicago demonstrations, is right in his contention that the brutal reaction of the Chicago police could have occurred in most other cities.

resentment. Most policemen are conservative, conventional, upwardly mobile working-class supporters of the American Way, who aspire for a better life for their families. Many of them seek to send their children to college. To find the scions of the upper middle class in the best universities, denouncing them as "pigs," hurling insults which involve use of the most aggressive sexual language, such as "Up against the wall, Mother F——," throwing bricks and bags of feces at them, is much more difficult to accept than any other situation which they have faced. Police understand as normal the problems of dealing with crime or vice. They may resent violence stemming from minority ghettos, but this, too, is understandable and part of police work. But to take provocative behavior from youths who are socially and economically much better off than they and their children is more than the average policeman can tolerate.

The deliberate effort to bait and provoke the police by contemporary New Left radicals is rather new in the history of leftist movements. The American Socialist Party in its early history actually pointed to the police department as a good example of the way the government could provide needed services efficiently. The Communists, of course, never described the police in this fashion, but in the twenties, European Communists concerned with attaining power rather than with symbolic demonstrations defined the police, like the rank and file of the military, as exploited working-class groups who should either be converted to the revolution or at least be neutralized. They directed propaganda to the self-interests of the police, calling on them to refuse to serve the interests of the ruling class during strikes or demonstrations. The European left has often sought to organize the police in trade unions, although it is, of course, also true that they have had an ambivalent attitude toward them. The police have been involved in brutal suppression of left-wing and trade-union demonstrations in Europe, which have made them the target of left-wing criticism and counterviolence. Nevertheless, the left there remembers that the police come from proletarian origins. During the May, 1968, student demonstrations and strikes in Italy, a leading Communist intellectual, Pier Paolo Pasolini, told the New Left students that in a conflict between them and the police, he stood with the police: "Your faces are those of sons of good families, and I hate you as I hate your fathers. The good breeding comes through. . . . Yesterday when you had your battle in the Valle Giulia with the police, my sympathies were with the police, because they are the sons of the poor" (quoted from the *Corriere della Sera* by Melvin Lasky in the August issue of *Encounter*).

Given the interest shown in the welfare of the police by sections of the European left, their membership in trade unions, and their working-class origins, it is not surprising that the political behavior of European police has been more ambivalent than that of their American compeers. On various occasions, segments of the police in Europe have shown sympathy for left and working-class forces, particularly where they have been serving under leftist governments for some time. This was true in Social Democratic Berlin and Prussia generally before 1932, in Vienna before

1934, and in parts of Republican Spain before 1936. The ambivalent attitudes of the police have shown up most recently in France, where a number of police unions issued statements after the May, 1968, events, denying responsibility for use of force against student demonstrators. The police organizations wanted it known that the government, not the police, was responsible for the vigor of the actions taken.

It is doubtful that the American New Left students will ever come to see the police in a sympathetic light, as exploited, insecure, alienated members of the underprivileged classes. As members of the first leftist youth movement which is unaffiliated with any adult party, they are unconcerned with the consequences of their actions on the political strength of the larger left-wing movement. To a large extent, their provocative efforts reflect the biases of the educated upper middle class. Lacking a theory of society and any concern for the complexities of the "road to power" which have characterized the revolutionary Marxist movement, they are prepared to alienate the police, as well as conventional working-class opinion, in order to provoke police brutality, which in turn will validate their total rejection of all social institutions. Hence, we may expect a continuation of the vicious circle of confrontation and police terror tactics.

Liberal moderates properly react to this situation by demanding that the police act toward deviant behavior much as all other professionals do, that they have no more right to react aggressively toward provocative acts than psychiatrists faced by maniacal and dangerous patients, that no matter what extremists do, the police should not lose their self-control. Such a policy is easy to advocate; it is difficult to carry out.

Furthermore, it ignores the fact that most of the police are "working-class" professionals, not the products of postgraduate education. As James Q. Wilson points out, "This means they bring to the job some of the focal concerns of working-class men—a preoccupation with maintaining self-respect, proving one's masculinity, 'not taking any crap,' and not being 'taken in.' Having to rely on personal qualities rather than on formal routines . . . means that the officer's behavior will depend crucially on how much deference he is shown, on how manageable the situation seems to be, and on what the participants in it seem to 'deserve.'" If society wants police to behave like psychiatrists, then it must be willing to treat and train them like psychiatrists rather than like pariahs engaged in dirty work. At present, it treats their job like a semiskilled position which requires, at best, a few weeks' training. Norman Kassoff of the research staff of the International Association of Chiefs of Police has compared the legal minimum training requirements for various occupations in the different American states. Calculated in terms of hours, the median minimums are 11,000 for physicians, 5000 for embalmers, 4000 for barbers, 1200 for beauticians, and less than 200 for policemen. The vast majority of policemen begin carrying guns and enforcing the law with less than five weeks' training of any kind.

The new tensions have increased the old conflict between the police and the liberals. For it must be said that liberals are prejudiced against police, much as many white police are biased against Negroes. Most liberals are ready to assume that all charges of police brutality are true. They tend to refuse to give the police the benefit of any doubt. They rarely denounce the extreme black groups and left radicals for their confrontationist efforts. They do not face up to the need for tactics to deal with deliberate incitement to mob violence. If the liberal and intellectual communities are to have any impact on the police, if they are to play any role in reducing the growing political alienation of many police, they must show some recognition that the police force is also composed of human beings, seeking to earn a living. They must be willing to engage in a dialogue with the police concerning their problems.

The New Barbarians

DANIEL J. BOORSTIN

For centuries, men here have been discovering new ways in which the happiness and prosperity of each individual revolves around that of the community. Now suddenly we are witnessing the explosive rebellion of small groups, who reject the American past, deny their relation to the community, and in a spiritual Ptolemaism insist that the U.S.A. must revolve around each of them. This atavism, this New Barbarism, cannot last, if the nation is to survive.

Because the New Barbarians seek the kudos of old labels—"Nonviolence," "Pacifism," "Leftism," "Radicalism," etc.—we too readily assume that they really are just another expression of "good old American individualism," of "healthy dissent," of the red-blooded rambunctious spirit which has kept this country alive and kicking.

Nothing could be further from the truth. We are now seeing something new under the American sun. And we will be in still deeper trouble if we do not recognize what has really happened. The New Barbarism is not simply another expression of American vitality. It is not simply another expression of the utopianism of youth. On the contrary. What it expresses, in tornado-potence, is a new view of America and of the world. It expresses a new notion of how the world should be grasped.

The Depression Decade beginning in 1929 saw in the United States a host of radicalisms, perhaps more numerous and more influential than at any earlier period of our history. Many of these were left-wing movements, which included large numbers of our academics, intellectuals, and men of public conscience, who became members or fellow travelers of groups dominated by Marxist ideas. They favored a reconstruction of American life on a base of socialism or communism. They had a great deal to do with promoting a new and wider American labor movement, with helping F.D.R. popularize the need for a welfare state, and with persuading Americans to join the war to stop Hitler. Although they fenced in American social scientists by new orthodoxies, they did have a generally tonic effect on American society. However misguided were many of the policies they advocated, these radicals did awaken and sensitize the American conscience. They confronted Americans with some facts of life which had been swept under the rug.

That was radicalism. And those of us who were part of it can attest to some of its features. It was radicalism in the familiar and traditional sense of the word. The word "radical" does, of course, come from the Latin "radix," meaning "root," and a radical, then, is a person trying to go to the root of matters.

Of course those radicals never were quite respectable. Their message was that things were not what they seemed, and that inevitably makes respectable people uncomfortable. But we would be mistaken if we assumed, as many do nowadays, that a radical is anybody who makes lots of other people uncomfortable.

What makes a radical radical is not *that* he discomfits others but *how* he does it. A drunk is not a radical, neither is a psychotic, though both can make us quite uncomfortable. Nor does mere rudeness or violence make a person a radical, though a rude or violent man can make everybody around him quite miserable. Nor is a man who is unjustly treated and resents it necessarily a radical. Caryl Chessman may not have been guilty as charged—yet that did not make him a radical.

The most vocal and most violent disrupters of American society today are not radicals at all, but a new species of barbarian. In the ancient world, "barbarian" was a synonym for foreigner, and meant an alien who came from some far-off savage land. He himself was "barbarous," wild, and uncivilized. He was a menace not because he wanted to reform or reshape the society he invaded but because he did not understand or value that society, and he aimed to destroy it.

The New Barbarians in America today come not from without, but from within. While they are not numerous anywhere—comprising perhaps less than two percent of our two hundred million Americans—they pose a special threat precisely because they are diffuse, wild, and disorganized. They have no one or two headquarters to be surveyed, no one or two philosophies to be combated. But they are no less rude, wild, and uncivilized than if they had come from the land of the Visigoths or the Vandals. The fact that they come from within—and are somehow a product of—our society makes them peculiarly terrifying, but it does not make them any the less barbarians.

We must not be deceived by our own hypersensitive liberal consciences, nor by the familiar, respected labels under which the New Barbarians like to travel. If American civilization is to survive, if we are to resist and defeat the New Barbarism, we must see it for what it is. Most important, we must see that in America the New Barbarism is something really new.

A first step in this direction is to cease to confuse the New Barbarians with the members of other, intellectually respectable groups which can and must claim tolerance in a free society. The New Barbarians are not radicals. This will be obvious if we recall the characteristics of the radicalisms that in one form or another have discomfited and awakened generations of Americans.

Radicalism in the United States has had several distinctive and interrelated characteristics:

1. Radicalism Is a Search for Meaning. The search for meaning is the search for significance, for what else something connotes. The socialist, for example, denies that the capitalist system of production and distribution makes sense; he wants to reorganize it to produce a new meaning in the institutions of property and in the economy of the whole society. The religious pacifist, if he is a Christian, seeks the meaning of society in the Christian vision of peace and the brotherhood of man. When the true radical criticizes society he demands that the society justify itself according to some new measure of meaning.

2. Radicalism Has a Specific Content. The radical is distinguished from the man who simply has a bad digestion by the fact that the radical's belief has some solid subject matter, while the other man is merely dyspeptic. A stomachache or sheer anger or irritability cannot be the substance of radicalism. Thus, while a man can be ill-natured or irritable in general, he cannot be a radical in general. Every radicalism is a way of asserting *what* are the roots. Radicalism, therefore, involves affirmation. It is distinguished from conservatism precisely in that the conservative can be loose and vague about his affirmation. The conservative is in fact always tempted to let his affirmation become mere complacency. But the true radical cannot refuse to affirm, and to be specific, although of course he may be utopian. The radical must affirm that *this* is more fundamental than *that*. One great service of the radical, then, is that by his experimental definitions he puts the conservative on the defensive and makes him discover, decide, and define what is really worth preserving. The radical does this by the specificity (sometimes also by the rashness) of his affirmation—of the dictatorship of the proletariat, of the Kingdom of God on earth, or of whatever else.

3. Radicalism Is an Affirmation of Community. It affirms that we all share the same root problems, that we are all in the same boat, though the radical may see the boat very differently than do others. For example, if he is a pacifist radical he insists that the whole society bears the blame for even a single man killed in war; if he is an anarchist radical he insists that the whole society bears the blame for the injustice of property and the violence of government. Radicalism, then, involves a commitment to the interdependence of men, and to the sharing of their concerns, which the radical feels with an especially urgent, personal intensity.

These are only general characteristics. Of course, there are borderline cases. We might be uncertain whether Henry George's Single Taxers or Tom Watson's Populists were real radicals. But a full-fledged radicalism, of the kind which can serve and has served as a tonic to the whole society, does have at least the three characteristics I have mentioned. There have been many such radicalisms in American History—from the Antinomians of Massachusetts Bay, through the Quakers of Pennsylvania, the Abolitionists and the Mormons down to the Jehovah's Witnesses and the Communists in our own day. But the most prominent, the most vocal, the most threatening, and the most characteristic disruptive movements in the United States within the last few years do not belong in this tradition. Whatever they or their uncritical observers may say to the contrary, they are not radicalisms. They do not exhibit the characteristics I have listed.

It is characteristic of the Student Power and the Black Power "movements" that in them the quest for meaning has been displaced by the quest for power. Among students, the Bull Session tends to be displaced by the Strategy Session. The "discussions" of activist students are not explorations of the great questions that have troubled civilized men as they come to manhood, since the days of the Old Testament and of Ancient Greece. They are not concerned with whether there is a God, with what is the true nature of art, or of civilization, or of morals. The Student Power Barbarians and the Black Power Barbarians pose not questions but answers. Or, as one of their recent slogans says: "Happiness Is Student Power." Their answer to everything is uncharmingly simple: Power. And to the more difficult questions their answer is: More Power.

These New Barbarians offer no content, no ideology, hardly even a jargon. While dissident students thirty-five years ago spoke an esoteric Marxist lingo, and debated "dialectical materialism," "the transformation of quantity into quality," etc., etc., the dissident students and Black Powerites today scream four-letter obscenities and expletives. While the radicals explored an intricate ideology in the heavy volumes of Marx, the cumbersome paragraphs of Lenin, and the elaborate reinterpretations of Stalin and Trotsky, today's power-seekers are more than satisfied by the hate slogans of Mao Tse-tung, Che Guevara, or Malcolm X. They find nothing so enchanting as the sound of their own voices, and their bibliography consists mainly of the products of their own mimeographing. They seem to think they can be radicals without portfolio. If they call themselves "anarchists" they have not bothered to read their Thoreau or Proudhon, Bakunin or Tolstoy. If they call themselves "leftists" they have not bothered to read Marx or Engels, Lenin or Trotsky. If they call themselves Black Power Nationalists, they mistake the rattle of ancient chains for the sound of facts and ideas.

Having nothing to say, the New Barbarians cannot interest others by *what* they say. Therefore they must try to shock by *how* they say it.

Traditionally, radicals have addressed their society with a question mark, but the new frustrates' favorite punctuation is the exclamation point! Having no new facts or ideas to offer, they strain at novelty with their latrine words. The Black Powerites, whose whole program is their own power, must wrap up their emptiness in vulgarisms and expletives. For racism is the perfect example of a dogma without content.

The appeal to violence and "direct action" as if they were ends rather than means is eloquent testimony of the New Barbarians' lack of subject matter. An act of violence may express hate or anger, but it communicates nothing precise or substantial. Throwing a rock, like hurling an epithet, proclaims that the thrower has given up trying to say anything.

These Student Powerites and Black Powerites are not *egalitarians* seeking a just community; they are *egolitarians,* preening the egoism of the isolationist self. Students seek power for "students," Negroes seek power for "blacks"—and let the community take the hindmost! Unlike the radicalisms which affirm community and are preoccupied or obsessed by its problems, the Student Power and Black Power movements deny any substantial community—even among their own "members." A novel feature of S.N.C.C. and S.D.S., too little noted, is the fact that they are, strictly speaking, "nonmembership" organizations. Members do not carry cards, membership lists are said not to exist. A person does not "join" as a result of long and solemn deliberation, he is not trained and tested (as was the case in the Thirties with candidates for membership in the Communist Party). Instead the New Barbarian simply affiliates, and stays with the group as long as it pleases him. "I'm with you today, baby, but who knows where I'll be tomorrow?" A desperate infant-instantism reveals the uncertainty and vagrancy of these affiliations. The leader better act this afternoon, for maybe they won't be with him tomorrow morning!

All these unradical characteristics of the New Barbarians express a spiritual cataclysm. This is what I mean by the Ptolemaic Revolution: a movement from the community-centered to the self-centered. While radicals see themselves and everything else revolving around the community and its idealized needs, each of these new frustrates tries to make the world revolve around himself. The depth and significance of this shift in focus have remained unnoticed. It has been the harder to grasp because it is in the nature of the New Barbarism that it should lack philosophers. Being closer to a dyspepsia than to an ideology, the New Barbarism has tried to generalize its stomachaches but has been unable to cast them into a philosophy. It is much easier, therefore, to describe the direction in which the chaotic groups comprising the New Barbarism are moving than to fix the precise position where they stand.

The New Barbarism, in a word, is the social expression of a movement from Experience to Sensation. Experience, the dictionary tells us, means *actual observation of or practical acquaintance with facts or events; knowledge resulting from this.* A person's experience is what he has lived through. Generally speaking, experience is (a) cumulative, and (b) communicable. People add up their experiences to become wiser and more knowledgeable. We can learn from our own experience and, most important, we can learn from other people's experiences. Our publicly shared experience is history. Experience is distinguished, then, by the very fact that it can be shared. When we have an experience, we enter into the continuum of a society. But the dramatic shift now is away from Experience and toward Sensation.

Sensation is personal, private, confined, and incommunicable. Our sensations (hearing, seeing, touching, tasting, and smelling) are what we *receive*. Or, as the dictionary says, sensation is *consciousness of perceiving or seeming to perceive some state or affection of one's body or its parts or senses of one's mind or its emotions; the contents of such consciousness.* If an experience were totally incommunicable, if I could not describe it to anyone else, if I could not share it, it would not really be an experience. It would simply be a sensation, a message which came to me and to me alone. Sensations, from their very nature, then, are intimate and ineffable. Experience takes us out of ourselves, sensation affirms and emphasizes the self.

What history is to the person in quest of experience, a "happening" is to the person in quest of sensation. For a "happening" is something totally discrete. It adds to our sensations without increasing our experience.

Experience and Sensation, then, express attitudes to the world as opposite as the poles. The experience-oriented young person suffers Weltschmerz—the discovery of the pain and suffering that are his portion of the world. The sensation-oriented suffers an "identity crisis": he is concerned mostly about defining the boundaries of that bundle of private messages which is himself. The experience-oriented seeks, and finds, continuity, and emphasizes what is shared and what is communicable. The sensation-oriented seeks the instantaneous, the egocentric, the inexpressible. The accumulation of *experience* produces the *expert*. Its cumulative product is *expertise*—competence, the ability to handle situations by knowing what is tried and familiar about them. And the name for accumulated experience is knowledge.

While sensations can be more or less intense, they are not cumulative. A set of simultaneous, intense and melodramatic sensations is not instructive, but it is shocking: we say it is *sensational*. Experience is additive, it can be organized, classified, and rearranged; sensation is miscellaneous, random, and incapable of being generalized.

Everywhere in the United States nowadays—and not only among the New Barbarians—we see a desperate quest for sensation and a growing tendency to value sensation more than experience. We note this in what people seek, in what they find, in what they make, and in what they like to watch. We note a tendency in painting to produce works which do not appeal to a common, shareable fund of experience, but which, instead, set off each viewer on his own private path of sensation. In the theatre and in movies which lack a clear and intelligible story line, the spectators are offered sensations from which each is expected to make his own private inward adventure.

An example of the current quest for the indescribable, the ineffable, the transcendent—aiming to maximize sensation rather than experience— is the current vogue for LSD and for other so-called "consciousness-expanding" drugs. Precisely speaking, they aim to expand not experience but *consciousness*. They aim somehow to increase the intensity and widen the range of the vivid, idiosyncratic self.

The special appeal of an LSD "trip" is that it leads to the ineffable: what one person gets is as different as possible from what is obtained by another. And it is all quite individual and quite unpredictable. "Instead of a communion," one psychologist explains, "it [the LSD state] is a withdrawal into oneself. The *religio* (binding together) is not visible here." This is how Richard Alpert, the archbishop of LSD, explains the sensations under the drug:

> "Nowhere" is Sidney's prediction of where the psychochemical (r)evolution is taking the "young people" who are exploring inner space. I prefer to read that word as NowHere, and fervently hope he is right— that LSD is bringing man back "to his senses". . . . Do not be confused! The issue is not LSD. . . . Your control and access to your own brain is at stake.

LSD sensations, Alpert insists, are "eyewitness reports of what is, essentially, a private experience." "It was," in the words of a girl who had just been on an LSD trip, "like a shower on the inside."

The search for sensation is a search for some way of reminding oneself that one is alive—but without becoming entangled with others or with a community. "I have never felt so intense, alive, such a sense of well-being. . . . I have chosen to be outside of society after having been very much inside. . . . My plans are unstructured in regards to anything but the immediate future. I believe in freedom, and must take the jump, I must take the chance of action." This is not the report of an LSD trip, but the explanation by a young white student of his sensations on joining S.N.C.C. The vocabulary of the Student Power movement reveals the same desperate quest for sensation. "Direct Action" is the name for spasmodic acts of self-affirmation. It is a way of making the senses scream. It matters not whether the "Direct Action" has a purpose, much less whether it can attain any purpose, since it gives satisfaction enough by intensifying the Direct Actor's sense of being alive and separate from others. "Direct Action" is to politics what the Frug or the Jerk is to the dance. It identifies and explodes the self without attaching the self to groups or to individuals outside. And now the "New Left" has become the LSD of the intellectuals.

The man who is pathologically experience-oriented will be timid, haunted by respectability. His motto is apt to be that posted over the desk of an English civil servant: "Never do anything for the first time!" On the other hand, the man pathologically obsessed by Sensation makes his motto: "Do everything only for the first time!"

All about us, and especially in the Student Power and Black Power movements of recent years, we see the pathology of the sensation-oriented. Contrary to popular belief, and to the legends which they would like to spread about themselves, they are not troubled by any excessive concern for others. Their feelings cannot accurately be described as a concern, and it is surely not for others. Their ailment might best be called *apathy.* For apathy is a feeling apart from others and, as the dictionary reminds us, *an indolence of mind.* The Direct Actionists, as President W. Allen Wallis of the University of Rochester has explained, "are the students who are truly apathetic." They do not care enough about the problems of their society to burn the midnight oil over them. Impatient to sate their egos with the sensations of "Direct Action," they are too indolent intellectually to do the hard work of exploring the problems to which they pretend a concern. Theirs is the egoism, the personal chauvinism of the isolationist self. Their "Direct Action" slogan means nothing but "Myself, Right or Wrong!"

These people I would call the *Apathetes.* Just as the Aesthetes of some decades ago believed in "Art for Art's Sake," so the Apathetes believe in "Me for My Own Sake." They try to make a virtue of their indolence of mind (by calling it "Direct Action") and they exult in their feeling-apartness (by calling it "Power"). Thus these Apathetes are at the opposite pole from the radicals of the past.

They abandon the quest for meaning, for fear it might entangle their thoughts and feelings with those of others, and they plunge into "Direct Action" for fear that second thoughts might deny them this satisfaction to their ego. Theirs is a mindless, obsessive quest for power. But they give up the very idea of man's need for quest. Instead they seek explosive affirmations of the self.

They deny the existence of subject matter, by denying the need for experience. How natural, then, that Youth should lord it over Age! For in youth, they say, the senses are most sensitive and most attuned. The accumulated experience of books or of teachers becomes absurdly irrelevant. There is no Knowledge, but only Sensation, and Power is its Handmaiden!

They deny the existence of time, since Sensation is instantaneous and not cumulative. They herald the age of Instant Everything! Since time can do nothing but accumulate experience and dull the senses, experience is said to be nothing but the debris which stifles our sensations! There must be no frustration. Every program must be instantaneous, every demand must be an ultimatum.

This movement from Experience to Sensation accelerates every day. Each little victory for Student Power or Black Power—or any other kind of Power—is a victory for the New Barbarism. Appropriately, the New Barbarism makes its first sallies and has its greatest initial successes against the universities, which are the repositories of Experience, and in the cause of Racism, which—whether it is Black or whether it is Aryan—is the emptiness to end all emptinesses.

Life
Imitates
Art

If there are no meanings, no values, no source of sustenance or help, then man, as creator, must invent, conjure up meanings and values, sustenance and succor out of nothing. He is a magician.
R. D. Laing in *The Politics of Experience*

Fashion is that by which the fantastic becomes for a moment universal.
Oscar Wilde

Introduction to Part Two

*I call Las Vegas the Versailles of America, and for
specific reasons. Las Vegas happened to be created after
the war, with war money, by gangsters . . . the first
uneducated, prole-petty-burgher Americans to have
enough money to build a monument to their style of life.
They built it in an isolated spot, Las Vegas, out in the
desert, just like Louis XIV, the Sun King, who purposely
went outside of Paris, into the countryside, to create
a fantastic baroque environment to celebrate his rule. It is
no accident that Las Vegas and Versailles are the only
two architecturally uniform cities in Western history. The
important thing about the building of Las Vegas is
not that the builders were gangsters but that they were
proles. They celebrated, very early, the new style of life of
America—using the money pumped in by the war to
show a prole vision . . .Glamor! . . . of style . . . long
after Las Vegas' influence as a gambling heaven
has gone, Las Vegas' forms and symbols will be
influencing American life . . . the new landmarks of
America, the new guideposts, the new way Americans get
their bearings. . .*

Tom Wolfe in *The Kandy-Kolored Tangerine-
Flake Streamline Baby*

Aestheticians and artists of the 1960s and 1970s may well look back on
their own era with some chagrin. In the 1950s the public and critics alike
were agreeable to accepting as bona fide art Rembrandts, Van Goghs,
Picassos, even Klees, works by Milton, Proust, and Durrell, grand opera,
legitimate theatre, and even certain selected "art" films. But the seventh
decade of the century changed that comforting certainty about the status
of art for once and for all. As early as 1965 young people in New York
City and San Francisco were smashing grand pianos to the accompaniment of eleven radios blaring away at full volume, each one turned to a
different station—and worse still, they were calling it a "Happening,"
"creative vandalism," a new art form. Overnight there mushroomed giant
Campbell soup cans, vinyl hamburgers, op art, pop art, kinetic sculpture,
musicals like *Hair* and *Salvation*, experimental films with titles like *Blowjob*
and *Blue Movie*—and all done in the sacred name of the Muse. Fashion
experts blithely assured us that the miniskirt was less sex symbol than

art form: the New Art of the switched-on sixties. Revolutionary and con-frontation theatre abounded, Happenings proliferated like spring leaves in fast movies, and Susan Sontag kept warning us at every turn against interpretation. Bernard Geis, publisher of *Valley of the Dolls* and similar best-sellers, proclaimed his theory of the Book-as-Artifact: cover, pages, print, incidental content, dust jacket, plus hype. Marshall McLuhan, in announcing the death of print and the print-oriented linear mentality, effectively ushered in an era of post-logical, post-literate, non-linear and non-verbal orientation. The Age of Pop was upon us: Versailles was *passé* and Las Vegas' time had come to shine. Yet in the midst of the New Theatre, the New Film, the New Books, and the New Sound, a few still small voices could be heard asking, like Schultz's Linus watching Snoopy waltz atop a toy piano: "Very nice. But is it art?"

Is it Art?: *that* was the aesthetic question of the sixties, and it still remains to be answered in the seventies. What is (was) Art? Or, perhaps more to the point, is (was) there any such thing as Art? Is there any aesthetic system inclusive enough, all-encompassing enough, to embrace both Las Vegas and Versailles, Donne and Ginsberg, Bach and the Beatles, Wyeth and Warhol, Sophocles and *Dionysus '69*? For one thing becomes increasingly clear as the New Art in all its various forms begins to surface: the old categories of painting, sculpture, literature, architecture, and music are now being expanded and redefined to include such mixed-media, multi-sensory forms as camp, op, and pop art, guerilla theatre, kinetic sculpture, posters, commercial and experimental films, acid and grease rock, country music, science fiction, "found" art, ethnic arts of all kinds, The Living Theatre, magazines, underground newspapers, jewelry, clothing, comic books, billboard poetry, ballads, computer music, theatre in the streets, mysticism in its various ramifications, television, and radio.

So what, amidst this plethora of new and evolving forms, can we say of the New Art? What kind of aesthetic values, if any, can we impose on this bewildering profusion of new aesthetic experiences? Although we have yet to develop that single great aesthetic system which will be to the New Art what the New Criticism was to the poetry of the fifties, at least three characteristics emerge as central to both the New Art and commentaries on it. Let us see how this is so.

1. Emphasis on self-expression for both artist and audience alike. To borrow Meyer Abrams' categories as outlined in *The Mirror and the Lamp*, we can designate most twentieth-century art as either expressive or pragmatic: either artist-oriented or audience-oriented, or perhaps both. Thus essayists in this section like Paul Williams ("How Rock Communicates") cite quotations from artists and composers to suggest that the focal point of rock and other pop music is the internal state of the composer or singer: "What you receive is part of the artist, it's alive," "You gotta have soul, baby, which means it's gotta be you you're passing on—people receiving parts of people, living matter, animate stuff," "They don't just say those things, they feel them." The New Art of the sixties thus moves in two apparently contradictory directions: on the one hand, toward works that "alienate" the audience, almost in a Brechtian sense, and, on the other, toward works that reach out, literally or symbolically, to the audience in order to involve its members in the artistic experience. The first category of art puts an aesthetic distance between the creator and his public by creating what Harold Rosenberg terms a "wall of incomprehension" between artist and audience, as in much op and pop art, theatre of the Angries, underground newspapers, and most Warhol films. This is the New Art which both Rosenberg and Alfred Kazin see as essentially boring: the art that presents a double façade. To its public it turns the aesthetic of the void, the total blank, while to the In-crowd it presents a universe of "shared opinions, acquaintances and incidents." This vacant front becomes in less-than-skillful hands the art of the put-on, the in-joke, the private game created for that precious intricate society which only the initiates know. It seeks its effect by angering, alienating, boring, or confusing its audience: its tools are repetition, the verbal or visual insult, the sly put-down, the knowing wink or nod.

By contrast there is that other art which reaches out to engulf and embrace its audience. Its key word is *involvement:* detachment or disinterest are signs of soullessness, "plastic" values, or neurosis. Thus it invites the audience to play an unwilling Pentheus to its creator's Dionysus and thus to join both artist and performers in a bacchanal of self-expression. Like its sister art of alienation, this art also features minimal content, is non-mimetic (the universe is relative to each viewer; thus, there is no stable reality to emulate), and implies that the work of art is nothing while the artist and audience are everything.

2. Anti-intellectualism and emphasis on immediacy and sensation. We already have seen that the "old art" (classical and Renaissance art through early twentieth century) took for granted that the purpose of art and criticism was to order existing reality and impose order on an often-chaotic universe. By contrast the New Art and the New Criticism assume that art exists in order to express a personal world view. Art thus becomes self-discovery and personal statement, expressive rather than mimetic or objective. Indeed, Ralph Carnes' criticism of reviewers like Pauline Kael concerns their inordinate interest in the biography of the producer or writer, the special effects, or the intentions of the producer rather than the form and content of the film itself. Thus, in its most extreme form the New Art may lead to a sort of aesthetic anarchy while less extreme cases stop with the assumption that one must "express" one's views at all costs. The New Art, unlike the old, is Dionysiac and orgiastic, not Apollonian and reflective or rational. It is interested in myth, ritual, magic, and incantation, as is appropriate for a society which is post-logical, post-literate, tribal, totemic, sensuous, and mystical. The art critic Dore Ashton has called it "the thinking that recalls rather than represents," implying that it summons up a collective unconscious or pre-conscious that deals in archetypes and myths rather than in literalisms.

The New Art is an expression of a chaotic post-war world, composed of fragments, myths, personal visions, dreams, nightmares, non-linear disjointed images, drug fantasies, the products of psychotherapy and hyp-nosis. Jerzy Grotowski in the *Tulane Drama Review* (1965) referred to "association images rooted in the collective unconscious"—a phrase that accurately reflects the sources of much of the New Art. Thus, for Paul Williams the important thing about rock music is not its complicated rhythms or sophisticated lyrics; it is, rather, the fact that rock music communicates by dream-states, unreal images, daydreams, and tenuous chains of association. Like Williams, Ronald Gross and Karen Murphy cite Bob Dylan and John Lennon as typical of this new generation of composer-singers apotheosized by the young largely because of their ability to understand youth's fragmented world. Rock, unlike the music of high culture, "is continuous with everyday life, not a departure from it" and thus succeeds with modern youth where conventional poetry and music fail. Youth holds a disjointed and chaotic world view that rock captures in its very rhythms as well as in its lyrics, and thus is commercially suc-cessful.

The *locus classicus* of the New Aesthetic is Susan Sontag's famous essay "Against Interpretation," which begins with this quotation from de Kooning: "Content is a glimpse of something, an encounter like a flash. It's very tiny—very tiny, content." Miss Sontag calls the earliest art "in-cantatory, magical, ritualistic." Yet its first theoretician, Aristotle, pro-posed a mimetic theory of art that has remained influential through cen-turies of art interpretation. Thus began the old form-content dichotomy that has plagued generations of artists and critics alike. This dichotomy is reflected in critical statements like "What *X* means is . . ." or "What *X* was really trying to say is . . ." Today, therefore, Miss Sontag concludes, content is "a hindrance, a nuisance, a . . . philistinism." To "interpret" is to impoverish and deplete the world in order to erect in its place "a shadow world of 'meanings.'" Thus she argues that we must replace interpretation with direct sensuous experience: "we must again experi-ence more immediately what we have." Films, she thinks, are the most exciting of all contemporary art forms because the sheer power and the overpowering nature of visual images overcome our urge to interpret. As for aesthetics, she concludes, we need a criticism that treats form as opposed to content; we need an aesthetics of "transparence . . . the luminousness of the thing in itself, of things being what they are." We need, in other words, to recover our senses: to see more, hear more, feel more, and "know" less. In the essay immediately preceding this introduc-tion ("The New Barbarians") Daniel Boorstin concludes that what experi-ence was for past generations, sensation is for the generation that came of age in the sixties and seventies. We are the new sensation-seekers, the new pioneers in a newly sensuous life-style, Boorstin implies, and our art and criticism reflect this shift in values.

As Alfred Kazin reminds us in "Art on Trial," twentieth-century art has long operated on the assumption that by honoring the unconscious, the spontaneous, the primitive, the childlike, the instinctive, and the sexual side of man, we could somehow mystically get ourselves back to the lost pre-industrial Eden, the garden without that serpent machine. Joni Mitchell's words "we've got to get ourselves/ Back to the garden" bear eloquent testimony to the implicitly Edenic assumptions of the New Art and its criticism. The assumptions are partly Freudian and Jungian, partly from Erich Fromm and Fritz Perls; in either case they celebrate the unconscious mind, myth, ritual, a fey childlikeness, play, magic, and incantation as ways of getting beyond the "plastic" world of capitalism and industry to the "real" one, the natural and spontaneous existence. The problem with the arts today, says Kazin, is that they may become merely trivial like our "hopelessly inflated and trivial" surroundings, playthings in an essentially egocentric civilization. He cites as an example the Warhol film *Chelsea Girls,* in which the entire script was ad-libbed. The problem was that after an hour or so all the lovely lanky birds and Eighth Avenue cowboys had run out of anything to say. Again the aesthetics of the void, the blank, "that new, schizoid stare which itself has become a hallmark of our times."

3. Emphasis on style. Leslie Fiedler in "The New Mutants" writes that we classify human beings according to their attitudes toward time as reactionary, conservative, revolutionary, or liberal. The decade of the sixties, however, has witnessed a new breed of youth whom Fiedler characterizes as non-participants in the past and "drop-outs from history" who reject both bourgeois and Protestant versions of humanism and see perpetual childhood as the end of life. This new race of new mutants, Fiedler suggests, are disconnected, alienated, mystically inclined, minority-group oriented, post-Puritan, and more sympathetic to madness than sanity.

Many of the assumptions of this new breed of youth, of course, are intimately linked with its sources and with its attitudes toward the culture that spawned it. Ralph Carnes' article " 'Fascinating, Captain Kirk' " relates the history of comic books and other media from the appearance of Superman comics to the present. Comic books gained popularity, he suggests, partially because of their oversimplified version of reality: in a Manichean world where good and might invariably conquered evil and weakness an electronic *deus ex machina* was a respectable way to solve problems. Today, he concludes, we live in a comic-book world peopled with comic-book figures who speak in easily identifiable word-balloons and appeal to our "comic-book mentalities," which still more than half-believe in the myth of the Simple Answer. Lindsy and Lawrence Van Gelder provide a further corroboration of Mr. Carnes' thesis in their essay, "The Radicalization of the Superheroes." The Van Gelders observe that in the mid- and late sixties, the predictable happened to the world of comic books: the heroes became radicalized and, as such, provided further fuel for the popular pseudo-revolutionary world view.

Thus, whatever else can be said for the New Art, one thing is clear: it is above all an art of style. John Corry's article on "The Politics of Style" (Part Three) suggests that today politics is less a matter of allying oneself with a particular political party or candidate than it is a matter of consciously choosing one's life-style. One adopts a certain way of talking, dressing, combing his hair, presenting an image to the world, and thus tacitly reaffirms certain ritual opinions. Art in the sixties was much like politics in this respect: it was created by, and simultaneously helped to create, its own ambience and life-style. Being a collector of Warhols and Jasper Johns and wearing Zandra Rhodes and Betsey Johnson designs indicated a certain world view that also hinted at vague sympathies with the Black Panthers and the California grape pickers. The 1960s, in fact, saw the transformation of "fashion" from mere clothing into a prepackaged and therefore easily accessible life-style which was symbolic not only of its wearer's socioeconomic standing and taste but also, and more important, of his political opinions, cultural ideals, aesthetics, and general life-style (see "The Glass of Fashion" in this section). Like everything else in the 1960s fashion came to be politically saturated and thus came to symbolize more than it explicitly stated. Styles sprang up from the Left Bank, from Chelsea and the Village, and progressed up the Rag Trade's Chain of Being until they finally reached the sacred precincts of the *haute couture* where they became, in Tom Wolfe's phrase, "radical chic." And so the New Art, like the new fashion, politics, and media, became more symbolic than literal, valued both for what it could tell us about its creator, producer, composer, or performer, and for what it revealed about its consumer. The art consumer who read the *East Village Other* and the *New York Review of* (Each Other's) *Books,* owned a reproduction of Robert Indiana's famous LOVE poster, looked to John Lennon, Leonard Cohen, and Mick Jagger as the new poets of the age, and enjoyed the sentimental lyrics of Rod McKuen and Kahlil Gibran was in all respects a different person from the one whose reading matter consisted of the *New York Times, Gentleman's Quarterly,* the *Wall Street Journal,* and who attended opening night at the opera and considered *The Graduate* an art film. Because everything today is politically saturated and has been so since the mid-sixties, the clothes we wear, the words we use, the newspapers and magazines we read (see Brackman's "The Underground Press"), the restaurants and coffee shops we frequent, the schools we attend, the styles of interior design we affect—all have implicit symbolic content and thus mirror those "unexpressed presuppositions" of which Alfred North Whitehead speaks.

This intense interest in style in turn leads to a consumer- and media-oriented art, created by and for a consumer society. Burt Korall in "The Music of Protest" suggests that rock protest lyrics at their worst become "abstract emotional substitutes for what is going on in the world": that singing protest songs creates in youth the illusion that they are actually protesting when what they are really doing is going to record shops and concerts. In "Music from the Conglomerates" (*Saturday Review,* 22 February, 1969), Hans Heinsheimer observes that recording companies with extravagantly antiestablishment names like "Kama Sutra Records" and "Buddha Records" are in fact owned by such staid firms as Viewflex, Inc. Similarly, Marshall Fishwick in "Folklore, Fakelore, and Poplore" describes three distinctly different new "iconographies" for the sixties and seventies. "Fakelore" he defines as the urban synthetic version of folk-lore, while poplore is chrome and kitsch transcendentalized by Madison Avenue. Genuine folk cultures, he points out, are rural, religiously-oriented, traditional, spontaneous, personal, oral, and sacred rather than secular. Fakelore, on the other hand, is none of these things: it is pseudo-folklore, like composed ballads and folk tales masquerading as real ones, and as such partakes of the nature of Boorstin's "pseudo-event": a planned, non-spontaneous event that is a self-fulfilling prophecy intended to be reported and reproduced *ad nauseam.* Fakelore is to folklore what the pseudo-event is to the real one, what a Sant' Angelo gyspy dress is to the original model, or what overalls and brogan shoes from Goldblatt's basement are to genuine rural versions of the same. On the other hand, poplore, much like the old folklore, avoids sentimentality and "artiness," preferring in-stead to derive its force from earthiness and "guts." Folklore mytholo-gizes; fakelore always de-mythologizes and destroys the supernatural, while poplore re-mythologizes and searches for a new ontology.

As early as 1966 Roger Vadim asserted that in the second half of the twentieth century youth has become a class. J. Marks in "The Hip Estab-lishment" assumes the validity of Vadim's pronouncement when he speaks of the creation of a new young power class with abundant money and leisure time that has helped to create and to affirm youth's tribal solidarity. Business capitalizes on this sense of "class": it both uses and creates the new "Hip Establishment," whose members act largely on specious distinc-tions of In and Out (one is reminded of the now-defunct *Eye* magazine's Up and Down escalators). Consequently, says Marks, we have the unique situation of a consumer market controlled by affluent and leisured youths who have terrific power and influence, a wide knowledge of the pop media, but a "terrible dearth of human experience."

It is this very emphasis on style that is the New Art's greatest asset and also its greatest liability. At its best the *avant-garde* has produced vital new art forms expressive of an urban and contemporary civilization instead of an ancient rural one. At its worst, however, the New Art may become merely the art of tedium, boredom, inexpressiveness, emotional disen-gagement, monotony, self-neutralization, obsession with details, and ab-stractness that Rosenberg accurately describes. The ultimate in this kind of boring New Art, Rosenberg says, is Warhol's *Blowjob* where we see the image of a "peculiarly blank" face throughout ninety minutes of film. It is interesting to note that Allen Ginsberg's reaction to the film was to be stirred to enthusiasm by the artist's "daring to be so blank."

The perfect legendary account of the New Art at its worst is the old fable of the emperor's new clothes in which only a child dares to proclaim the clothes invisible. The perfect contemporary analogue, however, is provided by R. Crumb's cartoon "Fritz the Cat." Fritz arrives back at the communal pad one night with two chicks in tow only to find his fellow animals stoned on dope as they listen in rapt attention to an anteater reading the dictionary. When Fritz and girls arrive the anteater has just begun the A's ("abaxeus, abaxial, aberedarlen, ablative, ablutant . . ."). The content is minimal, but every new word brings forth a fresh chorus of instant insights: "Tell it, man!" "Right on!" "O tell it to us good, baby!" "O wow!" "Great! Great!" "I see it, man! Yes!" "Great! Great! I see it all! Yes! GOD, yes!"

Valerie Carnes

The Sounds
of Silence

How Rock
Communicates

PAUL WILLIAMS

*A great many considerations and puzzles that one meets
sooner or later in all the arts find their clearest expression,
and therefore their most tangible form, in connection with
music.*

Suzanne K. Langer,
Feeling and Form

I know you deceive me; now here's a surprise . . .

Peter Townshend,
"I Can See for Miles"

*I have never consciously written a song through a personal
experience or an inspiration. I never write about things
that happen to me. A lot of writers will say they did a song
because they were in a certain mood but that's never
happened to me. I can write happy when I'm sad or sad
when I'm happy. I just get an idea and work on it.*

Smokey Robinson,
Interviewed by *Hit Parader*

I

I got up this morning and listened to "Heroes and Villains." Awakening
from deep sleep, unconsciousness spills hesitantly away, aspects of the
real slowly mixing in with the rest of your mind. . . . Last week I was at
Van Dyke Parks' home in the Hollywood Hills; the week before, chatting

with Brian Wilson at the Kennedy International Airport. He hadn't heard Van's album yet. He'd been surprised to read about *Smiley Smile* in *Craw-daddy!* When *Smiley Smile* came out, I wondered why "Heroes and Villains" didn't sound as good in stereo. Now I was listening to the single for the second time this morning. I stepped into the shower.

I don't know how I get these things on paper. Thoughts in my mind form words on a page through my fingers; concepts come together and generate ideas, and what can I point to to say, "I intended that"? The reader himself has no certain idea what goes on as his eyes touch the paper. He receives. I have given. But how?

How do we get from one place to another? (Now I'm thinking out loud.) Space is conquered by movement. Freedom of movement is granted by lack of restraint. There are things I can move through—water and air; there are things that detain me, like stone. I cannot walk through fire. How do we get from one place to another? We will ourselves to move through receptive media.

Then what are our vehicles for? They get us there safer, and faster, retarding our movement in time. We cover more space and less time. What is the vehicle for an image? A concept? Something that carries that concept, from here to there, in space and time. I hear music in New York that was recorded in Oklahoma; I hear it today and tomorrow; the musicians performed it last year. And the music itself is a vehicle, just like my words on the page. Pick up a concept, stick it in the music, send it on its way.

The medium. The medium. It's all pretty complicated. The medium carries the message, but that's not all there is to it. Some people relate to Bob Dylan's vision of the world. That doesn't have anything to do with the medium; that's something that's in his head. And now it's in your head. The music—the medium—delivered it intact.

But suppose you say you relate to the music itself. Now you're digging the package, right? But it's the music that communicates—the feeling you get from the melody, from the beat, from the sound of the words and all that interacting with the words themselves, the specific concepts. So maybe the package, the medium, *is* the message, since we can't quite separate Bob Dylan's vision from Bob Dylan's music. But . . . no, the music and the message aren't the same thing either. They aren't separable, but they aren't the same thing. You can't pry the painting from the canvas, but that doesn't mean the materials *are* the painting.

Communication is transportation (I'm just fooling around here; I wouldn't want to perpetrate *new* slogans). Time and space are things to pass through; art is the rearranging of the universe into patterns reflecting the artist's will. Message is a specific thing, a discernible thing. Will is not. Few artists deal with messages, few artists expect you to go at the physical body of their work with a scalpel and attempt to extract its essence. The artist's emotions and sense perceptions are transmitted by means of his work. He receives, and he sends so that you may receive. The medium is not important. The medium is inanimate, an object. What you receive—

not a message, not a specific, but a sum of messages, an emotion, a vision, a perception—what you receive is a part of the artist. It's alive. It's reborn in you. Music. The notes are not important. Virtuosity means nothing. No one cares how well you rearrange the objects. You gotta have soul, baby, which just means it's gotta be *you* you're passing on—people receiving parts of people, living matter, animate stuff. The medium *and* the messages it contains are just so much nothing, trees falling in the forest with no one to hear, unless there is human life on both ends of the line, sending, receiving, transferring bits of human consciousness from one soul to another. Communication is the interaction between our personal worlds.

Stepping out of the shower, I put on the Byrds.

Dear Trina:

That song by the Who, "I Can See for Miles," has meant more and more to me lately. I hear it in my mind. The song explodes in bursts of energy, from my brain, through my body, down the street by which I'm walking and out into the world, pulling me with its strength toward infinity. Peter Townshend's guitar rings harder and faster, and I can feel for centuries.

I first heard the song in September, thinking: "Ah. Hard rock. But not so advanced for the Who. . . ." It sounded like an exceptional performance of an unexceptional work, and I let it go at that. And then in October, all my jealousy and rage, the song rediscovered as a vent for my passion, earphones and violence "miles and miles and miles and miles and miles . . ."

November, Los Angeles, the Who on all the radios, especially one blasting moment of Proustian significance in the backseat of Rothchild's rented car, suddenly *the* record of the year, all meaning, all truth to my cross-country crossed-wires mind. You may take one giant step. Rock-and-roll has entered the realm of forever . . .

You know what I mean, that special feeling after the last words of a book, that goes on and on, extending that book and you across forever into now, the sudden unexpected sense of the real, the flash of power and togetherness in your mind. Perhaps something slips in Einstein's continuum, and for one quite certain moment you taste another level— we all know the desperate need to sustain that. And Townshend's achievement is somewhere along these lines.

But this is emotion, and you have asked me to explain. The last day in L.A., you wondering, "What does the music mean to you? What is it that you hear in it, how do you react?" I want to tell you, you have a need to know; but I wonder how far that question reaches, if even one book is enough to begin to answer it . . .

Recently some girl told me, while I rapped about the future of the universe, that she hadn't been able to think so far lately, it had been like a wall before her mind, and although now she got a little distance . . .

You remember how on Jane Street I couldn't write at all, only for deadline and even then I preferred my office; and moving up here has meant tens of thousands of words, something every day? It's because I can see the river, because looking out the window I have a feeling of open space, cars and lights below me, buildings, boats, New Jersey stretched beyond. My mind is open, free. I have a horizon. I can see for miles . . .

And the power of the song is all in musical perspective: if you sketch the railroad tracks you see them going on forever, there in your little ten-by-twelve frame, and Townshend not only makes you hear forever, there in his four-minute song, but pulls you into it, puts you out there with the immediacy and involvement that is rock. Kineticism was always limited, it couldn't really go on beyond the orgasm; but Pete discovered that, as in sex, the perfect union knows no timing, so in music you could direct that feeling, paint the railroad tracks just so . . .

And then last week I called it the song of the revolution; I didn't know why. Often a comment will come for no reason, just a feeling, a flash of future thought before it happens, the time machine in operation, a chunk of next week now.

But revolution to me is ecological, the big world-move toward human sense; and I was carrying on about my vision of what could be when this girl made her comment on her thinking, and, indirectly, on mine. Distance . . . thinking as a spatial function . . . looking out across the river and opening my mind. . . . It all came together, I don't know why I didn't connect these things before, the ability to think about the future and the freedom to see for miles and miles and miles and miles and miles . . . oh yeah . . .

And Townshend's song, which seemed about unfaithfulness back when that was foremost in my mind, could now become for me a statement to my world: "I know you deceive me, now here's a surprise . . . a joke on you . . . you're gonna lose that smile . . . I can see for miles and miles" . . . the ecological revolution, Frank Herbert's *Dune,* the need for incredible visionary perception that we may see all the contexts, put the world in perspective and work to straighten it out . . . Oh yes, it's my trip and not necessarily Townshend's (or Dylan's? "Let us not speak falsely now . . ."), but maybe this tells you something about what I hear in the music, how it affects me, the level it communicates on . . .

Anyway, I've been listening to "River Deep Mountain High" and feeling it everywhere and thinking about you. See you soon.

Love,
Paul

II

The Byrds go right at it. They are about as nice as you could be and still seem absolutely real, and few of us could think of groups we'd rather listen to. It's always what's there on the record that's stunning; not the quality or the cleverness of what's there, not the music or the intent of what's there, but the stuff itself—you hear it and you react, you feel good, you understand, you are entirely and personally involved. First you think: "Wow. I really love the Byrds," and then you maybe stop to think about why you love them or what it is that you think is so good. Maybe you never even know, but the important thing is, they always get to you.

Anyway, they always get to me. And I have a lot of friends who, for maybe a month after any given Byrds album comes out, walk around muttering "wow" and saying that when they really think about it, the Byrds are their very favorite rock group. And then they forget for a while, until another Byrds record appears; and of course it's not thinking about the Byrds that impresses them but hearing the Byrds. And isn't this how it should be?

The Byrds more than anybody today have mastered communication. Part of it is that they're not afraid. Not on any of the important levels. They try, but they're not very conscious of what they're "supposed to be" doing, and this is a saving grace. Such an ominous toy as the Moog becomes in their hands just a thing to make sound with at the beginning of "Natural Harmony." They aren't intimidated. They're in control, the music is completely theirs, there is no distance between man and machine because machine is appreciated as simply tool, extension of man, something to do things with. The same is true of the horns, strings, everything on *The Notorious Byrd Brothers*. The listener is absolutely not aware of strings on "Going Back," not because he can't hear them—they're right there—but because he's hearing the song. In the best art you cannot see the artist's handiwork. You can only feel his presence, in what you're perceiving, you're overwhelmed by that and not concerned with examining it. You relate. Sex can be much closer, more direct, than we think the word "close" means. So can looking at Picasso. So can listening to the Byrds.

Now that we are ready, now that they are ready, the Byrds do not ignore specifics. It is just the right time to sing about amphetamine, in the context of Memphis brass and waves of non-feeling; it is just the right time to follow that with further reflections on an overthought theme, going back, younger than yesterday, my back pages, underthought this time: a little bit of courage is all we lack, I'm going back. That means less and feels more. Vietnam is on this album. Vietnam is everywhere these days. Last year it would not have been proper, last year Vietnam and rock were not so close for us, we couldn't have made the bridge. This year some things are in all things, and the Byrds are us too, they feel that too, and what they feel is what's present on this album.

There is a natural progression, in my mind, from the Love album (*Forever Changes*) to the Dylan album(*John Wesley Harding*) to *The Notorious Byrd Brothers*. Self-awareness is the word I like to use, the artist aware of who he is and putting it right across, no distance, just presence. Horns, steel guitars, strings, rock stuff, harmonies, melodies, words, ideas, concepts, phrasing are all part of it, all more and more natural and invisible as the person of the artist takes shape, takes form, becomes present in the living room or wherever you listen, wherever you hear. Talking to a friend on the telephone, you get only voice, some words in straight line order, inflection of voice, and a lot of memory, a lot of consciousness of who this person is from all you knew before. Listening to the Byrds you have heard all those other albums, you know what you know, and you also have words in multileveled order, inflections, melodies, and rhythms, every sort of rich communication directly to/with you.

On a Byrds album how much distance is there between what the artist (several people, but singular on records) is trying to do and what he does? None at all, or none perceptible, or maybe we don't care what he was *trying* to do. He must have been trying to do this, he *did* this and it's incredible. No distance. Does this mean the medium's the message? No. Both those things are impersonal. This is all personal. The Byrds is the Byrds. The music and the group are the same concept, the same thing in our minds, the same thing on the record; the people are not the same as the music, but then the people in the Byrds are not the same as the Byrds, which is part of why they come and go so much. The Byrds is a true gestalt, successful insofar as six great albums and fifty-nine songs have been produced by that gestalt, successful insofar as that gestalt is known as a person to more people than most individuals are.

There is no distinction in time between Byrds albums; more than any other group they are as good on their first album, as appropriate now on their first album, as they are now on this album, and I suspect this album would have sounded perfectly fine back then, three years ago. The Byrds are now, the Byrds have always been now. They don't just say those things, they feel them, they get in and around and through all those things they say, and no one but the Byrds has more right to say . . . "that which is not real does not exist." . . . The Byrds have abolished time, for themselves, and for us all if we listen enough.

I'm really enthusiastic about this stuff. You could do me no greater favor than to read *Dune* and listen to the Byrds, be and grow well and perhaps communicate yourself when you are ready for it. Perhaps you're communicating now, and you'd forgotten. Remember the Byrds. They go right at it.

I'd like to review a book. You can get it in paperback. It's called *The Musical Experience,* the author's name is Roger Sessions, and you get it from Atheneum Books or the Princeton University Press. Roger Sessions is a composer and a professor of music at Princeton; he must also be a very fine man, because his book is not only brilliant but completely reasonable, and there are very few reasonable men writing on music or anything else these days. (The book was written in 1950; but there was quite a lot of confusion in the air even then.)

What Mr. Sessions does in these lectures prepared for his students, is to concern himself with what music really is to people; and he divides people, for the purposes of a discussion of music, into composers, performers, and listeners. "In the beginning, no doubt, the three were one. Later . . . the composer existed precisely because he had introduced into the raw material of sound and rhythm patterns that became recognizable and therefore capable of repetition. . . . The first performer was, in the strictest sense, the first musician who played or sang something that had been played or sung before. . . . Listening to music is the product of a very late stage in musical sophistication. . . . For the listener, music is no longer an incident or an adjunct but an independent and self-sufficient medium of expression."

The extent to which almost everything Sessions says about music in the abstract is applicable to rock music in particular is a healthy indication of the growth of rock as a modern art form, a lasting means of expression. Let me stop reviewing this book at this point, then, and instead report for you on that aspect of Mr. Sessions' approach which is most incredible and illuminating in terms of what I have been trying to talk about. Let me give you Roger Sessions on time:

> I am deliberately restricting the discussion here to primitive, direct, and simple responses to music. Even at this level, may we not say that the basic ingredient of music is not so much sound as movement, conceived in the terms I have indicated? I would even go a step further, and say that music is significant for us as human beings principally because it embodies movement of a specifically human type that goes to the roots of our being and takes shape in the inner gestures which embody our deepest and most intimate responses. This is of itself not yet art; it is not yet even language. But it is the material of which musical art is made, and to which musical art gives significance.

> If we appreciate these facts, we can understand the more readily why music is the art of sound. For of all the five senses, the sense of hearing is the only one inexorably associated with our sense of time. The gestures which music embodies are, after all, invisible gestures; one may almost define them as consisting of movement in the abstract, movement which exists in time but not in space . . .

Later in the book, he writes:

> It is interesting to consider how many of our technical terms apply originally to things seen rather than things heard, or to space rather than time. The word "form" or "architecture," for example, led to the once famous comparison of the sonata form with an arch. . . . The real flaw in such a comparison is in the fact that what we call "form" in the realm of time has nothing whatever to do with, and is in no real way comparable to, "form" as we know it in the realm of space. The one is fluid and its essence is fluidity; the other is static, and its primary requirement is stability.

Wow. Fluidity is, of course, available to the painter, to the visual artist dealing in any way with textures, but only the mobile arts can work from reference points in time. And only the visual arts can employ reference points in space. So the use of fluidity, movement, contrasts, repetition is very much an aspect of the medium in which the artist is working. Contrast, for example, is a fairly sophisticated technique in music, since it requires that the listener be involved enough to retain in his mind the events of one moment while listening to the events of the next. Hence the use of the first verse, second verse, break pattern in many rock songs —you have to get the listener used to something before you can effectively surprise him. Repetition, on the other hand, is as immediate in music as contrast is in painting—the orderly procession of a song in time really makes the word "cumulative" significant. Two great examples: Johnny Cash's "I Walk the Line," in which the absolutely unchanging guitar pattern, repeated throughout the song, creates affirmation; and the Rolling Stones' "Last Time," in which repetition of an unchanging guitar phrase is again used, but this time to create an atmosphere of doubt, uncertainty on a cosmic level. The key to the effectiveness of the guitar in each of these songs is its relationship to what's occurring in the vocal: in "I Walk the Line" the vocal is calm and constant, and the guitar backs it up; in "Last Time," Jagger shouts and pleads and cajoles and threatens, and the unresponsiveness of the guitar just becomes more and more ominous.

Film, ballet, drama are arts that employ both space and time; and there has been constant conflict in these arts (as in all others) between the artist's desire for freedom and his need for security. The greatest art has often been created by men who were severely and specifically limited in what they could do, but who did not feel that this in any way restricted or limited their ability to express themselves. Music has always had its advantages in this respect, as it is an art form absolutely incapable of spatial expression (save to the extent that it can be louder or softer within a given area) and therefore rather seriously restricted from the outset. The further limit imposed by top-40 radio (the birthplace and childhood home of rock music), that a song not exceed three or four minutes in length, has allowed artists who might otherwise be far too ambitious with far too little experience to really express themselves within a limited (from an objective point of view) form that is really (to the fledgling artist) as unlimited as any form of papyrus would be to the man who'd been trying to express himself by drawing in the air.

At this stage in its history, rock is breaking from restrictions placed on it in childhood, and I suppose we can say it is having a brilliant, though difficult, adolescence. It is discovering, in new ways every day, just what is really going on out there; and every new discovery is heralded as the final, unassailable truth. And perhaps (I hear it in the most recent music of the Kinks, the Who, the Byrds, the Beach Boys, Dylan) rock is just now beginning to discover that there are no unassailable truths, there is only greater and greater awareness of the universe. And of oneself.

In which case, Roger Sessions' is a good book to read. We have reached the stage where we know we're making music.

Let's take still another approach to this thing. My friend Bhob Stewart suggests that after *Bringing It All Back Home,* Dylan stopped calling his songs "Bob Dylan's 115th Dream" because he'd realized that *all* the songs were dreams, chains of seemingly related and unrelated sense perception,

stories told through the mind's attempt to connect all the worlds it perceives. "My songs are only dreams," says Donovan, "visiting my mind."
Dylan, who isn't so explicit, would probably not say "only." . . .

III

Dreams and insight are equally noted in waking. "Sunshine came
softly through my window today. . . ." Donovan, sitting on his bed, can
find the world a very certain place. He's bright-eyed enough to make
visiting his mind a highly smileable experience. Dylan, though he's gentle
—"these visions of Johanna have kept me up past the dawn"—can be a
frightening cuss to wake up to. Frightening because of what he says . . .
what he sees . . . and what he does. . . .

Jim Morrison, in concert before singing "Light My Fire," turns to the
audience and screams "WAKE UP!" Which is funny, because I doubt that
anyone thinks it a direct command (save Jim)—nothing about the Doors
sticks out enough to require special attention, and "WAKE UP!" is just
perceived as another part of what's there, whether the person is there
or not. The Doors make so many demands on their listeners that everyone
either dislikes them without knowing why or else assumes that anyone as
great as the Doors doesn't merely expect you to follow their directions.

Meanwhile, on what level of consciousness do we find Jody Reynolds?
"Endless Sleep" (Demon Records FF-1507) was a hit in the fifties that
Jody wrote himself (with Dolores Nance), all about Jody's melodramatic
baby, who walked into the sea after a lover's quarrel. There's a lot going
on here. . . . The beat is as unemotional as Jody's voice. . . . "I heard a
voice crying from the deep, 'Come join me baby in my endless sleep.' "

The Doors' "Moonlight Drive" comes to mind. But more than that,
notice how the chorus ends in the title of the song. This is the creation
of drama from the totally expected. Death—an everyday, once-in-a-lifetime
companion—is pretty exciting to your 1950's teenage rock fan; and words
that imply that somebody actually died are a source of great tension and
vicarious pleasure in a pop-rock context. So here we have this song with
its verse-chorus, verse-chorus, verse-chorus construction, and inevitably,
like taxes, at the end of each chorus we're gonna get the death sentence,
Jody is going to say "endless sleep." And he does. At the end of the third
verse he even refers to "*that* endless sleep," which goes to show that the
concept is an old friend by now. Historical tragedies work the same way—
you *know* what's going to happen at the end (of the play, of the chorus),
but each time you get really tense believing that somehow the impossible
will occur, the inevitable will be avoided, whoever it is will be saved.

Redemption is a familiar theme in early rock (unlike historical tragedies), so you can bet that Jody saved his girl. There's still a tense moment
when he's found her and holds her to him, and you don't know until the
chorus if this is necrophilia. But the last line is "I saved my baby from
that endless sleep"; and notice how, redemption or no redemption, the
chorus ends in the same fatal phrase. In fact, in some sort of wry emotion-
less comment on the whole thing, Jody ends the song by saying "endless

sleep" about six times; and the last thought you have before going down is that, repeated, "endless sleep" becomes "endlessly." The rest is silence. And Bob Dylan says (*11 Outlined Epitaphs*), "Anything that ain't got no end's just gotta be poetry one way or another."

But do you suppose there could be a more than coincidental relationship between waking, sleeping, dreaming, and the creative process? The Everly Brothers once posed the immortal question: what happens if you really did fall asleep at the movies, and nobody will believe you? How do you prove you weren't fucking? In a society that speaks only in euphemisms ("sleep together," as the Beach Boys almost dare to say in "Wouldn't It Be Nice") and communicates only in excuses, what do you do with the truth? Wake up, little Suzie, wake up. It's a funny but desperate song.

And then there's the Four Tops' masterpiece, "Shake Me, Wake Me," a song almost too real and terrifying to be listened to. . . . It is said that the most frightening thing about LSD is that for some people the "trip" recurs long after you're off the drug. That hasn't happened to me; but certainly the most frightening thing about "reality" is that sometimes you can't get rid of it.

And maybe you never never did dream before, maybe your mind can pull greater tricks on you than you think, maybe time and memory and waking and sleeping are so very mixed up, and the mind so very inaccessible, that certain silly rock songs are the closest we can come to knowing reality.

"Shake Me, Wake Me" nicely ties together the subject matter of dreams and waking with the theme of illusion versus reality. The singer wants someone to wake him later, but he's awake; he has closed his ears but he (now) hears everything that's said around him. Reality is on and can't be turned off. Tommy James and the Shondells pull the reverse trick on their listeners in a song called "Mirage"; the mere fact of Tommy's exclaiming, over your transistor radio or whatever, "just a mirage," is enough to make the radio, the song, and perhaps a good part of the afternoon vanish off the face of the earth. Just how real is a song on the radio to any given listener? If the song's singer disclaims its reality, isn't that enough to tip the balance? . . . Being *able* to turn off reality is also a pretty frightening number.

Except, of course, when practiced by the Beatles. The universally loved, always palatable Beatles couldn't frighten their way out of a wet paper bag, and anyway they prefer to take the attitude that this is a groovy bag to be in. ". . . and after all, I'm only sleeping." No one threatens their reality, because they refuse to really care about what's real and what is not. "Turn off your mind, relax and float downstream." Or, alternatively, "Shake it up, baby, twist and shout!" "Nowhere you can be that isn't where you want to be, it's easy." (If you take that attitude. Those of us who actually can remember being places we would rather never be again may wonder at the Beatles' absolutely indiscriminate absorption of the world. They consume more bulk than forty generations of rabbits, and manage to produce almost as much in return; and these are extremely admirable, though unenviable, accomplishments.) Doubts about reality, fear of the dark, are all very well for lesser rock groups; the Beatles are unshakable, which certainly contributes no end to their position as culture heroes, though it may someday detract from their standing as artists. There really isn't must distance between "Close your eyes and I'll kiss you" and "living is easy with eyes closed"; and if there is any distance the Beatles will be glad to make it up for you. They really have homogenized their universe. "With my eyes wide open, I'm dreaming. . . ."

"Before you slip into unconsciousness," begins Jim Morrison; "I gotta dream on," says Herman of the Hermits; and "All I've got to do is dream; dream, dream, dream," says Don or Phil Everly. Morrison comes back with ". . . some are born to sweet delight; . . . some are born to the endless night." Oh yeah, almost forgot the birth theme. Frank Herbert writes a novel called *Do I Wake or Dream?* Berkley Books retitles it *Destination: Void.*

But does arbitrarily relating all these songs and things through their common subject matter really get us anywhere? Good question, but—how do we usually relate things? What does get us anywhere? This is *my* thought-dream I'm spinning out for you; how does *your* chain of perceptions link together?

> *Dylan:* I am about to sketch you a picture of what goes on around here sometimes, tho I don't understand too well myself what's really happening.
>
> *Donovan:* What goes on? I really want to know.
>
> *Dylan:* I know no answers an no truth for absolutely no soul alive I will listen to no one who tells me morals there are no morals an I dream a lot.

A dream is a portrait, moving target for the mind. Waking is the shift from one level to another; here to there but not in space or time. This stuff is all important. And the hell of it is, rock really does communicate. It discusses this stuff in its own peculiar ways, and many an idea comes and goes without a conscious thought. Shifting, moving, existing, gone.

"Music is your special friend, dance on fire as it intends, music is your only friend" ["When you hear music, after it's over, it's gone in the air and you can never capture it again."—Eric Dolphy]. . . .

And more. How rock communicates is a mystery to me. Some days I stand in the shower till evening, pushing at songs in my mind.

"I've been in this town so long, so long to the city . . ." (Van Dyke calls from the Coast; just wants me to know it's all right) "I'm thick with the stuff" water running down the drain counterclockwise "to ride in the rough" Hudson day River at an end "And sunny down snuff I'm all right."

"By the heroes and villains . . ."

The Music
of Protest

BURT KORALL

Youth damns the past, defines the diseased present, and demands change. Their outrage and defiance takes various forms—from direct confrontation and protest, satire, love in the face of hate, to drugs and dropping out. What remains constant is a flood of commentary—youth taking the world's pulse and their own, using music to purge themselves, while increasingly irritating and provoking the forces of reaction. In essence, they function as an alarm clock for the country and march to the tune of their aspirations, hoping to attain sanity, reason, physical and mental mobility, love and, most important, realistic appraisal on a mass level.

Having overrun popular music and realized its power as a tool, they are cementing a link with an increasingly large audience through the country and the world. It is a matter of record that music representative of the tidal wave of youth sells more heavily than any other kind—and not only to youngsters. Cultural lag doesn't seem a problem in this era of multiple communication, even in more provincial areas.

The music of youth, like their clothes and hair styles, simultaneously singularizes and isolates them, while lending tribal strength. Nothing new; swing music of the 1930s and be-bop ten years later spawned analogous figures which, for simplicity's sake, we will call hipsters. They, too, had their own folkways, manner of dressing, language, and lived on the periphery of the establishment.

One major difference, however, separates today's rag-tagger from the hipster of old. Living away from the illness of the establishment is primary to today's young—at least until they can motivate some radical changes. The old-time hipster, on the other hand, put down the world as unbearably square but still was part of it. Politics and the expression of the need for radical metamorphosis were not his bag. Comfortable in his own orbit, where everything was familiar and relaxed, the hipster dismissed the square as funny and unfeeling. They couldn't dig him; they didn't know how. Proudly, but with a hint of finger-popping hostility, he ambled down Main Street in big town and small, flaunting his difference and his cool.

The rag-tag generation finds no humor in the mistakes and cop-outs of the conforming armies. Sleeping, easily fooled, bigoted people are a travesty, they say, and are responsible for the relative chaos in which we live. Anything but cool, youth senses what is wrong and how things should be. They find muscle in their growing numbers and the possibilities implicit in grouping for attack on the status quo, and in the attack itself. As for a sharply definitive sense of identity—that's another matter. The search continues. For the moment, the method, culminating in revelation, has not been found. The young of earlier generations fostered the idea that they knew who they were. "Today's youth have no such delusion," critic Albert Goldman declares. "But lacking any clear-cut sense of identity has only made them more keenly aware of everyone else's."

Cross-ventilation of ideas and techniques combined with the inner and outer ferment in the country have produced a radical change in popular music—now a fascinating, if sometimes troubled mixture of elements, which truly reflects our present position. What Goldman has deemed the "Rock Age"—the period in which we live—indeed has been a time of assimilation. Musically it has "assimilated everything in sight, commencing with the whole of American music: urban and country blues, gospel, hillbilly, Western, 'good-time' (the ricky-tick of the Twenties), and Tin Pan Alley. It has reached across the oceans for the sounds and rhythms of Africa, the Middle East, and India. It has reached back in time for the baroque trumpet, the madrigal, and the Gregorian Chant; and forward into the future for electronic music and the noise collages of *musique concrète.* By virtue of its cultural alliances, the Beat has also become the pulse of pop culture."

It remains to be determined whether music-song is a powerful, provocative instrument, which aids the cause of change. Does our contemporary musical amalgam, itself implicit protest against the limited popular music of the past, make its point?

There is widespread disparity of opinion concerning the cogency of musical protest. Critic John Cohen states that "topical songs are like newspapers; pertinent to the latest development, bearing the latest ideas, and ending up in the garbage can." It is his contention that "for young people in the cities, the topical songs have become abstract emotional substitutes for what is going on in the world; and although this can be a good factor when it stimulates people to action, more often it is a delusion." By making such connections, he explains, "topical songs blind young people into believing they are accomplishing something in their own protest, when, in fact, they are doing nothing but going to concerts, record stores, and parties at home."

Admittedly, protest music diminishes in impact once the crisis in question is past. It does, however, serve as a source of strength, unification, and expression when the battle is raging. Music's depth of importance within the civil rights movement earlier in this decade is a matter of history. It converted many to the cause in a manner that signs, demonstrations, and other means did not. Even more important, the songs solidified the chain of commitment among the followers. Northern writers, including the ever present Pete Seeger, Phil Ochs, Tom Paxton, and Len Chandler, among others, personalized the struggle, giving their own reactions to various situations. They spoke of injustices and what had to be done. The Southern freedom singers and writers, working within the Afro-American tradition, using gospel and rhythm and blues forms and songs, with lyrics to fit each occasion, also cut deeply and made their point, leaving an enduring mark. One has only to refer back to the tremendous effect of "We Shall Overcome."

At the base of today's musical protest, casting a giant shadow that sometimes goes unnoticed by current practitioners, are generations of black blues singers and players—disenfranchised, alienated, and imprisoned, who had their say, if sometimes obliquely, and broke through, using the only medium at their disposal, music. Equally influential in casting the current shapes and forms for contemporary comment were individuals of conscience and compassion who sang of injustice and helped people find answers to pressing questions in their songs.

The prototypical figure in the latter category is the late Woody Guthrie, a truth-teller about whom Tom Paxton had said: "The most important thing Woody gave us was courage to stand up and say the things we believe." A ramblin' man who wandered through his beloved land, he was devoted to causes—some deemed radical; however, with time on our side, it is plain to see that all Guthrie wanted to do was make us aware of the country's good points and bad, while bringing us closer to it. His thoughts, generally couched in simple, human terms, are accessible to all. Through more than 1,000 songs, he strung the history of the America he knew—from the deprivations of the Depression through the first post–World War II years, until his illness began to take hold of him and prove prohibitive on his talent.

Those who register complaint and desperation today are not far removed in spirit from Guthrie and other bards of yesterday, like black artists Big Bill Broonzy and Leadbelly, who spoke out of their experience and tried to bring mass focus to inequality and the number of sicknesses in the land. Today, however, the voices of dissent are louder, for cause; we cannot wait any longer for the rapport to develop whereby we can live with one another. It is either pass down an inheritance of absurd reality or change direction.

Amidst the hurt, disappointment, and hopelessness, there seems reason for limited optimism. The 1960s have been crucial years in the journey to a new reality. An extended period of silence, repression, and resultant welling up of feeling came to an end. A revolution broke out in music—and the other arts as well—paralleling the turmoil throughout the national and international structure. Folk artists in America again began speaking openly, following years of black lists and red channels. With the coming of Ornette Coleman and the emergence and development of John Coltrane, jazz again became a maverick. On the heels of an era concerned with consolidation and progressive rediscovery of roots, after the death of Charlie Parker in 1955, the ground breakers reached out, touching new bases. They provoked the young to look to their feelings. The music, though unfinished in many of its aspects and chaotic to the uninitiated, motivated a complete re-examination of existing guidelines, and challenges us to think about our lives and what the future will offer.

Some sage, for lack of a more ornate description, deemed it "The New Thing." An oversimplification, but appropriate for a sudden turning in the road. Bringing into play a variety of techniques from diverse musical and extra-musical sources, the practitioners mutate and revamp the jazz we know playing havoc on its identity. Exactly what will emerge remains to be heard; it's certain that jazz, by nature an evolving form, can never be the same. The revolution continues. To accept it wholly, completely discarding yesterdays, seems out of the question. To open one's self to its positive aspects and prospects is a necessity. A highly contemporary manifestation, it certainly has been instrumental in shaking jazz loose from a progressive case of nostalgia, a malaise which could envelop and incapacitate the music and its players.

It comes clear that it is no longer possible to separate music and life as it really is. Politics, sexuality, racial pride, deep and true feelings have entered popular music to stay. Our youth is central to this metamorphosis.

Bob Dylan has been *the* standard-bearer of the 1960s. A stylistic son of Woody Guthrie at the beginning of his career, he stepped forward in 1961 and initiated a stream of comment that continues to this day. Particularly at the outset he noted in no uncertain terms the hypocrisy of this country and the need for vigorous change. Using the narrative form, in the tradition of Guthrie, his first records echoed with the meaninglessness of life, the impossibility of racial inequality, the imminence of death, as man moved further and further from himself. It was time to take hold, NOW.

Deemed a poet by some, a prophet by others, a self-propelled mediocrity by still others, Dylan caught the tenor of the times in his songs. Innocence was a thing of the past. No longer was it possible to live with soda shoppe morality and answers which had nothing to do with pressing questions. He realized that isolation from true reality was as unbearable as the reality itself. Yet this did not prohibit him from immersing himself in surrealistic pessimism. After clearly indicting the world in his "Blowin' in the Wind," he turned to an inverted mode of writing, couching his point of view within a rush of words and images, oblique and abstract, often approaching hallucination: dreams more frightening than reality. This is the subterranean Dylan, living in song in a demimonde of "haunted, frightened trees"; dwarfs; clowns who seem blind; intransigent policemen. On occasion he surfaced to sing of love relationships (often unfulfilling) and to express youth's alienation from the older, reactionary generation who simply won't understand what it's all about, as on "It's Alright, Ma, I'm Only Bleeding." Dylan, the observer, would make things right if he could, but the governing forces block renewal of effort.

With the release early this year of *John Wesley Harding* (Columbia CS 9604), his first album after a silence of a year and a half, he gives evidence of having thrown aside the recent past in favor of rebirth and a new maturity. The electrified accompaniment that served his purposes prior to his near-fatal accident has been unplugged. His songs are concise rather than sprawling. The imagery, if still opaque, is not as dreamlike, nor just for him alone. His morality, accessible at every turn and almost religious in aspect, guides him in sharply defining good as opposed to that which is intrinsically evil. The nature of his songs and delivery are devoid of obvious artifice and the false "cool" and stances of the public person. Placing a heavy emphasis on country simplicity in vocally and instrumentally projecting his feelings, the songwriter-singer again acoustic-guitarist is back in the world. A new Dylan? Hardly. He's just a bit more direct, relaxed, open. His means and manner may change but he retains a unity of image. He is the questioning and needling voice of the 1960s.

Dylan's colleagues in the pop realm, like him, are the products of many influences and pressures. With few exceptions, their comment and mode of vocal and instrumental performances bear the marks of the black man —his inflections, mannerisms, and accents. But taken as a whole, popular music, 1968, reflects urban and provincial attitudes, sounds, and rhythms native to black and white, a spillover of techniques from traditional and contemporary classical music and foreign cultures. It is a democracy in sound—as free and flexible as the world we yearn for. It logically follows that the lyrics for this universal popular music would be as emancipated, outspoken, and diverse as the music itself.

This is very much the case. We have moved into wide-ranging application of words since swinging around the corner into the 1960s, with contexts running from the decisively concrete to abstraction. This is a considerable distance from the nonsense syllables and one-dimensional lyrics which characterized much of the song produce of the Fifties. The songsmiths aspire to be equal to the times.

Whatever the degree of accessibility of the wordage, the creator's need to link up with his audience is strongly sensed. Often, however, he will make the listeners work to achieve communion, benevolently allowing multiple interpretations of his message or lack of one, intimating that in life everyone doesn't see everything the same way. At their ultimate in surrealism and ambiguity, Dylan, the Beatles, and the acid rock groups— i.e., Jefferson Airplane—might initially cloud the mind with a crazy quilt of images. But they do draw you to them within the maelstrom and engage your capacities in a search that frequently is as exciting and fulfilling as the revelation that sometimes lies at the end of the trip. Observers have paralleled the experience with the drug turn on—an analogue not without basis in fact. The drug phenomenon *is* very much with us and figures in the music of youth. The maze and confusion out of which we try to make sense also structures the music and is part of its structure. Therefore, the music is singularly relevant, because it contains in its own form what's happening in and around us. If anything is true of contemporary popular music, it is the intent of its makers to set life to music.

Surprisingly, the prime movers are white—surprising only in that their black brethren have far more reason to build bandwagons. But there is reason for this. White people are freer and have less to lose. The black man generally remains repressed and is less inclined to show his true face—musically, anyway. Make no mistake, however, his protest is there for all who will take time to reach and find his soul. One has only to pay special heed to the sound and words of the blues.

· · ·

Admittedly, the turn of events in this decade has motivated the black man to speak more directly in his music, and to abandon to some extent the protective code and inside terminology of the past. Race pride and anger is felt in some of his songs, as well as the need to throw off strictured yesterdays. Lou Rawls, a modern black singer, with roots in gospel and the blues, gives urgent voice to these feelings in "They Don't Give Medals (to Yesterday's Heroes)"—a song by two white writers, Burt Bachrach and Hal David, which serves black aspiration well.

· · ·

Songs of burning inquiry, confrontation, and accusation are now written and performed by black people . . . and heard more and more often. Billy Taylor's "I Wish I Knew How It Would Feel to Be Free" has extraordinary currency and is increasingly performed and recorded. The musing, black folk artist-songwriter Richie Havens screams out the query, "Why must we wait until morning to wake up and BE?" in his scalding song, "No Opportunity Necessary, No Experience Needed." Otis Redding bemoans the lack of change in his hit, "Dock of Bay." James Brown, Soul Brother Number 1, raises his voice in the cause of black pride on his "Say It Loud —I'm Black and I'm Proud." Julius Lester, the literate and deeply expressive black songsmith and artist, takes a militant stance, espousing a strong front against the oppressor and the death of stereotypes: "Gonna get me a gun and shoot Aunt Jemima dead." Nina Simone often casts a skewering glance at bedridden society. Her record of Martha Holmes's "Turning Point," an eye-opening comment on the existing distance between the races, is a recommended experience. Perhaps the most touching song, rendering with rare clarity the situation in the black ghetto, is the relatively unheralded "Crackerbox Livin'," by Howlett Smith, as interpreted by singer Ernie Andrews in his Dot album, *Soul Proprietor.*

Inhibition on a really major scale, however, has not been broken. Black song, drenched in blues, with the throb and sob of the church at its core, remains a reflection of ephemeral Saturday night freedom—an act of love and despair, a flash of energy in a long darkness. Centering on black people's major source of strength—the love relationship, physically solidified—it soothes hurt and repairs dwindling dignity.

· · ·

The young, rebellious white, unlike his black counterpart, is unfettered. For him, however, this freedom is but part of an overall delusion. He feels trapped by the traditions and legacies of the past.

Confusion reigns. Truth and honesty are at a premium. A valid way of life is sought. To this end, the young explorer rolls across a wide spectrum of subject matter and musical means and mannerisms. He experiments with ideology and sounds, often shaping answers in the process. But they always are open to change; flexibility is part of the concept. Though his protest and comment is less centralized than his soul brother's, his objective is essentially the same. Hope is implicit in the negation of past and present mistakes—the hope for an apocalypse, which will make the blind see, the intractable feel, the world's fearful face change.

Fear is the underlying feeling motivating the young. It's everywhere, openly shared. "What's becoming of the children?" people ask in a Simon and Garfunkel song. "What has become of the world?" would be a more pertinent question. Moreover, if things go on the way they have, will it be here at all? Turmoil and violence, at every turn. A heavily theatrical and ritualistic rock group called The Doors, featuring lead singer Jim Morrison, is archetypical in its bold statement of the existing situation. Mounting a saturation bombardment attack in words, lights, and amplified sound, leveling listeners into submissiveness, the unit projects the fear embedded in the young, and all of us for that matter. Listen to "When the Music's Over."

. . .

Threading one's way through the mountains of recent recordings, the temper of the times and the matters of concern are multiply revealed. The Vietnam war is a primary subject. A yearning for peace is predominant. "Honor is without profit in its own country," declare The Split Level in the song, "Speculator," included in the group's recent Dot album. Kenny Rankin, a Mercury artist, singing Fred Neil's song, "The Dolphin," underscores the crucial fact: "Peace gonna come only when hate is gone." It seems indicated that songs will continue to pour from the cauldron until the situation in Southeast Asia is eased. Joan Baez inevitably will lead the voices of nonviolence and peace—just as inevitably as songs taking the opposite stance, like Barry Sadler's "The Ballad of the Green Beret," will be created.

The gap in understanding between young and not so young consistently is mirrored in music. Razor-sharp satirists, who laugh to keep from crying, like Frank Zappa's Mothers of Invention, define the situation with a sneering smile, lending it dimensions it would not otherwise have. In a song called "Mom & Dad," Zappa goes for the heart, querying parents. . . . Country Joe and The Fish, a San Francisco group deeply involved in today's swirl, also waves the ammonia bottle under the collective nose of America. Though its material has a comedic exterior and unit treatment deepens the satiric quality, these fellows aren't fooling around.

Loneliness also is a frequent song subject. . . . Confusion and the bureaucracy of life also crops up often, as on Arlo Guthrie's "Alice's Restaurant." The positive power of love to turn people away from their destructive proclivities is still another notable theme. ". . . plant them now, never a better time," Buffy Sainte-Marie says in her song, "The Seeds of Brotherhood." Record after record reveals the inner plight and acute sensitivity of today's youth and the world in which they live. The warnings are there to be understood.

In recent months, however, pop music of protest has taken on a much more affirmative tone. Songs define what might be, as opposed to expressing a condition. The recent assassinations of Martin Luther King and Robert Kennedy certainly contributed to this reversal. Seemingly artists and the industry as a whole have realized that there is no other alternative and concluded, exclusive of one another, to use music affirmatively, hopefully for a positive result.

Within a short space of time over a dozen items have been released— all statements of hope and faith in the underlying strength and possibility of the country. Included in this number are Laura Nyro's "Save the Country," James Brown's "America is My Home," a rash of inspirational songs—notably treatments of "The Impossible Dream" from *Man of La Mancha*—and the Kim Weston album, *This is America.*

Whatever the plight of America, its music indicates that the people are reaching out to find it and themselves. Some want revolution; others desire yesterday. Certainly things cannot stay the same. Take a look around. Listen to today's music. It's all there.

"All You Need Is Love. Love Is All You Need."

KAREN MURPHY and RONALD GROSS

> *Poets are the unacknowledged legislators of the world.*
> Shelley
> *We have to keep new sorts of music away from us as a danger to society.*
> Plato

I

Shelley wasn't talking about the books on the library shelf marked "Poetry." Rather, he meant language used at its most potent, to create and disseminate the notions of which kind of life is most worth living and which is most to be despised. And Plato knew that men were basically not what they knew, but how they felt their own existence. Today's young people find that the things they care about, and despise, and take delight in, are reflected and distilled most powerfully in the words and music of rock 'n' roll.

Two books of poetry were best sellers in America last year: the "Selected Poems" of Leonard Cohen and "Lonesome Cities" by Rod McKuen, the first a popular and respected rock songwriter and singer, the latter a popular *schlock* songwriter and singer. And the critics and purveyors of the fine arts have dutifully decided that if rock lyrics have meaning and importance to young people they must then be something more than just lowly entertainment. In recent months, scholarly symposia on rock lyrics have been held in New York at The New School for Social Research (as part of a course called "Expanded Poetry") and at Columbia University. Joshua Brackett, the nation's first "media ecologist," is writing a Ph.D. dissertation at N.Y.U. composed entirely of exegeses of rock lyrics. The literary magazines are falling over one another to take rock lyrics seriously; a Partisan Review writer recently compared the Beatles' lyrics to Shakespeare. Leonard Bernstein says of rock: "Many of the lyrics, in their oblique allusions and way-out metaphors, are beginning to sound like real poems."

Despite Cohen's and McKuen's books, and the fact that publishers are issuing histories of rock and anthologies of rock lyrics, it really isn't a very good idea to abstract rock lyrics from the accompanying music for isolated scrutiny. Rock is essentially an appeal to the gut sense of rhythm, intensely energy-releasing and sexual. In this respect rock magnifies a condition of all poetry. Even so cerebral a poet as T. S. Eliot said that meaning in a poem is like the piece of sirloin that the burglar slips the watchdog as he burglarizes the house: It keeps the reader busy while the poet does his work through the poem's rhythmic and sensuous qualities. Since Eliot, poetry has stressed this aspect more and more. The Beat movement was very much an insistence on the rhythmic and spoken basis of poetry, and more recent experimentation goes even further in stressing the sensory basis of poetic experience.

But rock lyrics are notably more than a nod to Sweeney's realization that "I've gotta use words when I talk to you." In fact, they are a quite remarkable departure from anything that has ever appeared before in American popular music.

Years ago, when he was just a semanticist instead of a beleaguered San Francisco college president, S. I. Hayakawa studied the lyrics of Tin Pan Alley songs and concluded that they gave listeners an idealized picture of love and marriage which was exactly congruent with the stereotypes of the advertising culture and severely discordant with reality. They were full of "wishful thinking, dreamy and ineffectual nostalgia, unrealistic fantasy, self-pity and sentimental clichés, masquerading as emotion."

. . .

If young people took such lyrics seriously, he warned, they would be headed for trouble when they projected them onto the tangle of real relations between men and women.

Today's rock lyrics are something else, though in the beginning (circa 1954) they were bad enough to make Tin Pan Alley look like a stronghold of realism and sophistication. The lyrics of the first rock superhit, Bill Haley's "Rock Around the Clock" . . . became a theme song of defiance; behind the idiotic lyrics kids heard: "We're going to rock around the clock —WHETHER YOU WANT US TO OR NOT."

The moronic metaphors that were common in early rock were transformed in the kids' minds, usually into a potent sexual code. . . .

These days, no topic of interest to young people is considered inappropriate for a rock 'n' roll lyric. Going beyond the spoon-moon-June of prerock pop, and the kiss-me-honey and parents-are-no-good of early rock, today's lyricists deal with politics (these are perhaps the least successful of the new rock songs), militarism, illegitimacy (there has recently been a tremendous boom in illegitimacy songs), miscegenation, prostitution, compulsive infidelity, the dangers and pleasure of drugs, the difficulties of rising above a slum background—the list could go on forever.

. . . For example . . . "Substitute," written by Peter Townshend, of The Who. The song arouses in the listener not only the cynicism that is explicit in the lyrics but also, ironically, a nostalgia for a love, and life, where "the simple things" are not "all complicated," a nostalgia enforced by the simple, throbbing hard-rock music.

· · ·

Rock lyrics tend, in other words, as one rock writer puts it, to "look at the rose through world-colored glasses."

A great deal of *schlock* pop is still written and makes up the bulk of the programming on AM-radio rock stations.

· · ·

Even the most stereotyped good-guy stations, however, have begun to program such songs as the haunting "White Room" by the recently disbanded group called Cream, which conveys in its music as well as its lyrics an elusive but terrifyingly real sense of alienation and emptiness.

· · ·

The most fashionable heavy topic for rock at the moment is revolution. The Rolling Stones brought revolution-rock (which had been sung for years by the Fugs, who are more revolutionaries than rock singers) into Top 40 stations with their "Street Fighting Man." . . . At the moment, the leading advocates of revolution-rock sing of political and sexual revolution as one and the same thing, as the MC5 do in their song "Kick Out the Jams." This lump-it-all-together approach was first popularized by the Doors.

· · ·

II

It is perilous to make qualitative judgments about something as personal and subjective as rock 'n' roll. But certainly some, if not all, of the best current rock lyrics are not about specific weighty subjects but attempts to convey the *feel* of today's world, or at least the part of it that affects young people. Two masters of this art are John Lennon and Bob Dylan. The Beatles and Dylan are idolized by kids today primarily because, without losing their ability to be specific, they seem to understand the essence, the totality, of a fragmented world, or, as the kids say, "where it's at."

The latest trend in rock lyrics seems to be an attempt to deal with complexity instead of merely capturing it. The first great song of this genre was the Beatles' "All you Need is Love."

· · ·

This simple song (deceptively simple? simple-minded?) marked a return to basics in rock lyrics. The Beatles' first big hit in this country, "I Want to Hold Your Hand," had been a simple-minded, not very hard-hitting number that did not become very popular until the Beatles had been given a massive dose of that pop publicity now called hype. However, unlike many groups which have floundered in too much money and hype, the Beatles lived up to publicity that was, on the evidence, at the beginning greatly exaggerated.

Not that they really changed; their early songs were deliberate attempts to reach a mass audience; once they had the audience, they played them like sitars. They could do this because they reflected changes in their audience as much as they caused them; perhaps it would be most accurate to say that they brought to the surface and rendered conscious and explicit ideas, trends and feelings that would have emerged anyhow, but in less vivid and self-confident forms.

The Beatles have offered social commentary ("Nowhere Man" and "Eleanor Rigby"), social satire ("Paperback Writer"), dreamy, druggy fantasy ("Strawberry Fields Forever") and surrealism ("Penny Lane" and "I Am the Walrus"). "I Am the Walrus" has perhaps the most bizarre and culture-critic-tempting lyrics of any rock song ever written.

· · ·

At the end of the last verse, amid a lot of chaotic noise, there is some conversation that is actually 17 lines from "King Lear."

What does it all mean? In "Glass Onion," a song from the Beatles' latest album, Lennon . . . in a recent interview in Rolling Stone magazine . . . adds: "The whole first verse was written without any knowledge."

The wild images in the song are not, in fact, connected in any logical way. There is no narrative meaning, no sirloin for the watchdog. But there is a larger, more important meaning: The quick flashing of disjointed phenomena reproduces the chaos of sensations in our world of information overload.

The high point of the Beatles' attempt to capture complexity, and the high point of the baroque period of rock in general, came with the release in June, 1967, of "Sergeant Pepper." Typical of the songs on the record is "Lucy in the Sky with Diamonds." When it was pointed out to Lennon that the initials of his title were "LSD," he denied any reference to drugs and said that his young son, Julian, had brought home a drawing from school that he said was called "Lucy in the Sky with Diamonds." In any case, "Lucy" came to symbolize a time of drugs, flower children, *art nouveau* and a dreamy, psychedelic escape from the real world.

· · ·

Then, while the critics analyzed Beatles songs in terms of Franz Kafka and Marshall McLuhan (though, as pop critic Richard Goldstein has remarked, "Is Ernest Hemingway responsible for Pete Hamill?"), the Beatles themselves moved on to a style called "The New Simplicity." In practice, it means a return either to basic nineteen-fifties hard-rock or to country music, but often with the simple lyrics parodied and the music complicated by elaborate electronic effects.

· · ·

III

While the Beatles write songs like "Revolution," which discourages violent Maoist rebellion, Bob Dylan is living what Lennon calls "his cozy little life." As the Beatles seem to be involved, just by their nature, in every trend or fad that affects young people, Bob Dylan is, by his nature, uninvolved, a very private person. It was not always so: In his old prerock days Dylan wrote songs with explicit social messages, like "Blowing in the Wind," "The Times They are A-Changing" and "Masters of War." But in his song "My Back Pages" Dylan renounces protest. . . .

Although he is socially aloof, Dylan is musically very much of his time. He was one of the first folk singers to go electric, to see the power of rock as a creative and persuasive medium. Like the Beatles, Dylan, too, had a baroque rock phase, typified by his "Subterranean Homesick Blues," a song that is similar to the Beatles' "Walrus" in that its disjointed, disparate images evoked disjointed, disparate, rapidly changing world. But whereas in "The Walrus" shadowy benevolent God/father figures wait in the background (the eggman, the walrus, and element'ry penguin), the background figures in "Subterranean Homesick Blues" are brutal or bureaucratic: a plainclothesman, a fireman, a frontiersman, a district attorney, a weatherman. All threaten the innocent and confused young person. . . .

Dylan's childishly compulsive rhymes suggest a closer affinity with amphetamines than with French verse forms, but "Subterranean Homesick Blues" must be counted poetry in that it reproduces, in articulate and structured form, a nightmare vision young people hold of the world.

On his latest album, "John Wesley Harding," a return to the basic country style that is now so fashionable, Dylan writes and sings of simple but dreamlike and often elusively allegorical individual relationships. One of the most compelling songs on the album, "I Dreamed I Saw St. Augustine," conveys the chief message of "Subterranean Homesick Blues," and one of Dylan's main themes—"Don't follow leaders." In the song, St. Augustine returns to earth in a state of anguish looking for lost souls. . . . Yet the innocent youth of "Subterranean Homesick Blues" has changed. Now the narrator accuses himself of being one of those who has martyred the saint. . . .

To the familiar question, "Do you think of yourself primarily as a singer or a poet?" Dylan gave an answer of sorts in a West Coast press conference a little over a year ago: "Oh, I think of myself more as a song and dance man, y'know." Despite this modesty (or false modesty), in a broad sense Dylan must be called a poet because, like the Beatles, he speaks of, and transforms, experiences vital to the consciousness of his listeners. A 20-year-old college girl says of Dylan: "I just feel, when I hear one of his songs, like he has been everywhere and he is sending us back pictures, but there is no one message for everybody; it's like clues, but clues to something that if it's pinned down, it'd be destroyed."

The Beatles and Dylan make light of any suggestion that they are poets, thus endearing themselves to their young audiences. But Jim Morrison, lead singer of the Doors, is an active candidate for simultaneous election to "Best Rock Poet" and "Biggest Sex Symbol" (no longer an incongruous combination).

A former Berkeley drama student, Morrison writes lyrics loaded with references to classical drama, which of course does not necessarily qualify them as poetry. In the Doors' second album, however, Morrison intones a short lyric called "Horse Latitudes" that, since it is spoken and unaccompanied by music, qualifies either as a poem or as nothing.

. . .

Intoned with pseudo-Elizabethan grandeur, "Horse Latitudes" conveys perhaps the desire of Mr. Morrison to have written a "real" poem more than it does an experience vital to him or anybody else.

If critics choose to elevate bad rock to the status of poetry, and to misinterpret rock lyrics in general, that is annoying but irrelevant, except insofar as it influences rock writers. But the rock lyricists seem to be catching on. Even Paul Simon, of whom Robert Christgau wrote, "He is the only songwriter [who] . . . writes about . . . the Alienation of Modern Man, *in just those words*," recently has come to realize that he writes better songs, and perhaps better poetry, when he stops worrying about Poetry.

. . .

Interestingly, as rock lyricists turn away from official poetry, many younger poets are now being seduced by the power of rock as a medium of communication and persuasion. Foremost among these poets, certainly, is Leonard Cohen, whose poetry sells better than most novels and whose rock record "The Songs of Leonard Cohen" is a best seller on both underground and campus circuits.

Cohen sings of a strange interior world where men and women really love each other but leave each other, often self-consciously relishing the pain of parting (it's still the men who do most of the leaving) and where sexual and Catholic images are intermingled. Throughout, there is a terrible ambivalence between the ringing deadness of one-night stands and the boring temptation of monogamy, a constant protesting that it is *perfectly healthy* to leave someone you love, which probably explains why Cohen is so popular with the ambivalent young.

One of his most affirmative songs, "Suzanne," has already achieved the status of a classic because it perceives a way out of this ambivalence. The narrator achieves a commitment to Suzanne (commitment has replaced orgasm as a status symbol) but hardly to domestic drudgery: Suzanne "gets" him mystically (she touches his "perfect body *with her mind*"; since the physical is so accessible, the mystical has become the sought-after goal). Notice how . . . as in most of Cohen's songs, religious and sexual images are cheerfully combined.

Like Cohen, Rod McKuen uses a persona whose essence is to wander forever solitary despite a real ability to love deeply. Apparently, McKuen manages to deal with the dichotomy that splits young people in a way that is meaningful to them, for with Cohen he is the most popular poet on campuses all over the country. Unlike Cohen, however, McKuen makes no attempt to face, let alone reconcile, complexities; nor does he worry much about language. . . .

Of the relationship between lyrics and poetry, Cohen says: "There is no difference between a poem and a song. Some were songs first and some were poems first and some were simultaneous. All of my writing has guitars behind it, even the novels."

Eric Cheyfitz, who writes poetry for *Stand, The Review* and *Per Se,* and lyrics for the jazz/classical-oriented rock group This Week Only, says: "The difference between writing rock lyrics and poetry is that eventually you can make much more money writing lyrics. Also, when you write rock lyrics you are formally limited by the melody and beat, and some phrases have to be changed because some words can't be sung in succession."

How do rock lyrics as a whole stack up against today's poetry? It would be easy to point out correlates in rock for many of the distinguishing characteristics of contemporary American verse: John Ashbery's surrealistic image sequences, Kenneth Koch's breezy humor, the projectivists' striving for a natural rhythm which reflects the patterns of American speech, the confessional poets' fascination with autobiography and personality.

Such a comparison would also reveal that nowhere in rock lyrics does one find anything to rival Robert Lowell's complex diction, Charles Olson's awesome erudition, Allen Ginsberg's vatic howl, Robert Creeley's limpid directness, or LeRoi Jones's Catullan bitterness.

But rock lyrics have some things, quite different but equally potent, going for them. First, the music. Ezra Pound said that music rots when it gets too far from the dance, and poetry atrophies when it gets too far from music.

Music can "carry" a lyric that has no logical meaning in itself and which might have no emotional meaning if it were simply printed instead of sung. This is true of the Beatles' "Walrus" [and] Van Morrison's "Brown Eyed Girl." . . . Somehow, within the context of the song, these lines are transformed into a poignant evocation of the things we remember of a lost lover.

Rock is nothing if not song, and rock lyrics shrivel when torn out of their musical context. Considered as a word/music whole, however, the range and depth of rock challenge the best of contemporary poetry, and certainly excel the work of routine Department of English poets-in-residence.

Because it hits with a musical punch, then, and because it is completely continuous with everyday life rather than a departure from it, rock lyrics get through to millions of kids and adults for whom conventional poetry is a closed book.

The hunger of the young for words to match the fervor, complexity and tone of their sensibilities has been fed not by poets in the usual sense, but by the rock lyricists. Whether or not rock lyrics are "really" poetry is not, after all, more than a matter of definition. What matters is not their verse techniques but their force and relevance.

Critic Donal Henahan cut to the core of the matter when he wrote: "In their own ways, the better popular and serious composers today are addressing themselves once more to life as it is actually lived, and if up to now one must admit that there has been a coarsening of sensibility, there has been a heightening of reality to compensate. The truths that Dylan rasps, that is, are for the moment more valuable for us than the truths that a less convulsed society found in Brahms. The truth-teller, in whatever guise, serves his own time well; listen, next time you have a chance, to the words of Dylan's 'The Times They Are A-Changing,' and admit what a clear prophecy they were of the last five years in America."

A heightening of reality, a telling of the truth, an utterance of prophecy —these, after all, are what poets have traditionally aspired to. To the degree that contemporary verse falls short of these ideals, and rock lyricists achieve them, the latter may be doing even more than taking their place in "real poetry." They may be reinventing it.

All the World's a Stage

The Unholy Ghost in the Machine: A Polemic Against Pop Criticism

RALPH L. CARNES

Recent popular criticism in the United States has become more and more a matter of individual Pop tastes, delivered in shimmering "Slickspeak;" and less and less a coherent, informative collection of assertions about the issues themselves. Like Stewart Alsop's "Pavlovian Liberals" (*Newsweek*, 10 February, 1969), what we can call the "Now Critics" sacrifice content and fact for flashy prose, catchy phonetic sequences, emotive language, and opinionated dicta that are largely unsupported by any recognizable canon of criticism. Much of the Now Criticism is merely pop commentary: it reflects the solipsism that is the hallmark of the Now Generation. It is cut off from the main stream of scholarly criticism, both historically and methodologically; it seeks neither to explain nor to elucidate. Its motives are transparently crass: to provoke, to tease, to infuriate, to confuse, to mislead, to obfuscate, and most important of all, to convince the reader that he too can become a part of Now, can be cool, hip, freaky, theoretical liberal and actual conservative, long gone and grooving in the slot, if only he will read Tom Wolfe, Pauline Kael, Ellen Willis, Robert Christgau, Jon Laudau, Michael Thomas, Abbie Hoffman, Paul Krassner, Roger Ebert, Eric Hoffer, William Buckley, Gary Wills, *ad confusiam*. Like the parade of Social Philosophers who guest on the Tonight Show, Pop Criticism and its Now Critics exist to fill up space, to kill time, to end thinking, to hold attention until the commercial.

The February, 1969 issue of *Harper's* magazine provides a classic of the genre with Pauline Kael's "Trash, Art and the Movies." Miss Kael's thesis, as far as it is possible to find it within the razzledazzle, seems to be threefold. First, bad low-budget films are better than bad high-budget films because they are less economically pretentious. Second, to be good, a movie doesn't need good action, good special effects, good directing, or good acting; it needs only a good idea. Third, and consequently, we shouldn't give Hollywood credit for making art films, no matter how good the film appears to be. All the rest is pretentious window dressing parading as cinema art.

If works of cinema art are to be judged according to the amount of money that did not go into their production; or, on the other hand if they are to be judged according to their place of origin or for their didactic potential, then movie criticism seems oddly stuck in an especially viscous mud, made of two parts American Plainstyle Grad-school in-group artiness; one part Protestant-Ethic-distrust of anything that smacks of wasting an honest dollar; topped off with a frosting of anti-hero, anti-myth, anti-romantic, alienated pseudo-existential weariness with anything that is similar to anything that has been done before. It is not criticism, it is a posture. It is formula aesthetics, written for formula audiences, only thinly disguised as serious criticism by a shiny verbal wrapper that lists its contents in dayglo color.

While in many cases the Now-Critic is in a better position than most to assess the significance of a particular work of popular art, there seems sometimes to be evidence of a compulsion not so much to miss the point but to *dis*miss the point of a major work because its contents do not fit a pre-salivated formula. This is precisely what appears to have happened in Miss Kael's otherwise perceptive article in *Harper's:* the content of *2001: A Space Odyssey* was either distorted or ignored for the sake of supporting an hypothesis concerning art films. There is no particular reasoning behind the selection of *2001,* except that comments not about the film but about the director's intentions (as related by Miss Kael) seemed to support the thesis of the article. Since the content of *2001* does not support her thesis, I suppose its presence in the article is simply irrelevant. However, although no analysis of the film is attempted, *2001* is condemned, largely on the basis of director Kubrick's presumptuousness in making such a film in the first place: ". . . a movie that might have been made by the hero of *Blow-Up* . . . it's fun to think of Kubrick really doing every dumb thing he wanted to do, building enormous science-fiction sets and equipment, never even bothering to figure out what he was going to do with them." The thing that is so abominably bad about such statements is not only that they are simply wrong, irrelevant, and misleading, but that they are probably taken as serious and legitimate criticism by hordes of people who haven't enough critical sophistication of their own to see through the rhetoric.

For the purposes of explication and comparison, let us take a look at *2001,* to see what the film itself seems to be saying. And that does not mean a review of Arthur C. Clarke's book of the same title. Mr. Clarke, a former Chairman of the British Interplanetary Society, and an inspired science-fiction writer on occasion (*Childhood's End* is unforgettable), did not do a great deal with the theme. A great deal of Miss Kael's criticism of the film is grounded in her reaction to the book, for the film itself does not evidence the easy solutions of the book. So let's forget about the book; after all, we are attempting a critique of the movie. Let's forget about the book and its stable of alien intelligences, super-beings, and such BEM ilk that control man's destiny. In short, let's remember our Brooks, Warren, Wimsatt, Beardsley and Frye and avoid the intentional and biographical fallacies. After all, unless we are seeking answers to ethical and epistemological questions, Mr. Clarke's book and Mr. Kubrick's "really doing every dumb thing he wanted to" are about as relevant to legitimate art criticism as the color of Richard Wagner's vest pockets.

I have seen *2001* seven times. By the third viewing, I was able to see past the special effects to the substance of the movie. It wasn't that the special effects were "dumb"; it was simply that they were all so incredibly right within the total context of the film, the temptation to dwell on them to the exclusion of other elements was too great to resist. I do not feel too badly about this: it is no sin to look at a painting first for its design, then for its color, then for its dynamics, and finally for the *kosmion* of unity that is constituted by the work as a whole. The illusion created by the effects were essential to the overall design of the film, which includes a progression from raw explicitness to pure metaphor. Such a progression from the apes to a symbolic Regency room would not have been possible unless the technical effects had been coldly realistic enough to allow us to effect what Coleridge called the "willing suspension of disbelief" about being in a movie house, watching actors play parts in a technical magic lantern that miraculously projected itself on a screen. Cinema itself, like all theater, is a kind of "trick." I see no reason to condemn it if the trick is a good one.

A good deal of the ballyhoo preceding the film had to do with the absence of dialogue. This provides us with a clue if we care to take the trouble of being sensitive to language. In the beginning (literally), language is simple and direct, consisting of grunts and shrieks. Within the proto-vocabulary, there are hunger noises, anger noises and fear noises, all explicit, obvious in their social function, and backed up (or explicated) with a cuff of the hand. The apes are herbivores. Their coats are tatty and their bodies are lean and passive. They are violent only verbally. When threatened by neighboring tribes, they do not fight; instead they perform a variety of antics including snarls and displays of uncovered teeth. Their lives, however mean, are peaceful enough. Small tapir-like creatures forage along with them unafraid. The Fall of the Ape-man comes with the introduction into his "garden" of what Miss Kael calls "the slab." No explanation is given for its appearance. It comes in the night and it disappears later. From the film itself there is no way we can guess the monolith's origin, anymore than the apes can understand its purpose. We, not the film (much less the book, which is completely extraneous), provide a link between the appearance of the monolith and the change in the ape-man's behavior. It is implied, perhaps, by the very appearance of the object; however, no explicit causal relation is indicated. We can tentatively take the monolith as a symbol to be explained later in the film. At any rate, what happened after the appearance of the monolith can be explained without reference to it. Herein lies the key to the monolith's symbolic function: it is not necessary to accept its causal function literally, since the apes could have discovered weapons without it while revealing no inconsistencies in their own behavior. The monolith, then, is a symbolic object, presented literally in a primitive, literal landscape, as an unknown—perhaps as *the* unknown.

The film's most powerful scene comes when the ape realizes that the bone lying in the pile before him can be used. His attention focuses on the bone. His head turns to one side as if to bring the idea itself into sharper focus. The bone is a tool. It is a tool for killing: a weapon. Robert Ardrey's *African Genesis* provides us with another key to the meaning here: when proto-man discovered that the femur of an antelope could be used to crack the skulls of the animals around him, Man was born. It is not a pretty thought, but then man has never been a pretty animal. When the ape grasps the bone, first with one hand, then with both, one can almost hear the thoughts grinding through his head. He lifts the bone once, again. Man raises himself upright for the first time, not to look at the stars or to his god, but to get enough momentum, enough kinetic force to smash the skulls in the boneyard, and thus to destroy his past life forever. The Fall is complete when Cain kills Abel: when the first ape is killed by one of his own kind. The coats are glossy now. The bellies are full. There is meat for the tapirs have become food. The Peaceable Kingdom is gone for good. It is not for nothing that the opening bars of *Thus Spake Zarathustra* are used here as a leitmotive that trumpets the transvaluation of all values.

2001 is an opera in four acts. It is performed on a Wagnerian scale. It is romantic, but only as a modern multi-media version of transcendentalism could be. When the ape-now-man tosses the bone-weapon into the air, a weapon whose punning phallic symbolism holds within it the seeds of man's future, the artificial satellite that we see after the instantaneous million-year leap is still phallic, still a weapon in its many uses and purposes, and still as deadly in its implications as the ancient femur. The ironic musical shift from Richard Strauss to Johann Strauss (a scene which Miss Kael calls "comic") is a shift from elemental explicitness to formalized meaninglessness.

Language as it is used by the people on the space station and at the moon base is almost purely ritual. When Dr. Heywood Floyd calls his daughter on the American-Express-Card-actuated radiophone (a scene which Miss Kael calls the "amateur-movie obligatory scene"), they do not communicate. They are too far removed from each other, both in space-time and within the limits of their language as well. The dialogue is banal. What else should it be? "Where is your mother?" "Where is the baby-sitter?" "What do you want for your birthday?" The theme of birth and family is important throughout the film, witness the cluster of apes with their young, General Floyd's daughter, Frank's birthday greeting on board the spaceship, references to the birth of the computer and the final rebirth of Dave. It is a theme of birth out of death, with symbolic over-lappings. The little girl wants a bushbaby for her birthday. Of course that fits: because a bushbaby is a type of small simian, a little ape. And thus the first act is linked again to the second.

Floyd's friend and her associates continue the ritual language in the lounge: "How are you?" "Would you like a drink?" "This is Doctor so and so . . ." (the formality of a Ph.D. both in fact and in address appears to indicate yet another facet of ritualization). The dialogue that follows is more than mere patter or mere film footage. It is a highly stylized language game, followed rigorously by the players, for the purpose of effecting the ritual of social interaction. There are rules and there are permissible responses. There are also taboos, chief of which is the sanction against the transference of genuine information about facts that exist apart from the ritual of the game. When the question is raised about the possibility of an epidemic on the moon base, the cardinal rule is broken and a new game begins, much the same as if the group were computerized and programmed to shift to a new game when extra-programmed questions were asked. The shift was instantaneous and predictable: "I'm sorry but I'm not at liberty to discuss that matter." When the question is asked again (a severe social error), the programmed response is repeated and the game is brought to a close. Dr. Floyd has checkmated his inquisitor with an ancient strategy: silence for the sake of security for all. The denouement is the finalization of the ritual and a return to the original game: "Well, are you sure you won't have that drink?" "Come to see us when you're back, and bring that lovely daughter of yours."

The scene in the conference room on the moon base follows the same pattern. Nothing is said that the participants do not already know. Dr. Floyd even prefaces his remarks with "I suppose you already know that. . . ." There is the inevitable photographer, polite applause, questions that do not require answers that are not already implicit in the questions— and the conference-game is over. On the flight to the monolith, there are more familiar games. "That was a fine speech you made today, General. It did a lot for morale." "Well, thanks. And I want you to know that you people are doing a fine job up here." Complete to the ritual swearing that always lubricates social situations between men in danger, whether they are in spaceships, cars, boats, submarines or tents: "I don't suppose you know what the damn thing is?" "I wish the hell we did." The inevitable hot coffee follows.

The similarity between the spacemen and the apes is obvious and revealing. If the monolith symbolizes the unknown, then there is no more reason for modern man to understand it than for the ape-man. The monolith is not merely an unknown object. It is a symbol of the mystery of the universe itself, and as such is inexplicable at any age, in any era. No answers are to be found when the monolith radiates a signal in the direction of Jupiter. The radio signal initiates a game of seek and find . . . hence the mission to Jupiter. Again, we hear the opening bars of *Thus Spake Zarathustra,* the leitmotive that heralds sudden and irrevocable change. It is as commanding as the *Ring's* Wotan motive; it is as elemental as Wagner's theme for the Root of all Matter. The monolith and its accompanying leitmotive serve as the film's most arresting symbol: not an artifact of an alien intelligence, anymore than a symbol for God. It is symbolic of Being itself, whether the sidereal universe, man's nisus toward the unknown, or the Hegelian World-Spirit objectifying itself symbolically through a faceless, black, geometric shape.

Act 3 begins on board a ship headed for Jupiter. The cast consists of several technicians who are in suspended animation, two crewmen, essentially featureless, who are "programmed" to effect the success of the mission (that is, to record and supervise the voyage, its orbit around Jupiter, and to act as volitional beings only if there is a computer failure). Frank and Dave, almost clinically pure and scrubbed, are accompanied by an HAL 9000 computer (H-A-L, short for Heuristically Programmed Algorithmic computer, is also one letter shy of, respectively, I-B-M). Ritual language games are of minimal importance here. Precise data, in the form of meters, lights, charts, dials and viewer-screens surround the men. They are as much "along for the ride" as the sleeping technicians, for their sole function during the flight seems to be that of a trouble indicator. They simply watch to see if the computer is running everything smoothly. They are cared for, pampered, fed, warmed, and counseled. It would be an easy mistake to think that the ship is a womb. But the ship is unmistakably male, both in shape and in function. It does not merely contain, it probes. And HAL is not merely a computer, he *is* the ship. His sensors are distributed throughout the ship, in much the same manner as the human nervous system. Conceptually, HAL is a model of man-as-machine. There is a linear connection between HAL and the antelope femur: the computer-ship is the logical conclusion of a mechanistic *weltanschauung* that was born in the primeval boneyard. The machine that man once contained now contains the man.

But HAL is more than computer-ship, for he becomes a sentient being. He is truly the "ghost in the machine" that Ryle attempted to lay to his rest. As such, HAL is perhaps symbolic of modern, scientific man himself: mechanistic man writ large, with metal skin, an electrical brain, and a sentience that mirrors the machine and hence itself. HAL's tragic flaw, the sin that he inherited from his creator, is that hubris that seems to generate from the irrational inference that actualizes hypotheses: "If I can think, I ought to think; if I can act, I ought to act; if I can decide, I ought to decide; if I can make my decisions alter reality, I ought to alter reality. I think, therefore I am. I am, therefore I act."

While HAL is programmed to effect the completion of the mission, he is also programmed to value the civilization that produced him. Veteran science-fiction aficionados will remember Isaac Asimov's Three Laws of Robotics: built-in safeguards against Frankenstein's monster. In order to complete the psychological workups on the crew, it would be necessary that HAL do more than record. The values that would indicate to HAL a "malfunction" in a crew member would also tell him that the success of the mission would mean the end of civilization as he knew it. As we discover later, HAL has data concerning the mission that is not available to the crew. He also has at his disposal more speculative ability than any man (if we define "speculation" as the review of probable inferences and possibilities). To complete the mission is to destroy Man. Not to complete the mission is to destroy the men of the crew. It is the presence of a paradox in the program, the contradiction between implicit values and explicit orders, that leads to the computer's apparent schizophrenia that brings Act 3 to its climax. It also provides a model for mechanistic man: schizophrenia is a term properly applied to the mental condition produced by contrary or contradictory programming. The all-important distinction between HAL and his electronic ancestors can be illustrated by the story of the Kalin-Burkhart logic machine. Built in 1947 by William Burkhart and Theodore Kalin, the machine was capable of solving simple logical problems; at least it would indicate with lights whether a proposition within an argument was true or false. Martin Gardner reports [*Logic Machines and Diagrams* (New York, 1958)] that when fed certain types of paradoxes, the machine would slip into an oscillating phase, hopping back and forth from "true" to "false." HAL, on the other hand, does not oscillate. He vascillates for a few moments, then by an act of will decides to take a course of action that will mean at once the death of the crew and the life of Mankind.

Dave's conversation with Frank about the possible need for disconnecting HAL is picked up as the computer reads their lips. Now the machine moves out of necessity: it must actualize the theoretical reflections concerning its paradoxical programming. The "solution" to the paradox immediately results in Frank's death. (Miss Kael refers to this death as "unexplained," and cites the opening scene of *You Only Live Twice* as much better, because "It had an element of the unexpected, of the shock of finding death in space lyrical." Lyrical?) The life functions of the technicians are stopped. Only Dave remains alive. When Dave outwits the computer and begins to disconnect HAL's higher brain functions, the computer says that it is afraid. As the brain is disconnected, circuit by circuit, HAL abreacts back to his "childhood" to his instructor at the factory. His final words betray not only the failure of a vast and complex mentality, but the love of man that led him to his end. It is a song: "Daisy, Daisy, give me your answer do. I'm half crazy, over the love of you."

The third act ends with the ejection of the pod, the ejaculation of the chromosome-carrying sperm cell, into the fluid of space-time. The journey through the space-time warp becomes a symbolic journey of the sperm through the womb and through the fallopian tubes. At the end, the source of life itself is found in an ovary that melds into pure symbolism. This is the part of the film that Miss Kael dismisses as a "trip" scene that is "not too good." To interpret this scene only as a trip is to miss the symbolism of the entire work completely. It is a "trip" all right, but to describe it as such, and with the connotation that that word carries is about on a par with responding to a volcanic eruption with "O wow."

The Edenic myth is asserted again as the downward flight ends. As our vision skims over an inchoate world, the field changes into color negatives. The hexamera, the six days of creation, are reiterated with the changing colors. The final shift leaves us and Dave to rest on the seventh day. The resting is done in a Regency room. The fourth and final act has begun, and we have moved from the stark naturalism of the first act to a sterile, artificial idealization of civilization: an architectural metaphor for a world-view that is about to come to an end.

The Regency room, unexplained, and explicitly inexplicable, is the final symbolic form of Western Civilization. At the end of man, a time when, within the context of the film rebirth is imminent, the Regency room provides a structure which is at once the past and the present. The eschatological significance of the room finds its locus in its very museum-like quality. It *is* the human past, with its art and its architecture, its sterile formalism reminiscent of the ritual conversations aboard the space station and at Clavius; and all too familiarly related in potential form to the complex sterility of the space ship. Although the room is impeccably done, it has all the warmth of a funeral parlor. It is dead, like the forms of the past it represents. But it is death in the expectation of a new life, as surely as Dave must undergo the final closing before his and man's rebirth come about. Time is telescoped, and as the protagonist sees himself, hears himself, in each successive almost-encounter with himself, time coalesces with all times past and all times present. The broken wine glass, a final ritual shattering of the past, the breaking of the amniotic sac, leads directly to the final ritual of Everyman: the gasps of a human body at the edge of death, the final desperate groping of Ancient Man, of ancient Everyman, reaching up toward the monolithic face of the Unknown. At that instant, like the almost-connected teardrops of Whitehead's successive presents, the transformation is made. Not resurrection, as Miss Kael tells us, but rebirth of a new entity out of the old being. There is no suggestion of the guiding hand of an alien life-form in this scene (must we take everything literally?). There is the monolith: a geometrical shape, for all of man's history denoting form, perhaps connoting purpose, perhaps symbolic of the introduction of Will into the Garden; but here life-in-death, a thing hoped for but not understood. When Everyman reaches for his most profound symbol, he is transformed, transmuted into a new form. The *Ubermensch* is born out of the dried leaves of ancient man. A star-child floats in its egg, floats through the fluid of space-time, its time come 'round again, toward Earth to be born. The planets again align themselves and the triumphant herald of *Thus Spake Zarathustra* announces the new Messiah. The myths of mankind, the hexamera, the Fall, the loss of primeval innocence, the coming of the Messiah, have all been worked out in a multimedia, multileveled allegory of modern man facing himself and an unknown future.

Miss Kael's final summary: "It has the dreamy somewhere-over-the-rainbow appeal of a new vision of heaven. *2001* is a celebration of cop-out. It says man is just a tiny nothing on the stairway to paradise, something better is coming, and its all out of your hands anyway. There's an intelligence out there in space controlling your destiny from ape to angel, so just follow the slab. Drop up."

In the immediate past, before the current union of bohemian and hipster, the list of certified Good Things included bare walls, candles burning in old Chianti bottles, ragged tennis slippers, stringy hair, self-conscious imitations of the Susan Sontag Look (essential for a female if she expected her intellect to be taken seriously), growing your own yogurt, verbal drivel for poetry, the myriad academic-plain-style activities that denoted intellectual cool; now add that marvelous extension of the American Middle Class yearning for instant everything: take grass and add a little rock. The contemporary edition leans toward revised (Edwardian) mod. Courreges out of Pucci, by the flea market. The historical solipsism of pop culture supports the limited vision of the Now Critics: the affirmation of the ascendancy of the Scene as the locus of all values assures the success of Pop Criticism, whatever and whoever its source may be. Harold Rosenburg outlined one aspect of the difficulty in the September, 1966 issue of *Vogue:*

> This ambiguity is present regardless of the mode in which the work is executed—it is as characteristic of paintings of zones and stripes, which allude to concepts favoured by a faction of critics, as of Pop films acted by a cast of pals or a sculpture consisting of a table covered with after-breakfast items. . . . Behind this barrier the band of initiates, pampered by semi-initiates, romps happily in an atmosphere as relaxed as socks on the bathroom floor. By erecting a wall of incomprehension between those in the know and humanity at large, the boring painting or performance serves to strengthen the inner unity of the various ideological, sex, and taste groups that constitute the world of the arts.

But isn't this criticism applicable to Pop Criticism itself? Isn't the Now Criticism itself a performance on the part of the critic, a work executed behind a barrier of incomprehension that follows the cult of personality on which it feeds? Part of my distress with the Now Critics has not so much to do with their lack of competence. I suspect that they, especially the better ones such as Pauline Kael, see quite clearly the meaning of good films, of good art. But art and art criticism, whether concerning movies, books, poetry or painting, all too frequently degenerates in the ritual game of words and clichés reminiscent of Heywood Floyd's conversation on the space station. If the purpose of writing is not to impart information, then it becomes mere ritual. The rules of the game are broken only by those vulgar enough to ask for genuine insight (hence the vulgarity of this article). And hence the absence of critical canons and hence the lack of interest in the cultural welfare of the reader-listener-viewer, as is evidenced by unconcern for facts but overweening concern for the performance of criticism. "Slickspeak," the language of the Now Criticism, is easily recognizable. The first five paragraphs of this article are faithful prototypes of the prevailing form.

In an age dominated by what Orrin Klapp calls heroes of the surfaces [*Heroes, Villains and Fools* (Englewood Cliffs, N.J., 1962)], the Now Critics provide an institutionalized mode of superficial acquaintance with the issues and answers of the pop scene. While claiming to provide the reader with insight, Pop Criticism, substituting description for analysis, offers a formula-conceptualization of current selected events, aesthetic judgements, and behavioral norms. It alleviates the need for the reader to make judgements about the arts or any other subject on the basis of his own ability to analyze and evaluate his experiences. The reader thus escapes the arduous responsibility of developing a sense of taste and judgement. All one needs to know can be found in Pop Criticism's Plumber's Manual for the Good Life. While it appears to inform the reader, "Slickspeak" attracts attention by the use of "catchy" popular expressions, in a style that is visual, tactile, non-analytic and non-reflective. The method (as illustrated in the beginning of this article) is *attack:* the abusive *ad hominem,* directed toward whatever idols are to be torn down. In some ways, the style borrows from billboard art: it can be read easily and quickly, before the sign passes from view.

The involvement offered by the Now Critics is not with works of art, nor is it with the problems of society that are sometimes used as vehicles for commentary. It is involvement with the authors, the directors, the wives, mistresses and lovers, in short, with the entire pantheon of Beautiful People who are our axiological archetypes. Thus it is possible for the reader-viewer-listener to experience vicariously and in seeming safety the dazzling lifestyles of his or her surface-hero. Hence it is of prime importance that the Now Critic provide information about the lives, thoughts, piccadillos and vices of the creators of art, politics, and the Scene. That this violates all the canons of good and responsible criticism is beside the point, since it is not the function of Pop Criticism to provide real insights about its alleged subject matter. What is provided is a pandering service for the vast multitude who would like to be Beautiful People themselves. The analogy with the theater brothel in Genet's *The Balcony* is, unfortunately, all too appropriate.

If Dave and Frank seemed sterile, it is because they provide a mirror image of ourselves. There was no authentic experience in the second and third acts of *2001.* Language did not carry information, it was merely ritual. Floyd did not talk to his daughter, he talked into a machine. Frank's parents wished him a happy birthday on a viewscreen. The food provided by the ship was pre-packaged; the range of choices was limited. Perception of location and condition was provided by instruments. The crew was protected from harm by life-support systems. The temperature was regulated. The water had been sterilized. All sharp edges had been rounded off. Fear had been conditioned away. Courses of action were determined prior to launch-time. The mission had been planned to the last detail.

Given the basic assumptions of a mechanistic world view, the finite number of logical possibilities opened by the introduction and adoption of the antelope femur had all been tried. It was not until the system itself failed that the possibility was raised not only for meaningful human action but of hope for something better in the future as well. HAL, the computer, the ship, the culture, sought to preserve man by eliminating the possibility of a new, alternative way of life. The Now Critics, by dwelling only on the specious present, by providing pre-packaged concepts for programmed audiences, have made newness trivial by making newness its own reward. Within a solipsistic world view, nothing is new or old, it simply *is*. And the ceremony of innocence is conducted by the priests of Pop Criticism.

Within the ritual the guru's word becomes law. And the gurus of the surface provide the life-support systems for the crew. Rock singers become sociologists, spaceship pilots become political theorists, college dropouts write treatises on psychedelic pharmacology, hippies and jet setters provide the new ethic: *ubiquita sexualis,* men's magazine publishers become social, philosophical and theological commentators, longshoremen replace Russell and Wittgenstein, ladies' magazines legislate automotive design, free universities discard content as irrelevant, and professors are admonished by uneasy administrators not to alienate their students by a show of competence. A clamor for "law and order" ignores the fact that authority is legitimated not by the rulers but by the ruled.

Something's happening, baby. A malfunction in the world's computer? Perhaps. Walter Karp (*Interplay,* March 1969) in an astonishing essay, "What's Wrong with the World?", has pointed out that it is possible for a man to be born, to grow up, to live out his years and die of old age, without ever having been required to make a single moral *decision* of his own. Gore Vidal, in "The Liberal Dilemma" [*Sex, Death and Money* (New York, 1968)] tells us that ". . . it does not take an unusually inspired prophet to note that once again the wheel of man's history has begun to turn and the human race is about to experience one of its periodic smashups." Perhaps we are about to trade Johann Strauss for Richard Strauss, again to break all the skulls in the boneyard. There is occasionally good criticism, but it is rarely remembered. The book as artifact describes the post-Gutenberg world with appalling accuracy. With no criterion besides Now, how does one tell the good critics from the bad?

Yes, perhaps a malfunction in the computer. But what of it? The computer has information inaccessible to us. HAL assuredly will detect any malfunctions, either in the ship or in us, and repair the difficulty with the laws of physics and the order of ritual. And in the meantime, we're all right aren't we? We're cared for, pampered, fed, warmed and counseled (well, at least most of us). Food is pre-packaged. Our instruments tell us where we are. Our life-support systems are working. If anything drastic goes wrong, HAL will take care of it. According to HAL, all systems are Go. There is every indication that the mission will be a screaming success. In every way. Groovy.

Are you sure you won't have that drink? How about a Soma?

The New Audience: From Andy Hardy to Arlo Guthrie

LARRY COHEN

According to the headline of an article that appeared late last May in *The New York Times,* buried with the film advertisements on page 36, "Young Writers Say They Don't Read." The five interviewed authors, all of whom were respectably under thirty, announced that they rarely if ever opened a book. "It's just easier to go to a movie and let it all wash over you," one of them said.

There were, of course, prominent exceptions to this impatient rule. Hermann Hesse and J. R. R. Tolkien both have large youthful followings. So does Kurt Vonnegut, Jr., who was singled out because "he writes cinematically." But most authors met a grimmer, much less cordial fate. Reading was regarded as an academic pastime, and most books were relegated to the level and enthusiasm of a chore. The article came to an abrupt close with one of those statements that must have chilled the warmest hardbound heart. One of the young writers, Sally Grimes, who had previously spent some time composing obituary notices for the *Philadelphia Bulletin,* committed her own cool piece of manslaughter by concluding: "I find I'm reading less and less. I really don't know why."

It occurs to me that the content of such a remark is less important than the tone with which it appears to have been said. Just think about what she's announcing. The death of literature? Hardly. The temporary disaffection of a substantial cross section of young writers (and young readers) with books? Maybe, despite the fact that the paperback market place is currently a veritable gold mine and new soft-cover publications such as *New American Review* and *US* have whopping, young readerships.

But listen to the statement rather than just its meaning. What resounds is something casual and half-shaded, something innocent and perhaps even unconscious. The remark sounds like an afterthought, as if the speaker was deaf to any echo. There is nothing guilty about such a confession, no sense that the Furies of Literature are about to swoop down upon her for heresy. It is the nonchalance that says everything, the pronouncement itself relatively little. For the mood to which Miss Grimes and the other young writers are subscribing may well be an accurate expression of a *new* sensibility, one which is defined in part by its very lack of guilt about not being well-read and, on the other hand, by its overtly positive enthusiasm about film. In its openness and bluntness, "I really don't know why" reflects 1969 and a large new audience.

These changes in emphasis are so recent that it's extremely difficult to pin down their source with any real exactitude. There are clues, however, and a quick personal flashback to four years ago, around the time I graduated from high school, brings to mind a different picture. The kids with whom I grew up were avid readers; some of them even lay awake late at night and sweated out plans for writing the Great American Novel. Vietnam and a pervasive drug scene were not substantial issues yet; like us, they were in their pubescent stages, and the day they would be taken for granted as realities seemed a long way off. Literature still had its grip on us and we on it. For, McLuhan and television notwithstanding, the primary frame of reference from which we derived our formal tastes and plans for the future was still verbal. Our own Great Expectations used writers like Ken Kesey, Thomas Pynchon, J. D. Salinger, and Nathanael West as models and sources of passionate discussion.

Significantly mitigating this classical orientation was a film course I took in my senior year with about thirty other kids. We spent the first part of a fall semester staring at supposedly familiar objects—a leaf or our thumb, for example—and discovered the hard way what Joseph Conrad meant when he argued that his purpose was to make us *see*. With our thumbs out of our mouths, we then began looking at films by Griffith, Chaplin, Eisenstein, and Welles. *Potemkin* and *Citizen Kane* served as textbooks; we dissected their sequences frame by frame and assimilated a new vocabulary, learning how a movie was put together and why it still worked decades later. While most of our friends were surrendering themselves to term papers on Milton or even to diagraming the perennial sentence, we were reading the late James Agee's movie criticism and screenplays, using Arthur Knight's *The Liveliest Art* to gain a historical context, and worrying about montage and nonlinear structures. In retrospect, we already were taking films personally and seriously.

By 1969, what has happened is simply this: the young audience for books has not so much shrunk as the young audience for motion pictures has appreciably grown and become more vocal. As a breed, the kids of the late Fifties and early Sixties—the ones who had avidly attended university creative writing courses or earnestly imagined themselves as editors for a New York publishing house—were now generally anachronistic. For that matter, almost no one I knew at college read anything beyond the required classroom texts. Students were now crowding and overfilling smoky lecture halls to see and "rap" about films—their theory and history—and in more than a few instances this new breed was also making 8 and 16 mm movies despite the cost of equipment.

One crucial difference between movies and the other arts was simple accessibility. Even in the cultural provinces of the Middle West, it was possible to see as many as a half-dozen films a week. (Francis Ford Coppola, the thirty-year-old director of *You're a Big Boy Now* and *The Rain People,* predicts that "movies will be sold like soup in the future," that "you'll be able to buy it in cartridges for $3 and play it as you would a record, at home.") In addition to sheer availability, films were answering the lusting college cry for "relevance," taking both their raw celluloid material and subject matters from today rather than the day before yesterday.

In this regard, *Blow-Up* functioned as the pivotal film; it radicalized the way in which many college students responded to film. More than three years after it first appeared, it remains a significant milestone in this country's awareness of motion pictures. Antonioni's tour of mod London was one of the first movies young people saw more than once. Its ambiguities, its mysteries, and its technological break-throughs brought them back to the theater again and again, converting them to the language of film. (Curiously and ironically, it even inspired some kids to become photographers.) Rather than just being one more foreign film, *Blow-Up* was a primer in technique.

In the process of this shift of focus off the writer and onto the film-maker, the literary gods lost many of their aspiring novices to a medium that was itself in a state of relative infancy. There was and is, of course, a set of both happy and notorious exceptions. Nabokov's *Ada* and John Fowles's *The French Lieutenant's Woman*—works of genius in my opinion —would be quickly purchased in spite of their prohibitive costs in hard-bound editions. Similarly, there would be large campus audiences for such national best sellers as *Portnoy's Complaint, Myra Breckinridge,* and *Couples.* The big money and larger audience, however, now belonged to film, and it is not surprising that all of these novels (with the understandable exception of *Ada*) are headed for the screen.

One key sign of film's evolution as the form that matters for young people today is the number of campus literary successes now being made into motion pictures. We already have witnessed several: Peter Brook's grainy 1963 adaptation of William Golding's book *Lord of the Flies;* Larry Peerce's pushy but humorous Sixties transplant of Philip Roth's 1959 novella, *Goodbye, Columbus;* and the soon-to-be-released film version of John Barth's *The End of the Road.* Even the indomitable classroom Shakespeare found himself ruthlessly pruned and feverishly revitalized for a young audience as the literally teen-age Leonard Whiting and Olivia Hussey became Romeo and Juliet. If the results in this latter case were a trifle goofy, seeing the star-crossed lovers played by kids against the background of director Franco Zeffirelli's lush visual imagery almost justified any irreverence.

As we enter a new decade, the possible list of properties based on collegiate favorites increases. A new company, United Screen Arts, has optioned Hesse's *Steppenwolf,* and Conrad Rooks, whose hallucinatory film-nightmare on drugs, *Chappaqua,* was released several years ago, is rumored to be preparing the same author's *Siddhartha* for the screen. Hillard Elkins, the producer of *Oh! Calcutta!,* is readying a movie version of *Cat's Cradle,* and other works by Vonnegut—including *Player Piano* and *Sirens of Titan*—are also scheduled. Some of these are tentative projects and may never make it to the screen. Their mere presence on the boards, however, suggests a different contextual base for American films in the future. With Tolkien's *Lord of the Rings* soon to go into production, can Richard Fariña's *Been Down So Long It Looks Like Up to Me* be far behind?

One industry journal recently estimated that "at least 70 per cent of box-office revenue comes from young people between 16 and 29," a statistic that indicates that the economy of motion pictures is quantitatively a matter of age. Thought of five years ago *only* as an entertainment form—with a separately delineated category for "art" house imports—movies are now *in* and regarded as a legitimate pursuit in America. In contrast, the more traditional arts such as theater and opera are shaky if not altogether ready to enter an old age home. The lines at the box office are a proof of sorts that film and film alone is attracting kids. Just as it is inconceivable that anyone would stand in line for two hours to see a play or purchase a book, it is taken for granted that one will wait this long to see *Midnight Cowboy* in a city like New York. Legitimate theater, with the exception of such youth-geared musicals as *Hair* and *Salvation,* exerts little if any appeal. And the one-week performance by the Who of their rock-media opera *Tommy* at the Fillmore East is the closest anyone under thirty will get to a tier at the Metropolitan.

To understand the kind of age polarization that has occurred, one has only to glance quickly at the lyrics of two songs: the title number from *Hello, Dolly!* and "Go to the Mirror" from *Tommy.* "It's so nice to have you back where you belong," sing the waiters in the long-running Broadway musical, articulating a nostalgia and a red-carpeted style of life that seems altogether foreign if not indulgent to the kids who witnessed Woodstock, the Vietnam Moratorium, and the March on Washington. In sharp contrast, the psychologically deaf, dumb, and blind Tommy sings, "See me, feel me, touch me, heal me" from the heavily amplified stage of the Fillmore, and the generations neatly split themselves right down the middle. One has fake cotton-candy dumplings in its mouth, while the other speaks of irresistible pinball wizardry from an electronically vibrant stage.

This polarization has been widely publicized, and the evidence is staggering in its abundance. It is now virtually impossible to pick up a national magazine without stumbling across a prominent article that discusses the "youth market" and the "New American film." One of the November issues of *Look,* for example, featured Daria Halprin and Mark Frechette, the two young nonprofessionals chosen by Antonioni for his first film in America, the soon-to-be-released *Zabriskie Point.* Earlier last fall *Newsweek,* with Arlo Guthrie gracing its cover, featured a story on Arthur Penn's *Alice's Restaurant.*

If the age bracket of the audience has been widely covered and debated in the press, it is also no secret that the major studios are in deep trouble and that Hollywood is running scared. Clearly, the old sorts of investments—the heavily insured, multimillion-dollar dinosaurs such as *Paint Your Wagon, Sweet Charity,* and *The Madwoman of Chaillot*—cannot hope to recoup their budgets at the box office and are suffering tremendous losses. Like the Norma Desmond of Billy Wilder's *Sunset Boulevard,* these films are now in a revealing close-up at the end of their staircase. They simply can't survive against the relatively low-budget, personal wave of films that *Easy Rider* typifies: a movie made for less than $500,000 that may well gross as much as $50-million in foreign and domestic sales.

Amid corporate power struggles, massive overheads, and the infusion of somewhat younger management, the studios are trying frantically to cater to this new audience. They are floundering because the only real precedents for youth films are the packages of American International Pictures—everything from the motorcycle and beach party formulas to *Wild in the Streets* and *Three in the Attic*—movies that were commercially successful and immune to critical reception. But a good film—and, to some degree, that is what is being demanded today—doesn't lend itself to readily identifiable denominators. The pseudo-politics of *Medium Cool* —the Democratic convention, the awkward restaging of Kennedy's assassination—make Haskell Wexler's film a work of serious intentions in spite of my strong reservations about its success. Used in Agnes Varda's *Lions Love,* the same issues are inane, if not in appallingly poor taste.

As a result of the youth craze, we are due for a series of films—some good, some bad—that reflect a Hollywood in transition. The year 1970 will witness the release of a mixed bag of pictures that are genuinely topical as well as those that will be lamentably foolish. MGM has completed *The Magic Garden of Stanley Sweetheart* from a screenplay by twenty-three-year-old Robert Westbrook based upon his own novel. The same studio is also preparing a screen version of James Simon Kunen's *The Strawberry Statement.* With its locale shifted from Columbia College to Oakland, the screenplay is an interesting blend of fiction and documentary by thirty-year-old playwright Israel Horovitz.

Joseph E. Levine, head of the company that released the phenomenally successful *The Graduate,* has dubbed Avco-Embassy's future banner as "New Faces of the '70s" and turned over the filming of the plague-ridden *Ski Bum* (from Romain Gary's novel) to three young graduate film students from UCLA. Haskell Wexler is readying production of *A Really Great Movie,* which Paramount describes as a film about two young college film-making students who are given the opportunity to make a major motion picture. Universal has the Berkeley-set *The Activist* in release. And only last month Radio City Music Hall, known for its tourists, kicking Rockettes, and tradition of Walt Disney fare, showed *Hail, Hero!,* perhaps the worst example to date of a film that tries to appeal to both pacifists and militants and rightfully pleases neither.

If *Blow-Up* was instrumental in attracting young people to film, the equivalent American landmark was Mike Nichols's *The Graduate.* Holden Caulfield, his worried future, identity-crisis, and traumas fairly intact, found a close screen ally in the person of Benjamin Braddock as played by Dustin Hoffman. Both characters assert the same basic appeal, a nervy and youthful cry against hypocrisy and false values that are captured lucidly by one word: *plastics.* What seems to me to be vital about the movie is that it signifies a phenomenon of rapport rather than a purely esthetic triumph; that it functions as a sociological replacement for Salinger despite its own confusions and impurities of self-conscious camerawork; that its score is by Simon and Garfunkel rather than Max Steiner.

This alliance with contemporary music has a great deal to do with the new look of American films and their success with a young audience. The Grateful Dead, Big Brother and the Holding Company, and John Barry's superb orchestrations contributed heavily to the impact of *Petulia*. And the two intentional or coincidental imitations of Nichols's film—the previously mentioned *Goodbye, Columbus* and *I Love You, Alice B. Toklas* —respectively used the Association and Harper's Bizarre for their title songs. When the team responsible for writing the latter movie made their directing debut this year with *Bob & Carol & Ted & Alice,* they appropriately ended what is in essence a middle-aged comedy with Dionne Warwick singing "What the World Needs Now Is Love."

There is a special category of movies in which the music and performer mean everything, and craft is less of a concern. D. A. Pennebaker's *Don't Look Back* opens with Bob Dylan holding placards for "Subterranean Homesick Blues" as the song is played on the soundtrack; it is a fresh, ingenious, and indelible image. But in spite of Pennebaker's attempts to have the camera be more than a passive recorder of a rock concert, the only interest in *Monterey Pop* is the roster of "stars": the Jefferson Airplane, Janis Joplin, and the Who. One feels inclined to reserve formal criticism because it somehow seems irrelevant, even in a simple exploitation film such as *Popcorn,* in which the audio performances by the Rolling Stones and Joe Cocker are virtually scuttled by the abysmal color visuals and self-conscious, intrusive camerawork. At this point, there is simply no conjecturing what the upcoming release of *Woodstock* by Warner Brothers will be like, but it clearly represents a much needed departure from the primitivism of its predecessors. It is described as a full-length color entertainment that makes use of split-screen techniques with up to six multiple images.

So much for the survey of the change, its physical and financial appearance. To borrow from the title of one of Richard Lester's early short subjects, the American cinema and its audiences are now running, jumping, and standing still—all at the same time. Some of this youthful insistence on relevancy has been invigorating and valuable in that it reflects an outcry against what is truly dated. It has brought us a vital (if not slightly late) awareness that film is primarily a director's medium. Consequently, kids and adults are becoming familiar with the names and works of Arthur Penn, Stanley Kubrick, Sam Peckinpah, and, of course, Mike Nichols. It has led to an appreciation of criticism: One spectator at this year's San Francisco Film Festival even asserted that the writings of critic Pauline Kael will survive the films of Sidney Lumet.

If we are lucky, this positive education will not stop with the director but will be extended to include an awareness of the components that define film-making: Nicholas Roeg's cool, alienating camerawork for *Petulia* (as well as the cinematography of such men as Lucien Ballard, Conrad Hall, William A. Fraker, Laszlo Kovacs, Pasquale de Santis, and Michael Nebbia); Dede Allen's major contribution as editor in *Rachel, Rachel* and *Bonnie and Clyde;* and Lawrence Marcus's brilliant screenplay of lacerated nerves and casual violence for *Petulia*.

Similarly, we are discovering just how a film-maker like Peter Yates can straddle two theoretically divided kinds of films—the entertainment and the so-called art movie. Superficially a cops-and-robbers film, *Bullitt* on closer examination yields a more complicated and fascinating set of structural parallels between the policeman and the killer. And his new film, *John and Mary,* transforms the banalities of an updated romance by complementing them with incisive visual details. By showing, for example, how Dustin Hoffman cracks his soft-boiled egg and eats it scooped out in the cup while Mia Farrow cracks and eats hers from the shell, by taking an overused device like the freeze-frame and showing how it can still be used humorously and originally, the British director draws attention to simple, illuminating bits of action instead of leaving the viewer to rely on dialogue to get his bearings.

On a more profound level, this youthful impact at the box office, if allied with a willingness to suspend old expectations and easy solutions, can lead to an appreciation of a film such as the current *Tell Them Willie Boy Is Here.* The second movie to be written and directed by the politically blacklisted Abraham Polonsky is remarkable (as was his 1948 *Force of Evil*) for its density of formal and moral texture, and in its eloquent union of image and sound. In its uncompromising attitude toward film and vision of a country that compromises its inhabitants, *Willie Boy* is a stunning achievement. The support of a new generation of filmgoers hopefully will elevate Polonsky to his rightful position as a unique force in American cinema: a man of ideas.

Young people's demands on the medium *can* take us in this direction. Yet, there is an equal if not greater chance that we are moving toward a mere embracing emphasis of today for the sake of today and a real irrelevancy. As Kunen puts it in *The Strawberry Statement,* "to say that youth is what's happening is absurd. It's always been happening. Everyone is nineteen, only at different times. This youth-cult scene is a disservice to everyone." His is a good, prematurely wise statement that foresees an inevitable and endless rash of "youth" films, imitations of some intangible quality that exists, after all, only in the mind. Like a Ponce de León in search of the magic fountain, the studios currently are equating being young with being talented with being profitable. I only hope the logic of this direction is reversed before the studios learn the hard way all over again that making bad films—young, old, or middle-aged—is no way at all.

The pair of films that I think genuinely reflect the end of this decade and the start of another are *Easy Rider* and *Alice's Restaurant.* As companion pieces of styles, attitudes, and approaches, they form a composite blow-up of what is happening in this country. They both take drugs for granted as a part of the grass ethic, and they are both possessed with a sense that we are becoming our own films. They are also intrinsically interesting in what they tell us about the interaction between audiences and movies, in the way the former sees itself on the screen.

Of the two, *Rider* works more obviously and is the more immediate film, applying the lyrics of Paul Kantner's song "We Can Be Together" by visually demonstrating that "we are all outlaws in the eyes of America." More than any film in recent memory, it generates its own pulse into the heartbeats of its predominantly under-thirty audience. The spirit of the movie is personal, even controversial. It says yes, it has been to this wave length of the United States before, and to prove that its age is ours, the soundtrack makes intensive use of contemporary rock—Steppenwolf, the Band, and Jimi Hendrix, among others. When Roger McGuinn sings "It's Alright Ma (I'm Only Bleeding)" near the end of the film, the audience and the movie have a viselike grip on each other. They go back a long way together, and I'm not altogether certain that anyone who wasn't weaned on Bob Dylan—whether three or thirty—can share the journey. Sometimes, the film says about itself, you just have to be there to understand.

Alice also utilizes music as its integral base, but directs it toward a more complicated, trickier, and eventually subtler end. Some of the soundtrack is simply music, like the appropriate and evocative "Songs to Aging Children Come," by Joni Mitchell. It is used as a quiet, melancholic background for a funeral sequence in the snow, a scene that owes a formal and emotional debt to the final part of François Truffaut's *Fahrenheit 451*. There are other songs including Pete Seeger's renditions of "Pastures of Plenty" and "The Car Song." The traditional hymn "Amazing Grace" becomes a generational link between a revival meeting and a youthful and communal Thanksgiving Day at Ray and Alice's church. And then there is the title song itself, the best expression of what the movie is really about. It articulates a cartooned life-and-death style, a giving and a taking, the good and bad times of a country in its logical but paradoxical youth. "You can get anything you want," says the song, "*excepting* Alice," suggesting the peculiar light and dark moods of an America and a film whose final shot will literally mimic this tension between lament and celebration.

The two films are similar in other ways. Both use nonprofessionals as well as trained actors; both are framed by the geography of late-Sixties America. *Rider* goes cross country on its fateful cycle journey to a whorish New Orleans, and along the harrowing way shows us places where the word police has a long "o," a vowel stretched out so far that it almost whistles like a rubber band. It is a land of motels with quickly turned on NO VACANCY signs as soon as its turned-on, long-haired riders arrive. And inevitably, it is a mental landscape full of crewcut goons with murderous aim if not intent.

Alice documents a lighter but hardly less scary America: a country of induction boards in which a young black veteran of the war has a hook instead of a hand; in which Arlo is violently abused for his hair and called a "hippie perversion"; in which Vietnam is pronounced Veetnam; and in which a solitary billboard from the Johnson administration still says "Keep America Beautiful! Cut Your Hair."

The crucial differences between the two films are not raw material but age and tone. For all intensive purposes, *Rider* is the first work of a young man (although Dennis Hopper is thirty-three and goes back to the days of

James Dean in the Fifties), and *Alice* is the sixth movie by a middle-aged man sincerely trying to bridge the considerable Great Divide. Hopper's vision is obsessed with death and prostitution from its very first minute on the screen; it senses persecution all around it, and it invites us to join in with our personal nightmares and experiences, our collective paranoia. It says that this is the way this country is, and, cleverly, it shows us the devastating fire and explosions in advance of their actual, sequential appearance that ends the film.

Undeniably, the movie is horribly effective; its own confusions even add a terrifying and inescapable logic. When the lawyer George Hanson (played brilliantly by Jack Nicholson) is killed, the loss is acute. The movie misses him; it came alive when he appeared, and in a curious way it seems to die when he does. Fonda's and Hopper's destruction elicits a strong response by virtue of the brutality of the act rather than by feelings for the individuals. Ours is a purely visceral reaction to murder, a response we even indulge in. But we have no time to think, no time to sort out the differences between the deaths. Despite whatever Hopper claims were his intentions, the film lurches out of control and so does the audience. There is a distinction that demands time to be thought out: namely, that Hanson was worth more alive than dead, and Wyatt and Billy become emotionally more valuable to us precisely *because* they die. It is a distinction few if any of us are able to make while still in the theater.

Alice also has its share of deaths: the passing of Woody Guthrie, of Shelley, of a whole way of life personified by the reconsecrated church. But unlike the brutal murders of *Rider,* both the man and boy die off-screen here. Their deaths are presented as a part of life rather than an end to it. Penn's film is vitally and compassionately interested in life and in a sense of humor as a style for coping, for living in Moratorium America without paranoia. Arlo's songs and manner are those of mild ridicule despite the disasters that shroud the film; the music and the style seem healthy, and they wear well.

In effectively suggesting these youthful but polar responses to domestic life, the two films are expressive landmarks for a medium and a country that are suffering growing pains. Hopper's seems more important right now because it slams in the gut, it is frequently right by sheer instinct, *because* it lacks subtlety. Penn's complex work—with its neat geometrical triangles, both religious and secular—strikes me as the more masterful and enduring motion picture. In its own way, *Alice* is a remake of the fifteen-year-old *Rebel Without a Cause* by Nicholas Ray. Yes, Arlo's hair is longer than James Dean's; he doesn't wear white socks, and the girls aren't as heavily lip-sticked as Natalie Wood. But what Penn is attempting is a translation into a late-Sixties style of the earlier film's anguish, vulnerability, and groping search for a surrogate family. And in linking Arlo with Dean's different but nonetheless similarly transcendent sort of articulateness, *Alice* suggests not only a way of being young in America, but also a possible way of being older. Arlo's grace takes us a long way from Andy Hardy.

Fiction and Film:
A Search
for New Sources

STEPHEN KOCH

The end of this dying, confounded decade of ours confronts anyone thinking even casually about the art of narrative with a blunt, and for Americans
relatively new, fact: it has become impossible to imagine any general
point of view—not even one based on strictly artistic criteria—within
which the art of fiction might seem more important than film. Even today,
such an assertion has a funny ring. On the razor's edge of the Seventies,
it bongs with an almost irritating banality, although not very long ago
(even a writer under thirty can remember when) it would have torn the air
like a shriek of treason. *Fiction?* A subordinate, unproductive art? As
compared to what? Hollywood? To most literary people, the idea remained
a crass outrage until at least 1965, when a succession of masterpieces
from Europe and decidedly remarkable American films finally made clear
to practically everyone that film had become the only narrative form that
mattered much.

In 1969, to insist on this point would merely submerge the obvious in
stridency. But think a moment: What American novel written in the Sixties
stands anywhere near (to pick off a list almost off-hand) *Jules and Jim,
Persona, Contempt, My Life to Live, Muriel, L'Avventura, Balthazar, Mou-
chette, Before the Revolution?* And these are movies that one admires
almost without qualification. What novels are even as interesting and
gratifying as the movies that fill the list of the decade's remarkable run-
ners-up: *Psycho, The Manchurian Candidate, A Hard Day's Night, Yellow
Submarine,* the much underrated *Reflections in a Golden Eye, Whatever
Happened to Baby Jane?,* or . . . ? But I'm just picking names out of the
air; a systematic effort would fill the column. The current relations of the
forms are a self-evident matter of vitality facing down enervation.

I see no reason to draw any apocalyptic conclusions from this, but the
recent history of the two brother arts makes it seem obvious in retrospect
that they have had this painful rendezvous from the beginning, that it has
been somehow implicit from the beginning in their artistic assumptions.
Things were easier once. It's almost embarrassing to repeat that Americans have only recently begun to think of film as art. In decades past, the
inane prejudice that it wasn't could always get its hype by merely con-
trasting the venal triviality of the Dream Factory with the uncontested
superiority of early-twentieth-century literary modernism. But with the exception of Beckett, that modernism has been fallow for almost thirty years,

since, say, 1941—the year both of Joyce's last book and of *Citizen Kane.* Since then, writing's prestige as High Art has been running largely on credit, academic credit at that. During the Fifties, this was understandable enough (given the general ignorance of European film). After all, *Rebel Without a Cause, Johnny Guitar,* and *Rear Window* are fine movies and all that, but they are something of a comedown after *Finnegans Wake.*

No more: The credit is exhausted. And to clinch the switch, last year we were presented with what looks very much like *the* masterpiece of the decade, emerging from nowhere else than Hollywood the Vile (via London) in the form of Stanley Kubrick's *2001: A Space Odyssey.* Kubrick's extraordinary masterpiece gathers into one dynamic image a major challenge to some of the assumptions that have dominated serious writing for at least a hundred years (and a challenge to the way those assumptions have affected film, as well), in a way that, say, Resnais's *Muriel* does not. *2001* is among the few great films that owe nothing at all to the assumptions of the middle-class psychological novel (as Resnais's film certainly does), entirely overlooking what is supposed to be the dominant preoccupation of "serious" modern narrative—the Self and its suffering—and substituting its own virile and deeply intelligent exploration of the human capacity for wonder. And that innovation creates another set of challenges. For example, though we've got used to assuming that "serious" art ought to partake of a set of "elitist," "adversary," "alienated" assumptions promoted by a certain kind of literary humanism, *2001* simply overlooks them all, which explains the hysteria of the critical reaction to it. It not only appealed to but overwhelmed a mass audience. Its politics are unnamable. It presents a complex and sometimes exalting image of that technology which we've been told again and again is inhuman and, therefore, the enemy of both art and the human spirit. All in all, ever since that ape leaped up in his exalting dance, crashing to pieces the dry bones of a dead animal, things haven't been the same.

And what's been happening to serious fiction while innovations like this have been emerging? For one thing, it has lost a big part of its best, most literate public to the movies, and *not,* as some rebarbative critics bitterly opine, because movies are "easy." (*Muriel, Balthazar,* and *Contempt* are not "easy" works.) People have lost interest because the middle-class psychological novel, which remains the only form our so-called serious writing takes, no longer has much to offer. And for a reason.

The reason is that the great tradition of modernist prose in English comes to an end in the work of Samuel Beckett—another ringing phrase, and though it may tinkle a bit with dogmatism, I'm convinced it isn't either really dogmatic or a mere matter of swallowing Beckett's own well-known views on the matter. It, too, has a kind of inevitable logic. Ever since Henry James, "serious writing" in English has been virtually defined as the rendering of consciousness through a self-conscious speaking voice. It has been the exploration and realization of the Self in words. As Isabel Archer sits beside the dead fireside in *Portrait of a Lady,* sensing the ghastly, geometric phantasm of her life's failure slowly rising to consciousness and fitting together before her, James is discovering, in Isabel's own self-discovery, the method, the *subject* of what was to be thenceforth the greatest fiction in English. Isabel's monologue is one of the great moments in the history of art, and near the end of it James exultantly exclaims, "Then, ah *then,* she *knew* where she was."

But when this tradition comes to an end in the gasping solitude of the last transcendent pages of *The Unnamable,* the conscious Self is singing a different tune: "Where I am, I don't know, I'll never know, in the silence you don't know, I can't go on, I'll go on." Here are sentences about *space* that demarcate the history of a kind of extreme self-consciousness in the twentieth century, the extreme self-consciousness that has been our best fiction's very life. From somewhere to nowhere; that is the trajectory of modern fiction, and, like all Beckett's works, *The Unnamable is* dominated by a single, horribly resonant, utterly penetrating insight: It is that consciousness meditating on itself alone is in fact meditating on death; that the *subject* of consciousness alone is death; that the life of consciousness alone is death.

The hero of contemporary fiction is the Nowhere Man, and his locale is the Nowhere Land, where he makes all his Nowhere Plans for Nobody. The Anguished Self is placeless and spaceless, and his art merely presents us year after year with a chronicle of self-humiliation, self-doubt, self-hatred, and (not to put too fine a point on it) masochism on a scale that I'm sure has been scarcely imagined since the fifteenth century. The heart of narrative is action, while our ideal seriousness is an account of impotence and the incapacity to act. That paradox has a certain richness, but it seems to me that its possibilities are utterly exhausted by Beckett's genius, and that we should take our greatest living writer seriously when he says it's time to put it to rest. In any event, it has stopped being interesting. Like some incorrigibly self-destructive friend, who first startles us with a sense of emotional urgency, whose situation then moves and even exalts us, but slowly begins to be an irritation because we've been to this same nowhere so many times before, our fiction has at last turned into one great big bore.

Mainstream modernism has died of complications implicit in a surfeit of subjectivity; it has died, literally, of inaction. But that's where movies and their extraordinary vitality come in. If the heart of narrative is action, the camera eye, poor, mindless fool, can't help but record those physical places, real spaces, real time within which action becomes real. More than that, condemned to this glassy objectivity, it can make them all flash into an autonomous life of their own. The blank camera eye is interested in action, and action alone, and that gives it certain obvious advantages as a narrative medium. But it has a less obvious bonus as a medium dealing with the emotional life. The foundation of emotion is the perception of physical reality, and the argument that the camera eye (the French word for lens is *objectif*) is enslaved by objectivity loses much of its conviction when one reflects on how very close the transformation of physical reality into a living artistic organism stands to both the basis of narrative and the emotional life itself.

Let's not be naïve: You don't have to swallow the Boy Scout Manual's definition of action to sustain this point of view. Dreams and fantasies are accounts of events, and, as the proto-narratives par excellence, they reveal a lot about the two arts they are so repetitively said to resemble. The *space* within which dreams occur is dynamic, cathectic, and brought to life by the dreamer's unfailing organic intelligence on the subject of detail. Moreover, though he is speaking in the self's purest known language, the dreamer is absorbed in the outside world, and almost every account of a dream begins by naming a *place* ("I was in my grandmother's house"), followed by a definition of how its space is perceived ("but the rooms seemed darker and bigger than usual"), and *then* one gets to the emotion ("and I felt lonely").

The dreamer's wondering and perplexed absorption in the world—*his* world—is film's forte. But it isn't enough to argue that film's organization of time and space gives this "objective" medium its "subjective" strength, since the point of art is something more than merely to set up a strong analogy to people's actual emotional lives. It is also a matter of endowing time and space with an autonomous artistic life of their own. In *Psycho,* when Anthony Perkins stabs the girl in that now classical shower stall, the hundred-odd separate shots that electrify the two minutes or so of her death show us not what the girl is seeing in her terror, nor what the murderer is seeing in his frenzy; they flash before us the spectacle of space terrorized, time in terror.

If it is to move beyond its current impasse (and why shouldn't it?), the novel has a lot to learn from all this, though the lessons might mean turning away from the masterpieces that have been its main source of strength and starting to pay attention to what has seemed until recently merely amusing trivia. Meanwhile, what does film have to learn from the novel? A little of the best fiction's integrity and artistic autonomy would do no harm, but one reason for the pre-eminence of *2001,* at least in *my* current thinking, is Kubrick's obvious decision that it had exactly nothing to learn from the novel. (Clarke's book, a very different kettle of fish, was written after the screenplay.) But I am speaking of *the* novel—the psychological novel —since the film's relation to science fiction is different, just as many "subliterary" genres currently have a vitality that "the" novel lacks. Two of the most gratifying novels I've recently read are Michael Crichton's *The Andromeda Strain* and Clarke's *Childhood's End* (what fabulous titles they make up!). Kubrick's film is nonetheless utterly cinematic, and one of its principal departures from the sci-fi form is to abandon the peculiarly verbal ploy of playing off amazement against a tendency to "scientifically explain" and rationalize events. (Hitchcock might take a clue from this, since murder mysteries use the same ploy: The very poor scene with the all-explaining psychiatrist at the end of *Psycho* is an uncinematic carryover from the novelistic method.)

Abandoning literature, *2001* represents a major departure from the main sources of cinematic energy in this decade. At least until around 1965, the "new wave" of France, for one, derived a great deal of its energy from discoveries about how to redeem certain features of the classical psychological novel for film. True, this is a factor that has often been overlooked because in the best work a cinematic procedure is so thoroughly achieved. But in its epistemological theme, its attitude toward the past, its extreme delicacy of character conception, and its breathtaking intelligence on the subject of perspective, Resnais's *Muriel* is perhaps the most successful Jamesian work of art since *The Golden Bowl*. (To preserve cultural hegemony, I suppose I ought to call it Proustian, but *Muriel's* emotional tone and its attitude toward objects more closely resemble the work of *our* genius.) Truffaut's *Jules and Jim* is another obvious example of an entirely successful cinematic transformation of the old novelistic ploy of a triangular situation that probes the mysteries of a personality, just as *The Soft Skin* is an almost entirely unsuccessful effort at the same thing. And then there's Godard.

As many critics have already pointed out, Godard's "literary" procedures are less an effort to "redeem" psychological narrative procedures than to play language against image in the name of a certain analytical, oblique intensity. To resort to a set of literary terms that necessarily make things inexact, Godard is much less interested in narrative than in poetry and criticism. True enough, until *La Chinoise* (more or less) "stories" did (more or less) appear in his movies, but they appeared almost inadvertently, the way a dancer sometimes simply has to walk from point to point on stage. Characteristically, his narratives are mere threads used to string a set of poetic moments into feature length; one example is his use for this purpose of the long journey, the odyssey, as in *Pierrot le Fou* and *Weekend.*

But Godard seems to be much less the critic than the poet, and, when he abandons poetry for his critical mood (in *La Chinoise, Deux ou Trois Choses que je sais d'Elle,* and above all the recent *Le Gai Savoir*), he courts a disaster that he gets up, down, and sideways in the last film, especially because he is enamored of a critical method—a phenomenologically oriented, structuralist critique of language—which (at least so far) seems catastrophically unsuited to the visual media. As *Le Gai Savoir's* amazingly presumptuous title suggests (it is taken from Nietzsche), Godard recently has fallen in dangerously above his head and is rapidly sinking into the familiar rant of a visually undynamic (not to say intellectually void) demagoguery when he ought to be crying for help.

The apparent exhaustion of innovating narrative ideas in the French by-now-not-so-new wave seems to suggest—I say only suggest—that, like fiction, film may also be at some new juncture, even in its current preeminence. One hastens to hedge that bet in favor of Resnais, however, since he shows no signs of any such exhaustion. Deplorably, his recent feature *Je t'aime, Je t'aime* may never be seen in America because the film has been bought by a major American studio and distributor that has decided not to release it. (Of course, it would be a film of interest to every serious moviegoer in America.) Bresson is certainly not exhausted either, and one can only hope that his remarkable *Une Femme Douce,* which has been bought by Paramount, will not meet the same oblivious, dust-gathering fate as *Je t'aime, Je t'aime,* though it's threatened that it will.

But generally speaking, European film seems sunk in a glum, fallow period, a fact reflected in this year's New York Film Festival, whose scouts cover European film with a fine-toothed comb that usually comes up with the finest productions of the year. This year it was a disappointment: The Italian cinema seems suddenly unproductive (I cannot take Pasolini seriously), while the French seem to be retreating into their own special variety of provincialism, both social and intellectual. Godard is where he is. Marguerite Duras's *Destroy, She Said,* a stuporously unsuccessful film, futilely attempts to bring to the silver screen some of the least interesting aspects of the new novel. (That *it* should be scheduled for major release, while *Je t'aime, Je t'aime* stands condemned and *Une Femme Douce*'s future dangles by a hair, staggers me.) Eric Rohmer's *Ma Nuit Chez Maud,* though terribly well made and conceived, is fundamentally an intensely provincial and bourgeois (I might even say Gaullist) work.

All this adds up not to a criticism of the festival, which remains one of the major bastions of cinematic seriousness in America, but to an observation of a certain, and perhaps not so sudden, petering out of its European fountainhead that produced the most important films of the Sixties. If two years ago somebody had told me that I would find Downey's *Putney Swope* or Schlesinger's *Midnight Cowboy* ("for all their faults" as Anna Livia says) altogether more impressive and exciting than the major Godard effort of the year, I would have laughed. Today, I'm not laughing, and I left Lincoln Center with Third Avenue on my mind.

If those sources are depleted, we'll have to look elsewhere for the best films of the Seventies: perhaps new European sources; perhaps (a sobering thought) America; perhaps the underground. But in the search for new sources, new ideas, I don't think that fiction needs to be anywhere near as protective of its autonomy as film. And it seems to me that literature has a great deal to learn from its big, brash, rich brother. Who knows —who can guess?—the outcome of this search for esthetic ideas, the fillip of obsession and accident, that the Seventies are so plainly demanding of both arts? Mired here in their history of brilliance and snotty squabbling, the brother arts stand at the opening of the decade giving the impression of being at the end of something, which is also, of course, the beginning of something, with everything left to be done.

The New Theater:
A Retreat
from Realism

JOHN LAHR

*There is a tendency to say that humanistic painting must
contain human figures, but why? Since human thought is
itself an abstracting process, there is no basic conflict
between abstraction and humanism.*

T. S. Eliot

The masquerade of democracy that America witnessed at the Democratic
convention will have its effect on all the arts, but most immediately on the
theater. The repressiveness of the society, the symbolic armaments with
which it smoothly protects itself from new ideas and fights off change are
stamped on a public imagination numb to brutality. The individual's integrity and even his words—so long upheld as a creative ideal on stage—
are mocked by the force of a state whose police can take both law and
justice into their own hands. The radical impulse toward which new theater
has been moving could only be intensified by the prospect of four more
years of tepid mediocrity. Ironically, the new theater emerging in the late
sixties will move into the intensely political and private battles which
abstract expressionism fought in the visual arts during the forties. Both
are radical departures from the texture of American life, both answer up—
in their own form—to the ethic of materialism, conformity, and a society
mechanized beyond the possibility of significant, individual political statement.

    The American theater, with its "picture stage," has ossified under a
concept of realism long discarded in other arts. In trying to find different
kinds of images, to forge a new relationship between the stage object
and the audience, the avant-garde theater work of La Mama Troupe, the
Open Theater, the Performance Group, and even Jerzy Grotowski's Polish
Lab Theater, which will tour America this fall, embodies the impulses of
abstract expressionism and must bear the same initial hostility from a
critical press whose values and sense of the world are threatened by their
work. They too, like Jackson Pollock, Hans Hofmann, Arshile Gorky, are
branded hoaxes—chic, obstruse, undisciplined. But this instinct shows
American theater tapping a healthy resource in much the same way as
medieval drama was—an outgrowth of its audience's plastic imagination
—wanting to see the drama of cathedral sculpture given three-dimen-
sional life. In the twentieth century, theater-makers are just realizing that
there is no longer the revealed (or revealing) word; they have become
fascinated with the process of creating theater which answers modern

needs. The creation itself becomes an act of religion. Their theater aspires to magic—a special kind of prestidigitation where images and ideas emerge in the act of *doing* them. Like the works of Pollock, de Kooning, and Gorky, this theater reflects their own eccentric and personal reconstruction of the world. This is not unreflective theater, although to some it seems sloppy; this is a moral theater, although some perceive it as merely self-indulgent. It is not without interest that Tom O'Horgan, the director of the La Mama Troupe, maintains, "What I've been working toward is a new naturalism where, like Pollock, part of the meaning is the gesture itself." The director becomes the choreographer and catalyst; the theater pieces aspire to the emotional totality of music. While some critics score this as exhibitionism, they neglect a modern world, spiraling in confusions, which pushes the creator away from a one-dimensional realism and also conventional techniques. As the brilliant English psychologist R. D. Laing has maintained in his book *The Politics of Experience:*

> If there are no meanings, no values, no source of sustenance or help, then man, as creator, must invent, conjure up meanings and values, sustenance and succor out of nothing. He is a magician.

Other media can tell a story or reproduce a precise fragment of life as it is seen. The new performance theaters want to go below that surface in much the same way that Pollack realized painting had to find its own specific impulse. "The modern artist," Pollack explains, "is living in a mechanical age and we have a mechanical means of representing objects in nature such as the camera and photograph. The modern artist, it seems to me, is working and expressing an inner world—in other words—expressing the energy, the motion, and other inner forces." The theater is much less malleable than painting; it is a clumsy art, full of extenuating circumstances and personal variables. Yet, to externalize some inner energy, some idea which cannot be verbalized in "human" language, is part of the new theater's intention. The stage not only acknowledges the object world, but also the special emotional life of the actor. Where Pollack attacked his canvas, painting an inner landscape, the techniques of improvisation bring this same interior quality to the surface of performance. The artist is no longer giving final order to the world, but externalizing his own immediate view of it. This is relatively new to theater (except for the great clowns of the American stage whose acrobatics often mirrored deeper intuitions), but not to painting. "The idea that nature is chaotic and that the artist puts order into it is a very absurd point of view, I think," observed Willem de Kooning. "All that we can hope for is to put some order into ourselves." This personalization of art offends the democratic theater critic who believes the theater belongs to the audience and not the creator. The new theater pieces are generally performed for small audiences (Grotowski has no more than eighty people at a performance) or in workshop. To a theater based on dollars and cents, this smacks of "amateurishness"; while the work may not always be outstanding, its impulse comes from a far greater need, where performing is not merely the inhabiting of a fictional personality but a process of self-discovery.

Performance theater has come under devasting attack in its first few years. *Futz, Tom Paine, Dionysus in 69* have been defined more by their detractors than by those who are seriously trying to build something new for the theater's future. Robert Brustein, who boldly called for a third theater in which "artistic license" was the alternative to "commercial appeal," used that language to support such shallow and easy political documents as *MacBird!* and *Viet Rock.* But the political impulse of new theater has gone farther than a criticism of society; it has created a theater which makes its own world and special rules for living in it. Having called for a revolution, Mr. Brustein throws up his hands in the face of a liberation from aesthetic principles at the core of his middle-class social concern. Discussing Tom O'Horgan's production of *Futz* in the *New Republic,* Brustein made his disclaimer for the movement he spawned in print:

> Two years ago, I spoke, in an article of a third theater which would combine (the words are Synge's) reality and joy: Let me say at once that this sort of thing is not what I meant at all. Mr. O'Horgan's theater strikes me as singularly joyless and mechanical—a theater which gives us eroticism without love, frenzy without energy, egoism without identity . . .

Whatever O'Horgan's excesses and failures in the production (there were many), he is on the side of experiment and evolution of the theater art. Mr. Brustein completely denies the process at work, shouting down innovation in the name of order, discipline, and conventional attitudes toward beauty and love. His white heat will not allow for growth, or worse still, acknowledge the possibility of new stage resources. Fortunately for the theater, the avant-garde has moved beyond the reformist caterwauling of *MacBird!* and *Viet Rock,* just as Jackson Pollock and his coterie eschewed social realism. The theater makes its statement—its isolation, its denial of the conventional contexts and responses of theater, is in itself a greater political gesture than name-calling. Melding the insights of new music and art into the stage experience is a destiny which was prophesied by Stanislavski who saw, as early as 1905, that realism on stage was a thing of the past. There must be a new kind of audience response and a new type of performing to conjure it:

> . . . realism and (depicting) the way of life have outlived their age. The time has come to stage the unreal. Not life itself, as it occurs in reality, but rather life as it is vaguely perceived in fantasies and visions at moments of lofty emotions. This is the spiritual situation that must be transmitted scenically, in the way that painters of the new school use cloth, musicians of the new trend write music, and the new poets, poetry. . . . The power of the new art lies in its combinations of colors, lines, musical notes and the rhyming of words. They create general moods that carry over to the public unconsciously. They create hints that make the most unobservant person create with his own imagination.

This, over a half century later, is the aesthetic toward which the performance theaters are developing. Their theater confronts the audience with its qualities as theater: energy, spectacle, movement, flesh, emotion. There is nothing between the stage action and the audience—no fancy seats, no romantic ideas or special lights, no scenery in the grand tradition. This confrontation is precisely the impulse of abstract expressionism, where the experience of paint—color, form, line—was the primary instinct. Pollack, in a letter, points out: "Abstracts painting is abstract. It confronts you. There was a reviewer a while back who wrote that my pictures didn't have any beginning or any end. He didn't mean it as a compliment, but it was. It was a fine compliment."

Pollock's elaborate network of drippings plunged the spectator into the spectacle of an artist drawing forth primal images on a barren canvas. The effect on the viewer is not meant to be logical or fully comprehended, but rather to communicate the energy, spontaneity, and risk of committing paint to canvas. "I think (the audience)," says Pollack, "should not look *for,* but look passively—and try to receive what the painting has to offer and not bring a subject matter or preconceived idea of what they are looking for." Pollack's breakthrough found a way out of the surrealist mythologies, in the same way that performance theater, with its emphasis on *doing,* is a response and an answer to the intellectual circle drawn by the drama of the absurd—itself a surreal canvas of Freudian implications and nightmare associations. A theater of performance makes a spectacle of physical risk, not only in its acrobatics, but in the individual type of acting it requires which is both personal and spontaneous. There is a jaggedness and a great possibility of failure, but the struggle becomes the real drama and something to keep alive. "As a director," explains Tom O'Horgan, "one of the main functions I find is to evolve procedures which will keep the real thing going. I keep playing the same game with myself, setting up very difficult situations for actors and then not solving them." The effect argues for confrontation of the performance with his audience; it attempts to evince a feeling, a response that is not programmed or contrived. This confrontation takes many forms. It can be by touch, which has been tried by the Open Theater *(Viet Rock)* and the Performance Group's *Dionysus in 69* where the performers coax spectators out of their environmental perches to join the bacchanal, and later offer the hope of a flesh-pile to anyone who will submit to massage. The confrontation can be created by the spectacle of movement as in the La Mama productions where the stage is filled with images of actions; the eye can never focus on one spot, nor can we expect experience to be translated to the mind (as in a proscenium stage) from one-point perspective. Bodies tumble and combine, slither across the stage, clasping around the neck, under the legs. In *Dionysus in 69,* a three-tiered environmental stage allows the performers to move around the audience, sustaining the artifice of the play while sweeping the audience into its intention. The picture which emerges is varied and weighty with implication because of this theater environment. Stimuli compete for the spectator's attention, as in life; the responsibility for choice and comprehension is thrust back to the audience's imagination. This impulse is meant, like abstract expressionism, not merely to confuse or bludgeon audiences, but to make them come alive. Speaking of Paul Foster's *Tom Paine,* Tom O'Horgan points out: "The world of Paul Foster's theater is a highly contemporary one, fragmented, burning hot and cold, offering data and facts, noncommittal, without solutions. The audience is made to feel the urgency of responsibility." The impulse is to stimulate response and thought, not simply spoon-feed an audience with a spurious "significance."

Abstract expressionism placed its greatest emphasis on the physical gesture of painting, the commitment of the artist to his *act.* "When you're painting out of your unconscious, figures are bound to emerge," Pollack explained. "We're all of us influenced by Freud, I guess. . . . Painting is a state of being. . . . Painting is self-discovery. Every good artist paints what he is." Pollack moving around his canvas, stretched beneath him on the floor, demanded spontaneity and directness in his work. Like him, and Hofmann, de Kooning gave special importance to speed of execution and autographic gesture. Their work became an act of immediacy and urgency. It became an event, the drama of an artist's self-discovery. "Painting, I think today—the more immediate, the more direct—the greater the possibilities of making a direct statement," Pollock maintained. Like performance theater, abstract expressionism emphasized action and its ritualistic overtones. In painting, the terms of discussion took on the language of theater, which the theater is only now fulfilling.

Describing Willem de Kooning's work, art critic Harold Rosenberg uses the language and instinct of a theatrical reporter:

> Through the action of de Kooning's brush, things, persons, scenes, feelings are recorded in shifting forms that record themselves in the eye of the spectator as on a strip of film; one, looking at a de Kooning, never sees the same image twice. . . . The gestures that brought the painting into being subsist in it not only through vestiges of energy—swipes of paint, splashes, smears—but through a constant forcing together of the visual ingredients of the painting. . . .
>
> De Kooning's performance is also an "act" in the arena of art history, a display of skill and imagination put on before an imaginary gallery of the great masters.

Painting never creates immediately for an audience; theater does, and performance theater not only strives for a similar improvisational revelation, but also a sense of acting against the framework of a larger theater history. Gesture, whatever its limitations in the new American theater, is meant to move the performer farther toward personal statement. Tom O'Horgan, discussing his approach to the actor, maintains:

> It is not easy to make a performer accept real freedom or responsibility on stage. Actors are ambivalent. "What am I supposed to feel

here? What's this about? Who am I?" All these things they can easily hide behind as actors. An actor can hide behind the old Method approach to performance where the author created a whole structure of personality and then the actor tried to inhabit it in some way. No actor is that clever. My own view is just to find a way to make people know who they really are as actors and to experience those things and not be afraid of them or hide. Hiding is what our whole acting school has been devoted to for the last ninety years. If an actor has trouble in knowing where those emotions are in himself, in understanding the buttons to push in himself, then he doesn't understand himself. My job is to set up little situations, games, traps—whatever you want to call it—which will make the actor respond to himself and the world honestly.

The impulse for honesty and self-evaluation is embodied in many of the performance theaters' events. Grotowski's theater has already defined the new aesthetic. "To play a part does not mean to identify with the character. The actor neither lives his part nor portrays it from the outside. He uses the character as the means to grapple with his own self, the tool to reach secret layers of his personality and strip himself of what hurts most and lies in his secret heart." The American events are slowly evolving methods of introspection. In *Tom Paine* the actors stop the play to discuss it, out of character, with the audience. In *Dionysus in 69,* an adaption of *The Bacchae,* they move from primitive rite to group therapy, where each actor talks about his fears as honestly as he knows how. Unfortunately, for all these theaters, the ability to know yourself intellectually is more highly developed than the physical presence which must still be attained. But the intention and resource for the theater is intriguing. Yet critics fault it before it has really begun. Witness Walter Kerr, who concluding his review of *Dionysus in 69,* captures the privacy of the new theater without understanding where it wants to go:

> It is only the actors who are liberated in this sort of meeting, and there is something arrogant, condescending, and self-indulgent about that. Clearly they enjoy the unleashing of their own inhibitions. During an impromptu aside on opening night, an actress was asked by another performer how she felt about dancing on the night of Senator Kennedy's death. She thought intensely for a moment, then answered, "I have to. It's my statement."
>
> But it is *her* statement, not ours She and her colleagues are in control of the master plan. They are free to do what they wish to do. We are only free to do what *they* wish us to do or invite us to do. That is not engagement. It is surrender.
>
> I'm still up tight.

The New York Times, June 16, 1968

In both painting and theater, anything that challenges conventional form is always branded self-indulgence or arrogance. These are, in a sense, the ingredients which create the climate for discovery. But Mr. Kerr, representative of a theater-wise generation trained in proscenium realism, gets hysterical (and nonsensical) when theater strikes out toward unstated emotions and nonverbal ideas. By his critical tenets, Gallileo's first glance at the heavens would be collegiate certitude; the impressionist's fragmentation of the canvas to experiment with light an infantilism not worth mentioning. In fact, actors have always had control over an audience's impulses; and in *Dionysus in 69,* where the Performance Group is examining the politics of ecstasy and its potential enslavement of the soul, it is not doctrinaire, but insidiously open to thought. But many Establishment minds are shut tight, not merely up tight.

In its retreat from realism, the performance theaters emphasize myth and ritual in an attempt to go beyond the perceivable, to something closer to the rhythms of contemporary life. They are not always successful, but their attempt asks new questions of theater which had been posed by abstract expressionists, who also "looked for authentic experience in primordial symbol and classic myth, seeking a significant rendition of a symbol no matter how archaic," as Dore Ashton has maintained. "Pollack, Gorky, Still, Gottlieb, Stamos, Tomlin, Rothko, Baziotes turned insistently back, deep into the past of civilization, to exercise the thinking that *recalls* rather than *represents.*" Pollack's fascination with totemic images was, according to Ashton, indicative of the abstract expressionists' attempt not to "use the unconscious—as did the Surrealists . . . [but to] portray themselves as spiritual wholes comprising ethical, conscious man and 'original' man with his primordial unconscious." Writing in *Possibilities,* the avant-garde magazine founded by painter Robert Motherwell and Harold Rosenberg, Mark Rothko emphasized an intention of abstract expressionism which has become increasingly the focus of new performance theater. Speaking of archaic creators' belief in the monsters they created, Rothko maintained:

> But with us, the disguise is complete. The familiar identity of things has to be pulverized in order to destroy the finite association with which our society increasingly enshrouds every aspect of our environment. . . . [Shapes must] have no direct association with any particularly visible experience, but in them one recognizes principles and passions of organisms.

How closely this emphasis on a mythological imagination approaches theater. At its best, Jerzy Grotowski's Polish Lab Theater speaks for similar associations. Grotowski has written:

> We are especially interested in an aspect of acting which has seldom been studied: the association of the gesture and intonation with a definite image. For example, the actor stops in the middle of a race and takes the stance of a cavalry soldier charging, as in the old popular drawings. *This method of acting evokes by association images deeply rooted in the collective imagination.*
>
> *Tulane Drama Review,* Spring, 1965

The stage archetypes, like the visual ones, transcend the society's strangle-hold on the facts of life. Ritual theater like Grotowski's forces the spectator back to his primordial past in order to comprehend his present. "Our culture, our language, our imagination are rooted in this darkness which science has called by different names," explains Eugenio Barba, a disciple of Grotowski. " 'Savage thought' (Lévi-Strauss), 'archetype' (Jung), 'collective representations' (Durkheim), 'categories of the imagination' (Mauss and Hubert), 'elementary thoughts' (Bastian). In the Theater Laboratory, the spectators are made to face the most secret, the most carefully hidden parts of themselves. Brutally thrown into the world of myths, they must identify with them in the light of twentieth-century men. Many experience the revelation as blasphemy."

The American performance theater is nowhere as accomplished or as certain of its direction as Grotowski is. If it has found the energy, the discipline of a totally committed revolution in theater is still to mature. Yet, mythology and a means of creating an iconography from the past aimed toward the future has dominated the new theater. Rochelle Owens, whose play *Futz* was the La Mama Troupe's first break with stage realism, creates fantasies which draw on Biblical and mythological impulses. *Istanboul* mixes Saracen and Christian images; *Beclch* evokes an African goddess with overtones of Greek mythology. In the same way, the Open Theater's newest production is a step beyond the somewhat figurative *America Hurrah* toward the evocation of old myths with new. *The Serpent* improvises on the Book of Genesis and uses these images in counterpoint with the assassination of Kennedy, confusing Adam in order to regain him. The Performance Group, likewise, has not only attempted to refurbish the Dionysian myth, but to extend it to a commentary on the orgiastic impulse in contemporary society, which breeds violence in its liberation. Whatever the content, the instinct is to push on toward the unexpressible and unattainable. This romantic notion (already a tenet of Grotowski's method: "Theatrical magic consists in doing publicly that which is considered impossible") expresses a hunger to get beyond the limitations of the finite world and its values, to confront larger questions with a thrilling dignity in action.

With American society bearing down heavily on the creative imagination, filled with a sense of its shame and horror at where the golden dream has led the nation—an unjust war, colonization at home as well as abroad, a violent self-satisfaction—the theater, like abstract expressionism, retreats into itself, not away from the world, but beyond it. The theater, thus far, has been fairly conservative in its departure from established conventions. The Performance Group's arena is still a center stage, not ready for Grotowski's total environment, where the audience is shuffled between patches of action, part of the artifice of the stage. As one English critic witnessing Grotowski's *Acropolis,* where the audience was surrounded by actors simulating inmates of a concentration camp, observed:

The actors moved around and behind you; you could smell their sweat. The pile of bronze metal pipes from which they gradually built an incinerator was within kicking distance. Every inch of acting space was precisely circumscribed, no superfluous movement tolerated from anyone. The critic who scribbled notes on his programme was committing an outrage equivalent to daubing paint on a canvas at an exhibition, as my neighbors quickly and rightly made me realize. The collective function of the audience was to sit still and symbolize the "civilized" world, helplessly witnessing gross crimes against humanity.

New Statesman, August 30, 1968

The search for new sounds and different music, the development of the body to externalize an inner state, the planning of the event to incorporate the audience creatively into the theatrical experience have still to be sufficiently developed in the flamboyant experiments in America. Yet, it is here, where the canker runs so deep, where the vitality and commitment have been so polarized by current events, that it may well flower as abstract expressionism did in reaction to oppressive times. If critics groan that they cannot hear, that they cannot understand, that the word is more important than the gesture, or that the process of improvised creation argues against the vitality of the theater, the performance theater, it must be recalled, is only just beginning—the theatrical equipment needed for effectiveness only now becoming apparent to both actors and directors. The groups need patience, but so do the audiences. In a society where consumers expect art, like detergent, to be new and improved with each package, performance theater will also need luck to accompany their diligence. Richard Schechner, answering Walter Kerr's backhand to *Dionysus in 69* in *The New York Times,* indicated the instinct of all the directors who are trying to move beyond the surface of American life to probe a more difficult and monumental imaginative reality:

> As a director I am not interested in free-for-alls. For every scenic situation there are rules. And if our work is well done it is no more haphazard than the formations of a professional football team.
> I readily admit that no American theater has yet achieved the necessary discipline and skills. But to reduce our attempts to the fiddling around of cop-outs, end-of-the-empire decadence, or sex-by-itself is to seriously misread and misunderstand what's going on.

In pure theater, as in abstract expressionism, there exists an ethic of transcience which upsets minds accustomed to false significance. Performance theater exists differently at each show; and the joy, for the audience, is watching something they know cannot be duplicated, which gives insight in a gesture, only to disappear. This ecstasy in creation is what Pollock understood in his painting:

> *Interviewer:* Well, actually every one of your paintings . . . is an absolute original.
> *Pollock:* Well—yes—they're all direct painting. There is only one.

New performance theater will undoubtedly create, in its ferment, an antithesis, sharing its presuppositions but seeking different means. Sam Shepard's cool, silent theatricality is an indication of the first response to performance theater which moves from action to a more passive reflective mode, in the same way that such artists like Ad Rheinhart, Barnett Newman, and Mark Rothko, while sharing with action painting an interest in a uniform pictorial field and a monumentality of pictorial order, moved toward a decelerated kind of painting—cool, illusionistic, minimal. It is too early to tell if performance theater will continue to follow the pattern set by abstract expressionists. But in discovering a similar cause and in seeking a way to create it, the performance theater holds the possibility of invigorating American theater with the fresh beauty, commitment, and thought that abstract expressionists bestowed on America's visual arts at an equally treacherous moment in history.

Andy Warhol, Won't You Please Go Home!

The Glass of Fashion: Reflections on Haute and Pop Couture in the Form of a Memoir

VALERIE CARNES

Youth is the one thing worth having. . . . It has its divine right of sovereignty. . . . a new Hedonism—that is what our century wants. . . . Youth! Youth! there is absolutely nothing in the world but youth!
> Oscar Wilde in *The Picture of Dorian Gray*

Good designers—like clever newspapermen—know that to have any influence they must keep in step with public needs . . . public opinion . . . and that intangible something in the air. They must catch the spirit of the day and interpret it in clothes before other designers begin to twitch at the nerve ends.
> Mary Quant in *Quant by Quant*

It's [fashion is] important from the standpoint of history because fashion reflects an era. If 2,000 years from now people want to know about us, they'll look at our clothes.
> Norman Norrell

One should either be a work of art, or wear a work of art.[1]
> From *Phrases and Philosophies for the Use of the Young*

[1] Quotations from: Oscar Wilde, *The Picture of Dorian Gray* (Baltimore, 1966), pp. 29–30; Mary Quant, *Quant by Quant* (New York, 1966), p. 85; Norman Norrell, as quoted in Marylin Bender, *The Beautiful People* (New York, 1967), p. 62; and *Phrases and Philosophies for the Use of the Young,* quoted by Susan Sontag, "Notes on 'Camp'," in *Against Interpretation* (New York, 1966), p. 279.

I

There is a certain scent recalls it to my mind: the smell of mock orange and lilac bushes after rain. I smell these and—magically—it is 1947 again and I am a little girl, sitting in my grandmother's dining room on a chilly April morning. It is cold sometimes in early spring in western Tennessee and this morning there is a fire sputtering in the black marble fireplace shooting sparks and cinders like fire-goblins onto the burnished brick hearth. "Oxydol brings you . . . Ma Perkins," the radio says, and the sewing machine hums and the early sun glints through the drawn lace curtains, making long shafts of dust motes where the sun-fairies play, my grandmother tells me at bedtime. If I throw my eyes just the least bit out of focus, I can see them even in the daytime. In the dining room are my grandmother, my great-aunt and my mother. The great claw-footed round oak table has been cleared and is covered with a bright melange of cloth and patterns. Somewhere far away in a place called Paris, France, they say, a man named Christian Dior is talking about the New Look. It must be something that all women want very much, because this morning my grandmother and mother and aunt are furiously letting down hems and making new dresses and suits in observance of this man's decree. For me it is all like stepping into one of my storybooks: the whiteness of my aunt's and grandmother's hair, drawn with long hairpins into elegant coils, and the darkness of my mother's curls, the thinness of the flowered voile and the softness of the fragile eggshell-colored wool, the dizzying pro-fusion of color, the ring of the china coffee cups when they touch the fluted saucers, the flurry of woman-talk, the sputter of the fire, the drone of the sewing machine, the bewilderingly bright heap of colored threads and scraps on the floor. I sit in my small red rocking chair with my doll and my needle and thread. My aunt gives me a large scrap of the thinnest of white organdy covered with pale purplish-pink sprigs of lilac like those outside the window. The cloth is so thin that it almost slips from my hands, and the flowers so pale that I can hardly see them when I hold the cloth to the light. I cut out a dress for my doll and sew it together with yellow thread and a big embroidery needle, making the smallest stitches I can make, just as my grandmother says I must. But I look at the hem of the sky-blue linen suit my mother is making: the stitches are so tiny that I can hardly see them. I can't make stitches that small or seams that straight. My head aches with the effort and the heat of the fire. Suddenly I feel myself small and clumsy and absurdly childish in this enchanted world of colored cloth and patterns and scissors and red tomato pin-cushions, of silver thimbles and thin, thin porcelain cups and steaming coffee and teacakes and gossip. Some day when I grow up I will be a woman too, and I will wear my hair brushed in a coil. I will be elegant and wise and wear wide-brimmed hats like my mother's, and wide skirts like the new one she wears now to go shopping, a flower garden of red and blue poppies and larkspur over a lace slip that whispers when she walks, and shoes with high heels and ankle straps. I will have a black coat like my grandmother's with real fur on the collar and cuffs and an ivory fan and a veil that makes spots before my eyes. And a black dress, a real black dress, with yards and yards of skirt, and silk dancing shoes. When I have the black dress I will know I am a grown-up woman.

II

We who grew into our childhood in the late 1940s heard of the New Look even as children. One day the streets of American cities, both large and small, were filled with women sporting broad padded shoulders and short straight skirts. The very next day, so it seemed, these same streets were jammed with women wearing long full skirts and narrow shoulders and pinched waistlines. Although Seventh Avenue manufacturers like Norman Norrell had been lengthening skirts for some time, only a Parisian like Dior could issue decrees with a tone of finality and make them stick. It was a natural reaction to the new prosperity, of course; the wartime restrictions on fabrics had been lifted only a short time before, and our mothers and grandmothers now had both the money and leisure to lengthen hems and to make and buy new spring clothes. It was a costly fashion adventure, but it imparted a fresh excitement to that postwar spring. Newspapers and magazines carried photographs and sketches of the new silhouette which we children faithfully reproduced in miniature costumes for our dolls. My favorite doll, Evelyn, named for the heroine of a soap-opera serial, had a new Oriental print dress with a halter top and wide skirt and gold metallic paper sandals and new white linen gloves— all courtesy of my grandmother.

With the advent of the New Look attention shifted from the female leg, where it had remained during the World War II era, to shapely calves, ankles, wasp waists, and bosoms. Décolletage (via sweaters and strapless evening gowns) was an important symbol of the era: it served to emphasize fashion's new focal points. The image of the desirable woman from the time of Dior's New Look to the celebrated Year of the Chemise in 1958 remained a sophisticated thirties-plus creature: established, poised, sophisticated, worldly-wise, with a touch of fashionable *ennui* about her knowing smile, and a mature contoured figure (about ten pounds overweight by sixties standards). She was usually pictured with languid black crepe dress, stiletto-heels, huge picture hat or fashionable turban, and cigarette dangling in a long holder. The consumer market of the late forties and fifties, however, introduced the vamp's keenest competition, the girl-next-door: the pretty, lively housewife who runs house, garden, washer, dog, kids, self, and hubby at peak efficiency all day and night and still has energy to spare; the Good Girl, the pretty, bubbly, vacuous blonde, cheerful, kind, energetic, empty-headed, and patently dull. Doris Day was her positive image and Marilyn Monroe the flip side —the good little-girl blonde gone bad and sexy. We watched various versions of this blonde mass-market washing machines, stoves, detergents, soaps, packaged foods, and mixes. The whole little-girl thing was due to get much worse, of course, but we never recognized the Frankenstein's monster that was about to erupt from the shapely thighs of Marilyn and

Doris. After all, blondes *are* certified Good Girls, aren't they? Doesn't every red-blooded American know that?

The New Look did something else for American women: it reinforced for them the total tyranny of Parisian *haute couture.* The great men of fashion had only to say the word and the American fashion market jumped through whatever hoops had just arrived from Europe. The latest word in fashion filtered down to the American masses engraved like Mosaic law on tablets of stone. The power of the Parisian *haute couture* was a myth that became stern reality for millions of American women in that spring of 1947. It was a hard lesson, and American women did not soon forget its significance. A decree from across the Atlantic could superannuate their carefully amassed and previously fashionable wardrobes overnight— planned obsolescence with a vengeance, that.

The New Look gradually, imperceptibly, became the Old Look as the forties ended and the fifties began. Now men were fighting in a place called Korea, and we listened on the radio at night to campaign speeches by Adlai Stevenson and General Eisenhower. A new presence entered our living rooms in the form of the new television set, and for nights on end we sat in total darkness staring at the flickering blue light on the omnipresent screen.

Fashion was not a matter of concern to us who grew into teen-agers in the fifties. As Frank Conroy has put it, we were teen-agers when to be a teen-ager was nothing. Adolescence was simply an awkward interval between childhood and maturity, when adulthood would rescue us from insignificance. We had our Elvis Presley and Pat Boone fan clubs, our 45 record collections, our autograph books and Bermuda shorts with clean white cotton knee socks and grey and brown and red and green wool knit socks, penny loafers and white socks, and dyed-to-match sweaters and skirts for school. Formal dances and talent shows were occasions to wear formal gowns with boned strapless tops and wide ruffled net skirts and flat-heeled black ballet slippers, and to compare our new décolletage.

The fifties had no teen-age ready-to-wear or couture market as such: we simply wore matching sweaters, preferably angora or cashmere, and soft tweed skirts, and moccasins, and sighed for the day that we would be thirty. Meanwhile we were waiting for the next big shift in fashion, hoping vainly that this time there would be something for us.

It was not long in coming. Just in time for our senior year in high school and freshman year in college came the Chemise. The Sack Look had replaced the New Look. To be sure, there had been rumblings of this daring new style as early as the first years of the fifties when Balenciaga had begun to loosen the wasp-waisted full-skirted New Look silhouette. But it was Hubert de Givenchy in 1958 who introduced us, via American designers and the growing ready-to-wear market, to the basic sack which was to dominate our early adult years. That summer there were innumerable sack jokes told by irreverent males while females of every age sewed again as they had not sewed since '47. Suddenly a "dress" consisted of two side seams, two very skimpy darts in front and back, a back seam, zipper, sleeves, neck binding, and hem. Emphasis was back to hips and legs again. The Look that fall was a skinny, flapperish silhouette, with a properly unfitted fit in bust and hips and nothing in between. It was a younger, freer shape than any we had previously seen, and we took to it like ducks to water. We turned them out in bewildering profusion that summer and fall, in bright wools, corduroys, silks, in somber tweeds and fragile wools, and in the bright new paisley patterns and synthetic fabrics. It was the Year of the Sack and the manufacturers were ebullient. Every department store reproduced them on every floor in every department: in the basement, $2.98 flower-printed sacks with bows across the hips; wool and tweed chemise jumpers and shirtdresses in the sportswear and junior dresses area; fragile wools and silks and jerseys in Better Dresses and crepe and satin chemises in Evening Apparel. Our new coats were pastel cashmeres or tweeds and had no buttons or belts, but fell open from the narrow lapels straight to the hem. For classes now we wore nylon hose and little spool-heeled shoes in bright suédes by Capezio, or leather moccasins and wool knee socks with soft loose long sweaters and skirts, and London Fog raincoats for bad weather.

In 1960 John Kennedy was elected President. We who were approaching our twenties were ecstatic: we saw the beginning of our time to shine. Not only this: if we bought an understated little-nothing A-line or H-line dress (a variation of the basic sack) in Cassini- or Givenchy-like pastels, a cloth coat with a round fur collar, teased our hair into a twenty-four-inch bouffant mane, carried a quilted bag with a chain handle, wore black mantillas to Mass, bought pillboxes to perch on our heads at just the right angles, pearls tucked inside a bateau neckline, medium heels, silk pants and matching Vera-like silk blouses for sportswear, and silk sheaths or sari prints for evening, we too could be just like Jackie and the Beautiful People. It was an institutionalized rich girl look and could be bought everywhere from Sears to Saks. We couldn't, of course, match the $50,000 *she* was said to have spent on clothes alone in the first sixteen months after the election—after all, no one could do that unless she wore sable underwear, could she?—but with time, and effort, and infinite pains and money, we too could attain The Look. This was just for weekends and lunch in town and family events, of course; for classes we affected madras wraparound skirts and blouses by Villager with flat little Peter Pan collars, or madras Bermudas and very clean white knee socks and dirty tennis shoes, beige carcoats lined with fake fur, and more London Fogs for wet weather. Or we went Beat and wore black leotard tops and somber tweed or dark solid shapeless skirts and black tights and ringed our eyes with black liner or kohl and wore white lipstick, smoked incessantly and wrote earnest bad verse in the style of Cummings and Eliot, and affected a sad-eyed soulful look like Europe dying. We pronounced ourselves Existentialists and talked importantly of Letters and planned to live on the Left Bank during junior year abroad.

By next year we were definitely post-Jackie, although we took our little-nothing A-lines and H-lines and our imitation Chanel suits back to campus with us, just in case, along with our Weejuns and coordinated Villager wraparound skirts and print blouses and cardigan sweaters. Once back on campus we hung them in the closet and forgot about them: instead we wore folksy versions of the basic sack once again, and let our hair grow long and straight, and bought Gibson guitars that we couldn't play. We affected deep rich earthy voices and continued ringing our eyes with dark shadow and black liner and wearing white lipgloss and drawing hollows in our cheeks with dark foundation. We all owned the Baez and Dylan canon and sat late into the night listening to all the answers that were blowing in the wind, and to the hard rain that everyone said was gonna fall.

It fell: in November of 1963 our youth was over, suddenly, abruptly, finally. There was no New Frontier after all, no common Round Table of black and white together, no King and Queen, no Arthur borne away by the dark queens to Avalon to be healed. So this was it: everything would come to this in the end. There was nothing, only those muffled drums beating in the brain for nights and nights on end, and Grane rearing at the head of the procession, snuffing the scent of our Siegfried's sudden death. We were just into our twenties, but suddenly we were old. We dragged the discarded Villager outfits from the backs of our closets and wore them until graduation thrust us out of that nightmare world and into another.

III

Nineteen-sixty-five: half the sixties gone already. Jackie was still in mourning, Folk and Beat were out, 007 was in, Bob Dylan had just sold out to the new electronic sound, and Lady Bird was wearing Adele Simpson creations in the White House. We felt strangely cheated, robbed of our youth.

Hot on the heels of the incredible Kennedy era came the James Bond craze. A 1965 issue of *Road and Track* featured a car advertisement showing a girl in her late twenties wearing a black leather trench coat, round black wraparound goggles *a la* Jackie, a small pearl-handled revolver held discreetly at her side, black mole to the left-hand corner of her enigmatically smiling mouth as she prepared for the inevitable KISS KISS BANG BANG finale to the international spy syndrome. That was how we all began to conceive of ourselves then: trench-coated, dark-glassed, enigmatic, disillusioned, waiting for the spy who would come in from the cold and love us for one brief night all the sweeter for its brevity. It was a sort of pop Hemingway ethic for the young women of the sixties who, having exhausted folk singing and existentialism, Beat and campus rah-rah, were more than ready for something new. We did not know it then, of course, but the handsome 007 and his assorted girls were the last adult fad for some time. Next year we would all be consigned to the Mary Janes and white socks we had worn at the age of twelve.

But now, unaware of the youth-quake brewing in Paris and London, we enjoyed our short fling at adulthood and mystery and admired 007 in silence, secure in the knowledge that even John Kennedy had admired Fleming immensely. Camelot and Spyland had come together briefly for the strangest romance of the century.

Like Camelot, Spyland was short-lived. Already in 1955 Mary Quant and Alexander Plunket-Greene, those terribly advanced darlings of the *avant-garde,* had opened a Bazaar on King's Road in Chelsea and hundreds of British pre-Mod teen-agers flocked to the narrow fitting rooms or tried on ready-to-wear skimp dresses before the open windows *sans* underwear, as Kay Kendall is said to have done, in order to achieve what was already growing into the Chelsea Look. The Look was not merely a matter of clothes: it was part and parcel of the England that swang like a pendulum—*Beyond the Fringe,* "That Was the Week That Was," *Queen* magazine, the Liverpool Sound, and terribly advanced, dishy, grotty, geary, trendy, kinky, kooky, mod, poove discothèques like Anabel's and Arthur's. London's two youth gangs, the Mods and the Rockers, locked in dubious battle for years, had finally gone their separate ways. The long-haired, dandified, slightly effeminate Mods with their flared striped pants and tough-looking birds finally won out over the leather-jacketed Rockers, and English "Mod" was officially born. Miss Quant's "glorious model girls," half human, half barely animated clotheshorse, tall, rangy, lanky, sexy, leather-booted, black-stockinged, miniskirted, became important symbols of the coming fashion era. England's most exportable commodity now came to be its "birds" and "dollies" who stood in the public eye for this curious, elusive, sudden uprooting of cultural, social, and sexual norms, the new "life is fabulous" philosophy and the new cool, the new refusal to be serious (read "hung-up") about anything. Modgirl had just arrived and Littlegirl was just around the corner. Folkgirl, Beatgirl, Spygirl, Jackiegirl and Prettygirl were Out. But it took almost ten years for the United States to pick up on the new trends *en masse.* Meanwhile we vacillated between our Villager outfits, our imitation flour-sack shifts, and the new black cloth trench coat, and waited . . .

In the spring of 1965 it began. *Vogue* that year showed André Courrèges' spare short little tunics and coats in pastels and whites with little white flat boots and astronaut baby bonnets and cowboy hats and giant zombie sunglasses on models with little-girl faces and figures. It seemed to us that spring like a mere ripple on the otherwise placid glass of fashion. Actually, it was the beginning of the end. Courrèges was still playing with Balenciaga's original chemise silhouette, and its A-line, H-line, and trapeze variations. This time, though, it was the whole proportion that was radically different: short skirt, long legs, flat heels, no bust or hips, flowing manes of Alice-in-Wonderland hair or cropped little-boy heads. The American ready-to-wear at last got the message and started producing. By the summer and fall of 1966 it was everywhere: flowered hip-huggers, ribbed Poorboy sweaters, vinyl and leather miniskirts, chain belts, knee-high vinyl boots, pantsuits, flat-heeled pumps, and little-girl dresses with puffed sleeves and scalloped hems mushroomed on every street across the country. A new breed of *jeunesse dorée* flowered across the United States and Europe with the spread of mini, micromini, and unisex fashion. With the coming of the miniskirt women's clothing became minimal, and girls compensated for the scantiness of their dresses by emphasizing accessories, fantastically painted faces, huge floppy hats, little-boy caps, manes of tawny hair *a la* Jane Holzer or geometrical Vidal Sassoon cuts, vinyl boots, patterned tights and stockings, leotards, false lashes, scarves, bags, costume jewelry, chain and braided belts, giant sunglasses, babushkas, falls, switches, hairpieces, wiglets, curls, braids, and ringlets. During the fall of '66 we shortened our Villager skirts by a good inch, bought a ribbed sweater, a gold chain belt, and opaque tights. It was a marvellous new and belated adolescence for the orphans of *Angst* and the Bomb. But where were the ivory fan and the long black dress with miles of skirt our grandmothers had promised us we could wear when we grew up?

IV

It had all begun, of course, back in the late fifties when Vladimir Nabokov's *Lolita* was first published. This tale of innocent pederasty not only immortalized America's first twelve-year-old nymphet and the original Dirty Old Man; it also created and crystallized a new national myth out of some very old ones. American men for decades had looked to younger women for fantasy bed-partners, largely because American wives tend to be such a wholesomely unappetizing crew. The myths grew up around the book and met their archetypes everywhere: businessmen taking long lunch breaks with pretty secretaries, wily co-eds seducing unsuspecting professors with weak tea, wilted flowers, and bad poetry. *Lolita* made the myth of the experienced child-woman into the dominant fashion and advertising theme of the sixties. Gone was the *femme fatale,* the kindly bitch, the prostitute with the heart of gold, the Lady Brett Ashleys and Moreau-ish, Monroe-ish vamps: here to stay for at least a generation was the innocent-looking little girl, at once whore and monster and fey adorable child, knowledgeable beyond her years, happy, excited, a tiny bit breathless, round saucer eyes opened wide and Taking It All In. The race was on: the Great Youth Hustle had already begun. But even in 1965 and '66 we were still living by the old fifties ethos and still hoped vainly for that magic slinky black creation that would turn us into an elegant woman. Little did we know that we were the Forgotten Generation, condemned to instant obsolescence by still-skinny teenyboppers in braces and pigtails, budding little silvergirls whose time had come to shine. By late 1965 and certainly by 1966 the country had most assuredly entered its Adoration of the Adolescent phase. Arrested development became the goal of every American woman. Legs (skinny and long) and arms (also skinny and long) were once again fashion's focal points; hips, busts, and waists were too, too gauchely *adult* for words. In February 1965, after seeing the European collections for the year, Eugenia Sheppherd decided Lolita was In and

Adult was Out: "The new leg is a little girl leg . . . delicately round but with absolutely no calf. . . . The new ideal leg is a round little pole. . . . Legs and arms seem to match, as they do with a child. The look is 100-proof Lolita." [2]

Lolita. Lo-lee-ta. Lolita, my love, my life. Suddenly she was everywhere: waiflike nymphets with matchstick legs and saucer eyes and long lank tawny-gold and auburn and fawn-brown hair romped, frugged, and jerked happily through the pages of *Vogue* and *Bazaar, Seventeen* and *Mademoiselle* and *Glamour* in little-nothing crepe and organdy discothèque dresses, pantsuits, leather and suede jeans, tough little jersey minidresses, point d'esprit and patterned tights, poorboy sweaters from Paris Left Bank boutiques, skimpy sweaterdresses from Biba's and Dorothée Bis, see-through knits from Canada and the United States. The paragon of the hour was *Vogue*'s vertically leaping nymphet. Mia Farrow, Chér, Julie Christie, Penelope Tree, Twiggy, Topsy Taylor, and Caterine Millinaire—"those attractive greedy little monsters who are up and about," [3] Diana Vreeland called them—were all part of the little-girl craze. High fashion began to Think Small: to be chic was to buy size 4 or 6 dresses from Jax, Splendiferous, Abracadabra, Paraphernalia, and Horse of a Different Color. European 12s and 10s were rumored to be American 8s and 6s. The ideal female type had regressed with the Jackie era to the woman of 25 to 35; now the *New York Times Sunday Magazine* carried pictures of wistful teen-agers with ironed hair, standing on one foot, and preadolescents in white knee socks and smocked baby-girl dresses that clearly appealed to the male desire to ravish (apparent) innocence. Hef's Playmates kept looking younger every month and spouting profundities like "I think the West Coast is a real groovey scene" or "I'd just like to find myself first and then maybe like get married." *Cavalier* spelled out the current fantasy by showing its fold-out girls clutching teddy bears and rabbits or cuddling a favorite doll.

Thus, as Roger Vadim has put it, in the sixties youth became a class, the one and only privileged class, with instant signs of recognition for the ones in the know. It was both axiomatic and predictable that pop and mod fashion should be adopted first by the young; it is also axiomatic that both American and European designers and manufacturers alike should wish to sell to as large a market as possible. The fact that half the population of the United States was under 25 caused everyone to assume that anyone over the magic age must wish to think young, be young, or lacking that, *act* young, *look* young, and above all, *buy* young. Old is ugly; Young is beautiful. Grow your hair, streak it blonde, or chop it off, Sassoon-style, paint on pouting moody child-heroine lips and eyes, skimp your body to Twiggy-like proportions and into the latest funky clothes. Resort, if you must, to plastic surgery, electrolysis, face-lifts, mini–face-lifts, massage, diets, but for heaven's sake, lady, STAY YOUNG. Part of the Look

[2] Bender, *The Beautiful People*, p. 74.
[3] *Ibid.*, p. 101.

now included an open-eyed, pleasant, but totally blank stare. Young women managed to erase every vestige of thought, imagination, or experience from their faces and thus achieved the final ingredient of the Look.

It was a heyday for the tyranny of youth. Elegance went on holiday; understatement was Out. Hyperbole, Camp, Op, Pop, and Mod were In. The fact that half the country's population was under 25 seems to have intoxicated not only the teenyboppers themselves but also the manufacturers, buyers, and owners as well. Now unlike the situation in 1947, fashion did not originate on Seventh Avenue or filter across the Atlantic from Savile Row and Paris's 8th *arondissement;* rather, it began in the Village, in Chelsea on King's Road and Carnaby Street, in Biba's in London, on the Left Bank of Paris instead of the Right, at Dorothée Bis and Laura, and in the new boutiques mushrooming in St. Tropez and the Rue de Sèvres, and worked its way up with dizzying speed into the pages of *Vogue, Bazaar, Mademoiselle, Glamour, Town and Country,* even *Realités,* and *Status* where the lanky little girl-children romped eternally in budding groves of newsprint. The boutique took America and Europe by storm. Wherever we traveled, to Denver's Larimer Square, to Winnipeg, to Chicago's Old Town, or Out of Sight in Dayton's in Minneapolis, we saw the formula boutique that fall of 1966: walls lined with aluminum foil, covered with posters in dayglo colors, buttons, boxed wax matches, old band and police uniforms, papier-maché fans, jewelry boxes, candle-holders, mirrors, lipstick tubes, peacock feathers, moth-eaten fur rugs and throws, paper flowers, peace symbols, beads, bells, skimpy little dresses with labels that said things like FAR OUT or CHARISMA or FUNKY or FREAKY, mock Tiffany paper lanterns hanging on tassled chains from the ceiling, rock music blaring from speakers, inexperienced salesgirls with blank looks and miniskirts, inflatable blow-up pillows and furniture, sleazy jersey and crepe dresses in skimpy sizes, chain belts and hardware of every conceivable kind, and dozens of predatory teen-age consumers packed into a few hundred feet of floor space, consuming. This was the formula for Instant Boutique in the sixties and it worked well, particularly during that fall of 1967. In Dayton's Out of Sight we bought fake fur rugs and peacock feathers and pheasant plumes, Bernhardt and Bonnie and Clyde posters and wax matches and tight satin blouses with billowing sleeves like a medieval poet's shirt, and carted them all home to redo our apartment and life-style. Just in case no one had yet got the point, *Esquire* in February 1967 did an issue featuring on the cover a pretty brunette of 25 or so (resembling us, we thought) sitting nude in a garbage pail. The caption asked the crucial question of the day: are American women finished at twenty-one? We shortened our skirts again for the third time and began looking for some new patterned tights. The Age of Aquarius was almost upon us.

V

It was during the middle and late sixties that fashion developed its four estates. At the top of the pop heap were representatives of the *haute couture:* Norman Norrell, Galanos, Jacques Tiffeau, Ben Zuckerman, Balenciaga, Mollie Parnis, Mainbocher, Pauline Trigere, Mme. Gres, Pierre Balmain—the last two unique simply by virtue of being the last of the couturiers to continue working solely for private clients. Of these great names, the ones most connected with pop couture were Yves St. Laurent, Pierre Cardin, and Courreges—the rest worked almost entirely with more conventional design and fabrics. Only slightly less influential were American designers such as Bill Blass, Kenneth Lane, Ken Scott, Oscar de la Renta, Donald Brooks, Geoffrey Beene, Chester Weinberg, Arnold Scassi, and Fernando Sarmi, all of whom were rather more interested in the other two Estates than the European couturiers. Following this Pop Chain of Being downward, the next estate consisted of "good" popular American designers who made clothes in the under-$200 price range: Don Simonelli for Modelia or STJ, Kasper for Joan Leslie, Stan Herman for Mr. Mort, Rudi Gernreich, Anne Klein, Eloise Curtis, Junior Accent, Junior Sophisticates, P. R. L., Claret, Youthguild, Elite, Victor Joris for Cuddlecoat, Betsey Johnson for Paraphernalia, Pinky and Diane for Hang Ups. Into this category also fell all clothes from boutiques and specialty shops like Chicago's Horse of a Different Color or Caravan and New York's Abracadabra or Wisdom and Folly, plus Mary Quant designs for J. C. Penney's, and clothes purchased abroad at Dorothée Bis, Laura, Biba's, or any of the Carnaby Street shops. Finally at the bottom of the line were the mass fashion houses, particularly those designing dresses for the under–twenty-one crowd: Jonathan Logan, Charisma, Crazy Horse, Leslie Jrs., Whistle Stop, Gay Gibson, Bobbie Brooks, and others. It was here that top designers' patterns were often "knocked off," or reproduced without proper credit, and in a greatly abbreviated and cheapened form; it was here, too, that fashion often began and worked its way up the Chain—here and in thrift shops, specialty stores, Army-Navy stores, resale shops, head shops, unposh little shops and men's boutiques like Chicago's Garment District and Man at Ease where the lanky golden girls bought well-cut jeans and sweaters and scarves. What makes the sixties unique in fashion history, however, is not the sources of fashion but rather the direction of influence. From 1965 to 1970 trends came not solely from *haute couture* downward; more often they came from the boutiques, the mass designers, the bohemian quarters like the Village, the Left Bank, or Chelsea, moved upward, and were finally copied by the legitimate couturiers themselves.

In the 1960s influence flowed also down to us middle-class, middle-income human beings via the women's magazines and via readily identifiable pantheons of pop goddesses. Diana Vreeland of *Vogue,* having correctly intuited that "the only thing people are interested in is people," [4] thereafter set out to create a myth of the Beautiful People. Today Miss Vreeland coyly disclaims her invention of the term which she says was originally a copywriter's idea, and adds, "I hate to see it misused. We mean people who are beautiful to look at. It's been taken up to mean

[4] *Ibid.,* p. 67.

people who are rich. We mean the charmers, but there is no harm to be rich."[5] The new heroines of the surface were usually both, however, as well as famous and of good family. Thus movie starlets like Jane Fonda, Raquel Welch, Barbra Streisand, Jean Shrimpton, and Julie Christie, young designers and hairdressers (Kenneth, Carita, Michael Kazin, Ken Scott, Princess Luciana Pignatelli, Consuela Crespi, Bill Blass, St. Laurent), movie makers, novelists, artists, rock musicians, and other *cognoscenti* of the Pop Establishment, as J Marks has christened them, and models Veruschka, Twiggy, and Penelope Tree rubbed shoulders with pop heroines like "Baby" Jane Holzer (Tom Wolfe's Girl of the Year for 1966, characterized by *Women's Wear Daily* in 1964 as "Switched On" and therefore somehow acceptable) and genuine Beautiful People, jet-setters, and professional sybarites (Jackie O., Lee Radziwill, Mrs. William Paley, Amanda Burden, Mrs. Frederick Eberstadt, Princess Irene Galitzine, Mrs. Winston F. C. ["Cee-Zee"] Guest, Louise Savitt, Charlotte Ford Niarchos, Mrs. Wyatt Cooper *et al.*). The latter group, sometimes referred to as "The Ladies," appears to be a genuine creation of the media, particularly of Miss Vreeland and *Women's Wear Daily,* in a sudden fervid zeal to raise conspicuous consumption and willingness to advertise one's clothing labels to the level of a pop art-form. Pop couture, the great leveller, had a marvellous way of erasing class distinctions. Thus Jane Holzer could say in 1964 that there's no class anymore: "Everybody is equal." The common denominators were hedonism, arrogance, contemporaneity, and a willingness to be photographed by the omnivorous press and to appear incessantly in pictures of every size and color.

And so it was that in 1966 and '67, inspired by pictures of our favorite idol Jacqueline emerging from a cab in front of La Grenouille in flowing locks, flat-heeled Puritan shoes by Roger Vivier (*the* Shoe of the Year, we later discovered), and miniskirt, we changed our life-styles and apparel one and for all. We became devotees of *Vogue* and *Bazaar* and read endless columns of advice on how to shrink a normal adult body with measurements of 36-24-36 into more respectably Twiggy-like proportions of 32-20-32. Nothing else would suit the stern Muse of Fashion. From these magazines we learned that fashion in the sixties included not only recognizing (and preferably owning) Gucci and Hermés handbags, a Pucci dress, an Elegant or Calderon belt, Charles Jourdan shoes, an Adolfo hat, and a Sant'Angelo gypsy dress; it also encompassed such seemingly irrelevant items as decorating one's home with unread $25 art books and unread European paperbacks with uncut pages, displaying a tolerant and benevolent appreciation of hippies and mind-expanding drugs, having an opening-night seat at *Hair* and *Che!,* keeping wildflowers mixed casually in La-Grenouille-like profusion in peasanty bowls on eighteenth-century chests, traveling to obscure Greek islands in the summer, as recommended by the last "Suzy Says" column, embracing meditation, wearing David Webb animal bracelets, burning Rigaud candles and incense, pass-

5 *Ibid.*

ing marijuana cigarettes on silver trays after a dinner party, lugging home amusing throwaways to "turn an Ugly into a Beautiful," in *Mademoiselle's* coy phrase, throwing parties in unexpectedly chic places such as barn lofts and abandoned gymnasiums, smiling knowledgeably at the name "Tigermorse," spending a two-week slimming session at the Golden Door, attending fashion luncheons at Bergdorf Goodman's and Ohrbach's, keeping Porthault linens on the bed, wearing tie-dyed Levis with fringed leather Indian belts, sporting hair streaked by Kenneth, and displaying a certain pop intellectualism, like Jackie O's.

Yé-yé and pop designers like Emmanuelle Khanh, Paco Rabanne, Sally Tuffin, Marion Foale, Mary Quant, Plunket-Greene, Christianne Baily, and Michele Rosier, "the Vinyl Girl," were ready to affirm along with Miss Rosier that "everything beautiful has the right to exist, the eccentric as well as the rational, provided it's cheap. . . . I prefer bad taste to good taste; it's gayer." [6] Miss Rosier was, of course, only voicing the fashion industry's equivalent of Miss Sontag's 1964 essay on camp in which she defined "camp" as dandyism in the age of mass-culture: a love of the exaggerated, a spirit of extravagance, style at the expense of content, antiserious art, vulgar and banal. From the pop decade that gave us Batman, Malcolm Byrd frugging in church aisles, JFK the Pop Politician and Jacqueline the Superconsumer, the Beatles, the Stones, and real purple Dynel hairpieces ("It's not fake anything . . .") sprang also Tigermorse vinyl dresses with HATE printed aft and LOVE fore. That was instant fashion when Bergdorf's bought it: instant *avant-garde* chic of the new rebellious nose-thumbing put-on kind. Youth, that new oppressed majority, could now demonstrate its social protest by operating and consuming from boutiques, hip apparel shops, specialty stores, poster shops, and other authentic by-products of the institutionalized antiestablishment.

Not only this: fashion in this era also meant the Robert Sculls' collection of Jasper Johns' beer cans and flag paintings, Warhol's Campbell soup can and of Baby Jane, who was photographed as Tom Wolfe says, "barebacked wearing a little yacht cap and a pair of 'World's Fair' sunglasses and holding an American flag in her teeth, so—so beyond Pop Art, if you comprehend." [8] The New Style, the New Chic . . . Peggy Moffitt, Rudi Gernreich's favorite model, had it, as photographed in the 20 July 1966 issue of *Queen* in a minidress of electric tangerine-flake geometric designs, mesh stockings, a Vidal Sassoon haircut with a black triangle under one eye. And so had Yves St. Laurent's bridal mannequins of 1966 with ruby lips and pink female torsos and blinking lights in their bridal bouquets. And so had Betey Johnson's "Noise dress" for "total environments" like Cheetah nightclubs and the Electric Circus. Those of us who had cherished romantic dreams of grown-up elegance resigned ourselves by the end of 1966. The world had gone irrevocably, unalterably, teen-age.

---

[6] *Ibid.*, p. 191.

[7] Sontag, "Notes on 'Camp'," pp. 277–243 *passim*.

[8] Tom Wolfe, *The Kandy-Kolored Tangerine-Flake Streamline Baby* (New York, 1965), p. 209.

VI

"If you're going to San Francisco, be sure to wear a flower in your hair." All that summer of 1967 the jukeboxes reminded us in the hopelessly square world of jobs and home and family of the new generation: the New Wave people in motion *en route* to the West Coast. By autumn every major news magazine in the country carried its full-page color spread on the hippies, the "wave makers," the drug cult, the new hedonists—no one was yet sure what to call them. In utter frustration at our middle-class provincialism we bought flared jeans, frayed the cuffs, found an old Army shirt at the nearest Army-Navy store, wore sandals despite the early chill of fall, stared by the hour at love beads by the light of department-store strobe candles, and meditated in the lotus position while listening to Sergeant Pepper's Lonely Hearts Club Band. "Lucy in the Sky with Diamonds" and "A Day in the Life" still can give us that vague alarming bittersweet feeling of an unhappy love affair, so much and so often did we contemplate the prospect of dropping out that brilliant fall. We returned briefly to the poses and gestures of our own Beat days, only this time instead of the Left Bank it was San Francisco that preoccupied the mind's eye. San Francisco! the new beautiful people, the real beautiful people, not the fake ones that *Vogue* talked about, freedom, communes, a chance to do one's own thing. Then December came. Our friends went to the Haight, and came back with the saddest of sad tales: the Haight was no more. The streets stood emptied of the flower children, the beautiful people had moved on, some back into the mountains, some on to communes in New Mexico. The Haight gone! It was like hearing that the shops on Carnaby Street were closing down. The end of one era, the beginning . . . of what? Reluctantly we buried the Sergeant Pepper album but continued on a strict course of meditation until spring of the following year.

1968: it was the best of times and the worst of times. Twice we sat in stunned silence before a television screen feeling the chill, familiar grip of a familiar horror: 1963 all over again. We watched the Presidential conventions the following August and marveled at the placid banality of the one, the senseless violence and short-sightedness of the other. Fashion that year was quieter, gentler. Switched-On seemed temporarily to have had it. *Elvira Madigan*–inspired ruffled dresses, frills, big hats, crisp organdies and laces, even a stray maxiskirt and midiskirt invoked a nostalgic mood. We rejoiced momentarily and toyed with the notion of rescuing Grandmother's ivory fan from the box in the attic. But a long-range Age of Elegance seemed as far away as ever. There were not only Elvira Madigan dresses, there were also Bonnie-and-Clyde dresses, striped gangster suits for both sexes, more psychedelia, clingy little jersey knits and more skimp dresses, thirties dresses fit for a Scott Fitzgerald heroine, forties dresses in funky cheap little cotton prints with draped shoulders and ankle-strap shoes, elephant pants, bare midriff outfits, unisex fashions, more chains, ropes, beads, belts, jackets, tinsel than last year. In the autumn we wore brown fake fur elephant pants with wide flared legs and a chocolate silk blouse with enormous sleeves, a violet velvet bolero trimmed in gold braid and enough chains and scarves to choke a horse. Miniskirts were still with us, but they were eclipsed by pantsuits and flared-leg elephant pants. Inspired by the Beatles' newest movie, "Yellow Submarine," the giant pants flowered in men's and women's boutiques alike. Men, having just gone through their Nehru and Eastern-inspired phases and having exploited the evening turtleneck for all it was worth, began a long flirtation with Hip Edwardian. For casual wear, flared pants took precedence over everything else. There were velvet jeans by Pierre Cardin, tweed flares for sport, dark flares for dress, freaky striped pants that scraped the ground in back when the wearer walked. For men and women alike, it was the Fall of the Accessory: clunky Minnie Mouse shoes, bags, scarves, chains, belts, bangles, collars, peace emblems, babushkas, mufflers, boots, stockings, sunglasses with colored lenses, and hardware of all sorts were the order of the day. Patchwork dresses brought the "rich peasant" look to the populace; designers like Sant'Angelo and Adolfo, to name only two, created the "rich hippie" look. There was also an Occult Look (metallic ball gowns trimmed with signs of the zodiac and other occult symbols), a Russian look, a Russian peasant look (subspecies of the first), a gypsy look, a Persian look, a Spanish gypsy look, a French peasant look, an incipient American Indian look, and an Afro look. It was fashion's Ethnic Phase, and fashion acquitted itself well. The Beautiful People blossomed forth in full fall regalia at New York's posh eateries, nightclubs, discothèques, private parties, and supper clubs in expensive patchwork, rags, and tatters. We began searching through Grandmother's scrap bag for bits of silk scraps and even began a patchwork skirt, which somehow never got beyond the first dozen irregular squares. Mod fashion was definitely losing its grip. It had entered its Eclectic Phase.

We who have lived out our twenties in the era of pop fashion, like Milton's Satan, can snuff the scent of mortal change on earth; we can detect, almost intuitively, when Seventh Avenue and Paris are preparing new goodies for us. As early as 1966 some Paris designers had been dropping hemlines, but nothing had yet come of it: women were not ready to give up their beloved miniskirts and kook clothes quite so soon. But by 1968 the youth cult was dead and we all knew it, felt it in our fashionably exposed bones. The Look had become institutionalized, thoroughly stylized. Clothing offered instant identification that was less important as body covering, man-bait or object of female envy than as symbols of a life-style. For the young and would-be young in the late sixties, fashion was theatre in the streets, an instant life-style, and often an instant politics (Left = Hip; Right = Straight), an easily accessible image, an identity statement, a way of "coming off" and selling oneself to the world that transcended its immediate practical and aesthetic value. It was human prepackaging for that most salable of sixties commodities: the elusive Self. It was also a "viable" life-style for a generation that seemed unable to manufacture its own—a generation for whom authentic existence had become a major obsession. Suddenly once-neutral items took on hidden sexual, political, and social connotations: leather boots and skirts, patterned tights, a fistful of rings, chain belts, flared trouser suits, sweater dresses, and poorboy shirts now provided instant recognition and that all-important self-expression. Merely by wearing these items millions of girls could now say wordlessly: I'm hip, I'm antiestablishment, I'm the New Girl, I'm fun, I'm with it, I'm in the know. Thus did fashion become THE Pop Art *par excellence* of the era. Men leaving the Art Institute with business suit and briefcase could be greeted by a *Seed* hawker with "The only good attaché is a dead attaché," while the next day in Old Town the same men in flared pants and dashiki would elicit smiles and V-signs from the same *Seed* sellers. In Chicago of 1969 we developed our uniforms for different parts of the city: dirty beige jeans and poorboy sweater, boots and head scarf for Hyde Park, expensive little knits and leather coats and boots for Rush Street, flared pants and sandals and Indian jewelry for Old Town, standard American mass-produced clothes for the Loop. To wear the wrong costume in the wrong part of town was a prime violation of social mores and assured one of jeers and catcalls and hostile looks from all passersby. No one looked at the clothes anymore: it was all symbolic anyhow, wasn't it? Living theatre in the street, instant life-style, instant recognition by others of the same mind? And meanwhile in Paris and Rome and London, on Seventh Avenue in New York, in little boutiques and antiestablishment establishments everywhere, the *haute* and pop couture were busy preparing the new symbols for us, the midi, the longuette, the New Proportion, the shiny new packages that will spell the official end of the Great Youth Hustle, the official end of an era.

VII

There they go, the Silvergirls!—past Melvin's down the sidewalk toward Mister Kelly's and the Flying Frenchman, past the lighted shops in the rain. Inside we mortals sit behind the screened sliding doors, watching the April rain drip in the budding trees, brushing the cinders from our eyes for a closer look at them as they go by. They travel in packs, out of some primitive hunting instinct, perhaps: the predatory nature of the beast asserting itself. On hot spring nights like this when the wet sidewalks are mosaics of Rush Street lights they walk by, tawny of hair, long of leg, short of skirt: the glittering goddesses gleaming like silver in the rain, preening their necks and smiling their small vacant smiles at the gaping boys behind the cafe doors, like Fitzgerald's Daisy, safe and proud above the hot struggles of the poor. You see them this season in tough little purple jerseys and platform sandals, snakeskin blouses and boots, leather shoulderbags dripping and flying fringe, bright beads of fake lapis lazuli and turquoise and coral, white ivory crosses, Indian headscarves, pantsuits and ancient frayed Levis and little white linen dresses with see-through grommeted sides, wide leather belts and new midi-raincoats, clunking and frugging, prancing and slinking and swinging down the street with their miles of leg and yards of hair. On winter mornings when the air is cold around the edges and the frost crystals glitter in the hard bright air, and Melvin's is almost emptied of its brilliant frisking kids, the Silver-girls are there again: well-cut beige and white flared pants covered with little fun furs and knitted caps and mufflers the color of eggshells, suede boots and leather gauntlets arming them against the cold, walking their Afghans past the nearly-empty shops. On tender spring evenings at five o'clock when the Michigan Avenue shops close you see them again, tanned arms laden with Bonwit's and Saks' shopping bags and parcels, eyes already hard and bright and predatory with visions of next season's treasures already dancing like gumdrops in their heads.

In the cafe I stir Sucaryl into my coffee, ever mindful of my constant starvation diet, and watch the April drops splash on the brick terrace. The beat of traffic and talk is electric, frenetic. Leaves grow on the trees in great green bursts like things in fast movies, the air sensuous, like an overripe fruit in the smoky haze of pollution that hangs like a visible weight over Big John and the Playboy Building. The stem of lilacs I stole from the park today is wilting fast, but one whiff and I am back like Proust to Combray with that bright confusion of thread and fabric, the fire, the flashing needles, the sheer unadulterated love of color and line and cloth and clothes, the hours of collusion and scheming and gossip and woman-talk, the coffee and tea-cakes and all the bright lost visions of myself as an elegant woman, grown-up, gracious, and infinitely wise. I've lost the hope of growing old elegantly just as I've lost the hope of growing to rival Veruschka's height or shrinking down to Twiggy's proportions. I'm too much the child of my own era, too much the creation of Villager shops and vinyl and hardware. I grow old, I grow old . . .

The raindrops splash heavily on the pavement now, clattering loudly on the roof above the cafe, whispering in the leaves dried by the sun. The crowds are pouring into Melvin's, the cheapest refuge from the rain in the glut of nightclubs and bars that line the street. Two silvergirls come in, sun-streaked hair beginning to wilt a little from the sudden shower. They sit down, order Cokes. The jukebox blares out its message—

LET IT BE, LET IT BE, LET IT BE, LET IT BE
SAIL ON SILVERGIRL, SAIL ON BY . . .[9]

"I'm going to get just six midiskirts and nothing more this fall. I mean, like then when they go out next year, like I could get something else . . ."

The purple jersey takes offense at this. "You got to get some boots. They have boots at Field's downtown, in the window on State Street."

"Oh. The lace-up things. Oh wow. Yeah. Maybe in August. But the boots will be finished by then, of course."

"I've got to get my hair streaked . . ."

LET IT BE, LET IT BE, LET IT BE, LET IT BE, SPEAKING WORDS OF WISDOM, LET IT BE.

[9] The Beatles, "Let It Be" (1970); Simon and Garfunkel, "Bridge Over Troubled Water" (1970).

". . . get them at Saks . . ."
". . . maybe the brown one at Bonwit's, I don't know . . ."
"Oh wow!"
". . . adorable long fringed bags in Old Town . . ."
". . . the new proportion . . ."
". . . Wild!"
"I'm having all the hems let out. I'm tired of them . . ."
". . . not where it's at . . ."

SAIL ON SILVERGIRL, SAIL ON BY . . .

"Let's get out of here . . ."
". . . bored . . ."
"The rain has stopped. You got any money?"

RAINDROPS KEEP FALLING ON MY HEAD. THEY KEEP FALLING. And what have they done to the rain?

They wander on, these lovely vacant creatures with eyes devoid of soul: the glorious girls Britain's Adel Rootstein once called the New Girl of the Sixties: tall, lean, tawny-haired, healthy, rangy, leggy animals with soft skins and no inhibitions, the Silvergirl in her ruddy golden mediocrity. Ah *jeunesse doreè!* The Look, the omnipresent Look! The Lolita Look, the Jackie Look, the Schoolgirl Look, the Goodgirl Look, the Badgirl Look, the Wet Look, the Mod Look, the Kinky Look. Lankygirl, Realgirl, Newgirl, Sportifgirl, Ethnicgirl, Hippiegirl, Peasantgirl, Romanticgirl, Silvergirl. Voices full of money, the jingle of it, the cymbals' song of it. . . . High in a white palace, the king's daughter, the silver girl. . . . Sail on, Silvergirl, sail on by. Don't you know that youth is, like . . . like the only thing in the world worth having? Youth, you know . . . I mean, a new hedonism, a total look, a life-style, you know, you pick your box and get inside and boom . . . there you are. A new hedonism . . . what our century wants. An instant Look! Instant Chic! Prepackaged! Youth! There is nothing, absolutely nothing in the world, but Youth. . . . I mean, what else IS there? The little black dress with real pearls? And dancing shoes and a fan? Really! That's been Out for years now. Or didn't you know?

That's it, Silvergirl. You tell 'em. Your time has come to shine, all right. But sail by fast, silvergirl, fast as you can. Better sail hard and fast. Go with the flow, hurry and keep up with the times. There's nothing worse than Yesterday's Now person Tomorrow.

Against Interpretation

SUSAN SONTAG

Content is a glimpse of something, an encounter like a flash. It's very tiny—very tiny, content.
                    Willem De Kooning, *in an interview*

It is only shallow people who do not judge by appearances. The mystery of the world is the visible, not the invisible.

                    Oscar Wilde, *in a letter*

The earliest *experience* of art must have been that it was incantatory, magical; art was an instrument of ritual. (Cf. the paintings in the caves at Lascaux, Altamira, Niaux, La Pasiega, etc.) The earliest *theory* of art, that of the Greek philosophers, proposed that art was mimesis, imitation of reality.

It is at this point that the peculiar question of the *value* of art arose. For the mimetic theory, by its very terms, challenges art to justify itself.

Plato, who proposed the theory, seems to have done so in order to rule that the value of art is dubious. Since he considered ordinary material things as themselves mimetic objects, imitations of transcendent forms or structures, even the best painting of a bed would be only an "imitation of an imitation." For Plato, art is neither particularly useful (the painting of a bed is no good to sleep on), nor, in the strict sense, true. And Aristotle's arguments in defense of art do not really challenge Plato's view that all art is an elaborate *trompe l'oeil,* and therefore a lie. But he does dispute Plato's idea that art is useless. Lie or no, art has a certain value according to Aristotle because it is a form of therapy. Art is useful, after all, Aristotle counters, medicinally useful in that it arouses and purges dangerous emotions.

In Plato and Aristotle, the mimetic theory of art goes hand in hand with the assumption that art is always figurative. But advocates of the mimetic theory need not close their eyes to decorative and abstract art. The fallacy that art is necessarily a "realism" can be modified or scrapped without ever moving outside the problems delimited by the mimetic theory.

The fact is, all Western consciousness of and reflection upon art have remained within the confines staked out by the Greek theory of art as mimesis or representation. It is through this theory that art as such—above and beyond given works of art—becomes problematic, in need of defense. And it is the defense of art which gives birth to the odd vision by which something we have learned to call "form" is separated off from something we have learned to call "content," and to the well-intentioned move which makes content essential and form accessory.

Even in modern times, when most artists and critics have discarded the theory of art as representation of an outer reality in favor of the theory of art as subjective expression, the main feature of the mimetic theory persists. Whether we conceive of the work of art on the model of a picture (art as a picture of reality) or on the model of a statement (art as the statement of the artist), content still comes first. The content may have changed. It may now be less figurative, less lucidly realistic. But it is still assumed that a work of art *is* its content. Or, as it's usually put today, that a work of art by definition *says* something. ("What X is saying is . . .," "What X is trying to say is . . .," "What X said is . . ." etc., etc.)

2

None of us can ever retrieve that innocence before all theory when art knew no need to justify itself, when one did not ask of a work of art what it *said* because one knew (or thought one knew) what it *did*. From now to the end of consciousness, we are stuck with the task of defending art. We can only quarrel with one or another means of defense. Indeed, we have an obligation to overthrow any means of defending and justifying art which becomes particularly obtuse or onerous or insensitive to contemporary needs and practice.

This is the case, today, with the very idea of content itself. Whatever it may have been in the past, the idea of content is today mainly a hindrance, a nuisance, a subtle or not so subtle philistinism.

Though the actual developments in many arts may seem to be leading us away from the idea that a work of art is primarily its content, the idea still exerts an extraordinary hegemony. I want to suggest that this is because the idea is now perpetuated in the guise of a certain way of encountering works of art thoroughly ingrained among most people who take any of the arts seriously. What the overemphasis on the idea of content entails is the perennial, never consummated project of *interpretation*. And, conversely, it is the habit of approaching works of art in order to *interpret* them that sustains the fancy that there really is such a thing as the content of a work of art.

3

Of course, I don't mean interpretation in the broadest sense, the sense in which Nietzsche (rightly) says, "There are no facts, only interpretations." By interpretation, I mean here a conscious act of the mind which illustrates a certain code, certain "rules" of interpretation.

Directed to art, interpretation means plucking a set of elements (the X, the Y, the Z, and so forth) from the whole work. The task of interpretation is virtually one of translation. The interpreter says, Look, don't you see that X is really—or, really means—A? That Y is really B? That Z is really C?

What situation could prompt this curious project for transforming a text? History gives us the materials for an answer. Interpretation first appears in the culture of late classical antiquity, when the power and credibility of myth had been broken by the "realistic" view of the world introduced by scientific enlightenment. Once the question that haunts post-mythic consciousness—that of the *seemliness* of religious symbols—had been asked, the ancient texts were, in their pristine form, no longer accept-able. Then interpretation was summoned, to reconcile the ancient texts to "modern" demands. Thus, the Stoics, to accord with their view that the gods had to be moral, allegorized away the rude features of Zeus and his boisterous clan in Homer's epics. What Homer really designated by the adultery of Zeus with Leto, they explained, was the union between power and wisdom. In the same vein, Philo of Alexandria interpreted the literal historical narratives of the Hebrew Bible as spiritual paradigms. The story of the exodus from Egypt, the wandering in the desert for forty years, and the entry into the promised land, said Philo, was really an allegory of the individual soul's emancipation, tribulations, and final deliverance. Inter-pretation thus presupposes a discrepancy between the clear meaning of the text and the demands of (later) readers. It seeks to resolve that dis-crepancy. The situation is that for some reason a text has become unac-ceptable; yet it cannot be discarded. Interpretation is a radical strategy for conserving an old text, which is thought too precious to repudiate, by revamping it. The interpreter, without actually erasing or rewriting the text, *is* altering it. But he can't admit to doing this. He claims to be only making it intelligible, by disclosing its true meaning. However far the inter-preters alter the text (another notorious example is the Rabbinic and Christian "spiritual" interpretations of the clearly erotic Song of Songs), they must claim to be reading off a sense that is already there.

Interpretation in our own time, however, is even more complex. For the contemporary zeal for the project of interpretation is often prompted not by piety toward the troublesome text (which may conceal an aggression), but by an open aggressiveness, an overt contempt for appearances. The old style of interpretation was insistent, but respectful; it erected another meaning on top of the literal one. The modern style of interpretation excavates, and as it excavates, destroys; it digs "behind" the text, to find a sub-text which is the true one. The most celebrated and influential modern doctrines, those of Marx and Freud, actually amount to elaborate systems of hermeneutics, aggressive and impious theories of interpreta-tion. All observable phenomena are bracketed, in Freud's phrase, as *mani-fest content*. This manifest content must be probed and pushed aside to find the true meaning—the *latent content*—beneath. For Marx, social events like revolutions and wars; for Freud, the events of individual lives (like neurotic symptoms and slips of the tongue) as well as texts (like a dream or a work of art)—all are treated as occasions for interpretation. According to Marx and Freud, these events only *seem* to be intelligible. Actually, they have no meaning without interpretation. To understand *is* to interpret. And to interpret is to restate the phenomenon, in effect to find an equivalent for it.

Thus, interpretation is not (as most people assume) an absolute value, a gesture of mind situated in some timeless realm of capabilities. Interpretation must itself be evaluated, within a historical view of human consciousness. In some cultural contexts, interpretation is a liberating act. It is a means of revising, of transvaluing, of escaping the dead past. In other cultural contexts, it is reactionary, impertinent, cowardly, stifling.

4

Today is such a time, when the project of interpretation is largely reactionary, stifling. Like the fumes of the automobile and of heavy industry which befoul the urban atmosphere, the effusion of interpretations of art today poisons our sensibilities. In a culture whose already classical dilemma is the hypertrophy of the intellect at the expense of energy and sensual capability, interpretation is the revenge of the intellect upon art.

Even more. It is the revenge of the intellect upon the world. To interpret is to impoverish, to deplete the world—in order to set up a shadow world of "meanings." It is to turn *the* world into *this* world. ("This world"! As if there were any other.)

The world, our world, is depleted, impoverished enough. Away with all duplicates of it, until we again experience more immediately what we have.

5

In most modern instances, interpretation amounts to the philistine refusal to leave the work of art alone. Real art has the capacity to make us nervous. By reducing the work of art to its content and then interpreting *that,* one tames the work of art. Interpretation makes art manageable, comfortable.

This philistinism of interpretation is more rife in literature than in any other art. For decades now, literary critics have understood it to be their task to translate the elements of the poem or play or novel or story into something else. Sometimes a writer will be so uneasy before the naked power of his art that he will install within the work itself—albeit with a little shyness, a touch of the good taste of irony—the clear and explicit interpretation of it. Thomas Mann is an example of such an overcooperative author. In the case of more stubborn authors, the critic is only too happy to perform the job.

The work of Kafka, for example, has been subjected to a mass ravishment by no less than three armies of interpreters. Those who read Kafka as a social allegory see case studies of the frustrations and insanity of modern bureaucracy and its ultimate issuance in the totalitarian state. Those who read Kafka as a psychoanalytic allegory see desperate revelations of Kafka's fear of his father, his castration anxieties, his sense of his own impotence, his thralldom to his dreams. Those who read Kafka as a religious allegory explain that K. in *The Castle* is trying to gain access to heaven, that Joseph K. in *The Trial* is being judged by the inexorable and mysterious justice of God. . . . Another *oeuvre* that has attracted interpreters like leeches is that of Samuel Beckett. Beckett's delicate dramas of the withdrawn consciousness—pared down to essentials, cut off, often represented as physically immobilized—are read as a statement about modern man's alienation from meaning or from God, or as an allegory of psychopathology.

Proust, Joyce, Faulkner, Rilke, Lawrence, Gide . . . one could go on citing author after author; the list is endless of those around whom thick encrustations of interpretation have taken hold. But it should be noted that interpretation is not simply the compliment that mediocrity pays to genius. It is, indeed, *the* modern way of understanding something, and is applied to works of every quality. Thus, in the notes that Elia Kazan published on his production of *A Streetcar Named Desire,* it becomes clear that, in order to direct the play, Kazan had to discover that Stanley Kowalski represented the sensual and vengeful barbarism that was engulfing our culture, while Blanche Du Bois was Western civilization, poetry, delicate apparel, dim lighting, refined feelings and all, though a little the worse for wear to be sure. Tennessee Williams' forceful psychological melodrama now became intelligible: it was *about* something, about the decline of Western civilization. Apparently, were it to go on being a play about a handsome brute named Stanley Kowalski and a faded mangy belle named Blanche Du Bois, it would not be manageable.

6

It doesn't matter whether artists intend, or don't intend, for their works to be interpreted. Perhaps Tennessee Williams thinks *Streetcar* is about what Kazan thinks it to be about. It may be that Cocteau in *The Blood of a Poet* and in *Orpheus* wanted the elaborate readings which have been given these films, in terms of Freudian symbolism and social critique. But the merit of these works certainly lies elsewhere than in their "meanings." Indeed, it is precisely to the extent that Williams' plays and Cocteau's films do suggest these portentous meanings that they are defective, false, contrived, lacking in conviction.

From interviews, it appears that Resnais and Robbe-Grillet consciously designed *Last Year at Marienbad* to accommodate a multiplicity of equally plausible interpretations. But the temptation to interpret *Marienbad* should be resisted. What matters in *Marienbad* is the pure, untranslatable, sensuous immediacy of some of its images, and its rigorous if narrow solutions to certain problems of cinematic form.

Again, Ingmar Bergman may have meant the tank rumbling down the empty night street in *The Silence* as a phallic symbol. But if he did, it was a foolish thought. ("Never trust the teller, trust the tale," said Lawrence.) Taken as a brute object, as an immediate sensory equivalent for the mysterious abrupt armored happenings going on inside the hotel, that sequence with the tank is the most striking moment in the film. Those who reach for a Freudian interpretation of the tank are only expressing their lack of response to what is there on the screen.

It is always the case that interpretation of this type indicates a dissatisfaction (conscious or unconscious) with the work, a wish to replace it by something else.

Interpretation, based on the highly dubious theory that a work of art is composed of items of content, violates art. It makes art into an article for use, for arrangement into a mental scheme of categories.

7

Interpretation does not, of course, always prevail. In fact, a great deal of today's art may be understood as motivated by a flight from interpretation. To avoid interpretation, art may become parody. Or it may become abstract. Or it may become ("merely") decorative. Or it may become non-art.

The flight from interpretation seems particularly a feature of modern painting. Abstract painting is the attempt to have, in the ordinary sense, no content; since there is no content, there can be no interpretation. Pop Art works by the opposite means to the same result; using a content so blatant, so "what it is," it, too, ends by being uninterpretable.

A great deal of modern poetry as well, starting from the great experiments of French poetry (including the movement that is misleadingly called Symbolism) to put silence into poems and to reinstate the *magic* of the word, has escaped from the rough grip of interpretation. The most recent revolution in contemporary taste in poetry—the revolution that has deposed Eliot and elevated Pound—represents a turning away from content in poetry in the old sense, an impatience with what made modern poetry prey to the zeal of interpreters.

I am speaking mainly of the situation in America, of course. Interpretation runs rampant here in those arts with a feeble and neglegible avant-garde: fiction and the drama. Most American novelists and playwrights are really either journalists or gentlemen sociologists and psychologists. They are writing the literary equivalent of program music. And so rudimentary, uninspired, and stagnant has been the sense of what might be done with *form* in fiction and drama that even when the content isn't simply information, news, it is still peculiarly visible, handier, more exposed. To the extent that novels and plays (in America), unlike poetry and painting and music, don't reflect any interesting concern with changes in their form, these arts remain prone to assault by interpretation.

But programmatic avant-gardism—which has meant, mostly, experiments with form at the expense of content—is not the only defense against the infestation of art by interpretations. At least, I hope not. For this would be to commit art to being perpetually on the run. (It also perpetuates the very distinction between form and content which is, ultimately, an illusion.) Ideally, it is possible to elude the interpreters in another way, by making works of art whose surface is so unified and clean, whose momentum is so rapid, whose address is so direct that the work can be . . . just what it is. Is this possible now? It does happen in films, I believe. This is why cinema is the most alive, the most exciting, the most important of all art forms right now. Perhaps the way one tells how alive a particular art form is, is by the latitude it gives for making mistakes in it, and still being good. For example, a few of the films of Bergman—though crammed with lame messages about the modern spirit, thereby inviting interpretations—still triumph over the pretentious intentions of their director. In *Winter Light* and *The Silence,* the beauty and visual sophistication of the images subvert before our eyes the callow pseudo-intellectuality of the story and some of the dialogue. (The most remarkable instance of this sort of discrepancy is the work of D. W. Griffith.) In good films, there is always a directness that entirely frees us from the itch to interpret. Many old Hollywood films, like those of Cukor, Walsh, Hawks, and countless other directors, have this liberating anti-symbolic quality, no less than the best work of the new European directors, like Truffaut's *Shoot the Piano Player* and *Jules and Jim,* Godard's *Breathless* and *Vivre Sa Vie,* Antonioni's *L'Avventura,* and Olmi's *The Fiancés.*

The fact that films have not been overrun by interpreters is in part due simply to the newness of cinema as an art. It also owes to the happy accident that films for such a long time were just movies; in other words, that they were understood to be part of mass, as opposed to high, culture, and were left alone by most people with minds. Then, too, there is always something other than content in the cinema to grab hold of, for those who want to analyze. For the cinema, unlike the novel, possesses a vocabulary of forms—the explicit, complex, and discussable technology of camera movements, cutting, and composition of the frame that goes into the making of a film.

8

What kind of criticism, of commentary on the arts, is desirable today? For I am not saying that works of art are ineffable, that they cannot be described or paraphrased. They can be. The question is how. What would criticism look like that would serve the work of art, not usurp its place?

What is needed, first, is more attention to form in art. If excessive stress on *content* provokes the arrogance of interpretation, more extended and more thorough descriptions of *form* would silence. What is needed is a vocabulary—a descriptive, rather than prescriptive, vocabulary—for forms.[1] The best criticism, and it is uncommon, is of this sort that dissolves considerations of content into those of form. On film, drama, and painting respectively, I can think of Erwin Panofsky's essay, "Style and Medium in the Motion Pictures," Northrop Frye's essay "A Conspectus of Dramatic Genres," Pierre Francastel's essay "The Destruction of a Plastic Space." Roland Barthes' book *On Racine* and his two essays on Robbe-Grillet are examples of formal analysis applied to the work of a single author. (The

---

[1] One of the difficulties is that our idea of form is spatial (the Greek metaphors for form are all derived from notions of space). This is why we have a more ready vocabulary of forms for the spatial than for the temporal arts. The exception among the temporal arts, of course, is the drama; perhaps this is because the drama is a narrative (i.e., temporal) form that extends itself visually and pictorially, upon a stage. . . . What we don't have yet is a poetics of the novel, any clear notion of the forms of narration. Perhaps film criticism will be the occasion of a breakthrough here, since films are primarily a visual form, yet they are also a subdivision of literature.

best essays in Erich Auerbach's *Mimesis,* like "The Scar of Odysseus," are also of this type.) An example of formal analysis applied simultaneously to genre and author is Walter Benjamin's essay, "The Story Teller: Reflections on the Works of Nicolai Leskov."

Equally valuable would be acts of criticism which would supply a really accurate, sharp, loving description of the appearance of a work of art. This seems even harder to do than formal analysis. Some of Manny Farber's film criticism, Dorothy Van Ghent's essay "The Dickens World: A View from Todgers,' " Randall Jarrell's essay on Walt Whitman are among the rare examples of what I mean. These are essays which reveal the sensuous surface of art without mucking about in it.

9

Transparence is the highest, most liberating value in art—and in criticism—today. Transparence means experiencing the luminousness of the thing in itself, of things being what they are. This is the greatness of, for example, the films of Bresson and Ozu and Renoir's *The Rules of the Game.*

Once upon a time (say, for Dante), it must have been a revolutionary and creative move to design works of art so that they might be experienced on several levels. Now it is not. It reinforces the principle of redundancy that is the principal affliction of modern life.

Once upon a time (a time when high art was scarce), it must have been a revolutionary and creative move to interpret works of art. Now it is not. What we decidedly do not need now is further to assimilate Art into Thought, or (worse yet) Art into Culture.

Interpretation takes the sensory experience of the work of art for granted, and proceeds from there. This cannot be taken for granted, now. Think of the sheer multiplication of works of art available to every one of us, superadded to the conflicting tastes and odors and sights of the urban environment that bombard our senses. Ours is a culture based on excess, on overproduction; the result is a steady loss of sharpness in our sensory experience. All the conditions of modern life—its material plenitude, its sheer crowdedness—conjoin to dull our sensory faculties. And it is in the light of the condition of our senses, our capacities (rather than those of another age), that the task of the critic must be assessed.

What is important now is to recover our senses. We must learn to *see* more, to *hear* more, to *feel* more.

Our task is not to find the maximum amount of content in a work of art, much less to squeeze more content out of the work than is already there. Our task is to cut back content so that we can see the thing at all.

The aim of all commentary on art now should be to make works of art—and, by analogy, our own experience—more, rather than less, real to us. The function of criticism should be to show *how it is what it is,* even *that it is what it is,* rather than to show *what it means.*

10

In place of a hermeneutics we need an erotics of art.

Art on Trial

ALFRED KAZIN

Thoreau said that every generation abandons the old like a stranded vessel. This is a biological law in the arts as well. The new generation brings in the new men needed to change things. Often it takes just one man. But perhaps the attention paid to the generaion gap points up an anxiety that is not so much competitive—between the generations—as it is an anxiety among young and old alike to ride with the times, to make the most of this violently changing, always exciting time, to get at the center of so much new energy and to identify with it. Something indescribably marvelous yet possibly terrible is going on for hundreds of millions of people. We all feel it. There is almost too much power around—for good and evil. The sense of our own power is heavy on the imagination.

Art changes all the time, but it never "improves." It may go down, or up, but it never improves as technology and medicine improve. All the wisdom we have collected about art has never helped the ungifted man to create. I read somewhere that science is a way of making the ordinary man intelligent. You cannot say of art what you can say of science—that it does grow on itself, that it creates a body of knowledge from which the individual can learn creativity.

Art changes only when remarkable persons—with a new technical language that is like a new human instinct—enter the picture. And when one such person does that, as we know from the influence of Eliot, Joyce, Picasso, Stravinsky—the next generation seems to live on him. Of course the historian, later on, will cite the sense of the age that such people possessed. But the uniqueness of the art language that makes the change makes it difficult for us to say, later on, just what is the relation between creativity and the age. It is the artist who illuminates the age, not the other way round.

On the other hand, when there is a lot of excitement in the arts, possibilities in new materials, new techniques, visions of new space to be filled, when there are extensions of perception, it is easy to feel that great things are going on—or should be. The sense of a vast cooperative undertaking in our time, with our sense of space, is overwhelming. But the more immediate and abundant our technical power, the more we lose the naïve, spontaneous imagination. Then we feel hemmed in by the power world that we have made and that is constantly reshaping us—we rebel against the impersonality that we see all around us and fear in ourselves. So imagination today may be all too often the opposite of what we Freudians think imagination is. For a long time we have all assumed that by honoring the "unconscious," the "spontaneous," primitivism, childhood, and sex, we would find our way back to the lost pre-industrial paradise.

In point of fact, I believe that in our culture, the imagination gets more and more sophisticated, self-conscious, abstract, intellectualized, manipulative. We are Prometheans who have stolen fire from the heavens for ourselves—and there are no gods to punish us. I view twentieth-century "modern" art as a prolongation of Romantic aspiration—the hero of our drama is still the individual in all his self-confrontation. The Romantics upheld individual experience and understanding in protest against the classical cult of the general. But though we honor the irrational, the dream-like, the "original" impulse, the attempt gloriously launched in the first twenty-five years of this century to win the mind away from a wholly acquisitive culture is more inspiring as history than as present fact.

Art can stand any tyranny, said the Russian critic and writer Andrei Sinyavsky—it cannot stand eclecticism. There are just too many ways of "knowing" these days for the artist to feel like a whole man. One of the most telling comments on what art is considered to mean nowadays occurred when Sinyavsky went on trial in a Soviet courtroom and had to—tried to—explain to his judges that when a character in a novel makes a statement, the author is not to be identified with that statement. Sinyavsky tried to explain to these people that the anti-Semitic remarks of a character in a book by his fellow-defendant, Yuli Daniel (himself a Jew), are not his, but those of people he has invented.

As I read the testimony given in that Soviet courtroom, I felt that art was on trial before the state. I remembered the exchanges during the McCarthy period between Arthur Miller and the Congressmen. I thought of the argument that goes on all the time between teachers of literature and really hep students. *Why* is art important? *Why* is *King Lear* more important than a clever comic strip? Our students have all been taught to take a poem apart, but not why a poem is different and so important. Art in our modern sense, expressive, radical, world-building art, the art of Lawrence, Eliot, Faulkner, Joyce, Proust, Stevens, Klee, Picasso, Stravinsky—the art that shattered more bourgeois ways of thinking than the Russian Revolution—this has become more and more difficult to practice in a world in which the imagination is shamed by the predominant rules of rationality and coerced by so many suspicious powers that be. And distrust of the imagination, uncertainty about what it is, fear of being stuck with a loser—keeps many an independent artist from the innocent eye that he really needs.

Of course a lot of people are trying to get back to "spontaneous imagination" by way of cultivated disorder—LSD is now only one of many short circuits to "feeling like an artist." There is also a carefully cultivated violence in certain arts. But these pale imitations of freedom, these postures of hatred, these super-defiant hints of just how wicked the artist could still be, if only the squares would let him—these are just part of the swinging scene. To be an artist is now a bourgeois ideal. But Lawrence said, "Never trust the artist; trust the tale."

Money is more important than ever, but there's no longer any prestige in amassing money. Art now has a brighter luster than gold—not really, of course, but so it seems to many parched and disenchanted souls weary of the business cycle and the war cycle. And even if you don't succeed in writing a good poem, you exhibit psychic freedom and impress the undergraduates. Allen Ginsberg used to be a poet; now he's a swami, a guru, the poet showing himself and declaring himself and encouraging others to show themselves and declare themselves. The writing of *poems* will perhaps not count as much. But Ginsberg is no threat to the state; and the loss of some possible poems, in our day when journalism as "history" dominates literature, is just white marks on snow.

The problem with the arts is that they may be becoming *trivial.* That is why I have this picture in my mind of dear Andrei Sinyavsky in a Soviet courtroom, trying to convey to his judges just what writing is about. He is paying for that failure with a harsh, possibly fatal sentence to a prison camp. Now despite the relative freedom we have in this country, our rulers, too, are more and more spoiled by power, quick to accept dominion over things they don't understand. I think of all the care, calculation, money, and insensitivity that went to burn up those three astronauts, and I don't have to ask what we care about as much as we care about conquering "outer space." It certainly isn't "art." We don't respect art enough for it to shape our personal culture, our moral decision.

SUPERMARKET EXCITEMENT

This writer living in New York today is not much impressed by the great new revolution in the arts. There's just too much slag. The excitement is in New York itself, in the stream of money pouring new hope into so many people, the constant change of fashion, the pop culture on display in all those Madison Avenue galleries and East River apartments, in the excitement that grabs on to the hope that art can mimic our hopelessly inflated surroundings. But how can you tell the dancers from the dance?

The action critic today is infatuated with the energy that seems to be pervading the art scene. Like the people who speak of getting "turned on," this new language in the arts can be very exciting. Obviously this feeling for advanced new rhythms everywhere has created some vital things. But what I'm talking against here is the state of mind that still sees art as self-expression. What the *self* gets out of making a work of art (especially when it doesn't make one) is irrelevant. In any event, modern literature is never directly about this conventional, social self, but uses it as a starting point for true self-investigation. Eliot said that poetry is not the expression of personality but the renunciation of personality. And that flies in the face of the American craving for unlimited self-satisfaction. In this whirligig we live in, this America so full of new buildings, automobiles, roads, supermarkets, in the midst of this glut, one does get sensations of enormous excitement and possibility. Modern times! Modern art! Modern, all modern! What a beautiful, exciting motion all around us! These instincts, these fleeting connections, may be expressed in art. When they are, I hope to recognize them. But I don't think that looking over the railing of a modern supermarket and looking at so much plenty, commotion, such a wild mix-up as America presents to us, makes one an artist because this disorder makes one *feel* like an artist.

My friend Jules Feiffer tells the story of a young lady wandering the fields of an artist colony. She had a large pad and paint box, and someone asked her, "Are you a painter?" She drew herself up haughtily and said, "What does the medium matter?"

Art is a very old habit with mankind, an old-fashioned way of *making* certain things. Literature, when compared with science, seems extraordinarily conservative. It can't really use the promptings to new fashion that have been sounded here. The "eclectic"—the distracting—make for too many substitutes. Marshall McLuhan is a clever man, but look at him now, selling his ideas, preaching that the medium is the message. So far as he's concerned, he's right. The medium in pop hamburgers *is* the work of art. And all this tries to justify its salesmanship as intellectual parody, even "self-parody," designed to make you see the artist or publicist as a critic of these new media, when obviously he's enchanted by them. So there are writers who claim that America is in such a terrible state that only "black humor" will do justice to the horror. But our society doesn't disgust them in the least—it delights them, especially when it supports enthusiastically these lively, would-be subversions.

The question I ask myself is: can art say anything to the overwhelming power that rules us just now? What is the relation of art to power? Can it—with use to itself—criticize power?

Matthew Arnold said that poetry is a criticism of life. Tolstoy was so sickened by the poverty he saw everywhere that he decided it was wrong to write novels; they couldn't touch the worldly powers that permitted injustice, and justice mattered. These nineteenth-century ideas of good and evil cannot be dismissed. Sartre, who is ahead of most living writers in thinking out the writer's duty to his fellowmen, even suggests that it may be wrong to write advanced literature for a few intellectuals when most of the world's people are illiterate and hungry.

In America advanced artists and their propagandists like to identify their alienation from existing society—which only wealthy hedonists can afford—with social protest. I was bored to death by Andy Warhol's *The Chelsea Girls;* it seemed to be a preposterously unlimited exercise in self-indulgence. What is most striking about it: when those fabulously good-looking girls and Eighth Street cowboys were invited to ad-lib—hour after hour!—they had nothing to say. The intellectual poverty of these human dolls is striking. What had any of that to do with power, poverty, war, oppression? It was just a camp home movie with a blown-up review that identified the picture with the sense of outrage many artists feel about Vietnam.

Of course that's not true. The arrogance of our leaders hasn't been and can't be touched by the arts, no matter how angry they get. Probably nothing that artists do can ever touch Johnson and Rusk in the least. But let's not pretend that the new erotic art, whose real interest and achievement is to tell the squares what sexual Milquetoasts they are, is any challenge to the money and privilege that keep our society what it is.

Ours is an ugly civilization. Our cities are ugly, our mass houses are designed by welfare workers and engineers, the very air in our great cities is poisoned. Over two hundred American boys are being killed every month in Vietnam. While the rich are getting richer, and money gets more and more important in every aspect of life, the poor—especially the Negro poor—irritate the affluent and the comfortable as the wretched always irritate the prosperous. The great books of the past showed the selfishness, vanity, and destructiveness of mankind. We are just as selfish and vain as the bourgeoisie we read about in Balzac. Where is the man who will describe *us* as we are? We look at soldiers being killed on our television screens, and we eat and drink as we look. Literature hasn't done a thing to improve our minds or our hearts.

Sartre said that to think of Proust during the war was to imagine a very fat lady in a tight velvet dress putting one bonbon after another into her mouth. American artists are more political than Proust ever was, but on me, at least, many American productions—advanced, commercial, super-Broadway, off-off-Broadway—have the same effect. They are sensitive to the disgust in the air, but they don't touch on the lives we really lead. Nathanael West wrote *Miss Lonelyhearts* because he still believed that to concentrate on so much suffering would somehow serve to shame people —to change them. I heard a speaker say how exciting it was to look down into a supermarket, to appreciate the disorder and vulgarity of panties and packaged bread being sold off the same shelves. More and more we are able to take the sacrifice in Vietnam of so many young men, the poisonous smoke in the air, the packaged panties and packaged bread—because the abundance of so much experience is exciting, even "aesthetic." No wonder that Robert Lowell's new poems are haunted by the Roman Empire. We are a madly heedless, domineering civilization. In this context, art is a plaything.

A FEW
GOOD THINGS

All the wisdom that runs so fluently about art in our time is, like so much talk about art, irrelevant to its real interest. Its real interest is the gift of the maker: *making* is what "poetry" means. The gift shapes the work, which means that it's beyond the artist's feeling ill or well, happy or unhappy. Of course some profound individuality of spirit influences the creative deed. No one who loves Bach, Michelangelo, Shakespeare, Blake, can miss the exceptional human person behind their works. The will to fame, the personal self-expressiveness or self-healing of the artist, has nothing to do with the value of what he makes.

Obviously it's getting more and more difficult for the writer to find a quiet place in his own mind and heart to write a book from. There are too many rival claims. But art, in any generation, still consists of the making of a few good things. Let me point out that this particular time has produced some very good poets—Lowell, Roethke, Berryman—some very fine novelists—Mailer, Bellow, Flannery O'Connor, J. F. Powers, Ralph Ellison— some extraordinary essays by James Baldwin.

Nothing is a substitute for genuine literary achievement. When it's there and exists solidly for the rest of us, we take heart—it helps us to live. As a teacher, I never get over the fact that a few people out of the 'twenties still provide essential spiritual ground for young Americans worrying about the draft and sickened by Vietnam. In this wildly sputtering, spurting, powerful, all-too-powerful country of ours, sometimes the only oasis for young people is a poem by Eliot or Frost, a story by Joyce, read in class.

Virtuosos of Boredom

HAROLD ROSENBERG

At first encounter, masterpieces of this century are likely to fatigue the reader or spectator rather than to tempt him. Not that Joyce or Stein, Schoenberg or Varèse, Mondrian or Pollock ever *intended* to bore their publics. Even Kafka, with whom tedium is a spiritual substance, is never purposely uninteresting; the greyness of his narratives is lighted by distant cries and by subsurface jests. *The Castle, Finnegans Wake,* the *Cantos, Déserts,* are difficult works; but to confuse difficulty with tediousness, as is done by conservative critics, is merely to exalt a taste for the facile and the familiar. The audience of modern art might legitimately complain that its sensibilities have been ignored but not that it has been put upon.

Recently, however, an aesthetic of boredom has been gaining prestige in all the arts as the most advanced approach of the moment. Tedium has become a goal, either as an affirmatively calculated effect (as in compositions of John Cage or "underground" movies of interminable length and homemade awkwardness) or as the inevitable consequence of the deliberate elimination of all qualities likely to be attractive to the mind, the senses, or the imagination (as in the wave of "reductive" paintings and sculptures). Samuel Beckett, declares a critic, Leo Bersani, in the spring issue of *Partisan Review,* "has been developing in his novels more and more effective strategies designed to make us find them unbearable." His current canvases, announces a well-known painter, present "cold zones, mostly reduced to black and white, from which have been excluded, to the maximum possible degree, lyricism, humanity, and warmth of expression." Examples of similar intent can be multiplied each week from among new films, concerts, dance recitals, even lectures.

Art has always run the risk of boring some people, and all people under adverse psychological conditions—it was Poe's great contribution to criticism to point out that a reader's genuine poetic response was limited to a matter of minutes. What is distinctive of today's art is that boredom is no longer left to chance. The new works insist on their utter plainness. Today, it is the artist, not some hostile critic, who underlines the non-presence in the work of every insight, feeling, or association that might make it interesting.

One might confirm the boredom of concerts of a pair of reiterated sounds or of exhibitions of purged canvases to the extent of staying away from them, but the motives behind such works are thoroughly intriguing. In painting, "inexpressive" art arose as a reaction against the intensity of Abstract Expressionism, particularly its Action painting aspect. The emotional disengagement of the artist from his work was conveyed in the sleekness of Pop Art and of Optical painting, the machine-shop spirit of kinetic sculpture, the rationalized impersonality of various forms of geometric and colour-field abstraction. The deletion of one layer of individuality after another has, as is customary in art, followed a steady logical progression. Pop reflected the artist's environment in dead pan; Op proclaimed his affiliation with the laboratory; current shaped canvases and "primary structures" have brought his back to the wall of the $2 + 2 = 4$ of space, "flat" and "deep." In accompanying movements the spectator has passed from the imaginative tension of Action painting, through the amused relaxation of Pop clichés, to the dazzle of Op, to, finally, the bafflement and boredom of paintings and sculptures denuded of sensibility.

As already indicated, however, the aesthetics of boredom extends over a far wider range than present developments in painting. Indeed, Abstract Expressionism has been a stubborn aberration in the drift in all the arts toward monotony, repetitiveness, and shedding of content. For years commentators have been proclaiming the continuous erosion that has been reducing to the vanishing point the mighty ego of the Romantics and of "inner-directed" man. With the ultimate neutralization of the self, any choice is futile and, as in the "chosiste" novels of Robbe-Grillet, human beings and events are alike mere extensions of *things*. The steady attrition of the qualities of man and nature, this view holds, determines both the direction of the arts and their meanings. Works closest to zero, or in Beckett's phrase the "endgame," are the most profound. In sum, the aesthetics of boredom and the quality-purged works of art are offshoots of the literature of alienation which has flooded Western civilization since World War II. Though its coolness appears as the antithesis of Existentialist anxiety, both have essentially the same source.

Action painting was an attempt to overcome the individual's loss of identity by concentrating on the act of creation and self-creation as the exclusive content of painting. It discarded recognizable subject matter, compositional harmony, and, on occasion, colour and drawing. It retranslated form and motif in order to make them serve the artist as the figure of contemporary man faced with anonymity. Affectless art begins with the negations of Action painting but, resigning itself to loss of identity, it denies the creative act, too, as a fraud and a self-deception.

Confronted by dance recitals consisting of random shufflings, sculpture exhibitions of toneless polyhedra, the audience experiences that combination of lassitude and impatience known as boredom. "How do we know," asks a writer in *Art News* about an Andy Warhol film, "anything was going on at all in *Blowjob?* All we saw was the image of a face, peculiarly blank." The point is not, as Allen Ginsberg is reported to have felt, to be stirred to enthusiasm by the artist's daring to be so empty. It is rather that the audience is being bored bears witness to the sober truth—that of the universal vacancy. Its ennui is a sign of philosophical profundity and of insight into the modern world.

Boredom is also an evidence of aesthetic virtue. It is proof that the artist has made no concession to popularity or success. In being bored the audience comes as close as possible to behaving as if it were not there. In the midst of America's hectic art boom the tiresome art work evokes the heroic days of modernism when art was created without thought of the spectator's response, and the artist was solitary and free. Andy Warhol does not ignore his audience but deprives it of peaceful enjoyment of its visual platitudes. With his genius for giving what one critic has called "a ratty look" not only to paintings but to the glamour-media of advertising and the news photo, the comic strip, the film, the discothèque he is a veritable Leonardo of boredom.

Through its Puritanism, boring art is associated with "pure" art, in the sense of art that is self-contained, obeys its own laws, and exists solely in and for itself. "In painting of this persuasion," writes an art critic of *The New York Times,* hailing the significance of paintings "deduced" from the shape of the stretcher to which the canvas is attached, the metaphorical element in art, or indeed all reference to anything that suggests the interpretation or transmutation of experience, is totally and cheerfully rejected, and a complete divorce is effected between the work of art and its commerce with the world of extra-artistic meaning." This rather cumbersome statement could describe the art for art's sake of the last century, except that for the concept of beauty there has been substituted the concept of the void. The virtuoso of boredom is a neo-aesthete who cares for nothing but art and strives for an art that cannot be cared for.

Collective boredom deliberately induced is a species of scandal. It is a way of committing a nuisance, an act of assault, albeit one in which the victim collaborates. Boring the audience is a device favoured by artists moved to revenge upon society, for example, on account of hardships suffered because of sexual peculiarities.

Also, art that is boring is almost invariably an art of double meanings, one (the blank) for the public, the other (winking references to friends, intimate incidents, shared opinions) for the family of insiders. This ambiguity is present regardless of the mode in which the work is executed—it is as characteristic of paintings of zones and stripes, which allude to concepts favoured by a faction of critics, as of Pop films acted by a cast of pals or a sculpture consisting of a table covered with after-breakfast items. The work is a masquerade that keeps the stranger at arm's length, yet prevents him from taking his leave by hinting at a significance that is never disclosed. Its impenetrable surface defeats him psychologically and humiliates him as a hopeless Philistine.

Behind this barrier the band of initiates, pampered by semi-initiates, romps happily in an atmosphere as relaxed as socks on the bathroom floor. By erecting a wall of incomprehension between those in the know and humanity at large, the boring painting or performance serves to strengthen the inner unity of the various ideological, sex, and taste groups that constitute the world of the arts.

The aesthetics of boredom are inconceivable without the enormous efflorescence of critical and interpretive writing in all the arts that has marked the cultural boom and the expansion of the universities since World War II. From the moment of its appearance, a painting, novel, or play is appropriated as an object of dissection by academically trained specialists with professional and intellectual interests of their own and equipped with a vocabulary increasingly more complex and self-sufficient. Several years ago, in a widely read article, Saul Bellow cried out against "deep readers" who refused to allow a work of literature to mean what it said—subsequent antagonism to *Herzog* came in large part from critics who found it too interesting to require their services.

To the critic the bareness of a work is an opportunity to display his powers of exegesis and to top other critics who might have given up the work as hopeless. In a recent instance, an art reviewer who had championed "minimal" art finally threw up her hands before the "literality, repetition, and boredom" of a sculpture exhibition of containers in rudimentary shapes; she was promptly challenged by another reviewer who expatiated for columns on the visual subtleties and depth of conception which she had missed in the objects in question. The ideal situation from the point of view of the new critics would be for works of art to vanish completely and for nothing to be left but the critical interpretation.

Today, no degree of dullness can safeguard a work against the determination of critics to find it fascinating. Even when boredom is the artist's explicitly stated objective, his intention will be frustrated by decorative inlays from the critical workshop. "It is . . . disconcerting," protests Bersani, "to read so many admiring, undaunted analyses of a significance for which Beckett . . . expresses only boredom and disgust. . . ." While Robbe-Grillet in a preface to one of his novels pleads with the reader to swallow the bald facts without interpretive dressing, "to see in it only the objects, actions, words, and events which are described, without attempting to give them either more or less meaning than in his own life, or his own death."

Nothing is boring to the specialist practicing his vocation. Under close scrutiny, an inch of skin or a page of the telephone book will yield wonders of accidental combination, alphabetic pattern, symbolic suggestion. Nor does boredom exist for the partisan or the promoter. The speeches of Stalin contained an infinity of wisdom for the Stalinist and the emotional possibilities of Father's Day are inexhaustible to the public-relations representative. One who denies the reality of boredom confesses to being dedicated to a cause or to having something to sell.

Boredom is experienced only by persons whose attentiveness is tuned to the human scale without the distortion of professional ambitions. It is an effect of disrupting the normal movement between the self and the external world. One is bored when the mind is forced back upon itself or when it is trapped in a situation which it is powerless to affect. Art inspired by the aesthetics of boredom embodies the prevalence of this disruption between the "I" and things in contemporary mass society. It is the mirror of the repetitiveness, unexpressiveness, the abstractness, the obsession with detail of daily life. The "message" of this art—and lacking pleasure, it is in all instances an art with a message—lies in urging its own rejection as a first step in the development of a free individual sensibility.

Words
Words
Words

The Language
of Nowspeak

VALERIE CARNES

I

Now that much of the sound and fury over hippies, yippies, flower power, student power, Berkeley, Chicago, and Columbia has begun to die away, and pot, acid, and speed have become as much household words as the name of Spiro T. Agnew, it is time at last for a long look at the language of the current youth movement. For at least one thing becomes increasingly clear as the underground begins to surface: the much-celebrated generation gap of the sixties was—and still *is*—largely a linguistic gap existing between standard English and Nowspeak, the language of the Movement, the youth under thirty and their over-thirty sympathizers.

To accept even the mildest form of the linguistic relativity thesis entails the admission that one's world view is to some extent relative to his language system. Clearly the world view of a twenty-one-year-old radical whose universe is built around large categories labeled "pigs," "heads," "the System," and "the Revolution" will manifest itself quite differently from that of his Establishment counterpart who still operates in terms of more conventional classes: "liberals," "conservatives," "Commie rats," "anarchists," "Democrats," "Republicans." The very existence of the language that I have christened Nowspeak affirms the existence of a large and active youth Underground. It also institutionalizes the subculture of Beatles and Stones and Fugs and Ché Guevara-ism, of "Hair" and Tarot cards, witches and warlocks, acid and grass, and gives it in the public eye a local habitation and a name. Hippies, hipsters, beats, pushers, and heads have been part of the Scene for a very long time—since the 1920s, in fact; it is their group names that remind Peter Schrag's Forgotten Americans of these embarassing Presences in a stolidly sentimental and conformist culture.

Thus for Movement and Establishment alike the language becomes symbolic. It does not only "stand for" or "point to" the subculture: it *is* the subculture. This fact should remind us of Paul Tillich's useful distinction between a sign and a symbol: the sign, he says, points the way to the thing, but the symbol participates in it. Nowspeak is a symbol of the life-style of the emerging subculture and also serves as the System's plumber's-manual guide to that life-style. It is symbolic in this sense both for those who use it and those who do not. Users align themselves against non-users. Nowspeaking youth draw a sense of solidarity and community from the language that represents their chosen style while the Establishment feels itself to be the nation's annointed people in part because it still speaks standard English. Non-users, presenting their case in conventional pig-Americanese, argue that Movement lingo is mindless, non-expressive, illiterate, obscene, and meaningless, while the other side argues with equal fervor that all the assertions and experiences of youth are incapable of verbal expression. As one girl recently put it, "If you've been there, you'll know it, and you don't need to talk about it." In the opening bars of *Their Satanic Majesties* the Stones urge their listeners to "open your heads, let the pictures come." Indeed, one of the hidden premises of Nowspeak is the assumption that there are many classes of experience which cannot and should not be verbalized. The act of verbalization is itself a dodge, a corruption of the experience, a "sell-out" or "cop-out" from the pure moment of sensation. I am well aware of the irony implicit in this study. This is not an essay on the language of the youth culture but instead on abstractions from that language as it is spoken, transposed onto the printed page. The most important characteristic of the language is that it is spoken, not written, and is therefore in a constant state of flux. Yet paradoxically the very nonverbal nature of the language is symbolic of the world view it both influences and reflects—anti-rational, action-oriented, visual, tactile, highly sensuous, primitive, ritualistic, colorful, emotive, solipsistic, and so always the language of the present moment, the immediate Scene, the place where the action is, or was—in short, the language of Now.

The primary source of Nowspeak is of course the language of other American bohemian movements. Nineteen-twenties bohemianism—Parisian expatriates, winos, Braque, Picasso, Hemingway, Stein and her beloved Alice B. Toklas, the rash of "little" magazines, and Zelda and Scott, those lovely lost children of Prohibition playing in the fountains at the Plaza—established the standard bohemian style and attitude: a sadly romantic, fatalistic, cosmopolitan, nonconforming, and lost generation of street-cafe and attic subcultures, writing poetry out of a golden alcoholic haze. Came the 1930s, and hipsters, jazz musicians, and an authentic hard-core drug underground began unwittingly to build the language that the young rebels of today's suburbia still speak. Jazz usages yielded such important terms as *action* (a general term for whatever is happening at the time), *bad* (for something very good, especially a woman), *blast* (get high), *bomb* (a failure), *bread* (money), *bug* (to annoy or disturb), *bust* (arrest), *cat* (any human being, especially a swinger), *chick* (a girl), *come down* (from a high), *cool* (ignore, snub, become less intense about a person or thing), *cut out* (leave), *dig* (understand or comprehend, in an emotional sense), *fag* (homosexual), *far out* (very advanced, ahead of its time), *funky* (basic, earthy, down-home), *groove* (a predilection or enjoyable thing), *head* (drug user), *lay* or *lay on* (to give or say), *make it* (have success), *put on* (to make fun of or ridicule without letting the victim know), *scene* (particular place or atmosphere), *stoned* (high or drunk), *turn on* (to get someone high on pot or to interest someone in a specific thing) and *wild* (remarkable). A high percentage of these terms still are in Nowspeak usage today.

Underworld language, which has found its way into Nowspeak, dates back to the time when the entire drug scene was largely confined to the fringes of society—the ghetto, the bohemian settlements, the underworld—and drug users were more or less forced by economic and social exigencies to live a life of petty crime. From this indigenous subculture come the standard slang terms referring to drug use: *cap* (drug capsule), *head* (user of drugs), *H, horse, shit, smack, duji* (heroin); *Mary Jane, MJ, pot, tea, grass, boo* (marijuana); *coke, snow, snowbird* (cocaine and its users). Most of these words are prepsychedelia and therefore refer to the more conventional drugs that were standard bohemian and ghetto fare from the twenties and thirties into the fifties and sixties—hashish, marijuana, heroin, cocaine, opium, benzedrine. Also from that nebulous area where underworld jargon coalesces with black ghetto talk come words dealing with the relations of the drug user and petty criminal with the police: *hit* (to be arrested), *bust* (to make an arrest, often for illegal drug use, as in "He got busted for possession last night"), *heat, fuzz,* or *the Man* (police), *uptight* and *strung out* (in desperate financial straits, usually as the result of intensive or prolonged drug use). One interesting term with underworld connotations is *straight*. A common word in homosexual and criminal society, it was first used to mean not with the particular "in" crowd in question (hence, heterosexual in one case, non-criminal in the other). Later the meaning became generalized so that the word now can refer to anyone who is not "with" a particular scene; hence, conventional, ordinary, not in the know, not "hip," generally "out of it." A more recent variant is more specific and less derogatory; it means "temporarily off drugs, clean for the moment," as in "Once I was straight for three days."

"Soultalk," the language of urban ghetto blacks, has become an increasingly important element in the vocabulary of the Nowspeaker, probably because of the heightened social consciousness of the Movement and its intense identification with minority groups of all kinds. Black "hip" and "soul" talk has added to Nowspeak such important words as *man* (generalized term of address, as in "Man, you're blowing my mind"), *ball* (to have sexual intercourse), *the Man* (the police; more generally, any Establishment figure, preferably white, in a position of power), *mother* (short for motherfucker, a term of derision and often hatred), *cat* (any male human being, especially a hip one), *hip* (with it, cool, in the know, under control), *hipster* (hip cat), *shit* (drugs in general), *tell it* or *tell it, man, lis'en at him, nigger* (in a soulful affectionate sense, not a condescending or derogatory one, as in "He's the baddest nigger I ever saw"), *something else* (pronounced *sum'pn else*), *police* (pronounced *po-lice*), *stuff* (heroin or the vagina), *bag* (originally, in the thirties, graft paid to the po-lice; now, a person's vocation, hobby, fancy, whimsy, or caprice, as in "that's your bag, man"), *strung out, uptight, cop* (originally an abbreviation for copulation, but by 1955 a synonym for the verb "to get," especially in relation to pot, hard drugs, hot goods, pistols), *boss* (something extraordinarily good or great, later replaced by *groovy, tough, beautiful,* and *out of sight*), *kill 'em* (for "give 'em hell," not as an expression of malice or violence). Other classics that often overlap into underworld and "beat" diction of the fifties and that have by now wandered into Nowspeak include *solid, cool, jive* (as noun), *jive-ass, thing, swing,* and *swinging* (the sixties added *swinger*), *pimp, dirt, freak, heat, right on* (term of approbation), *piece, sheet* (a jail record), *squat, square, stash, lay, mire, gone, smooth, joint, blow, play, shot, hassle, chick, junkie, bitch* (girl), *tight* (friendly), *O. D.* (overdose), *soul, soulfood, gig.*

Perhaps the single most important contribution of the black hipster is the word *baby* (pronounced "bay-buh," *a la* Janis Joplin), used in address to another, highly masculine, black male. Claude Brown offers this explanation of the elusive term in *Manchild in the Promised Land:*

> The first time I heard the expression "baby" used by one cat to address another was up at Warwick in 1951. Gus Jackson used it. The term had a hip ring to it, a real colored ring. The first time I heard it I knew right away I had to start using it. It was like saying, "Man, look at me, I've got masculinity to spare." It was saying at the same time to the world, "I'm one of the hippest cats, one of the most uninhibited cats on the scene. I can say 'baby' to another cat, and he can say 'baby' to me, and we can say it with strength in our voices." If you could say it, this meant that you really had to be sure of yourself, sure of your masculinity. . . . The real hip thing about the "baby" term was it was something that only colored cats could say the way it was supposed to be said. . . .

Haight-Ashbury summer of 1967, with the subsequent growth of the youth Underground and the more amorphous Movement, popularized and brought to the surface dozens of terms like these that had once been indigenous black soultalk in the thirties, forties, fifties, and early sixties, then found their way into the vocabularies of the children of affluent upper–middle-class WASP society. That the drug culture itself followed precisely the same pattern, out of the ghetto and into suburbia, is significant, for it suggests that the daily life-style of the Harlemite hipster and pusher was transformed into a middle-class elitist cult tinged with mystical overtones largely by the use of a bona fide drug-and-underworld language.

The hipster who came into prominence in the thirties and forties and finally sprang full-blown from the media in the fifties and sixties was a young male, often black, who was "hip" (originally, "hep" to the beat), extraordinarily aware, in the know, especially about jazz, drugs, and the street scene. The word "hippie," which came into national prominence in 1967, was being used in Harlem in the early 1950s to describe the uptown white who played at being a black hipster. Robert George Reisner's *The Jazz Titans* (1960) defines a "hippie" as a young person who is trying to put on hip airs but doesn't quite make it—thus, one who may be overly hip. Malcolm X's *Autobiography* recalls a similar incident: "A few of the white men around Harlem, younger ones whom we called 'hippies,' acted more Negro than Negroes. This particular one talked more 'hip' talk than we did" (p. 94).

Beat language of the fifties drew on all these sources—soultalk, jazz, drug, underworld and homosexual slang, hipster and hippie language. It incorporated all of these and yet, paradoxically, was unlike any of them. Norman Podhoretz in an early essay, "The Know-Nothing Bohemians" (reprinted as the first reading in this volume), comments on the "urban, cosmopolitan bias" of twenties' bohemianism, whose ideals were "intelligence, cultivation, spiritual refinement." By contrast bohemianism in the thirties, with its abundance of card-carrying Communists and Marxists, was colored by political radicalism, intellectual seriousness, and social reform. Podhoretz succinctly sums up the difference between earlier and later bohemianisms. The 1950s "beat" ethos, he comments, was hostile to civilization, worshipped primitivism, instinct, energy, "blood," was "cool" but mystical, irrational, spontaneous, anti-language, anti-analytical, and fascinated perennially, like Ginsberg's "angel-headed hipsters" and Kerouac's Dharma bums, with violence, drugs, Dada, surrealism, wine, and madness. Interestingly enough, the word "beatnik" was media-created: its genesis coincided with the furor over the Russian satellite Sputnik, and thus were the beats subtly and erroneously identified with Communist tendencies. The word "beat" itself referred at least in part to the ubiquitous jazz beat that was so much a part of the fifties Scene; it also meant, according to Kerouac, "beatified" or "beatific," suggesting a kind of frantic hip holiness in the beat stance. For the uninitiated it also meant disgust with middle-class philistinism and provinciality, utter disgust and exhaustion with the straight scene.

Beat language, like the Nowspeak of the sixties, was relatively simple. Adjectives were pared down to an eloquent few: *great* (greatest), *tremendous, crazy, mad, wild, groovy*. Nouns and verbs were simple and expressive: *bread* (money), *crash* (to sleep, from an old Hell's Angels' term that means "to die"; may also be used to refer to a temporary residence or sleeping space, as in "He's running a crash pad for pot heads"), *joint* (a marijuana cigarette), *roach* (the butt end of a joint), *pad* (place of residence, as in "Duke, they blowin' pot like mad up at Mildred's pad," from the R. Crumb cartoon, "The Adventures of Fritz"). Slang terms for drugs also were common beat usage, perhaps as a means of avoiding the fuzz: *MJ, pot, tea, grass, H, horse, shit, O, smack* and so on.

A merger between the beat culture and the folk song and the various war–civil rights–free-speech protests of the early sixties brought the Movement as it then existed out of Greenwich Village and the Haight onto the college campuses and coffee shops and into the media. The Berkeley Free Speech Movement (FSM) institutionalized and sanctioned the use of four-letter words as an authentic gesture of protest; civil rights demonstrations publicized words like *sit-in, demonstration, nonviolence, passive resistance,* SNCC, CORE, NAACP, *civil disobedience* and *God is on our side* (both phrases from Thoreau's famous tract), *happening, love-in,* and *riot.* The folk-singing phase of the movement, centering around sad-eyed lady of the lowlands Joan Baez and early pre-electronic Dylan, was the aesthetic equivalent of social and political nonviolence. In it was the ageless lure of wild cold woods and wind and salty sea, snow-white doves and long black veils, cruel ladies and love-sick knights, and forlorn maidens haunted by restless ghosts. It was poignant, sad, archaic, funny, and full of a simple moral outrage at war and racism; yet it was also cruel with a kind of barbarous innocence, the savage tenderness of the most ruthless of the Scottish Child ballads. And of course since beauty hurts Mr. Vinyl it could not and did not last. Although folk singing added few new words as such to the growing lexicon of Nowspeak, it introduced a down-home earthy lowdown shackdown niggerbaby blues plainness of style that set the cultural stage for the earliest of hippie life-styles.

In the mid-sixties the long-standing feud of British Mods and Rockers culminated in the cultural victory of Mod and so introduced a newly self-conscious element into the indigenous American youth cult. Magically the Scene shifted from Newport to Carnaby Street and Baez and Dylan were replaced overnight by Justin and Twiggy. Boutiques mushroomed in the most Establishment of department stores and funky sleazy minifashions, bell-bottoms, elephant pants, wide belts, boots, vinyl skirts, picture matches, fans, Tiffany paper lanterns, op, pop, the Liverpool sound, Victoriana, discothèques, light shows, go-go girls, vinyl hamburgers, and burgeoning Campbell soup cans spelled out the new message in dayglo colors: COME ALIVE, YOU'RE IN THE PEPSI GENERATION. Limp-haired and limpid-eyed Lolitas, chock full of vitamin pills and orange juice, put on granny glasses, French yé-yé knits, and little white vinyl boots. Boys adopted the Teddy Boy look and tried vainly to resemble John Lennon. The style of the hour was J. C. Penney transcendentalized by Quant and Courrèges, and the media responded fittingly with a shiny new slickspeak: "where it's at," "the action generation," "the Now people," "the Pepsi generation," "the Beautiful People," "camp art," "happenings" (which included such questionable activities as smashing grand pianos with hammers while, in the background, thirteen radios blared *forte fortissimo* and painted go-go girls did action paintings on the side). Some of this jargonese was simulated British slang (girls were "birds" or "model girls," thanks to Twiggy and Mary Quant), and if they wore *minis* or *microminis,* they were *kooky, kinky,* and had "the knack" (after a British art film of that name). It was the heyday of the microcosm, the diminutive, a mod mod mod Lilliputian world for all the Little People. Everything from the poor-boy skinny-rib sweater to Vesuvius erupting was "fun," "crazy," "super," "marvellous," "fantastic" or "groovy." Clothes were fun things. Shoes were to fall in love with. Makeup was super stuff. Discothèques were fun places. Arnel was when. Yé-yé. Yeah. Yeah. Yeah.

Hippie summer of 1967, heralded by the Human Be-In in San Francisco and by the haunting imperative issuing from every jukebox across the nation, instructing the new generation to wear a flower in its collective hair, saw the first full-scale surfacing of the new-style Underground of the sixties. By August of 1967 every major magazine from *Playboy* to the *Saturday Evening Post* was preparing its own lead article on the hippie phenomenon, complete with full-color photographs of lush paradisal landscapes where lank golden girls ran barefoot forever through the Koda-chrome grass, their long manes tumbling in the wind, light shows and artlessly painted bodies gyrating in time to invisible acid rock bands, gaunt gurus wordlessly holy on acid, celluloid flowers, newspaper posters, head shops, Diggers, Hell's Angels, Leary and Ginsberg leading mantras, and bespectacled bearded boys with beads and bells and Digger hats and bloodshot eyes that seemed to see beyond the world they never made to some better secret cloud–cuckoo-land green with the sweet aroma of burning grass. The ceremony of innocence had begun, and from every-where the summer hippies converged on the Haight. When they arrived they found a prefabricated culture waiting for them: buttons, a ready-made dress style, head shops full of groovy merchandise, records, drugs, crash pads, free stores, free food, free love, free rock and an instant name, "hippies." To go along with all this there was, not surprisingly, a language. With very minor variations it was 1920s bohemian, thirties hipster-drug-soultalk out of fifties beat by way of folk-protest-rock-yeah-yeah-mod-yé-yé, and all systematized and solidified by the ever-present media. The hippies' chief contribution to Nowspeak was in the area of drug euphemisms. Many of these were the old reliables of the twenties and thirties resurrected for the occasion: *pot, tea, boo, horse, O, joint, roach, grass, fix, connection, stash.* Others were relatively new, having sprung up like the holy mush-rooms of Mexico in response to the new and popular psychedelics or "head" drugs: *hallucinogenic, buzz, flash, crash, LSD, acid, STP, speed, crystals, downer, bummer, freak-out, freaked out, freak* (as noun: acid freak, print freak, speed freak, motorcycle freak), *head, breakthrough* (also a military and scientific term), *trip, trip out, doing one's own thing, bag, groove.* Many words used to describe the effects of the psychedelics were phrases taken over from descriptions of the state of alcoholic inebriation: *high* (in a state of euphoria achieved by drugs or alcohol; as a noun, the state itself, or more generally, an overall sense of joy or well-being, as in "When I was on a high I thought I would found this groovy scene, see, 'Teen-age Evangelism' "), *stoned* (excessively high on drugs, "I want to save that for later when we're stoned") and so on.

Significantly, many "In" phrases at the time were implicit mechanical metaphors like Timothy Leary's famous injunction to "tune in, turn on, drop out"—figures of speech that are all drawn, implicitly or explicitly, from radio or television. "Turned on," used as an adjective, meaning high or under the influence of drugs or, more generally, receptive to drugs or to experience of any kind, especially that of an unconventional nature, illustrates the tendency of such words to broaden their range of possible meanings. (We already have noted that early jazz usage limited the "turn-on" to drugs and Charlie Parker's horn.) Another electronic-mechanical metaphor is the word *vibe,* short for *vibrations.* Like *turned on* it also has a more generalized meaning than merely the implicit mechanical metaphor: it may refer to the atmosphere or spirit of a scene or person, or to the cosmic forces present in a particular setting. Thus a person, scene, event, or general situation is said to send out *good vibes* or *bad vibes,* depending on the speaker's reaction. Witches and warlocks were much prized on the Haight-Ashbury scene in 1967 for their ability to psych out good vibes. The term thus suggests a coalescence of electronic and cosmic-mystic metaphors of popular occultism. Mysticism and the occult also added *guru, yoga, meditation* (one was said to be "on meditation"—an obvious transfer of the drug metaphor to a nondrug experience), *sadhana* (Hindu equivalent of one's own thing), *karma* (destiny), *horoscope, zodiac, warlock, witch, sitar, mantra, hare krishna, maharishi, swami, mandala, veda, Gita, om,* and the elusive *vibe.*

It is difficult to overestimate the importance of the hippie subculture that began in 1967. It gave disaffected American youth, disillusioned by an ugly and senseless war and by a growing credibility gap, a rallying point and a locus of their new self-image. It also gave rise to a whole horde of movements that were and still are only tangentially related to hippiedom, but somehow still acquire guilt or innocence by association: SDS, student power, antiwar protest groups, YIPPIE (Youth International Party), the Chicago demonstrations of 1968, disturbances at Columbia, Harvard, Cornell, and San Francisco State, the Woodstock music festival, and the People's Park episode in Berkeley, 1969. Out of each of these small movements has arisen a set of chants, slogans, words, and phrases that for one reason or another caught on and became part of the language system: "all power to the people," "up against the wall, mofo," "into the streets," "down with pigs," "student power," "zap the world with love," "chicks up front," "give a flower to a cop," "Ho, Ho, Ho Chi Minh," "Hey, hey, LBJ," "Right on!" Specific events have also added to this new idiom. Thus Abbie Hoffman in a passage from *Rights in Conflict* describes the origin of the two terms *pig* (cop) and *Yippie* (Youth International Party member), which became the semantic poles of the Chicago riots in the summer of 1968: "There we were, all stoned, rolling around the floor . . . yippie! . . . Somebody says oink and that's it, pig, it's a natural, man, we gotta win" (p. 29).

As the passage above illustrates, much of the language was an authentic response to an immediate situation; some of it, however, was media-created or was given national prominence by the media: *name of the game, the generation gap, the credibility gap, where the action is, never trust anyone over thirty, the In Crowd, the Now Generation, the new morality, where it's at, the flower children, flower power* (this one attached to a photograph of a pig-hippie confrontation in San Francisco where the hippies zapped the barrels of the cops' guns with flowers), *charisma, tell it like it is* (possibly a corruption of the black "tell it" or "tell it, man"), *the Beautiful People* (originally a *Vogue-Bazaar* jet-set term transferred to the under-thirty crowd sometime during that eventful summer of 1967). Buttons contributed their share of slogans, too: "Save water, shower with a friend," "War is harmful to children and other living things," "Draft beer, not students," "Reality is a crutch," and "Frodo lives" and "Welcome to the Middle Earth," an in-signal for Tolkien lovers everywhere. Pop psychiatry and sociology contributed *confrontation, meaningful relationship* (*Newsweek*, 3, February 1969, calls this one a substitute for "campus sex"), *hang-up* (any psychological problem; also, any intense or consuming interest in anything), *strung out, relate, relevant, irrelevant* (said to be true of all academic pursuits), *therapy, shrink* (a psychiatrist, as in Arlo Guthrie's "Shrink, I wanna kill"), "group" (for group therapy), *group dynamics, T-group* (sensitivity-training session), *communicate, communication, nude therapy, body language, life-style, crisis, dialogue* (or *meaningful dialogue*) and *commitment*.

II

It should be obvious from a look at the sources above that any attempt to systematize the language of Nowspeak is doomed to failure. The language is "post-Gutenberg," is primarily spoken and only secondarily written, and thus does not take kindly to the printed page. Moreover, precisely because it *is* a spoken language, it is changing at a much faster rate than standard English and is therefore subject to continual revision. Today's In signal may be tomorrow's dead metaphor. Changes in vocabulary and syntax are passed on by word of mouth within inner circles of the nebulous "Movement" and eventually filter out to the farthest fringes with some effect on the media *en passant*. A study of this sort needs constant revision; otherwise it cannot keep pace with the rapid rate of change in the language of this important and growing subculture. Nevertheless, an attempt at classification of the types of words and phrases most used by American youth under thirty may prove useful at this juncture. For the sake of clarity a systematic outline incorporating the conventional parts of speech will be used with the full and ironic realization that such an outline is itself an imposition of an artificial structure on a highly unstructured and loosely-formed language.

A. Nouns

1. Nouns used to identify the enemy of the Movement: *the Establishment, the Man* (any authority figure, particularly the police), *narcs* (narcotics agents), *pigs* (or *fascist pigs*), *motherfuckers, pig-fuckers, uptights, straights, the Right, over-30s, fascists, racists, conservatives, sell-outs, the System, game-players, imperialist lackeys, capitalists (capitalist pigs), turned-offs, warmongers, hawks, the Administration* (national or academic), *hung-ups, fuzz, heat, attack squad*.

2. Nouns used to identify the Movement and its members, as opposed to the enemy: *the Movement, the New Left, the anti-Establishment, the In Crowd, the Now Generation, the Now People, the youth cult, freaks, with-its, hippies, yippies, the head community, the Underground, teeny-boppers* (high school students, often in a derisive sense), *radicals, peaceniks, smarts, heads* (or *cool heads, good heads*), *cop-outs, drop-outs, flower children, militants, pacifists, spades, brothers, revolutionaries, the Revolution, baby, chicks, niggers* (as term of approbation or approval: see section I), *blacks, the beautiful people, cats* (beat usage), *hips, connections, dealers, pushers, users* (of drugs), *kooks, kinks, Diggers* (hippie social workers named after seventeenth-century English farmers who gave food to the poor), *Hell's Angels, groupies* (girls who attach themselves to pop rock singers).

3. Nouns and noun phrases used to identify certain activities or to suggest what's going on at a particular moment in a particular place. Many of these, as we already have seen, are media-produced: *be-in, sit-in, love-in, human be-in, teach-in, demonstration, revolution (The Revolution), happening, guerilla theatre, guerilla warfare, confrontation, flower power, session, trip, good (bad) bag, riot* (police, student, black, ghetto), *action, where the action is, where it's at, kicks, the Scene, commune, gig* (originally a musical term, now any activity such as a light gig or a drug gig. Contrast with *bag,* someone's thing, a deep obsessive involvement, as a Beatles' bag, a speed bag), *piece of the action* (originally a criminal term used to describe someone muscling in on your territory), *put-on, freak-out, light show, what's happening, power* (student, black, flower, to all the people), *the Age of Aquarius.*

4. Drug terms, usually nouns or adjectives or a combination of both. In this class of words belong the standard drug-underground and "hip" or "beat" drug jargon that has been in existence for several decades, and has reference largely to the conventional, non-psychedelic drugs: marijuana, hashish, kif, opium, heroin, cocaine. Included in this class are *MJ, pot, boo, tea, grass, H, horse, duji, snow, shit, smack, hash, coke, head, lid* (ounce of MJ), *connection, drop, fix, joint, roach, hype* (hypodermic needle). In addition to the old standards the following terms have also come on the scene: *amphetamine* (pep pills in straight usage: *benzedrine, dexedrine, methadrine), acid* (LSD: lysergic acid diethylamide, the initials of which were popularized in the Beatles' "Lucy in the Sky with Diamonds"), *toke* (to take a puff or hit on a joint), *acid-funk* (LSD-induced depression), *acid rock* (rock and roll with psychedelic orientation), *cyclert* (magnesium hydroxide and per-moline, a memory stimulant), *dime bag* (a $10 bag of MJ), *DMT* (dimethyl tryptamine, a hallucinogenic drug), *downs* (downies or barbiturates), *freak rock* (acid rock), *hard drugs* (addictive drugs), *head drugs* (psy-chedelic drugs), *nickel bag* ($5 bag of marijuana), *owsley* (the Rolls-Royce of the LSD capsules, named after its inventor, Augustus Owsley Stanley III), *quarter bag* ($25.00 bag of marijuana), *run* (amphetamine

high), *scag* (heroin), *soft drugs* (hallucinogenic drugs), *spaced* (originally, an amphetmine high; now, any drug high), *speed, STP* (a recently discovered hallucinogen; the *East Village Other* reports that the initials may stand for "serotonin triphosphate"; *Time* believes that STP may be chemically described as 5-methoxy-NN-dimethyltryptamine; says *Innerspace,* "Where LSD is general, STP is specific, exposing you to pure molecular energy, beyond mysticism, beyond love, beyond Maya: IT"), *tea-totaller* (a purist in matters of drug use who refuses commercially-processed grass or other commercial drugs; the sort of diehard who will still be rolling joints lovingly and ritualistically by hand long after the rest of the world is turned on by commercial preparations), *yellow submarine* (a barbiturate capsule), *head shop* (place selling psychedelic merchandise), *snappers* (amyl nitrite ampoules), *crystals* (methedrine or meth: Denver is called "Crystal City" because of the great amount of meth available there), *Acapulco gold* (or simply *gold,* a high-grade Mexican marijuana), *trip, bummer* (bum trip), *brick* (a litter of uncut marijuana, as in "He has a couple of bricks coming in from Mexico soon"), *buzz, flash, breakthrough, backwards* (tranquilizers; any central nervous system depressant), *benny* (benzedrine), *cannabis* (Indian hemp, hash, MJ), *forwards* (speed), *key* or *ki* (about 2.2 pounds of any drug, usually pot, compressed into brick form), *matchbox* (a small amount of marijuana, enough for about five to eight joints).

5. Besides the words describing the enemy, the Movement, and the Scene, and the accompanying drug terms, there are many proper nouns with charisma and connotative power that have come into prominence in recent years as a result of the youth movement. Like Stewart Alsop's over-thirty Pavlovian intellectual liberal, the Nowspeaker divides the world into certified Good Things and People and certified Bad Things and People. There are names with negative charisma: LBJ, "the Hump," Mayor Daley, Madison Avenue, Wall Street, Joe McCarthy, Judge Hoffman—in short, any member or artifact of the Establishment. To respond favorably to these names is a sure sign of having sold out to the System. On the other hand, there is another semantic set composed of culture heroes, things, and organizations with positive charismatic power: Black Panther, Hashbury, Hobbits, Ché Guevara, Huey P. Newton, Bobby Seale, Janis Joplin, Norman Mailer, Eugene McCarthy, Eldridge Cleaver, John Lennon, Yoko Ono, the Stones, the Doors, Sergeant Pepper, Jerry Rubin, Big Brother, Timothy Leary, Allen Ginsberg, Herbert Marcuse, CORE, CADRE, Friends, YIPPIE, Paul Krassner, Fritz the Cat, Tom Hayden, Rap Brown, Ravi Shankar, Abbie Hoffman, the Blackstone Rangers, and so on.

B. Adjectives and words used adjectivally

1. Derogatory terms used to describe the enemy: *square, uptight, fascist, racist, out of it, not with it, not where it's at, plastic, unreal, structured, conservative, pluty* (plutocratic), *Establishment* (as adjective,

as in "You're so Establishment, Mother"), *tense* (serious or dangerous), *heavy* (may be disparaging, or may simply indicate dismay at great depth and apparent complexity as in, "That's a heavy scene, man" or "I'm into some heavy stuff now"), *uncool* (connected in some way with the Scene but unable to cope with all its happenings and hassles), *hung-up* (all enmeshed in some psychological problem, a *bag* of some kind, and thus unable to swing), *straight* (in its narrow sense, a person who isn't in the know or In about some scene, such as drugs, homosexuality, protest, or guerilla theatre; more broadly, it refers to a person or scene not connected with or very aware of the Now world—most parents, college officials, mass media, and politicians are *straight*).

2. Terms of approbation used to describe members of the youth cult: *hip, wild, freaky, real, with it, sexually enlightened, swinging, unstructured, gutsy, cool* (in tune with the Scene, implies flair and finesse in moving within this scene and coping with contingencies and vicissitudes), *funky* (wild, uninhibited, down-home earthy), *groovy* (pleasant in a "with it" way), *trendy, turned-on, spaced* (or *naturally spaced* outside the conventional realm of things; as a drug metaphor, it means totally disoriented), *boss, "George," out of sight* (excellent, beyond compare), *beautiful* (all-purpose term of approval; a favorite Now accolade is "You're a beautiful person"), *electric, far-out, crazy, frantic, clean* (temporarily free of drugs or money, though not straight), *fun* (as in "She's a fun person" or "it's a fun scene"), *up, high, super* (gives intensive force, as a superminiskirt is a micromini), *tripped out, tough, sexy.* A Yippie flyer distributed during the Chicago demonstrations of 1968 calls for "a generation of people who are freaky, crazy, irrational, sexy, angry, irreligious, childish and mad" and thus sums up the emotive force of many of the Good Thing adjectives (see *Rights in Conflict,* p. 68).

C. Verbs

One of the linguistic paradoxes of Nowspeak is that, while it is an action language for an action generation, designed to mirror a world always caught in the instant of becoming, nevertheless common usage reveals only a small number of verbs used with any regularity. The verbs fall into two main classes: common verbs that are part of everyday Americanese, used by the Nowspeaker in a special, often metaphorical sense, and less common verbs, often more gutsy, slangy, onomatopoeic, colorful words than conventional verbs. Many of these verbs commonly govern certain nouns or prepositions or appear as part of phrases fixed by custom and usage: *trip out, go up, come down, cop out.* For the sake of clarity the whole verb phrase when necessary will be listed here with variants.

1. Common verbs:
  a. *be* (strung out, uptight, high, stoned, tripped out, in a bag)—an all-purpose verb describing any state of being that the speaker wants to convey. As a noun, appears in compounds like *be-in, human be-in.*

b. *blow*—to smoke, as in "to blow pot like mad." To perform well musically or verbally. To leave. To experience homosexual intercourse or heterosexual oral-genital contact. *To blow one's mind,* to experience any strange or stimulating mental or psychic sensation, particularly one with consciousness-expanding or hallucinogenic overtones; to consciously experience stark amazement about a particular happening or situation; thus, to be totally overwhelmed by a new perception, whether on or off drugs. As a derogatory term, it means to experience an astonishing or anger-provoking experience, similar to *bad vibes* or a *bad trip,* as in "Man you're blowing my mind." Yippie literature prior to the Chicago demonstrations speaks of burning down the city in an effort to "blow their [the public's] minds."

c. *bring (down)*—to cause to come off a high; hence, to cause a lapse from euphoria, happiness, or well-being as in the Beatles' song, "She says that livin' with me is bringing her down."

d. *bug*—to annoy or perturb, as in "this scene really bugs me."

e. *burn*—to rob, to be shot or arrested.

f. *bust*—to arrest; *(to get* or *be) busted*—to be arrested by the pigs.

g. *come* (down)—to wear off a high. *Come (on)*—to adopt an approach, attitude, or life-style, as in "He comes on too strong," "He comes on uptight."

h. *cut* (out)—to leave, as "I'm cutting out."

i. *dig*—to understand or comprehend, to experience a feeling of joyous rapport with, as in "I dig you," "I dig that groovy scene," "they dug the idea of people coming to Chicago and grooving there."

j. *do* (up)—to enjoy a thing; a general term of action, as in "Let's do up this scene." To *do* (one's own) thing—to do whatever the Nowspeaker feels is necessary, right, and appropriate to his own life-style, peace of mind, and physical and spiritual well-being.

k. *drop* (out)—to remove oneself voluntarily from a scene, especially from society (straight society) at large. To *drop* acid—to take LSD, as in "I dropped my first acid in Paris," "I dropped 250 mikes (micrograms) last night." As a noun, *to make a drop,* to deposit grass, acid, or speed or another drug with another head, hopefully in a stash out of sight of the pigs.

l. *go* (up)—to get high, as in "I go up on grass." *Go down,* same as *bring down,* as in the Beatles' song, "Happiness Is a Warm Gun." Also, *to go*—to act without inhibitions, as in "Go, man."

m. *make*—general term which may refer to a chick (balling her), a scene, a drop, or a hit. To *make it*—to succeed, to groove with some scene, as in the Simon and Garfunkel song, "I know I'm . . . not really making it." *To make the scene*—much like *groove* (see *groove).*

n. *lay* (something) on—to give, as in "Lay some bread on me," or "he laid some acid on me last night." Sometimes simply *lay it on me, man*—roughly equivalent to *tell it, man.*

o. *put* (on)—to freak (someone) out, often with hallucinogenic overtones; to make fun of or ridicule without the victim's knowledge. To *put down,* to criticize, reject, disparage; also to stop some action or habit. As a noun, a *put-down* is the perfect Now squelch.

p. *tell* (it)—exclamation taken over from Southern black speech; indicates enthusiastic approval: "tell it" or "tell it, man" are the most common forms.

q. *sell* (out)—to go over to the enemy camp, for fun or profit, with strong derogatory overtones. Getting a Ph.D., a haircut, or a job with the grey-flannel-suit crowd are all forms of selling out to the Establishment. As a noun, a *sell-out* is one who has renounced the Movement and joined the System.

2. Less common verbs with specialized meanings:

a. *ball*—from black speech. To have sexual intercourse, as to *ball* a chick. Less specifically, to *ball* is to have a good time, to groove.

b. *buy* (out, me)—to sell out to the Establishment.

c. *cool* (it)—to come off it, to exhibit cool, to act in a less intense, more disinterested, less strung-out manner; to taper off, ignore, or snub, as in "I'm cooling on Jim," "I'm cooling it with the Stones bag," "You better cool it."

d. *cop*—to get, buy, steal, make a permanent loan of, or "liberate" an object. To *cop out*—to give up, succumb to conventional pressures, depart the Scene, sell out to the Establishment.

e. *cope*—to handle ordinary tasks in straight society while tripping.

f. *crash*—to come down hard and fast from a psychedelic high; also, to sleep or to reside briefly. As an adjective, a *crash* pad, a place to sleep for a night or several nights.

g. *deal*—to sell drugs.

h. *flash*—to experience an intense pleasurable sensation with hallucinogenic overtones; also, to hallucinate, as in "When I was stoned on acid I flashed this heavy scene." As a noun, *to have a flash,* to experience a hallucinogenic state during which some thing or person is clearly seen.

i. *flip*—to go wild. "Then he flipped his wig (lid)."

j. *fly*—to get with the drug scene, be high on drugs.

k. *freak* (out)—to engage in wild, uninhibited irreverent behavior; thus riots are said to "freak out the pigs." To have fun. To change something radically (painting a bus in psychedelic dayglo colors is freaking the bus). To experience a bad trip. As a noun, a *freak-out* or *freak* is anyone who engages in a particular life-style: a beach freak, speed freak, acid freak, print freak. May be a term of endearment, as in Arlo Guthrie's famous greeting "Hi, freaks!"

l. *gas*—to excite or overwhelm.

m. *groove*—to move with the Scene in a fun, uninhibited style; to move in harmony with the universe, as in "grooving with the (Village, Hashbury, Old Town, San Francisco) scene."

n. *hassle*—to engage in a squabble, trouble, heated disagreement, or discussion, as in "I just don't want to hassle the draft board."

o. *hit*—to request money or sexual favors.

p. *hold*—to have drugs on your person or close at hand; hence, Big Brother and the Holding Company.

q. *hustle*—to bend effort to bring about something such as money, permission from parents or authorities, or sexual surrender of a partner.

r. *pick* (up on)—to obtain, feel, understand, appreciate, as in "I picked up on the Stones' last album."

s. *psych* (up)—to be excited in anticipation of something. *Psych out,* to figure out by intuitional rather than logical means, as in "I psyched out the scene," "I psyched out the prof the first day," "He psyched me out."

t. *push*—to sell drugs or other illicit items and services; more broadly, to make any active attempt to manipulate your environment.

u. *rap*—to achieve rapport through conversation, especially of the stream-of-consciousness type, as hip speakers say, "nonlinearly," letting conversation drift where it will, aimlessly, rather than directed to conclusions; as in "He spent three hours rapping to me about you." Also, more specifically, to talk rapidly and compulsively while high on amphetamines.

v. *score*—to attain success in drugs or sex, get what you want, as in "I scored with that chick." To procure concrete goods or services or external recognition.

w. *screw*—to have sexual intercourse. More generally, to blow someone's plans, as in "The prof screwed me on that quiz."

x. *split*—to leave, to go, as in "He split the scene."

y. *spook*—to give off bad vibes, to blow one's mind, often with mystical and/or derogatory overtones. Thus Abbie Hoffman in an account of a meeting between the Chicago *Seed* group, and some New Yorkers recalls, "In the original schedule I wrote 'Wednesday —police riot' and that spooked them" (*Rights in Conflict*, p. 37).

z. *stone(d)*—used as past participle; high on drugs, completely out of control.

aa. *swing*—to enjoy oneself in grooving with a particular scene, often in a sexual sense; to be a spontaneous effective participant in any ongoing thing.

bb. *trip* (out)—to take hallucinogenic drugs for the purpose of in- ducing hallucinations, visual effects, heightened sensory experiences; to be *tripped out* refers to the sort of psychic disorientation that one experiences while *on a trip*. Used as in "While I was tripping I be- lieved that the only way to get a cup of coffee was to drop the phone in the mashed potatoes."

cc. *tune* (in)—to groove, to be in harmony with a certain scene.

dd. *turn* (on)—to get high on drugs. To turn (someone else) on to something, to introduce him to and create an interest in drugs, music, or some other activity.

ee. *zap*—to hit in a figurative sense, to overwhelm, to get directly to another person, to present (something) in a memorable way, as in "to zap the pigs with flowers," "zap the world with love."

ff. *zen-in*—to interest, read a mind, know intuitively.

gg. *zonk* (out)—to trip out or totally fascinate.

D. Expletives

The Movement is largely responsible for bringing to public attention and into the media such hitherto-forbidden words as *shit, screw, mother- fuckers, asshole* and others. *Fuck* is usually used in a generalized sense, not so much as a reference to sexual intercourse as a sort of verbal nose-thumbing at society and social mores, as in "Go fuck yourself," "Up against the wall, mofos." Significantly, most of the metaphors are implicit anal metaphors; few are explicitly sexual in nature. A parallel is found in "acid rock" music, in which the double entendre is not pri- marily sexual but drug-oriented.

One interesting aspect of Nowspeak is that there are no adverbs of any note, no subordinate conjunctions, few connectives—in short, little else besides the nouns, verbs, adjectives, and expletives named above. Many of the words double as two parts of speech at once: *head,* for example, is both noun and adjective, as in "He's a groovy head," "an acid head," or "the head scene." *Trip* and its variants become noun, adjective, or verb, depending on usage: "on a trip," "tripped out," "to trip out." However, besides the common nouns, adjectives, and verbs there are only three other important categories of words: prepositions, phrase markers, and coordinating conjunctions. The most common prepositions are "in," "into," "on," "off," and "out of." *Into* for the Nowspeaker connotes the act of doing or producing something or the state of participating in some scene: "He's into speed," "She's into posters now," "They're into the drug scene," "I'm into heavy stuff." *Rights in Conflict* offers two examples from Abbie Hoffman: "Many people are into confrontation. The Man is into confrontation" (p. 72) and "They're the Left, they're into heavy words, words mean something—I'm into emotion, I'm into symbols and gestures and I don't have a program" (p. 34).

Similarly, "in" connotes purposeful involvement in some activity, as in the 10 February 1969 issue of *Time,* which quotes the editor of *Ramparts* as saying, "We went in to hang the CIA," "We went in to hang the Saigon government." The preposition *on* is generally used in a specific sense to denote being involved in the use of a certain drug: "he's on speed now," "they're on opium," "I'm holy on acid." One of the striking facets of the meditation bag that swept the country during the winter of 1967–68 was the use of the term *on meditation*—obviously a drug metaphor that had extended itself to a non-drug activity.

The most common phrase markers are seemingly meaningless phrases that serve as punctuation marks in the long rambling elliptical sentence structure of Nowspeak, "I mean," "you see," "see?" "like," "man," and "dig?" I say "seemingly meaningless," for their very incoherence and open-endedness is quite significant. It is as if no Nowspeak sentence is ever quite finished; all statements seem to trail off into a string of ellipses. The well-formed formula (WFF) of symbolic logic that completely expresses a single proposition $[(P \supset Q) \cdot (R \supset X) \therefore (P \supset X)]$ is no longer the prevailing mode of discourse, because logical propositions themselves are no longer the prevailing mode. Nowspeak does not set forth propositions: it creates emotive states, excites, turns on, titillates, soothes, cajoles, puts on, puts down, freaks out, grooves, and blows its listeners' and readers' minds. What Nowspeak does not say often is far more significant than what it says, and in this respect it is poles apart from standard English.

The usual coordinating conjunctions are *and, but,* and *or.* In the absence of subordinate conjunctions, which place one thing in a grammatically subordinate or inferior position to another, either temporally, logically, or causally, and thus imply choice or value judgments (this is the famous Hemingway style), Nowspeak at its worst can read like a bad parody of *Across the River and Into the Trees.* Perhaps we can even see reflected in Nowspeak's plethora of compound and run-on sentences, its fierce emphasis on social and ideological equality, its dogged insistence that anyone's opinion is as good as anyone else's, and a genuine reluctance to make verbal value judgments about matters of rank and order. Nowspeak thus lends itself well to a rambling, stream-of-consciousness elliptical style which is partly the rhythm of modern advertising slogans ("Arnel is when . . .", "Winston tastes good like a cigarette should"), partly a written transcription of colloquial speech ("that spooked them, I mean they, these people were kids, you know," *Rights in Conflict,* p. 37), and partly an authentic and indigenous new prose sty!e. The style of the hour is characterized by the use of highly conventional if colorful figures of speech ("in a bag," "spaces me out," "out of sight"), a high incidence of run-on, compound, and open-ended sentences, and the incantatory, almost mantra-like repetition of certain words and phrases that serve to fill in those freaky holes in time, in your head, in the world out there. Wild. Groovy, you know, like I mean. Oh, wow.

III

Like any language system, Nowspeak has its own value system built into it. The language serves several purposes at once: it is a code to freak out the ever-present Establishment, it solidifies the feeling of community among this tenuously-bound subculture and assures its members that the Underground, the Movement—even the Revolution—really do exist, even if it's only in your head, and finally, it polarizes present-day society into linguistic camps and thence into social and political camps that follow from these linguistic sets. It is no great revelation to anyone that the world looks quite different to a young man who thinks of everything from cutting his hair to negotiating with the college administration in terms of "selling out to the System" than it looks to his father, who is scarcely aware that there is a System, much less that he is himself a part of it. A common geographical space and roughly coincident chronology is practically all that the two share: their politics, morality, aims, ideology, aesthetics—in short, their culture—are quite different, and the difference often starts and ends with the variance in languages. Ludwig Wittgenstein has hypothesized that the words that are used to describe aesthetic judgments play a very complicated but very definite role in the culture of a period. To describe their use or to describe what you mean by a cultured taste, you have to describe a whole culture. Since an entirely different cultural game with different rules is played in different ages, fully to describe a set of aesthetic rules means to describe the culture of a period. The fact that the Nowspeaker's highest accolades are "groovy," "wild," "beautiful!" "out of sight," and "naturally spaced" as opposed to his father's or professor's "very intelligent," "cultivated," "sensible," "successful" or "well-rounded" means something far more significant than merely the choice of one word over another: it means a totally new aesthetics and hence a whole new value system for the subculture.

Part of the point of the new aesthetic, of course, is that it is moving toward a non-verbal orientation. Contentless courses, meditation, yoga, chanting, drugs, T-groups, nude therapy, action painting, onstage nudity, touch therapy, group gropes, guerilla theatre in the streets, seances, satanism, be-ins, body langauge, dancing, rock festivals, proclamations of the Age of Aquarius and everywhere action, action, action—all these signs of the times are indications that McLuhan's retribalized youth are trying desperately to develop ways of communicating with something other than words. It is not only the old politics, the old imperialism, the old morality, the old society that is under attack; it is rationality and language itself. To present the Now people with carefully-worded logical arguments against their world view is only to compound the irony. Words are a large part of what their revolt is about. If language is a tool of the Establishment, then to present a linguistic argument to the Now people is already to have sold out to the System.

But the wheel of civilization has not yet turned full circle, and we are living literally in a transitional age between the old culture when intelligence was verbal almost by definition and the new nonverbal total-experience aesthetic. It is possible, then, to make one further step beyond our examination of the language and say that from an analysis of Nowspeak we can draw a number of valid inferences about the culture that it describes: its latent but intense romanticism, its folkishness and tribal qualities, its highly emotive nature, its solipsism, its "this-here-now-ness" and orientation toward the present existential moment, its connotative and reductive aspects. Let us see how this is so.

Perhaps the most striking quality of Nowspeak is that it is a highly romantic language, designed to mirror what all romanticisms ultimately mirror: the revolutionary transvaluation of all values. Thus the verbs of Nowspeak express action in onomatopoeic, slangy, quick and brittle phrases exploding like small balloons over the heads of some giant Superman or Phantom: *cop out, zap, zonk, sell out, bust, tune in, hit, flip, crash, groove.* They are comic-book and cartoon-time verbs for a TV generation. Among the most-quoted quotes of the Movement is the saying of Mao Tse-Tung, "Act first, then think, then act, then think, then act." Nowspeak is an action language for an action generation naturally "spaced" on the power of the moment. Print is irrelevant, hopelessly linear and static; it doesn't move, doesn't swing, groove, jiggle, gyrate, rock, or roll. Worst of all, it can't keep up with the Scene, can't go where it's at or where it's just been. Only with pure spontaneous action can things not fall apart and the center hold just a little longer.

Nowspeak nouns express a world view that is divided, like the world of the ancient Manicheans, into the powers of light and the powers of darkness, the Beautiful People and the System. The powers of darkness are identified with authority, uptightness, non-grooving, stodginess, and age: *the Man, the Establishment, pigs, sell-outs, game-players, uncools, hung-ups, fascists.* The powers of light in Nowspeak become *the New Left, the Movement,* the "good people," the In Crowd, the Underground, the Scene, the Age of Aquarius. Adjectives express superlative approval ("Beautiful!" "Wild!" "Freaky!") or describe emotional excesses of disapproval ("fascist pigs!" "You're uptight, man, you're blowing my mind, don't hassle me," "That's a heavy scene, man," "Oh no, you don't want grim, man; you want grim, you go to Chicago"). The vast and amorphous movement that gave birth to Nowspeak shows the same characteristics as nineteenth-century English, French, and German romanticisms: energy, boldness of thought, emphasis on creativity, the adulation of the new, the cult of personalities and the hero of the surface, stress on spontaneity and freedom of expression, anti-mechanistic and anti-scientific tendencies, supernaturalism, strangeness, a glorification of all sensory experience, the exaltation of wild freaky individualism, nonconformity, social responsibility, and the cult of sensibility. Nowspeak reflects to a greater or lesser degree all these romantic tendencies. The words as we have seen are highly emotive, intensional rather than extensional, connotative rather than denotative, expressive rather than emotionally neutral; and their impact is fully realized only by the "cool head" community of participants in this new cult of sensibility. Words furnish a kind of verbal shorthand to communicate to others who are also hip to the Scene: they know, for example, that *happening* refers to an event that's a trip of some kind for its participants and implies the excitement of something meaningful going on with a possibility of wonder and surprise; that you can get a *contact high,* or vicarious buzz, from interacting with someone who's up on drugs; that to *turn on* means to come alive and carries with it the implication that ordinary straight society creates people who are not alive and must be switched on to exist in any real sense. They also realize that *where it's at* refers to the whole physical or psychological locus of real and significant activity going on at some place and time, as opposed to the ritual and sham of the Establishment scene, and are hip to the implicit theatrical overtones of *Scene* itself: it suggests the whole of a setting and the action occurring with it—the physical setting plus mood (vibes) plus people (the theatrical analogue is set plus props plus staging plus actors plus script plus prompters *ad infinitum*). But there is no way that the straight world can know all these things unless it too switches on, psychs out the vibes, and goes.

All Western romanticisms are Edenic in impulse and origin, for all presuppose the fact of the Fall, symbolically if not literally, and all affirm the necessity of returning to the primordial Garden before the intrusion of the serpent machine. There are accurate and often chilling parallels to be drawn between the present youth cult in the United States and similar nineteenth- and early twentieth-century European cults with their fierce Rousseauism, their revolutionary cries for liberty, fraternity, equality, their *Sturm und Drang,* Pantisocracies, lyrical ballads, Satanism, Gothicism, *Volkgeists* and *Wanderlust.* The life-style of the young in twentieth-century America is also romantic, tribalized, and folkish, comprised of one part beat-academic–plain-style–Susan-Sontag–bricks-and-boards–white–washed-walls-authentic-products of cottage-industry–Chianti-drinking–yogurt-growing ethos; one part light-show–Quant-by-quant–psychotic-acid-freak-rock-stoned media-bag; and two parts idealized peasant and tribal ethos–hence the long hair, the fierce tribal loyalties, the barefoot hippie girls drifting artlessly through endless meadows of the mind, beards, mustaches, sideburns, dashikis, tatty racoon coats, caftans, beads, bells, buttons, sandals (always the sign of the bohemian in Weejun'd America), Afros, Digger hats, minis, maxis, boots, and Indian headbands. Marshall McLuhan in a recent *Playboy* interview (March 1969) comments perceptively on what he calls the retribalization of American youth: "Our teenage generation is already becoming part of a jungle clan. . . . Sexual freedom is as natural to newly tribalized youth as drugs. . . . LSD and related hallucinogenic drugs . . . breed a highly tribal and communally oriented subculture, so it's understandable why the retribalized young take to drugs like a duck to water." The natural-man, tribal, folkish, Edenic aspect of the youth cult figures heavily in its language. There is a freer use of sexual, anal and other "taboo" terms and four-letter words: the language is simpler, the vocabulary is cut to a bare minimum, and there are many coined words, themselves authentic products of the Movement. Adjectives and nouns that denote approval are terms that express the ability to lose one's inhibitions, to move in a natural, uninhibited un–hung-up manner, to go where the action is and move with it, to put oneself in touch with cosmic rhythms—in short, to psych out the scene, feel its vibes, and then groove with it.

As we have seen, Nowspeak relies heavily on connotative power rather than denotative meaning for its impact. The greatest problem in compiling the short glossary in Section II was that of definition. Many of the terms, I found, could not be adequately defined in words. I could talk around them, use them correctly in context, sense their power when I heard them or read them, but an exact definition always eluded me. The "definitions" I finally settled on are less definitions than a sort of translation or paraphrase of their approximate meanings. Many of them can best be defined in context. Nowspeak at its worst can be a slick, vague, repetitive, and frustrating Hipspeak that smacks of the hard sell and fast deal quite as much as of the new morality and aesthetic. At its best, however, it is gutsy, emotive, colorful, and highly expressive of a whole range of thought and action that conventional English simply cannot express. Webster's offers us no exact equivalent for "pig" or "uptight" or "sell-out" or for the depth of ridicule and contempt that the terms convey, nor for the wildly enthusiastic approbation that lies behind "out of sight!" "spaced!" "freaky!" or "beautiful!" A friend of mine, recently turned twenty, spent a frustrating half-hour trying to describe to a gathering of cool heads the experiences of a recent acid trip and finally lapsed into "Oh, wow! If you only knew . . . like wild! freaky scene, man, just this freaky scene. . . . Oh, wow . . . spaced out . . . like you know, stoned . . . if you just knew, I mean, if you only knew." More intimate acquaintance with the dictionary would not have helped him communicate the incommunicable, for the experiences he was describing lie, for the moment at least, far beyond the pale of ordinary Sally-Dick-and-Jane reality. No wonder, then, that Nowspeak is against reason, against interpretation, against language itself: how else could it survive? Similarly for the use of taboo words, for it is a means of expressing utter disdain for ticky-tacky Establishment values to use obscenity in describing some of its more hallowed members and institutions.

If we think of the movement as McLuhan does in terms of a return to a romanticized primitive tribal ethos, we must also recognize that this language serves as an in-group sign, the verbal equivalent of a secret handclasp, a password that simultaneously gives solidarity to the inner circle and freaks out and excludes non-users, the ubiquitous Establishment. This use of language reminds us of Kenneth Burke's theory of language as gesture, for Nowspeak is indeed a sort of symbolic nose-thumbing at the Establishment—a complex and fun way of saying "Screw you" in a linguistic set that only the initiates know. Nowspeak is the code that the System must break, and as such it unites the various branches of the nebulous movement with an often specious sense of community. Nowspeak appears deceptively simple; actually, it is quite complex and involves many subtleties of syntax and style. Since it is spoken, not written, it is transmitted and its conventions established by word-of-mouth communication. The only sure way to establish current usage is to be in constant contact with speakers, for the language changes daily and today's In phrase is liable to be tomorrow's tired-out cliché. A written version of the language is at best only an approximation of its spoken form. Youth-oriented magazines such as *Cavalier, Ramparts,* and *Evergreen* realize this and effect in their writing style a skillful synthesis between ordinary English and authentic Nowspeak by repeating key words in contexts that indicate the cultural sympathies of the editors. Dust jackets, theatre marquees, and record jackets also let the young audience know by verbal sleight-of-mouth that the designer or producer was "where it was at" when the artifact in question was produced. By succumbing to the hip sell and buying the product the young consumer is invited to join the cool community where he, too, can be Norman Mailer-ed, Maxwell Taylor-ed *ad nauseum.*

By nature Nowspeak is sensation-oriented rather than experience-oriented, solipsistic rather than chronological or historical. While typical standard English sentence structure is chronological ("It was raining," "They left with us on Tuesday," "He used to drop by for drinks on Wednesday nights"), Nowspeak is non-chronological, non-temporal, a language of, for, and about the present moment. It is a process language designed to express the shifts, the swift reversals, the kaleidescopic flux, the insecurities and ephemera of an electric kool-aid acid world. Like the Hopi Indian's tongue, Nowspeak is designed to tell us only that "it is summering," not that "it is summer": witness the number of words that describe ongoing or continuing action (*happening, Scene, where it's at, swinging*). Thus the language is geared toward making what the American philosopher Charles Hartshorne has called "this-here-now" statements about immediate actions and present states of being. To listen to the Now people rapping or to read an underground newspaper is to live briefly in the historical present. Few if any of the verbs are in the past tense, and most of the sentences are short, simple declarative statements directed less toward imparting information than toward creating a mood or emotion. Most of the statements are action-directed imperatives ("screw in the streets," "kill the pigs," "stop the trial") or exclamatory-declarative statements with a pithy, down-home epigrammatic brevity about them ("All power to the people," "This is a racist culture," "The streets belong to the people"). Daniel J. Boorstin, writing for the October 1968 *Esquire,* calls the Movement "the social expression of a movement from Experience to Sensation"—the shift from cumulative and communicable observation of or acquaintance with facts and events to simple awareness of perception which by definition is personal, private, highly confined, and essentially incommunicable. "What history is to the person in quest of experience," he writes, "a 'happening' is to the person in quest of sensation. For a 'happening' is something totally discrete. It adds to our sensations without increasing our experience." Perhaps we can see in the sensation-orientation, the "this-here-now"–ness of Nowspeak and its speakers a popularization of pseudo-Whiteheadian process metaphysics. This new pop philosophy mirrors the shift in contemporary world view from traditional substance-attribute metaphysics to a *weltanschauung* where things fall apart, the center cannot hold, movies-within-films-within-metaflicks are cinematic commonplaces, and today's pop idol is tomorrow's Nowhere Man. Once-credible reality was shattered with the dreamy lyricism of early grass and acid rock ("Strawberry fields forever") and now like Humpty-Dumpty's egg, the pieces of this cosmic Chinese puzzle cannot be put back together. Nowspeak reflects all these things: for a fragmented and incoherent time it offers us a pastiche-lingo whose silences and ellipses are more eloquent than its words.

Nowspeak, like most subculture languages, is more incantation than analysis or definition and thus relies heavily on word connotation rather than denotation. We already have noted the proper names that have charisma and evocative power. Certain other words and phrases also have it: "The Revolution," "power (supply: black, student, flower)," "the System," "the Movement," "kill pigs," "do your own thing." Men have died for less clearly defined terms than these. Nat Hentoff in the April 1969 *Evergreen* tells the story of a recent meeting of young liberal teachers in New York that quickly degenerated into a name-calling contest on the word "racist." The fact that the word was left undefined during the meeting was irrelevant. The evocative power of the word was enough. The important thing about words like the Movement and the Establishment is not that anyone can point to referents for them, but that they are sufficient in emotional force to generate their own new myths as they gather the tribes about them. For the Nowspeaker, as for Lewis Carroll's Humpty Dumpty, the word can mean anything that pleases the speaker at the time: for example, the word *uptight,* which seems to change meanings with the seasons. Claude Brown in "The Language of Soul" (*Esquire,* April 1968) remarks that the word came into use about 1953 in Harlem and meant being in financial straits. In time, it came to be popular with junkies to describe their perpetual condition of needing money for the next fix. In the early sixties when "uptight" was first making its way into under-thirty jargon, a younger generation of people in black urban communities of the East revived the word with a new meaning: "everything is cool, under control, going my way." For the Nowspeaker "uptight" may be either a term of approbation ("everything is proceeding according to plan," "I have it all psyched out," "I'm cool, I'm hip") or of derision (as an equivalent to "square," "uncool," "not with it"). Once again, it is not the denotative power of the word that counts (*uptight* may denote two completely antithetical states, depending on its usage); it is the connotation of the word, the manner of uttering it, the occasion, the context, and the emotive force that determines the word's meaning in a given situation.

Stanley Kripner's paper before the International Society of General Semantics in August 1968 suggested that what the youthful user of "head drugs" learns from his earliest drug experiences is no very specific knowledge or information: instead he learns a new semantic set proper to the occasion ("spaced out," "groovy," "freak out," "high," "crash," "turned on"). To put the matter in good linguistic terminology, we might say that the Nowspeaker often mistakes the map for the territory; he speaks intensionally rather than extensionally, evocatively and incantatori-ally instead of analytically and rationally. Both in popular and a McLuhan-esque sense of the word, Nowspeak is a "cool" language—indefinable, vague, often imprecise, requiring rigorous audience participation to fill in the holes in the content. Thus for the Nowspeaker the medium is quite literally the message.

Like George Orwell's famous Newspeak, Nowspeak is essentially a reductive language intended to facilitate rather than stimulate thought by limiting the possible alternatives that can be articulated within the language set. Designed for instant speech, minimum thought, and instant replay, it is built around an implicit two-value logic that denies or disregards the possibility of compromise or alternative systems. It is easy for America's retribalized youth to think in terms of these neat polar opposites—pig and Yippie (the poles of the 1968 Chicago confrontation), New Left and Es-tablishment, System and Revolution—for it provides a comfortable means of instantly categorizing all the possible experiences that one might have. For the Nowspeaker the world is all black or white with no redeeming shade of grey in between. Black is beautiful and white is a sell-out. The student is a nigger. All power to the people, death to pigs. Down with the System; up, up, and away with the Beautiful People. Reason is bad, feeling is good. Act, think, act, think, then act, act, act. Nietzsche's prophetic transvaluation of all values has at last come to pass. The lack of a middle ground, a middle term somewhere between the extremes of total conform-ity and total assault on the culture, makes it impossible for Nowspeak to reflect with accuracy any world other than one drawn in the starkest of blacks and whites. There is, for example, no such animal as "pig-hippie" for that would be an animal as anomalous and absurd as Suzanne Langer's "rabbit-dog." One must be one or the other, never both at once. Thus, for all its dayglo colors, its newspaper taxis and marshmallow people, plasti-cene ponies and insanity's horse adorning the skies, the world of Nowspeak is a strangely sinister, almost medieval world, a battlefield where the chil-dren of light and the sons of darkness, the Now Generation and the Oldthinkers, play out the psychedelic *psychomachia* to the finish. The lines were drawn long ago with deadly clarity, and it may be too late to turn back the clock. As Gore Vidal reminds us in the final essay of *Sex, Death and Money,* the wheel of civilization is once more beginning to turn and most of us can only watch in morbid fascination as the flower kids in this strangest of all Children's Crusades are pied-piped away by the idol of the hour.

Yet the case for language may not be totally lost. It may well be this polarizing tendency of Nowspeak that will spell its end as the ruling subculture jargon. All philosophical systems have built into them certain basic assumptions that substantially limit the types of statements possible within each system. The same can be said of languages, for the verbal set of any culture (or subculture) determines to a great extent the limits of its possible assertions, its knowledge, its ideology, its perceptions, and hence its achievements. Like the heroine of Vilgot Sjöman's *I Am Curious (Yellow)* we all are feeling the need to smash our tidy op art cardboard archives with all the groovy letters and slogans and In words pasted all over the slick surface, and to find a new box with new labels for our collective files. Already hip young journalists, politicians, students, teachers, playwrights, poets, and critics are beginning to chafe at the restrictions of a language designed for incantation and slogans rather than for thoughtful analysis and action. Nat Hentoff's *Evergreen* article speaks of the New Left's "prison of words," and, after analysis of such phrases as Herbert Marcuse's "discriminative tolerance," Hentoff concludes that it is a polite euphemism for "elitist authoritarianism"; that "all power to all people" means not what it seems to say, but rather implies the implicitly snobbish view, "all power to me and everyone else who believes exactly as I do." For the first time perhaps in this decade we are beginning to look behind the words to the things and ideas, to search out hidden paradoxes ("All power to all people," and "America is a nation of fascist pigs," for example, are slogans as compatible as "Buddha is and is not"—and about equally meaningful).

Nowspeak has served its function and served it well and faithfully. Despite obvious limitations of its own, it has freed standard Americanese from the impoverishment of Webster's, Madison Avenue, pop psychiatry, military-industrial jargon, academese, and koffee-klatch-and-pizza-late-late-show TV. It has introduced a colorful, freaky, rhythmic, whimsical, gutsy, outrageous, "sexy, childish, irreligious and mad" element into a language that was giving signs of languishing in its prime. It has elevated the jargon of the hipster, the black, the drug pusher, bohemian, beat, hippie, and general rebel with or without a cause to the status of legitimate usage and has infused instant glamour and expressiveness into the speech of millions (both the *New York Times* and David Brinkley have noted a special affinity for *uptight*). In a very real sense, Nowspeak is itself the pop poetry of the new age just as rock is its lyric voice. Yet in an equally real sense the greatest strength of Nowspeak lies in its power and need to be superseded. C. D. Burns put it this way in an essay called "The Sense of the Horizon" (1933):

The experience of any moment has its horizons. Today's experience, which is not tomorrow's, has in it some hints and implications which are tomorrow on the horizon of today. . . . However wide it may be, that common world also has its horizon; and on that horizon new experiences are always appearing.

That Nowspeak's horizon is Now is significant: that is at once its lifeblood and its death knell. Already the neon lights have burnt out on Carnaby Street, the Beatles have gone their separate ways, the Haight stands emptied of its brilliant frisking flower children, the orchard gone to ashes, and the dry leaves swirl like fallen Lucifer's host in the People's Park. Sergeant Pepper's buried; he will not come out of his grave. The summer people have taken to the streets, and the old hippies have fled into the mountains, feeling some new wind brewing in them as they breathe. And which of us knows what rough beast of a newer Nowspeak, its hour come 'round at last, slouches toward San Francisco to be born?

Folklore, Fakelore, and Poplore

MARSHALL FISHWICK

> *From legends men draw all the ideas necessary to their existence. They do not need many, and a few simple fables will suffice to gild millions of lives.*
>
> Anatole France

Folklore is the country mouse talking. Taken to the city, cheapened by charlatans and opportunists, folklore became fakelore, as the mass took over from the folk. To some, the sad tale ends here. But wait—there's another mutation. Using the new urban material with its chrome and kitsch, imaginative artists, ad men, and scriptwriters are developing a poplore which is as true to its environment as was folklore to an earlier one. Call it poplore, and ask if it doesn't complete the circle.

Folklore is material handed on by tradition—oral or active; by mouth, practice, or custom; folk song, folktale, Easter eggs, dance step, or knocking on wood. To try for an eloquent oversimplification: Folklore is oral history transmuted into poetry. Scholars will accept no short definition, of course. In fact, the more one investigates, the more convinced he is

From August 26, 1967 *Saturday Review*. Copyright © 1967 Saturday Review, Inc. Reprinted by permission of Marshall Fishwick and Saturday Review, Inc.

that they won't accept *any* definition. The *Standard Dictionary of Folklore, Mythology, and Legend* lists twenty-one. Key words in the twenty-one "standard" definitions are "oral," "transmission," "tradition," "survival," and "communal." But there is no central agreement or emphasis. Experts have filled more than seventy volumes of the *Journal of American Folklore* without agreeing on what their subject is.

If we have trouble defining folklore, we can say where it is found— among isolated groups who have developed their own distinctions and stability. This isolation may be not only spatial, but occupational, religious, racial, linguistic, or a combination of the five. The enclave of provincial culture may be in the Kentucky mountains or among sailors, the Pennsylvania Dutch, Gullah Negroes, or French-Canadians. A family might be the crucial, isolated unit, as with certain ballads. The central thread is plain; we are speaking of folk cultures that are essentially rural and religious, in which behavior is traditional, spontaneous, and personal. The sacred prevails over the secular. Status, rather than the open market, determines the economy. All folklore is orally transmitted, but not all that is orally transmitted is folklore.

The connection between genuine European folklore and American variations is well documented and convincing. One of the best known examples is "Barbara Allen," a ballad that crossed oceans and mountains with ease. The essential tale is that of a young girl who scorns her lover, Sweet William (or Willie, Sweet Jimmy, Young Johnny, or Jimmy Grove). Pepys praised a rendition by the celebrated London actress, Mrs. Knipp, in 1666. He would have been surprised to know that generations later Americans were singing:

> Way down South where I came from
> Is where I got my learning.
> I fell in love with a pretty little girl
> And her name is Barbey Ellen.

Then there is "The Twa Sisters" who became "Sister Kate" in the New World. This time a jealous girl pushes her younger sister into a mill stream for stealing her suitor. The European version has the miller, who recovers the body, perform magic on various parts of the corpse; in America this aspect was dropped, and the story became a children's game. Magic was transformed into merriment, and folklore prevailed.

In "The Gypsy Laddie," a fair lady gives herself to a roving gypsy. Her lord returns, finds her gone, chases after and rescues her, and hangs fifteen of the gypsies. In adaptations which have come to light in Virginia, the retribution and hanging are omitted. Instead, the lady decides to cast her lot with the roaming vagabonds—a decision that might well have appealed to the hard-pressed trailblazers moving into frontier territory:

> "How can you forsake your house and land
> How can you forsake your money O?
> How can you forsake your sweet little babe
> To go with the gypsy laddie O?"

"O, I can forsake my house and lands
O, I can forsake my money O,
O, I can forsake my sweet little babe
To go with the gypsy laddie O."

She was used to a feather bed
And servants all around her,
And now she has come to a bed of hay
With gypsies all around her.

Similarly, "The Three Ravens" was revamped on this side of the Atlantic into "The Three Crows." Back in the Appalachians you might still hear the macabre song, which moves forward with the bareness and directness that marks enduring ballads:

There were three crows sat on a tree
As black as any crows could be.

One of these crows said to his mate
"What shall we do for food to eat?"

"There lies a horse in yonder lane
That has been only three days slain

We'll sit upon his bare backbone
And pick his eyes out one by one."

Vestigial remains of Old World folklore fascinate scholars. The English expert Cecil J. Sharp (1859–1933) tramped through the Blue Ridge Mountains in 1918, finding "for the first time in my life a community in which singing is as common and almost as universal a practice as speaking." Harvard's Francis J. Child assembled a monumental five-volume collection of migratory *English and Scottish Popular Ballads,* while A. K. Davis, Jr., was finding in Virginia fifty-one British ballads still sung lustily by wood-choppers and whisky-makers. Visiting isolated mountain pockets, Vanderbilt's George Pullen Jackson was able to show that white spirituals were the progenitors of many famous Negro folk tunes. But plainly the main trend was toward urbanism, consolidation, homogenization. Patterns of folk culture changed rapidly. "After 1860 the homespun yarn never again became nationally intelligible," Richard Dorson notes. "A century later, literary scholars and folklorists would unearth specimens as antiquarian curiosities."

This same scholar coined the word "fakelore" (*American Mercury,* March 1950) to refer to and denigrate the contrived efforts of hucksters and jokesters who hid behind the word folklore. Imitating ballads and folktales had been in vogue at least since the eighteenth century; but Heine, Rossetti, Wordsworth, and Meredith wished their imitations to be accepted as literature. Fakelorists wished their work to pass as folklore.

They insisted that Paul Bunyan—a prime example of the pseudo-hero—was a genuine folk character, created by the people themselves. "The people, the bookless people, they made Paul and had him alive long before he got into books," said Carl Sandburg, waxing eloquent amid the native corn. "Paul is as old as the hills, young as the alphabet." Actually, the Paul most Americans knew was younger than Sandburg's *Chicago Poems.*

Studying the meager Bunyan material in 1920, Constance Rourke concluded that there was no live prototype for Bunyan, a conclusion with which Professor Daniel Hoffman concurred a generation later. Paul owed much of his fame to a free-lance advertising man, William B. Laughead, hired by the Red River Lumber Company to sell their products. When other ad men and promoters joined in, Paul came to symbolize the cult of bigness and power in a booming chauvinistic democracy. He mirrored a bumptious, optimistic nineteenth-century robber baron—the collective state of mind of people whose primary task was the physical mastery of nature. Bunyan was *company* fakelore—in a business civilization, the most likely to succeed.

Meanwhile, a plethora of phony folk heroes and villains flooded our books, movies, and TV screens. *Life* published a "remarkable new series" (starting in August 1959) on "The Folklore of America" which was mainly fakelore. Pecos Bill didn't come from the Wild West, but from the typewriter of Edward ("Tex") O'Reilly. Annie Christmas's spicy saga can be traced not to the New Orleans brothels but to the typewriter of Lyle Saxon. Margaret Montague dreamed up Tony Beaver. Daddy Joe was contrived by Stewart Holbrook, Big Mose by Herbert Asbury, Whiskey Jack by Charles Brown, and Strap Buckner by Florence Barns. Jeremiah refined fakelore by combining the appeal of sailors and cowboys—his "Bowleg Bill" specialized in riding giant tunas. "Maybe the scholars have been following a false lead," Bernard De Voto wrote in 1955. "Maybe popular literature isn't a folk art at all." By then factory-made folklore had blazed a trail across American journalism, advertising, and entertainment like a jet plane racing across a cloudless blue sky.

One of the first writers to deal with the consequence of this cultural gimmickery was Walter Lippmann. As early as 1922, in *Public Opinion,* he gave examples of "oversimplified patterns" in American life that gave us ways to defend our prejudices by seeming to give definitiveness and consistency to our daily experience. For years thereafter Lippmann pointed to pseudo-events (the fakelore of journalism) which "ignore the world outside and concentrate on the pictures in our heads." In so doing, Lippmann piqued most of the master image-makers (including, most recently, Lyndon B. Johnson). It remained for Daniel Boorstin, in his curiously underestimated book called *The Image; or, What Happened to the American Dream* (1962), to dissect a pseudo-event: (1) It is not spontaneous, but planned and planted; (2) It is planted to be reported and reproduced; (3) It is tied in with a self-fulfilling prophecy.

Thus fakelore is to folklore what the pseudo-event is to the real event. And thus the emergence, in the Eisenhower years, of a new Gresham's law of American public life: counterfeit happenings will always drive spontaneous happenings out of circulation. Poison tastes so sweet that it spoils our appetite for plain food. When the gods want to punish us, they make us believe our own advertising.

In such a climate, folk songs ran in out of the hot noonday sun to the air-conditioned comfort of nightclubs. The authentic folk song style—described by Cecil Sharp as "austere, high-pitched melody, rigidly and undemonstrably performed"—was turned into something "charming, senti-mental, sweet." To put it more bluntly, the guts were removed from folk music. Alan Lomax, a leading folk song collector, noticed that when Aunt Molly Jackson sang to country folks in Oklahoma, they called it the most beautiful music they had ever heard. When she repeated the program for city children, they compared her singing to a cat's yowling.

To the first audience, the folk "gapped-scale" and modal intervals were still familiar; to the second, raised on mass media kitsch, one had to adjust the intervals, remove the harshness, and electrify the guitar. But the music and lore of the Elvis Presley era dwelt in a strange no-man's-land. It aped and honored the old folk idiom and metaphor, like the "colonial home" in suburbia which had a fireplace, spinning wheel, and picket fence—complete with electric stove, sewing machine, and televi-sion. No one summed up this cultural schizophrenia better than Marshall McLuhan:

> The past went that-a-way. When faced with a new situation, we tend always to attach ourselves to the objects, to the flavor of the most re-cent past. We look at the present through a rear-view mirror. We march backwards into the future. Suburbia lives imaginatively in Bonanzaland.

"Years ago," McLuhan—the most original exponent of the Age of Cir-cuitry—told Gerald E. Stearn in a recent interview, "I abominated ma-chinery, cities, everything except the most Rousseauistic. Gradually I became aware of how useless this was and I discovered the twentieth-century artists had a different approach and I adopted it." What McLuhan had done was study folklore; discern and reject fakelore, then discover poplore. He had, in a single lifetime, gone through the whole cycle I am trying to describe and document.

One should not think that the new poplore is the antithesis of tradi-tional folklore; they are much more alike than either is like fakelore. Pop is not slick but savage; in musical terms it avoids the chromatic scales of the nightclub and uses the old Greek musical modes. Both folklore and poplore avoid sentimentality, reject the "arty" approach for the earthy one, draw from primary materials, colors, and emotions. The line of force connects more with the stomach than the cerebellum. Consider this verse from the folk song about Old Joe Clark:

Old Joe Clark killed a man
   Killed him with a knife;
I'm damn glad he killed that man—
Now I'll have his wife.

Hold it up against . . . "A Day in the Life," from the Beatles' . . . album, banned by the BBC.

. . .

The lights have changed, the world has changed, and the young are moving out into realms their parents will never ever enter. The young have always done this, of course; only to return and occupy the stable, conservative positions they once decried. Here is the big difference: The generation which has just moved out may never come back.

The folk-fake-pop division I suggest is no neat thing, and many bits of data don't fit into the pattern. Much genuine folklore and folk music remains, for example, in distant valleys. Perhaps factories and computer centers will create a new vigorous folklore of their own; perhaps the notion that folklore is dying out is itself a kind of folklore.

Poplore may lack both the vitality and significance I attribute to it—only time will tell. But from the information and insight available at this moment, I believe that Warhol, Rosenquist, Oldenburg, and Segal *have* changed the course of American art. Men will continue to enjoy Molière, Shakespeare, and Ibsen; but now that we have been a part of "happenings," the theater will never be the same. Playwrights can no longer work in isolation, since they confront a group on either side of their message. Everything is interdependent. Once the audience and performer have been wed, who can put them asunder?

The plastic and performing arts have found a way to be involved in modern life, and to speak its idiom. Having been boxed in by the Shakespeare syndrome for centuries, contemporary theater has broken out of the square, first into the round, now into orbit. Jazz has moved from hot to cool and now to all-encompassing—into the musical melting pot with Dixieland, swing, blues, country, Western, country-Western, mountain, gospel, Nashville, bluegrass, rock'n'roll, folk rock, raga rock, baroque, ballad. From a kaleidoscopic variety of subforms comes the new sound of poplore: a celebration of the new, plugged-in, revved-up psychedelic global village in which we must somehow find our way. What does it celebrate? Oriental painting, African sculpture, cave drawings, computer clicks; firepower, flower power, horsepower? The old traditional lines and barriers are disappearing. Art schools teach electronics, wiring, and glass blowing. "Light artists" use aluminum, polyesters, and motors to create objects that beep, buzz, and pop.

No longer are used-car lots, billboards, and hot dog stands part of the Wasteland. They are raw material for visual involvement—part of the "environment" (a key word in poplore). Environments are not passive wrappings, but active, invisible processes. The entire environment can be seen as a work of art, or as a teaching machine designed to give us maximum perception. Propaganda is the invisible, invading environment of electronic information, swallowing up all ideologies just as a frog swallows flies. The ideologies are not the propaganda; they merely keep it snapping and make it croak.

Just who first used the terms poplore, pop art, and pop music isn't clear. The question is academic. New art doesn't come from doctrines but from performances.

Long before and after the Old Testament, folklore allowed us to mythologize our culture. Fakelore destroyed the supernatural and demythologized our lives. The job of poplore is to remythologize them.

Man is the only being who asks questions about being—about the power, surge, logos of reality. Power plus structure equals a life of being. Poplore seems to be searching for a new ontology. In so doing, it becomes both vital and outrageously pertinent. This is not to claim that all of pop culture is defensible, let alone significant. Probably only 5 per cent will survive. But can we ignore gold nuggets because there's lots of fool's gold around?

The point of view of poplore can be expressed theologically. God is neither *in* hand (bumptious assumption of romantic optimists) nor *out* of hand (gloomy contention of romantic pessimists), but *at* hand—nearby, close, now. The most appropriate response is neither to gloat nor despair, but to probe.

How are we to conceive of this new Age of Circuitry? Think of your mind as a telephone switchboard—organized and programed for specific connections. In comes the signal. The mind plugs in the reaction—click. Society has programed you. So has your family, church, school, government—each adding a new set of predictable circuits. How's that for a description of daily routine?

Not so good, say pop-rock singers like Bob Dylan—via disturbing new songs.

. . .

Music is crucial to the whole pop revolution. Here, as nowhere else, the kids have succeeded; they write, sing, record, buy, judge, and discard music that's of, by, and for kids. The sound? Lots of lip, lots of bass . . . music not meant to be read, but absorbed.

The old boys are horrified. "Grunts, moans, offbeat slappings, eerie animal whinings," a critic complains. "Squeaks and slurs like a short-wave radio trying to pick up Vladivostok during a sunspot storm." Volume for its own sake; monotonous rhythm; "I am a rock! I am an island!"; "Sgt. Pepper's Lonely Hearts Club Band"; "Would you love me anyway, would you have my baby?" How much are we expected to put up with?

The teasing reply of Bob Dylan: "Something is happening and you don't know what it is—do you, Mr. Jones?"

The New Mutants

LESLIE A. FIEDLER

I

A realization that the legitimate functions of literature are bewilderingly, almost inexhaustibly various has always exhilarated poets and dismayed critics. And critics, therefore, have sought age after age to legislate limits to literature—legitimizing certain of its functions and disavowing others—in hope of insuring to themselves the exhilaration of which they have felt unjustly deprived, and providing for poets the dismay which the critics at least have thought good for them.

Such shifting and exclusive emphasis is not, however, purely the product of critical malice, or even of critical principle. Somehow every period is, to begin with, especially aware of certain functions of literature and especially oblivious to others: endowed with a special sensitivity and a complementary obtuseness, which, indeed, give to that period its characteristic flavor and feel. So, for instance, the Augustan Era is marked by sensitivity in regard to the uses of diction, obtuseness in regard to those of imagery.

What the peculiar obtuseness of the present age may be I find it difficult to say (being its victim as well as its recorder), perhaps toward the didactic or certain modes of the sentimental. I am reasonably sure, however, that our period is acutely aware of the sense in which literature if not invents, at least collaborates in the invention of time. The beginnings of that awareness go back certainly to the beginnings of the Renaissance, to Humanism as a self-conscious movement; though a critical development occurred toward the end of the eighteenth century with the dawning of the Age of Revolution. And we may have reached a second critical point right now.

At any rate, we have long been aware (in the last decades uncomfortably aware) that a chief function of literature is to express and in part to create not only theories of time but also attitudes toward time. Such attitudes constitute, however, a politics as well as an esthetics; or, more properly perhaps, a necessary mythological substratum of politics—as, in fact, the conventional terms reactionary, conservative, revolutionary indicate: all involving stances toward the past.

It is with the past, then, that we must start, since the invention of the past seems to have preceded that of the present and the future; and since we are gathered in a university at whose heart stands a library[1]— the latter, like the former, a visible monument to the theory that a chief responsibility of literature is to preserve and perpetuate the past. Few universities are explicitly (and none with any real degree of confidence)

From *Partisan Review,* Fall 1965, Vol. 32, no. 4. Copyright © 1965 by Partisan Review.
[1] "The New Mutants" is a written version of a talk given by Mr. Fiedler at the Conference on the Idea of The Future held at Rutgers, in June, 1965. The conference was sponsored by Partisan Review and the Congress for Cultural Freedom, with the cooperation of Rutgers, The State University, New Brunswick, New Jersey.

dedicated to this venerable goal any longer. The Great Books idea (which once transformed the University of Chicago and lives on now in provincial study groups) was perhaps its last desperate expression. Yet the shaky continuing existence of the universities and the building of new college libraries (with matching Federal funds) remind us not only of that tradition but of the literature created in its name: the neo-epic, for instance, all the way from Dante to Milton; and even the frantically nostalgic Historical Romance, out of the counting house by Sir Walter Scott.

Obviously, however, literature has a contemporary as well as a traditional function. That is to say, it may be dedicated to illuminating the present and the meaning of the present, which is, after all, no more given than the past. Certainly the modern or bourgeois novel was thus contemporary in the hands of its great inventors, Richardson, Fielding, Smollett and Sterne; and it became contemporary again—with, as it were, a sigh of relief—when Flaubert, having plunged deep into the Historical Romance, emerged once more into the present of Emma Bovary. But the second function of the novel tends to transform itself into a third: a revolutionary or prophetic or futurist function; and it is with the latter that I am here concerned.

Especially important for our own time is the sense in which literature first conceived the possibility of the future (rather than an End of Time or an Eternal Return, an Apocalypse or Second Coming); and then furnished that future in joyous or terrified anticipation, thus preparing all of us to inhabit it. Men have dreamed and even written down utopias from ancient times; but such utopias were at first typically allegories rather than projections: nonexistent models against which to measure the real world, exploitations of the impossible (as the traditional name declares) rather than explorations or anticipations or programs of the possible. And, in any event, only recently have such works occupied a position anywhere near the center of literature.

Indeed, the movement of futurist literature from the periphery to the center of culture provides a clue to certain essential meanings of our times and of the art which best reflects it. If we make a brief excursion from the lofty reaches of High Art to the humbler levels of Pop Culture— where radical transformations in literature are reflected in simplified form —the extent and nature of the futurist revolution will become immediately evident. Certainly, we have seen in recent years the purveyors of Pop Culture transfer their energies from the Western and the Dracula-type thriller (last heirs of the Romantic and Gothic concern with the past) to the Detective Story especially in its hard-boiled form (final vulgarization of the realists' dedication to the present) to Science Fiction (a new genre based on hints in E. A. Poe and committed to "extrapolating" the future). This development is based in part on the tendency to rapid exhaustion inherent in popular forms; but in part reflects a growing sense of the irrelevance of the past and even of the present to 1965. Surely, there has never been a moment in which the most naïve as well as the most sophisticated have been so acutely aware of how the past threatens momentarily to disappear from the present, which itself seems on the verge of disappearing into the future.

And this awareness functions, therefore, on the level of art as well as entertainment, persuading quite serious writers to emulate the modes of Science Fiction. The novel is most amenable to this sort of adaptation, whose traces we can find in writers as various as William Golding and Anthony Burgess, William Burroughs and Kurt Vonnegut, Jr., Harry Matthews and John Barth—to all of whom young readers tend to respond with a sympathy they do not feel even toward such forerunners of the mode (still more allegorical than prophetic) as Aldous Huxley, H. G. Wells and George Orwell. But the influence of Science Fiction can be discerned in poetry as well, and even in the polemical essays of such polymath prophets as Wilhelm Reich, Buckminster Fuller, Marshall McLuhan, perhaps also Norman O. Brown. Indeed, in Fuller the prophetic–Science–Fiction view of man is always at the point of fragmenting into verse:

men are known as being six feet tall
because that is their tactile limit;
they are not known by how far we can hear them,
e.g., as a one-half mile man
and only to dogs are men known
by their gigantic olfactoral dimensions. . . .

I am not now interested in analyzing, however, the diction and imagery which have passed from Science Fiction into post-Modernist literature, but rather in coming to terms with the prophetic content common to both: with the myth rather than the modes of Science Fiction. But that myth is quite simply the myth of the end of man, of the transcendence or transformation of the human—a vision quite different from that of the extinction of our species by the Bomb, which seems stereotype rather than archetype and consequently the source of editorials rather than poems. More fruitful artistically is the prospect of the radical transformation (under the impact of advanced technology and the transfer of traditional human functions to machines) of *homo sapiens* into something else: the emergence—to use the language of Science Fiction itself—of "mutants" among us.

A simpleminded prevision of this event is to be found in Arthur C. Clarke's *Childhood's End,* at the conclusion of which the mutated offspring of parents much like us are about to take off under their own power into outer space. Mr. Clarke believes that he is talking about a time still to come because he takes metaphor for fact; though simply translating "outer space" into "inner space" reveals to us that what he is up to is less prediction than description; since the post-human future is now, and if not we, at least our children, are what it would be comfortable to pretend we still only foresee. But what, in fact, are they: these mutants who are likely to sit before us in class, or across from us at the dinner table, or who stare at us with hostility from street corners as we pass?

Beatniks or hipsters, layabouts and drop-outs we are likely to call them with corresponding hostility—or more elegantly, but still without sympathy, passive onlookers, abstentionists, spiritual catatonics. There resides in all of these terms an element of truth, at least about the relationship of the young to what we have defined as the tradition, the world we have made for them; and if we turn to the books in which they see their own destiny best represented *(The Clockwork Orange,* say, or *On the Road* or *Temple of Gold),* we will find nothing to contradict that truth. Nor will we find anything to expand it, since the young and their laureates avoid on principle the kind of definition (even of themselves) for which we necessarily seek.

II

Let us begin then with the negative definition our own hostility suggests, since this is all that is available to us, and say that the "mutants" in our midst are non-participants in the past (though our wisdom assures us this is impossible), drop-outs from history. The withdrawal from school, so typical of their generation and so inscrutable to ours, is best understood as a lived symbol of their rejection of the notion of cultural continuity and progress, which our graded educational system represents in institutional form. It is not merely a matter of their rejecting what happens to have happened just before them, as the young do, after all, in every age; but of their attempting to disavow the very idea of the past, of their seeking to avoid recapitulating it step by step—up to the point of graduation into the present.

Specifically, the tradition from which they strive to disengage is the tradition of the human, as the West (understanding the West to extend from the United States to Russia) has defined it, Humanism itself, both in its bourgeois and Marxist forms; and more especially, the cult of reason —that dream of Socrates, redreamed by the Renaissance and surviving all travesties down to only yesterday. To be sure, there have long been anti-rational forces at work in the West, including primitive Christianity itself; but the very notion of literary culture is a product of Humanism, as the early Christians knew (setting fire to libraries), so that the Church in order to sponsor poets had first to come to terms with reason itself by way of Aquinas and Aristotle.

Only with Dada was the notion of an anti-rational anti-literature born; and Dada became Surrealism, i.e., submitted to the influence of those last neo-Humanists, those desperate Socratic Cabalists, Freud and Marx —dedicated respectively to contriving a rationale of violence and a rationale of impulse. The new irrationalists, however, deny all the apostles of reason, Freud as well as Socrates; and if they seem to exempt Marx, this is because they know less about him, have heard him evoked less often by the teachers they are driven to deny. Not only do they reject the Socratic adage that the unexamined life is not worth living, since for them precisely the unexamined life is the only one worth enduring at all. But they also abjure the Freudian one: "Where id was, ego shall be," since for them the true rallying cry is, "Let id prevail over ego, impulse over order," or—in negative terms—"Freud is a fink!"

The first time I heard this irreverent charge from the mouth of a student some five or six years ago (I who had grown up thinking of Freud as a revolutionary, a pioneer), I knew that I was already in the future; though I did not yet suspect that there would be no room in that future for the university system to which I had devoted my life. Kerouac might have told me so, or Ginsberg, or even so polite and genteel a spokesman for youth as J. D. Salinger, but I was too aware of what was wrong with such writers (their faults more readily apparent to my taste than their virtues) to be sensitive to the truths they told. It took, therefore, certain public events to illuminate (for me) the literature which might have illuminated them.

I am thinking, of course, of the recent demonstrations at Berkeley and elsewhere, whose ostensible causes were civil rights or freedom of speech or Vietnam, but whose not so secret slogan was all the time: *The Professor is a Fink!* And what an array of bad anti-academic novels, I cannot help reminding myself, written by disgruntled professors, created the mythology out of which that slogan grew. Each generation of students is invented by the generation of teachers just before them; but how different they are in dream and fact—as different as self-hatred and its reflection in another. How different the professors in Jeremy Larner's *Drive, He Said* from those even in Randall Jarrell's *Pictures from an Institution* or Mary McCarthy's *Groves of Academe.*

To be sure, many motives operated to set the students in action, some of them imagined in no book, however good or bad. Many of the thousands who resisted or shouted on campuses did so in the name of naïve or disingenuous or even nostalgic politics (be careful what you wish for in your middle age, or your children will parody it forthwith!); and sheer ennui doubtless played a role along with a justified rage against the hypocrisies of academic life. Universities have long rivaled the churches in their devotion to institutionalizing hypocrisy; and more recently they have outstripped television itself (which most professors affect to despise even more than they despise organized religion) in the institutionalization of boredom.

But what the students were protesting in large part, I have come to believe, was the very notion of man which the universities sought to impose upon them: that bourgeois-Protestant version of Humanism, with its view of man as justified by rationality, work, duty, vocation, maturity, success; and its concomitant understanding of childhood and adolescence as a temporarily privileged time of preparation for assuming those burdens. The new irrationalists, however, are prepared to advocate prolonging adolescence to the grave, and are ready to dispense with school as an outlived excuse for leisure. To them work is as obsolete as reason, a vestige (already dispensible for large numbers) of an economically marginal, pre-automated world; and the obsolescence of the two adds up to the obsolescence of everything our society understands by maturity.

Nor is it in the name of an older more valid Humanistic view of man that the new irrationalists would reject the WASP version; Rabelais is as alien to them as Benjamin Franklin. Disinterested scholarship, reflection, the life of reason, a respect for tradition stir (however dimly and confusedly) chiefly their contempt; and the Abbey of Theleme would seem as sterile to them as Robinson Crusoe's Island. To the classroom, the library, the laboratory, the office conference and the meeting of scholars, they prefer the demonstration, the sit-in, the riot: the mindless unity of an impassioned crowd (with guitars beating out the rhythm in the background), whose immediate cause is felt rather than thought out, whose ultimate cause is itself. In light of this, the Teach-in, often ill understood because of an emphasis on its declared political ends, can be seen as implicitly a parody and mockery of the real classroom: related to the actual business of the university, to real teaching only as the Demonstration Trial (of Dimitrov, of the Soviet Doctors, of Eichmann) to real justice or Demonstration Voting (for one party or a token two) to real suffrage.

At least, since Berkeley (or perhaps since Martin Luther King provided students with new paradigms for action) the choice has been extended beyond what the earlier laureates of the new youth could imagine in the novel: the nervous breakdown at home rather than the return to "sanity" and school, which was the best Salinger could invent for Franny and Holden; or Kerouac's way out for his "saintly" vagrants, that "road" from nowhere to noplace with homemade gurus at the way stations. The structure of those fictional vaudevilles between hard covers that currently please the young (*Catch 22, V., A Mother's Kisses*), suggest in their brutality and discontinuity, their politics of mockery something of the spirit of the student demonstrations; but only Jeremy Larner, as far as I know, has dealt explicitly with the abandonment of the classroom in favor of the dionysiac pack, the turning from *polis* to *thiasos,* from forms of social organization traditionally thought of as male to the sort of passionate community attributed by the ancients to females out of control.

Conventional slogans in favor of "Good Works" (pious emendations of existing social structures, or extensions of accepted "rights" to excluded groups) though they provide the motive power of such protests are irrelevant to their form and their final significance. They become their essential selves, i.e., genuine new forms of rebellion, when the demonstrators hoist (as they did in the final stages of the Berkeley protests) the sort of slogan which embarasses not only fellow-travelers but even the bureaucrats who direct the initial stages of the revolt: at the University of California, the single four-letter word no family newspaper would reprint, though no member of a family who could read was likely not to know it.

It is possible to argue on the basis of the political facts themselves that the word "fuck" entered the whole scene accidentally (there were only four students behind the "Dirty Speech Movement," only fifteen hundred kids could be persuaded to demonstrate for it, etc., etc.). But the prophetic literature which anticipates the movement indicates otherwise, suggesting that the logic of their illogical course eventually sets the young against language itself, against the very counters of logical discourse. They seek an anti-language of protest as inevitably as they seek anti-poems and anti-novels, end with the ultimate anti-word, which the demonstrators at Berkeley disingenuously claimed stood for FREEDOM UNDER CLARK KERR.

Esthetics, however, had already anticipated politics in this regard; porno-poetry preceding and preparing the way for what Lewis Feuer has aptly called porno-politics. Already in 1963, in an essay entitled *"Phi Upsilon Kappa,"* the young poet Michael McClure was writing: "Gregory Corso has asked me to join with him in a project to free the word FUCK from its chains and strictures. I leap to make some new freedom. . . ." And McClure's own "Fuck Ode" is a product of this collaboration, as the very name of Ed Saunders' journal, *Fuck You,* is the creation of an analogous impulse. The aging critics of the young who have dealt with the Berkeley demonstrations in such journals as *Commentary* and the *New Leader* do not, however, read either Saunders' porno-pacifist magazine or *Kulchur,* in which McClure's manifesto was first printed—the age barrier separating readership in the United States more effectively than class, political affiliation or anything else.

Their sense of porno-esthetics is likely to come from deserters from their own camp, chiefly Norman Mailer, and especially his recent *An American Dream,* which represents the entry of anti-language (extending the tentative explorations of "The Time of Her Time") into the world of the middle-aged, both on the level of mass culture and that of yesterday's ex-Marxist, post-Freudian avant-garde. Characteristically enough, Mailer's book has occasioned in the latter quarters reviews as irrelevant, incoherent, misleading and fundamentally scared as the most philistine responses to the Berkeley demonstrations, Philip Rahv and Stanley Edgar Hyman providing two egregious examples. Yet elsewhere (in sectors held by those more at ease with their own conservatism, i.e., without defunct radicalisms to uphold) the most obscene forays of the young are being met with a disheartening kind of tolerance and even an attempt to adapt them to the conditions of commodity art.

But precisely here, of course, a disconcerting irony is involved; for after a while, there will be no Rahvs and Hymans left to shock—anti-language becoming mere language with repeated use and in the face of acceptance; so that all sense of exhilaration will be lost along with the possibility of offense. What to do then except to choose silence, since raising the ante of violence is ultimately self-defeating; and the way of obscenity in any case leads as naturally to silence as to further excess? Moreover, to the talkative heirs of Socrates, silence is the one offense that never wears out, the radicalism that can never become fashionable; which is why, after the obscene slogan has been hauled down, a blank placard is raised in its place.

There are difficulties, to be sure, when one attempts to move from the politics of silence to an analogous sort of poetry. The opposite number to the silent picketer would be the silent poet, which is a contradiction in terms; yet there are these days non-singers of (perhaps) great talent who shrug off the temptation to song with the muttered comment, "Creativity is out." Some, however, make literature of a kind precisely at the point of maximum tension between the tug toward silence and the pull toward publication. Music is a better language really for saying what one would prefer not to say at all–and all the way from certain sorts of sufficiently cool jazz to Rock'n'Roll (with its minimal lyrics that defy understanding on a first hearing), music is the preferred art of the irrationalists.

But some varieties of skinny poetry seem apt, too (as practised, say, by Robert Creeley after the example of W. C. Williams), since their lines are three parts silence to one part speech.

. . .

And, of course, fiction aspiring to become Pop Art, say, *An American Dream* (with the experiments of Hemingway and Nathanael West behind it), works approximately as well, since clichés are almost as inaudible as silence itself. The point is not to shout, not to insist, but to hang cool, to baffle all mothers, cultural and spiritual as well as actual.

When the Town Council in Venice, California was about to close down a particularly notorious beatnik cafe, a lady asked to testify before them, presumably to clinch the case against the offenders. What she reported, however, was that each day as she walked by the cafe and looked in its windows, she saw the unsavory types who inhabited it "just standing there, looking—nonchalant." And, in a way, her improbable adjective does describe a crime against her world; for non-chaleur ("cool", the futurists themselves would prefer to call it) is the essence of their life-style as well as of the literary styles to which they respond: the offensive style of those who are not so much *for* anything in particular, as "with it" in general.

But such an attitude is as remote from traditional "alienation," with its profound longing to end disconnection, as it is from ordinary forms of allegiance, with their desperate resolve not to admit disconnection. The new young celebrate disconnection—accept it as one of the necessary consequences of the industrial system which has delivered them from work and duty, of that welfare state which makes disengagement the last possible virtue, whether it call itself Capitalist, Socialist or Communist. "Detachment" is the traditional name for the stance the futurists assume; but "detachment" carries with it irrelevant religious, even specifically Christian overtones. The post-modernists are surely in some sense "mystics," religious at least in a way they do not ordinarily know how to confess, but they are not Christians.

Indeed, they regard Christianity, quite as the Black Muslim (with whom they have certain affinities) do, as a white ideology: merely one more method—along with Humanism, technology, Marxism—of imposing "White" or Western values on the colored rest of the world. To the new barbarian, however, that would-be post-Humanist (who is in most cases the white offspring of Christian forebears) his whiteness is likely to seem if not a stigma and symbol of shame, at least the outward sign of his exclusion from all that his Christian Humanist ancestors rejected in themselves and projected mythologically upon the colored man. For such reasons, his religion, when it becomes explicit, claims to be derived from Tibet or

Japan or the ceremonies of the Plains Indians, or is composed out of the non-Christian sub-mythology that has grown up among Negro jazz musicians and in the civil rights movement. When the new barbarian speaks of "soul," for instance, he means not "soul" as in Heaven, but as in "soul music" or even "soul food."

It is all part of the attempt of the generation under twenty-five, not exclusively in its most sensitive members but especially in them, to become Negro, even as they attempt to become poor or pre-rational. About this particular form of psychic assimilation I have written sufficiently in the past (summing up what I had been long saying in chapters seven and eight of *Waiting for the End*), neglecting only the sense in which what starts as a specifically American movement becomes an international one, spreading to the *yé-yé* girls of France or the working-class entertainers of Liverpool with astonishing swiftness and ease.

III

What interests me more particularly right now is a parallel assimilationist attempt, which may, indeed, be more parochial and is certainly most marked at the moment in the Anglo-Saxon world, i.e., in those cultural communities most totally committed to bourgeois-Protestant values and surest that they are unequivocally "white." I am thinking of the effort of young men in England and the United States to assimilate into themselves (or even to assimilate themselves into) that otherness, that sum total of rejected psychic elements which the middle-class heirs of the Renaissance have identified with "woman." To become new men, these children of the future seem to feel, they must not only become more Black than White but more female than male. And it is natural that the need to make such an adjustment be felt with especial acuteness in post-Protestant highly industrialized societies, where the functions regarded as specifically male for some three hundred years tend most rapidly to become obsolete.

Surely, in America, machines already perform better than humans a large number of those aggressive-productive activities which our ancestors considered man's special province, even his *raison d'être*. Not only has the male's prerogative of making things and money (which is to say, of working) been preempted, but also his time-honored privilege of dealing out death by hand, which until quite recently was regarded as a supreme mark of masculine valor. While it seems theoretically possible, even in the heart of Anglo-Saxondom, to imagine a leisurely, pacific male, in fact the losses in secondary functions sustained by men appear to have shaken their faith in their primary masculine function as well, in their ability to achieve the conquest (as the traditional metaphor has it) of women. Earlier, advances in technology had detached the wooing and winning of women from the begetting of children; and though the invention of the condom had at least left the decision to inhibit fatherhood in the power of males, its replacement by the "loop" and the "pill" has placed paternity at the mercy of the whims of women.

Writers of fiction and verse registered the technological obsolescence of masculinity long before it was felt even by the representative minority who give to the present younger generation its character and significance. And literary critics have talked a good deal during the past couple of decades about the conversion of the literary hero into the non-hero or the anti-hero; but they have in general failed to notice his simultaneous conversion into the non- or anti-male. Yet ever since Hemingway at least, certain male protagonists of Amercan literature have not only fled rather than sought out combat but have also fled rather than sought out women. From Jake Barnes to Holden Caulfield they have continued to run from the threat of female sexuality; and, indeed, there are models for such evasion in our classic books, where heroes still eager for the fight (Natty Bumppo comes to mind) are already shy of wives and sweethearts and mothers.

It is not absolutely required that the anti-male anti-hero be impotent or homosexual or both (though this helps, as we remember remembering Walt Whitman), merely that he be more seduced than seducing, more passive than active. Consider, for instance, the oddly "womanish" Herzog of Bellow's current best seller, that Jewish Emma Bovary with a Ph.D., whose chief law is physical vanity and a taste for fancy clothes. Bellow, however, is more interested in summing up the past than in evoking the future; and *Herzog* therefore seems an end rather than a beginning, the product of nostalgia (remember when there were real Jews once, and the "Jewish Novel" had not yet been discovered!) rather than prophecy. No, the post-humanist, post-male, post-white, post-heroic world is a post-Jewish world by the same token, anti-Semitism as inextricably woven into it as into the movement for Negro rights; and its scriptural books are necessarily *goyish,* not least of all William Burroughs' *The Naked Lunch.*

Burroughs is the chief prophet of the post-male post-heroic world; and it is his emulators who move into the center of the relevant literary scene, for *The Naked Lunch* (the later novels are less successful, less exciting but relevant still) is more than it seems: no mere essay in heroin-hallucinated homosexual pornography—but a nightmare anticipation (in Science Fiction form) of post-Humanist sexuality. Here, as in Alexander Trocchi, John Rechy, Harry Matthews (even an occasional Jew like Allen Ginsberg, who has begun by inscribing properly anti-Jewish obscenities on the walls of the world), are clues to the new attitudes toward sex that will continue to inform our improbable novels of passion and our even more improbable love songs.

The young to whom I have been referring, the mythologically representative minority (who, by a process that infuriates the mythologicaliy inert majority out of which they come, "stand for" their times), live in a community in which what used to be called the "Sexual Revolution," the Freudian-Laurentian revolt of their grandparents and parents, has triumphed as imperfectly and unsatisfactorily as all revolutions always triumph. They confront, therefore, the necessity of determining not only what meanings "love" can have in their new world, but—even more disturbingly—what significance, if any, "male" and "female" now possess.

For a while, they (or at least their literary spokesmen recruited from the generation just before them) seemed content to celebrate a kind of *reductio* or *exaltatio ad absurdum* of their parents' once revolutionary sexual goals: The Reichian-inspired Cult of the Orgasm.

Young men and women eager to be delivered of traditional ideologies of love find especially congenial the belief that not union or relationship (much less offspring) but physical release is the end of the sexual act; and that, therefore, it is a matter of indifference with whom or by what method ones pursues the therapeutic climax, so long as that climax is total and repeated frequently. And Wilhelm Reich happily detaches this belief from the vestiges of Freudian rationalism, setting it instead in a context of Science Fiction and witchcraft; but his emphasis upon "full genitality," upon growing up and away from infantile pleasures, strikes the young as a disguised plea for the "maturity" they have learned to despise. In a time when the duties associated with adulthood promise to become irrelevant, there seems little reason for denying oneself the joys of babyhood—even if these are associated with such regressive fantasies as escaping it all in the arms of little sister (in the Gospel according to J. D. Salinger) or flirting with the possibility of getting into bed with papa (in the Gospel according to Norman Mailer).

Only Norman O. Brown in *Life Against Death* has come to terms on the level of theory with the aspiration to take the final evolutionary leap and cast off adulthood completely, at least in the area of sex. His post-Freudian program for pan-sexual, non-orgasmic love rejects "full genitality" in favor of a species of indiscriminate bundling, a dream of unlimited sub-coital intimacy which Brown calls (in his vocabulary the term is an honorific) "polymorphous perverse." And here finally is an essential clue to the nature of the second sexual revolution, the post-sexual revolution, first evoked in literature by Brother Antoninus more than a decade ago, in a verse prayer addressed somewhat improbably to the Christian God.

. . .

Despite the accents of this invocation, however, what is at work is not essentially a homosexual revolt or even a rebellion against women, though its advocates seek to wrest from women their ancient privileges of receiving the Holy Ghost and pleasuring men; and though the attitudes of the movement can be adapted to the anti-female bias of, say, Edward Albee. If in *Who's Afraid of Virginia Woolf* Albee can portray the relationship of two homosexuals (one in drag) as the model of contemporary marriage, this must be because contemporary marriage has in fact turned into something much like that parody. And it is true that what survives of bourgeois marriage and the bourgeois family is a target which the new barbarians join the old homosexuals in reviling, seeking to replace Mom, Pop and the kids with a neo-Whitmanian gaggle of giggling *camerados*. Such groups are, in fact, whether gathered in coffee houses, university cafeterias or around the literature tables on campuses, the peace-time equivalents, as it were, to the demonstrating crowd. But even their program of displacing Dick-Jane-Spot-Baby, etc., the WASP family of grade school primers, is not the fundamental motive of the post-sexual revolution.

IV

What is at stake from Burroughs to Bellow, Ginsberg to Albee, Salinger to Gregory Corso is a more personal transformation: a radical metamorphosis of the Western male—utterly unforeseen in the decades before us, but visible now in every high school and college classroom, as well as on the paperback racks in airports and supermarkets. All around us, young males are beginning to retrieve for themselves the cavalier role once piously and class-consciously surrendered to women: *that of being beautiful and being loved.* Here once more the example to the Negro— the feckless and adorned Negro male with the blood of Cavaliers in his veins—has served as a model. And what else is left to young men, in any case, after the devaluation of the grim duties they had arrogated to themselves in place of the pursuit of loveliness?

All of us who are middle-aged and were Marxists, which is to say, who once numbered ourselves among the last assured Puritans, have surely noticed in ourselves a vestigial roundhead rage at the new hair styles of the advanced or—if you please–delinquent young. Watching young men titivate their locks (the comb, the pocket mirror and the bobby pin having repaced the jackknife, catcher's mitt and brass knuckles), we feel the same baffled resentment that stirs in us when we realize that they have rejected work. A job and unequivocal maleness—these are two sides of the same Calvinist coin, which in the future buys nothing.

Few of us, however, have really understood how the Beatle hairdo is part of a syndrome, of which high heels, jeans tight over the buttocks, etc., are other aspects, symptomatic of a longer retreat from masculine aggressiveness to female allure—in literature and the arts to the style called "camp." And fewer still have realized how that style, though the invention of homosexuals, is now the possession of basically heterosexual males as well, a strategy in their campaign to establish a new relationship not only with women but with their own masculinity. In the course of that campaign, they have embraced certain kinds of gesture and garb, certain accents and tones traditionally associated with females or female impersonators; which is why we have been observing recently (in life as well as fiction and verse) young boys, quite unequivocally male, playing all the traditional roles of women: the vamp, the coquette, the whore, the icy tease, the pure young virgin.

Not only oldsters, who had envisioned and despaired of quite another future, are bewildered by this turn of events, but young girls, too, seem scarcely to know what is happening—looking on with that new, schizoid stare which itself has become a hallmark of our times. And the crop-headed jocks, those crew-cut athletes who represent an obsolescent masculine style based on quite other values, have tended to strike back blindly; beating the hell out of some poor kid whose hair is too long or whose pants are too tight—quite as they once beat up young Communists for revealing that their politics had become obsolete. Even heterosexual writers, however, have been slow to catch up, the revolution in sensibility running ahead of that in expression; and they have perforce permitted homosexuals to speak for them (Burroughs and Genet and Baldwin and Ginsberg and Albee and a score of others), even to invent the forms in which the future will have to speak.

The revolt against masculinity is not limited, however, to simple matters of coiffure and costume, visible even to athletes; or to the adaptation of certain campy styles and modes to new uses. There is also a sense in which two large social movements that have set the young in motion and furnished images of action for their books—movements as important in their own right as porno-politics and the pursuit of the polymorphous perverse—are connected analogically to the abdication from traditional maleness. The first of these is nonviolent or passive resistance, so oddly come back to the land of its inventor, that icy Thoreau who dreamed a love which ". . . has not much human blood in it, but consists with a certain disregard for men and their erections. . . ."

The civil rights movement, however, in which nonviolence has found a home, has been hospitable not only to the sort of post-humanist I have been describing; so that at a demonstration (Selma, Alabama will do as an example) the true hippie will be found side by side with backwoods Baptists, nuns on a spiritual spree, boy bureaucrats practicing to take power, resurrected socialists, Unitarians in search of a God, and just plain tourists, gathered, as once at the Battle of Bull Run, to see the fun. For each of these, nonviolence will have a different sort of fundamental meaning—as a tactic, a camouflage, a passing fad, a pious gesture—but for each in part, and for the post-humanist especially, it will signify the possibility of heroism without aggression, effective action without guilt.

There have always been two contradictory American ideals: to be the occasion of maximum violence, and to remain absolutely innocent. Once, however, these were thought hopelessly incompatible for males (except, perhaps, as embodied in works of art), reserved strictly for women: the spouse of the wife-beater, for instance, or the victim of rape. But males have now assumed these classic roles; and just as a particularly beleaguered wife occasionally slipped over the dividing line into violence, so do the new passive protestors—leaving us to confront (or resign to the courts) such homey female questions as: *Did Mario Savio really bite that cop in the leg as he sagged limply toward the ground?*

The second social movement is the drug cult, more widespread among youth, from its squarest limits to its most beat, than anyone seems prepared to admit in public; and at its beat limit at least inextricably involved with the civil rights movement, as the recent arrests of Peter DeLissovoy and Susan Ryerson revealed even to the ordinary newspaper reader. "Police said that most of the recipients [of marijuana] were college students," the U.P. story runs. "They quoted Miss Ryerson and DeLissovoy as saying that many of the letter packets were sent to civil rights workers."

Only fiction and verse, however, has dealt with the conjunction of homo-sexuality, drugs and civil rights, eschewing the general piety of the press which has been unwilling to compromise "good works" on behalf of the Negro by associating it with the deep radicalism of a way of life based on the ritual consumption of "pot."

The widespread use of such hallucinogens as peyote, marijuana, the "mexican mushroom," LSD, etc., as well as pep pills, goof balls, airplane glue, certain kinds of cough syrups and even, though in many fewer cases, heroin, is not merely a matter of a changing taste in stimulants but of the programmatic espousal of an anti-puritanical mode of existence—hedonistic and detached—one more strategy in the war on time and work. But it is also (to pursue my analogy once more) an attempt to arro-gate to the male certain traditional privileges of the female. What could be more womanly, as Elémire Zolla was already pointing out some years ago, than permitting the penetration of the body by a foreign object which not only stirs delight but even (possibly) creates new life?

In any case, with drugs we have come to the crux of the futurist revolt, the hinge of everything else, as the young tell us over and over in their writing. When the movement was first finding a voice, Allen Ginsberg set this aspect of it in proper context in an immensely comic, utterly serious poem called "America," in which "pot" is associated with earlier forms of rebellion, a commitment to catatonia, and a rejection of conventional male potency.

· · ·

Similarly, Michael McClure reveals in his essay, *"Phi Upsilon Kappa,"* that before penetrating the "cavern of Anglo-Saxon," whence he emerged with the slogan of the ultimate Berkeley demonstrators, he had been on mescalin. "I have emerged from a dark night of the soul; I entered it by Peyote." And by now, drug-taking has become as standard a feature of the literature of the young as oral-genital love-making. I flip open the first issue of yet another ephemeral San Francisco little magazine quite at random and read: "I tie up and the main pipe [the ante-cobital vein, for the clinically inclined] swells like a prideful beggar beneath the skin. Just before I get on it is always the worst." Worse than the experience, however, is its literary rendering; and the badness of such confessional fiction, flawed by the sentimentality of those who desire to live "like a cunning vegetable," is a badness we older readers find it only too easy to perceive, as our sons and daughters find it only to easy to overlook. Yet precisely here the age and the mode define themselves; for not in the master but in the hacks new forms are established, new lines drawn.

Here, at any rate, is where the young lose us in literature as well as life, since here they pass over into real revolt, i.e., what we really cannot abide, hard as we try. The mother who has sent her son to private schools and on to Harvard to keep him out of classrooms overcrowded with poor Negroes, rejoices when he sets out for Mississippi with his comrades in SNCC, but shudders when he turns on with LSD; just as the ex-Marxist father, who has earlier proved radicalism impossible, rejoices to see his son stand up, piously and pompously, for CORE or SDS, but trembles to hear him quote Alpert and Leary or praise Burroughs. Just as certainly as liberalism is the LSD of the aging, LSD is the radicalism of the young.

If whiskey long served as an appropriate symbolic excess for those who chafed against Puritan restraint without finally challenging it—temporarily releasing them to socially harmful aggression and (hopefully) sexual self-indulgence, the new popular drugs provide an excess quite as satisfactorily symbolic to the post-Puritans—releasing them from sanity to madness by destroying in them the inner restrictive order which has somehow survived the dissolution of the outer. It is finally insanity, then, that the futurists learn to admire and emulate, quite as they learn to pursue vision instead of learning, hallucination rather than logic. The schizophrenic replaces the sage as their ideal, their new culture hero, figured forth as a giant schizoid Indian (his madness modeled in part on the author's own experiences with LSD) in Ken Kesey's *One Flew Over the Cuckoo's Nest.*

The hippier young are not alone, however, in their taste for the insane; we live in a time when readers in general respond sympathetically to madness in literature wherever it is found, in established writers as well as in those trying to establish new modes. Surely it is not the lucidity and logic of Robert Lowell or Theodore Roethke or John Berryman which we admire, but their flirtation with incoherence and disorder. And certainly it is Mailer at his most nearly psychotic, Mailer the creature rather than the master of his fantasies who moves us to admiration; while in the case of Saul Bellow, we endure the theoretical optimism and acceptance for the sake of the delightful melancholia, the fertile paranoia which he cannot disavow any more than the talent at whose root they lie. Even essayists and analysts recommend themselves to us these days by a certain redemptive nuttiness; at any rate, we do not love, say, Marshall McLuhan less because he continually risks sounding like the body-fluids man in *Dr. Strangelove.*

We have, moreover, recently been witnessing the development of a new form of social psychiatry[2] (a psychiatry of the future already anticipated by the literature of the future) which considers some varieties of "schizophrenia" not diseases to be cured but forays into an unknown psychic world: random penetrations by bewildered internal cosmonauts of a realm that it will be the task of the next generations to explore. And if the accounts which the returning schizophrenics give (the argument of the apologists runs) of the "places" they have been are fantastic and garbled, surely they are no more so than, for example, Columbus' reports of the world he had claimed for Spain, a world bounded—according to his newly drawn maps—by Cathay on the north and Paradise on the south.

In any case, poets and junkies have been suggesting to us that the new world appropriate to the new men of the latter twentieth century is to be

---

[2] Described in an article in the *New Left Review* of November–December, 1964, by R. D. Laing who advocates "ex-patients helping future patients go mad."

discovered only by the conquest of inner space: by an adventure of the spirit, an extension of psychic possibility, of which the flights into outer space—moonshots and expeditions to Mars—are precisely such unwitting metaphors and analogues as the voyages of exploration were of the earlier breakthrough into the Renaissance, from whose consequences the young seek now so desperately to escape. The laureate of that new conquest is William Burroughs . . .

I Read the
News Today,
Oh Wow

"Fascinating, Captain Kirk": The Cultural Impact of Pop Media

RALPH L. CARNES

Assume standard orbit, Mr. Sulu. All hailing frequencies
open, Lt. Uhuru. Meet me in the transporter room,
Mr. Scott, Bones. Mr. Spock, you're in command.

Sometimes, when the grown-ups were sitting in the cool shadows of the living room after the Sunday meal, I would slip away to the broomsage patch by grandma's house with my arms full of books. I would lie under the sticky cottonwood tree, on patches of grass amidst the yellowing broomsage, and read and read and read. Sometimes, I would hear a droning in the air. I would look up and see a yellow Taylor Cub, or a Waco biplane, or maybe even an autogyro. I would settle back against the bank of grass, munch my Three Musketeers bar, and instantly be wafted away to a land where knights were always strong and brave and true, heroines were always young and lissome, and evil-doers were always punished in the end. They were the children's classics: Dickens and Hawthorne, *Wind in the Willows* and *The Wizard of Oz*, *The Secret Garden*, *The Five Little Peppers*, *Winnie the Pooh*, *The Five Little Martins*, Tom Swift's adventures, *The Little Lame Prince,* and Howard Pyle's *Book of Pirates.* Nobody ever read Horatio Alger anymore, because back there in the primordial chaos of the Thirties, we no longer thought success was possible.

On Saturday afternoons, I would go to my Aunt Flossie's house. She kept homemade cupcakes in the cupboard, and her house always smelled fresh, like the old-style pink Lifebuoy soap. Uncle Frank was forever tinkering with some kind of Rube Goldberg contraption; and Aunt Flossie seemed to float through the house with her long dresses trailing on the rugs. I would gather up two or three cupcakes and go to the sun porch to read. The sun porch shelves held a complete set of Raggedy Ann and Raggedy Andy books. And as I lay reading on the window seat, surrounded by golden shafts of sunlight that carved lines through the myriad dust particles in the air, I would seem to float down babbling brooks, walk through fields of red and yellow poppies, make wind sandwiches, and sit on a grassy hillside with Raggedy Ann while her chocolate candy heart dried in the sun.

They were my personal Golden Days, of course, filled with sunny air and soft breezes and flowers strewn along the pine forest paths of my home. My grandfather's flower garden stretched for three hundred feet alongside the yard. It was bordered to the south by a rippling broomsage patch. The house had twelve rooms and a tin roof that pattered in the rain. White pebbles from the riverbank lined the walkways. At night, the tall grandfather's clock sounded like a carriage rolling down cobblestone streets (maybe carrying Bob Cratchit or Little Nell), creaking and whirring as it prepared to chime. Sometimes, I would turn on the light and read after my parents had gone to bed. My father had been a newspaperman in a tiny southern town. I was surrounded by words and stories. I would stay awake with all my books (they covered the bed) and read until my eyes were dry with sleep. Reluctantly, I would turn off the light and settle back against the feather bed. Later, when we lived in my grandmother's house, my bed was in a dormer, and I could see the lights of the town winking off at midnight. I imagined Uriah Heep sneaking through the darkened village. On clear nights, I would look up at the stars, at far Antares, deep red against the horizon; and Arcturus above was glossy white. Sometimes I could see the fine diadem of Corona Borealis. Jupiter and Saturn were flooded with reflected light. The moon would slowly rise, spreading its stronger light like a veil over the dimming stars. Years later, Ray Bradbury would teach me that I was one of the "Book People." Truffaut would make a movie of Bradbury's *Fahrenheit 451,* almost too late to catch the few of us left. It was not a great box-office success. Still later, Fredric Brown would tell me that the Lights in the Sky are Stars; and I would go to college, rescued from being another of the South's "good ole boys" by the unlikely pantheon of Science Fiction writers, Bradbury, Asimov, Clarke, Sturgeon, Simak, Kornbluth (how now, *Marching Morons?*), Heinlein, Van Vogt, Boucher, Campbell, Zenna Henderson, del Ray, and most of all by a man named Montag, the name of paper, sprung full-blown from Bradbury's imagination.

Rheumatic fever ended the golden years. The aroma of ripening broomsage and the softness of Aunt Flossie's tufted window seat were replaced by the antiseptic smells of rubbing alcohol, rubber hospital sheets, needles, and things that stick and sting and ache. The dull pain in my chest was a portent of the years of convalescence ahead. The last short summer months of 1938 were the end of the age. That summer, my pal Lord Daniel and I, we tied our threads to the Junebug's leg and flew the summer away. And then one morning, when the first crisp chill of autumn was in the air, as I lay in my bed and smelled the salty goodness of frying sausage, I thought that in a few minutes my mother would call me from the kitchen and I would spend a lazy Saturday morning eating biscuits, eggs, sausage and sorghum syrup. But when I tried to get up, I found that my right leg was bent beneath me, the knee joint frozen overnight with rheumatoid arthritis. It did not straighten for months. The Little Lame Prince was trapped in the tower, without his magic flying cloak.

I huddled beneath the patchwork quilt and lay my head against my mother's side. Frost covered the windows of the ten year old Nash coupe. I could hear the transmission whining beneath the seats. My father wore a heavy wool sweater with leather-reinforced elbows. My mother tried to shield me from the cold as best she could. The car had no heater. I remember vividly the inside of that old convertible. The meters trembled within their glass cases; and during our twenty mile trip to Villa Rica, I sorted out all of the sounds of the car: the click of the valves, the hiss of the carburetor, the whizzing of the generator. I followed the energy with my ears through the transmission, down the drive shaft to the differential, then out to the right rear wheel whose tire blipped across the asphalt expansion joints that framed the concrete highway.

When we parked in front of the doctor's office, we were early for my appointment. My father carried me into the downstairs drugstore for a Coca-Cola. We sat at a little porcelain-topped table and sipped our "fountain cokes." On a shelf by the candy counter lay the doomsday book of children's literature: "Action Comics" had at last arrived in Villa Rica, Georgia. On the cover, in full color, a man in a blue suit with a red cape flew through the air. Below him, people pointed and gasped. So did I. My father paid the necessary dime, and in an instant Rumpelstiltskin was gone in a puff of smoke. And with him went all the richness of his world. No more pirates. No more Dickensian universes in the back streets of London. No more dark and stormy nights, with castles on their heaths. No more witches feeling something wicked this way coming. The galaxy of the imagination had given way in my feverishness to the tight orbit of a costumed super-hero, zooming across the face of a comic book. The world of literature had suddenly become so simple that a child could understand it.

I had a brief respite from my chronic illness the next year (no thanks to my medical care; my rheumatic fever was diagnosed as tonsilitis. I have tried for three decades to make physicians take seriously the fact that what they call my "miraculous" remission of arthritic symptoms came only twelve hours after an aging Negro woman had plastered my swollen joints with hot poultices made from the roots of poke salad plants.) But I had to rest twice a day, and little or no exercise was allowed. Often I was brought home from school half exhausted. But no matter, I had my comic books! In fact, I had a comic book business. My father's news-paper had long since been swallowed by the depression. Now his radio repair shop was failing. I sold old radio batteries from a "Radio-Flyer" wagon, to be burned in the town's pot-bellied stoves (it cleans out the flue). Sometimes, I brought in more money than my father did with his radio shop. New comics sold for a dime. But a nickel would buy a used comic book with the cover on, or two with the covers off. I traded one with the cover off for one with the cover on. I made a small profit and I got to read all of the comic books.

It was a world of easy identification, of straightforward problems with straightforward solutions. *Action Comics* were "Action" comics. While credibility might be strained, one's imagination had it easy. For me it was especially enticing, because I could escape my illness and my little town with no effort whatever. I could BE Superman. All I had to do was lie in my bed at night, close my eyes, and there I was: Clark Kent, mild-mannered reporter for the Daily Planet. I could rush into an empty store-room, rip away the clothes that covered my blue and red suit, and leap out the window to fly through the sky ("Up, up and away!"). On other nights, I would imagine myself walking out of the office building in which I (Billy Batson) worked, stepping into the shadows and saying softly, "SHAZAM!" Instantly, I would be transformed into Captain Marvel (not the alien freak that Marvel Comics currently has, the real Captain Marvel, gang, the one with the red suit and the white cape, with the golden rope around his shoulders). There were others too. There was Captain Marvel Junior, who said "CAPTAIN MARVEL" instead of Billy Batson's "SHA-ZAM." There was Plastic Man, the Spectre, the Human Torch, the Sub-Mariner, Tarzan, Hawkman, Captain America (you didn't really think Peter Fonda invented that name, did you?), the Flash, the Spirit (only for the real connoisseurs amongst us), and the Dynamic Duo, Batman and Robin. It was not until I was a senior in college that I learned about Dr. Frederic Wertham's thesis (in *Seduction of the Innocents)* that Bruce Wayne and Dick Grayson lived in a homosexual dream fantasy. A homo-what? Holy Seduction! All I ever saw were two people who had dedicated their lives to fighting crime. Just like Mr. Hoover, gang. Just like any-body would if they were strong and loyal and just and true like Batman and Robin. Gee Whiz, Doc, crime fighters fight vice, they don't practice it! Next we'll be told to take cold showers and run around the block before reading Wonder Woman comics. Gee Whiz! Golly! Boy Howdy!

The newspapers belonged to daddy, but the comic books belonged to us. We knew all of the characters personally. I could walk up and down the streets with Mickey and Goofy. I could swing from limb to limb with Tarzan. With no effort at all, I could be and be with all of the characters I'd seen. It was as if I could move along the page with them, skipping from frame to frame, with word balloons above my head. All you had to do was say, very softly, "SHAZAM." No, the seduction of the innocents was neither violent nor sexual. It was worse than that. Our imaginations were simpli-fied into word balloons.

Before I became ill, Lord Daniel and I had a standing date to go to the Grand Theater on Saturday mornings. It never occurred to me that Lord Daniel sat in the balcony because the manager made him sit there. It also never occurred to me that I could not sit there with him. He was black and I was white. The supposed significance of that fact escaped me. To me, Lord Daniel simply lived on the other side of grandma's broomsage patch, and he was my best friend. Once inside the theater, the blackness made such grown-up concerns doubly meaningless: here we each lived in our own private world, watched the chimerae cross the screen and recite their lines, and merged our consciousnesses with the images we saw. After the show, Lord Daniel and I would leave, stop at Baby Hat Roberts' cafe to get a Three Musketeers bar, and run stealthily single file down the narrow bottle-cap encrusted alleyway, across the cafe's back lot, through the culvert, across the field of broomsage to Grandma's house.

We were the Durango Kid, Bob Steele, George O'Brien, Hopalong Cassidy and Windy, Tom Mix, the Sons of the Pioneers, Gene Autry, Flash Gordon, Ming, Dr. Zarkhov, and Tarzan of the Apes. We lived in a simple fantasy world where no one worried about two dimensional characters. We provided the fleshing out ourselves. What boy of the time didn't take the largest towel in the bathroom, tie it around his neck, and make mighty leaps down the slopes of sandpiles? And who among us didn't get a lickin' for swinging around in trees clad only in Jockey shorts? Some of the movies led to even greater troubles for us: "Hello chief? This is Larry Doyle. Listen, I've got a hot tip on the Purple Gang. Yeah. Okay, I'll be right over." Let's see, this key starts it. Here's the emergency brake. Oh, Oh. Oh no! Wow! Crash!

Henry? Henry Aldrich!

During the long illness that began in the fall of 1940 there were times when I could not hold a comic book in my hands. My father built a book prop and encouraged me to read "something worthwhile" again. I had nothing but time, so in a two month flurry I read the entire 1910 edition of the *Encyclopedia Brittanica*. The doctor winced when I greeted him with questions about the nature of microcephalia (under "Neuropathology," vol. 19, p. 433). My father and I had a private joke that involved verses made from the volume names ("A to AUS, Santa Claus"; "CON to DEM, Out on a limb"; "MUN to ODD, Dig in the sod." We could never do anything with "HUS to ITA."). I built model airplanes for a while—Hi-Flyer, Guillow and Strombecker kits—but eventually it became too tiring. Years later, I recaptured the past by spending three years on a Curtiss-Hawk P6E (twenty-one coats of dope, with movable controls from the cockpit). Eventually, comic books returned as an effortless time-killer. But one can't read all day. And I was there all day. And all night, all week, all year.

It was a small Stewart-Warner table model with a brown bakelite case that had been broken four times and glued back together with airplane glue. It had a marvelous dial, with lights and string behind the numbers.

The voice would say, "Don't touch that dial. You are tuned to 750, the voice of the South." At the time, I wondered how he knew my radio was tuned to 750. When the long weeks stretched into months, the radio characters became auditory comic books. The hours of the day were neatly divided into fifteen minute segments, each filled with familiar friends. Before long, I knew all of the programs and all of the plots. Ma Perkins had a lumber yard and a daughter named Fay. Jim Brent was a doctor on "Road of Life." And there were the others: "Pepper Young's Family," "Our Gal Sunday," "Right to Happiness" with Papa David and the Slightly-Read Bookstore, "Portia Faces Life," "Young Widder Brown," Lorenzo Jones (who reminded me of Uncle Frank), Stella Dallas, and the whole squalling bunch of soap operas. At night, there were Hop Harrigan, Little Orphan Annie, Tom Mix, and all of the comic book characters. Later in the evening, we listened to Lum and Abner, Amos and Andy, and beloved Fibber McGee. At noon, a voice would say "It's a beeyootiful day in Chicago." It was time for the "National Farm and Home Hour." Some of the shows survived the advent of television, but it wasn't the same. The names are dead now, like the shows they signify. It has become poor taste to bring up Old Radio.

Back then, however, I would lie awake at night and construct alternate plots for the shows. I would revel in the luxury of fright from "Inner Sanctum" and "Lights Out" (does anybody else remember "The Chicken Heart"?). Like the comic books, the radio shows were so simple that even a child could understand. The radio had done for drama what comic books had done for literature. The super-heroes of radio belonged to us in the same way that the super-heroes of comic books belonged to us. We understood them. We saw the characters as real people. We lived their life-styles in every sandlot in America. At first, I thought that it was my illness that caused me to identify with the comic book characters as much as I did. But we all did it back then. The other kids read the comics and listened to the shows without being bedridden. They were designed for us without our knowledge. They were like manna from heaven. They answered every need, every desire. So we listened to the shows and bought the comics. And we bought Little Orphan Annie Milkshake Mugs, and secret decoder rings, comic-scopes, and Lone Ranger Masks. We faithfully cut out boxtops and sent them to Battle Creek, Michigan, in exchange for ray guns and periscopes, cap pistols, boats, cars, balls, nets, gloves, knives, and skates. We bought bicycles and bows and arrows, bats and chewing gum, candy and soap, cereal and cereal and cereal. For it just wasn't right to listen to Tom Mix without Shredded Ralston. And it wasn't right to listen to Little Orphan Annie without drinking Ovaltine. Hadn't the announcer told us that if it weren't for Ovaltine, Orphan Annie wouldn't be on the air? None of us could even think of being disloyal. So we bought things. And we bought more things. And more, and more and more and more things. Hmmmmmmm.

When television came to Atlanta, Georgia, suddenly living room lights went out one by one all over the neighborhood. The first people near us to own a set were the Prices. We would sit in their living room, fumble over dinners, and watch ghostly figures skitter across the tiny screen. It was an electric comic book! Some of the adventure series followed the grand tradition: "Captain Video," "Tom Corbett, Space Cadet," the children's shows. All were filled with characters who could have operated perfectly with word balloons over their heads. The adult shows fared no better. We had a new gadget, but dramatically it wasn't even on a par with the old radio shows. We all sensed it, but the novelty alone was enough to hold our attention at first. Then the better shows came—"Omnibus," "Odyssey," "Studio One"—and went.

The tone of living began to change. Our traditionally elaborate dinners gave way to thin, packaged "TV dinners." We sat goggle-eyed in the semi-darkness of our living rooms, literally parts of the circuitry of the television set. Conversation declined. Living room furnishings began to be designed around the tube. The most vivid impression that I remember is that of the utter simplicity of it all. For all that it really mattered, now we could *see* the characters; and we could *see* the newscast being read; and we could *see* the orchestras play and the people being asked questions about trivia for prizes. We could also see the political conventions. We believed in TV more than we had believed in radio for reasons that are embedded in our very language: "You gotta show me!" or "Seein' is believin'." We saw. And some of us believed. No one seemed to remember the counter-maxim, "The hand is quicker than the eye." It was about this time that Newton Minow called television a "vast wasteland." We had a whole new line of comics now: there were Jack Paar comics, William Bendix comics, Ozzie and Harriet comics, Jackie Gleason comics, and Gunsmoke comics. It was no accident that some of the shows were published in comic book form to be vended from the supermarket shelves.

After a two year escape from television on my motorcycle, I discovered science fiction and rediscovered literature.

I worked on the evening shift at an Army supply depot, pushing buttons on IBM machines. I hated the job almost as much as I loved my motorcycle (not more, else I would not have worked and could not have bought the machine). I was not a good employee at all. There was something about standing in front of an IBM machine for eight hours a night, reading endless lists of numbers and catchy nomenclatures ("Socks, olive-drab, No. 11, reinforced toe, 14,283 prs."), listening to an office full of post-menopausal females complaining about their husbands and their drab lives, eating sack lunches, pulling shredded cards from recalcitrant machines...there was something about the job that kept it from sustaining my interest. I am sure that my supervisor was as happy to see me leave as I was to go. It was not a happy time, hammering out dollars in Nebelheim. One of the problems was my store of "crazy ideas." As my supervisor put it one day, "rocket ships to the moon my ass, git them cards sorted and git that report out." That was the day I inadvertently sent the teletype test-deck to Washington instead of the day's report. Oh well.

Each morning, I arrived at home between one and two A.M. I would read until I heard my parents' alarm clock go off. I would then place my books back on the shelf and pretend to have been asleep. There, in the stillness of the winter nights, I recaptured my sense of awe and wonder about my world. How does one go about thanking someone for giving back one's imagination? How can I ever repay Ray Bradbury for *The Martian Chronicles, The Illustrated Man,* or *Fahrenheit 451?* I imagine Bradbury would say "no thanks necessary. Welcome back to the Book People."

Two years later, after a dreary day of pushing IBM buttons in the basement of a downtown bank, I started up the stairs to my apartment. When I was about halfway up the stairs, I had one of those incredible and terrifying experiences that seem always to happen to other people. It was as if my imagination had suddenly expanded to infinity. It was as if I had come out from under an anaesthetic. Everything stood out in sharp clarity around me. I felt an accelerating expansion of my personal universe, as if every past experience had become connected, thus laying before me a veritable universe of chance and choice. I stumbled the rest of the way up the steps, entered the house, and announced that I was resigning my position in the bank in order to enroll in college. The next day I resigned and started the machinery that was to put me into school within two months. I could hardly wait for classes to begin. I became a freshman at twenty-four.

Every day brought a new revelation, a new set of experiences that had to be collated with the things I knew. There was a thrilling sort of voluntary naïveté about my feelings. But some of my classmates exhibited a peculiar indifference to learning. I could not understand it at all since the classes were terrifically exciting to me. I'm sure that Professor Numan thought me rabid when I asked for extra work in freshman English. The crispness and light that surrounded the Emory University campus seemed to provide a physical counterpart to the atmosphere in the classes. There was a certain clarity of mind at Emory, a certain intangible, a finely chiseled lucidity of thought and of purpose that I have seen on no other campus. I would sit on the library steps when the first leaves were falling in the autumn, waiting for classes to begin. I would walk through the stacks of the library in tears, wishing to read all of the books at once, wanting to know all the scholars' works immediately, aching to become a part of all that I saw around me. I had to work full time at night in order to meet expenses. I lied to the administration about the number of hours I worked so that I could go to school full time also. They were years of picaresque adventures: I seemed to be moving from episode to episode, from class to class. After well over a decade I still remember the individual classes, the unabashed dedication of some of the professors, and the sadness I felt at the end of each quarter when I knew that another episode was over, never to be lived again. I was always the last to leave. I always made it a point to thank the professor for the course. It seemed the least I could do.

I remember a certain late-spring day, as I sat in the office of the Graduate Institute of the Liberal Arts, when I realized that I was again to be deprived of my classes and my professors for an entire summer. Thomas J. J. Altizer had just ridden away on a red Honda 305. His new book was out. Gregor Sebba and Jim Smith were planning the departmental seminar for the fall. Joseph Conant and I were talking about the subtle change in Pentheus' speech (in a good translation or in the original) when Dionysus gains control over him. Out of the back office came Herbert Benario, bearing an empty coffee cup, and intoning with mock sonority "Greeks, Greeks, Greeks! Bah; The Romans, my friends. Rome. That's where the grandeur was!" He filled his coffee cup and retreated to his cubicle. Our catcalls followed him as he chuckled to himself. Mrs. McKay, the secretary, gave up and went to lunch. I threw myself into an impossible translation of the *Bacchae* in an irrational effort to stretch the quarter subjectively. Time would not stretch. The next night, on schedule, I returned to my post as assistant ambulance driver for another dreary summer of work in a local funeral home. That evening, it seemed that all the souls in the mortuary were more alive than I. When the summer was over, the intellectual vacuum of the funeral home made a doubly bad joke of the feeling of resurrection on returning to school. I was back in the real world. There was nothing two-dimensional about Professor Doby, or Professors Benjamin, Cuttino, Jordan, or Hartshorne. The spell was cast again. As I walked between the pines and oaks on the Emory campus, and smelled the crisp autumn air, I knew, for however brief a time, I had returned home.

At length, when I had ground out an acceptable dissertation for the Institute, I left Emory for good. I taught for three years at a small college in Atlanta before leaving for a miserable year and a half of teaching in south Alabama. I had studied my lessons well. I knew the skeleton of knowledge. Teaching provided the bones with flesh. At Oglethorpe College, in the outskirts of Atlanta, Professor Harry Dobson breathed life into it all.

We called him Papa. He was a colleague (at least officially; actually, nobody was in his league). I attended his music history classes for a year. It was completely fortuitous that I met him. We talked about music over lunch one day during summer school. He invited me to sit in on his Wagner course. I did not know that my life was to change again as a result of that year; that the change would be as irrevocable as the change initiated on the steps of my apartment eight years before. It wasn't simply that he knew his field. Nor was it that he had merely a specific teaching method that captured our imaginations. It was, strangely enough, that there seemed to be something more to him than we could grasp. He provided the answer inadvertently one day when he compared Bergit Nilsson to Kirsten Flagstad. Papa said, "The singer with great talent always gives you the very best, the limit of her capacity to give; the genius always gives at least the same amount, but always has far more in reserve. The intuition that there are reserves possessed which never need be called is the intuition of the person's genius."

When he taught his classes, it was not that music was being taught there. It was, rather, that Music was there. We felt that we were sitting in the presence of Music, of Poetry, of Drama, of Literature, Philosophy, and Art. All the years of study seemed merely a prelude to our friendship. Again, as on the steps eight years before, I felt expanded, transfigured, as I sat, day by day, listening to Papa's world unfold. The shadows that I had seen but dimly back there in my halcyon college days, now came full view with a completeness and with a force of authenticity that made my previous understanding seem curiously pedantic and sentimental. We would sit and talk for nine hours at a time, about Wagner, about Puccini, about Mozart, about tonal theory and technical problems in musicology, about Picasso and Degas, Milton and Chaucer, Yeats and Dylan Thomas, Russell and Whitehead, Ayer and Wittgenstein. Of course, he knew about them all ("of course" sounds facetious here, but then again, he *did* know about them all; and it was not a dilettante's acquaintance, but a scholar's knowledge).

The morning after (the pun is intended) one of our marathon talks (when I had ridden about in my VW most of the night after taking him home, trying to assimilate all that I had learned), instead of the intellectual pallor that ordinary associations have led us to expect, I would find that the previous day's conversation had merely been the overture for the new day's performance. After a meticulous explication of the libretto under study, Papa would turn on the stereo set, and stand by the window while Sieglinda's eyes met Siegmund's, watching me out of the corner of his eye to see if I caught the subtle change in Sieglinda's leitmotive, and chortling when I did. Looking back over the years, the sense of strangeness has not left. Indeed, it is as if we have merged somehow, as if the gestalt formed back there in 1963 lives in and of itself.

Years later, as I sat with my wife in a creaking house, a blizzard threading its wind through the walls, making the rooms cold around the edges, I remembered Papa's parting words. "Isn't this wonderful?" he said, his books and opera albums held to his heart. "All of these great works and the great men who created them? It is all that I live for. It is all I have ever lived for. It is all that is worth living for. I read five books a week just to stay alive. I read for them. It is the least I can do." He was 71 when he said that. Eventually, Papa was retired to make way for a younger man who "could relate to the students." On the day of his retirement, the university, perhaps finally realizing, however dimly, who had been in their midst for all those years, bestowed upon him an honorary doctorate. The standing ovation that he received from hundreds of worshipful students and alumni was no more than Professor Doctor Harry Dobson had deserved from the beginning.

But what of his world? What of the world of golden shafts of light streaming through a Victorian music room? What of that world of great minds and great works, of drama and irony, complexity and depth? Is it so irrelevant now? For the sake of relevance, my wife and I searched through sixty magazines per month for three years. We maintained Papa's reading schedule "just to stay alive" in a barren North Dakota countryside laced with snow and ice and bitter cold. It was the least we could do. And in the end, we saw what we had suspected and dreaded all along. We lost, we did, Papa and Valerie and I. We've lost because of the danger that the last few pages of this essay have creaked with age and aging values. The gentle and childlike conceptions of children's books and children's thoughts, refined by learning and experience, "improv'd by tract of time" into music and literature and poetry, art and philosophy, seem all but gone, else the reader would not have been impatient with the apparent sentimentality of the last few paragraphs, the painfully personal remembrances of cupcakes and the way to Aunt Flossie's house, or the embarassingly revealing affection for Papa. A sneaky trick? Poisoning the well? A circumstantial *ad hominen?* You bet. It's a heavy scene.

Of course the comic books have won. Before he escaped, Bradbury's Montag looked each night at a magazine of pictures with no words. Books are forbidden in *Fahrenheit 451*'s not so distant future. We showed Truffaut's film of *Fahrenheit 451* to a group of honors students in a large midwest state university. They couldn't see the point: "Why does everybody get so excited over a bunch of dumb books?" It's so difficult, you see, what with irony and all that. "Why can't people just say what they mean? Why spend all that paper saying what could have been said on one page?" The fact that this group of students had all placed in the upper 25 percentile of the College Board exams made their reaction even more alarming. The comic books have won.

But does it seem that there was ever any other way to look at things? Is there any corner to which the comic book mentality has not reached? What we need is a groovy hero, okay? And this guy could take over the government, okay? And he would clean up the air and the lakes and the rivers, and end the war in Vietnam, you dig? Yeah, but if he was a REAL man, he would get rid of them pinko communist brats, right? An' he would straighten out what's wrong with this country, get me? (a) Oh wow (b) By God   if the right man got into office, he could (a) turn over the country to the people and we could all live in love and communication, relating to each other and realizing ourselves as persons, not gettin' all hung up on possessions and rules and that shit, smoking dope and groovin' on flowers and trees and sayin' what we please and doin' our thing as long as it don't hurt nobody and as long as it don't keep nobody from doin' their thing, okay? (b) turn the country back over to the real Americans, by God, who respect the flag and don't use no damn obscene language, and are willin' to fight for what they believe in and what they know is right, and then we could get people who are willin' to do an honest day's work and not go around with alla that hair and dirt and funny clothes, not havin' any respect for anything sacred no more. Choose one.

Choose it wisely, for the investment is high. Your choice carries a ready-made, prefab life-style with it, complete with accessories. There are millions still to be made on the hip sell. If you catch the returning straight market, you might cash in on next year's in-scene. All you need is the life-style, the details will work themselves out. Pick a life-style today. Be a super-hero. Get 'em while they're hot. Only a soul for a new one. Half a soul will buy a used one with the cover on or two with the covers off. You've nothing to lose that you haven't already lost, right? Okay? POP WORLD-VIEW INC. has the whole line:

Revolution Comics, with Ché and Tom and Jerry and Mark
Hard Hat Comics, with Construction Man
Kennedy Comics, with Teddy and the Camelots
SDS Comics, with Weatherman
Witch Comics, with Bernardine and Uglygirl
Panther Comics, with Ghettoman
Commune Comics, with Earthman
Freak Comics, with Abbie and Yippieman
Dope Comics, with Acidman
Sex Comics, with Hornyman
Silent Majority Comics, with Suburbanman
Nixon Comics, with Spiroman
Congressional Committee Comics, with Rhetoricman
Sensitivity Training Comics, with Threatenedman

And there's DOOM COMICS, and ECOLOGY COMICS, and LIBERAL COM-ICS and CONSERVATIVE COMICS, ROCK COMICS, HUNTLEY-BRINKLEY COMICS, DISEASE COMICS, RADIATION COMICS, GUERILLA THEATER COMICS, GURU COMICS, and many, many more. And don't forget, right around the corner is a groovy carnival. Cooger and Dark, isn't it, Ray? It's the egress of the show.

And even the *good* comics don't last, no matter how well conceived the Enterprise.

Are you all right down there, Captain?
Yes, I'm all right Mr. Spock. It's a mess, but the Prime
Directive says don't interfere. Beam me up and let's
get back to our own time.
Fascinating, Captain. Fascinating.

The Radicalization of the Superheroes

LINDSY VAN GELDER and LAWRENCE VAN GELDER

*I began to see that Superman was a punk, that Superman
didn't relate to replenishing the earth, like Huey Newton
and other real people do. In essence, Superman is a
phony and a fake. He never saves any black people in this
country in any comic book stories.*

Bobby Seale, Chairman, Black
Panther Party, in *Seize the Time*

Not any more, Chairman Bobby. Superman's been getting his thing together.

Where kryptonite, ray guns and the inspired madness of generations of evil fiends toiling in the shadow of spider webs to the echo of demented laughter have failed, *tsuris, angst* and guilt have conquered.

It will never be the same again with Superman, nor with the others of the caped and cowled legions that fill the pantheon of superheroes. No longer is it possible to go home again to the golden age of comic books, to the safe, secure, predictable world of superheroes menaced by no more than an occasional natural disaster, a monster lurching amuck, a pointy-shoed hood, a Kraut lieutenant, or—God forbid—the loss of their secret identity.

Buying a comic book today is spending fifteen cents for the *New York Times* with four-color art and guys in capes playing the role of The Wasp, an exercise in futility usually assigned by the *Times* on a rotating basis to John Lindsay, Nelson Rockefeller and Richard Nixon. (Nixon, who wishes the golden age of Commie-zapping would return, sometimes farms out his assignments to his sidekick, Spiro Agnew.) To turn the pages of comic books today is to revisit not the old world of good and evil and of virtue triumphant on a field of craven yeggs, but to plunge to the nostrils in the bleeped-up world of today.

Here they are, folks: See the blacks sitting in at the State Office site at 125th Street; see the cops straining at the leash; see the Young Lords seize a building and take service on an injunction; see whitey try the old hog-wash and watch him fail; take a look at a sky raining a pox of filth and rivers resembling closeups of Campbell's Chunky soups.

Is it Metropolis, where good old Clark Kent and his spine of *gehackte leber* used to conceal the impervious *kishkas* of Superman? Is it Gotham, where Bruce Wayne and his adorable ward, Dick Grayson, used to don their Bat duds under the old manse?

Hell, no, it's New York, no matter what they call it. And when today's superheroes travel a bit they find people starving in Appalachia, politicians and public officials wallet-high in sellouts, homicidal hippie-cultists fomenting race-war, American Indians still trying to find the treat in a treaty, and heroes of Hollywood Westerns practicing virulent super-patriotism instead of The Method.

Do the superheroes fare any better than our politicians in finding the solutions to bigotry, oppression, corruption, pollution and inequality? The answer is no. Like ordinary humans elevated to power, the best they can do is raise the questions, point the way, and hope.

But the recognition of the limits of power among the superheroes, and beyond that their accelerating social consciousness, their deepening anxiety, the proliferation of their neuroses, their increasing involvement in issues with no clear solutions, and most of all, their burgeoning radicalization, have restored excitement, interest and merit to a once-crippled industry.

Comic books, damned by parents, reviled by psychologists, denounced from pulpits and nearly borne away on a riptide of criticism in the mid-fifties, are in the throes of revolutionary change.

Children and the young at heart who stood by the superheroes in the years of their travail and ostracism, who endured their fantastic irrelevance and patent absurdity, who witnessed their brief deification on the altar of camp, have long known that the change was in progress. Today the pace is quickening, and those who turned away from the unreal world of comic books a decade or more ago may well find themselves surprised–and perhaps outraged—at the new politics of pulp.

Like other members of the establishment, superheroes are finding themselves on the receiving end of tough questions raised not by the yokels who used to ask, "Who was that man?" or "Is it a bird, a plane . . .?" In a de-emphasis on inter-galactic exploits, the superheroes are facing questions raised on blighted urban streets by angry blacks, troubled whites and concerned, embittered social workers.

Remember Green Arrow, the technological Robin Hood of the comic books, and Green Lantern, the ray-slinger? Radicalization overtook them last spring, in the form of a shabby black man who appeared while the two superheroes were arguing the merits of rescuing a fat, white slumlord from a gang of bottle-heaving kids. To Green Lantern, the kids were "anarchists."

Then the black man turned up, "I been readin' about you," he said. "How you worked for the Blue Skins. And how on a planet someplace you helped out the Orange Skins. And you done considerable for the Purple Skins. Only there's skins you never bothered with—the black skins! I want to know—how come? Answer me that, Mr. Green Lantern!"

His powerful body slumped, his hands open helplessly, his head bowed, Green Lantern whispered: "I . . . can't."

Since then, Green Arrow and Green Lantern have taken off on an Easy-Rider-type tour of the country. "Listen," Green Arrow told his super-colleague, "forget about chasing around the galaxy, and remember America! It's a good country . . . beautiful . . . fertile . . . and terribly sick! There are children dying . . . honest people cowering in fear . . . disillusioned kids ripping up campuses! On the streets of Memphis a good *black* man died . . . and in Los Angeles, a good *white* man fell. Something is wrong! Something is killing us all! Some hideous moral cancer is rotting our very souls!''

In their travels, Green Lantern and Green Arrow have helped poor whites in Appalachia topple a corrupt mine-owner, tangled with a Charlie Manson-style cult on the West Coast, defended an Indian tribe from white man's greed, and gone on trial for conspiracy before a madman who binds and gags them, makes his own rules and bears a suspicious resemblance to Abbie Hoffman's favorite judge.

A month or so ago, good old Superman, in a retrospective episode in issue No. 393 of *Action Comics,* found himself asking the operator of a storefront academy, "You mean you left college to bury yourself in this SLUM just to educate these hoodlooms?''

Superman found himself hearing, "These slum kids have auto dumps instead of playgrounds . . . fire hydrants instead of swimming pools . . . people here have to scrounge around for a bare existence! Could *you* survive in this *jungle* without super-powers? While you're off preventing disasters on remote worlds, who prevents disaster in your *own* backyard? It's time you did something for *these* people!''

So Superman turned on with his heat vision and his steel fists to demolish a block of abandoned tenements. Then he told the ghetto folks to try a little self-help to finish the rebuilding job themselves. "Remember,'' he thundered, "as American citizens, you've got a mighty super-power of your own—the vote!''

Jimmy Olsen—you remember Jimmy, that gutsy, eager kid who has been a cub at the *Daily Planet* for about 30 years—well, Jimmy recently exposed "the secret slumlord of Metropolis,'' a wealthy philanthropist.

What's more, Jimmy led a delegation of blacks who dumped roaches and rats on the slumlord's front lawn during a radical chic party. And Lois Lane—dear Lois, who used to spend her time harboring suspicions about Clark Kent and hankering for wedlock with Superman—well, she's musing about the oppression of women these days.

Batman has been turned into something of an urban guerrilla, and Robin has finally been shipped off to college, where the action really is.

Green Arrow and Green Lantern have also helped the Justice League of America—the superheroes' equivalent of SDS, including Superman, Batman and Black Canary—to fight for ecology. Their adventure begins with a tip from a night watchman at a dockside factory replete with billowing black smoke and gushing slime. "What that factory was manufacturin' was nothing but pollution,'' says the night watchman. "It was there deliberately to foul the air and water.''

An appeal by the superheroes to the city manager brings the fascist-pig rebuff: "Take your bleeding heart and get out. That factory brings in thousands in taxes. We need the money. That conservation stuff is a lot of bunk.''

The superheroes discover that the pollution factory is the creation of mutants from another planet who have destroyed their own world, evolved into pollution-breathers and are now seeking new worlds to pollute and colonize. In the end, the creeps are routed, and Green Arrow and his girlfriend, Black Canary, stroll by the riverside in postcombat bliss. Black Canary says she is happy that the superheroes have saved Earth. Green Arrow looks over his shoulder at the factories, still belching smoke into the night sky.

"Did we?" he asks. "I wonder . . ."

Green Arrow's skepticism is typical of the new radicalized superhero. The new Politics of Pulp is not simple—if it were, Superman could put himself out of business by razing the slums, replenishing the soil, ending poverty and bestowing everlasting peace and prosperity in a single issue. Instead of turkey-basket liberalism, the superheroes are confining themselves to making clear that the future of the earth will be determined by its people.

Mixed in with the politics is another recent development—the super hangup.

Superman, who made his debut in 1938 and is now an untrustworthy over-30, is but one in a ward of *angst*-ridden comics characters. "He's here, but he can't belong," explains Carmine Infantino, the editorial director for National Periodicals, the DC Comics group, whose ranks include the veteran man of steel, Batman, Green Lantern, Green Arrow and the Flash, to name a few.

According to Infantino, upcoming Superman adventures will focus increasingly on the Krypton-born Superman's sense of alienation on Earth. The change has already begun. Recently the man of might worked himself to the verge of the dread Excedrin headache when he contemplated his inability to have a normal family life (Lois' impatient availability notwithstanding).

"I'm Superman," the old boy *kvetched* as he flew through the skies. "The wealth of the world is at my command. I have powers beyond the dreams of mere mortals. Yes, I'm the man who has everything! But what wouldn't I give to have a son like Dan!"

Another new gimmick will pepper Superman's supermind with a soupçon of schizophrenia. At the touch of some exotic variety of kryptonite, an antimatter Superman emerges, a dormant dark side of his personality whose each awakening drains his energies, stirs conflict and threatens destruction to the real Superman and the world.

Even Clark Kent, the mild-mannered newsman, is being updated. Gabe Pressman may not like this, but Clark Kent is invading television. God only knows what's going to happen should the two ever descend on Mario Procaccino at the same time, but Clark is just a working man, and the *Daily Planet* has been taken over by a conglomerate with broadcasting interests.

Wonder Woman, the Amazon in the star-spangled suit who used to zip around bouncing bullets off her bracelets, has lost her super powers completely, but gained admission to the ranks of liberated superheroines. Like Black Canary and Black Widow, she is a karate ace who depends on no man but romances with several. The Invisible Girl's husband helps her with the housework and shares the child care.

Even Lois Lane bitches when city editor Perry White passes her over for a dangerous assignment. "That's not fair, Perry," she grumbles. "You're discriminating against me because I'm a woman! I protest!"

The *angst,* guilt and awareness now beginning to afflict the DC superheroes have raged for years among their principal rivals for the affections of comic-book lovers, the Marvel superheroes.

This trend-setting group, spawned by the remarkable Stan Lee, boasts the Fantastic Four, quarreling among themselves and losing money on the stock market; Invisible Girl and her husband, Mr. Fantastic, fretting about the lack of time they can devote to their infant son; the Incredible Hulk, wandering the earth and cursing his ugliness; Daredevil and Captain America, trying to cope with perplexing romantic lives; and the extraordinary Spider-Man.

Spider-Man, the favorite superhero on college campuses, owes his powers to radioactivity and his *tsuris* to acne, trouble with his grades, difficulty with his girlfriends and a chronic shortage of money.

Not every superhero has gone radical, however. One of Marvel Comics' most interesting creations is Iron Man, the comics' answer to Richard Ottinger, who hews to his millions and his guilty white liberalism.

When not encased in the outfit that gives him his name, Iron Man is Tony Stark, a munitions magnate who inhabits a mansion, pals around with U.S. senators, keeps a few skyscrapers in his portfolio and operates a foundation. Tony was just another guy with the looks and assets of Howard Hughes until he went to Vietnam about ten years ago and was blown to pieces. Escaping death, Tony fashioned for himself a ferrous maxi, the technocrat's dream-suit of valves, blasters, transistors, computers and other gadgetry. Iron Man is the New Capitalist Hero—the triumph of military-industrial know-how and good-guy instincts over the forces of evil and a damaged heart. He spends a lot of his time fighting duels with Castro-like Caribbean leaders and pitting his skills against Soviet superheroes who fight dirty.

Between punches, he is given to Silent Majority sermonettes, like "Lucky for you, I'm not a Red—I can't continue to attack a helpless enemy" and "You made the worst mistake a Red can make—you challenged a foe who isn't afraid of you."

But Iron Man can be challenged right here in America. One recent adventure—published not long after police cleared black militant squatters from the State Office Building site at 125th Street—pits Iron Man against a Pantheresque superhero named Firebrand.

The story begins with a flaming clenched fist searing through a fence erected on the site of a new community center financed by the Iron Man Foundation. "Anything the Man puts up, I'm ready to tear down," announces Firebrand.

The next day, Tony Stark and City Councilman Lyle Bradshaw arrive for groundbreaking ceremonies, only to find that Firebrand and the militants have occupied the land. "This is gonna be a *community* center, man!" a brother in a beret tells the white cops. "Well, *we're* part of the community, dig it? And we're stayin' until we get listened to.

"No ground's gettin' broken, no construction's gettin' done until *we* have some say in what goes here! Maybe a community center is good for a lotta white consciences, but it ain't what the blacks on the North Side want!"

Councilman Bradshaw promptly rips up the militants' list of demands —for black construction workers and black control of the center's functions—and orders the cops to clear them out.

"I won't allow an irate minority to bully the North Side community out of something it so obviously needs," fumes Bradshaw. "You can't reason with animals!"

A riot ensues, and Firebrand and Iron Man take to the rooftops for a little *mano a mano.* "You'd like to believe that I'm just part of a neat little criminal plot," Firebrand raps as he clobbers. "A commie, a pinko! . . . Well, I'm just an all-American boy, Iron Man. One of those wide-eyed innocents who started out to make this nation a 'better place.' I sat in for civil rights, marched for peace and demonstrated on campus . . . and got chased by vicious police dogs, spat on by bigots, beat on by 'patriots,' choked by tear gas and blinded by Mace, until I finally caught on . . .

"This country doesn't WANT to be changed! The only way to build anything decent is to tear down what's here and start over!"

Stunned, Iron Man returns to the brick-tossing melee below and convinces the cops to leave and allow the militants twelve hours to do the same. He and a few moderate blacks—who have been denounced as Uncle Toms—go to Bradshaw's office and try to work things out. Bradshaw is adamant and accuses the group of "knuckling under to criminals"—at which point Firebrand bursts through the window, shouting: "The people won't wait any more! We're not waiting to have the world handed to us! It's ours for the taking." In the scuffle that follows, Firebrand blows open the councilman's safe, revealing that Bradshaw is the secret head of the realty and construction firms that stand to profit from the center.

As Bradshaw is carted off in cuffs, Firebrand hurls his parting shot at Iron Man. "I'll wait to fight another day. History's on *my* side!" As Firebrand zips off, a cop asks Iron Man if he feels he has failed by not capturing the supermilitant.

"It's not Firebrand's escaping that bothers me," says the shaken liberal. "It's wondering where the rest of us went wrong—that someone like him should have to come into being at all!" He walks off brooding, iron head down.

Firebrand is just one of a squad of superblacks ripping around in the pages of Marvel Comics. There is the Falcon, who looks like Jim Brown, lives in Harlem and preaches against extremists of both races. There is also T'Challa, the Black Panther, an African prince who teaches Afro-

American studies in his civilian guise and is given to agonizing over whether his true place is in the ranks of superheroes with his white friends or among his own people. In Marvel Comics, blacks are even villains as well as students, cops, reporters, love story principals and just about anything else anyone is likely to be.

Stan Lee, the inventive Marvel editor, has had blacks in his stories for so many years that he can say with justification, "I don't even think its worthy of comment."

Like GM and Ford, Marvel and DC (National Periodicals) stand in the forefront of an industry dominated by half a dozen publishers responsible for estimated sales this year of more than 300 million comic books under at least 200 different titles. The industry is committed to general appeal. National Periodicals as well as Magazine Management, the parent concern of Marvel, puts out a general line that embraces romance and whimsy. Readers looking for a little of the old innocence will find Archie, Jughead, Veronica and Betty still cavorting between shiny covers, along with Casper the friendly ghost, the Disney characters and an assortment of Western characters and hot-rod fetishists.

But the trend toward topicality that has captured the affections of a sophisticated new generation of readers seems clearly traceable to Marvel's Lee, a tall, bearded man who looks like Rex Harrison and regards himself as the world's most prolific short-story writer.

Lee entered the comics business 30 years ago as a seventeen-year-old office boy and found himself an editor before he was eighteen. About ten years ago, he began introducing "real life" to Marvel's pages. "I was bored sick with what we were doing," he recalls. He began to deal with the comic-book adventures as "fairy tales for grownups. I thought, 'If a guy were superpowerful, how would he exist in the real world?' "

It was the kind of question that led to rent troubles for superheroes, girl trouble and a lot of lip from people who think a guy in a crazy-looking costume is a guy in a crazy-looking costume and not a superhero. "It would naturally follow," says Lee, "that we seem to be radical."

Imagination and topicality are taking comics in a direction that brooks no pussy-footing and borrows heavily from the headlines. In a recent issue of Daredevil, a bomb explodes in the Hilton Hotel (Walter Cronkite is at the scene) during a demonstration against Spiro Agnew. The bomb turns out to be the work of a maddened right-wing Hollywood film actor who hopes to discredit the peace movement. Agnew puts in frequent appearances in today's comics. On one occasion, Iron Man turns to Thor as the two arrive at a superheroes' summit meeting and quips: "From the glum looks on their faces, Thunder God, I'd say that something big is up. Either the earth's been invaded . . . or Spiro Agnew just made another speech!"

How far the imagination can go is limited by the Code of the Comics Magazine Association of America, a document adopted by the major publishers on October 26, 1954, when juvenile delinquency was a major problem and comics had been pilloried for their violence, gore and sexiness.

Both Stan Lee and Carmine Infantino, at 45 another veteran of the comics' travails, would like to see the code liberalized. Reminiscent of the old Hays code that rigidly constrained the motion picture industry for many years, the Comics Code sets strict standards for its subscribing members.

Its seal, imprinted on the covers of the subscribing publications, whose titles account for well over 90 per cent of all comic books sold in the country, is a sign of adherence to provisions governing advertising and the portrayal of crime, evil, bloodshed, violence, profanity, obscenity, religion, nudity, marriage and sex.

"Some of it," says Infantino, a newly appointed member of the eight-member board that represents publishers, distributors, engravers and printers, "is ridiculous."

Infantino, who joined National Periodicals about 25 years ago and used to draw Batman, is now campaigning for an end to restrictions on stories involving narcotics. "I feel very strongly about it," he says. "I don't believe in hiding your head in the sand."

Lee, too, would like to see a change. "I feel that comics could do much good as far as helping kids avoid the danger of drugs."

But Leonard Darvin, a lawyer who is the code administrator, believes it is a poor idea. The power to change the code in respect to narcotics rests with the board, but the 60-year-old Darvin can remember when the wave of revulsion against the industry's excesses swept away more than 30 publishers and dumped circulation from a peak of about 650 million in 1953 to about 200 million within a few years.

Each month he reviews about 100 comic books for adherence to the code, and recommends necessary pre-publication changes. Although he frowns on any change in the code with respect to narcotics, he can foresee changes that would at least liberalize some provisions on sex to reflect, if only slightly, the new permissiveness in motion pictures.

Although Lee and Infantino would like to see a liberalization that would permit them to reflect the world of the 1970s more accurately, neither finds it remarkably difficult to exist within the code's provisions.

"The world," observes Lee, "is a little more liberal now."

And radical, too.

The Underground Press

JACOB BRACKMAN

I

"Newspapers create and feed the illusions we live by. Instead of instructing us, instead of telling us what's wrong with the country, they stuff our vanity."

Poet Allan Katzman lifted one foot onto a desktop in his claustrophobic city room and stroked his beard reflectively. "The press is losing its power to report spontaneous events," he went on. "But it's gaining a new power —to *create* events; to turn news gathering into news *making.* The papers of pseudo events, news leaks and press releases offend no one; they take no moral stand. They are just . . . neutral. They furnish our boring and repetitive lives with boring and repetitive 'news.' "

Katzman is cofounder of a biweekly newspaper in Lower Manhattan called *The East Village Other.* The *Other* doesn't separate fact from opinion. Its journalism is unabashedly, militantly interpretive: pro pot, peace, sex, psychedelics and subversion; anti most of what remains in switched-off American society. Since 1964, some two dozen similar "underground" papers have sprung up across the country. A few died fast. The rest are now growing at an astonishing clip—to a collective circulation pushing 270,000 in three years, with no sign of slowing down.

Katzman's dismissal of the establishment press sounds mild next to the gripes of other underground proprietors. Their charges run from "bland" or "ignorant" all the way to "fascist," "hypocritical" and "brainwashery." Paul Krassner, head man at *The Realist,* talks about an "escalation of bullshit," and John Wilcock, nationally syndicated underground columnist, insists that "big-city dailies are a corrupt advertising medium; they've forfeited their right to be called newspapers."

"They've let the people down and they've lost the people's confidence," Wilcock says. Like his fellow workers, he believes the demands of modern capitalism have proved inimical to a free exchange of information and ideas. "Most papers—even the holy *Times*—are up to their necks in old money and official connections. Their job is to keep certain blocs and certain ideas in power. Like, they'll write about pot 'dope fiends' like the *Daily News* did 30 years ago. But pot's part of *your* scene . . . how can you believe a paper when you *know* it's feeding you lies?" From the vantage point of hip, the establishment media have only three reactions to a groovy scene: Ignore it, put it down or exploit it.

"So where can people who want to bust out of monolithic culture discover one another?" rhetorically asks Ed Sanders, editor of a subunderground magazine. "Assembly places and media are controlled by the creeps. Establishment papers are demented; like a diplomatic mission in a foreign country—you have to ass-kiss your way in. And who can they speak for? They've no idea what it means to live in a slum on the edge of a city. A paper and its audience need a living relationship, like an organism, a tree. And you can get that now, because cultural migrations are happening in the country and pockets of protesting people are filling up the vacuums. A cat from the Village, say, can plug into a similar underground in cities all over."

Ranting about the establishment press, underground spokesmen may well come on like A. J. Liebling might have after an acid freak trip. But their vision of a "new life out there," no longer able to stomach that old press, is undeniable. Hippies, anarchists, New Leftists, teeny boppers, artists, gypsies, groupies, pacifists, nihilists and heads—they comprise a new audience, eager to subscribe to a new journalistic product. Next to the mass readership (25,000,000 for *Reader's Digest,* 6,700,000 for *Life,* 2,000,000 for the New York *Daily News*), the underground seems a pitifully small, impotent phenomenon. Yet its press has taken root in a climate unhealthy for entrepreneurial journalism—more than 400 papers have folded in the last 20 years. And as a cultural fifth column pressing a covert war of infiltration, it may have something to say about the directions of mass society. Psychedelic drugs, disbelief in the Warren Commission, *nouveau* poster art, interracial sex, Happenings and militant protest were accepted aspects of the underground scene, after all, long before they received attention from Henry Luce.

The underground newspapers have not come into being to amplify establishment coverage. They wish to supply an antidote—a frontal assault on all morale boosting in conventional media. Thus, a full-page *East Village Other* cover photo recently grafted L.B.J.'s head onto the body of a Nazi storm trooper.

This sort of opening for a lead story is not unusual:

> Sometime in March, in Paris, in a courtroom of the world, the dead will speak; burned flesh will ooze upon the witness chair; the wounds of the tortured will reopen and missing fingers point as America the Beautiful stands accused of war crimes, and there is no one willing to defend her . . .

Ultraradical rhetoric, however, is but a portion of the underground staple. On the lighter side, *EVO* has run a regular housewifey column, "High on the Range" ("stimulating" recipes calling for marijuana or hash); a reader correspondence section called "tripstripstrips" (a psychedelic show and tell); Timothy Leary's column, "Turn On/Tune In/Drop Out" (Norman Vincent Peale to the generation of mutants); irregular cartoon strips (such as *Sunshine Girl*); "Where It's At" (the hipster's calendar of events); a photo feature dubbed "Slum Goddess" (a Poverty Playmate from the tenement next door); and some editorial rumblings, aptly entitled "Poor Paranoid's Almanac."

These are just the mainstays. Recent 20-odd-page issues have featured articles covering germ warfare in Vietnam, the antibrassiere movement, Cardinal ("Hawk") Spellman, the abortion circuit, an impeach-Johnson campaign, trepanation (drilling a hole in the cranium for "permanent turn-on"), a "desert call" to U.S. troops, mass skinny-dipping, apocalyptic tattooing and Nelson Rockefeller ("Pickpocket Robber Baron"), as well as occasional fiction and poetry. Also, the "Personal" columns of *EVO* reveal more of the life style of the underground than do the articles, whether offering lessons on the sitar or happily promiscuous sexual relationships.

A newspaper, finally, is a vision of the world. The young underground press is struggling to counter with its own vision—now loving, now wildly messianic, now passionate and venomous, now withdrawn in disgust— against what it claims to be the repressive, monolithic vision of the "establishment blats." Most often, the new rebel papers might be writing about another planet altogether. Where the establishment press has L.B.J., Romney, Reagan and Bobby Kennedy, the underground papers have Staughton Lynd, Mario Savio, Tom Hayden and Louis Abolafia. The establishment makes folk heroes of Bob Hope, Natalie Wood, Sinatra, Twiggy, Jackie, the Beatles, Doris Day, Pat Boone, Truman Capote and Johnny Carson. The underground does the same of Ken Kesey, the Grateful Dead, USCO, Madalyn Murray, William Burroughs, Albert Ellis, Alan Watts, Meher Baba, Che Guevara, Ravi Shankar and the Kuchar brothers. The establishment is haunted by the ghosts of Lincoln, Jefferson, John Kennedy, Churchill, Pope John and Eleanor Roosevelt; the underground, by the ghosts of Jesus, Aldous Huxley, Lenny Bruce, Charlie Parker, Malcolm X and A. J. Muste. E.P. critics write political analyses of literature. U.P. pundits pour out literary analyses of politicians. Establishment papers go to weddings, banquets, Broadway shows and testimonials; underground papers, to acid tests, love-ins, light works and free-beaching. The E.P. spies on Liz and Dick, Pat and Luci; the U.P., on Mick Jagger and Marianne Faithfull, Ginsberg and Orlovsky. The E.P. learns from Dr. Spock, Admiral Rickover, John W. Gardner; the U.P., from Wilhelm Reich, A. S. Neill and Maria Montessori. The establishment battles narcotics, homosexuals, subversives, free love and extremism, and fosters Medicare, the Peace Corps and the transit authorities. The underground battles HUAC, the Pentagon, the CIA, corporations, university administrations, and seeks legalization of abortion, marijuana and miscegenation. Every now and then, the *San Francisco Examiner,* say, and the two-year-old *Berkeley Barb* cover the same story. The *Examiner* says "bearded leftists"; the *Barb* says "dissident elements." The *Examiner* says "a local right-wing organization"; the *Barb* says "a local hate group." The *Examiner* says "the civil rights situation in Oakland"; the *Barb* says "brutality and segregation in Oakland." The *Examiner* says "protest march"; the *Barb* says "pilgrimage." The *Examiner* says "riot"; the *Barb* says "confrontation." The *Examiner* says "police officers re-established order"; the *Barb* says "fuzz suppressed."

II

One spring in Eisenhower America, just halfway through the torpor of the 1950s, Norman Mailer helped launch a weekly newspaper in New York City, which he named *The Village Voice.* From Dan Wolf (still editor) came the idea for the paper; from Ed Fancher (still publisher) came most of the initial capital; and from Mailer—not a little disheartened at the critical attacks on his third published novel—came some fitful work around the newsroom and—in the fourth month of the *Voice*'s infancy—a column, filled with his special brand of brave, tormented narcissism.

"At heart, I wanted a war," Mailer mused later, "and the Village was already glimpsed as the field for battle." His guerrilla attacks on the "tight sphincter" of the Village community lasted through 18 issues. When he began, the *Voice,* almost unknown, was losing a thousand dollars a week. It took the paper eight years to climb out of the red. But when Mailer quit, complaining to readers of "grievous errors" in the setting of his prose, it was already a conversation piece throughout the city.

Mailer admitted even then that the friction between himself and the editors ran deeper than typography. Some years later, he wrote of their clashing dreams for the paper: "They wanted it to be successful; I wanted it to be outrageous. They wanted a newspaper that could satisfy the conservative community—church news, meeting of political organizations, so forth. I believed we could grow only if we tried to reach an audience in which no newspaper had yet been interested. I had the feeling of an underground revolution on its way, and I do not know that I was wrong."

From this early dialectic of editorial hip and square emerged an inevitable compromise: an inveterately liberal, often courageous, occasionally capricious journal, not yet hipster, not yet radical, not yet reaching out into the caves on the edge of the city, but stoutly declining the "snow jobs" of the establishment press. Mailer's success formula (the defiant rejection of all success formulas) was outvoted. It was, as ever, the sad destiny of his intelligence to be ready for revolution before the troops were ready; and it is doubtful that the hip paper he envisioned could have survived as handsomely as did the *Voice.* His premonition of underground stirring, however, was far from mistaken.

The *Voice* grew and by its side, if never quite encompassed by it, hip grew. Then, in the mid-Fifties, repelled by the vacuous complacency of Ike society, the folklore of Beat spread over the highways, along the rails, from New York, through Mexico, to San Francisco and back East across the campuses. Kerouac and Ginsberg were its prophets and Madison Avenue provided free promotion. As yet, the communities of dissent were insufficient to support an actual newspaper. But underground publications, some mimeographed almost on the run, a few persisting staunchly into the Sixties, began to spring up in large cities: *Combustion* in Toronto (perhaps the first high-class, large-scale mimeo network), *Beatitude* in San Francisco, *Magazine, My Own Magazine, C, Mother, Entrails, Intercourse.* In the past 15 years, many hundreds—no one knows precisely how many—of different fringe publications have been privately distributed, sold over the counter at disreputable bookstores or hawked on the streets of New York, Los Angeles, San Francisco, Chicago, Detroit, Montreal and Toronto. While the *Voice* constructed its civilizing bridge between the most gifted of the underground and the establishment's legitimate frontier, the mimeographed magazines supplied the meat to the caves. Leaning heavily toward unrevised poetry, sex (especially homosexuality and fetishism), scatology, mysticism and exhibitionism, they printed stuff that would turn most *Voice* readers bluish green. The legitimate frontier never read them; the establishment never heard of them.

Then, in 1958, a 26-year-old flop comedian named Paul Krassner founded *The Realist,* a hippie-dippie urban marriage of *I. F. Stone's Weekly, Confidential* and *Mad.* Almost from the beginning, the Magazine of Irreverence, Applied Paranoia, Rural Naïveté, Neuter Gender, Criminal Negligence, Egghead Junkies (Krassner kept changing his mind on the masthead) abounded in wit and style. Krassner demonstrated that literacy was not tantamount to squareness. *"The Realist,"* commented one New York writer with considerable glee, "is the *Village Voice* with its fly open."

The magazine had its predecessors, of course, a sort of eternal political underground: Lyle Stuart's ongoing *The Independent,* with 15,000 monthly subscribers, forever lambasting censorship and the Church; George Seldes' *In Fact,* attacking establishment politics and its press; M. S. Arnoni's *Minority of One;* and half a dozen other serious, independent journals of dissent. Similarly, another half-dozen more lighthearted sheets made appearances around the country: Victor Navasky's *Monocle,* in the late Fifties (which continues to publish sporadic special issues); a West Coast paper called *The Idiot; Aardvark* out of Chicago; and a self-proclaimed debunker named *Horseshit,* published by California's "Scum Press."

But Krassner, once he shed a disproportionate anticlericalism, covered the total scene. No subject—spouse swapping, abortion, famous junkies, Walter Jenkins, Stevenson's "assassination," Luci's wedding night, J. F. K.'s "body snatchers" or his "first wife"—was too hot for him. And no one had given the press as hard a time since Liebling. He was dissident, abstract, topical, personal, scatological, crusading, hip and funny all at once. He persuaded you on one page and put you on in the next. He refused to be restricted, he refused to be predicted, he refused advertising and, with it, most of America's social mythology. Circulation rose from 600 to 150,000—and Krassner estimates his current readership at a quarter of a million.

Yet if the underground had found an iconoclastic voice, *The Realist* was no newspaper. Perhaps the times were still not sufficiently ripe for the ballsy press that Mailer had envisioned a few years earlier; perhaps the community of hip had not yet so solidified as to sustain a real journalism of its own.

But as the country rounded the corner of the Sixties, she seemed to imbibe some rejuvenating potion. Suddenly, spiritual senility was out and even the hucksters were thinking young again. With Eisenhower's exit from the international scene, the great leaders—Mao, Chiang, Khrushchev, Franco, De Gaulle, Adenauer and Macmillan—were confronted with an American entry some 30 years their junior; and, a bit to the south, a bearded hell-raiser, Fidel Castro, became another symbol of the new youth. On the home front, it wasn't long before the scruffy underbelly of the Pepsi generation let forth some embarrassing growls. Sahl, Bruce, Gregory, Rickles and others helped Krassner bury the notion that there were still cows too sacred for roasting. Beat, a trifle weary of the open road, settled into urban coffeehouses and campus common rooms for marathon talk. As rallying places were found, young dissidents began to discover one another and the concerns that united them.

Kerouac faded off to Long Island and Florida; Ginsberg went abroad for a time—to India and eastern Europe; others of their ranks turned paunchy with success or failure. The old underground of Eisenhower America yielded to a series of new coalescent movements. Female contraception—widespread precocious use of diaphragms and, more dramatically, the pill—did more to actualize a moral and sexual revolution than had endless libertine talk. The suburbs scarcely finished clucking over the college sex scandals of the early Sixties before the college drug scandals made headlines. No sooner was marijuana ubiquitous on large campuses than psychedelics mushroomed, and undergraduates could get hold of treated sugar cubes as easily as pot. Jazz—the cool and bitter background to beat conversation—gave way to a frenetic, funky, exultant sound, ultimately to a visceral marriage of folk and rock. Improvisational communal dancing declared open war on decorum and inhibition.

But youth would not be bought off with the freedom to fornicate, bugaloo and get high. The Berkeley uprising, analyzed to distraction in print, reputable and otherwise, demonstrated that an organized youth underground could win impressive support and shake up conventional institutions if not blast them to pieces. More openly now, disaffiliates shot society the finger; militants mobilized for action. As the old peace movement flickered with the atomic-testing ban and Kennedy's ostensible triumph in the Cuban missile crisis, its remains enlisted in the cause of civil rights. The marches, the sit-ins, the Mississippi project helped undermine the assumption that long-stagnant conditions could not be changed. As SNCC and CORE accelerated their campaigns in the South, SDS launched community organization projects in Roxbury, Newark, the District of Columbia, Oakland, Chicago and Cleveland. The poverty program stirred potential ghetto leadership to a consciousness of fraud and deprivation. In the face of rampant domestic rot, the escalating Vietnamese war became a double outrage. Rarely had the tranquilizing words of the establishment seemed so foreign to its deeds, and the growing community of hip developed a deep cynicism.

Whether asocial or passionately social in his vision, the hipster came to resent what he regarded as mass culture's attempts to trick him in every sphere. Holden Caulfield, an emblem of sensitive youth in the Eisenhower years, experienced dismay at well-intentioned "phonies." But Holden never realized how dangerous the phonies could become. The new generation emerged with an obsessive wariness, a loathing of hypocrisy.

Given a new youth, a new bohemia, a new iconoclastic humor, a new sexuality, a new sound, a new turn-on, a new abolitionism, a new left, a new hope and a new cynicism, a new press was inevitable.

III

Meanwhile, a few of "the littles," which used to steer wide of politics and sociology altogether, started editorializing. *The Floating Bear,* a semi-monthly sheet edited by LeRoi Jones and Diane Di Prima, called itself a newsletter and printed some reviews and comment to back up its experimental poets. Ed Sanders' *Fuck You / A Magazine of the Arts* declared itself dedicated to—among other things—"pacifism, national defense through nonviolent resistance, unilateral disarmament, multilateral indiscriminate apertural conjugation, anarchism, world federalism, civil disobedience, obstructors and submarine boarders, peace eye, the gleaming crotch lake of the universe, the witness of the flaming ra-cock . . . mystical bands of peace-walk stompers, total-assault guerrilla ejaculators, the Lower East Side *meshuganas,* vaginal zapping, the LSD communarium, God through cannabis, hashish forever, and all those groped by J. Edgar Hoover in the silent halls of Congress."

Sanders also penned occasional editorials, inverse parodies of the reasoned, moderate tones used in establishment papers. One, urging repeal of marijuana laws, called for "fringe attacks: pot-ins at Governmental headquarters, public forums and squawking, poster walks, hemp-farm disobedience. In New York: with a number too large and prestigious to ignore, a multithousand joint light-up on the steps of city hall—FORWARD! THIS IS OPERATION GRASS!" Another political "position paper" began:

> It makes us puke green monkey shit to contemplate Johnson's war in Vietnam. Lyndon Baines is squirting the best blood of America into a creep scene. Kids are "gook-bricking" in Asia without thought, without reason, without law . . .

This editorial concluded with a call for "a demonstration of peace by tender fornicating love-bodies . . . a group screw zapped around the world." (A relatively new sheet, *Gargoyle,* has promised to print "what Ed Sanders rejects"; and back numbers of earlier Sanders editions are already premature collector's items, going for ten dollars a copy.)

If some of the mimeo mags oozed only occasionally into political territory, others planted their tents on that enemy ground. *Resurgence,* one of the farthest out, was established as the literary organ of the Resurgence Youth Movement ("a new anarchist movement based on the world revolution of youth and the birth of a new psychedelic Afrasian-American soul"). Founded in the summer of 1964, blatantly, hysterically subversive, *Resurgence* reads like the rantings of a soapbox poet-zealot:

> surrealysics: :pataphism: :panultraneo: :underdogma: :negativentropy: : Resurgence has not yet defined any limits. We may be three billion persons, we may be a negative universe reaching out across the void. . . .

> Revolution is the total destruction and creation of society. . . . All science and art is crap. We will not submit and we will not coexist.

The magazine envisions a planet on the very brink of apocalypse (the epithet "burnbabyburn" is etched here and there in its margins; grotesque dragons glower over its text). "Logic and metaphysics to the torch," it cries. "Turn our culture upside down and cut its head off. Go wild. Go naked." But there is some intelligence behind its mystical, venomous ravings, and to call its authors and audience "out of touch" would not serve any purpose. Their delusions are evident enough from the vantage point of the mainstream. But in London, members of the Industrial Workers of the World have joined with the Resurgence Youth Movement to start a similar magazine for revolution called *Heatwave;* in Amsterdam, anarchist publications are issued by *Provo;* in Brussels, by *Revo.* This fall, R. Y. M. began a new bulletin called *New Man,* to feature "regular columns and reports from the intergalactic struggle," which it plans to "build into a newspaper to reach tens of thousands of young people, students, workers, dropouts, all over the world."

> What is the Provotariat? Provos, beatniks, *pleiners, nozems,* teddy boys, rockers, *blousons noirs,* hooligans, *mangupi, stiljagi,* students, artists, misfits, anarchists, ban the bombers . . . those who don't want a career and who lead irregular lives . . . THE PROVOTARIAT IS A GROUPING OF SUBVERSIVE ELEMENTS. . . . It exists in a society based on the cult of "getting on." The example of millions of elbow-bargers and unscrupulous go-getters can only serve to anger the Provotariat. We live in a monolithic sickly society in which the creative individual is the exception. Big bosses, capitalists, Communists impose on us, tell us what we should do, what we should consume. . . . They will make themselves more and more unpopular and the popular conscience will ripen for anarchy. . . . THE CRISIS WILL COME.

The "Provotariat," of course, lives in the throes of a sort of lunacy. So alienated from the cultural mainstream, so robbed of influence, the woolliest imagine themselves preparing the barricades for massive hostilities. But even those less trapped by the helpless fantasy of systemicide continue to believe, in the vaguest of terms, that America is destined to crumble by virtue of her own malignancy. They foresee some contemporary parallel to the fall of ancient Rome—the rise of African or Asian nations, perhaps, the isolation of the United States in a Communist world, a right-wing take-over followed by popular uprising, an inevitable erosion of corrupt institutions.

The apocalyptic delusion takes many forms: religious, moral, sociological, international, racial; all help sustain an underground that feels itself vilely repressed. Until two years ago, no newspaper had ever expressed such frustrations, or such dreams.

IV

By avoiding the peculiar preoccupations of the true underground, *The Village Voice*'s circulation rose from 20,000 to 75,000 in the past three years—with one quarter of its papers sold outside the metropolitan area. When the *Voice,* not even *bar mitzvahed* yet, dumps on Bobby Kennedy, his office phones up the next day. It is still decidedly a community newspaper—embroiled in local skirmishes for reform Democrats, schools, zoning laws—but it judged early in the game that Greenwich Village was not a community like any other. Rather, it billeted, in remarkably close quarters, much of the vanguard of American fashion, art, politics and theater and was, therefore, worthy of representation to the world "out there." Establishment papers sent reporters on forays into the world of the Village, of course, but they came as aliens, ogling the natives, scooping titillating items that might amuse the uptown folks and give them something to cluck about over their breakfast coffee. *Voice* reporters lived their beats; covering civil rights, off-Broadway, the Pop scene or a neighborhood campaign, they wrote, essentially, about themselves and about their friends. When they broadened their sights, they tended—where *The Nation, Commonweal* or *New Leader* sounded faintly old, tired and square—to be in touch with what was happening. And so the *Voice,* bolstered by almost weekly gains in advertising, shows signs of becoming the first national organ for insurgency in politics and the arts.

The *Voice* opened up the territory. The papers that moved in to occupy it were, in one sense, children of the radical mimeo sheets and, in another, children of the *Voice.* Some were promising, some were mentally defective. But all reacted against the conservatism of their *Voice* parent; they swore at birth enmity to compromise.

Modeled quite frankly after the *Voice,* the *Los Angeles Free Press* was the first organ of the new underground. The idea for the paper, and an initial investment of $15, came from Art Kunkin, a 39-year-old tool-and-die man from Brooklyn. When Kunkin asked permission to promote plans for a liberal-bohemian weekly at the 1964 Renaissance Pleasure Faire, a friend suggested he put out a dummy issue for the Faire, and in two frenetic weeks he collected enough money and material for a 5000-edition, eight-page tabloid. Dressed as Robin Hoods and 15th Century peasant girls, Kunkin and a merry band of college students gave their papers away as wandering peddlers, attracted a lot of sympathy and a little financial support and, on a fairly hand-to-mouth basis, built the *Free Press* to a paid circulation of 50,000 in three years.

In New York, Walter Bowart, a painter, and Alan Katzman founded the *East Village Other,* a 16-page tabloid that made the *Voice* read like *The Wall Street Journal.* They were quickly joined by John Wilcock, who'd done a weekly *Voice* column for nearly 11 years.

"Wolf and Fancher run their paper with an iron hand," Wilcock says. "I'd discover new things, the *Voice* would sit on them for a while and then promote them when they became fashionable. I was on to hallucinogens seven or eight years ago. They discouraged my writing about Albert Ellis, Lenny Bruce and nudist camps. You know where they advertise? *The New York Times Book Review.* It's clear where they stand. Their average reader is 30-odd years old. He's not interested in changing society. *EVO*'s average reader is ten years younger. We have no taboos. We'll publish anything people write or draw." *EVO* reacts to the relative stodginess of the *Voice* much as the *Voice* began in reaction to a garden-club/sewing-circle weekly called *Villager,* which had been "Reflecting the Treasured Traditions of This Cherished Community" with a New Englandy town-crier flavor since early in 1933.

"We're no community paper," insists Katzman, now managing editor of *EVO.* "We're a world-wide movement for art, peace, civil rights, morality in politics. There's a new population under 34—economically powerful, with the weight of numbers as well as of ideas—reacting to what they aren't getting from the press. They're not getting interpretation; they aren't even getting the facts. 'Kennedy was killed by a crazy man,' they're told. 'Only crazy people kill Presidents of the United States. No one has anything to gain.' If the media don't get a tighter grip on what's happening, they're going to lose a lot of these people to us."

"Us" does not refer simply to *EVO* itself but to a whole new spectrum of underground newspapers, united in their editorial war on what they call "the new oppression." Each publication, at bottom, represents an extension of the personalities of its editor and cronies. *EVO* seems to reflect the vision of second-generation hip, still believing in the Good and True and Real, but no longer surprised at new instances of corruption. It is most aware of an international brotherhood of dissent, and underscores kinship with subterraneans in Paris, London, Bulgaria, Japan, India and elsewhere; it prints "dirtier" cartoons and photo montages; and, while some of its colleagues are still talking Zen, *EVO* is into witchcraft, cannibalism, macrobiotics, astrology, aphrodisiacs, electric-charge machines, theocracia, existential psychotherapy and political independence (secession, emigration) for the underground. The editors, to be sure, sneer at the charge that their paper is "far out." "We're creative artists," Wilcock says. "We represent our milieu, people pushing the boundaries—and exploring beyond them. We're not interested in shocking anyone, just in reaching the guys who don't think automatically, who feel like us, dig us. We give them a forum and ammunition." Possibly because *EVO* is confident and familiar with its audience, its tone is more clipped than hysterical.

Until quite recently, the West Coast papers had an even more frantic sound, the scruffily wholesome quality of a single generation's remove from the middle class. (A front-page lead in the *Free Press* refers to "such greats as Freud and Dr. Kinsey"; nutty little marginalia and subscription plugs, reminiscent of *Mad,* fill out short columns.) Whereas *EVO*'s orientation is decidedly psychedelic, the *Free Press* is urban political, in the *Voice* tradition. (Its layout, also, is borrowed directly from the *Voice.*) Where *EVO* tends to cop out on Manhattan problems, the *Free Press* is thick in the L. A. fray, especially on race (Kunkin ran an extended series on Watts after the riots) and poverty. The *Free Press* has been joined recently by three more L. A. papers: *The Provo,* a little tabloid; *The Oracle of Southern California;* and the full-size, *Free Press*—like *Los Angeles Underground.*

Max Scherr, a 51-year-old New Leftist who, before founding the *Berkeley Barb,* ran a local bar called Steppenwolfe, takes a more global slant than Kunkin. Scherr tends to trap himself in the simplicities of radical rhetoric and, mixing up the Big Issues into a sexintegration-peacehigh bundle, commits the fatal error of unintentional humor. The *Barb* is a "cause" paper (backing, for instance, the Committee to Fight Exclusion of Homosexuals from the Armed Forces), but its tenor is almost pastoral —Scherr is obviously more interested in grape pickers than in the Negro ghetto.

During the school year, an antibureaucratic weekly called *The Paper* has been coming out of Michigan State in East Lansing, despite "harassment" from a "puritan" president and university administration (who've had their hands otherwise full, explaining CIA involvement in MSU's Vietnam-aid project). Michael Kindman, the 22-year-old Merit Scholar who founded *The Paper,* rallied several full-scale campus protests on its behalf.

And with no credential beyond a high school diploma, a 19-year-old refugee from the *Free Press* named Harvey Ovshinsky returned to his home town, Detroit, last year to start his own "organ for hippies, liberals and anarchists." *The Fifth Estate,* so far, isn't much more than a hick cut-and-paste job of pilfered material: the evil-eye motif, Tim Leary's column from *EVO,* cartoons and unclassifieds" from the *Free Press,* etc. *The Fifth Estate* is one of the shortest, most derivative and least professional-looking of the papers, replete with unreadable gray type, spelling mistakes and malapropisms. One recent issue contained an uninspired arts column (Kulchur list plus pep talk), endorsement of a local peace candidate, a SNCC press release, protest against Dow Chemical Company and religious Christmas stamps, and three articles on Bob Dylan. Another covered its back page with a mock WANTED poster for an undercover narcotics agent, offering a reward of "one pound, U. S. grass to anyone who can drop 1000 micrograms of LSD into this man's misdirected body." Ovshinsky is devoted to *The Fifth Estate,* however; it is reaching a heretofore ignored audience and is improving.

Previously, such frayed-shoestring ventures scrounged desperately for money and copy. *The Newspaper* in Boston, *The Journal* in Santa Barbara and others all tried to hop on the underground express after Kunkin's success, but each of them failed.

About a year ago, however, a half-dozen such papers formed a loose alliance, the Underground Press Syndicate, with grandiose plans. Since then, 20 additional papers—weeklies, fortnightlies and monthlies—have joined their ranks and the syndicate expects to pick up others by the end of the year. Some already exist—*The Kansas Free Press,* the *Lake Shore Gazette* in Chicago (aimed, actually, at enlightened *bourgeoisie*) and *The*

Fire Island News. A *Time*-style newsmagazine of the underground from Manhattan is currently in the works. Negotiations with college papers are under way; and even high school students are beginning to issue unauthorized and uncensored extracurricular publications, such as Detroit's *South Hampton Illustrated Times* (known to the student body as *SHIT*).

The Underground Press Syndicate, like a jazz combo, offers a framework for improvisation. Any member paper (membership costs $25 annually) is free to pick up features, cartoons, news or whatnot from any other member paper, without remuneration. A single national agency solicits ads for all of them. All revenue goes back into the common fund. If and when nonmember papers want to run U.P.S. articles, they pay for them; that money goes into a fund earmarked for setting up a telex, teletype and telephoto wire service between San Francisco, Los Angeles, Chicago, New York, London, etc. "That we may all together become well informed and in turn inform the public on a larger scale bothers those who would want us to remain ununited," declares an *EVO* editorial. "Let us then bother everyone; irk them, poke them, tickle them, sway them till they understand that what bothers us bothers everyone."

"This system will make it three times as hard for the middle-class press to suppress the things we're talking about," Katzman predicts. The syndicate envisions a growing demand for its brand of coverage—from AP, UPI, college papers and TV-radio networks—which the establishment press will be unable to satisfy. In turn, more attention will be focused on the syndicate papers themselves. From there, the sky is the limit. Wilcock, for example, foresees a network of short-range pirate radio stations, outside FCC jurisdiction—a sort of Radio Free America—broadcasting underground gospel to the fettered, yearning masses. Katzman dreams of a giant Consumer's Union paper, which would undermine the dichotomy between employers and workers, uniting all in consumerhood, a living entity independent of state and producers. ("We will eat the food! We will wear the clothes! We will drive the cars!" Katzman rhapsodizes.)

Many such quixotic notions are predicated upon a fierce sense of *us* against *them.* ("They" are alternately known as "the enemy," "the evil forces," "the shadow" and "the world of up-tight fear.") But while *EVO* rants about "fascist narcos," while the *Barb* and the *Free Press* bewail the excesses of "slug-happy fuzz" or "Gestapo storm troopers," a newer West Coast entry, *The Oracle,* sends emissaries to the local police chief "to test the power of love." Finding him "intelligent, amiable and receptive," they are now dickering for a plan by which police may use the words and mystique of an ancient Indian mantra to disperse the hippie multitudes.

This sweet-tempered scheme is typical of *The Oracle,* a handsomely designed bimonthly ("approximately") from the Haight-Ashbury district of San Francisco. *The Oracle* is the gentlest and loveliest of the underground papers. Decorated with multicolored collages, woodcuts and psychedelic paintings; filled with quasi-religious Hindu myths, hymns to nature, spiritual introspections, astrological charts; sponsoring movements out of the city, into the surrounding woods and farmlands (such as "Seedpower," a transcendentalist new youth kibbutz); *The Oracle* seems often to be moving beyond resentment—toward mellow, joyful resignation. Now hyper-intellectual (it calls teeny boppers "preinitiate tribal groups . . . in evident and nostalgic response to technological and population pressures"), now lyrical (half of its letters to the editor are "LOVE-HAIGHT" poems), it laughs at the absurdity of the straight scene without any aggression at all.

Waiting is.
Meditation is action,

soothes its "Gossiping Guru," who expresses the hope that Berkeley's "campus radicals will get the message and start singing. . . . by entering the political arena against the establishment one only succeeds in lowering his level of consciousness to that of his opponent." Already, in the few short months that it has spread its gospel, *The Oracle* has changed the face of the underground press, bringing love messages to hard-hippie *EVO* and psychedelic illustrations to drier, issue-oriented papers such as the *Barb*.

The Oracle's meager "news coverage" is supplemented, at the Haight, on an almost hourly basis by an auxiliary hippie group that calls itself The Communication Company. This mimeograph operation forms the benevolent propaganda arm of The Diggers, originally a handful of generous local poets who provided free highs, food, lodging and spiritual guidance to impoverished visitors, but by now expanded to include large numbers of roving "flower people" and denizens of communal pads—"the invisible government" of Haight-Ashbury. The Communication Company produces topical leaflets within 30 minutes, day or night, and circulates them throughout the district in another 30. So far, it has distributed close to 1000 different, multicolored "publications"—ranging from poetry to position papers for the sharing gospel ("Freedom means everything free," "If you're not a Digger, you're property"), to where-and-when announcements for the next "spontaneous demonstration of joy," to warnings of impending busts.

On the Haight, hippies virtually control the scene. They feel, therefore, less persecuted, less paranoid, more relaxed—and their press reflects this sense of communal well-being in "waves of cellular trans love energy vectors." But elsewhere in the country, too, the rash of be-ins, fly-ins, love-ins, sweep-ins and megapolitan peace-pipe powwows has been bringing the new youth together with the promise of a great "gathering of the tribes" into viable communities. Public areas (such as Provo Park in San Francisco and Tompkins Square in Manhattan) have been appropriated for "freaking freely." Diggerlike cadres have sprung up in various cities (New York alone now boasts the Drop-Ins, The Real Great Society and The Jade Companions). And new underground papers give voice to the communal dream.

V

Readers of establishment papers may express themselves most genuinely in lovelorn letters; underground readers appeal to each other directly through classifieds. Not surprisingly, personal ads tend to be as freewheeling as the publication in which they appear. The *Voice* has always screened notices carefully. Its "Village Bulletin Board" rejects explicit appeals for sexual companionship, although more than a dozen presumably sophisticated dating services, mostly computer, advertise in the paper. Their Bulletin Board, typically, is encrusted with notices for avant-garde films, theater events, social get-togethers, publications and *objets d'art.*

Classifieds in the underground press fall between extremes of licentiousness, with West Coast ads leaning more toward tribal scenes (nude beach parties, Lonely Genitals Club, Sexual Freedom League functions, group acid tests) and East Coast ads, toward individual setups ("Keep me high and I'll ball you forever, Samantha"); drugs ("Attention new pot-heads, jippies, A-heads, junkies and thieves. 'Goody' Cardinelli will con you if possible. Bill Healy is a fingerman. I'm serious. Fight burn artists and finks by publishing names of known rats."); oddball cults ("GOUR-METS: Delicious Recipes for Preparing Human Flesh"); and cryptic personals ("Wrote your number on a Sarno cream puff *again* and ate it. I'll call my analyst tomorrow."). Midwest ads are tamer. Share-my-pad propositions ("Desirous of meeting buxom, beddable, stacked, sophisticated swinger"), perhaps the most prevalent form of personal, read like souped-up, adolescent refugees from *The National Enquirer.* (The *Enquirer's* editor, who considers *EVO* "in bad taste," claims *their* ads "must meet certain high standards.") But subterraneans are quick to insist that hippie advertisers are a different breed of cat entirely.

"Once I saw an ad in the *Enquirer* that said, 'I'd like to meet a girl who doesn't read this sort of paper,'" Paul Krassner recalls. "Most of these people would probably rather advertise in *The New York Times.*" (The *Times* rejected a help-wanted ad for an *EVO* salesman.) Krassner himself experimented with a "Department of Personal Propaganda" and then expressed some journalistic embarrassment at phrases like "Open-minded attractive females only" and "Will answer every letter" and "Photo (optional) returned." Rather than risk an integrity crisis over the question of censorship, he dropped the feature after a single issue. That was sad, for even though, as Krassner admits laughingly, *"Realist* readers were just as horny as anybody else," they offered more imaginative self-interpretations than most lonely-hearts, e.g.:

> Divorcee and kids: 25; attractive; I. Q. 135; intuitive-correlative and abstract-objective thinking-wise; can and do recondition self at will; extreme (and controlled) emotional range; culture-free to great extent. Like: s-f, horsing, sensual music, learning, individuals, sex, creating, existence. Dislike: cold, literature, past and present history, people en masse, boundaries. Want mate sans legality, equal or superior in sanity, freedom, potential.

"These people aren't necessarily hard up," Krassner insists. "I've got friends who use classifieds. It's a screening device. And if, say, you want to plug into a couple-swapping underground, where else can you go?"

"We're used to thinking a guy who advertises for a chick has to be a loser," says the girlfriend of an *EVO* columnist. "But that's where it's at now. Frontal. Direct. He may be really groovy. Look, if I had dressed this way five years ago—tank top, bright colors, spider stockings, huge earrings—you'd have thought I was a whore. But now I'm acceptable. Society picks things up from its fringes—and changes."

Underground proprietors, too, hope to shift the center of social gravity leftward. Ed Sanders, who also edits the *Marijuana Newsletter* (which quotes prices on the grass exchange), and whose successful shock-rock Fugs may be clearing the way for a new sort of top-40 sound, appeared on the cover of *Life*. He's an important prophet for freaking with a purpose.

"Anyone can go live in an ashram somewhere," he says. "But once you pick up the telephone, once you accept the existence of the A & P, you've *got* to get involved. Otherwise you're a psychopath. The social game is just a matter of energy sources. Now we pretend a benign political life at home and go wreaking violence all over the world. The underground tries to dull the impulse toward violence and redirect the energy into sexual and creative channels. Take pot; a highly sophisticated substance, a miracle drug. Tied in with *sex,* not violence. A sexual and philosophical union of people who turn on and have radical economic views can become a power bloc—libertarian socialism—but you've got to pound your idea into the culture. . . . You may be 'weird' and 'far out,' but you're effecting change. Once they understand you're not violent, they can't use violence against you. These newspapermen are gentle people. No fists. So you're a freak for five years, and then a radical for another ten, and then you're conservative and some other Turks are howling at the gates. We'll devote our whole lives to this campaign, because what's freaky today will be frazzled tomorrow. If you can affect just one generation of young people, you save the world for 30 or 40 years; you get people to take LSD, make love with their eyes open. For every protester, there are ten secret supporters. Get them out in the open and you cool the whole scene."

To learn what is happening, to form a personal judgment of America, we must rely heavily upon the testimony of the press. We know the defense briefs by heart. In the face of overwhelming economic and sociopolitical impotence, the underground press seeks to prepare a case for the prosecution. Its witnesses are mostly a strident, frowzy lot, bitter for all their talk of love, unruly, perhaps even a bit mad. But they are, at last, demanding to take the stand. And they have quite another story to tell.

The Hip
Establishment

J MARKS

In the same way that adults believe that youth is wasted on the young, kids believe that power is wasted on the old. The young are determined to do something about it. As a result, young people all over the world have drastically and forcefully contested the nature of conventional values. The dissent of the young seems to amount to a generation of idealists turned militant and fighting a full-scale war against established institutions.

The power of the youth army is not just its vast numbers. Heretofore we have been impressed by its unity and common goals. Now, however, the relativity of truth has become a major factor and the powerful youth forces have splintered. Ideals are no longer homogeneous: The pacifists on communal farms who dream of sexual and psychological liberation through drugs and commune-ism have little in common with the college militant-activist who dreams of social and political liberation through confrontation and civil disobedience. The breakdown of values within the youth camp has created the same kind of insecurity that has often made room for despots in Establishment society. The age of tyrant kids is upon us. Some of them will be good leaders and some of them will be cranks and brutes.

The young power class is a Hip Establishment: created intentionally by certain money interests, created unconsciously by a lot of fashion-following adolescents, and manufactured egotistically by a select group of hip angels turned devious. What it amounts to is a generation determined to preserve the unity of young people by the formation of a power class that prescribes dogmas of taste, morality, political purpose, and artistic aims with more authoritarian insistence and often with more bitterness than the old Establishment.

Some of the seventeen-year-olds who have been catapulted to early success and who have had a taste of power and fame are becoming hateful jaded brats who don't know just what to do with success. They have power and influence, they have talent but a terrible dearth of human experience. Their prose, in particular, is vitriolic, and their rigid distinctions between what is "pure" and what is "impure," what is "in" and what is "out," are ridiculous and pretentious. The *Los Angeles Free Press,* king of the underground newspapers, said, "The Byrds are for the birds!" in their death-dealing review of a rock album by a formerly big-time group. *Rolling Stone,* a San Francisco newspaper, once wrote adoringly of Jim Morrison—the theatrical lead singer of the famous rock group called The

Doors—and then put him down mercilessly as a hype because of his teeny-bopper success.

London's *International Times* (*IT*) asked: "What can YOU do to help bring about a more loving society?" It recommended: "Open up new channels of communication so that the established media will no longer be able to impose a blanket of silence on your views." The notion is beautiful. But it is ironic since the new channels of communication, namely, the underground press and radio, are steadily closing down all expression of opinion beyond their approved dogmas. The *East Village Other* (*EVO*) began in part as a counter to the Establishmental attitudes of *The Village Voice,* which, way back, began publication to refute the Establishment views of *The New York Times.* Recently, *RAT* came into existence as a newspaper hoping to liberalize the conservative political views of *EVO.* (Didn't H. G. Wells predict all this at the end of the movie *Things To Come?*)

Business has also helped to create a Hip Establishment. It uses popular concepts as the basis for selling anything to the kids. It uses the new language and the new youth ideals in television, radio, and magazine advertising, using these hip elements in their private lives because it's commercially as well as socially valuable to appear to be part of the hip scene. Business has bastardized the new slang, the new imagination, and the new ideas. It has made acts and words and expressions that originally were genuine and significant seem absurd and insignificant through their promotional shucks. Business is cashing in on the unpleasant fact that weekend hippies exist and that many young people feel a compulsion to join a "movement" that they don't clearly understand. While business may disapprove of the realities of the youth movement, it is cashing in on the "saleable part of the poison," as one ad man said.

Business is not the only factor responsible for the decline of the individual power of the hip ideal. Businessmen can only make bread where there is a market, and the people who really created the market are frequently and sadly the rock musicians who had an enormous influence on the young but who rarely had the least notion of what the youth rebellion was all about intellectually, artistically, or spiritually. They wanted to make it big and rich. Most of them believed in music, but that's about all—except, of course, for their own fantastic egos, which a dozen or more major record companies inflated with a constant stream of overheated air. Many rock stars play the Hip Establishment game.

"It's the most vicious, mean, and competitive business in the world," the former editor of a major youth magazine told me sadly. "They like to characterize themselves as not being show business, blah-blah-blah . . . but actually they're worse than all of those show-biz types put together. I could easily name five or six people who control success and failure in the rock scene ruthlessly. On a whim they can slice people apart and screw up a whole career."

There are also the people who *really* believe in the new values and who pioneered many of the new concepts of morality, politics, music, art, theatre, and literature. But when they got some attention, they got hung up on private ego trips. Many of the leaders of the young have fought very hard for a channel of communication. Now that they have it, they have become the same kind of people they warned us against. Their vice is in their efforts to create a world in their own image. Wasn't that the chief flaw in the lives of our parents?

The Hip Establishment reaches out just like the Adult Establishment before it: bringing ratings and incurable moneymindedness to FM radio. There is a new media monopoly—the underground press—whose chiefs often gloat at the demise of the competition when a writer or newspaper is busted; the Bill Graham conspiracy, which gently threatens to turn the Fillmore into the ruling Copa of Rock (is there still room for an eighteen-year-old kid with a guitar?); the rock circuit international, whereby concert promoters also own record companies, nightclubs, ballrooms, and every other facility necessary to a rock group; nudity as underground super-sale. Is it any longer really a matter of liberty or has it become simply a matter of salesmanship?

Will we live forever with Vacuum Art, that faddish kind of décor? Posters, lightshows, things that go blink in the dark, and almost anything else sold at the thousands of headshops of the world—VACUUM ART—bring up the other people. The kids who are mean and inert and frustrated and violent. They have also helped to create the Hip Establishment. They follow trends and fads without the least personal, emotional, or intellectual motivation except the age-old motive of scoring sexually and socially at any cost. Cut-down hot rods and street fights have given way to mod threads and freaky discothèques. The nouveaux hip far outnumber the young people who have been the centre and source of the youth revolution, but their importance perhaps rests in their capacity for *followship* rather than leadership. It takes many convinced but uninformed followers to create a movement. And the Hip Establishment is distinctly a social movement.

This is not to say that the Hip Establishment is a worse disease than the one it set out to cure. Many elements of this new power class are unique and imaginative. Much of the new dogma is an improvement over the older generation's conceptions. It is only awkward for a generation of what seemed to be anarchists to become the same kind of clan as the social order against which it revolted. We thought we were going to be free—much like the Frenchmen who fought the Revolution—instead we ended up in new chains. Perhaps Jerry Rubin summed it up best in his article in the English underground magazine called *Oz* when he asked desperately: "Are we a new brotherhood or are we just a tangle of organizations and competing egos? What will happen when we reach age thirty and forty?"

"The answer," Mr. Dylan said long ago, "is blowin' in the wind."

Bringing
It All
Back Home

In all this I feel a grave danger, the danger of what might be called cosmic impiety. The concept of "truth" as something dependent upon facts largely outside human control has been one of the ways in which philosophy hitherto has inculcated the necessary element of humility. When this check upon pride is removed, a further step is taken on the road towards a certain kind of madness— the intoxication of power which invaded philosophy with Fichte, and to which modern men, whether philosophers or not, are prone. I am persuaded that this intoxication is the greatest danger of our time, and that any philosophy which, however unintentionally, contributes to it is increasing the danger of vast social disaster.

Bertrand Russell

Introduction to Part Three

CALIBAN

I

In the beginning was the island:
fresh springs, brine pits, both barren place and fertile,
green grasslands, bees, sweet honeycombs,
berries, mushrooms, brown pignuts, forests, birds,
fens, pits, rocks, sounds, and sweet airs
that give delight and hurt not.
No human hand plucked berries ripe and swollen,
no human eye surveyed this island Eden,
no tongue, godlike, dared call it good or evil.
For master of this isle and king by birth
I Caliban, the natural son of Sycorax,
mooncalf and freckled whelp of witchhag dam,
black mummer playing on an island stage,
alone as king I graced the isle in beauty.
Alone I lived: there was no right or wrong,
did mine own thing, yelped, whimpered, and careened.
Then came bookloving Platonist Prospero,
displacéd duke of Naples, governor,
philosopher-king as his blind books had called it,
with staff and volumes to usurp mine isle.
Sycorax had warned me against his kind,
usurping all the ends of nature to
his will to System. And me the freckled whelp
hagborn, accursed with brutish shape,
what should I do against him? I'd seen him tame
the tempests with his magic, calm the waves.
In short, I was afraid. Co-opted by his system
King Caliban was displaced. When first he came here
he strok'd me and made much of me, and gave me
water with berries, taught me sun and moon,
I showed him all the qualities of the isle,
fresh springs, brine pits, both barren place and fertile.
Curses on him! curse his Platonic prattle!
and curse me too, mind-raped by Prospero,
for I am all the subjects that he has, and here he sties me
in this hard rock, whilst he does keep from me

the rest o' th' isle. Keeps me from
the fair Miranda. I had peopled else
this isle with Calibans. The land belongs to people.
This isle belongs to Caliban its king.

II

First it was the words: he was hung up on words.
At night I could hear him gabbling letters from those books,
all old and black and red. Trying to cram
his knowledge down my throat.
Then it was names: he named everything in sight.
He used to wake me, nights, with his naming of things.
It was fig tree, windflower, foxglove, poppy, hazel,
Sweet William, sourgrass, St. John's warts,
watercress, pignut, mushroom the livelong day.
O Tangiers loon, woodlark, o kildeer crying,
small chopping sparrow, olive meadowlark:
so calved the grassy clods, the flocks arose
fleeced and bleating to fellow spring in fleece,
tigers, stags, ocelots rose like moles
throwing the earth in hillocks as they came.
The shining fields were full of animal voices
and Prosper spoke to me in cloven myths
that mastered being, ordered all
this wild unknowing, tamed
the jungle in me, watched
my summer flesh that wintered with the trees.
And as the sky was hatching out the earth
a land formed in me and the Word was born.
He said that I must learn to speak, to spell,
to carry water, sweep and cook and fetch:
he spoke to me as 'twere a thing most brutish:
"What, ho, slave! You, Caliban!
Thou witch-hag whelp! Thou earth, thou! Speak!"
That other, fairy rumpkisser, Ariel
he called "fine apparition, dainty Ariel." This puppet
sold his own birthright for a place at court,
co-opted by an empty pledge of freedom.
Just words, all empty rhetoric.
The sunrise and the sunset, spring and fall,
the turning of the year, the bogs and fens
is the only philosophy Caliban can know.

III

As I had said, I'm subject to a tyrant,
a sorcerer that by that cunning theory
cheated me of that isle that once was mine.

Witch Sycorax with age and envy
was grown into a hoop. Banished from Argiers
this blue-eyed hag was hither brought with child,
locked howling Ariel in a cloven pine. Now Caliban,
the nigger of the isle, doth fetch in wood,
make fires, and serve in offices that profit them,
the System I despise.
The springs belong to people,
this island's mine by Sycorax my mother,
and yet he steals it from me. He taught me language
my profit on't's this:
I know to curse. The red plague rid you
for learning me your language. I call upon you
all the infections that the sun sucks up
from bogs, fens, flats, on Prosper fall.
Curse you old man. Curse you. Then Caliban
fell on some heavenly beings that were crying,
"Open your mouth: here's that will give you language, cat."
So blew my mind, expanded consciousness,
opened my eyes. So knelt I to Stephano,
the brave god that bears celestial liquor,
and thus I kneel to *him.* Will show him springs,
pluck berries, fish, bring wood, dig pignuts.
A plague upon the tyrant that I serve!
I'll bear *him* no more sticks, but follow *thee,*
Pied Piper with the glorious jug of rum,
a lotus-eater Caliban's become!

> 'Ban, 'Ban, Ca— Caliban
> Had a new master, got a new man.
> Freedom, high-day! high-day freedom!
> freedom, high-day, freedom, freedom!

This isle belongs to the people: so says my master;
this day we'll call it Peoples Isle: I Caliban
have a new master, rule a new land.

IV

When Ferdinand and Miranda were to marry
he made this pageant, see, of the old gods
like Iris, Juno, Ceres, all the deities
the System worships, senseless now to me.
Then he stood up: he said that this rough magic
he'd here abjure (abjure? what word is that?),
he called for heavenly music from the deep
and broke his staff and drowned his magic book,
and called on elves of standing lakes and groves
and Jove, of course (these old men always do).

Said something about clearer reason that
I did not understand and do not now. That is
the kind of speech that makes me want to puke.
Why did he do it? Now he's powerless.
I'd never give up power once I had it,
I witchhagchild, I freckled Caliban,
care not for reason and an old man's books.
Then the old man said we're made of dreams,
the show had all been spirits and the globe itself
would disappear, leave not a rack behind.
(What was he up on? pignuts, berries, brine-springs?)
Then straight away confessed that he was mad. "Sir, I am vexed," he
said, those were his words. "Bear with my weakness. My old brain
is troubled." He didn't have to tell us he was muddled.
But ideas are only in your head anyway.

So yesterday I told Stephano
that 'twas a custom of his to nap there, afternoons: there we may brain him,
(having first seized his book) or with a log
batter his skull, or punch him with a stake. Or burn
the island down. Remember
first to possess his books and burn them:
without them he's but a sot. He's just like us.
All hate him rootedly as I. Burn but his books
and liberate his house, his brave utensils.
Let's make the isle a liberated zone.
His house shall belong to the people. The isle is Caliban's.
Take to the fields, take to the streets with singing.
This night shall Caliban reclaim his lands.

V

Now Stephano and Trinculo go with me
to do that good mischief, make this isle
Stephano's own forever, and I Caliban
forever his footlicker.
O' night we'll steal into old grandsire's cell,
save generations hence from co-optation
by grey paternalistic rapists. "Fight your nature,"
he once said. "Trust not your intuition. Trust reason,
not sensation. Be men, not animals.
Work within systems, be genteel, and cultured,
just, humane, rational, scholars like myself.
Apollo and not Bacchus is your god."
More of an old man's foolish dreams, no doubt.
Old Prosper dreams tonight beside his fire;
his dreams reveal the Caliban who seethes,
mates with Miranda, roams the isle once more,

kindles bonfires with branches and brown pignuts,
roars in the pits and leaps with little goatcries
among the grasslands and the honeycombs.
Subdues the isle, burns Prosper in his bedstead,
remembers I am king and he the fraud.
I'll not be forced by Shakespeare now to sue
for grace and bend the suppliant knee.
I Caliban am free, am my own man.
It's action's needed here, not words,
and Caliban will act and act again.

Thus the witch-child with others finds the means
to overthrow and take back Peoples' Isle,
to make a new world, man, our own new world,
rid once for all of systems, codes, pretenses,
language and logic, empty theory,
learning and culture: all the eldern bullshit
that once corrupted virgin Caliban.

And once again it will be beginning
when Caliban is king.

Valerie Carnes

Things Fall Apart, the Center Cannot Hold

Are We in the Middle of a Revolution?

ANDREW KOPKIND

I

Revolution is a serious business. It is not the Dodge Rebellion, the miniskirt revolt, or the McCarthy movement, however beneficial or entertaining those campaigns may have been. People talk now about the coming of the revolution as they would discuss the arrival of the latest hurricane; it is thought to be imminent, or upon us, or just blowing by. But real revolution is a wind of longer passing.

It is at once the most tragic and redeeming social experience. It is what societies do instead of committing suicide, when the alternatives are exhausted and all the connections that bind men's lives in familiar patterns are cut. Death and transfiguration is the ultimate human drama; revolution combines those two acts in a single transcendent scene.

Whatever else may be going on in America, it is not very much of a revolution. Despite some unruliness, a few perilous moments, and a great deal of intramural bickering, the strongest fortresses of "the system" remain in the hands of the same élites that have held power for years. The only change is that the capability of those hands can now be questioned. But Ralph Nader and his irate consumers have hardly dented General Motors. The New Left and the Yippies will find the Cook County Democratic machine still running. All the power of poor people's organizations, community-control projects, and black economic development schemes have failed to impede the extravagant growth of corporate capitalism at home and abroad in this generation. RAT does not threaten the hegemony of The New York Times; Luckies outsell grass; Andrew Cordier still outranks Mark Rudd in anybody's hierarchy of power.

By usual definition, revolution means the displacement of the rulers by the ruled, a redress of the imbalance of power in a social system. The classic model—a seizure of the state in violent struggle—is of course unthinkable in America now. Potential revolutionary classes—black people, students, blue-collar workers, hippies—are either ill-placed or ill-disposed for such battle.

If there is a revolutionary program in anyone's head, it involves action along all kinds of fronts to soften the system—by blowing kids' minds, frightening the comfortable classes, organizing the oppressed, questioning the legitimacy of everything. But that would be only a preliminary stage; plans and programs would have to grow out of the experience. The Declaration of Independence detailed tyranny but presented no formula for constitutional democracy. Marx carved up capitalism but laid out only the foggiest conception of a Communist state.

Conventional politics should be the last place to look for revolutionary change, and with only one possible exception—the distressing example of the Wallace campaign—no exercise of electoral politics has carried revolutionary values along with it. As the midnight choo-choo left Alabam', it carried an implausible coalition of rich Goldwaterites, *petit-bourgeois* Birchers, battered blue-collar workers and agonized rednecks. The passengers harangue against the "liberal Establishment," which Wallace identifies quite correctly as the power base of both the Republican and Democratic parties. Wallace supporters may entertain fantasies of replacing the Establishment's welfare bureaucrats, bankers, foundation managers, internationalist businessmen and union leaders with their own numbers. If they could do it, the result would be a revolution of a kind— a kind of American Fascism. But the Wallace movement is strongest where America is least vulnerable—in the decaying rural South or the shrinking near-slums of the blue-collar North—and it can amount only to a permanent (if permanently dangerous) minority.

Across the center spread, the left margin of politics is even thinner. The McCarthy campaign was conceived (if not plotted) as an *anti*-revolutionary reform movement, to "channel protest" into the two-party system, to strengthen the Democratic liberals, and to replace evil and incompetent managers with humane and wise ones—at the head of the same machine.

The effort had many advantages: It gave large numbers of people the believed effective. Most of those people may never go further than a "peace" campaign within a major party, but they are now concerned opportunity to *fail* in a last "test" of the only political methods they enough to set themselves up as a buffer zone between the stern forces of law-and-order and the radicals. But throughout its long winter and spring, the campaign never developed the first plan or promise for dismantling and restructuring the institutions which give rise to white racism and militarism—the effects of which the McCarthyites so clearly disliked.

Understandably, they focused their attack on segregation and unequal opportunity, and on the war in Vietnam. But the war which they sought to end is only the deformed child of too-healthy parents: the Joint Chiefs and the defense intellectuals, Lockheed Aircraft and I.B.M., the Rand Corporation and the A.F.L.-C.I.O., the nice and the nasty, the actively conniving and the merely complicit. Sterilization of the parents might have been revolutionary; abortion of the child could not be.

Segregation and unequal opportunity are only expressions of the racist element in all aspects of national life. It may have nothing to do with personal prejudice. The fact that in most big cities most domestic maids are black is a fact of racist economy in a class society, whether the mistress of the house is a member of a civil-rights organization or not. The certainty that black children will receive inferior educations is determined by racism. Urban riots, however "unpolitical" they may seem, are responses to racist political structures. Though they may be unaware of the relationship, the affluent suburbanites built their comfortable homes and careers at the expense of those in the ghettos. The suburbs get better public services, cheaper insurance, convenient domestic labor, classy culture, good education and political power—and the slums lose out in "competition." To "revolutionize" the role of blacks would require commitments of resources, sacrifices of status and the drastic re-allocation of priorities which politics as currently constituted is unable to make. "Socialism" would perhaps be a beginning, but only that. Obviously, McCarthy was far even from that first step, as the Robert Kennedy campaign—with all its "urbanism"—was, too.

The only reallocation of power which the McCarthy campaign seemed to propose was in favor of the suburban liberal "New Class." That would have been small change indeed: The same people have been accumulating power for 30 years. If they are to get even bigger slices of the power pie, they will have to take it away from those without the means to hold on: blacks, poor whites, the underemployed. For example, as McCarthy's well-educated liberals (the candidate's own characterization of his supporters) asserted power in Democratic organizations, they preempted political space from the militant and poor of both races, who had either to stay in subservient positions or else drift into fractional and irrelevant sects. The left is much less cohesive today than it was a year ago, in some measure because the McCarthy campaign took power—in terms of money, energy, publicity and numbers of people—away from the racial base. Last winter, there were perhaps hundreds of thousands of woebegone liberals ready to desert the Democratic party for more militant political action outside the narrow two-party framework. McCarthy successfully stopped the movement of that base—perhaps only temporarily—by giving it creative play therapy in Democratic primaries. But we have only to sniff the air to notice that McCarthy did nothing to reduce the power of the right.

It is where the conscientious and well-surrounded McCarthy liberals find themselves in the social universe—not what they fancy in fashion and style—that gives them an unrevolutionary role. With the best intentions and warmest sympathies, they will work to keep control of resources in their own hands. In a wholly different context, Marx described the same mentality 120 years ago:

> They desire the existing state of society minus its revolutionary and disintegrating elements. . . . They naturally conceive the world in which it is supreme to be the best; and they develop this comfortable conception into various more or less complete systems. . . . They wish for a *bourgeoisie* without a proletariat.

Replace the old-fashioned terminology with trendier words, and it is easy to understand McCarthy's list of putative Cabinet members: Rockefeller, Gardner, Thomas Watson and the rest of that able crew were aboard. None could be counted exactly revolutionary cadre, and McCarthy had the wit and sensitivity to deny a revolutionary role for himself. But his campaigners were less discreet. Last spring, they were talking about "the McCarthy revolution," which had accomplished, among other things, the termination of the war and a "bloodless coup" in the White House. What they forgot was that even if McCarthy, by some miracle, had won the Democratic nomination, the same interest groups and classes would stay in power. That may be all right, but it's not revolution.

II

The art of holding onto power is the American system's special grace. The trick is to make reform seem so tantalizingly close as to dull the edge of militancy and force the purest revolutionaries into the peripheries of political action. Dissent has a political function as well as a constitutional position; it legitimizes and supports the status quo. Only the dumbest establishments practice open suppression of dissidence; what Marcuse calls "repressive tolerance" is far more effective: In practice, it is the art of letting dissident minorities say whatever they please within a system loaded in favor of the most powerful élites. The dissidents let off steam; the controllers keep power. A shirt-sleeve walk through a riot area works better than a police charge—and for the same ultimate objective.

America is cleverest when it protects its oppositions and neutralizes them: by buying them (War on Poverty), channeling them (Clean for Gene) or marketing them (turn on with cars). The last method is the most fun— and the most profitable. To a society that is suffering from too much internalized repression already, the sale of vicarious liberation can bring a bonanza in cash returns. Radicals, hippies and "black-power extremists" have only to sit by the phone or collect their mail these days while the invitations pour in. Newspaper syndicates are searching for lefties to run alongside their regular columnists on the editorial pages of a hundred provincial papers. The mass-circulation magazines can't seem to get enough of S.D.S. Hearst is publishing a head magazine for the straights. The performing rebel is urged to tell it like it is and do his own thing— *pour épater les bourgeois*. Media fortunes will be made or broken on a company's ability to swing with the liberation movements. It is all proof enough that this is not a revolutionary situation; if it were, Tom Hayden wouldn't be on television, Country Joe and the Fish would be underground, and Eldridge Cleaver would be shot.

Sometimes it seems that if Tom Hayden, Country Joe and Eldridge Cleaver did not exist, America would have had to invent them. And so— in a way—America *did* invent them: to satisfy revolutionary longings. They are aphrodisiacs in the air-conditioning system, hallucinogens in the water supply. To the extent that the forces they represent can be contained, society is safe. But if the forces reach a critical mass, the mild hype becomes hell broken loose. Repressive tolerance is an exquisitely subtle game.

If society invented the actors, the forces they are acting out are inevitable. They were unleashed by the inexorable progression of basic drives in the American experience. Centralization of bureaucratic power led to movements for "participatory democracy." Oppression of black people had to produce a freedom movement. There is a straight line from Victorian prohibitions to the intersection of Haight and Ashbury. It would have been odd, and tragic, if the war in Vietnam had not stimulated the antiwar protest.

Why they all happened now—and together—is the intriguing political question. There may be no one answer, as there certainly is no single approach: The theory of overcontribution of causes seems to apply, and it is practically futile to assign weights to factors. But the historical outline is fairly clear. Two streams of radical response to very real conditions began to come together in America at the beginning of the nineteen-sixties. The first was the struggle of the black underclass against the classic forms of political tyranny and economic exploitation expressed as racism and poverty. The second was the struggle by middle-class whites against the newer forms of institutional oppression and manipulation expressed as personal alienation and cultural emptiness: In other words, the simple desire of people to maintain a sense of their own importance and hold onto their values in a superorganized world of bigness and impersonality.

What led the two streams into confluence was a shared sense of powerlessness. All at once, it seemed to occur to blacks, poor whites, students, farm workers, technologists and just ordinary uncategorizable people that they had no influence over "the decisions which affect their lives."

The forms that radicalism has taken are familiar enough to everyone: There are the student revolutionaries, the hippies, the drug-heads, the middle-class marchers, the black nationalists and other less virulent types fading out into the gray center. Among them there are scores of ideological bits and pieces, some amounting to no more than a phrase and others comprising a regular *Weltanschauung*. Chunks are borrowed from one or another foreign model or historical example, and strains spring as well from native American soil. But what unites them all is more interesting: a common thread of values and needs that people in this tech-nologized, overproductive, postindustrial land seem so desperately to lack. Participation, recognition, loving, honesty, caring; the list is so "corny" that the values must be expressed in cooler clichés: "Do your thing," "Like it is," "Listen, whitey," "Share in the decisions," "Make love, not war."

The thread is woven in no particular pattern throughout all the areas of disaffection. Single events or a series of them occasionally make it very clear. The four kids who sat in at a lunch counter in Greensboro, N.C., in 1960 were enacting the *idea* of individual effectiveness in a pure and simple form. For the decade of the nineteen-fifties at least, no one had dreamed that one person could effect change by beating on the anonymous and impassive system. It was not so much that people had wanted to be "silent" in that generation; they had no notion that speaking out would make the slightest difference.

The roots of radicalism in both its major streams and all its forms lie in that existential ground that the Greensboro kids plowed. The politics came later, and is of secondary importance for understanding (although of primary importance for the strategy of change). What it meant to be "under 30" (in 1964) was to identify yourself with that surge of resistance against the old values. Whatever supported or legitimized them became a fair target: university administrations and their I.B.M.-card rules, political machines and their hypocritical reforms, college professors and their self-justifying intellectualism, parents and their suburban aspirations, unions and their unfulfilled promises. When the kids and the blacks excoriated America in four-letter words, they were talking of more than the war or segregation. They meant that America had lied to them— and in a way that was the original sin.

Separately or together, the radical streams seemed to have no real revolutionary potential. It was hard to conceive of a strategy for radical reconstitution of America. Some looked to Marx or Castro or American Populism, but none of those was seen then, or now, to be singularly ap-plicable. The "center" of the system was too securely in control, at once too flexible and too commanding to allow the development of mass action.

But the history of the last three years is the chronicle of the "center's" disintegration, of the failure of the methods of political liberalism to cope with systematic disorders. The mediating institutions that have been dominant from the New Deal through the Great Society delayed the day of confrontation but could not remove the causes. In their last incarnations the mediators were antipoverty programs, peace offensives, methods for humane riot control, urban-renewal projects, counterinsurgency schemes, foreign-aid grants, antisegregation laws, the McCarthy campaign, "dove" candidacies, the "politics of joy"; in short, most of the things which editorialists from *The New Republic* to *The Times* endorse. All of them sought to reduce the real conflicts of our lives, and all of them were inadequate. The rising sense of hopelessness and helplessness this summer—the widespread fear that there were no more "alternatives"—

followed from the realization that the mediating forces were out of commission.

The crisis of the society is expressed in the resistance of its rebels, but the rebels did not cause the crisis. White racism was prevalent before Watts, the advancing empire was ruinous before Vietnam, violence was immanent in the American character before Chicago. The black insurgents, the Vietcong and the antiwar demonstrators did not manufacture the evils they opposed. They brought those evils into sharp relief when the mediators proved incapable of finally keeping the images hazy.

There is a real failure of the left in America, but it follows the collapse of the middle. Radicals can provide no believable alternatives for many of the people spinning out of the center as the vortex widens and deepens. The Wallace campaign has captured some—notably Northern blue-collar workers—by providing a racist focus for their several complaints. An independent "fourth-party" McCarthy campaign might have done the same for disaffected liberals, but McCarthy was not interested in the job. The white radicals have no program to appeal to the working class or to newly radicalized middle-class adults. Black militants do not appeal organizationally to the mass of black people.

That may be too bad, but the left should not bear all the blame. America does that to its radicals. It fragments and isolates them, illegitimizes and scorns them. However rebellious children may be, they have their parents' genes; American radicals are Americans. They cannot easily cross class lines to organize groups above or below their own station. They are caught in the same status traps as everyone else, even if they react self-consciously. If they must spend all day outwitting the Red-baiters, they have little time for anything else. If they can prove their point about America only by confronting it, they must take themselves out of action— in jail or hospital emergency room—when they should be digging in for hard work. If they cannot get a useful education—for life-changing instead of life-adjustment—in the classrooms, they must take it in the streets or on the campuses, and that is risky business.

III

Diseases kill when therapy fails. Symptoms express morbidity, but they are logically irrelevant to its cause. If some kind of "fascism" comes to America—as too many of all persuasions now fear and hope, as a way of self-vindication—it will be because institutional therapy failed to cure a complex of morbid "social diseases."

With each passing Wallace rally during the campaign and each new indication of incompetence by the middle's managers, that awful day has seemed closer. But radical change from the right is probably not much more likely than from the other side. A period of crackdown is not the same thing as an age of fascism. Any analysis of the rise of Hitler or Mussolini, or of the O.A.S. in France, suggests that one or two critical factors are missing in the American situation. For one thing, American economic institutions are seen to be in tip-top shape. For another, there is no readily available army of the dispossessed large enough, and at the right social levers, to threaten or seize state power. Neither Hitler's *Lumpen* or General Salan's troops have actual counterparts in the United States. Welfare cutbacks and a hard line on street politics under the next Administration will not pull America together, but—in the absence of any new economic or military crisis—the process of disintegration should not greatly accelerate.

As the stock market booms and the new cars roll out of Detroit, economic problems loom small, but the military problem is still engrossing. It has many aspects, but the fundamental question is whether militarism can be checked by democratic control, whether the power of armies need be applied to the extension and maintenance of American political and economic influence over two-thirds of the world. It is not only, as many critics have said, that America is a world cop; America is a world robber. It appropriates national resources and national identity, imposes governments and values, covets profits and independence. Empires have a habit of acting that way: The U.S. could no more let the Dominican Republic (in its sphere of influence) assert independence than the Soviet Union could let Czechoslovakia take its "independent" strategic position on the frontiers of the Russian sphere.

The urge to empire is supported by the whole political economy of a nation. Whoever wrote General Eisenhower's warning about the "military-industrial complex" deserves global recognition. That's it—and the playing of musical chairs in directors' boardrooms does not change the functionally imperial role of the firm.

The long-term military problem is enormous and perhaps insoluble. The short-term one—the war—is enormous but probably soluble. Vietnam has had such a devastating effect on America that the mere cessation of hostilities will end only a few of the agonies. That the Johnson Administration did not accede to the pressure of major sectors of business, the press, the Democratic party and the general public and settle the thing long ago is tribute of a kind to the power of the defense establishment. A President who wants to end it next year, or the year after that, will have to contend with the same countervailing force, and it may cost him billions for a missile build-up and defense-systems spectaculars to comfort the old "complex" for its loss of face. For the rest of us, the comfort will be cool.

What the war has done to the society—quite apart from the cost in lives—is only beginning to be understood. It introduced politics to a generation which had been taught that politics—in the ideological sense —was dead in America. The war's duration and pointlessness have "radicalized" some numbers, if not hordes, of previously bored and apathetic liberals. That process is easy to describe in terms of personal perception: (1) The war is an unfortunate necessity. (2) The war is an unnecessary aberration of U.S. foreign policy. (3) The war is one of many mistakes. (4) The war is one mistake in a generally unprotested pattern of interventions. (5) The war is a product of the same political structure and the same economic relationships that "institutionalize" racism, brutalize the poor and alienate the middle classes, and creates that oppressive reality of powerlessness which is at the bottom of it all. (6) Pig! (7) Brother . . .

Not everybody goes all that distance. The radicalizing process depends on many variables of background and station in life, and it is rather more experiential than rational. The McCarthy delegates in Chicago, for instance, were poised in midprocess when the Democratic National Convention opened. The police charges put many of them in a personal confrontation with authority which in one explosive moment stripped a layer of myths from their conception of America. Some have described it almost in psychoanalytic terms: "I had this sudden insight," or "I didn't know I felt that way," or "Why can't other people understand?"

Millions of others were carried along to lesser degrees by the television coverage, and the pictures reinforced other images that had been registering for many months. Grant Park meant more after three years of burned Vietnamese villages; Mayor Daley's cops somehow hark back to Bull Connor's. The shock of recognition is a potent force.

Marches, vigils, teach-ins, draft-refusal rituals and the myriad protests of these protesting years have involved a sizable fraction of the population, personally or once-removed. No one is quite the same after he has marched in a demonstration, however tame, and it is at least half as good to hear about the adventure from a close relative or friend. Legitimacy mounts, and one experience can be transplanted to another "issue" via the familiar forms. The 200 parishioners who walked out on Cardinal O'Boyle's anti–birthcontrol sermon in a Washington cathedral were to some unknown degree spiritual heirs of the peace marchers and the freedom riders.

The war works its devastation in conjunction with other pressures in the society, and their combined effect increases exponentially month by month, according to some unsolved synergistic equation. The social cost of racism, the war and bureaucratic corporatism is far greater than their simple sum. For instance, the cost of pursuing the war compels reductions in even the modest programs of the War on Poverty, thus sharpening the sense of exclusion in the black ghettos. That surely contributes to the black uprisings, which in turn exacerbate tensions already produced by the war alone. The resultant threat of social crisis leads to demands for "law and order," which in turn drive blacks and whites farther apart, separate generations and renew class antagonisms.

So much is moving and shifting that it is hard to catch more than a glimpse of the action as it passes by. Events tumble upon one another like theatrical happenings, and the sequence of things is lost: Logic is another casualty of political disintegration. In a situation of such fluidity the events themselves have less intrinsic than contextual meaning. Senator McCarthy's good showing in the New Hampshire primary (who remembers that he lost in the popular vote, to a write-in candidate?) and Robert Kennedy's subsequent entrance into the Presidential campaign were thought to have "caused" President Johnson's March 31 speech of retirement and deescalation. But it is dangerous to draw tight causal relationships. Those political events were set in the context of the N.L.F.'s stunning Tet offensive and the world gold crisis—which were related phenomena themselves.

There is something happening, as Dylan sang, but we don't know what it is, at least not exactly. People are right when they sense something new in their lives, even if they cannot touch it or see it. Sexual freedom, the kids, the riots, assassinations: They all seem to be related, but the bonds are obscure.

To look for the links between those surface effects is inevitably unrewarding. The connections are all underground, in a root mass of rapidly growing and changing new relationships, of men to men and institutions among themselves. For four decades the material basis of American life has been in the process of real transformation, from classic industrial development to the "new system" of postindustrialism, or postcapitalism, or technologism, or whatever it's called. The politics, ideologies, mores and life patterns of the old system obviously cannot work well with the new. Marx, again:

"Does it require deep intuition to comprehend that man's ideas, views and conceptions, in one word, man's consciousness, changes with every change in the conditions of his material existence, in his social relations and in his social life?"

Work has new meaning, personal space is compressed, leisure looms large, consumption has a different function. Notions change accordingly: Good taste becomes prudery, adjustment is conformism, surplus is waste, success is self-indulgence, status is paralysis, pragmatism is hypocrisy, welfare is slavery.

Those who hold steadfastly to the old values are true conservatives; those who only sense the new are worried liberals; those who see the whole pattern very clearly are radicals, and they don't know what to do about it.

Whether any of the preconditions for a political revolution on top of the basal changes now exist is most difficult to say. Classical revolutionary theory—Marxism, for instance—provides a useful method of analysis but few helpful hints for prediction, which explains the prevalence of *neo*-Marxists in postindustrial countries. Marxism rather disastrously missed the boat by predicting proletarian revolution, and it is up to theorists now either to dismiss the working class or redefine it as a revolutionary agent (both tacks are taken).

Where we are now is far from that point at which a revolutionary "agency" seizes state power.

. . .

Cultural change has been far more successful than the political kind; the radical movement has moved from Lenin to Lennon in one generation. It is easily spread by a thousand rock stations and the big record companies, and it is carried by the winds that blow the burning grass. Not for nothing has *The Wall Street Journal,* for one, questioned the wisdom of antimarijuana laws. Apart from any inherent injustice, enforcement is turning an entire class of pre-élite kids against established authority. If the House Un-American Activities Committee had any sense, it would leave Dave Dellinger alone and investigate Big Brother and the Holding Company.

"The Great Bourgeois Cultural Revolution" can change people's lives in a way, but it is too easily manipulated by the same old economic forces, and the pot and the music end up reinforcing their positions of control. Any revolutionary content is soon drained, and all that remains is a new style.

Only political change can build the new (or rediscovered) cultural values into the life of the society. For the first time in years, people have begun to talk seriously about such change taking place. Half a year ago the issue of revolution was not considered quite legitimate for conversation, even on the left. Only this summer did white radicals begin to refer to themselves as "revolutionaries" with less than total irony. They are looking for "allies," in the spiritual more than the material sense, in Western and Eastern European movements, as well as in Cuba or Vietnam. Anyone hacking away at the American empire from abroad is an ally of those chipping away from within.

The problem is where to start chipping. The revolutionaries, of all degrees, are as baffled as anyone else. If the need for change is obvious, the strategy remains obscure. Whether they can hold out for very long in the face of little or no success is still more problematic. They need patience now (later, after the revolution, they will need irony, as the hero said in *La Guerre Est Finie*). But their genius so far has been the ability to redefine "success." It consists no longer in electing a militant city councilman or passing a local antidiscrimination law, in paralyzing the Selective Service System or occupying a college hall. The objective really is closer to the Beatles': to "free minds" by forcing people to re-examine their beliefs about their world.

That has been a more successful campaign than anyone would have thought possible. Street fighting is only one tactic. There are a thousand projects yet untried, and radicals of all types are finding support for their efforts in their own haunts. Education and electoral politics were clear initial targets; the press and the mass media may be next. No one need plot the attacks. One wave can break on several shores. The kids in Chicago, for instance, touched many reporters at the core of their consciences. One result has been the publication of a new Chicago monthly paper by journalists who objected to their papers' convention coverage. In Washington, some young reporters are talking about refusing to cover events or write stories when to do so would violate their own political commitments. People are finding allies everywhere.

At an impromptu street rally in Paris last May, I heard a student speaker from atop a car remind his fellows: "The unique and essential enemy is America." To him it meant the America that is on everybody's back, spreading herbicides in Indochina and sociology at the Sorbonne and spies in Africa. To his American revolutionary ally, the enemy is the system that victimizes its own people. Both revolutionaries share an affection for (and derive inspiration from) American imagination, spontaneity and energy. They love the music and the movies, the style and the sweep of American adventure. The Frenchman might easily reject it all in a critical moment; the American cannot throw it all away—not the kids with the cops, the underground press with the TV networks, the hard rock with the Muzak, Harlem with Scarsdale, the High Sierras with the automobile graveyards. To be a revolutionary is to love your life enough to change it, to choose struggle instead of exile, to risk everything with only the glimmering hope of a world to win.

A Yippie
Manifesto

JERRY RUBIN

This is a Viet Cong flag on my back. During the recent hearings of the House UnAmerican Activities Committee in Washington, a friend and I are walking down the street en route to Congress—he's wearing an American flag and I'm wearing this VC flag.

The cops mass, and boom! all of a sudden they come toward us. I think: Oh, man, curtains. I am going to be arrested for treason, for supporting the enemy.

And who do the cops grab and throw in the paddy wagon?

My friend with the American flag!

And I'm left all alone in the VC flag.

"What kind of a country is this?" I shout at the cops. "YOU COMMUNISTS!"

Everything is cool en route to Canada until the border. An official motions me into a small room and pulls out a five-page questionnaire.

"Do you use drugs?" he asks quite seriously.

"Yeah," I say.

"Which?"

"Coca Cola."

"I mean DRUGS!" he shouts.

"Coca Cola is more dangerous for you than marijuana," I say. "Fucks up your body, and it's addictive."

"Have you ever advocated the overthrow of the Canadian government?" he asks.

"Not until I get into Canada."

"Have you ever been arrested for inciting to riot?"

I reply no, and it is true. In August I was arrested in Chicago for something similar, "solicitation to mob action," a violation of a sex statute.

Finally I ask the border official to drop out. "Man, your job is irrelevant," I say. "The Canadian-American border does not exist. There are no such things as borders. The border exists only in your head.

"No state has the right to ask me these questions. The answers are mine. Next thing I know you guys will be tapping my brain!"

I try to get the cat to take off his uniform right there. But he refuses, saying, "I've got a job to do and a family to support."

So goes the cancer of the Western world: everyone just doing his "job." Nobody learned the lesson of Eichmann. Everyone still points the finger elsewhere.

America and the West suffer from a great spiritual crisis. And so the yippies are a revolutionary religious movement.

We do not advocate political solutions that you can vote for. You are never going to be able to *vote* for the revolution. Get that hope out of your mind.

And you are not going to be able to buy the revolution in a supermarket, in the tradition of our consumer society. The revolution is not a can of goods.

Revolution only comes through personal transformation: finding God and changing your life. Then millions of converts will create a massive social upheaval.

The religion of the yippies is: "RISE UP AND ABANDON THE CREEP-ING MEATBALL!!"

That means anything you want it to mean. Which is why it is so power-ful a revolutionary slogan. The best picket sign I ever saw was blank. Next best was: "We Protest————!"

Slogans like "Get out of Vietnam" are informative, but they do not create myths. They don't ask you to do anything but carry them.

Political demonstrations should make people dream and fantasize. A religious-political movement is concerned with people's souls, with the creation of a magic world which we make real.

When the national media first heard our slogan, they reported that the "creeping meatball" was Lyndon Johnson. Which was weird and unfair, because we liked Lyndon Johnson.

We cried when LBJ dropped out. "LBJ, you took us too literally! We didn't mean YOU should drop out! Where would WE be if it weren't for you, LBJ?"

Is there any kid in America, or anywhere in the world, who wants to be like LBJ when he grows up?

As a society falls apart, its children reject their parents. The elders offer us Johnsons, Agnews, and Nixons, dead symbols of a dying past.

The war between THEM and US will be decided by the seven-year-olds.

We offer: sex, drugs, rebellion, heroism, brotherhood.

They offer: responsibility, fear, puritanism, repression.

Dig the movie *Wild in the Streets*! A teenage rock-and-roll singer campaigns for a Bobby Kennedy-type politician.

Suddenly he realizes: "We're all young! Let's run the country ourselves!"

"Lower the voting age to 14!"

"14 or FIGHT!"

They put LSD in the water fountains of Congress and the Congressmen have a beautiful trip. Congress votes to lower the voting age to 14.

The rock-and-roll singer is elected President, but the CIA and military refuse to recognize the vote. Thousands of longhairs storm the White House, and six die in the siege. Finally the kids take power, and they put all people over 30 into camps and give them LSD every day. (Some movies are even stranger than OUR fantasies.)

"Don't trust anyone over 30!" say the yippies—a much-quoted warning.

I am four years old.

We are born twice. My first birth was in 1938, but I was reborn in Berkeley in 1964 in the Free Speech Movement.

When we say "Don't trust anyone over 30," we're talking about the second birth. I got 26 more years.

When people 40 years old come up to me and say, "Well, I guess I can't be part of your movement," I say, "What do you mean? You could have been born yesterday. Age exists in your head."

Bertrand Russell is our leader. He's 90 years old.

Another yippie saying is: "THE GROUND YOU STAND ON IS LIBERATED TERRITORY!"

Everybody in this society is a policeman. We all police ourselves. When we free ourselves, the real cops take over.

I don't smoke pot in public often, although I love to. I don't want to be arrested: that's the only reason.

I police myself.

We do not own our own bodies.

We fight to regain our bodies—to make love in the parks, say "fuck" on television, do what we want to do whenever we want to do it.

Prohibitions should be prohibited.

Rules are made to be broken.

Never say "no."

The yippies say: "PROPERTY IS THEFT."

What America got, she stole.

How was this country built? By the forced labor of slaves. America owes black people billions in compensation.

"Capitalism" is just a polite schoolbook way of saying: "Stealing."

Who deserves what they get in America? Do the Rockefellers deserve their wealth? HELL NO!

Do the poor deserve their property? HELL NO!!

America says that people work only for money. But check it out: those who don't have money work the hardest, and those who have money take very long lunch hours.

When I was born I had food on my table and a roof over my head. Most babies born in the world face hunger and cold. What is the difference between them and me?

Every well-off white American better ask himself that question or he will never understand why people hate America.

The enemy is this dollar bill right here in my hand.

Now if I get a match, I'll show you what I think of it.

This burning gets some political radicals very uptight. I don't know exactly why. They burn a lot of money putting out leaflets nobody reads.

I think it is more important today to burn a dollar bill than it is to burn a draft card.

(Hmmm, pretty resilient. Hard to burn. Anybody got a lighter?)

We go to the New York Stock Exchange, about 20 of us, our pockets stuffed with dollar bills. We want to throw real dollars down at all those people on the floor playing monopoly games with numbers.

An official stops us at the door and says, "You can't come in. You are hippies and you are coming to demonstrate."

With TV cameras flying away, we reply: "Hippies? Demonstrate? We're Jews. And we're coming to see the stock market."

Well, that gets the guy uptight, and he lets us in. We get to the top, and the dollars start raining down on the floor below.

These guys deal in millions of dollars as a game, never connecting it to people starving. Have they ever seen a real dollar bill?

"This is what it is all about, you sonavabitches!!"

Look at them: wild animals chasing and fighting each other for the dollar bills thrown by the hippies!

And then the cops come. The cops are a necessary part of any demonstration theater. When you are planning a demonstration, always include a role for the cops. Cops legitimize demonstrations.

The cops throw us out.

It is noon. Wall Street. Businessmen with briefcases and suits and ties. Money freaks going to lunch. Important business deals. Time. Appointments.

And there we are in the middle of it, burning five-dollar bills. Burning their world. Burning their Christ.

"Don't! Don't!" some scream grasping for the sacred paper. Several near fist-fights break out.

We escape with our lives.

Weeks later *The New York Times* publishes a short item revealing that the New York Stock Exchange is installing a bulletproof glass window between the visitors' platform and the floor, so that "nobody can shoot a stockbroker."

(In Chicago 5,000 yippies come armed only with our skin. The cops bring tanks, dogs, guns, gas, long-range rifles, missiles. Is it South Vietnam or Chicago? America always overreacts.)

The American economy is doomed to collapse because it has no soul. Its stability is war and preparation for war. Consumer products are built to break, and advertising brainwashes us to consume new ones.

The rich feel guilty. The poor are taught to hate themselves. The guilty and the wretched are on a collision course.

If the men who control the technology used it for human needs and not profit and murder, every human being on the planet could be free from starvation. Machines could do most of the work: people would be free to do what they want.

We should be very realistic and demand the impossible. Food, housing, clothing, medicine, and color TV free for all!!

People would work because of love, creativity, and brotherhood. A new economic structure would produce a new man.

That new structure will be created by new men.

American society, because of its Western-Christian-Capitalist bag, is organized on the fundamental premise that man is bad, society evil, and that: People must be motivated and forced by external reward and punishment.

We are a new generation, species, race. We are bred on affluence, turned on by drugs, at home in our bodies, and excited by the future and its possibilities.

Everything for us is an experience, done for love or not done at all.

We live off the fat of society. Our fathers worked all-year-round for a two-week vacation. Our entire life is a vacation!

Every moment, every day we decide what we are going to do.

We do not groove with Christianity, the idea that people go to heaven after they are dead. We want HEAVEN NOW!

We do not believe in studying to obtain degrees in school. Degrees and grades are like money and credit, good only for burning.

There is a war going on in the Western world: a war of genocide by the old against the young.

The economy is closed. It does not need us. Everything is built.

So the purpose of universities is: to get us off the streets. Schools are baby-sitting agencies.

The purpose of the Vietnam war is: to get rid of blacks. They are a nuisance. America got the work she needed out of blacks, but now she has no use for them.

It is a psychological war. The old say, "We want you to die for us." The old send the young to die for the old.

Our response? Draft-card burning and draft dodging! We won't die for you.

Young whites are dropping out of white society. We are getting our heads straight, creating new identities. We're dropping out of middle-class institutions, leaving their schools, running away from their homes, and forming our own communities.

We are becoming the new niggers.

I'm getting on a plane en route to Washington. An airline official comes up to me and says, "You can't go on this airplane."

"Why not?" I ask.

"Because you smell."

That's what they used to say about black people, remember?

They don't say that about black people anymore. They'd get punched in their fucking mouths.

Our long hair communicates disrespect to America. A racist, shorthair society gets freaked by long hair. It blinds people. In Vietnam, America bombs the Vietnamese, but cannot see them because they are brown.

Long hair is vital to us because it enables us to recognize each other. We have white skin like our oppressors. Long hair ties us together into a visible counter-community.

A car drives down the street, parents in front, and 15-year-old longhair kid in back. The kid gives me the "V" sign! That's the kind of communication taking place.

Within our community we have the seeds of a new society. We have our own communications network, the underground press. We have the beginnings of a new family structure in communes. We have our own stimulants.

When the cops broke into my home on the Lower East Side to arrest me for possession of pot, it was like American soldiers invading a Vietnamese village. They experienced cultural shock.

Fidel Castro was on the wall. They couldn't believe it! Beads! They played with my beads for 20 minutes.

When the cops kidnapped me in Chicago, they interviewed me as if I had just landed from Mars.

"Do you fuck each other?"

"What is it like on LSD?"

"Do you talk directly with the Viet Cong?"

The two generations cannot communicate with one another because of our different historical experiences.

Our parents suffered through the Depression and World War II. We experience the consumer economy and the U.S.A. as a military bully in Vietnam.

From 1964 to 1968 the movement has been involved in the destruction of the old symbols of America. Through our actions we have redefined those symbols for the youth.

Kids growing up today expect school to be a place to demonstrate, sit-in, fight authority, and maybe get arrested.

Demonstrations become the initiation rites, rituals, and social celebrations of a new generation.

Remember the Pentagon, center of the military ego? We urinated on it. Thousands of stoned freaks stormed the place, carrying Che's picture and stuffing flowers in the rifles of the 82nd Airborne.

Remember the Democratic Convention? Who, after Chicago, can read schoolbook descriptions of national political conventions with a straight face anymore? The farce within the convention became clear because of the war between the yippies and the cops in the streets.

We are calling the bluff on the myths of America. Once the myth is exposed, the structure behind it crumbles like sand. Chaos results. People must create new realities.

In the process we create new myths, and these new myths forecast the future.

In America in 1969 old myths can be destroyed overnight, and new ones created overnight because of the power of television. By making communications instantaneous, television telescopes the revolution by centuries. What might have taken 100 years will now take 20. What used to happen in 10 years now happens in two. In a dying society, television becomes a revolutionary instrument.

For her own protection, the government is soon going to have to suppress freedom of the press and take direct control over what goes on television, especially the news.

TV has dramatized the longhair drop-out movement so well that virtually every young kid in the country wants to grow up and be a demonstrator.

What do you want to be when you grow up? A fireman? A cop? A professor?

"I want to grow up and make history."

Young kids watch TV's thrill-packed coverage of demonstrations—including the violence and excitement—and dream about being in them. They look like fun.

Mayor Daley put out this television film about Chicago. It had cops beating up young longhairs. In one scene, the cops threw a tear-gas canister into the crowd, and one demonstrator picked it up and heaved it right back.

Who do you think every kid in the country identified with?

Then the announcer said the chiller: "These demonstrations are Communist led! . . ."

Communism? Who the hell knows from Communism? We never lived through Stalin. We read about it, but it doesn't affect us emotionally. Our emotional reaction to Communism is Fidel marching into Havana in 1959.

There is NO WORD that the Man has to turn off your youth, no scare word.

"They're for ANARCHY!"

Damn right, we're for anarchy! This country is fucking over-organized anyway.

"DON'T DO THIS, DON'T DO THAT, DON'T!"

Growing up in America is learning what NOT to do.

We say: "DO IT, DO IT. DO WHATEVER YOU WANT TO DO."

Our battlegrounds are the campuses of America. White middle-class youth are strategically located in the high schools and colleges of this country. They are our power bases.

If one day 100 campuses were closed in a nationally coordinated rebellion, we could force the President of the United States to sue for peace at the conference table.

As long as we are in school we are prisoners. Schools are voluntary jails. We must liberate ourselves.

Dig the geography of a university. You can always tell what the rulers have up their sleeves when you check out the physical environment they create. The buildings tell you how to behave. Then there is less need for burdensome rules and cops. They designed classrooms so that students sit in rows, one after the other, hierarchically, facing the professor who stands up front talking to all of them.

Classrooms say:

"Listen to the Professor.

"He teaches you.

"Keep your place.

"Don't stretch out.

"Don't lie on the floor.

"Don't relax.

"Don't speak out of turn.

"Don't take off your clothes.

"Don't get emotional.

"Let the mind rule the body.

"Let the needs of the classroom rule the mind."

Classrooms are totalitarian environments. The main purpose of school and education in America is to force you to accept and love authority, and to distrust your own spontaneity and emotions.

How can you grow in such an over-structured environment? You can't. Schools aren't for learning.

Classrooms should be organized in circles, with the professor one part of the circle. A circle is a democratic environment.

Try breaking up the environment. Scream "Fuck" in the middle of your prof's lecture.

So, we organize a University of the Flesh. Four of us go into a class-room. We sit in the middle of the class. The lecture is on "Thinking."

Thinking!

We take off our shirts, smoke joints, and start French kissing. A lot of students get nervous. This goes on for 10–15 minutes, and the professor goes on with his lecture like nothing is happening.

Finally a girl says, "The people there are causing a distraction, and could they either put their shirts back on or could they please leave."

And the prof says, "Well, I agree with that. I think that if you're not here to hear what I'm saying . . ."

We shout: "You can't separate thinking from loving! We are hard in thought! !"

And the prof says, "Well, in my classroom I give the lessons."

Scratch a professor deep and you find a cop!

Fucking milquetoast! Didn't have the guts to throw us out, but in his classroom, HE GIVES the lesson. So he sends his teaching assistant to get the cops, and we split.

We must bring psychological guerrilla war to the University.

The mind is programmed. Get in there and break that bloody program!

Can you imagine what a feeling a professor has standing in front of a class and looking at a room full of bright faces taking down every word he says, raising their hands and asking him questions? It really makes someone think he is God. And to top it off, he has the power to reward and punish you, to decide whether or not you are fit to advance in the academic rat race.

Is this environment the right one for teacher and student?

Socrates is turning in his grave.

I was telling a professor of philosophy at Berkeley that many of his students were wiser men than he, even though he may have read more books and memorized more theories.

He replied, "Well, I must take the lead in the transfer of knowledge."

Transfer of knowledge! What is knowledge?

How to Live.

How to Legalize Marijuana.

How to Make a Revolution.

How to Free People from Jail.

How to Organize Against the CIA.

When a professor takes off his suit and tie, and joins us in the streets, then I say, "Hey man, what's your first name? You're my brother. Let's go. We're together."

I don't dig the "professor" bullshit. I am more interested in a 15-year-old stoned dope freak living on street corners than I am in a Ph.D.

There is anti-intellectualism in America because professors have created an artificial environment. That is why the average working guy does not respect professors.

The university is a protective and plastic scene, shielding people from the reality of life, the reality of suffering, of ecstasy, of struggle. The university converts the agony of life into the security of words and books.

You can't learn anything in school. Spend one hour in a jail or a courtroom and you will learn more than in five years spent in a university.

All I learned in school was how to beat the system, how to fake answers. But there are no answers. There are only more questions. Life is a long journey of questions, answered through the challenge of living. You would never know that, living in a university ruled by the "right" answers to the wrong questions.

Graffiti in school bathrooms tells you more about what's on people's minds than all the books in the library.

We must liberate ourselves. I dropped out. The shit got up to my neck and I stopped eating. I said: NO. NO. NO!! I'm dropping out.

People at Columbia found out what it felt like to learn when they seized buildings and lived in communes for days.

We have to redesign the environment and remake human relationships. But if you try it, you will be kicked out.

You know what professors and deans will say? "If you don't like it here, why don't you go back to Russia!"

A lot is demanded of white, middle-class youth in 1969. The whole thing about technological and bureaucratic society is that it is not made for heroes. We must become heroes.

The young kids living in the streets as new niggers are the pioneers of tomorrow, living dangerously and existentially.

The yippies went to Chicago to have our own counter-festival, a "Festival of Life" in the parks of Chicago, as a human contrast to the "Convention of Death" of the Democrats.

I get a phone call on Christmas Day, 1967 from Marvin Garson, the editor of the *San Francisco Express-Times,* and he says, "Hey, it looks like the Peace and Freedom Party is not going to get on the ballot."

I say, "I don't care. I'm not interested in electoral politics anyway."

And he says, "Let's run a pig for President."

An arrow shoots through my brain. Yeah! A pig, with buttons, posters, bumper stickers.

"America, why take half a hog, when you can have the whole hog?"

At the Democratic convention, the pigs nominate the President and he eats the people.

At the yippie convention, we nominate our pig and after he makes his nominating speech, we eat him. The contrast is clear: Should the President eat the people or the people eat the President?

Well, we didn't kill our pig. If there is one issue that could split the yippies, it is the issue of vegetarianism. A lot of yippies don't believe in killing and eating animals, so I had to be less militant on that point.

We bring Pigasus to Chicago, and he is arrested in Civic Center. The cops grab him. They grab seven of us, and they throw us in the paddy wagon with Pigasus.

The thing about running a pig for President is that it cuts through the shit. People's minds are full of things like, "You may elect a greater evil." We must break through their logic. Once we get caught in their logic we're trapped in it.

Just freak it all out and proclaim: "This country is run on the principles of garbage. The Democratic and Republican parties have nominated a pig. So have we. We're honest about it."

In Chicago, Pigasus was a hell of a lot more effective than all those lackeys running around getting votes for the politicians. It turned out that the pig was more relevant to the current American political scene than Senator Eugene McCarthy. I never thought McCarthy could reform the Democratic party. Hell, McCarthy barely got into the convention himself. He had to have a ticket. That's how controlled the damn thing was. Finally, we forced McCarthy out into the streets with the people.

The election was not fair because every time we brought the pig out to give a campaign speech, they arrested him. It happened in Chicago, in New York, in San Francisco, even in London.

The yippies asked that the presidential elections be canceled until the rules of the game were changed. We said that everyone in the world should vote in the American election because America controls the world.

Free elections are elections in which the people who vote are the people affected by the results. The Vietnamese have more right to vote in the American elections that some 80-year-old grandmother in Omaha. They're being bombed by America! They should have at least some choice about if, how, and by whom they are going to be bombed.

I have nothing in particular against 80-year-old grandmothers, but I am in favor of lowering the voting age to 12 or 14 years. And I am not sure whether people over 50 should vote.

It is the young kids who are going to live in this world in the next 50 years. They should choose what they want for themselves.

Most people over 50 don't think about the potentialities of the future: they are preoccupied with justifying their past.

The only people who can choose change without suffering blows to their egos are the young, and change is the rhythm of the universe.

Many older people are constantly warning: "The right wing will get you." "George Wallace will get your momma."

I am so scared of George Wallace that I wore his fucking campaign button. I went to his campaign rally—all old ladies.

There are six Nazis who came with black gloves and mouthpieces, looking for a fight. And two fights break out. Two guys with long hair beat the shit out of them.

I am not afraid of the right wing because the right wing does not have the youth behind it.

"Straight" people get very freaked by Wallace. "Freaks" know the best way to fuck Wallace up. We support him.

At Wallace's rally in the Cow Palace in San Francisco, we come with signs saying "CUT THEIR HAIR!" "SEND THEM BACK TO AFRICA!" "BOMB THE VIETNAMESE BACK TO THE STONE AGE!"

When we arrive there is a picket line going on in front of the rally. I recognize it is the Communist Party picketing.

What? Picketing Wallace?

I walk up to my friend Bettina Aptheker and say, "Bettina, you're legitimizing him. You're legitimizing him by picketing. Instead, support him, kiss him. When he says the next hippie in front of his car will be the last hippie, cheer! Loudly!"

We have about two hundred people there, and we are the loudest people at the rally. Every five seconds we are jumping up and swearing, "Heil! Hitler! Heil! Hitler!"

Wallace is a sick man. America is the loony bin. The only way to cure her is through theatrical shock. Wallace is necessary because he brings to the surface the racism and hate that is deep within the country.

The yippie Fugs spearheaded the anti-war movement of the past five years by touring theaters and dance halls shouting into a microphone: "KILL, KILL, KILL FOR PEACE! KILL, KILL, KILL FOR PEACE!"

Wallace says aloud what most people say privately. He exposes the beast within liberal America. He embarrasses the liberal who says in one breath, "Oh, I like Negroes," and then in another breath, "We must eliminate crime in the streets."

Remember what Huey Long said: "When fascism comes to America, it will come as Americanism."

Wallace may be the best thing for those of us who are fighting him. You can only fight a disease after you recognize and diagnose it. America does not suffer from a cold: she has cancer.

The liberals who run this country agree with Wallace more than they disagree with him. George tells tales out of school. The liberals are going to have to shut that honest motherfucker up.

Do you dig that most cops support Wallace? Cops—the people who make and enforce the law in the streets! Wallace speaks FOR them.

Isn't that scary? Can't you see why blacks are getting guns and organizing into small self-defense units? Wouldn't you, if you were in *their* situation? Shouldn't *you* be?

Make America see her vampire face in the mirror. Destroy that gap between public talk and private behavior. Only when people see what's happening can they hear our screams, and feel our passion.

The Vietnam war is an education for America. It is an expensive teaching experience, but the American people are the most brainwashed people in the world.

At least the youth are learning that this country is no paradise—America kills infants and children in Vietnam without blinking. Only professional killers can be so cool.

If you become hip to America in Vietnam, you can understand the reaction against the red-white-and-blue in Latin America, and you can feel why China hates us.

They are not irrational—America is.

Wallace is a left-wing agitator. Dig him. He speaks to the same anxiety and powerlessness that the New Left and yippies talk about.

Do you feel overwhelmed by bigness, including Big Government?

Do you lack control over your own life?

Are you distrustful of the politicians and bureaucrats in Washington?

Are you part of the "little people"?

Wallace stirs the masses. Revolutions should do that too.

When is the left going to produce an inflammatory and authentic voice of the people? A guy who reaches people's emotions? Who talks about revolution the way some of those nuts rap about Christ?

Wallace says: "We're against niggers, intellectuals, liberals, hippies."

Everybody! He puts us all together. He organizes us for us.

We must analyze how America keeps people down. Not by physical force, but by fear. From the second kids are hatched, we are taught fear. If we can overcome fear, we will discover that we are Davids fighting Goliath.

In late September a friend calls and says, "Hey, I just got a subpoena from HUAC."

I say, "Yeah? I didn't. What's going on here? I'm angry. I want a subpoena too."

It's called subpoenas envy.

So I telephone a confidante to the Red Squad, a fascist creep who works for the *San Francisco Examiner,* and I say, "Hey, Ed, baby, what about HUAC? Are they having hearings?"

He answers, "Well, I don't know. Are they?"

"Well, my friend just got a subpoena," I say. "I'd like one, too. If you can manage it."

He says, "Call me back in a few hours."

I call him back that afternoon and he says, "Well, I just talked to HUAC in Washington, and you are right. They are having hearings, and they are looking for you in New York."

"In NEW YORK? I've been in Berkeley a week! You guys are sure doing a shitty job trying to save this country!"

We exaggerate the surveillance powers of cops. We shouldn't. They are lazy. Their laziness may be the one reason why America doesn't yet have a totally efficient police state.

The cops were not lazy in Chicago. They followed "the leaders" continuously, 24 hours a day. If you are trailed by four cops just six steps behind you, you can't do very much.

But the people really doing things—why, the cops didn't even know who they were!

Pigs cannot relate to anarchy. They do not understand a movement based on personal freedom. When they look at our movement, they look for a hierarchy: leaders, lieutenants, followers.

The pigs think that we are organized like their pig department. We are not, and that's why we are going to win. A hierarchical, top-down organization is no match for the free and loose energy of the people.

As the pigs check with their higher-ups to find out what to do next, we have already switched the tactics and scene of the battle. They are watching one guy over there, and it is happening over here!

I come to the HUAC hearings wearing a bandolero of real bullets and carrying a toy M-16 rifle on my shoulder. The rifle was a model of the rifles the Viet Cong steal and then use to kill American soldiers in Vietnam.

The pigs stop me at the door of the hearings. They grab the bullets and the gun. It is a dramatic moment. Press and yippies pack us in tightly. The pigs drag me down three flights of stairs and remove the bullets, leaving the gun, Viet Cong pajamas, Eldridge Cleaver buttons, Black Panther beret, war paint, earrings, bandolero, and the bells which ring every time I move my body. My costume carried a nonverbal message: "We must all become stoned guerrillas."

The secret to the costume was the painted tits. Guerrilla war in America is going to come in psychedelic colors. We are hippie-guerrillas.

In HUAC's chambers Abbie Hoffman jumps up and yells out, "May I go to the bathroom?" Young kids reading that in their hometown papers giggle because they have to ask permission every time they want to go to the bathroom in school.

The message of my costume flipped across the country in one day: an example of our use of the enemy's institutions—her mass media—to turn on and communicate with one another.

I wore a Santa Claus costume to HUAC two months later in a direct attempt to reach the head of every child in the country.

Our victories are catching up with us: America isn't ready to napalm us yet, but the future doesn't look easy.

From June to November 1968, when I was helping to organize the demonstrations against the Democratic convention in Chicago, I experienced the following example of Americana: New York pigs use a phony search warrant to bust into my apartment, question me, beat me, search the apartment, and arrest me for alleged felonious possession of marijuana; a pig in Chicago disguises himself as a biker to "infiltrate" the yippies as an agent provocateur and spy; he busts me on a frame-up, "solicitation to mob action," a felony punishable by five years in the pen; the judge imposes $25,000 bail and restricts my travel to Illinois; then the Justice Department in a document to a Virginia court admits that it maintains "electronic surveillance . . . of Jerry Rubin . . . in the interests of national security."

To try to suppress youth, Nixon will have to destroy the Constitution.

We will be presumed guilty until proven innocent.

Our privacy will vanish. Big Brother will spy on all of us and dominate our lives.

Every cop will become a law unto himself.

The courts will become automatic transmission belts sending us to detention camps and prisons.

People will be arrested for what they write and say.

Congress will impose censorship on the mass media, unless the media first censors itself, which is more likely.

To be young will be a crime.

In response, we must never become cynical, or lose our capacity for anger. We must stay on the offensive and be aggressive: AMERICA: IF YOU INJURE ONE, YOU MUST FIGHT ALL.

If our opposition is united, the repression may backfire and fail. The government may find the costs too heavy.

Don't think, "They can never get ME."

They can.

You are either on the side of the cops or on the side of human beings. YIPPIE!

Addicts and Zealots: The Chaotic War Against Drug Abuse

MARION K. SANDERS

Nineteen-seventy may well be remembered as the year of the great drug panic, the year when addiction was a permanent theme in the press and on TV and when government officials and office seekers made instant headlines by pledging a "massive attack" on the problem. People old enough to recall previous waves of hysteria about drugs and similar promises of action view these pronouncements with cynicism verging on despair. They concede, however, that something new has been added. The image of the addict has changed. Suddenly, he is seen not merely as a criminal derelict. He may, it turns out, be a young child who not only knows how to tie a tourniquet around his arm and stick a needle in his vein but also sells drugs to his schoolmates.

Last December young Walter Vandermeer died of a heroin overdose two weeks after his twelfth birthday. Since then New York newspapers have published a daily body count of OD fatalities, a phrase which no longer needs explanation. Although the vast majority of the victims— young and old—are slum dwellers, affluent America is also represented on these grisly lists.

With mounting evidence that this plague can no longer be quarantined in the ghettos, there is less talk about "getting the addict off the streets" and more about what can be done to salvage him. One result is that the treatment of addicts has become a growth industry with proponents of various theories fiercely vying for public funds to support their enterprises. This competition, it should be said, is not motivated by greed. Treating addicts is heart-and-back-breaking and generally unprofitable work. It is a task for zealots.

Over the past several months I have taken a firsthand look at what some of them are doing in New York, heroin capital of the U.S.A. where half of the nation's addicts are believed to live. Appropriately, this city has been the chief proving ground and battle ground for rival theories about the cause and cure of addiction.

Paralleling the vogue for "sensitivity training" and other forms of group psychotherapy is the current enthusiasm for programs which apply similar strategy to addiction. Known as "therapeutic communities," these are modeled after Synanon, which was launched in Santa Monica, California, twelve years ago. Its founder, Chuck Dederich, an ex-alcoholic, propounded the theory that the addict can change his faulty behavior patterns only by voluntarily joining a sternly disciplined but loving pseudo-family. There he must be guided by ex-addicts who have unique insight into his weaknesses and evasions and provide living proof that his habit can be overcome. This is accomplished through a "self-help" regime which includes plenty of physical work plus the now-familiar techniques of group dynamics which have given such words as "encounter" and "confrontation" a special meaning.

Among those attracted to Dederich's ideas were two psychiatrists, Dr. Daniel Casriel of New York and Dr. Efren Ramirez of Puerto Rico. With the blessing of city officials, Dr. Casriel obtained a grant from the National Institute of Mental Health to set up on Staten Island a privately operated Synanon-type institution to be known as Daytop Village.

Almost immediately, the project ran into a predictable difficulty—a dearth of the skilled and reliable ex-addicts needed to run it. After many months, the right man was found, David Deitch, a talented Synanon graduate. Under his leadership Daytop flourished. A play performed by Daytop residents became an off-Broadway hit in 1968 and offered persuasive evidence to hundreds of theatergoers that "The Concept" (its title) actually worked.

In 1966, Mayor John Lindsay invited Dr. Ramirez to come to New York to coordinate and expand the city's battle against narcotics. Preceded by glowing reports of his success in treating addicts in his native Puerto Rico with a mix of the Synanon formula and his own brand of existential psychiatry, Dr. Ramirez found the going rough in New York. The black community which most needed help turned its back on any program headed by a Puerto Rican. The medical establishment was affronted by the claim that nonprofessional therapists could succeed where it had failed. In fact, few ex-addicts went into action, for scarcely any could meet the educational requirements of civil service. The acquisition of buildings and equipment was mired in municipal red tape. Dr. Ramirez departed after a stormy year, turning the job over to his deputy, Larry Alan Bear, who now heads the city's Addiction Services Agency.

A resourceful administrator with keen political antennae, Bear, a lawyer by profession, has forged rapidly ahead on the path Ramirez charted. The city now operates a chain of therapeutic communities known as Phoenix Houses, as well as a growing network of storefront outposts aimed at reaching young people, and has embarked on a program of prevention through schools and community organizations. With the help of a private foundation, emergency purchases can be made quickly. A new civil-service category, "addiction specialist," has been established with minimum formal educational requirements. Part of the cost of operating the Phoenix Houses is met by having residents who are on welfare contribute their welfare checks.

Bear has had to expend much of his considerable energy defending his efforts against the sniping of private-program operators who miss no opportunity to aggrandize their own projects by denigrating all others.

The most strident has been the psychiatrist Dr. Judianne Densen-Gerber who opened up her own treatment center, Odyssey House, in 1967.

Like the majority of philanthropies nominally under private auspices, most "private" addiction treatment programs in New York are heavily dependent on government support. Odyssey's "Mother House," with seventy residents currently in treatment, has received $770,000 from the state since its inception. Last summer Dr. Judy, as she is known to her charges, moved some 35 adolescent heroin users into an abandoned convent previously occupied by nine nuns, and applied to the state for an additional $250,000 to operate a separate facility for adolescents there. She was turned down on the grounds that no further funds were available for private agencies in the current fiscal year and that Odyssey House was not licensed to care for children. Subsequently she was hauled into court for violating city building regulations. In a press interview she blamed her troubles on the "malevolence" of politicians.

A non-stop talker with an ample bosom and an ego to match, Dr. Judy appeared last winter at a televised legislative hearing with a puny twelve-year-old boy, Ralph de Jesus, seated on her lap. The audience was moved to tears as he told his story which included mainlining (injecting into the vein), mugging, and pushing to support his habit. The next day I visited the shelter where Ralph was spending his fourth day of abstinence and found him sitting forlornly on his bunk. "It was kinda scary," he said of his television debut. Shortly afterwards he left the shelter. A *New York Times* reporter tracked him down in his South Bronx home and asked him whether everything he had said at the hearing was true. "Some of it," Ralph replied.

While Dr. Judy has performed a service in sounding the alarm about a tragically neglected problem, her methods are open to criticism. By pre-empting the limelight she has diverted public attention from much more extensive efforts, particularly the city's sixteen Phoenix Houses where nearly 1,000 addicts, ranging from young adolescents to middle-aged men and women, are currently in treatment.

Each house is run by a small paid staff of ex-addicts with the help of residents nearing the end of their treatment. Residents do all the work of the place, starting out as each new house is opened by making a dilapidated building habitable through a strenuous roach-and-rat extermination campaign, plastering, partitioning, painting, rewiring, and replumbing. Cooking, cleaning, and all maintenance work are also done by residents, who start out on the lowliest tasks such as KP and scrubbing toilets. They are promoted to clerical and administrative jobs as they demonstrate progress by carrying out assignments responsibly, and by personality changes which are tested at encounter sessions, held three times a week.

There are three cardinal rules: no chemicals; no violence; no threats of violence. Infractions are dealt with by demotion to a lowlier work squad or by what are known as "learning experiences." The minor offender may incur a "haircut"—that is, a public reprimand or temporary ostracism by the group. At Phoenix House and similar centers, you also see young men and women going about their tasks with large cardboard signs dangling from their necks hand-lettered with such phrases as, "I am a baby," "I must stop testing the program," "I am a liar." There are boys with shaved heads and girls with their hair stuffed into stocking caps. ("We don't shave the girls' hair, it means too much to them emotionally," I was told. "They tried it on one girl at Daytop and she went into the bathroom and cut her wrists.")

Phoenix Houses, like most therapeutic communities, are coeducational except for the sleeping quarters on the upper floors. There is an easy camaraderie among residents, and one hears over and over again identical phrases about the merits of the program and about "responsible concern" for one's fellows which includes reporting their misdeeds or "wrong attitudes" at encounters. Visitors are welcome at "wake-up sessions" held at eight in the morning, where coffee is served to an accompaniment of songs and impromptu speeches or readings from the day's newspapers. All residents must attend, since learning to get out of bed at a fixed hour is a basic step in moving out of the benumbed, erratic life of addiction.

Outsiders are not generally encouraged to attend encounters both because an alien presence might inhibit their spontaneity and because the tone and content of the dialogue are likely to be jolting to anyone who has not undergone "sensitivity training" or its equivalent.

Such is, in truth, my own experience when I find myself seated on a hard wooden chair in a circle along with a dozen young people—black, white, and Puerto Rican. All wear long-sleeved blouses or sweaters, the uniform of the mainliner whose needle-striped and abscess-scarred arms are the permanent badge of his affliction. Leader of the group is Charlotte, a pretty blond college dropout who is ready for "reentry" after eighteen months of treatment. There are several other fairly advanced residents. The rest are candidates for admission to Phoenix House. This is an "induction encounter" designed to test their readiness.

The air is thick with cigarette smoke as a verbal barrage is directed at a handsome sloe-eyed Negro youth who persists in mumbling almost inaudibly despite exhortations to "speak up" and "contribute some input." Charlotte finally goads him into reciting a halting memoir with much prodding from the rest of the group.

"My name is Raymond. . . . I'm twenty-two. My father died when I was six."

"What do you remember about him? Did you like him?"

"He was big and husky. . . . He worked in a chemical plant. Once when my mother wouldn't buy me a cap pistol he got it for me. . . . My mother remarried."

"How did you feel about your stepfather?"

"He was mean to me. He yelled at me when I didn't straighten up my room . . . stuff like that . . . I don't like nobody to yell at me."

"What did you do? Just sit there and listen like you do here?"

"Well, I stumble when I talk so I don't talk good. One of my brothers got killed. He got hit in the temple with a stick. . . . My oldest brother has been in and out of jail most of the time. My mother didn't want that to happen to me. . . . She died in the hospital when I was fifteen or sixteen. I was smoking reefers then, staying out nights. . . . The dean caught me and threw me out of school. I was running in the street for a year . . . started shooting dope. I went to live with one of my sisters. . . . I stole from her. I took a portable TV, a record player, and her watch. I always meant to get her another watch but I never did. . . . When my niece got married there were a lot of wedding presents in the house. I stole them. My sister threw me out. I moved in with my other sister. She axed me in. I took her camera. And her watch. An eighty-dollar watch. Not the TV . . . it was too big to carry. I got picked up by the housing detectives. My sister come to court with me. . . . I got probation. Then I'm picked up on possession."

"You keep blowing a good thing."

"That's right."

"Well, you got an advantage here. Who you got to look bad before? We're all just a bunch of dope fiends. Inside we're all babies. We say to ourselves, it hurts. Who has to hurt? I can get high. How do you see yourself today?"

"I see myself as a liar, a thief, and a dope fiend."

For Raymond, this degree of candor is rated as progress. With what seems savage intensity the group now turns on Dolores, a plump, swarthy girl who has been in and out of several treatment centers—a common pattern. Her last sojourn was at Boerum Place, a recently opened city facility for children, where she was sent because she is only fifteen. She walked out after less than a week. Dolores is given to turning her head away and giggling at some private joke.

"Why you split from Boerum Place?"

"All those little kids. I didn't like it. I want to be back in Phoenix with my friends."

"You're inconsistent. You're selfish."

"What you want me to do?"

"Talk about your hang-ups."

"I don't have no hang-ups."

"You're a lying bitch. One guy split from this program because of you. There's a lifetime ban on somebody like you—a split-ee. You're like a cancer. You sound fucking poisonous."

"I thinks she's dealing."

"Maybe she's a spy from another program."

"She's a spoiled brat with a cute little female body."

"You liked it on Hart's Island [another treatment center] where there were two hundred boys and thirty girls?"

Dolores responds with a nostalgic giggle.

"You know what a whore is?"

"I know. But I'm not a whore. Sure, I turned tricks when my boyfriend didn't have money for dope. He got me tricks. But I'm not a whore."

"Then why you go around balling everybody? You couldn't fuck at Boerum so you went out to shoot dope and get down with Tom. . . ."

Though their prospects of success seem dim, Raymond and Dolores will probably be admitted whenever space is available. In fact many applicants are no more promising. Few addicts spontaneously seek salvation in a place where they know they will be under close surveillance by their fellows even though the front door is unlocked. Most come because of pressure from parents, on order from the court, or because their welfare checks will be cut off unless they go into treatment. Others simply find the rigors of street life temporarily unbearable.

Since they have taken on an assignment that is inherently so risky, the therapeutic-community advocates object strenuously to being judged by the "numbers game." They prefer not to mention that more than half of those who enter drop out quite early. When they cite a "success rate" of 90 per cent or better—as do Odyssey, Phoenix, and Daytop for example— the base they are using is the handful of residents who have run the full course and who can be checked a year or more after they leave.

A high proportion of their graduates remain in addiction work as staff members. The most extreme example of this trend is Synanon, which, on the theory that no ex-addict can cope with the realities of the square world, encourages its members to remain permanently hooked on Synanon, spending the rest of their days in one of several outside business enterprises operated by alumni on Synanon property and enjoying lifetime membership in a utopian society.

Some do leave, to be sure. Along with the graduates of other programs, many ex-addicts have proved themselves highly effective therapists and forceful lecturers who have a unique credibility for young audiences. They also tend to attribute almost divine powers to group dynamics, which is, in fact, by no means the sole or even the most promising therapy for drug addiction.

There is, indeed, considerable evidence that the most effective treatment that could be used on a large scale is not psychiatric but medical— a technique known as methadone maintenance. It grew out of experimental work begun in the late 1950s by Dr. Vincent Dole of Rockefeller Institute, a distinguished metabolic researcher. Seeking an entirely new approach to the drug-abuse problem, he teamed up with Dr. Marie Nyswander (now Mrs. Dole), who had spent twenty frustrating years treating addicts with the methods of classic psychiatry. After trying a variety of possible antidotes to heroin they chose methadone, a synthetic opiate developed in Germany during World War II when morphine was scarce. Small doses of methadone block the craving for heroin. The Dole-Nyswander experiments showed that if the dosage is gradually stepped up, the euphoric effects of heroin are also blocked. Though it is a narcotic, methadone, taken by mouth, causes virtually no undesirable reactions.

When he reaches the "maintenance level," the patient comes to the hospital daily to drink his dose of methadone dissolved in Tang under the watchful eye of a registered nurse. (At a later stage he comes once a week to pick up his supply.) He leaves with her a urine specimen to be checked for drug usage by means of a test developed by Dr. Dole which has become the standard method of policing all therapy programs.

A number of New York hospitals now offer methadone-maintenance therapy under the general direction of the Morris Bernstein Institute of Beth Israel Hospital, the program's main base. To be admitted, patients must be eighteen or older, with at least a two-year history of addiction and a record of arrests and failure in other types of treatment.

Statistically monitored by the Columbia University School of Public Health and Administrative Medicine since its inception, methadone maintenance has rolled up an impressive score, with a better than 80 per cent success rate. As of September 1969, 2,205 individuals had been admitted to the program. Of these, 18 per cent dropped out. The rest remained in treatment and after three years only 2 per cent had been rearrested; 96 per cent were in school or gainfully employed (as compared to only 29 per cent on admission) and none had become readdicted.

Figures like these do not impress doctrinaire believers in the therapeutic communities, who consider methadone a "cop-out," simply substituting one addiction for another. Dole, Nyswander, and their followers do not deny that their patients are dependent on methadone. Addiction, they say, is a disease for which the addict needs medication, just as a diabetic requires insulin and the cardiac patient digitalis. So long as he takes it only by mouth and in the proper dosage, the patient can lead a normal life. On the basis of experiments with animals Dr. Dole has propounded the theory that narcotics addiction causes metabolic changes in the body which necessitate lifetime treatment. This view (disputed by other researchers) stirs heated emotions in the anti-methadone forces who point to the considerable number of ex-addicts who have managed to remain "clean" for a good many years by other means. They also hint darkly at a vast illicit traffic in methadone, known on the street as "dollies" (Dolophine is the trade name of methadone in tablet form). Addicts are known to use dollies to cut back a habit that has grown too expensive. Though there is at present no evidence of an extensive illegal trade in methadone, it obviously should not be dispensed like aspirin and it is hazardous—as is almost any drug—if injected. Furthermore, the end of his drug craving is only the beginning of rehabilitation for the addict who needs—and is given, under well-organized programs—continuous help in finding a job and otherwise adjusting to the square world. Methadone is being misused in some bogus programs hastily set up to convince taxpayers that the drug problem is being dealt with.

The guerrilla war between New York's addiction experts took a novel turn last March. One morning at four o'clock, the *New York Post* city desk received a call from a man identifying himself as Dr. Thomas Butler of Roosevelt Hospital. He reported two deaths due to methadone: one man, he said, had hanged himself in jail after receiving a methadone injection in a hospital; the other had been found dead in his home after renewing his methadone supply. The caller was at pains to say that "methadone acts as a depressant whose use has not been carefully researched. It can often do more harm than good." He was so quoted in the story that was published after a check with the police confirmed the fact that the deaths had indeed occurred.

The next day, the *Post's* able medical reporter, Barbara Yuncker, decided that the matter needed further investigation. Her sleuthing revealed that Roosevelt Hospital had never heard of Dr. Thomas Butler and that no such name is listed in the state medical directory. Furthermore, the medical examiner's office, which did not perform autopsies until many hours after the story was phoned to the *Post,* flatly said that neither death could be attributed to methadone. The small dose given intravenously to one man in the hope of easing his withdrawal agonies would have been more likely to cause a high than a depression. The other man—who was being phased out of a maintenance program at Harlem Hospital because of alcoholism—succumbed to massive bleeding from a ruptured spleen apparently suffered when he fell in an alcoholic convulsion. The perpetrator of this hoax has not been found.

Upon assuming command of New York's addiction services, Dr. Ramirez promptly withdrew all city funds from the methadone program, which he found ideologically obnoxious. The project has since been supported entirely by the State Narcotics Addiction Control Commission. Known by those it touches as NACC or the Rockefeller Program, this agency also underwrites a number of city projects and private agencies and provides films, pamphlets, and speakers to schools and other worried organizations including some prestigious business firms. In addition NACC has spent in the neighborhood of $150 million to construct and equip thirteen large institutions where currently some 4,800 addicts are kept securely under lock and key and, in theory, are rehabilitated at the same time. The plan was largely modeled after the Rehabilitation Center set up with high hopes in Corona, California, in 1961. Follow-up studies conducted there indicate that three years after leaving the institution only 16 per cent of its former population are "reasonably free" of drugs.

On the basis of early returns, New York State is unlikely to do better. In effect these institutions scoop up the bottom of the barrel, the addicts suffering from many aberrations who have repeatedly failed in voluntary programs. They arrive angry, embittered, generally devoid of any motivation to change.

"Some come back here two and three times," I was told by Stephen Chinlund, a young Episcopalian minister who a year ago took over the direction of one of the state-run facilities for women, the Manhattan Rehabilitation Center. Previously he directed two voluntary addiction programs—Exodus and Reality House. "They don't stay in any treatment voluntarily," he said ruefully, "so we have to try to do our best for them this way."

Mr. Chinlund must be credited with trying hard. He has shaken up the staff and has taught the security officers, who are known as counselors, to lead group-therapy sessions. He put the residents to work redecorating the building, a former motel; the well-furnished double bedrooms and dining halls are physically more attractive than the girls' dormitories in some Ivy League women's colleges. There are classrooms, both academic and vocational, where residents spend three or four hours a day. But now that there are no more walls to paint, they have long wearisome hours with nothing to do but sleep, eat, and look at TV, locked on a single corridor. Because all routine maintenance work is done by paid staff, there is no work program and no way of rewarding good behavior through promotion to more responsible tasks, as is done in the therapeutic communities. Nor is there any comparable peer pressure to enforce rules. Minor infractions are punished by depriving the culprit of a cherished privilege such as the pre-bedtime snack. Intractable individuals are sent to "detention," a euphemism for solitary confinement. The intellectual and educational level of most residents is low, as is the emotional boiling point. Many are lesbians, a frequent concomitant of drug addiction in women.

Despite the odds against them, some souls are saved. I talked, for instance, with one wispy black woman who had returned of her own volition for a second stay. "I just wasn't ready the last time," she said, showing me a photo of her twenty-year-old son with whom she hopes to live. "Now I think I can make it. I've learned to type and I've got a good job waiting for me."

Immediately afterward I am buttonholed by a hard-eyed platinum blonde. She bats her half-inch fake eyelashes as she recites her grievances against counselors who play favorites, against the boredom of her life here and the meanness of the judge who sentenced her just because her boyfriend was found stabbed to death three days after she had left him. "I could get parole now," she says, "but I don't want no aftercare. I'll do my time here and then I want to just disappear and lead my own life."

As with other commodities, the traffic in narcotics is a matter of supply and demand. In Harlem, there is a buyers' market in heroin. Prices are at an all-time low and the quality is said to be better (*i.e.,* less adulterated) than ever before—a fact which may account for the mounting death rate from overdoses. The rise in youthful addiction may well be the result of a sales campaign deliberately aimed at the teen-age and juvenile market; innovative packaging—the $1 and $2 bag—has been designed for this trade. (The $5 bag is the adult size.) Because of overstocked inventories, heroin—long sold strictly for cash—may be bought on credit. When an addict says, "The man's about to ice me," he means that he is so heavily in debt to his dealer that he fears for his life. And in all probability if he does not pay up he will be stabbed or pushed off a roof.

In a six square-block section of central Harlem, a militant tenants' organization, after conducting a door-to-door census last year, has concluded that 80 per cent of the population is addicted and that on every block there are at least twelve "shooting galleries" where addicts congregate for their daily fix.

The leader of the tenants' group is Mrs. Beraneece Sims, a soft-spoken gray-haired black woman whose gentle manner cloaks a seething rage and an iron will. A few months ago she set up her own addiction program, calling it "The Community Thing." Sitting in her shabby office—a store on Lenox Avenue acquired simply by "occupying" it—one gets a perspective on the narcotics problem quite different from the view downtown.

Mrs. Sims sees the "hard-core addict" not as a single stereotype but as two distinct breeds. The older ones, whom she calls the "Bible Belt type" have usually had some stabilizing family ties which gave them the rudiments of a value system. Although they are professional thieves, forgers, shoplifters, passers of bad checks, they seldom resort to violence and they do not operate in their own community. "They would rather be sick in the street than do that," she says. Because they hustle downtown, they are not perceived in Harlem as dangerously antisocial characters. Their loot, which finds eager customers at bargain prices, is regarded as a kind of tithe on white society and there is even a certain admiration for the skill with which they practice their specialties. Some, for instance, have perfected the art of walking out of department stores in broad daylight carrying off two portable TV sets. Others are "cattle rustlers" who steal meat to order for housewives, charging them half the market price. (The real experts swap labels in the store so that the purchaser winds up paying half the price of a porterhouse for the chuck steak she gets.)

These older addicts, along with all other ghetto residents, view with horror the new, younger breed—the mugger or the purse snatcher who has not even the skills of the professional thief but is simply a ruthless predator preying on his own people. "These adolescents came along when our community fabric had fallen apart," Mrs. Sims says. "What can you expect when you don't have to walk half a block for a fix, when dealing in drugs is the easiest money in Harlem?"

The Community Thing has acquired squatter's rights to a row of venerable buildings which were scheduled for demolition, and is using them for its own therapy program. On one door is a sign, "Come into my house, child." Here are lodged some twenty addicted youngsters ranging in age from seven to fourteen.

"We don't believe in encounters, confrontation—all that," she says. "Not for our children anyway. They have been damaged too much. They need to find out who they are, to develop some pride and purpose, they need *habilitation* not rehabilitation. We take them off drugs, cold turkey. Then we try to find out what their *thing* is and get them busy at it."

For some, the thing is "growing something." This spring a steep slope in a nearby park glowed with tulips and daffodils planted on land terraced and cultivated by some of the children who are being taught by a volunteer landscape gardener.

Any addict who makes a "soul decision" to change may join The Community Thing, even though the decision may be merely to cut back his habit. All are encouraged to go to work or to school and to get involved in community-action programs. Some become scouts for the drug program, roaming the streets, housing projects, tenements, and playgrounds in search of "copping" youngsters.

"We also use addicts who are not going to change themselves but who want to help us anyhow," Mrs. Sims explains calmly. "We need them most for our Special Child Detail Squad. They are the ones who help us find the pawned children."

"Pawned children?"

"When an addicted mother owes her dealer more than she can ever pay, she might become a pusher. Or she might go to work in a factory where they package heroin. If she is really desperate she may pawn her child to the dealer. She hopes she'll be able to redeem it someday, but she never does. If it's an infant the dealer may sell it to a childless couple. The eight-, nine-, and ten-year-olds become pushers and sometimes the boys work as homosexual prostitutes, the little girls as prostitutes for 'specialty sex acts.' Only an addict can find these children for us. An ex-addict is respected but he's not trusted like the one who's still using."

Except for a mini-grant of a few thousand dollars from the state, The Community Thing has been supported entirely by contributions, mostly from Harlem people. "Our addicted brothers and sisters understand, as we all do, that we've got to save our children or we're finished as a race, *finished,*" Mrs. Sims says. "Some of the older addicts give us 15 per cent of their take every week. That's mighty generous you know—they have that much less left for a fix. The numbers people help us too."

The ideal way to solve the drug problem would be to cut off the supply. But as Americans sadly learned during Prohibition, a multimillion-dollar business operated by organized criminals, who corrupt public officials ranging from the cop on the beat to the highest levels of government, presents a formidable law-enforcement problem. It is not solved by the sporadic seizure of smuggled drug shipments or periodic arrests of dealers and pushers.

"A big collar makes a big noise," said a Harlem clergyman. "But these fellows are just straw bosses. We want to know who's the big plantation boss sitting back with his mint julep, raking in the millions."

On rare occasions one of these overlords is seized and a temporary panic in the street follows. "I remember a time like that back in 1965," an ex-addict told me. "The story was that the cops had collared a big gumbah of Frank Costello's and made a deal with him. They agreed to let him go home safe to Italy if he would get the heroin out of Harlem. Forty-eight hours later, 116th Street was full of addicts puking in the gutter, lighting bonfires, throwing their money around. You literally couldn't get a fix. Of course, this only lasted a week or so."

The federal Narcotics Bureau has recently been transferred from the Treasury to the Justice Department, which, with the help of local crime commissions, has sent an unusual number of Mafia bosses to jail in New York and New Jersey. However, the drug traffic is no longer a Mafia monopoly; free-lancers from Latin America have moved in and dominate the cocaine-smuggling industry whose trail begins in the coca bushes of Peru and Bolivia and moves into the United States via Miami.

Most heroin originates in the poppy fields of Turkey, where part of the crop, grown chiefly for conversion into medicinal morphine, is sold at much higher prices to the bootleg market. It is refined into heroin in Marseilles. There the American importer may pay $5,000 to $15,000 for a kilo, which, when cut, will bring in $250,000 at retail after passing through a chain of jobbers and dealers each of whom skims off a profit. The earthquakes which recently struck the Turkish poppy fields may somewhat shrink the supply. Pressure could also be exerted on France, Turkey, and other exporters to cut off the traffic at the overseas source.

Meanwhile vigilante groups in some drug-infested communities are waging their own wars against dealers and pushers. Others clamor for higher mandatory jail sentences for drug offenders, despite abundant evidence that this has never been an effective weapon against crime. A few politicians urge us to adopt the British system, under which all criminal sanctions are abolished and doctors prescribe freely to all addicts the drugs they need. This proposal was widely touted in the 1950s by liberal critics of the punitive philosophy of Harry J. Anslinger, longtime chief of the Bureau of Narcotics.

Even at that time it was apparent that what might work in Britain, with a minute addicted population, was irrelevant to the monstrous American problem. Most of Britain's addicts then were well-to-do people who were introduced to morphine during a painful illness. Within the past few years the drug problem in England has escalated as a new breed of addicts have proved adroit at hoodwinking several doctors into supplying them and then selling the surplus. Many British experts concede that their system is in disarray. For the tragic fact is that, though a few addicts may be able to function despite their habit (one per cent of American doctors are said to be addicted), heroin turns most people into befuddled, stuporous, totally disorganized and unproductive members of society.

Even if the heroin supply could be totally dried up, addicts would find something else to shoot into their veins. This is the view of most experts in the field, particularly those who have made it their mission to work with adolescents—many from prosperous homes—who sniff glue, gulp pills, and inject subcutaneously (skin-pop) or into their veins (mainline) barbiturates, amphetamines, and almost anything else they can lay their hands on.

"They would shoot Carbona or peanut butter once they're really strung out on drugs," says Brendan John Sexton who founded and directs Encounter, a day-care therapy center for young addicts in New York. After conquering a drug problem of his own five years ago, Sexton, now in his mid-twenties, started his project by recruiting in the psychedelic coffee shops and on the streets of Greenwich Village. Encounter's fame has since spread to campuses and high schools across the country, and the project, housed in an old loft building, is filled to capacity from early morning to late evening. It serves as a kind of clubhouse for its clientele, who are prodded into returning to school or finding jobs while they continue treatment.

Sexton has found the Phoenix-Daytop techniques extremely effective in dealing with young people from the age of thirteen or so on up. "Encounters aren't a cure for addiction," he said. "The problems these kids have aren't drugs. They are really messed up, and so are most of their parents. Encounters are a way of learning to cope with your real problems."

To illustrate the point he handed me a copy of Encounter's house organ, published strictly for intramural distribution. It contains a good deal of rather childish poetry as well as autobiographical sketches of several young, middle-class drug abusers. After promising to omit identifying details, I was given permission to quote from them. Here are two sample excerpts:

I grew up in suburbia. My family was middle-class but it felt like poverty row. They bought all the things they couldn't afford like cars and TVs and houses by skimping on things like food, clothing, and education. Like any dumb kid growing up in the Fifties I left the woods surrounding my house alone. I grew up in front of a 9-inch TV set. "My Little Margie" was my role model. . . . My parents got divorced when I was a junior in high school and I spent a lonely senior year with my mother complaining about how bad my father was for leaving her for a younger woman. When I visited my father occasionally, I learned how badly she had treated *him*. . . . I stayed in college for two years but I got tired of working my way through and never having any money to spend. I went to New York and worked for a while as a bank teller and a sales clerk. I spent a lonely year trying to fit in with the single-swinger bar set. I got so desperate to find a boyfriend that I gave up my apartment so I would have to find someone to live with. I did. He was an ex–medical student anxious to introduce me to the world of drugs. Within six months I was shooting amphetamine with him every day and taking any other drug I could get my hands on. It went downhill rapidly with violent arguments, hassles for drugs, pipe dreams about getting off them, and finally suicide attempts. . . . Bellevue . . . other hospitals . . . jail. When I got out on parole I heard about Encounter. Slowly, I'm learning how to live. . . .

From the beginning of my school career I was a rebel loner. I read a lot—fifteen to twenty books a month. I decided I was smarter than everyone else but I was miserable. . . . When I got to college I kept trying to learn more about people and emotions. This plus loneliness led to dope. I had read about it and wanted to try it, so I got a job in a hospital and stole drugs. . . . One summer I had a job in New York.

That was when I got turned on to amphetamine. I shot on and off for ten months . . . sometimes every two hours. . . . When I went back to college I knew I had to stop because it fucked me up so much but every once in a while the urge got too strong. . . . I started taking smack [*heroin*] and barbiturates. I had a bad accident while fucked up on barbs so that was out. . . . I realized smack was the next thing I'd get into and I was scared. I knew I'd find out that it was maybe more destructive than the others. That was when some people from Encounter came to our campus. . . .

Because he is young, un-square, and speaks with the authority of first-hand experience of the hip scene, the pressure of peer groups, the excitement of a "high," and the miseries that follow, Sexton is unusually effective as a therapist and as an ambassador of good sense to school and college audiences. He is the anonymous star of a documentary film, *The Seekers,* which is generally regarded as one of the better visual tools available for use in drug-prevention programs aimed at adolescents.

"Kids have heard all about bad LSD trips; they aren't scared by horror posters and pamphlets and they are really turned off by the phoniness of most of the so-called educational materials," says Robert Fox, an energetic auburn-bearded young sociologist who runs the state's drug-education program. By way of an example, he described an anti-drug film recently shown in a high-school assembly. In the first reel the young heroine comes home from school to find her mother is out. To assuage her loneliness the child smokes a cigarette. Scene two finds her seeking companionship among some pot-smoking teen-agers. And in the finale she has reached the depths of degradation—mainlining. The climax of the film is a close-up of a bloody syringe as she shoots heroin into her arm.

"Most of these kids have tried a joint themselves and they know this isn't the way it happens," Fox said. "There wasn't any discussion afterward—except in the corridors. A movie is only useful if it leads to a meaningful discussion."

He conceded that it takes a highly skilled leader to turn the discussion into something other than an interminable rap session about the hypocrisy of martini-swilling adults who refuse to legalize pot. It is a dead-end argument in which the grown-ups point to the proven fact that most hard-drug users smoked marijuana earlier in their careers. The kids, who have heard this one all too often, rejoin that millions of pot-smokers never become pot-heads or junkies. And of course they are right.

This irrelevant dialogue is not likely to end until our anti-marijuana laws are revised at least to remove criminal sanctions from possession. It might be wise also to consider the possibility of handling marijuana as we do another potentially dangerous drug—alcohol—through licensed outlets. This would at least make it possible to exercise some control over quality, which now ranges from virtually innocuous "subway pot" (said to consist of dried oak leaves plus a marijuana-like fragrance) to hashish, a potent hallucinogen also derived from the hemp plant. Presumably, marijuana advertising would be banned from TV and radio. This would set a valuable precedent which might help us rid the home screen of one prevailing and ominously seductive cause of the current "drug ambience" (another factor, of course, is the pop-rock drug-glorifying scene)—the ingenious commercials which sell us drugs to pep us up, calm us down, and indeed to handle all of life's crises by popping a pill in our mouths. Children who start looking at TV at the age of two are estimated to have spent eight thousand hours in front of the tiny screen by the time they enter school. Like marijuana, mood-influencing drugs are not physically addictive: that is, people who stop using them suffer no withdrawal symptoms. But they can cause psychological dependence—which as any cigarette or diet-pill addict has learned is no minor matter.

Most of the experts working on the addiction problem take the hard line on marijuana (although all agree that the present savage penalties for its use are atrocious). They are also profoundly worried about the spreading abuse of barbiturates and amphetamines, which have been found to result in brain damage that is sometimes irreversible. Most intractable of all is the LSD psychosis which can recur unpredictably months after the last bad trip.

The treatment of very young addicts is still largely unexplored territory. Dr. Marie Nyswander is currently experimenting with a few children by giving them very small doses of methadone which she hopes eventually to withdraw altogether. She is not yet ready to report on this project. Little scientific attention has elsewhere been focused on this increasingly pressing problem.

The present danger is that the expansion of vitally needed therapy and prevention programs will be bogged down in acrimonious debate about methods. One of the least discussed but most effective has been religious conversion. The Black Muslims, for example, have persuaded large numbers of their followers to forsake drugs. An evangelical spirit also sparked another grass-roots program in Harlem, the Addicts' Rehabilitation Center. Its director, James Allen, found his own salvation from drugs through the Manhattan Christian Reformed Church.

Clearly what is now needed is an objective evaluation of the different approaches which show some promise of success. In New York, the ideological barriers between competing programs have made it impossible to do this.

New York's loss, however, has proved Chicago's gain. Last year Dr. Jerome Jaffe, a remarkably open-minded psychiatrist formerly on the staff of Albert Einstein Medical College, fled New York's addiction feuds. Financed by the state of Illinois, he is directing in Chicago the country's first multi-modality addiction program. Patients are assigned, according to their needs, to therapeutic communities, psychotherapy, methadone maintenance, or treatment with one of the non-addictive narcotic antagonists such as cyclazocine. If the patient is not progressing in one treatment, he is shifted to another without animus since no one has a vested interest in any particular method. The program is being monitored by the National Institute of Mental Health. And the results are awaited with almost breathless interest. Conceivably, they might even cause peace to break out in New York.

The Politics of Style

JOHN CORRY

It happened sometime in the early 1960s, and although no one can say exactly when, it may all have begun in that magic moment when Robert Frost, who always looked marvelous, with silver hair, and deep, deep lines in his face, read a poem at the inauguration of John F. Kennedy, and then went on to tell him afterwards that he ought to be more Irish than Harvard, which was something that sounded a lot better than it actually was. Hardly a man today remembers the poem, which was indifferent, anyway, but nearly everyone remembers Frost, or at least the sight of him at the lectern, which was perhaps the first sign that from then on it would not matter so much what you said, but how you said it. When the arts arrive in politics this way, surely neither style, nor show business, can be far behind, and if the Left must now suffer John Wayne, then the rest of us must put up with Jane Fonda, and the high keening sound you hear over the landscape is the sound of anguish, which is our newest form of artistic and political expression. My own favorite publication in keeping track of these things is *The Village Voice,* which is a prosperous weekly put out in New York, and also a prominent example of advocacy journalism. As a practical matter in advocacy journalism, the most important thing is neither how well you write, nor how well you report, but what your position in life is, and a good many people at the *Voice* write mostly about themselves, although sometimes they write about each other, and about how they *all* feel about things. One way or another this can be wonderfully entertaining, even if a political writer at the *Voice* may sometimes sound as if he has been greatly influenced by *The Sorrows of Young Werther,* and even if when he is deepest in his anguish he suffers from what Martin Luther would have called the sin of pride. The best thing about the *Voice,* though, is that it not only reports on what the cultural and political radicals are doing, it also popularizes it, and it does it better than its less intelligent imitators, who are legion around the country. A good argument for reading the *Voice,* in fact, is to read it not only for what it says, but for what it is, and for what this can tell you about our own slow return to the Dark Ages.

The *Voice,* for example, is good at keeping you up on things like Women's Liberation and the Black Panthers, and even though the Panthers think of Women's Lib as a distraction, and of its members as unfit for a serious revolution, which makes the Women's Lib ladies a little mad, the two organizations have more in common than is ordinarily supposed. For one thing, the members of both tantrum a lot. For another, neither the Panthers, nor the ladies, care much for themselves and they both have great doubts about whether or not they can make it in life. They wear oppression like both a badge and an excuse, and they do not seem to be seriously engaged in anything other than being oppressed, and in telling everyone else about it. Being oppressed, sad-assed, and sorry can be a way of life, just like any other, and just like anyone else the Panthers and the Women's Lib ladies will fight hard to keep their way of life. This may not matter much with the ladies, but the Panthers are something else again. They are black Stalinists who wear funny clothes, talk nasty, and scare the hell out of the Justice Department. Even in the best of times, Washington has trembled easily, and now the Panthers *really* are being oppressed, and this makes it tough on all the rest of us. (One of the dreary things we must live with now is the quality of both the oppressed and the oppressor in America. John Mitchell has no class, but then neither do some of the people he most dislikes. The only correct response to the Chicago conspiracy trial was to send $10 to the defendants' defense fund, and then to hope that Jerry Rubin and Abbie Hoffman would be hit lightly by a passing truck.)

One way or another, white America will try to turn the blacks into song and dance men, and one way or another some blacks will respond. The Black Muslims, despite their nuttiness, got on to this pretty early, and elected to wear suits and ties, promote middle-class virtues, and leave the white radicals alone. The Panthers did not, becoming the new song and dance men, and furnishing a great deal of entertainment for the white radicals, who became the new crackers. The radicals, and the liberals who find diversion in the Panthers, are telling the Panthers that they really are not good enough to make it, and that they will never be much good at being anything other than oppressed. "We will have our manhood even if we have to level the face of the earth," Huey Newton told the Panther convention, and this is not so much inflammatory as it is sad, a confession that the Panthers do not have something that the other boys in town take for granted. The new patronage toward the blacks is to agree when the militants say that the world is simply too much for them, and neither the Panthers, nor their supporters, would ever suggest that a Panther could become, say, a doctor. (Similarly, the male supporters of Women's Lib cannot see how a girl who has just crashed a men's bar, or thrown her bra away in an exquisite gesture of protest, and then marched down Fifth Avenue to tell us about it, can ever be anything but a member of Women's Lib. Neither, though, can I.) The Panthers are the natural sons of Stepin Fetchit, who was never thought of as being able to be anyone or anything else, either, and they are not the heirs to Nat Turner, which is what they keep telling us they are. The new patronage demands that we say something about black rage, and this is not much removed from saying, Man, they really do have a sense of rhythm. Either concept can rob a man of his humanity, and there are blacks all over America who think the Panthers are a marvelous joke on the whites, but they wouldn't want their daughter to marry one, either. *Soul on Ice* simply was not a very good book, and Cleaver said nothing in it that his betters hadn't been saying for years, and more intelligently, too. Frederick Douglass said it all more than one hundred years ago, and then later there was Richard Wright, Du Bois, Ellison, and a whole lot of other people who are not read as much now as they ought to be.

My favorite analyst at the *Voice* on these and other matters is Jack Newfield, a New Left columnist and speaker, who is also one of the finer deadpan humorists of our time. In a recent story, Newfield disclosed that the Liberal party of New York was really a machine, and that it had a boss, and that it had done things that it ought not to have done. A great many people in New York had suspected this for some time, but Newfield's great contribution was his mock outrage, and the absolutely wonderful way he got you to share his sense of discovery, never once tipping his mitt that he was not going to say anything new at all. Somewhere in the story he wrote that "the Liberal party was fathered twenty-six years ago by that most conservative of passions—anti-Communism," and this was a marvelously funny thing for a political analyst to say, too, probably getting big fat chuckles from Koestler, and the shades of Richard Wright and Silone. Newfield does this kind of thing quite often, and as comic masterpieces there has been nothing quite like them since the time Calvin Coolidge was putting on Sioux war bonnets, and staring inscrutably into the silent cameras. In a literary sense, however, Newfield sometimes dilutes his comic gifts by going in rather heavily for soul. This is all right for some people, but Newfield has an unfortunate tendency to write about his favorite politicians in approximately the same terms that Louisa May Alcott wrote about Beth, and sometimes he can sound a little sappy. Still, the old comic genius does come through from time to time, as it did, for example, in this wonderful passage from a recent eulogy he did on Robert Kennedy: "And then, later that night, Kennedy would tell me and David Halberstam how much he loved people who worked hard with their hands, how much he preferred the white poor of West Virginia and Gary to the Manhattan intellectuals 'who spend their time worrying about why they haven't been invited to some party.' " Newfield's audacity here is staggering. At great risk, he goes for a chuckle, and as an old ironist he pulls it off, simply by reminding us of just how much poor white trash, and how many smart Manhattan folks the Senator actually did hang around with. Newfield's talents, considerable as they are, however, do not travel well to other publications. In a story in *New York* magazine in which he nominates Ramsey Clark for President, Newfield spends an intolerable amount of time saying he doesn't feel well, mentioning his friends, and then wondering aloud if he should take the assignment and write the story. As a way of building suspense this is not much, and it is hardly any surprise when Newfield decides on page 3 that he will go ahead and do the story, anyway. Then, after comparing Clark to Gary Cooper, Will Rogers, Lincoln, and St. Francis, and giving him all the better of it, too, Newfield decides that he would make a hell of a President, but that the country may not deserve him. With that kind of promotion, a politician hardly needs any enemies at all.

At bottom, Newfield is a moralist, which is also what so many young people are today, and moralists, who are not necessarily idealists, have always been hell on the rest of us. A moralist refers everything back to himself, and that is what makes the young, particularly the young radicals, so stupefyingly dull, when they are not being simply unpleasant. Politics needs not be a demanding profession, which is one reason it attracts the people it does, and the moralists among the politicians usually have been found on the Right. Strom Thurmond, for example, is uncluttered with either ideas, or a sense of ambiguity, but he has a high sense of purpose, and he is a moralist. The liberals, however grievous their other faults, are more cynical about things, and they lack that high sense of purpose, which makes them easier to get along with. It is chilling to think of the radicals forming a third party, although the suggestion is much put about these days, because the radicals might easily capture and dominate the liberal Democrats, and then go on to bury us all in righteousness, snobbery, and bad manners. Those prudent persons who have never hoped for much from politics, anyway, except perhaps a little less noise, and some decent kind of socialism, would be left with nowhere to turn to at all. This is a good reason for the liberals to become honest men, and to save us before it is too late.

If you were fortunate enough to have had something like the flu on Moratorium Day last year, which would have freed you from the necessity of attending any of its demonstrations, you could have lain in bed all day watching a succession of speakers on television, nearly all of whom said this was the wrong war in the wrong place, and so on, and some of whom offered plans for withdrawal. These were liberals, speaking at length. The radicals said this was a sick society, which was true, although probably not for the reasons they thought. (No one mentioned that Nixon was doing pretty much what Kennedy and McCarthy had proposed the year before.) All that any public person could decently have done on Moratorium Day, however, would have been to rise, say that we must leave Vietnam now, and then sit down.

No one did, and no one expected it, because this is a time of involvement, and of the awful need to convince others of our involvement. What is more dreadful, we must prove it, too, which is an absolutely sure way of obscuring any issue, and of letting loose wild aberrations on the land. For the liberals, involvement is a matter of style, and not necessarily of commitment. For the radicals, involvement is a matter of position. That is, the question on the Left will not be whether one Panther knocked off another Panther, the question will be, Do you or do you not support the Panthers? The question will not be whether or not the Democratic process is at work in Cuba, the question will be, Are you in favor of the people? It is all very vexing, and it means that if you do not support the Panthers you are a racist, and if you have reservations about Fidel you are an imperialist.

People who write letters to the *Voice* catch on to this, and if they are going to question something that Cleaver, say, or Huey Newton, has said, they customarily begin by disclaiming any racism on their own part. This is the kind of attitude that spreads, and now we can show our interest in equal rights for women only by paying careful attention to some of the marvelously empty-headed chicks in Women's Lib. It is what the moralists have led us to, and it is better to beware of them. There are still some of us who feel discomfort when an artist believes he must drape his canvas in black to show he is against Vietnam, or racism, or Agnew, and there are those of us who wish, without knowing exactly why, that prominent people would wail privately, and not publicly, about whatever injustice is bothering them. The politics of protest and anguish is virtually mindless, requiring very little of a person, and it is practiced by some very great charlatans. Most of all, however, it is the amateurs who give it a bad name, and the worst amateurs of all are the fancy people, and the people in the arts. When the arts and politics join, the one debases the other, and radical politics debases worst of all.

Moralists look at life in a simple way, which artists ought not to do, and along the Left, in general, and among advocacy journalists, in particular, simplicity is a very great virtue indeed. Consequently, for every oppressed, the Left must find an oppressor, the problem being that in real life it is not always easy to settle on which one is truly the bastard. In the Nigerian-Biafran war, the moralists on the Left said it was Nigeria, deciding not to recognize that for every relief shipment that the Nigerians kept out of Biafra, the Biafrans turned one back, too. (The publicists of the Right also jumped all over Nigeria, a rare instance of moralists who ordinarily are far apart in everything coming together on something. Biafra had a very clever public-relations operation.) Then there were the Young Lords, an organization of Puerto Rican militants, much beloved by the *Voice,* who seized the First Spanish Methodist Church in East Harlem. Religion, you understand, is the oppressor, unresponsive to the needs of the community, an arm of the Establishment, and so on, and the Young Lords went about the work of the Revolution by sitting in, and seizing, the First Spanish Methodist Church. Nothing much happened, of course; it was the Young Lords' style that counted, and their style was sufficient to ensure their standing among the radicals, and to send little tingles along the liberals' spines. Not many of the people who tingled, however, had ever been in a Protestant church in East Harlem, and there was something marvelous about the Revolution taking over this church, which was the kind of beleaguered place where the parishioners would gather together and debate the wisdom of saving their money, and buying a coffee urn for the church basement. The thing you must understand about advocates of the Revolution, and of liberal causes, in general, is that their warmth toward the Revolution, or the causes, increases in proportion to the distance they are removed from them. (The South, of course, has been telling the North this for years.) The parishioners of the First Spanish Methodist Church, who were poor and Latin, were not noticeably enthusiastic about having their church taken over, and it would have been wonderfully entertaining for all of us if the Young Lords had occupied a Reform Democratic club, or the beaches of East Hampton in August, or, say, *The Village Voice* itself.

Nonetheless, the Young Lords, being Puerto Rican, have a chance of keeping their revolution honest and intact in a way that the Black Panthers do not. The liberals and radicals hardly know the Puerto Ricans at all, being mostly accustomed to seeing them as busboys, doormen, and delivery boys, and these are not roles that easily lend themselves to romantic visions. Moreover, too many Puerto Ricans have a reputation of being positively jolly, and their rage and suffering have not yet intruded themselves into the popular culture. Consequently, the Young Lords are more likely to be left alone, and are more or less free to be what they want to be. This is a great break for them, although there is still the danger that, having made it in *The Village Voice,* the Young Lords will now make it into *Vogue,* or *Harper's Bazaar,* which are something like uptown *Village Voices,* and therefore well worth looking at from time to time. They teach you something about style, and about how it can reach out and diminish us all, and something about politics, too. It is not just that Arthur Schlesinger reviews movies for *Vogue,* which gives both him and the magazine a cachet neither would have alone, it is also that *Vogue* and *Harper's Bazaar* are always searching for something, anything, new and then writing kicky little paragraphs about it. If Gauguin were painting in Tahiti today, *Vogue* or *Harper's Bazaar* would almost certainly come upon him, intruding as they do on things that should be most private, and offering them up without a hint of the loneliness, pain, and commitment that actually go with them.

This is the way it is with politics, too, and when *Vogue* or *Harper's Bazaar* touch on things political or sociological, they will always be things that touch the liberal's interest. With the exception of William Buckley, who is apparently a monarchist, the conservatives and their causes have no real style. John Lindsay is sometimes proposed as a possible leader of a new coalition of liberals and radicals for no apparent reason other than his *looking* as if he ought to be the leader. Ramsey Clark, who has no particular style, which is good, almost certainly will have one invented for him. It is the way things work now, and Clark's style will be made up of innocence, detachment, and a disdain for politics, all of which are qualities that would make him a disaster as a President. Eugene McCarthy went through the primary campaign like a dyspeptic Jesuit, which captivated a great many people, and neatly hid the fact that he never said very much. This, of course, put him one up on most politicians, who say too much, but McCarthy blew his moral superiority by being uppity. None of this mattered, however, because he had style. "Muskie reminds me of Ed Sullivan," Newfield writes in the *Voice,* "relaxed, pleasant, and totally hollow and conventional." Here Newfield gives it all away, saying that Muskie has no style, and so therefore he has no character, either. This is the kind of elegant contempt for people that is exercised by *Vogue* and *Harper's Bazaar,* and it is what unites them with the moralists on the Left, and it is what sometimes sends very fashionable people to drift about in the radicals' world. If the fashion magazines were to do something on a dragger fisherman in Maine he would have to have a Barcelona chair on his poop deck, and if they were to do something on a carpenter in Oregon he would have to have a Giacometti by his workbench. Their message is that you must have something extra going for you, or else you do not matter much. In other words, you must have style, which means you must be something other than yourself.

The fashion magazines themselves are prominent examplars of this. For one thing, the clothes they show are remarkably ugly, and excruciatingly self-conscious, and a woman who wears them will not look like a woman, and in fact she may hardly look like a person. She will, however, be full of style, which is presumably the only reason that anyone would buy things of such consummate ugliness. Just so, there is a plague of ideologies and therapies being visited on us these days, and, like the ladies' clothes, they compete in telling us that we can, and should, be something other than what we are. They are offered to us as part of the pursuit of happiness, and they will cheat us if we forget that a mild state of pain is our most natural state, and that some of the deficiencies we are trying to overcome are deficiencies in what long ago was called the human condition. The junkiest of the ideologies and therapies begin as idle people's toys, and then they become stylish, which is what makes them attractive, and sends our poor shriveled selves lusting after them, and then confuses us as to what they are really all about. It is like the girls in Women's Lib who talk about their distaste at being thought of as sex objects, which is really a conceit on their part, and then go on to raise this into an ideology, having serious debates all the way along about the propriety of sleeping with a man. There is not much new in this, and for years perfectly nice, ordinary American girls have been telling one another that they would never go to bed with anyone who didn't love them, without ever giving much thought to turning the notion into a national movement. In these dark days, however, people join gangs, and what once were private pleasures, and private pains, are now public pastimes.

Consequently, there is Esalen, and sensitivity training, and mass therapies, and other group gropes beyond number, and they are all getting to be bloody bores. The *Voice* is filled with paid notices put in by swamis and yogis who are at loose ends, and there are elaborate advertisements that offer the services of computers to help you find a date. This is the old lonely-hearts thing dressed up by IBM, and the people who subscribe to it must be not so much horny as they are helpless. The cry heard most often is a cry for help, or, more likely, a snivel, and where it will end nobody knows, and there is not the slightest indication that it ever will. Letting it all hang out is supposed to be good for you, but the privilege is being abused, and most people's sensibilities are not that interesting, anyway. Masters and Johnson, and Dr. David Rubin are spreading themselves thin across the land, Masters and Johnson all technical and dull, Dr. Rubin all smarmy and smirky, and they are picked up by people who have had perfectly nice sex lives, never even having heard of fellatio, but now absolutely certain that they can't go on without it. This is the other side of the consumer society, and it means that there are no end of ways in which Americans can be manipulated, and made to feel there is something wrong, and that whatever it is can be solved by something, or someone other than themselves.

This impoverishes us, and we are being intruded upon, and things that were once private and worthwhile are being pushed out into the open, where they can do nothing but shrivel and die, or at least leave us wondering what it was that we once saw in them. It is like the new pornography in the movies, serving up breasts and buttocks like heaps of pasta, and excising eroticism and its pleasures more neatly than any missionary who ever served God by draping a Mother Hubbard over some poor girl in the Fijis. We lose our freedom to be ourselves, to be whatever it was we decided to be in our most secret depths, and we lose our capacity for finding salvation in the small forms of kinky behavior that at least were our own. Whatever we were before is no longer good enough, and we seem to be afraid to be alone. As sorry a thing as buggery, which two honest men might once have sanctified by committing decently and privately, is now being flaunted, and the homosexuals are forming liberation leagues. The politics of protest and anguish slops over into our private lives, and it is worth noting that Women's Lib got its big impetus not from Betty Friedan, but from the girls of SDS, who, politics failing, were determined to nibble us to death in other ways.

When the moralists on the Left talk about alienation, they are talking about emptiness, which is hardly ever an interesting phenomenon, even though it is now considered to be a weapon in the cultural and political revolution. Alienation, in fact, is getting passed into the popular culture as something of a virtue, and this may be the most dreadful thing of all because now we are beginning to celebrate it. *Easy Rider,* in its simple-minded way, was about alienation, and its heroes were two monosyllabic junkies who were wedded to their motorcycles. The critics loved it. They loved *Diary of a Mad Housewife* even more, and this was about three nitwits, any one of whom would have suffered a collapse if ever faced with a real problem. The housewife herself was an emptier vessel than even Scarlett O'Hara, although the movie seemed to be saying that she was a human being, full of true pain, who had fallen victim to circumstance. She was, however, mostly a twerp.

Alienation, or emptiness, was once a solitary preoccupation, which at least gave it some dignity, but now it is practiced by whole groups and classes of people. We may all bore one another to death this way, and the young, who are the most self-conscious about their alienation, can be the most boring of all. They are narcissistic, some of the time withdrawing all of the way into their own and each other's heads, and all of the time fluttering indecently between acceptance and rejection of all the rest of us. In warm weather in Washington, Georgetown is beset by clouds of hippies. They clog the sidewalks, and sell underground newspapers, and sometimes they strike out for freedom by chalking something about the Vietcong on a garage wall. Mostly, however, they stand about, mumble to one another, and drive the people in Georgetown nuts. If the hippies had a sense of history, or of irony, they could enjoy themselves hugely doing this, knowing that they were bringing to Georgetown some of the world that its resident politicians had helped to create. The hippies do not know this, however, and they come to Georgetown because of its charm, which is the charm that comes only from affluence. There is something depressing, and even offensive about this. The hippies represent a culture that pretends to deliver us from the malfeasances of affluence, but it does not, and the hippies are enchanted by nothing so much as the charm and grace they find in Georgetown. Nevertheless, if they stay on there they will destroy it. First there are the head shops, and then the tourists, and then the crummy gin mills. The radical culture is still only a reflection of the conventional one, and somewhere in that there ought to be a lesson for all of us.

Meanwhile, there is no sign that the radical culture will disappear, and radical politics will be with us forever, getting carried along, as it always has been, on its own tide of dogma, righteousness, and fervor. This generation of radicals may end up being distinguished from other generations of radicals only by its style, and by its marriage with the world of fashion, which is a thought that makes it worthwhile to return one last time now to *The Village Voice.* Carter Burden, a City Councilman in New York, was once apotheosized by *Vogue* as one of the "Beautiful Burdens," the other beautiful Burden being his wife. This ought to be a stigma for any politician, but Burden is persevering, and this year he acquired the controlling interest in *The Village Voice.*

Haydn-Marat Dylan-Sad: Dafining a Ganratin

JACK NEWFIELD

Tom Hayden, the Thomas Jefferson of the New Left, and at twenty-eight the author of two important books, has written:

> What is desperately needed is the person of vision and clarity, who sees both the model society and the pitfalls that precede its attainment, and who will not destroy his vision for short-run gains, but instead, will hold it out for all to see, as the farthest dream and perimeter of human possibility.

. . .

Hayden and Dylan personalize the two most important moods and movements of the generation still under thirty: the politics of resistance, and the art of the absurd. Hayden and Dylan are the modern equivalents of Marat, the utopian revolutionary, and Sade, the poet of nihilism; linked by the common outrage against what is, but divided by contradictory visions of how to forge what might be. They are what Emerson called "representative men," and Hegel called "zeitgeists."

Hayden, the seminal architect of SDS (Students for a Democratic Society), left graduate school to become its organizer and has lived, since 1964, with the wretched of Newark. He would agree with Marat when he says, "Against nature's silence I use action. . . . I don't watch unmoved, I intervene and say this and this are wrong. The important thing is to pull yourself up by you own hair, to turn yourself inside out, and see the world with fresh eyes."

Dylan, who abandoned narrow political protest songs in 1964, in order to explore the surreal, the absurd, and the hallucinatory, would agree with Sade, who answered, "Why should you care about the world outside? For me the only reality is imagination, the world inside myself. The revolution no longer interests me."

I know that 75 percent of the "Now Generation" cares only about fraternities, drive-ins, and football. But that has been true of all generations, including those baptized by the pop sociologists as Beat, Lost, Silent, and Now. Minorities give all generations their characters. Less than one million young people participated in social action during the 1930's, but they are remembered now, not the majority untouched by political passion, or motivated only by commercial ambition. So it is today that the New Left, symbolized by Hayden, and the absurd artists and juke box poets, symbolized by Dylan, will give this generation its historical character. And not the button-down opportunists of the Young Democrats, the jingle-hucksters of Madison Avenue, or the dreamless millions, already programmed for safe jobs, dull marriages, and what Thoreau once called "lives of quiet desperation."

Hayden and Dylan, born one year apart, in the adjacent heartland states of Michigan and Minnesota, are *Zeitgeists* because they have let themselves be vulnerable to the traumas which have most shaped this generation, a generation whose collective biography is inscribed in the names of blood-stained places: the Bay of Pigs, Mississippi, Dallas, Watts, and Vietnam. And because they are both young Americans, *in extremis,* Hayden and Dylan are most repelled by arbitrary authority, the mass media, hypocrisy, status, and compromise. Neither one is a liberal Democrat with a nine-to-five job.

For all its paradoxes, lack of program, and anti-intellectualism, the New Left is the most hopeful political movement in the country because it knows certain crucial things the rest of the country does not yet know.

It knows, for one, that the liberalism of the unions and the ADA (Americans for Democratic Action) is exhausted and without relationship to the new agents of change. It was the ADA's generation of liberals who executed Caryl Chessman, invaded Cuba, sold out the Mississippi Freedom Democrats, sent the state police onto the campus at Berkeley (and Madison and Brooklyn), accepted covert money from the CIA to subsidize their cold war unions and organizations, and made Vietnam a charred monument to their paranoid anti-communism.

The New Left also knows the limits of mere legislation and bureaucratic programs. A poverty program became the patina of the Great Society, but more Americans are on welfare today, and live in slum housing today, than when LBJ was inaugurated. Two civil rights bills have been passed, but Negroes are poorer and more bitter now than ever before. The under-thirty radicals know that *values* and *attitudes* must be changed before new laws do anything more than polish the illusion of reform; they know that justice is more important than Professor Daniel Patrick Moynihan's sacred "stability," and that justice will only emerge from more, not less, conflict.

The New Left knows other things too, that the editors of *Time,* LBJ's cabinet, and Freedom House do not. They know that if the Vietnam war is not wrong, *then nothing is wrong;* that marijuana is pleasurable and does not lead to heroin; that the *New York Times* does not print the truth all the time; that anti-communism is now a greater threat to American democracy than communism; that people riot because they are poor, not because Rap Brown tells them to.

Generations, however, are not defined by their rhetoric or by their abstract insights, but by their deeds and their impact on the general culture. And it is here that the young radicals have made and altered history.

If Christ began with only twelve followers, and Fidel began in the Sierra Maestra with less than fifty, the modern civil rights movement began with the four Negro freshmen who sat-in in Greensboro, North Carolina, on February 1, 1960. If SNCC, the freedom rides, and the Mississippi Summer Project had not flowered from that seed, there would never have been civil rights bills passed in 1964 and 1965, nor a Negro sitting today in the Mississippi State Legislature. If SDS had not organized a march of twenty thousand against the Vietnam war on April 17, 1965, Senators like Fulbright, Kennedy, and McCarthy would not now be so bold in their dissents. If the Free Speech Movement had not challenged Berkeley's computerized bureaucracy, the "Multiversity" would not now be the subject of dozens of symposia. If Tom Hayden, Herbert Aptheker, and Staughton Lynd had not traveled to Hanoi in December of 1965, the courts would never have had a chance to declare the State Department's ban on free travel illegal. If *Ramparts* magazine had not exposed the secret life of the Central Intelligence Agency, God knows what might have happened.

Any generation that has grown up listening to Jack Ruby, CIA recruiters, Eichmann, George Romney, Andy Warhol, Richard Speck, and Lyndon Johnson must have a sense of the absurd. And so it has been that the absurd artists have given the under-thirty generation its second characteristic vision—that of comic-apocalyptic chaos and absurdity. They find it in the songs of Dylan, the Beatles, the Mothers of Invention, and Phil Ochs; in the fiction of Joseph Heller, Thomas Pynchon, J. P. Donleavy, Terry Southern, and Ken Kesey; in films like *Morgan* and *Dr. Strangelove*; in the poetry of Allen Ginsberg, the comedy of Lenny Bruce; and the cartoons of Jules Feiffer. The immense underground popularity on the campuses of novels like *Catch-22* and *One Flew Over the Cuckoo's Nest* mirror a generation's perception that logic, rules, and order explain less and less about a culture that puts Martin Luther King, Joan Baez, and Ken Kesey in jail—and Lester Maddox, General Hershey, and Ronald Reagan in power. Or a culture that can send 525,000 troops to Asia, but not eight-two voting registrars to Mississippi.

The only analogies for that are Kesey's novel, where the inmates of a mental hospital are healthier than the guards, or Yossarian, who screams at his colonel in *Catch-22:* "Crazy! What are you talking about? You're the one who's crazy!"

That's how the young feel, when literally the most sensitive and dispassionate adults in the land—Senator Mansfield, Eric Sevareid, James Reston, etc.—emotionally condemn their demonstrations against the war but admit, ever so calmly, that the war is wrong and that dissent (in the abstract) is nice. It is this irony that makes Dylan's lines like, "To live outside the law you must be honest," and "Don't follow leaders, watch the parkin' meter," appear so prophetic. Or Hayden's remark that "It has been the most respected liberals who have caused most of our problems and disillusioned me the most." James Reston sounding like a "good German" is what C. Wright Mills meant by "crackpot realism."

Four years ago a leader of SDS tried to convince me that the Warren Report was a fraud, that the NSA (National Student Association) was being secretly financed by the CIA, that I shouldn't vote for Lyndon Johnson because he would follow the same policy as Barry Goldwater in Southeast Asia, and that a washed-up Late Show actor would soon become governor of the nation's largest state. I told him he was crazy. But it turns out that it is America that is crazy.

"All the lonely people, where do they all come from?" ask the Beatles.

"Not with my life you don't," chant the draft resisters of SDS.

"I can't get no satisfaction," sing the Rolling Stones.

"Burn, Baby, Burn," chant the ghetto children of Malcolm X.

"You don't know what's happening, do you, Mister Jones?" taunts Dylan.

These expressions of rebellion and chaos reflect the deepest feelings of the generation that has grown up absurd, listening to Dean Rusk explain why we are in Vietnam.

Sartre said of blood-sick France, during the Algerian war: "Ours is the age of assassins." And perhaps that is the truest epitaph for this American generation, that before its thirtieth birthday it has witnessed the assassinations of John Kennedy and Malcolm X and the murder of a nation ten thousand miles away.

Twenty Centuries of Stony Sleep

The Dark Heart of American History

ARTHUR SCHLESINGER, JR.

The murders within five years of John F. Kennedy, Martin Luther King, Jr., and Robert F. Kennedy raise—or ought to raise—somber questions about the character of contemporary America. One such murder might be explained away as an isolated horror, unrelated to the inner life of our society. But the successive shootings, in a short time, of three men who greatly embodied the idealism of American life suggest not so much a fortuitous set of aberrations as an emerging pattern of response and action—a spreading and ominous belief in the efficacy of violence and the politics of the deed.

Yet, while each of these murders produced a genuine season of national mourning, none has produced a sustained season of national questioning. In every case, remorse has seemed to end, not as an incitement to self-examination, but as an escape from it. An orgy of sorrow and shame becomes an easy way of purging a bad conscience and returning as quickly as possible to business as usual.

"It would be . . . self-deceptive," President Johnson said after the shooting of Robert Kennedy, "to conclude from this act that our country is sick, that it has lost its balance, that it has lost its sense of direction, even its common decency. Two hundred million Americans did not strike down Robert Kennedy last night any more than they struck down John F. Kennedy in 1963 or Dr. Martin Luther King in April of this year."

I do not quarrel with these words. Of course two hundred million Americans did not strike down these men. Nor, in my judgment, is this a question of a "sick society" or of "collective guilt." I do not know what such phrases mean, but I am certain that they do not represent useful ways of thinking about our problem. Obviously most Americans are decent God-fearing people. Obviously most Americans were deeply and honestly appalled by these atrocities. Obviously most Americans rightly resent being told that they were "guilty" of crimes they neither willed nor wished.

Still, it is not enough to dismiss the ideas of a sick society and of collective guilt and suppose that such dismissal closes the question. For a problem remains—the problem of a contagion of political murder in the United States in the 1960s unparalleled in our own history and unequaled today anywhere in the world. If we minimize this problem, if we complacently say it is all the work of lunatics and foreigners, that nothing is wrong and that our society is beyond criticism, if we cry like Macbeth: "Thous canst not say I did it; never shake/Thy gory locks at me," then we lose all hope of recovering control of the destructive impulse within. Then we will only continue the downward spiral of social decomposition and moral degradation.

Self-knowledge is the indispensable prelude to self-control; and self-knowledge, for a nation as well as for an individual, begins with history. We like to think of ourselves as a peaceful, tolerant, benign people who have always lived under a government of laws and not of men. And, indeed, respect for persons and for laws has been one characteristic strain in the American tradition. Most Americans probably pay this respect most of their lives. Yet this is by no means the only strain in our tradition. For we also have been a violent people. When we refuse to acknowledge the existense of this other strain, we refuse to see our nation as it is.

We began, after all, as a people who killed red men and enslaved black men. No doubt we often did this with a Bible and a prayer book. But no nation, however righteous its professions, could act as we did without burying deep in itself—in its customs, its institutions, and its psyche—a propensity toward violence. However much we pretended that Indians and Negroes were subhuman, we really knew that they were God's children too.

Nor did we confine our violence to red men and black men. We gained our freedom, after all, through revolution. The first century after independence were years of incessant violence—wars, slave insurrections, Indian fighting, urban riots, murders, duels, beatings. Members of Congress went armed to the Senate and House. In his first notable speech, in January 1838, before the Young Men's Lyceum of Springfield, Illinois, Abraham Lincoln named internal violence as the supreme threat to American political institutions. He spoke of "the increasing disregard for law which pervades the country; the growing disposition to substitute the wild and furious passions, in lieu of the sober judgment of Courts; and the worse than savage mobs, for the executive ministers of justice." The danger to the American republic, he said, was not from foreign invasion:

> At what point then is the approach of danger to be expected? I answer, if it ever reach us, it must spring up amongst us. It cannot come from

abroad. If destruction be our lot, we must ourselves be its author and finisher. As a nation of freemen, we must live through all time, or die by suicide.

So the young Lincoln named the American peril—a peril he did not fear to locate within the American breast. Indeed, the sadness of America has been that our worst qualities have so often been the other face of our best. Our commitment to morality, our faith in experiment: these have been sources of America's greatness, but they have also led Americans into our error. For our moralists have sometimes condoned murder if the cause is deemed good; so Emerson and Thoreau applauded John Brown of Osawatomie. And our pragmatists have sometimes ignored the means if the result is what they want. Moralism and pragmatism have not provided infallible restraints on the destructive instinct.

America, Martin Luther King correctly said, has been "a schizophrenic personality, tragically divided against herself." The impulses of violence and civility continued after Lincoln to war within the American breast. The insensate bloodshed of the Civil War exhausted the national capacity for violence and left the nation emotionally and psychologically spent. For nearly a century after Appomattox, we appeared on the surface the tarnquil and friendly people we still like to imagine ourselves to be. The amiability of that society no doubt exerted a restraining influence. There were still crazy individuals, filled with grievance, bitterness, and a potential for violence. But most of these people expended their sickness in fantasy; the Guiteaus and the Czolgoszs were the exception. These years of stability, a stability fitfully recaptured after the First World War, created the older generation's image of a "normal" America.

Yet even in the kindly years we did not wholly eradicate the propensity toward violence which history had hidden in the national unconscious. In certain moods, indeed, we prided ourselves on our violence; we almost considered it evidence of our virility. "Above all," cried Theodore Roosevelt, "let us shrink from no strife, moral or physical, within or without the nation, provided we are certain that the strife is justified." That fatal susceptibility always lurked under the surface, breaking out in Indian wars and vigilantism in the West, in lynchings in the South, in labor riots and race riots and gang wars in the cities.

It is important to distinguish collective from individual violence—the work of mobs from the work of murderers; for the motive and the effect can be very different. There can, of course, be murder by a mob. But not all mobs aim at murder. Collective violence—rioting against what were considered illegal British taxes in Boston in 1773, or dangerous Papist influence sixty years later, or inequitable draft laws in New York in 1863, or unfair labor practices in Chicago in 1937—is more characteristically directed at conditions than at individuals. In many cases (though by no means all), the aim has been to protest rather than protect the status quo; and the historian is obliged to concede that collective violence, including the recent riots in black ghettos, has often quickened the disposition of those in power to redress just grievances. Extralegal group action, for better or worse, has been part of the process of American democracy. Violence, for better or worse, *does* settle some questions, and for the better. Violence secured American independence, freed the slaves, and stopped Hitler.

But this has ordinarily been the violence of a society. The individual who plans violence is less likely to be concerned with reforming conditions than with punishing persons. On occasion the purpose is to protect the status quo by destroying men who symbolize or threaten social change (a tactic which the anarchists soon began to employ in reverse). A difference exists in psychic color and content between spontaneous mass convulsions and the premeditated killing of individuals. The first signifies an unstable society, the second, a murderous society. America has exhibited both forms of violence.

Now in the third quarter of the twentieth century, violence has broken out with new ferocity in our country. What has given our old propensity new life? Why does the fabric of American civility no longer exert restraint? What now incites crazy individuals to act out their murderous dreams? What is it about the climate of this decade that suddenly encourages—that for some evidently legitimatizes—the relish for hate and the resort to violence? Why, according to the Federal Bureau of Investigation, have assaults with a gun increased 77 per cent in the four years from 1964 through 1967?

We talk about the legacy of the frontier. No doubt, the frontier has bequeathed us a set of romantic obsessions about six-shooters and gun fighters. But why should this legacy suddenly reassert itself in the 1960s?

We talk about the tensions of industrial society. No doubt the ever-quickening pace of social change depletes and destroys the institutions which make for social stability. But this does not explain why Americans shoot and kill so many more Americans than Englishmen kill Englishmen or Japanese kill Japanese. England, Japan, and West Germany are, next to the United States, the most heavily industrialized countries in the world. Together they have a population of 214 million people. Among these 214 million, there are 135 gun murders a year. Among the 200 million people of the United States there are 6,500 gun murders a year—about *forty-eight times* as many.

We talk about the fears and antagonisms generated by racial conflict. Unquestionably this has contributed to the recent increase in violence. The murders of Dr. King and Senator Kennedy seem directly traceable to ethnic hatreds. Whites and blacks alike are laying in arms, both sides invoking the needs of self-defense. Yet this explanation still does not tell us why in America today we are tending to convert political problems into military problems—problems of adjustment into problems of force.

The New Left tells us that we are a violent society because we are a capitalist society—that capitalism is itself institutionalized violence; and that life under capitalism inevitably deforms relations among men. This view would be more impressive if the greatest violence of man against man in this century had not taken place in noncapitalist societies—in Nazi Germany, in Stalinist Russia, in precapitalist Indonesia. The fact is that every form of society is in some sense institutionalized violence; man in society always gives up a measure of "liberty" and accepts a measure of authority.

We cannot escape that easily. It is not just that we were a frontier society or have become an industrial society or are a racist or a capitalist society; it is something more specific than that. Nor can we blame the situation on our gun laws, or the lack of them; though here possibly we are getting closer. There is no question, of course, that we need adequate federal gun laws. Statistics make it evident that gun controls have some effect. Sixty per cent of all murders in the United States are by firearms; and states with adequate laws—New Jersey, New York, Massachusetts, Rhode Island—have much lower rates of gun murder than states with no laws or weak ones—Texas, Mississippi, Louisiana, Nevada.

Still, however useful in making it harder for potential murderers to get guns, federal gun legislation deals with the symptoms and not with the causes of our trouble. We must go further to account for the resurgence in recent years of our historical propensity toward violence.

One reason surely for the enormous tolerance of violence in contemporary America is the fact that our country has now been more or less continuously at war for a generation. The experience of war over a long period devalues human life and habituates people to killing. And the war in which we are presently engaged is far more brutalizing than was the Second World War or the Korean War. It is more brutalizing because the destruction we have wrought in Vietnam is so wildly out of proportion to any demonstrated involvement of our national security or any rational assessment of our national interest. In the other wars we killed for need. In this war we are killing beyond need, and, as we do so, we corrupt our national life. When violence is legally sanctioned for a cause in which people see no moral purpose, this is an obvious stimulus to individuals to use violence for what they may maniacally consider moral purposes of their own.

A second reason for the climate of violence in the United States is surely the zest with which the mass media, and especially television and films, dwell on violence. One must be clear about this. The mass media do *not* create violence. But they *reinforce* aggressive and destructive impulses, and they may well *teach* the morality as well as the methods of violence.

In recent years the movies and television have developed a pornography of violence far more demoralizing than the pornography of sex, which still seizes the primary attention of the guardians of civic virtue. Popular films of our day like *Rosemary's Baby* and *Bonnie and Clyde* imply a whole culture of human violation, psychological in one case, physical in the other. *Bonnie and Clyde,* indeed, was greatly admired for its blithe acceptance of the world of violence—an acceptance which almost became a celebration. Thus a student in a film course in San Francisco noted:

> There is a certain spirit that belongs to us. We the American people. It is pragmatic, rebellious, violent, joyous. It can create or kill. Everything about *Bonnie* and *Clyde* captures this spirit.
>
> John Brown was motivated by this spirit and it has scared the hell out of historians ever since. The Black Panthers have it. Cab drivers, musicians, used car salesmen and bus drivers understand it, but doctors, dentists and real estate salesmen don't.

Television is the most pervasive influence of all. The children of the electronic age sit hypnotized by the parade of killings, beatings, gunfights, knifings, maimings, brawls which flash incessantly across the tiny screen, and now in "living" color.

For a time, the television industry comforted itself with the theory that children listened to children's programs and that, if by any chance they saw programs for adults, violence would serve as a safety valve, offering a harmless outlet for pent-up aggressions: the more violence on the screen, the less in life. Alas, this turns out not to be necessarily so. As Dr. Wilbur Schramm, director of the Institute of Communication Research at Stanford has reported, children, even in the early elementary school years, view more programs designed for adults than for themselves; "above all, they prefer the more violent type of adult program including the Western, the adventure program, and the crime drama." Experiments show that such programs, far from serving as safety valves for aggression, attract children with high levels of aggression and stimulate them to seek overt means of acting out their aggressions. Evidence suggests that these programs work the same incitement on adults. And televiolence does more than condition emotion and behavior. It also may attenuate people's sense of reality. Men murdered on the television screen ordinarily spring to life after the episode is over: all death is therefore diminished. A child asked a man last June where he was headed in his car. "To Washington," he said. "Why?" he asked. "To attend the funeral of Senator Kennedy." The child said, "Oh yeah—they shot him again." And such shooting may well condition the manner in which people approach the perplexities of existence. On television the hero too glibly resolves his problems by shooting somebody. The *Gunsmoke* ethos, however, is not necessarily the best way to deal with human or social complexity. It is hardly compatible with any kind of humane or libertarian democracy.

The problem of electronic violence raises difficult questions of prescription as well as of analysis. It would be fatal to restrain artistic exploration and portrayal, even of the most extreme and bitter aspects of human experience. No rational person wants to re-establish a reign of censorship or mobilize new Legions of Decency. Nor is there great gain in making the electronic media scapegoats for propensities which they reflect rather than create—propensities which spring from our history and our hearts.

Yet society retains a certain right of self-defense. Is it inconceivable that the television industry might work out forms of self-restraint? Beyond this, it should be noted that the networks and the stations do *not* own the airwaves; the nation does; and, if the industry cannot restrain itself, the Communications Act offers means, as yet unused, of democratic control.

We have a bad inheritance as far as violence is concerned; and in recent years war and television have given new vitality to the darkest strains in our national psyche. How can we master this horror in our souls before it rushes us on to ultimate disintegration?

There is not a problem of collective guilt, but there is a problem of collective responsibility. Certainly two hundred million Americans did not strike down John Kennedy or Martin Luther King or Robert Kennedy. But two hundred million Americans are plainly responsible for the character of a society that works on deranged men and incites them to depraved acts. There were Lee Harvey Oswalds and James Earl Rays and Sirhan Bishara Sirhans in America in the Thirties—angry, frustrated, alienated, resentful, marginal men in rootless, unstable cities like Dallas and Memphis and Los Angeles. But our society in the Thirties did not stimulate such men to compensate for their own failure by killing leaders the people loved.

Some of the young in their despair have come to feel that the answer to reason is unreason, the answer to violence, more violence; but these only hasten the plunge toward the abyss. The more intelligent disagree. They do not want America to beat its breast and go back to the golf course. *They do want America to recognize its responsibility.* They want us to tell it like it is—to confront the darkness in our past and the darkness in our present. They want us to realize that life is not solid and pre-dictable but infinitely chancy, that violence is not the deviation but the ever-present possibility, that we can therefore never rest in the effort to prevent unreason from rending the skin of civility. They want our leaders to *talk* less about law and order and *do* more about justice.

Perhaps the old in American society might now learn that sanctimony is not a persuasive answer to anguish, and that we never cure ourselves if we deny the existence of a disease. If they learn this, if they face up to the schism in our national tradition, we all will have a better chance of subduing the impulse of destruction and of fulfilling the vision of Lincoln —that noble vision of a serene and decent society, united by bonds of affection and mystic chords of memory, dedicated at last to our highest ideals.

1918—1968: Is the World Safer for Anything?

HENRY STEELE COMMAGER

"The anniversary of Armistice Day should stir us to great exaltation of spirit because of the proud recollection that it was our day, a day above those early days of that never-to-be-forgotten November which lifted the world to the high levels of vision and achievement upon which the great war for democracy and right was fought and won." So wrote the dying Woodrow Wilson on the fifth anniversary of that day which had concluded the war to end war and to make the world safe for democracy.

Surely the world had a right to exult when this greatest and most terrible of wars dragged to its weary end. Militarism had been crushed, aggression frustrated, tyranny ended, injustice rectified, democracy vindicated and peace assured; for now, after centuries of yearning and striving, men of good will had set up a league to preserve peace. No more wars, no more tyranny—mankind had at last sailed into the safe harbors of peace.

Rarely in history have such high hopes been dashed so low, and Wilson added to his tribute the bitter lamentation that the glory of Armistice Day was tarnished by the recollection that "we withdrew into a sullen and selfish isolation which is deeply ignoble . . . cowardly and dishonorable." So we did, but we were not alone in selfishness or dishonor. Even before the guns fell silent over the stricken battlefields of Europe, the great coalition that had won victory had come apart. Russia, defeated and desperate, had plunged into Communism; and the other partners, each with its own fears and ambitions, glared at each other over the conference tables; while Germany, embittered by defeat, plotted vengeance; and the most ancient of empires fell apart. "Authority was dispersed," wrote Winston Churchill, "the world unshackled, the weak became the strong, the sheltered became the aggressive, and a vast fatigue dominated collective action."

Nineteen-eighteen did not usher in the millennium, it ushered in a half century of conflict—turbulence, war, revolution, desolation, and ruin on a scale never before seen or even imagined. It was a half century that leveled more cities, ravaged more countries, subverted more societies, obliterated more of the past, endangered more of the future, cost more lives, and uncovered more savagery than any time since the barbarians swarmed over Western Europe. Ancient nations were overthrown, empires fragmented, principles of law subverted, and traditional standards of morality repudiated. The era which was to have seen the end of war ushered in instead the most terrible of wars, which rose to a climacteric in the most terrible of weapons; the era which was to have seen the triumph of democracy saw instead the triumph of tyranny; the era which was to have witnessed the triumph of science over inveterate ills heard instead the hoofbeats of the Four Horsemen of the Apocalypse.

Once again the blood-dimmed tide was loosed, and the world was sucked into war. Once again the "freedom-loving" nations triumphed; once again men of good will came together to set up a league that would preserve peace; once again major powers were excluded from the new organization—China, Japan, Germany—while those who controlled it used it as a stage on which to indulge their rivalries and voice their grievances. The great powers glared at each other with ceaseless animosity. Soon the hottest of wars was succeeded by the coldest, and we had Robert Frost to remind us that "for destruction ice is also great and would suffice." During the whole quarter century after the fall of Italy, Germany, and Japan, war and violence were continuous: in India and Pakistan, in Israel and the Arab lands, in Greece and Turkey, in Algiers and Tunisia, Hungary and Berlin, Cuba and Haiti, Argentina and Bolivia, the Congo and Nigeria, Laos and Indonesia. If the great powers did not grapple with each other in global wars, they consoled themselves, as it were, with local wars in Korea and Vietnam, and with arming themslves for Armageddon.

How can we explain this long succession of blunders and tragedies almost without parallel in history? How could men whose resolution and courage had triumphed over mortal peril, whose skills and resourcefulness had enabled them to master nature, fail so greatly? They could control the great globe itself, but not themselves; solve infinite problems, but not finite; penetrate to the stars, but neglect the earth on which they stood. Noble in reason they doubtless were, infinite in faculty, like a god in apprehension, but in action more like a dinosaur unable to adapt to an unfamiliar environment than like an angel. The contrast between intellectual talents and social accomplishments seemed to make a mockery of free will; the contrast between expectations and realities threw doubt on the theory of progress.

There were, no doubt, particular and immediate causes for the collapse of order after the first war. That war had bled victors and vanquished to exhaustion; it had killed off potential leaders of the new generation; it had left a heritage of confusion for victors and bitterness for defeated; it had launched Communism in Russia and revolution elsewhere; it had fatally weakened Britain's hold on her empire; it had left Americans baffled and disillusioned and prepared to embrace isolationism.

The Second World War had wasted even more human material, and moral resources than the First, and had shattered, even more violently, the existing pattern of political life. But these are excuses rather than explanations. After all, Europe had been afflicted by previous wars, but had recovered and returned to her traditional position. And after all, the United States had been exempted from the wrath of both the great wars and had emerged from both with her resources unimpaired, yet she too suffered the malaise that afflicted the Old World. We must seek deeper causes for a change in the currents of history so great that it resembles rather a change in the tides of Nature herself. Nor are these hard to find.

First, and most fundamental, among the causes of our malaise is one that we stubbornly refuse to recognize: the emergence of the forgotten, the neglected, the disparaged, the impoverished, the exploited, and the desperate; one-half of the human race came out of the long dusk that hid it from our view and into the bright light of history. Here is not only the greatest revolution of our time but, by almost any test, the greatest revolution since the discovery of America and the shift in the center of gravity from the Mediterranean to the Atlantic and beyond. "The people of Europe," said Woodrow Wilson at the close of the first war, "are in a revolutionary state of mind. They do not believe in the things that have been practiced upon them in the past, and they mean to have new things practiced." That proved to be true of Russia—a truth even Wilson failed to recognize—and it proved even more true of the vast, heaving, turbulent peoples of Asia and Africa.

Stirred by the Wilsonian principle of self-determination after the First World War, and released by the breakup of the great empires and colonial systems after the Second, these peoples threw off their ancient bondage and struck for equality. Now they are determined to close, in a single generation, that gap of centuries which separated them from the peoples of the West—to close it peacefully if that is possible, otherwise through revolution and violence. They are determined to wipe out the century-old inferiority, the exploitation, the bondage which the West imposed upon them; to conquer poverty, ignorance, disease that afflict them disproportionately; and to take their equal place among the nations of the world. No wonder the whole globe is convulsed by this prodigious upheaval. The failure of the West, and particularly of the United States, to understand and cooperate with this revolution is a greater blunder, by far, than the earlier failure of Europe to understand the significance of the American Revolution, or of the West, including the United States, to understand the significance of the Russian Revolution. It is a failure of global dimensions.

This was a revolution of two large continents—three if South America is included—against two smaller. No less ominous, it was a revolution of the colored races against the white. The exploitation, the inferiority, the bondage which the West had imposed upon Asia and Africa was racial as well as geographical. The subjugation of colored peoples by white had gone on for centuries until Europeans, in Old and New Worlds, came to assume that it was part of the cosmic order of things. White Europeans committed genocide against the native races of the Americas in the sixteenth and seventeenth centuries, destroying ancient civilizations, wiping out, by war and disease, perhaps ten millions of Indians—one of the great holocausts of history. White Europeans filled the ranks of labor in the New World by enslaving millions of Africans—a business in which all the civilized nations of Europe engaged. White Europeans invaded Asia, imposed their will on old and proud peoples, and ruled over them with arrogance and violence. Nor was racial exploitation confined to Asia and Africa: It was carried to the New World and flourished for two centuries as slavery and for another as social and economic subjugation.

Here, then, is the second great cause of our current malaise: the racial revolution—a revolution which takes protean form in different countries and continents but has, almost everywhere, two common denominators: the refusal of all colored peoples to wear any longer the badge of inferiority which whites have fastened on them, and the inability of most whites, in American and in Europe, to acknowledge their responsibility and their guilt or to realize that this long chapter of history is coming to an end.

One of the great paradoxes of history is that the revolt of the non-Western world against the West is being carried on with tools and principles fashioned by the West. The tools are science and technology; the principles are those of modern nationalism. Here is a third fundamental explanation of the crisis of our time: the ravages of nationalism. For ours is, indubitably, the great age of nationalism: Within the past quarter century, some sixty nations have been "brought forth" while older nationalism has been given a new lease on life.

In its earlier manifestations—in the eighteenth and early nineteenth centuries—nationalism tended to consolidate, to centralize, to mitigate particularism and parochialism, and to encourage administrative efficiency and cultural unity, especially in the United States, Italy, and Germany. But almost from the beginning—in the Old World and in Spanish America—nationalism stimulated fragmentation along racial, linguistic, and religious lines; almost from the beginning it exacerbated chauvinism, imperialism, and militarism. Whether in the long run the advantages of political efficiency and cultural self-consciousness will outweigh the disadvantages of national antipathies and cultural chauvinism still remains to be decided. But it is difficult to avoid the conclusion that the nationalism of our own time is profoundly dangerous.

Alas, the new nations that have emerged from the disruption of empires have imitated, or adopted, all the worst features of the old. Small, they yearn to be large; weak, they pile up armaments; vulnerable, they seek alliances; insecure, they develop into police states; without political traditions, they hover constantly on the brink of civil war or anarchy; without viable economies, they are dependent on richer neighbors; without cultural unity, they manufacture an artificial culture and impose it by force; striving convulsively to be independent, they become increasingly dependent and threaten the peace of their neighbors and of the world. How many recent crises have been precipitated by their ambitions and quarrels—quarrels exploited, all too often, by the great powers: the crisis of Berlin and East Germany, the recurring crises of Arab-Israeli relations, the crises of Cyprus, of the Congo, Algiers, Nigeria, Rhodesia, the crisis of India and Pakistan, of North and South Korea, of Indonesia and Laos and Vietnam.

These new countries, it will be said, are but following the bad example of the older nations of the West. This is true enough, but with two fateful differences; first, the new nations are committed to ideologies that involve them with fellow believers everywhere and engage them in larger quarrels; and, second, that they are operating in a world shadowed by nuclear clouds.

For the triumph of malevolent over benevolent nationalism, the great powers—and most of all the United States and Russia—bear a heavy responsibility. Far from curbing competitive nationalism, they have abetted it. To the new nations of Asia and Africa they provided lavish military aid —the largest portion of American aid after the war, for example, was military. They interfered high-handedly in the internal affairs of these new nations. They built up networks of alliances designed to bring small nations into the orbit of large; they tried to divide the world into two armed camps with no room for neutralists. Nor did they for a moment curb their own chauvinism, their own commitment to military solutions of world problems, their own traditional nationalism and traditional sovereignty.

Closely related to the revolutionary upsurge of underprivileged peoples and the equally revolutionary impact of the new nationalism was the revolution precipitated by science and technology, and the rising expectations which it nourished. For the first time in history, science and technology seemed to bring the good life within the reach of men and women everywhere—the end of hunger, the wiping out of contagious diseases, the prolongation of life, security from the elements, the preservation and development of natural resources, the pleasures of learning and of the arts. In the twentieth century, it was at least reasonable to hope that the burdens which had for so long afflicted mankind would be lifted.

Once again, expectations were to be disappointed. The gap between what men imagined and what they enjoyed had always been deep; now the gap between what men were taught to expect and what they actually received seemed intolerable. The machinery of life grew ever more elaborate, but the products of that machinery became less and less gratifying. At the end of a generation of unparalleled advance in science and technology, mankind found hunger more widespread, violence more ruthless, and life more insecure than at any time in the century.

Nor was this disappointment confined to the backward peoples of the globe: Even in America, which boasted almost limitless resources and the most advanced technology, poverty was familiar in millions of households, white as well as black; cities decayed, the countryside despoiled, air and streams polluted; lawlessness, official and private, was contagious; and war and the threat of war filled the minds of men with hatred and fear.

The symbol—more than the symbol—of this failure of science to bring expected rewards was the discovery and exploitation of nuclear energy. To release the energy of the atom was assuredly one of the greatest achievements in the history of science, and one that held out possibilities almost limitlessly benign. Instead, the United States and after her, competing powers, concentrated their scientific talents on harnessing atomic energy for war. As Churchill wrote prophetically in 1929: "Without having improved appreciably in virtue or enjoying wiser guidance, mankind has got into its hands for the first time the tools by which it can unfailingly accomplish its own extermination. That is the point in human destinies to which all the glories and toils of men have at last led them." Nor was there any assurance that those who stood at the levers of control would refuse to use these weapons of infinite destruction if they thought their own survival was at stake. After all, Americans had used them in 1945; after all, Americans, Russians, Chinese, and Frenchmen were carrying on continuous experiments to achieve even greater destructive power. And after all, prominent statesmen, not least those in the United States, did not hesitate to shake the raw head and bloody bones of nuclear destruction at intransigent opponents elsewhere on the globe. And if it could be said that only madmen would actually carry out such threats, the inevitable reply was that two madmen, Hitler and Stalin, had fought their way to power in the recent past, and that as yet the resourcefulness of mankind had not devised any way of preventing a repetition of this monstrous situation.

Finally, consider one of the great paradoxes of our day: at the time of the triumph of the experimental method in science, we should abandon it in the realm of politics. Clearly, one of the causes—and one of the manifestations, too—of our malaise is the rejection of the practical, the relative, the organic view of society and politics, and the embrace of the doctrinaire, the absolute, and the static. The substitution of ideological for realistic policies is the hallmark of much of modern political philosophy, but it has not heretofore been characteristic of the American. In the name of doctrinaire notions of Aryan superiority, Hitler was prepared to bring down a Götterdämmerung upon his own country and the world; in the name of doctrinaire Marxism, the Soviet was prepared to subvert all other governments; and in the name of "containment," the United States seems prepared to bustle about the globe putting down subversion and revolution. Our commitment, to be sure, has not been wholehearted; and the almost instinctive distaste of the American people for ideological principles has inspired widespread protest against the new departure. But even as the bankruptcy of the ideological approach to the great convulsive problems of the world becomes clearer, we seem to adopt the same approach to the issues of domestic politics.

There is nothing more implacable than ideological enmities or crusades—witness the religious wars of the sixteenth and seventeenth centuries—and one explanation of the peculiar ferocity of so many of our modern wars, even the American, is the ideological or quasi-religious character. Ordinary rivalries and conflicts involve interests and issues that can be settled by negotiation and compromise. But ideological conflicts are moral, and honorable men find it difficult to compromise on principles or negotiate about morals. Woodrow Wilson had a more doctrinaire mind than Franklin Roosevelt, but Wilson could call for "peace without victory" while Roosevelt insisted on "unconditional surrender."

The three great powers that glare ceaselessly upon each other now, and whose conflicts shake the globe, are all committed to ideological positions which they find difficult to compromise. The leaders of all three nations know—as religious fanatics of the seventeenth century knew—that they are the pure of heart, that their cause is just, that they stand at Armageddon and battle for the Cause. Naturally, all three atempt to rally the smaller nations to their side, to enlist them in their crusades; and all are inclined to believe that those who are not with them are against them. None can tolerate deviation from the true faith. The Russians put down Hungarians and Czechs who transgress the scriptures; the Chinese punish dissenters even at the cost of civil war; the Americans will tolerate deviation in Guatemala or Santo Domingo and in Cuba only because they have succeeded in isolating it.

The ideological approach took over even in the American domestic arena—in politics, race relations, education, and elsewhere. It stigmatized the crusade of Joseph McCarthy against subversives, real or imagined; it sustains the ceaseless zeal of the House Un-American Activities Committee through the years in its search for Communists in government or in the universities; it provides moral fervor to George Wallace's arguments for white supremacy and logic to opponents of open-housing who proclaim that God is white. It characterizes, alike, students who think that the universities are all corrupt and fit only to be burned because they do not instantly involve themselves in current affairs, a Vice Presidential candidate who thinks all demonstrations are pernicious, and Senators who are prepared to subvert the Constitution because Supreme Court judges do not automatically respond to obscenity with moral fervor.

The symptom of ideology is impatience, and its offspring is violence. Those who see the great turbulent issues of politics or law or society in simple terms of right and wrong are impatient with compromise or concession and even with reason. Impatience characterizes much of American life in the second half of the twentieth century: impatience of the young with the old, and of the old with the young; impatience with due process of law; impatience with old ideas rooted in tradition, and with new ideas that lack the authority of tradition; impatience with those who are neutral, and those who are independent; impatience with the machinery of adjudication and arbitration; impatience with any solutions short of utopian.

And with impatience goes violence. This is natural enough: When men no longer believe in reason, when they no longer have confidence in the potentialities of history, they naturally turn to violence for the solution—or the liquidation—of their problems. Russia resorted to violence to get rid of the embarrassment of independence in Czechoslovakia; South Africa resorted to violence to dispose of the awkward fact of the predominantly Negro population; the Arabs have no communications with the Israelis except by acts of violence; the United States elevates aimless violence against Vietnam to a philosophy. The connection between violence and ideology is not fortuitous but consequential.

In all of the great changes and development that have characterized the last half century and condemned it to disorder, the United States has played a prominent part. It shared the failure to appreciate and support the great revolution of the underprivileged peoples; it shared—and indeed exemplified—the subordination of colored peoples to white; it stimulated and supported self-determination after the first war, and the breakup of ancient empires after the second; and did nothing to mitigate the ravages of chauvinistic nationalism. It devoted a major part of its scientific energies to war and the preparation for war, and exalted the role and the power of the military. It embraced an ideological approach to the great problems of international politics and sought to imprison in ideological straitjacket the turbulent tides of history. In most of this Americans departed from their own traditions and betrayed their own character. Is it too much to hope that we will return to our traditions and rediscover our true character?

The Forgotten American

PETER SCHRAG

There is hardly a language to describe him, or even a set of social statistics. Just names: racist-bigot-redneck-ethnic-Irish-Italian-Pole-Hunkie-Yahoo. The lower middle class. A blank. The man under whose hat lies the great American desert. Who watches the tube, plays the horses, and keeps the niggers out of his union and his neighborhood. Who might vote for Wallace (but didn't). Who cheers when the cops beat up on demonstrators. Who is free, white, and twenty-one, has a job, a home, a family, and is up to his eyeballs in credit. In the guise of the working class—or the American yeoman or John Smith—he was once the hero of the civics book, the man that Andrew Jackson called "the bone and sinew of the country." Now he is "the forgotten man," perhaps the most alienated person in America.

Nothing quite fits, except perhaps omission and semi-invisibility. America is supposed to be divided between affluence and poverty, between slums and suburbs. John Kenneth Galbraith begins the foreword to *The Affluent Society* with the phrase, "Since I sailed for Switzerland in the early summer of 1955 to begin work on this book . . ." But *between* slums and suburbs, between Scarsdale and Harlem, between Wellesley and Roxbury, between Shaker Heights and Hough, there are some eighty million people (depending on how you count them) who didn't sail for Switzerland in the summer of 1955, or at any other time, and who never expect to. Between slums and suburbs: South Boston and South San Francisco, Bell and Parma, Astoria and Bay Ridge, Newark, Cicero, Downey, Daly City, Charlestown, Flatbush. Union halls, American Legion posts, neighborhood bars and bowling leagues, the Ukrainian Club and the Holy Name. Main Street. To try to describe all this is like trying to describe America itself. If you look for it, you find it everywhere: the rows of frame houses over-looking the belching steel mills in Bethlehem, Pennsylvania, two-family brick houses in Canarsie (where the most common slogan, even in the middle of a political campaign, is "curb your dog"); the Fords and Chevies with a decal American flag on the rear window (usually a cut-out from the *Reader's Digest,* and displayed in counter-protest against peaceniks and "those bastards who carry Vietcong flags in demonstrations"); the bunting on the porch rail with the inscription, "Welcome Home, Pete." The gold star in the window.

When he was Under Secretary of Housing and Urban Development, Robert C. Wood tried a definition. It is not good, but it's the best we have:

> He is a white employed male . . . earning between $5,000 and $10,000. He works regularly, steadily, dependably, wearing a blue collar or white collar. Yet the frontiers of his career expectations have been fixed since he reached the age of thirty-five, when he found that he had too many obligations, too much family, and too few skills to match opportunities with aspirations.
>
> This definition of the "working American" involves almost 23-million American families.
>
> The working American lives in the gray area fringes of a central city or in a close-in or very far-out cheaper suburban subdivision of a large metropolitan area. He is likely to own a home and a car, especially as his income begins to rise. Of those earning between $6,000 and $7,500, 70 per cent own their own homes and 94 percent drive their own cars.
>
> 94 per cent have no education beyond high school and 43 per cent have only completed the eighth grade.

He does all the right things, obeys the law, goes to church and insists —usually—that his kids get a better education than he had. But the right things don't seem to be paying off. While he is making more than he ever made—perhaps more than he'd ever dreamed—he's still struggling while a lot of others—"them" (on welfare, in demonstrations, in the ghettos) are getting most of the attention. "I'm working my ass off," a guy tells you on a stoop in South Boston. "My kids don't have a place to swim, my parks are full of glass, and I'm supposed to bleed for a bunch of people on relief." In New York a man who drives a Post Office trailer truck at night (4:00 P.M. to midnight) and a cab during the day (7:00 A.M. to 2:00 P.M.), and who hustles radios for his Post Office buddies on the side, is ready, as he says, to "knock somebody's ass." "The colored guys work when they feel like it. Sometimes they show up and sometimes they don't. One guy tore up all the time cards. I'd like to see a white guy do that and get away with it."

WHAT COUNTS

Nobody knows how many people in America moonlight (half of the eighteen million families in the $5,000 to $10,000 bracket have two or more wage earners) or how many have to hustle on the side. "I don't think anybody has a single job anymore," said Nicholas Kisburg, the research director for a Teamsters Union Council in New York. "All the cops are moonlighting, and the teachers; and there's a million guys who are hustling, guys with phony social-security numbers who are hiding part of what they make so they don't get kicked out of a housing project, or guys who work as guards at sports events and get free meals that they don't want to pay taxes on. Every one of them is cheating. They are underground people—*Untermenschen.* . . . We really have no systematic data on any of this. We have no ideas of the attitudes of the white worker. (We've been too busy studying the black worker.) And yet he's the source of most of the reaction in this country."

The reaction is directed at almost every visible target: at integration and welfare, taxes and sex education, at the rich and the poor, the foundations and students, at the "smart people in the suburbs." In New York State the legislature cuts the welfare budget; in Los Angeles, the voters reelect Yorty after a whispered racial campaign against the Negro favorite. In Minneapolis a police detective named Charles Stenvig, promising "to take the handcuffs off the police," wins by a margin stunning even to his supporters: in Massachusetts the voters mail tea bags to their representatives in protest against new taxes, and in state after state legislatures are passing bills to punish student demonstrators. ("We keep talking about permissiveness in training kids," said a Los Angeles labor official, "but we forget that these are our kids.")

And yet all these things are side manifestations of a malaise that lacks a language. Whatever law and order means, for example, to a man who feels his wife is unsafe on the street after dark or in the park at any time, or whose kids get shaken down in the school yard, it also means something like normality—the demand that everybody play it by the book, that cultural and social standards be somehow restored to their civics-book simplicity, that things shouldn't be as they are but as they were supposed to be. If there is a revolution in this country—a revolt in manners, standards of dress and obscenity, and, more importantly, in our official sense of what America is—there is also a counter-revolt. Sometimes it is inarticulate, and sometimes (perhaps most of the time) people are either too confused or apathetic—or simply too polite and too decent—to declare themselves. In Astoria, Queens, a white working-class district of New York, people who make $7,000 or $8,000 a year (sometimes in two jobs) call themselves affluent, even though the Bureau of Labor Statistics regards an income of less than $9,500 in New York inadequate to a moderate standard of living. And in a similar neighborhood in Brooklyn a truck driver who earns $151 a week tells you he's doing well, living in a two-story frame house separated by a narrow driveway from similar houses, thousands of them in block after block. This year, for the first time, he will go on a cruise—he and his wife and two other couples—two weeks in the Caribbean. He went to work after World War II ($57 a week) and he has lived in the same house for twenty years, accumulating two television sets, wall-to-wall carpeting in a small living room, and a basement that he recently remodeled into a recreation room with the help of two moonlighting firemen. "We get fairly good salaries, and this is a good neighborhood, one of the few good ones left. We have no smoked Irishmen around."

Stability is what counts, stability in job and home and neighborhood, stability in the church and in friends. At night you watch television and sometimes on a weekend you go to a nice place—maybe a downtown hotel—for dinner with another couple. (Or maybe your sister, or maybe bowling, or maybe, if you're defeated, a night at the track.) The wife has the necessary appliances, often still being paid off, and the money you save goes for your daughter's orthodontist, and later for her wedding. The smoked Irishmen—the colored (no one says black; few even say Negro)—represent change and instability, kids who cause trouble in school, who get treatment that your kids never got, that you never got. ("Those fucking kids," they tell you in South Boston, "raising hell, and not one of 'em paying his own way. Their fucking mothers are all on welfare.") The black kids mean a change in the rules, a double standard in grades and discipline, and—vaguely—a challenge to all you believed right. Law and order is the stability and predictability of established ways. Law and order is equal treatment—in school, in jobs, in the courts—even if you're cheating a little yourself. The Forgotten Man is Jackson's man. He is the vestigial American democrat of 1840: "They all know that their success depends upon their own industry and economy and that they must not expect to become suddenly rich by the fruits of their toil." He is also Franklin Roosevelt's man—the man whose vote (or whose father's vote) sustained the New Deal.

There are other considerations, other styles, other problems. A postman in a Charlestown (Boston) housing project: eight children and a ninth on the way. Last year, by working overtime, his income went over $7,000. This year, because he reported it, the Housing Authority is raising his rent from $78 to $106 a month, a catastrophe for a family that pays $2.20 a day for milk, has never had a vacation, and for which an excursion is "going out for ice cream." "You try and save for something better; we hope to get out of here to someplace where the kids can play, where there's no broken glass, and then something always comes along that knocks you right back. It's like being at the bottom of the well waiting for a guy to throw you a rope." The description becomes almost Chaplinesque. Life is humble but not simple; the terrors of insolent bureaucracies and contemptuous officials produce a demonology that loses little of its horror for being partly misunderstood. You want to get a sink fixed but don't want to offend the manager; want to get an eye operation that may (or may not) have been necessitated by a military injury five years earlier, "but the Veterans Administration says I signed away my benefits"; want to complain to someone about the teen-agers who run around breaking windows and harassing women but get no response either from the management or the police. "You're afraid to complain because if they don't get you during the day they'll get you at night." Automobiles, windows, children, all become hostages to the vague terrors of everyday life; everything is vulnerable. Liabilities that began long ago cannot possibly be liquidated: "I never learned anything in that school except how to fight. I got tired of being caned by the teachers so at sixteen I quit and joined the Marines. I still don't know anything."

AT THE BOTTOM
OF THE WELL

American culture? Wealth is visible, and so, now, is poverty. Both have become intimidating clichés. But the rest? A vast, complex, and disregarded world that was once—in belief, and in fact—the American middle: Greyhound and Trailways bus terminals in little cities at midnight, each of them with its neon lights and its cardboard hamburgers; acres of tarpaper beach bungalows in places like Revere and Rockaway; the hair curlers in the supermarket on Saturday, and the little girls in the communion dresses the next morning; pinball machines and the *Daily News,* the *Reader's Digest* and Ed Sullivan; houses with tiny front lawns (or even large ones) adorned with statues of the Virgin or of Sambo welcomin' de folks home; Clint Eastwood or Julie Andrews at the Palace; the trotting tracks and the dog tracks—Aurora Downs, Connaught Park, Roosevelt, Yonkers, Rockingham, and forty others—where gray men come not for sport and beauty, but to read numbers, to study and dope. (If you win you have figured something, have in a small way controlled your world, have surmounted your impotence. If you lose, bad luck, shit. "I'll break his goddamned head.") Baseball is not the national pastime; racing is. For every man who goes to a major-league baseball game there are four who go to the track and probably four more who go to the candy store or the barbershop to make their bets. (Total track attendance in 1965: 62 million plus another 10 million who went to the dogs.)

There are places, and styles, and attitudes. If there are neighborhoods of aspiration, suburban enclaves for the mobile young executive and the aspiring worker, there are also places of limited expectation and dead-end districts where mobility is finished. But even there you can often find, however vestigial, a sense of place, the roots of old ethnic loyalties, and a passionate, if often futile, battle against intrusion and change. "Everybody around here," you are told, "pays his own way." In this world the problems are not the ABM or air pollution (have they heard of Biafra?) or the international population crisis; the problem is to get your street cleaned, your garbage collected, to get your husband home from Vietnam alive; to negotiate installment payments and to keep the schools orderly. Ask anyone in Scarsdale or Winnetka about the schools and they'll tell you about new programs, or about how many are getting into Harvard, or about the teachers; ask in Oakland or the North Side of Chicago, and they'll tell you that they have (or haven't) had trouble. Somewhere in his gut the man in those communities knows that mobility and choice in this society are limited. He cannot imagine any major change for the better; but he can imagine change for the worse. And yet for a decade he is the one who has been asked to carry the burden of social reform, to integrate his schools and his neighborhood, has been asked by comfortable people to pay the social debts due to the poor and the black. In Boston, in San Francisco, in Chicago (not to mention Newark or Oakland) he has been telling the reformers to go to hell. The Jewish schoolteachers of New York and the Irish parents of Dorchester have asked the same question: "What the hell did Lindsay (or the Beacon Hill Establishment) ever do for us?"

The ambiguities and changes in American life that occupy discussions in university seminars and policy debates in Washington, and that form the backbone of contemporary popular sociology, become increasingly the conditions of trauma and frustration in the middle. Although the New Frontier and Great Society contained some programs for those not already on the rolls of social pathology—federal aid for higher education, for example—the public priorities and the rhetoric contained little. The emphasis, properly, was on the poor, on the inner cities (*e.g.,* Negroes) and the unemployed. But in Chicago a widow with three children who earns $7,000 a year can't get them college loans because she makes too much; the money is reserved for people on relief. New schools are built in the ghetto but not in the white working-class neighborhoods where they are just as dilapidated. In Newark the head of a white vigilante group (now a city councilman) runs, among other things, on a platform opposing pro-Negro discrimination. "When pools are being built in the Central Ward—don't they think white kids have got frustration? The white can't get a job; we have to hire Negroes first." The middle class, said Congressman Roman Pucinski of Illinois, who represents a lot of it, "is in revolt. Everyone has been generous in supporting anti-poverty. Now the middle-class American is disqualified from most of the programs."

"SOMEBODY HAS TO SAY NO . . ."

The frustrated middle. The liberal wisdom about welfare, ghettos, student revolt, and Vietnam has only a marginal place, if any, for the values and life of the working man. It flies in the face of most of what he was taught to cherish and respect: hard work, order, authority, self-reliance. He fought, either alone or through labor organizations, to establish the precincts he now considers his own. Union seniority, the civil-service bureaucracy, and the petty professionalism established by the merit system in the public schools become sinecures of particular ethnic groups or of those who have learned to negotiate and master the system. A man who worked all his life to accumulate the points and grades and paraphernalia to become an assistant school principal (no matter how silly the requirements) is not likely to relinquish his position with equanimity. Nor is a dock worker whose only estate is his longshoreman's card. The job, the points, the credits become property:

> Some men leave their sons money [wrote a union member to the *New York Times*], some large investments, some business connections, and some a profession. I have only one worthwhile thing to give: my trade. I hope to follow a centuries-old tradition and sponsor my sons for an apprenticeship. For this simple father's wish it is said that I discriminate against Negroes. Don't all of us discriminate? Which of us . . . will not choose a son over all others?

Suddenly the rules are changing—all the rules. If you protect your job for your own you may be called a bigot. At the same time it's perfectly acceptable to shout black power and to endorse it. What does it take to be a good American? *Give the black man a position because he is black, not because he necessarily works harder or does the job better.* What does it take to be a good American? Dress nicely, hold a job, be clean-cut, don't judge a man by the color of his skin or the country of his origin. What about the demands of Negroes, the long hair of the students, the dirty movies, the people who burn draft cards and American flags? Do you have to go out in the street with picket signs, do you have to burn the place down to get what you want? What does it take to be a good American? *This is a sick society, a racist society, we are fighting an immoral war.* ("I'm against the Vietnam war, too," says the truck driver in Brooklyn. "I see a good kid come home with half an arm and a leg in a brace up to here, and what's it all for? I was glad to see *my kid* flunk the Army physical. Still, somebody has to say no to these demonstrators and enforce the law.") What does it take to be a good American?

The conditions of trauma and frustration in the middle. What does it take to be a good American? Suddenly there are demands for Italian power and Polish power and Ukrainian power. In Cleveland the Poles demand a seat on the school board, and get it, and in Pittsburgh John Pankuch, the seventy-three-year-old president of the National Slovak Society demands "action, plenty of it to make up for lost time." Black power is supposed to be nothing but emulation of the ways in which other ethnic groups made it. But have they made it? In Reardon's Bar on East Eighth Street in South Boston, where the workmen come for their fish-chowder lunch and for their rye and ginger, they still identify themselves as Galway men and Kilkenny men; in the newsstand in Astoria you can buy *Il Progresso, El Tiempo,* the *Staats-Zeitung,* the *Irish World,* plus papers in Greek, Hungarian, and Polish. At the parish of Our Lady of Mount Carmel the priests hear confession in English, Italian, and Spanish and, nearby, the biggest attraction is not the stickball game, but the *bocce* court. Some of the poorest people in America are white, native, and have lived all of their lives in the same place as their fathers and grandfathers. The problems that were presumably solved in some distant past, in that prehistoric era before the textbooks were written—problems of assimilation, of upward mobility—now turn out to be very much unsolved. The melting pot and all: millions made it, millions moved to the affluent suburbs; several million—no one knows how many—did not. The median income in Irish South Boston is $5,100 a year but the community-action workers have a hard time convincing the local citizens that any white man who is not stupid or irresponsible can be poor. Pride still keeps them from applying for income supplements or Medicaid, but it does not keep them from resenting those who do. In Pittsburgh, where the members of Polish-American organizations earn an estimated $5,000 to $6,000 (and some fall below the poverty line), the Poverty Programs are nonetheless directed primarily to Negroes, and almost everywhere the thing called urban backlash associates itself in some fashion with ethnic groups whose members have themselves only a precarious hold on the security of affluence. Almost everywhere in the old cities, tribal neighborhoods and their styles are under assault by masscult. The Italian grocery gives way to the supermarket, the ma-and-pa store and the walk-up are attacked by urban renewal. And almost everywhere, that assault tends to depersonalize and to alienate. It has always been this way, but with time the brave new world that replaces old patterns becomes increasingly bureaucratized, distant, and hard to control.

Yet beyond the problems of ethnic identity, beyond the problems of Poles and Irishmen left behind, there are others more pervasive and more dangerous. For every Greek or Hungarian there are a dozen American-Americans who are past ethnic consciousness and who are as alienated, as confused, and as angry as the rest. The obvious manifestations are the same everywhere—race, taxes, welfare, students—but the threat seems invariably more cultural and psychological than economic or social. What upset the police at the Chicago convention most was not so much the politics of the demonstrators as their manners and their hair. (The barbershops in their neighborhoods don't advertise Beatle Cuts but the Flat Top and the Chicago Box.) The affront comes from middle-class people—and their children—who had been cast in the role of social exemplars (and from those cast as unfortunates worthy of public charity) who offend all the things on which working class identity is built: "hippies [said a San Francisco longshoreman] who fart around the streets and don't work"; welfare recipients who strike and march for better treatment; "all those [said a California labor official] who challenge the precepts that these people live on." If ethnic groups are beginning to organize to get theirs, so are others: police and firemen ("The cop is the new nigger"); schoolteachers; lower-middle-class housewives fighting sex education and bussing; small property owners who have no ethnic communion but a passionate interest in lower taxes, more policemen, and stiffer penalties for criminals. In San Francisco the Teamsters, who had never been known for such interests before, recently demonstrated in support of the police and law enforcement and, on another occasion, joined a group called Mothers Support Neighborhood Schools at a school-board meeting to oppose—with their presence and later, apparently, with their fists—a proposal to integrate the schools through bussing. ("These people," someone said at the meeting, "do not look like mothers.")

Which is not to say that all is frustration and anger, that anybody is ready "to burn the country down." They are not even ready to elect standard model demagogues. "A lot of labor people who thought of voting for Wallace were ashamed of themselves when they realized what they were about to do," said Morris Iushewitz, an officer of New York's Central Labor Council. Because of a massive last-minute union campaign, and perhaps for other reasons, the blue-collar vote for Wallace fell far below the figures predicted by the early polls last fall. Any number of people, moreover, who are not doing well by any set of official statistics, who are earning well below the national mean ($8,000 a year), or who hold two jobs to stay above it, think of themselves as affluent, and often use that word. It is almost as if not to be affluent is to be un-American. People who can't use the word tend to be angry; people who come too close to those who can't become frightened. The definition of affluence is generally pinned to what comes in, not to the equality of life as it's lived. The $8,000 son of a man who never earned more that $4,500 may, for that reason alone, believe that he's "doing all right." If life is not all right, if he can't get his curbs fixed, or his streets patrolled, if the highways are crowded and the beaches polluted, if the schools are ineffectual he is still able to call himself affluent, feels, perhaps, a social compulsion to do so. His anger, if he is angry, is not that of the wage earner resenting management—and certainly not that of the socialist ideologue asking for redistribution of wealth—but that of the consumer, the taxpayer, and the family man. (Inflation and taxes are wiping out most of the wage gains made in labor contracts signed during the past three years.) Thus he will vote for a Louise Day Hicks in Boston who promises to hold the color line in the schools or for a Charles Stenvig calling for law enforcement in Minneapolis but reject a George Wallace who seems to threaten his pocketbook. The danger is that he will identify with the politics of the Birchers and other middle-class reactionaries (who often pretend to speak for him) even though his income and style of life are far removed from theirs; that taxes, for example, will be identified with welfare rather than war, and that he will blame his limited means on the small slice of the poor rather than the fat slice of the rich.

If you sit and talk to people like Marjorie Lemlow, who heads Mothers Support Neighborhood Schools in San Francisco, or Joe Owens, a house painter who is president of a community-action organization in Boston, you quickly discover that the roots of reaction and the roots of reform are often identical, and that the response to particular situations is more often contingent on the politics of the politicians and leaders who appear to care than on the conditions of life or the ideology of the victims. Mrs. Lemlow wants to return the schools to some virtuous past; she worries about disintegration of the family and she speaks vaguely about something that she can't bring herself to call a conspiracy against Americanism. She has been accused of leading a bunch of Birchers, and she sometimes talks Birch language. But whatever the form, her sense of things comes from a small-town vision of national virtues, and her unhappiness from the assaults of urban sophistication. It just so happens that a lot of reactionaries now sing that tune, and that the liberals are indifferent.

Joe Owens—probably because of his experience as a Head Start parent, and because of his association with an effective community-action program—talks a different language. He knows, somehow, that no simple past can be restored. In his world the villains are not conspirators but bureaucrats and politicians, and he is beginning to discover that in a struggle with officials the black man in the ghetto and the working man (black or white) have the same problems. "Every time you ask for something from the politicians they treat you like a beggar, like you ought to be grateful for what you have. They try to make you feel ashamed."

WHEN HOPE
BECOMES
A THREAT

The imponderables are youth and tradition and change. The civics book and the institution it celebrates—however passé—still hold the world together. The revolt is in their name, not against them. And there is simple decency, the language and practice of the folksy cliché, the small town, the Boy Scout virtues, the neighborhood charity, the obligation to support the church, the rhetoric of open opportunity: "They can keep Wallace and they can keep Alabama. We didn't fight a dictator for four years so we could elect one over here." What happens when all that becomes Mickey Mouse? Is there an urban ethic to replace the values of the small town? Is there a coherent public philosophy, a consistent set of beliefs to replace family, home, and hard work? What happens when the hang-ups of upper-middle-class kids are in fashion and those of blue-collar kids are not? What happens when Doing Your Own Thing becomes not the slogan of the solitary deviant but the norm? Is it possible that as the institutions and beliefs of tradition are fashionably denigrated a blue-collar generation gap will open to the Right as well as to the Left? (There is statistical evidence, for example, that Wallace's greatest support within the unions came from people who are between twenty-one and twenty-nine, those, that is, who have the most tenuous association with the liberalism of labor.) Most are politically silent; although SDS has been trying to organize blue-collar high-school students, there are no Mario Savios or Mark Rudds—either of the Right or the Left—among them. At the same time the union leaders, some of them old hands from the Thirties, aren't sure that the kids are following them either. Who speaks for the son of the longshoreman or the Detroit auto worker? What happens if he doesn't get to college? What, indeed, happens when he does?

Vaguely but unmistakably the hopes that a youth-worshiping nation historically invested in its young are becoming threats. We have never been unequivocal about the symbolic patricide of Americanization and upward mobility, but if at one time mobility meant rejection of older (or European) styles it was, at least, done in the name of America. Now the labels are blurred and the objectives indistinct. Just at the moment when a tradition-bound Italian father is persuaded that he should send his sons to college—that education is the only future—the college blows up. At the moment when a parsimonious taxpayer begins to shell out for what he considers an extravagant state university system the students go on strike. Marijuana, sexual liberation, dress styles, draft resistance, even the rhetoric of change become monsters and demons in a world that appears to turn old virtues upside down. The paranoia that fastened on Communism twenty years ago (and sometimes still does) is increasingly directed to vague conspiracies undermining the schools, the family, order and discipline. "They're feeding the kids this generation-gap business," says a Chicago housewife who grinds out a campaign against sex education on a duplicating machine in her living room. "The kids are told to make their own decisions. They're all mixed up by situation ethics and open-ended questions. They're alienating children from their own parents." They? The churches, the schools, even the YMCA and the Girl Scouts, are implicated. But a major share of the villainy is now also attributed to "the social science centers," to the apostles of sensitivity training, and to what one California lady, with some embarrassment, called "nude therapy." "People with sane minds are being altered by psychological methods." The current major campaign of the John Birch Society is not directed against Communists in government or the Supreme Court, but against sex education.

(There is, of course, also sympathy with the young, especially in poorer areas where kids have no place to play. "Everybody's got to have a hobby," a South Boston adolescent told a youth worker. "Ours is throwing rocks." If people will join reactionary organizations to protect their children, they will also support others: community-action agencies which help kids get jobs; Head Start parent groups, Boys Clubs. "Getting this place cleaned up" sometimes refers to a fear of young hoods; sometimes it points to the day when there is a park or a playground or when the existing park can be used. "I want to see them grow up to have a little fun.")

CAN THE COMMON MAN COME BACK?

Beneath it all there is a more fundamental ambivalence, not only about the young, but about institutions—the schools, the churches, the Establishment—and about the future itself. In the major cities of the East (though perhaps not in the West) there is a sense that time is against you, that one is living "in one of the few decent neighborhoods left," that "if I can get $125 a week upstate (or downstate) I'll move." The institutions that were supposed to mediate social change and which, more than ever, are

becoming priesthoods of information and conglomerates of social engineers, are increasingly suspect. To attack the Ford Foundation (as Wright
Patman has done) is not only to fan the embers of historic populism
against concentrations of wealth and power, but also to arouse those who
feel that they are trapped by an alliance of upper-class Wasps and lower-
class Negroes. If the foundations have done anything for the blue-collar
worker he doesn't seem to be aware of it. At the same time the distrust of
professional educators that characterizes the black militants is becoming
increasingly prevalent among the minority of lower-middle-class whites
who are beginning to discover that the schools aren't working for them
either. ("Are all those new programs just a cover-up for failure?") And if
the Catholic Church is under attack from its liberal members (on birth
control, for example) it is also alienating the traditionalists who liked their
minor saints (even if they didn't actually exist) and were perfectly content
with the Latin Mass. For the alienated Catholic liberal there are other
places to go; for the lower-middle-class parishioner in Chicago or Boston
there are none.

Perhaps, in some measure, it has always been this way. Perhaps none
of this is new. And perhaps it is also true that the American lower middle
has never had it so good. And yet surely there is a difference, and that
is that the common man has lost his visibility and, somehow, his claim on
public attention. There are old liberals and socialists—men like Michael
Harrington—who believe that a new alliance can be forged for progressive
social action:

> From Marx to Mills, the Left has regarded the middle class as a
> stratum of hypocritical, vacillating rear-guarders. There was often
> sound reason for this contempt. But is it not possible that a new class is
> coming into being? It is not the old middle class of small property
> owners and entrepreneurs, nor the new middle class of managers. It is
> composed of scientists, technicians, teachers, and professionals in the
> public sector of the society. By education and work experience it is
> predisposed toward planning. It could be an ally of the poor and the
> organized workers—or their sophisticated enemy. In other words, an
> unprecedented social and political variable seems to be taking shape
> in America.

> The American worker, even when he waits on a table or holds open
> a door, is not servile; he does not carry himself like an inferior. The
> openness, frankness, and democratic manner which Tocqueville de-
> scribed in the last century persists to this very day. They have been a
> source of rudeness, contemptuous ignorance, violence—and of a cre-
> ative self-confidence among great masses of people. It was in this latter
> spirit that the CIO was organized and the black freedom movement
> marched.

There are recent indications that the white lower middle class is coming back on the roster of public priorities. Pucinski tells you that liberals
in Congress are privately discussing the pressure from the middle class.

There are proposals now to increase personal income-tax exemptions from $600 to $1,000 (or $1,200) for each dependent, to protect all Americans with a national insurance system covering catastrophic medical expenses, and to put a floor under all incomes. Yet these things by themselves are insufficient. Nothing is sufficient without a national sense of restoration. What Pucinski means by the middle class has, in some measure, always been represented. A physician earning $75,000 a year is also a working man but he is hardly a victim of the welfare system. Nor, by and large, are the stockholders of the Standard Oil Company or U.S. Steel. The fact that American ideals have often been corrupted in the cause of self-aggrandizement does not make them any less important for the cause of social reform and justice. "As a movement with the conviction that there is more to people than greed and fear," Harrington said, "the Left must . . . also speak in the name of the historic idealism of the United States."

The issue, finally, is not *the program* but the vision, the angle of view. A huge constituency may be coming up for grabs, and there is considerable evidence that its political mobility is more sensitive than anyone can imagine, that all the sociological determinants are not as significant as the simple facts of concern and leadership. When Robert Kennedy was killed last year, thousands of working-class people who had expected to vote for him—if not hundreds of thousands—shifted their loyalties to Wallace. A man who can change from a progressive democrat into a bigot overnight deserves attention.

Should I Assume America is Already Dead?

SEYMOUR KRIM

I don't know Abbie Hoffman but I know the people around him: Jerry Rubin (whom I had just met that day, small, beaded, self-possessed and distant when I made one of the futile nominating speeches for his vice presidency at the 1968 N.Y. Peace & Freedom Party Convention on the basis of his intelligence as shown in the underground press): John Wilcock, Ed Sanders, Tuli Kupferberg, and Paul Krassner. They are all writers, radicals, activists, and all have very quick and creative minds. But when I say they are writers I should qualify that and say WORDMEN, because the self-imposed isolation of writing as opposed to performing in public, doing Their Thing before an audience they can actually see responding to them, has come to seem like what Abbie would call "masochistic theatre."

Why jerk yourself off when you can ball? I can hear John or perhaps Ed say. Why artificially lock yourself up in a room when the action is out on the unpredictable and chance-ridden streets? Why sanctify the written word when it grows stale by the time you put it down (let alone get it printed) compared to the immediacy of the spoken one? I have to except Wilcock from this generalization, of course, because he is all journalist, possibly a great one, certainly the most independent and consistent underground newspaperman of my own generation, in spite of occasional crank infatuations. But even John's use of words is impatient, immediate, functional; I know he is suspicious of "writing" and wants a style as close to speech as he can get it, and, since I am involved in the human gamble of trying to have an impact on events through the use of written language at the intensity of art, I find John's work utilitarian rather than ultimate. It is excellent to its purpose but not memorable: my obsession is for a para-journalism that combines soul and straight fact in such a way that the reader is challenged, persuaded, invaded, and literally powered into positioning himself in relation to the new future that the act of writing has just created.

In other words, in this time of increasingly direct action, I am still trying desperately to hang on to my faith in the written word, make it highly contemporary, see where it differs from the spoken word (the latter perceived through the ear and gesture while the written word uses that great organ, the eye, as well as the invisible ear), and I am shaken by Abbie Hoffman's fascinating handbook of Yippie survival tactics, *Revolution for the Hell of It,* where he says flatly that "words are horseshit." "Action," he tells me, "is the only reality; not only reality, but morality as well." How, I ask myself, do Tuli Kupferberg and Ed Sanders relate to this concept when they began as poets with a deep involvement in language (Sanders in particular, as opposed to Tuli's dry and knifing wit, has already added to our language with his "grope" imagery and all the squack-squarf-poons-comp animal wildness that went into *Fuck You*/A Magazine of the Arts) and now seem more than willing to subordinate it to the musical action of their rock group, The Fugs? Yes, I know, Sanders talks and freaks his verbal vision on stage and both of them write lyrics—"Kill for Peace," etc., now apparently offered as pop poetry in *The Fugs' Songbook*—which communicate a definite anarchistic point of view that supplements the work they were doing when they wrote words on paper for the eye; but the necessary theatricality of their being rebel ENTERTAINERS doesn't allow them to explore this language for its own sake. A song has built-in limitations and the lyric is only part of the experience; how do they rationalize their dream as poets by putting these words only into half-action? The answer is probably that they need a participating audience at almost any price, the problem of all serious modern writing, but the cost is high and disturbing when writers themselves think of print as prison and

Al Jolson replaces Dylan Thomas as an example of genuine communication.

I will get back to Abbie in a moment, since his brand of nonverbal activism (and yet to add to the paradox he has gone and written a book with words to give credence to his ideology!) seems to me central to what's happening out on those streets of the imagination, but in the privacy of my own mind I am sorely troubled by the downgrading of the written word on the part of writers-turned-activists. To be frank about it, I think it represents a turning away from everything that literature is supposed to have embodied and the implications of the "uselessness" of the written word cut deeply into my own existence.

My conscious life, and I'm now a month shy of being 47, has been bound up with that printed word from the beginning; and since I came of spiritual age in the late thirties, when the American novel was the most vital creative outpouring in this culture, I identified every hope of my own being with prose, and now I'm stuck with it in a revolutionary time (in every sense) where TV, film, new theatre, and the climax of all these dynamic visual forms, "body confrontation"—the very physical presence of the living man—seems to be of much more reality to the radical leadership of the new generation than the abstractions of written language. But I have a deeply vested interest riding here, not only for me but for every writer my own age, and out of that total investment I have tried to match the needs of action by putting my own body and being in the way of the reader by means of gut commitment right before his eyes; I have tried to be physical in my work at least, if not out on those mythic streets, and if I continue to write prose (and what choice do I have after 25 years if only to maintain my identity, make a living, collect some of the ego-dues I think are legitimately owed me because of risks far beyond the call of expediency?) I want to increase my involvement with each word so that the person on the other end KNOWS he is undergoing an experience and hardly an abstraction at all.

I say all of this to show that not only Abbie but the present writer and hundreds like him are enormously sensitive to the irrelevance, right now, of what we used to call "literary writing" as opposed to survival expression; and I mean that last phrase in every sense, running from one's craft to one's life—they are all the same. The communication of our day that will truly reach others has to come out of the abyss where men and women are struggling for their sense of purpose and the existential reality of the instruments they use, like the written word, or it will be communication from another age. But Abbie and his team are so tuned in to sensations, trips, the notion that "fantasy is the only truth," that I wonder if a writer like me is assumed to be a heavy fool for taking the pains to try and tell the truth about himself in a literal way as a means of establishing contact; and then getting something going, in the sense that the artistic authenticity of his statement (or lack of it), is the measure of what will happen to it as an act in society that has to be reacted to.

But of what value is my goddamn theory and my practice, I have to ask myself, when a generation of PRINCIPLED nonreaders like Abbie (if I can trust what he tells me) couldn't care less? Of course the answer must be that I will continue to do this private brand of communications work if only for myself, to keep my own record straight no matter if I have no other readers but my own pair of eyes when I pick up a pencil to edit what I have written. But even my limited confidence has been damaged, frankly, by the thought that I might be pounding my typewriter, my being, in a void when the people I want to reach out to (and I would like to get a word-relationship going with everyone, but as a man being borne forward on a collision course with death I would also very much like to hold the young out of such middle-aged weakness as wanting "to count" and being "important") are more involved in motherfucking, defying, getting terrorist kicks, getting their heads smacked, jamming the radio rather than receiving, the entire noisy apocalypse described by Abbie this way: "When you're involved you don't get paranoid. In a riot I know exactly what to do."

Abbie's generation, or let's say the generational view that he brings to a sharp zinging point (since at 31 he's considered "old" I've been told), is geared to visible action in a way that my literary generation never was; I came of age after the Communist zenith in this country had already passed and given us writing that was inferior, using the most generous standards, to the work produced by the more complex, Trotskyite-socialist group that clustered around the *Partisan Review,* and which was not afraid of being ambivalent, ambiguous, plunging into the entire mess of themselves and the world without easy answers. I nevertheless broke with the cerebral style of the *PR-Commentary* crowd a decade ago because I couldn't move in every important sense under its insulated intellectual netting and got turned on to my own particular motorcycle of word-action via the well-caricatured Beat Generation. As I turn around and look back from the rush of the present activism—the making of new history that has me backed against the wall of myself, especially the values raised by Abbie's book—I see the Beats as the primitive or at least unsophisticated center of radical energy for so much that has come to threatening full flower now; the personal anarchism toward "the Establishment" (let's sink that word!), the white nigger conspicuousness as a result of long hair and short bread, panhandling, dope, concern with the East, communes, new dress, so much that has now become a casual reality for what Abbie calls "the St. Marx (Pl.) dropouts."

But through all of this transition in America from Beats to Yippies, one man's concern (this one's) was not so much with outward change but the liberation within that could allow him to say his say with more freedom, openness, fullness, and depth—with no taboos or hangups as to subject matter, using confession when necessary, new and more vivid imagery, even a more "religious" personal-journey tone without being accused (as I often was in pre-Beat days) of narcissism and solipsism. What I am saying is that the explosion that has been set off now, and I feel that its momentum is going to travel through the seventies without letup, was, in its beginnings, part of my Beat second life, and perhaps that's why I'm so conscious of it and so equally conscious of my own double view toward it: the fact that I'm not a wholehearted member (as in a broad sense are John and Tuli, neither kids, with perhaps Paul Goodman as a foster father and Allen Ginsberg, Tim Leary, Bill Burroughs, etc., as parent figures) and the obvious reality that I'm worried about my own future as writer-man in relation to this sweeping emphasis on life-action instead of word-action. Or, to take Abbie very seriously in this context, the new need to be an "artist" (as he legitimately calls himself) out in public, to be an artist in the flesh, to make the Word flesh without hiding indoors behind a machine but "wearing a flower in your fist"—like Abbie.

The fresh chutzpah and flair of his stance impresses me so much that I feel I have to justify my own indoor years and say to myself and to him that I, too, have wanted to put my life on the line almost as a way of re-deeming the idea of LITERATURE from aimlessness and shrinkage into the second-rate; just as I have always backed off from the temptation of writing "fiction" and possibly making a nice score because the form seemed to me too easy, riskless, evading my equivalent of the street reality, no "body confrontation," no blood, challenge, embarrassment, pain, exposure—in other words, none of the danger that is the very name of experience today. I might have been wrong in that decision, and it may very well have come (as young writers have told me) from a restricted idea of what a novel, or a post-novel, can be; but at least by my own standards of significance I have never succumbed to a less real "fiction" when I could dramatize the area of fact I had lived through and which might have a direct effect on other beings who enter into a trust with me when they read my words. I say this not to boast, for I have nothing to boast about in the mood that is upon me now, but to show that writers can risk their skins in their own way as much as brave young men like Abbie and Rubin who lie down in front of National Guard tanks, face the House UnAmerican Activities Committee dressed like Revolutionary War soldiers or clothed in the American flag; or like the pig-bearers who broke up a pro-Humphrey meeting in 1968 by bearing that animal's head upon a plate in simple nakedness and knocking the liberal wind out of such a self-righteous type as Shelley Winters, who was shocked all the way to the bank, as they say. I don't see such actions as "crude and childish"— as I've heard them put down in the so-called mature literary-intellectual community—but rather as a unique combination of political imagination and courage. Living Revolutionary Theatre, that's the name of Abbie's game, and it's a thousand times less melancholy, grim, overserious, hungup on warts and decimal points of being, introspective, the whole bad bag of Self, than my own (and my generation's) microscopic inspec-tion of experience has been.

It's a relief for someone like me to swing and cheer with Abbie's clear and uncomplicated prose—he has no need to impress because he thinks words are no important things and uses them to tell succinctly where he's at, which is everywhere ("I am the Revolution") at once—and it gives my heart a great lift by making reality both a simpler and more potentially rewarding place than I have known it. Dear Ankey, Beverly, Peter, Willie, Weldon, Rhoda, all my dead tormented suicide friends, couldn't you have waited to read Abbie and gotten the tonic injection that I have gotten? Were you all in error to have found your lives hell when you could just as well have found them great—"One learns reality is only a subjective experience," says Abbie confidently, "it exists in my head"—and now you've paid for a downbeat view WHEN IT COULD JUST AS WELL HAVE BEEN THE OTHER?

Yes, possibly, hopefully, but that well-known voice within, a nagging voice which I don't want to hear, says, "But is Abbie's view reality as you have known it, is this existential gaiety about 'fucking the system,' owning the streets, balling on roofs, seeing visions of Bob Dylan in treetops, the so-called politics of ecstacy, is this the real thing for you?" The answer that comes back, that I don't particularly want (who wants difficulty above pleasure?) is no, not for me, much as I'd like to think in this technicolor cartoon-strip style, it doesn't do justice to the thousand stubby details of being alive which have always been a fascination to me even when they were painful. Abbie wipes them out too blithely (but what a fine, defiant wipeout against life's invalidism!) with his new moral and tactical short cuts which make short shrift of layers of experience that preoccupy less glamorous people. For example, he convincingly tells me why the Old Left is "shitting in its pants" (because they don't understand the simultaneous bombardment of contradictory experiences), but he doesn't tell me how to live successfully with another human being, whether I should replace my glasses with contact lenses, whether I should have an operation for hemorrhoids or try to get by with Preparation H. He gives me the world on a psychedelic platter but he almost entirely leaves out the SUBSTANCE of one's personal life that continues to dog one all of one's days. It is that substance, that reality, that march through the glue of actuality that I'm stuck with, as are millions of people, and when I look to buoyant Abbie for help he is sitting on a window ledge megaphoning down instructions on how to manipulate the media. Abbie, I don't want to manipulate the media, I want to get by with a little help from my friends!

And yet as I see Abbie's attitude toward our anachronistic society and its absurdities gaining power and belief, penetrating the mass media because of his and his friends' ingenuity and fearlessness, penetrating the phony armor of our reactionary official personages (Mayor Daley, Captain Fink, James Wechsler, deposed LBJ, people in positions of public authority who used to frighten me because they were alien and tough), I realize that right as I might be about where Abbie lets me down I have been timid and self-conscious about confronting institutions that NEED an Abbie to yank their pants down, and I embrace him for his guiltless political homosexuality.

Further, can it be that my own and my N.Y. Jewish literary buddies' bias toward American experience—wanting to be a member of this nation in a central sense rather than the outsiders we felt like as adolescents, identifying ourselves with the warming mythos of the country through Whitman and Melville and Hart Crane and Wolfe, rather than resisting like mensches until it could prove itself to us as something more than promises, romantically digging its variety and even the shape of its evils as part of the magnitude of the great picture—has become dated, of nothing but sentimental (non) value, a shell disguising what is really going on? I have to accept this as a possible charge against my vision, my point of view, the very identity that I have conceived for myself, and when I feel the moral crime of my possibly unreal madness toward this country in Abbie's throwaway remark, "Assume America is already dead," I wonder if I have been putting myself on all these years and must now pay for it. Abbie is right—different views of reality or not, I am the proof in the head-searching he puts me through—when he says of the Yippies and himself: "We are dynamiting braincells. We are putting people through changes. The aim is not to earn the respect, admiration, and love of everybody—it's to get people to do, participate, whether positively or negatively."

Abbie has gotten men to participate—jesus, yes—he has knocked me off my balance, made me question my own relevance, dig once again for my own sense of what is real; and yet he has done all of this through the pissed-upon written word which I must take more fanatically than he because to me it MUST contain the fluid of life, intelligence, purpose, while to Abbie it's only a backhanded means to action. I and those like me have none of those escape hatches except that printed word which he rightfully demeans from his point of view. But don't forget that he also tells me that people over 40 don't know how to live with antitheses such as his booting out the word while exploiting it, that juggling these illogics is the "secret" of the revolutionary-pop scene, so it is less important to me to seize on his own inconsistencies (as I sense them) than to profit by his vision and measure what I and those like me have tried to do against its surprising luminousness. It seems to me, in the light of the imaginative flare that Abbie has shot up, that I and my most diehard literary friends have failed to see through many of the compromised arrangements that have taken place at the "top" of American life; that the longing in ourselves "to make it" has corrupted us in varying degrees into accepting bourgeois achievement, heavy and dull, that Abbie no longer takes seriously. He uproariously laughs at institutions which we also have attacked —the easy target of the *Times,* Time-Life, NBC, CBS, Pentagon, police, Congress, all of it—but the revealing thing is the difference in EMPHASIS, the informal grace and detachment in his style as compared to the heat and emotional fervor from our side. What one sees in the mirror of Abbie's absurdist approach is that we have apparently been much too straight in taking on these cultural monsters; we took them at their own values, so to speak, credited them with a middle-class straightforwardness of motive, the making of money, which Abbie almost vomits up because it seems to him a defamation of existence in front. They are his stone, unashamed enemy—his living principles are the abolition of all private property, money, and the setting up of totally free institutions and stores that you and I use at will—and this belly-anarchism of his beautifully simplifies his behavior; there is no wavering at the source if again I can trust him from his words.

Added to this, Abbie seems to feel none of the self-accusatory guilt that those of us brought up in the delicate strands of middle-class personal relationships (family especially) still feel even today toward those who may have persecuted us; there is in his book, to me, a COOLNESS, even a ruthlessness, which I envy but cannot emulate and still keep kosher, and through Abbie I suddenly really see Mark Rudd, the SDS, The Up Against The Wall Motherfuckers, their human examples like Che, Ho Chi Minh, Mao, Castro, etc., but all converted into an American style (and language!) which in this tough form has never really been on our scene before. And as far as "Amurrica" goes—which is the way the young slashers mock it but, cornball Yid that I am, I truly can't—keep in mind that Abbie was almost a post-Bomb all-American Boy, not awkward, introverted, "tormented," which was almost the sacred passport of admission into our literary world. Speaking from his cool pride Abbie tells me that he was always a competitor, a medal-winner in almost everything he took on (from hustling pool to stealing cars to modern dance), and it is the joining of this self-confident, extroverted, almost hip businessman's URGE TO WIN with his revolutionary disbelief at everything that I and thousands like me once assumed was normality, that makes me watch him sharply —to the point where I'm already exploiting him as a probe into my own cancers.

But in case you think that I underrate myself unfairly, am too generous at my own expense, which I know I'm not, let me say that Abbie also makes me understand conclusively that words are not "horseshit"; because each item that he has taught me has come through his own WRITTEN language. It carries everything about him (I can read writing, I believe, the way a fortuneteller can read palms): his facile, psych major IQ, the lack of texture in his prose which means the lack of deep sensuality in the man, his genuinely mod combination of humor and insane determination, the extraordinary combining processes of his head where the cues he has picked up from Artaud, McLuhan, Dylan, Che, Hollywood, TV, Lenny Bruce, the Beatles, Mailer, Ginsberg, Heller (all his influences are very "right," but it is fair odds that he will one day be dated by them even as right now he is ahead of the pack) become metaphors for him to bounce points off you. What a user you are, Abbie, as I hope you'd be the first to admit! But the very significant thing, which should never be forgotten, is that Abbie Hoffman has brought the thinking of a cocky non-verbal cat ("Jerry Rubin is a writer, but I know I can whip him publicly because I'll use any means necessary") to those sneaky little words, and just by doing that has made a really fresh contribution to an art that he sneers at. More than that, much more than that to me, he has, by going in a new direction—organizing a new cross section of thoughts that create a genuine blueprint for his own synthesis of dada-acid-flower revolution, setting down his unclichéd, unselfconscious, clear and perky prose—given someone else an IMPORTANT EXPERIENCE which confirms to that person, finally, the nature of his own contribution as opposed to Abbie's.

I finally come out of Abbie's high, quick, funny, smart, slightly thin world, confident that I must take myself as seriously as I ever have ("People who take themselves too seriously are power-crazy, if they win it will be haircuts for all," Abbie tells me, and I agree and still know I must do what I have to do) in order to communicate to readers as a person who is squeezed into doing the boldest part of his living in words. I write out of necessity, just the way Abbie acts, but my old-fashioned grind is still a means of commitment in this day of instant Abbies, and the way I know I can do it, throwing my body wrapped in the very horseshit words that make man man before any tanks that can be invented, reassures me that the doubts which often sweep my being about the purpose of my trip and the limitations of my ability are less important than I thought when I started this piece. Abbie's book, for deep emotional reasons, brought out every spectre I have feared about writing, age, being out of it, being out of action, seeing John and Tuli and Ed and Rubin take the Word into the public arena and putting me uptight with envy and self-doubt until I screwed the paper into the machine once again for the ten thousandth time out of having NO PLACE ELSE TO GO with my head; then Abbie really straightened me out, at least for now, and I know he's an East Side medicine man in the sense that Creeley once said of Kerouac that he had "healing hands."

Slouching Toward Bethlehem To Be Born

What's Wrong with the World?

WALTER KARP

There is one political question, of great moment, which has never been precisely formulated, and we are in danger of answering it without even knowing that it has been asked. The question is this: do men, as a matter of ascertainable fact, want serious demands made upon their courage, loyalty, generosity and understanding? Do men, in other words, care to be moral beings, and do we prefer a life that might penalize us somehow for being craven, faithless or ungenerous? If we do not, then there is nothing radically wrong with the world. It is being fashioned in every way to suit us. If we do, then there is a great deal wrong with the world, and it is getting worse.

The situation, in brief, is that the world beyond our doorstep runs fairly well without us. It produces our food, collects our garbage, names our streets, defends our shores, educates our children, upholds public order. And it does all this without calling upon any moral virtues whatever in the vast majority of its inhabitants. Beyond the circle of friends and family— in the world, that is—what moral qualities we have, or lack, are quite irrelevant. The system—with some interesting exceptions—will plod on just the same.

All the world now asks most of us to do is wake up in the morning when the alarm clock rings and get to work on time. It also demands a large number of small negations, such as not evading our taxes, not robbing and killing, not breaking the ordinary rules of society merely out of pique, and, of course, not lying in bed after the alarm clock sounds. These demands, on the whole, are not very complex.

The world also asks that we do our work more or less proficiently. The sum total of proficient performances accomplishes a huge proportion of

From *Interplay*, March 1968. Reprinted by permission of *Interplay*, the Magazine of International Affairs.

the world's moral work for us. We can take, as the obvious example, charity. A half-million, or perhaps two million trained social workers dispense necessities to the deserving poor, but these workers are not, as individuals, performing charitable acts or anything remotely resembling charitable acts. (If they did, they would disrupt the system.) Even if every welfare worker were as tightfisted as Volpone, the poor would not be a whit more hungry. The workers need only be efficient; the Department of Welfare as a whole performs the charitable act. Abysmal swine could run any conceivable Bureau of Goodness, but as long as they were efficient swine and obedient swine, the good work would be done. This, in general, is the way the world works. We decided to make individual man morally irrelevant perhaps three centuries ago, when kings put uniforms on their unpredictable warriors and valor was made a product of the military system itself.

There is some exaggeration in this, but not much; in a century it will be quite accurate, for this is the way we are tending. Outside the circle of our families, most of us are jobholders doing work that demands our skill and patience, but only rarely and incidentally what might be called our moral qualities. Now and then we may have to stand up to the boss with some show of courage, or, being a boss ourselves, weigh the moral niceties of firing an employee with a large family to support. In little neighborhood groceries, shopkeepers must decide on occasion whether or not to extend credit to a housewife with an ailing husband. This list of moral occasions could certainly be extended. Still, it does not make a life. As it stands, most of us are morally irrelevant most of the time. We are neither leaders nor followers; we don't need the loyalty of others, and they do not need ours. We do not judge and we pass no sentences. No community asks us to shun a pariah and no pariah asks us to defy those who shun him. We can hold views about everything, but we need never stand up and defend them. As for our families, the police protect them.

THE MORAL PROFESSIONS

If we overlook details, there are not many kinds of work that are, through and through, morally demanding; that is, work which a bad man would normally do badly. I can think of only three: teaching, police work, and politics—plus, perhaps, the legal profession. Teachers, policemen and politicians do most of the moral work—and all of the dirty work—still left in individual hands. Interestingly, these are all occupations that are heartily distrusted by the people at large. The reason is obvious. Those who fail as teachers, policemen, and politicians are likely to be moral failures and so must bear the odium. No such odium attaches to the salesman who fails to sell merchandise, or to any other person who fails by bungling some technical task or other. Incompetence is not deemed morally reprehensible, at least not yet. The day it becomes a cardinal sin we will have arrived at a moral dispensation more accurately fitted to our condition.

Even among these three occupations, the world shows its powerful tendency to make an individual's moral qualities irrelevant. Work that might depend on a foolish, knavish man is considered too dangerous to preserve and we accept remarkably flimsy excuses for discarding it. To eliminate the teacher, there are an increasing number of impersonal and mechanized substitutions: teaching machines, closed-circuit television, standardized tests, stereotyped lesson plans and standard operating procedures in general. Even with these, the teacher remains a morally dangerous person and so we have introduced the trained and standardized "guidance counselor." His job is to apply set rules for smoothing over difficulties that arise in the classroom—which is to say, he is a pseudo-moral agent brought in to cut down the range of a teacher's moral responsibilities. He limits the dangers inherent in having a fallible human being in a morally demanding place. These educational measures are taken, we are told, because good teachers are costly. That we, the richest people in history, can believe this so readily, shows how profoundly we are in accord with the deepest intent of these measures, which is the restriction of teaching as a human activity. For what other reason could anyone contemplate the introduction of a teaching *machine?*

In police work, the means are even simpler. The policeman who walks his beat is being replaced—as an economy measure, we are told—by the policeman patrolling in a squad car. The end, the unstated and most unconscious reason for the change is the same, however: a morally rooted task is to be replaced by its mechanical facsimile. The policeman on the beat is a man upon whom moral demands are incessantly made. He knows the people in his neighborhood; they know him. He must decide daily, with Solomon's wisdom, whether some thieving street urchin deserves to be booked or dragged, repentant, back to his family. He must decide whether some member of the neighborhood is breaking an ordinance, or whether, in the case at hand, the ordinance is breaking the man. If the policeman is a bully or a scoundrel, the whole neighborhood will suffer. His role is complex and demanding because he is, in the strict meaning of the term, a peace officer. He is there to keep peace, which may even mean winking at the law, or deciding whether catching a fleeing thief is worth the risk of winging a stray bullet into a member of the neighborhood. The policeman in the squad car, on the other hand, is not a peace officer. He is a criminal-catcher. He does not belong, in any sense, to a neighborhood, but merely floats about a vicinity, swooping down whenever he spies a lawbreaker. This may or may not be efficient, but it certainly narrows his moral responsibility—*au fond,* the reason he was put in a squad car.

Politics is a more complicated matter, but when have we ceased longing for the day when politicians would be replaced by administrators, technicians and experts? Marx prophesied that the day would come; the rest of us only hope that it will. For a jobholder, a real effort of imagination is required to understand a politician's life. He inhabits an exotic community so perplexing in its moral demands that the rest of us suspect he is a crook.

To conclude and to repeat, if men care to be moral beings, then we are all morally underemployed.

Before returning to our opening question, a few assumptions ought to be clarified. First, I have stressed moral *demands* because I take it for granted that moral qualities do not exist unexercised. A man can scarcely be held courageous, for example, if his courage is never called upon. Indeed, if a man dwelt in a moral vacuum all his life, what moral qualities he possessed would be anybody's guess, including his own.

Second, I am not here concerned with whether men are naturally good —or bad. I am only asking whether we care to live a life such that good and bad, virtuous and vicious, were qualities that more often mattered.

Third, I take for granted that there is no substitute for necessity, which is why I spoke of morally demanding work and not morally demanding play. Men's moral qualities have to be needed for the world's work or the call upon them is either a hobby (as in a parachute club) or a swindle. Men rightly resent large corporations that lay claim to their employees' total loyalty. This is not because men are inherently disloyal, but because these companies do not need all our loyalty. They are only being hoggish.

It is only within the circle of intimacy—friendship, marriage and family —that moral demands are now subtly and ceaselessly made. It is impossible in marriage, for example, to be morally neuter. There is no "proficiency" in it. To fail as a husband is to fail as a man, and this is so, of course, for women as well. The smallest want of generosity will be mercilessly exposed; nothing can long conceal a cold heart. Until a person marries, he may not discover, or even suspect, his capacity for spitefulness. Or forbearance, for we also discover in the circle of intimacy virtues we did not know we had. In his friendships and family, a man learns something of what he is and what he is capable of. For this reason, a man frequently finds that the most rewarding, taxing and memorable event of his life was a love affair, the complexities of a brief romance having taught him more than 15 years of selling stationery, or supervising the typing pool, or teaching graduate courses.

A CONTEMPORARY SHIFT

This shift in our conception of individual moral response is a consequence of the organization of modern life. The circle of intimacy has become a more interesting, exacting and more dangerous place than the world, for it demands so much of us and the world so little. This comparative advantage is not just due to the world growing less demanding. The truth is, we have made intimacy a hundred more times more demanding than it ever was before. Being morally irrelevant in the world, we have sought a compensatory moral life in the circle of intimacy. Nothing suggests how strongly men wish to be moral beings than this profound transformation.

Men once looked upon their homes as their bulwark and sustainer, the means to other ends. Athenians likened domestic life to a dark cave from which men emerged into the noon light of the agora, refreshed for citizenship. To make too much of it was dangerous. Cicero warned that an excessive pleasure in the marital bed distracted a man from his public duties. The circle of intimacy was conceived as an island of safety, not of danger. It was held nourishing, but not exalting, and certainly not arduous. Conceiving it that way, men doubtless found it that way and saw little that was perplexing in intimacy. Montaigne, that most personal of men, termed marriage a "sort of conscientious delight" and rarely spoke of his own; friendship was simply a good, disrupted by death or the follies of kings. Jane Austen, that most skeptical of ladies, assumed that when an upright man and a kind-hearted woman were wed, her story was at an end. We doubt this in our bones, knowing a thousand pitfalls that await the couple. Our skepticism begins where hers leaves off.

CLOSING
THE CIRCLE

We today cannot look upon intimacy as an island of safety. In such a case, given the organization of the world, we would have nothing to be. Instead, we have had to fashion a moral vision more consistent with our condition, which is that of moral irrelevance to the world. We have had, first of all, to claim intimacy as the locus of the very highest good. "Only connect," as E. M. Forster once said, giving the motto for our time. We have also had to make the capacity for intimate relations the highest virtue, the virtue by which all others are weighed. We tend to look, therefore, on those who thrive in the world, yet fail in intimacy, as failures. When someone said of Charles I that, although a bad king, he was a good father and husband and so a good man, Macauley retorted that a bad king is a bad man. He spoke out of an older morality now called into question. We have had, in addition, to make moral excellence in the circle of intimacy as difficult to attain as virtue in the world had once been. It must be made a matter of constant striving. A great number of modern minds, not otherwise agreeing, have worked toward these ends, as if in unison. Men do not lack for long the doctrines they require.

All analytical psychology, for example, can be viewed, morally speaking, as a means to these ends, perhaps the very prime means. The first task this psychology performed was to throw open to the most withering scrutiny all those intimate relations that had once been regarded as above suspicion. It can detect in certain wives, apparently loved by their husbands, surrogate mothers inspiring a childish affection; it will see in admired husbands, the simulacrum of a woman's too-admired father. It will find, then, in the seemingly straightforward relations of intimacy, crooked pathways, diseased passions and falsity of every kind. There is no safety here.

Analytical psychology can judge of intimate relations this way—and it is a harsh way by past standards—because it takes as its starting point a more perfectionist notion of *successful* intimacy: of "mature" or "genital" love, or personal "rapport," or the "ability to communicate" and to "give" of oneself, these being the key moral terms of the doctrine. They serve, or have the effect of serving, as exalted and exclusive moral standards, since we are measured, psychologically, entirely by our failure to live up to them. They define the highest virtues, and the virtues they define—in essence, the capacity for personal love—can only be manifested in intimacy. The world would, and does, deform them. They are also virtues extremely difficult to attain, for what does the belief in the universality of neurosis mean except the universal failure to attain them? Somewhat like the concept of honor, they tell us what we must strive for, while warning us that we cannot strive too hard. Also, analytical psychology makes it plain that there can be no avoiding the effort. As its explanatory principles demonstrate, our failures in intimacy are the fruit of all that we are and have been, the failure to which all our other failings are tributary. What we are and can become as men, we are and can become only at home, where a thousand pitfalls await us. Thus the circle of intimacy is made a morally demanding and dangerous place. This is why our authors describe it so attentively.

An intellectual historian might usefully trace, in the writings of our time, the variations in this new exacting ethics of intimacy. A great deal of elaboration, experimentation and eloquence goes into the fabrication of a living moral system and it is the work of many gifted men. The psychologist speaks, with a clinician's experience, of mature or genital love; the poet of the redemptive power of personal love. The analytical theorist lays down that the hunger for power and prestige are deformed substitutions for an affection not found in intimacy; the novelist traces the subtle corruptions of worldliness in his characters, and measures its effects on their capacity for love. The conforming write pious homilies on the domestic hearth, while moral radicals tell us that all that a man is and can be is demanded of him in the sexual act alone. Variations are many, but all agree in this: the only genuine moral demands on a person will be found in the circle of intimacy.

KNOWING THYSELF

Ernest Hemingway, one of our few influential teachers who went outside this ethical system, confirmed its strength. He called upon men to leave the circle of intimacy with their teeth clenched and prepared for nothing except falling gracefully under superior force. He assumed, that is, that men do not inhabit the world, but only make occasional raids upon it. This viewpoint, given the prevailing view of intimacy, was singular enough to affect many men deeply. According to Mr. Schlesinger, President Kennedy himself believed that "grace under pressure" was the highest virtue. As President he conceived each act of the Soviet Union as a test of *his* courage and grace, an apprehension which testifies not only to Hemingway's influence, but to the moral vacuum that his teachings filled. Political men cannot be guided by the ethics of intimacy, and so an American President, like many lesser men, had to seize on the little else that was offered.

That we have attempted to make the circle of intimacy a morally exacting place suggests strongly that men wish to be moral beings and to live in such a way that their moral qualities matter greatly. If we did not so wish, we could have left the circle of intimacy as we found it. It may be, though, that this recasting of intimacy suffices, and that it is just as well that we have the world, with all its glories and miseries, off our backs. In that case, no political question arises. Or, rather, it has been answered, for we are lifting the world from our backs more or less automatically. On the other hand, it may be that our need for a morally demanding life is too intense to be accommodated entirely within even the modern circle of intimacy; in that case, the political question does arise.

A dreadful uncertainty about one's personal identity is held to be a characteristic malady of our time. A gnawing, oppressive anxiety is another; a sense of alienation from the established order of things a third. These maladies, however pervasive, are not fundamental. They are symptoms of the organization of life and its attendant moral underemployment of people. Perhaps, to this account, a fourth ailment might be added— monotony, that enduring life-monotony whose relief is the wholesale consumption of passive amusements. Moral demands, at any rate, are absorbing. Who would not prefer to spend the night plotting revenge rather than watching television? This is why public men hate to return to private life.

Regarding the loss of identity: we are what we do, but suppose we have too little to do? Suppose that our moral capacities were not sufficiently called upon in the course of our lives? We would not know very well who we were. We might hold various hypotheses regarding ourselves, but whether they were true or not we could not say for certain. Seeking assurances, we would look for reflections of ourselves in other men's eyes, and find sly signs of our worth in chance encounters and superficial tests. A limitless vanity would be our lot. We would be like men shut up in a hall of distorting mirrors, trying to decide which mirror to trust and knowing desperately that we can trust none of them. We could have no sure sense of identity, for men know themselves when they know what their moral nature is, whether generous wherever generosity has mattered, loyal where loyalty was rightly called upon, and so on through the range of virtues or failings. This ignorance of one's moral nature is not bliss. There are men among us half-crazed with worrying whether, in some final definitive way, they will prove to possess courage. They want to know the worst and be done with doubting, for doubting itself brings maddening unease. Falstaff, after all, was a merry coward, since he knew, with complete knowledge, that danger was not his métier, just as merriment, which was his, was not other men's.

Regarding anxiety: this malady seems to be, essentially, a deep pervading fear that on any given tomorrow we will be proven worthless. It is a phantom fear, for men are not worthless, far from it. Every man (almost), given the chance, has his métier and season, occasions in which his particular virtues are needed and gratifying to exercise. There are men who falter and fumble in action, yet who are just and delicate in their judgments of others. There are men bigoted and crude-minded, who are yet swift and sure in action; and men who cannot persist loyally in common enterprises but who can stand bravely alone under public obloquy. In some circumstances, they are men of virtue; in others, failures and worse.

For this reason sudden shifts of circumstance become especially revealing. On such occasions we swiftly learn what the half-buried people around us can do. When the electric lights went out a few years ago, just such a moral illumination played over the whole curious scene. The stock clerk, known only for his idle chattering, appears in the dark, tangled streets directing traffic with calm concentration; on the stuck, stricken train, the fat, pasty sales clerk shows admirable resources of usable good spirits; the business executive, so calm within the carapace of his office, falls to pieces from a bruised conceit. In truth, if the electricity failed more often in the great cities, the discipline of corporations would be shaken. Men would come to know each other too well to abide by the timid rules of office life. The day after the great blackout, police discovered that the crime rate had gone down sharply, especially among juveniles. This baffled the police, who always assume that the darker the streets, the more cars will be stolen. The truth was that the "missing" delinquents probably found the darkness too exhilarating and too full of occasions for gallantry for them to bother about stealing cars, their ordinary anodyne for boredom and waste.

Men have, potentially at least, their métier, where their mettle shows well and matters much. But suppose that the man who is just in his judgments is never called upon to judge, has no occasion that requires him to discriminate finely. Suppose that the man swift in action is condemned to watch televised football games, and that the man who can stand alone is asked to do nothing but get to the office on time. And suppose that a man of steadfast loyalty finds no leader and no enterprise demanding his loyalty and steadfastness. This is what it means to be morally irrelevant to the execution of the world's work. It is also the condition for anxiety; we are deprived of serious occasions in which we might know ourselves worthy. Unlike Falstaff, we will not find our métier. We possess nothing to dispel the phantom fear of our worthlessness except, perhaps, the shaky conceit that some unexercised virtue is especially ours, if we can maintain even that solace in the face of the long years when nothing happens.

This corrosive anxiety, it is worth remarking, is not ordinary fear bred of ordinary hazards. Nor is it due to the "pressures" of modern life or its "hectic pace." We are not made anxious for having to catch trains and watch clocks. In Norway, under the Nazi occupation, a curious health improvement took place which shows the truth of these remarks. Despite the tension, the peril and the taut suspense of this new life under the Nazis, the rate of death due to heart ailments drastically decreased. This was an apparent paradox, because the corrosions of anxiety had long been held a factor in the incidence of heart disease. A partial explanation of the paradox turned out to be dietetic. Norwegians during the war ate far less fatty foods than normally, and from this medical researchers were led to discover the role of fats in promoting heart disorders. A full explanation, however, would also add that anxiety, despite the tension of the occupation, had decreased also. Norwegians had more to fear, but less to be anxious about. Moral demands were ceaselessly made in the occupied towns, and conditions for knowing one's worth multiplied accordingly.

To look a Nazi officer in the face, to speak up for some trifling customary right, to help a distressed friend, to decide in hushed councils whether some neighbor had become a collaborator, or had forgivably succumbed to overwhelming pressure—these and countless other moral demands were being made every day. Men discovered qualities in themselves that they never suspected—and I am talking about ordinary moral acts and not of heroic resistance. Such dense moral experience dispelled the phantom of worthlessness, and so the peacetime anxiety of life declined and with it the heart disease mortality rate. It must be said, however, that suffering a military occupation is a poor way to cure our ills.

There is, lastly, the malady of alienation, now much discussed. What is this sense of alienation, after all, if not the subjective realization that we are morally irrelevant to the world? To lament one's alienation is to complain, in the most direct way, of that irrelevance. Who would feel so estranged from the established order of things if his loyalty, his courage and much else that was good in him, were directly called upon to sustain it? It is the malady characteristic of youth, just as anxiety is the malady of men in their prime. The young feel possessed of virtue and so feel acutely their moral irrelevance, while older men, having been for so long irrelevant, face the phantom fear of worthlessness.

Anxiety, loss of identity, alienation and boredom: these are maladies that give rise to others. David Riesman has rightly termed us "other-directed men," and now we can better understand what this means. We can see that the fateful weakness of the other-directed man is *not* that he takes his guidance and his assurance from the opinions of others. He is not timid and conforming because he heeds the views of his fellows. This is an incomplete description. After all, what did "honor" mean for so long, if not the wish to shine before one's peers and to win their high approval? No, it is not the opinions of others that enfeebles us, but the fact that these opinions are based upon appearances and not upon real virtues called forth and seen. It is because our moral qualities are anybody's guess and that it becomes fatal to wear the wrong suit. Who would care so much about his neighbor's style, manner and habits if he knew what his real moral qualities were? But we are morally irrelevant and half-buried, so we judge by trifling signs and emblems and force other men to live by them. It is this which makes conformity destructive and the opinions of others a petty tyranny.

THE DEAD END

We can see, too, the real meaning of Ortega y Gasset's "mass-man," who demands everything of the world like a gluttonous child, and nothing of himself. Slipshod, passive, a consumer of merchandise, an unthinking reed, he is the morally irrelevant man seen through the wrong end of a telescope. Ortega's mass-man makes puerile demands on the world—but why not? We have framed the world to dispense goods as automatically as possible. Why, then, should ordinary men look upon it as a delicate creation constantly in need of regeneration? Why should they make demands upon themselves, and exercise virtues that nobody needs? Men are too sensible—and life too difficult— for individuals to invent difficulties for their own sake. What is not truly needed will not be forthcoming. The rest is idle moralizing or occupation for cultists. Yet one-eyed greed and slothful passivity are repulsive, and if the organization of life produces such traits in abundance, it is one more mark against it.

If this account is correct (though nothing in it is proven), man's moral irrelevance lies at the heart of our most characteristic ailments and deformations of spirit. We have made the circle of intimacy difficult and demanding, but it does not suffice. It does not enable us to find ourselves, to discover our worth and to feel our connection with the established order of things. This suggests a partial answer, at least, to the question I raised at the beginning: do men care to live in such a way that their moral qualities matter greatly? The partial answer is that we do need, urgently, to live in such a way that our moral qualities matter, and that, in organizing the world as we have, we have been taking a heavy toll in wasted lives and blighted spirits.

A WAY OUT

What, then, is to be done? How can we make men's moral qualities more relevant to the work of the world? This is a political question and, practically speaking, it is partly resolved when men begin to ask it, for when numbers of men are set upon a task, great resources of ingenuity and imagination will come into play. The prime thing is to see, whenever anything is decided, that whatever deepens and widens the moral demands made upon us is a good in itself. This is no small thing, because much looks different when judged in this light—as, for example, teaching machines, however efficient, and local poverty councils, however inefficient, because the former eliminates a morally demanding occupation, and the latter creates a small circle of power and yet another circle of moral demands that extends far beyond the council itself. Because teaching, policing and engaging in politics are morally demanding tasks, we should increase, in whatever way feasible, the number of these, although the teachers need not work under boards of education, or the guardians under police bureaucracies, and the politics need not be left to professionals.

Of all the practical possibilities, politics is the most hopeful. Nothing else calls forth men's qualities so urgently and so fully, and nothing spreads moral demands among so many. Politics, whenever it is local and visible, creates not only leaders, but personal followers. It places real demands upon loyalty, produces crises that test individuals, makes principles something to stand up for, gives us men to judge and to be judged by, and offers occasions for courage, steadfastness and generosity. Whatever creates political life and activity—in neighborhoods, corporations, campuses, wherever—will do much to reduce men's irrelevance and all that this irrelevance means. We must forget efficiency for a while. It is not that fallible, contending men will accomplish tasks better, but that they are better men for doing them. This should be the guiding principle, for to bring men's moral qualities back into the world's service is a need more drastic than perhaps now appears.

We stand at what amounts to a crossroads, with all the force of momentum driving us to continue in a straight line as before. Yet if we continue in this way, something must eventually rupture, and it is worth thinking what this might be. My own guess is that there will come a time, in some future wonderland of plenty, perhaps Mr. McLuhan's "global village," when men, grown ignorant of the world and of themselves, will rise out of their passivity and find a moral relevance of a terrible and destructive kind. They will find their selfhood, their worth and their peace in the roar of massed crowds and the tramping feet of marching hordes— and by then they will be badly equipped to make things better.

The Liberal Dilemma

GORE VIDAL

It seems only fifty-nine minutes ago that John Kenneth Galbraith's liberal hour struck. Freed of narrow prejudice, uninspired by the conventional wisdom, willing to institute reforms tending in the direction of a greater democracy, the American leadership had finally made its "long-term commitment to the realities." Dissenters from liberalism were few and predictable—Right-wingers obsessed with conspiracy and mistrustful of fluorine. Except for an occasional eccentric, the educated, the energetic, and the hopeful were dedicated to making things better. Everyone was pragmatic and no one was dogmatic; the New Frontier could be crossed and the Great Society built. But as the thirty-sixth President learned the hard way, there is no lasting consensus this side of the grave.

The liberal Center did not hold, and for some time now liberalism has been at bay. At alarmingly regular intervals that most liberal of professional public servants, Dean Rusk, has been picketed by the educated, the energetic, and the hopeful because, as one of them explained recently at an ad hoc meeting in New York's Bryant Park: "We're demonstrating against the American establishment, against the liberal fascists." The phrase "liberal fascist" is almost as unthinkable as "Christian atheist." Admittedly Mr. Rusk's dream of making Southeast Asia safe for liberalism has called into question certain of his methods, but to question so cruelly the ultimate worthiness of his ideals and the generosity of his vision would have been unthinkable a few seconds ago. After all, Dean Rusk is a former foundation head.

Some try to discount these attacks as signs of "immaturity" among the young (not to mention Communist infiltration), and so disregard them. But lately the attacks on liberalism have been mounted from other, more respectable quarters. "Liberalism," observed Whitney M. Young, "seems to be related to the distance people are from the [Negro] problem." Apparently Northern well-wishers who had been willing to go South to stir up the red-necks were reluctant to confront conditions in their home cities. Youth, generally, is disaffected. The National Student Association is now confronted by the Students for a Democratic Society. These dissidents believe that "the liberal program of NSA is inadequate to bring about the meaningful social change that is necessary to create a truly democratic society in America." In other words, liberalism and true democracy are incompatible. Even that traditional *arrière-garde* institution the American theater has taken note of the disrepute into which liberalism has fallen. In the words of Clive Barnes, the new play *The Niggerlovers* "seems to be making the point that white liberalism is merely the mirror image of white racism, and that one could not exist without the other." While the protagonist of the comedy *Scuba Duba* is, according to Mr. Barnes, "a good white Partisan Review liberal reader whose wife has gone off with a Negro, and he finds himself—quite sincerely—spilling out the most obscene racist hatred." On the other hand, the bold and tactless Dr. William Shockley believes that scientific attempts to determine intelligence differences between Negroes and whites are systematically thwarted by "inverted liberals." With equal disdain, both Left and Right dismiss today's liberal as an ineffective, guilt-ridden, hypocritical masochist, resembling nothing so much as one of Jules Feiffer's cartoon characters whose inner frustrations and confusions can be read at inordinate length on one of those huge balloons to which the shakily-drawn head seems diminutive afterthought.

Words like "liberal" and "conservative" are of course notoriously difficult to define. More to the point, they are impossible to apply accurately to individuals who tend to vacillate from issue to issue, depending upon health, age, weather, and the stock market. It should be noted, however, that there has never been much liberal sentiment in our middle-class society. Americans are about evenly divided between conservatives and reactionaries. The late President Kennedy was a conservative; former President Eisenhower was a reactionary. Neither was radical, if only because each was a shrewd politician who had learned the famous paradox of our system: to do anything one must obtain power but to obtain power one must do nothing.

In any case, major politicians dislike political labels. An exception was Barry Goldwater, who took pleasure in the word "conservative" and all that he thought it stood for. But even he used to say in private that it was a shame, really, they couldn't come up with some other word to describe man's best instincts, since the word "conservative" had been hopelessly traduced by sinister liberals. Now the word "liberal" has also become anathema to those militant social reformers who are presently converging upon the center stage of our national life.

Two events have caused this change: the President's war in Asia and the Negro minority's struggle for economic parity with the white majority. The war in Asia became active at the end of the Kennedy administration, and though many liberals like to place the full blame upon Lyndon Johnson and his Texas reactionaryism ("There's an old saying down in Texas, if you know you are right, just keep on coming and no gun can stop you"), from the beginning the war has been prosecuted and escalated by such liberal officials as Rusk, Bundy, and Rostow, with considerable assistance, at least in the early stages, from all sorts of liberal outriders, most of whom can now be found on quiet campuses, writing memoirs, and waiting for the Kennedy restoration. But their early complicity in a war which today's young activists find not only ugly but irrelevant to American interests made many people suspect, perhaps unjustly, that these particular liberals prefer the pompous show of power to truth or right action. Recently, the stern Andrew Kopkind dismissed *all* liberals as "a sorry lot; they spent the late forties and early fifties feeding Communists and radicals to the McCarthy-ites (the *other* McCarthy), came briefly to glory in the days of the New Frontier, and suddenly were deposed by the onrush of history and the whim of President Johnson." Even those liberals who have remained out-side the bright circle of power appear dim to the young and restless, who grow each day more frustrated by a war that they can find no moral basis for, a war in which many of them have refused to serve, a war that should go away but does not. As a result, there is now a strong movement to mount the barricades and bring the whole structure down—hypocritical liberals, paranoid Texans, greedy salesmen, gobbling consumers . . . smash the whole works and begin again. The war has split the country like no other issue in modern times, except that of the Negro revolution.

For more than a generation conservatives have tended to blame white liberals for artificially creating discontent among the Negroes. In the thir-ties and early forties it was an article of faith that the Negroes only began to get uppity when Eleanor Roosevelt started giving them ideas (the Eleanor Clubs met regularly in order for maids to compare notes on how best to burn dinner, overstarch shirts, and generally behave in a sassy manner). It would be nice if this were true. Actually Mrs. Roosevelt and her fellow travelers tended to follow events, not lead them. It was not the liberals but the Second World War which gave ideas to the illiterate sharecropper and the pool-hall hustler, to the janitor and the day laborer, to all of those who were suddenly wrenched from what seemed to be their immutable humble condition and allowed to taste new pleasures and dignities they not unnaturally liked. What war began the television commercial continued in the postwar world. Not to have the money to buy the gadgets a whole nation worshiped was too cruel a deprivation to be borne. And so, in response to the growing discontent of the poor, liberal whites and militant Negroes forged a series of alliances which led to various postwar reforms, culminating in the apotheosis of Martin Luther King during the dreamy golden Eisenhower years.

But though liberals saw to it that, on paper at least, Negroes were finally able to enjoy most of their Constitutional rights, the expectations of the Negroes as a whole were simply not met by society. Despite much talk of justice and fair deals, the liberals could neither shatter the walls of prejudice nor make effective programs to ensure for the Negro his share of consumer goods. To date every Federal aid program has been a bust. The fault is not the liberals nor even that of those entrenched reactionaries who control so many Congressional committees and prefer the expensive slaughter of Asians to the less ambitious task of bettering conditions at home. The fault is more one of effective organization than of deficient will. Federal agencies begin with great energy and excitement, then metamorphose into vast existential organisms entirely oblivious to the purpose for which they were founded. According to Daniel P. Moynihan, "The Federal government is good at collecting revenues, and rather bad at disbursing services." He has even gone so far as to propose Federal financing of programs that would be *entirely* administered at the local level. This positively Manichean heresy is gaining considerable support among disturbed social meliorists.

Meanwhile, those liberals who raised such hopes a decade ago are now being blamed by the Negroes for everything from the failure of the Head Start educational program to the proliferation of rats in the slums. Essentially moderate Negro leaders like Floyd McKissick of CORE are now forced by the rising passions of their constituency to lash out at all whites, with particularly bitter emphasis on the failure of the reformers.

Last Labor Day's confrontation between white liberals and Negro activists at Chicago was a splendidly comic and highly dangerous affair. The National Conference for the New Politics began hopefully with talk of running the Doctors King and Spock for President and Vice President. But this project was torpedoed by a Negro minority called the Black Caucus. Headed by James Forman of SNCC, the Caucus took charge of the conference and rammed through a thirteen-point program calculated to distress all but the dizziest of Black Muslims. Nevertheless, in an ecstasy of masochism, the white majority allowed the black minority to have its will and, as one observer remarked, "the walls of the Palmer House dripped with guilt." Mr. Forman and his brightly costumed goons brought a nice touch of African democracy to Mayor Daley's Chicago. Tactically, Mr. Forman and the Mayor could learn quite a lot from each other but, unfortunately, they may soon have no common language since Mr. Forman's group now urges blacks to learn Swahili even though a speaking knowledge of English might be more helpful. In any event, it was made plain that should the liberals wish to start a third party in order to end the war in Vietnam and make a decent society for both black and white, they would have to proceed without the most active of the Negro groups. Strained relations between the races are now developing into non-relations which, some believe, are prelude to what Rap Brown happily refers to as a "guerilla war against the honkie white man."

If nothing else, the troubles last year have convinced even the most indifferent of the white majority that one tenth of a nation is seriously disaffected. The problem now is what to do. Certain Negro leaders equate the current situation with that of Africa in the last years of the colonial empires, and they believe that the white imperialist war lords can be overthrown by Mau Mau tactics. But the colonial analogy is a false one. Whites outnumber blacks in the United States; they control the country's wealth; they are not about to be driven into the sea. As a result, the rhetoric of the day grows more and more violent while the "solutions" proposed become less and less realistic. CORE currently favors an optional society. Those Negroes who find too demoralizing the white devil's company can take refuge in all-black communities; those Negroes who can tolerate a mixed environment will be allowed to live wherever they like among the whites, who, needless to say, will *not* have the right to segregate themselves.

The threat of nuclear catastrophe abroad and race war at home has convinced many of the need for a drastic change not only in American policy but in the institutions which make and execute that policy. The New Left is on record as wanting not to "capture the present power structure but to parallel it." The tactics of parallelization are often beautifully weird but by no means ineffective. For instance, between a liberal (conservative) candidate like Pat Brown and a conservative (reactionary) candidate like Ronald Reagan, the rule is to support the reactionary since he is bound to be repressive in his methods and so bring the day of revolution that much closer (it should be glumly noted that the policy of supporting the worst man was much employed during the declining years of the last but one French Republic). To the radical, the real enemy is the liberal who delays the revolution by limiting the excesses of the unenlightened.

Needless to say, the tactics of the radicals may prove to be more successful than their aims. Human institutions are fragile affairs at best, and easily smashed. But what is to take the place of those we now possess? It is not enough to be against unjust wars and in favor of the good life for all citizens. Almost everyone shares those simple liberal sentiments; in fact, they are Constitutional. The trick is how to stay out of unjust wars if one's country is, no matter how innocently, a world empire? Or how best to ameliorate the lot of millions of citizens against whom there are innumerable irrational prejudices not susceptible to legislation? These are

problems not easily handled in a quasi-democracy where a majority probably approve of unjust wars (do you favor the overthrow of Godless Communism by force?), and keeping their dusky brothers away from switch-
blade knives, white girls, and the competitive labor market.

Yet in a society of conflicting interests the only democratic way in
which matters can be improved is through politics, and politics means
the compromising of extremes in order to achieve that notorious half loaf
which the passionate and the outraged never find sufficient. Though
Americans are not, usually, passionate and outraged in everyday life, at
heart we are still instinctively Puritan with exaggerated notions of good
and evil, and a theoretic dislike of compromise. As a result, we have
always regarded with a certain contempt the working politician who
wheels, who deals, who does not truly believe. Fortunately, through sloth
and indifference, we have evolved a system of government which is often
inadequate, sometimes corrupt, always hypocritical, yet enormously successful at ensuring for most of its citizens political stability and a wide
prosperity quite unknown to the majority of nations. But now our great
Affluency is threatened from within as well as from without and, as always,
crisis provokes the irrational response and makes attractive the extreme
gesture. Summon a new Constitutional Convention, cries the Right wing,
and sanctify once and for all the holy rights of private property, while putting the shiftless in their place. Undermine the system so that it will collapse, whispers the Left, and then reassemble the pieces, making something altogether new and pure, with justice for all but the unjust, even
though the unjust are the majority.

In sharp contrast to those who would move and shake the society to its
foundation are the men and women who have opted out. Whether known
as hippies or Diggers or just plain "beautiful," they are not merely a
current fad, to be succeeded by goldfish eaters or flagpole sitters. Their
defection is important, and if the present society does not change, their
numbers will grow. Unable to find work worth doing, or a community in
which human connections can be made, thousands of men and women
have withdrawn from the consumer society and formed groups where
worldly possessions are shared, and where individuals can attempt to give
to human life a value which the society around them quite obviously does
not. For it is hardly a secret that in our vast megalopolises man's traditional relationships have broken down. The family is not, to say the least,
what it was, while grotesque overpopulation has smashed the old human
scale of community and substituted for it a frightening world of frightened
strangers with nothing in common save a dread of the anonymous others.
It is not surprising that the delinquent youth as well as the professional
criminal finds it easier than ever to kill. Since there are so many people,
born to no purpose and put to no use, what can it matter? There are
plenty more where the victim came from. The young are peculiarly victimized by city life. Unable to find values worth emulating, they become
bored, listless, hostile. Those who join gangs are at least making the
effort to be human, even in joint destructiveness. At every level agora-

phobia is prevalent. To this general malaise, the hippies have responded gently, the gangs violently, the conservatives with irrelevant platitudes, the radicals with threats of murder in the streets and the smashing of the society as it is presently organized.

At the center of all these passions is that odd man out the liberal whose temporizing influence is dismissed as mere sinister (or dextrous, depending upon the adjective-giver) shilly-shallying. It is enough to make the ADA weep. Yet the boredom with liberal values is understandable, for we are moving into strange territory, and it does not take an unusually inspired prophet to note that once again the wheel of man's history has begun to turn and the human race is about to experience one of its periodic smashups. After all, nearly half of those born since the race began are now alive, and there is not enough food for them to eat.

Since 1959, the so-called Third World's population has been increasing at the rate of twenty-six per thousand per annum, while increased food production can feed only fifteen of those twenty-six. According to agronomists, at some point between 1974 and 1980 world famine will occur, and there is now no way of avoiding it despite talk (but of course no large-scale action) of extracting food from the sea, etc. It is even too late for enforced birth control if such a thing were possible, which of course it is not since every human being has the God-given right to add as many new people to the world as he wants though the whole race starves as a result. Recently the fearless Dr. Shockley proposed *total* birth control, with the Bureau of the Census determining which couples might be allowed to add new citizens to the tax rolls. Something on this order will doubtless come to pass in time, but it will be too late for the present generations. Only disease, famine, and war can reduce our doubling billions to manageable size. Disease we have nearly eliminated; famine we are beginning to suffer and will continue to suffer on the largest scale; war may finally prove to be nature's way of restoring the balance between us and an environment we have poisoned and used up.

It is no accident that in this falling time, anthropology should be the most looked-to of the sciences. From Claude Lévi-Strauss to Konrad Lorenz, the latest texts are studied eagerly, almost desperately, as we attempt to understand precisely what sort of animal man is, and what his ecological fate may be. We are told that our aggressiveness is innate (as most parents discover, the will of the permissively brought-up child is quite as fierce as that of his overdisciplined brother): nature's way of assuring the survival of the fittest. Aggression is a characteristic of our species, and the secret of our success. But under certain stresses, our healthy aggressiveness (origin of love and music, architecture and the Olympic Games) becomes irrational and violent. On a large scale the result is war, an activity which many used to regard (the liberal Theodore Roosevelt for one) as an enormous stimulus for good. And it is true that in the wake of war, great economic and social advances are often made: the West German industrial comeback, the American Negro's new sense of himself. Even in the slow lazy times of peace, human societies (like certain human paranoids) need the idea of the Enemy to keep them alert and inventive. What earthly government would now be in space were it not for fear of Them?

Since a ritual hostility to members of other tribes is the normal condition of our race, one cannot view the future with much optimism. Significantly, we are one of the few mammalian species that have no inhibition about killing their own kind. Also, unlike the sensible rat, we do not respond to overcrowding by automatically ceasing to breed. Therefore, able to kill one another with ease yet not able to control the making of babies, it would appear that a kindly and ever-resourceful nature has programmed us for war. In which case the grand collision that so excites the radical temperament may be at hand, and we are launched upon necessary nightmare: the elimination of half the race in order that the rest may survive and begin again.

It is a tribute (though a small one) to the liberal temperament that it tends to be unnatural. Trying to make things better, trying to compromise extremes, trying to keep what we have from falling apart, the liberal goes about his dogged task; and in times of relative stability he can occasionally succeed in making improvements. Certainly he knows that, as Hegel put it, "Nothing happens unless individuals seek their satisfaction in the issues of their society." But when the cry of "blood" begins, as it seems to do at least once a generation, the liberal's voice is no longer heard and he himself looks altogether absurd, the maverick lemming who tries to climb the hill rather than join his excited peers in their long deadly swim. Yet each acts as he must, and if those structure-minded anthropologists are correct, our behavior is entirely predetermined. In which case, by acting as though man's condition can be improved, the liberal simply demonstrates his predictability, his constant variation to the common theme, and does what he must since there is nothing else for him to do and no world elsewhere.

Rituals: The Revolt Against the Fixed Smile

MELVIN MADDOCKS

In the spring of 1627, the Pilgrim settlement at Plymouth was scandalized when a rather different American named Thomas Morton decided to show the New World how to celebrate. At Merry Mount, which may have been America's first counterculture community, Morton erected a Maypole—80 feet of priapic pine—and by his own account "brewed a barrell of excellent beare" to be distributed with "other good cheare, for all commers of that day." Other good cheare included Indian girls, according to "a song fitting to the time and present occasion" written by the host himself:

Lasses in beaver coats, come away,
Ye shall be welcome to us night and day.

Myles Standish, that well-known non-womanizer, accompanied by America's first vice squad, interrupted the revels, which were subsequently described by Plymouth Governor William Bradford as "the beastly practices of the mad Bacchinalians." Morton eventually was busted, placed in the stocks and returned to England in a state of mortifying near starvation.

It is only simplifying history, not distorting it, to suggest that on May Day 1627, the struggle for the American soul was settled once and almost for all. Score: Ants, 1; Grasshoppers, 0. The devil had been unmasked as the imp of play, the demon who made song and dance the pulsebeat of life. And so the men in the gray Puritan suits went their unmerry way: sober, industrious, thrifty, starkly Protestant, with absolutely no use for Maypoles. For Maypoles meant not only untrammeled festivity but something of larger significance: rituals. And rituals meant not only feelings and passions but coded repetitions of the past—things that New Man had come to the New World to escape. On May Day 1627, cool, clear American voices of reason said a firm no to all that.

The no was firm, but it was not, and could not have been, final. As Philosopher George Santayana, looking at the American Puritan through half-Spanish eyes, noted: "For the moment, it is certainly easier to suppress the wild impulses of our nature than to manifest them fitly, at the right times and with the proper fugitive emphasis; yet in the long run, suppression does not solve the problem, and meantime those maimed expressions which are allowed are infected with a secret misery and falseness." Nearly $3\frac{1}{2}$ centuries later, the Merry Mount case no longer seems so open and shut. Not only could contemporary man use a Maypole in his blighted Garden of Eden, but he is just beginning to realize the damage caused by not having one. Consider those maimed excuses for Merry Mount that have come to serve, ever so ineptly, as its substitute. On New Year's Eve (Oh, God! A year older and what have we accomplished?) the children of Myles Standish are condemned to gather with noisemakers, paper hats and lamp shades, and out of sheer embarrassment get smashed. The stocks could not hurt worse than such gross incompetence at ritual gaiety. Every New Year's Eve, Thomas Morton is avenged.

Is this really so small a price to pay, this emptiness of heart? In between un-Mortonlike holidays—the Christmas ringing with carols to shop by, the Easter that means chocolate bunnies and an annual visit to the church of one's unfaith, the Labor Day spent dourly traveling to nowhere along clogged highways—there occur other public rites, as grimly forgettable as scenes in a bad home movie. The lady with a champagne bottle, weighed down by her furs and obligatory Fixed Smile, whacks like an inept murderer at the prow of a receding ship. The politician, equipped with a trowel and the Fixed Smile, gobs mortar on a cornerstone, or noshes his way along the campaign trail.

America's unacknowledged but cheerlessly compulsive rituals make up a montage of trivia that boggles the eye. Brother Masons shake their In-group hands. Boy Scouts extend *rigor mortis* salutes. Shriners vibrate their fezzes. Drum majorettes goose-step. Plastic Miss Americas and Nixon's Graustarkian palace guard seem to pass together in surreal review, followed by that parody of Roman triumph, the Veterans Day parade —all paunch, sourly dispirited bugle blasts, and flat feet hitching to keep step. The banal, hand-held camera pans on, showing no pity. There go the Rose Bowl floats; where does the papier-mâché end, where do the people begin? Here come the shaman-orators and all the Babbitt snake dancers. Dear Lord, another political convention!

The gift for ritual is not exactly prospering in the 20th century; secularity, urbanism, technology—all contrive to separate modern man from the kind of community that encourages, even demands, a sense of ceremony. But is this the best that America can do for a bill of rites? Other people's rituals tend to release them—as they should. Rituals are society's unwritten permission for civilized man to express primitive emotions: fear, sexuality, grief. Other people's rituals invite them to be more human in public —more themselves—than they dare to be in private. Greek Zorbas whirl like fertility gods, Irishmen keen at their friends' funerals or even the funerals of strangers. Americans smile their Fixed Smile: the smile as antismile—no pleasure, no love, no silliness. The smile that tries to hide the face of American Gothic and only betrays it. The smile that says, "I cannot be myself in public."

Lately a ghastly doubt has begun to mock us, and it refuses to go away. We aren't sure, but we wonder: Is a sense of ritual—a sense of formal, sanctified public ceremonial—the preliminary state to a special kind of wisdom, a higher seriousness of the heart than Puritan hearts can ever know? Through some hideous gaffe did the anti-Maypolers reject not the devil but one face of God? By being so busy conquering nature that they could not celebrate it, by insisting with prim spiritual pride on reason, did the first Americans cut us all off from the more chaotic but deeper rhythms of life?

When his first child is born, an American father finds how criminally inadequate it is to pass out cigars. When his father dies, an American son discovers that the national habits of grief and commemoration are even worse. A son honors his father by buying a cosmetic job from an undertaker who was a stranger to the living face. Mass-produced casket, mass-produced headstone, all-purpose prayers. Amen.

At the life-and-death occasions, the common-sense, I-can-do-it-myself American bumps up against the humbling truth: rituals teach men how to behave at the best and the worst moments of their lives. If one has learned no way to behave—or only a superficial way—the meaning of those moments, the meaning of life itself, hangs in jeopardy. The greatest of the American watchers, Alexis de Tocqueville, put his finger on the risk. No-frills rugged individualism, he warned over a hundred years ago, not only makes "every man forget his ancestors, but it hides his descendants and separates his contemporaries from him; it throws him back forever upon himself alone and threatens in the end to confine him entirely within the solitude of his own heart."

But now a new tribal generation has arrived. It knows nothing of Merry Mount because it knows nothing of history. But in its blood runs Morton's cursed inspiration. It is determined to raise a Maypole. With beads and real Indian headdress and peace symbols, Woodstock Nation wanders the countryside looking for its own Merry Mount: the perfect rock festival.

No one can begin to understand the young people—including the young people—until one astonishing fact is grasped: they are not kicking against the System because they think it has too many values, but because they think it has too few—and those too thin. In its preoccupation with doing, the System has let the big moments, the festive moments, the very bright and the very dark moments—the ritual moments—get away. The System has just hustled on past with its Fixed Smile in place. And for this, the young are not about to forgive it.

Woodstock Nation is staging a kind of reverse revolution, it may be the first young generation to demand more rather than less ritual. And despite its ignorance, despite its boorishness, the revolution of the children is becoming the education of us all. For though they have not made the fathers trust their values, they have made them distrust their own. Young and old, we are all developing a new respect for ritual. We are learning that knowledge without the ritual element of wonder is barren and self-mocking. We are beginning to understand that the need for ritual is a human constant, not just a craving of primitive Indians and decadent Englishmen, and that if good rituals are not invented, bad rituals happen.

Almost 20 years ago, Dr. Rollo May (*Love and Will*) speculated whether modern man, suffering "in our commercial and industrial society from a suppression of fantasy life and imagination," would seize upon "new forms of magic." His prophecy has come true with a vengeance. At the profoundest levels, as well as at the most trivial, we hunger to ritualize our everyday lives. Like a humorless orgy, the Living Theater spills its rites of the stage into the audience and finally into the street. The young read as holy writ Allen Ginsberg's *How to Make a March/ Spectacle.* Protests against war, or even air pollution, find men in saffron robes with shaven heads carrying joss sticks and chanting the *Hare Krishna.* For other instructions, people consult the *I Ching*—including how to stage a new-life-style marriage. The mood reaches even the middle-aged, who tentatively toy with beards and hair styles—the least radical forms of period costuming—and adopt sensitivity training as a kind of labor-relations device. With a fever to be relevant, priests and ministers are bringing religious services into the coffeehouse, the factory, the supermarket. More often than not, the music that enhances these mod liturgies comes from an electric guitar pulsating to a rock beat. Once again, "Make a joyful noise unto the Lord" is our collective text.

What all this suggests is that a touch of madness is in the air and Americans have, as usual, gone from one extreme to the other. In *The Making of a Counter Culture,* Historian Theodore Roszak protests: "We begin to resemble nothing so much as the cultic hothouse of the Hellenistic period, where every manner of mystery and fakery, ritual and rite, intermingled with marvelous indiscrimination." Rituals threaten to be the next epidemic. Consider the games of ritual that people play: group-encounter institutes, hippie communes, mate-swapping clubs—all with varied seriousness are peddling salvation to the Fixed Smilers. The medicine men are setting up their booths. You want to be yourself in public? Have they got a ritual for you! Mysticism has become a carnival sell. Right on, scientology.

The '70s are seeing the American launched on a curiously un-American quest. He has order—the order of the machine and the punch card, the order he once thought he wanted—and he is sick to death of all the well-oiled predestination. He is off and hunting for a richer order than technology can provide, a more organic sense of meaning. Confusedly, belatedly, he is searching for something very like his soul. No one has a right to feel very optimistic about the prospects. If young people associate the Fixed-Smile syndrome with Viet Nam, older Americans see behind all the Dionysian huggermugger the face of Charles Manson. And they sense that what the children are saying to the fathers is this: We will put the Maypole back up, even if it kills us—and you.

By the most insufferable of history's practical jokes, "letting it all hang out" could produce the same results as holding it all in. Instead of Salem witches, the California breed; instead of the Ku Klux Klan, the Weathermen. If Plymouth without Merry Mount was a mistake, Merry Mount without Plymouth could be a disaster. The country that began with theocracy could end with demonology. But such an end would be cheap parody. Rituals are not quick cures for civilization and its discontents. Nor are they self-indulgence for psychic escape artists. Rituals are ultimately the SOS of terrorized hearts trapped between knowledge of their own mortality and ignorance of the dark and quite possibly hostile universe about them. What they are desperately signaling for is a deal. They are the new compact that man tries to make with reality after the death of his illusion that he is God.

America began as a ritual of rebirth—the world's best publicized new beginning. Now the original American Dream is dying by bits and pieces, and that is our panic. Do the new rituals represent fumbling attempts to initiate a second beginning? Is all the writhing and the agony, all the violent self-division, the schizophrenia of an old self dying, a new self being born? Are we witnessing, at last, the erratic rites of America's coming of age? Of its coming to a self-awareness chastened by defeats into being more human? It is too soon to speculate—even to dream a second dream. One's hope is so guarded that it dares express itself only as these tentative questions. All that can be said now is that most Americans find themselves in a kind of no man's land, between Plymouth and Merry Mount, between Middletown and Woodstock. Between too much reason and too much passion. Between the impulse to act and the impulse to be.

According to Hawthorne's short story *The Maypole of Merry Mount,* the peal of a psalm from Plymouth would occasionally collide with "the chorus of a jolly catch" from Merry Mount and echo in a splendid confusion of styles. Suppose a little band of displaced Americans had lived exactly in the middle, in that no man's land between culture and counter-culture. Suppose they had listened to that collision of psalm and catch tune for weeks, for months. Would the double echo have ceased to be two competing sounds? Would one new sound have fallen in the ear, with a new rhythm and harmony of its own, neither hymn nor May dance: a third way?

We will be the first to know, for 343 years afer May Day 1627, we have become those displaced Americans. We are the people that both sides warned against.

The New Girl

JOHN CLELLON HOLMES

I

A virgin coed, on being asked why she is taking the pill, explains that just as she wants to feel absolutely free to say yes without fear of pregnancy, so she wants to be sure that when she says no she isn't using this same fear as a cop-out. A lyrically graphic book of poetry about sexual euphoria, composed largely in love's forbidden language, is the object of an obscenity action in San Francisco, and its author is neither Allen Ginsberg nor Henry Miller but a pretty young poetess in tank top and hip-huggers. A clear-eyed maiden in patterned stockings lists her five civil rights arrests with the same quiet pride with which her older sister once listed her sorority affiliation. A high-fashion model, earning $50,000 a year, takes ten months off to gypsy around Europe with a hippie poet, making the *Provo* scene in Amsterdam, living on bread and wine on the beach at Iviza, and comes home to resume her career with no more scars to her psyche than the secretary of the past brought back from her proverbial two weeks of man hunting in the Poconos. A plain girl from a plain neighborhood in Brooklyn, driven by the urge to sing but refusing to accept the old showbiz rule that plain girls are doomed to being funny (so many Cass Dalys or Martha Rayes), creates an eerie beauty out of her large nose and aquiline features, inspiring thereby a whole style of kookie chic. Serious actresses, who have "done time" at the Actors Studio, appear fully nude in films or Happenings and do not feel like exhibitionists, much less whores. A folk singer devotes part of the fortune she has amassed with her ethereal, May-moon voice to the establishment of a school for the teaching of nonviolent direct action. A young socialite, bored by the charity-bazaar organizing and cotillion chaperoning that were the fate of her kind in other years, appears in underground movies, pals around with working-class minstrels from Liverpool and, far from being ostracized by her set, leads the march of Park Avenue down to the East Village.

Though these young women and their counterparts do not yet represent the numerical majority of their generation, there are strong reasons for believing that they constitute the advance guard of a new female attitude, an attitude that heralds the most profound change in femininity since the suffragettes, a change that is creating nothing less than a New Girl (the counterpart of the New Young Man), a girl with the very interests—sexual freedom and psychedelics, skindiving and the swim, Bobby Kennedy and Bobby Dylan, the New Left and civil rights—that so sharply distinguish that young man from his elders. Like all advance guards, this New Girl is pioneering the territory her sisters will eventually colonize; and what has happened to her may well happen to all young women tomorrow. What has happened is the emergence, at long last, of the Postfeminist Girl.

What Joan Baez and Baby Jane Holzer have in common is not a similar

424 Slouching Toward Bethlehem To Be Born

moral or political attitude, any more than what Barbra Streisand shares with poet Lenore Kandel is an identical life style or clothes taste. Indeed, young women today are astonishingly diverse in their solutions to the question of how they want to live and toward what ends. What they all share, however, is a radically new relationship to the stereotypes that have defined womanhood heretofore—those stereotypes of wife, mother, spinster, courtesan, whore or ball breaker that were the only options offered to women in the past, roles that were conceived by men for the most part and reflected male attitudes that had their source in male needs. What the New Girls of today all exhibit in their various ways is an impatience with these roles and a rejection of the traditional idea that women, unlike men, are somehow supposed to be *fulfilled* by the roles they play, among which they would include the historically most recent, and emotionally least fulfilling, role of all (created by women themselves)—that of the feminist.

If the New Girl's impatience with role playing seems curious to some men, it is because these men forget that oppressed groups, in order to survive, are forced to act out the image of themselves that their oppressors find most acceptable. The Negro's evolution in America, for instance, could be described as a process of Stepin Fetchit turning into "Bojangles" Robinson turning into Harry Belafonte turning into Dick Gregory—all of which succeeding "images" revealed more about the white man's changing attitudes toward the Negro than the Negro's actual attitudes toward himself.

Women, it must be remembered, have been full citizens of the U.S. for less than 50 years—only half as long as Negroes. Before 1920, they had little choice but to become so many *Little Women, Sister Carries* or *Madame Bovarys*. And, like Negroes, women's social emancipation (at least in terms of real equality of opportunity) remained, until recent years, largely a matter of a constitutional amendment that carried about as much weight as the paper on which it was printed. Also like Negroes, the psychic liberation of women from all the subtle hangovers of chattel status in the past has taken considerably longer. Its achievement may be only now in sight, and perhaps the most persistent hangover of all has been feminism itself.

"Psychologically, feminism had a single objective: the achievement of maleness by the female." So wrote Marynia Farnham and Ferdinand Lundberg in *Modern Woman, the Lost Sex*. For the feminist played a role no less thwarting to her development as a human being than the patient helpmate or compliant mistress whom she hoped to supplant. If her aims were positive, the attitude behind them was deeply negative. Though she was always loudly defending female rights, she was actually preoccupied with attacking male privileges. Her crusades for birth control, for the right to smoke and drink in public and for an abolition of the double standard in sex and business stemmed largely from her sense of outrage at injustice, rather than from a desire to live more fully, more experimentally, more permissively. And the feminist attitude did not vanish with the passage of the 19th Amendment, which granted women the vote.

In the 1920s, for instance, the emancipated woman bound down her breasts, chopped off her hair and stood at the speak-easy bar, knocking back bootleg with the men and thereby acting just like all strangers in a new church: She watched what the other guy was doing and imitated him. As an example, Lady Ashley (heroine of Hemingway's *The Sun Also Rises)* reserved her ultimate contempt for the male character who "wanted me to grow my hair out. . . . He said it would make me more womanly," because her aim, of course, was to be *less* "womanly" in the feminine sense, associated, as that was, with the hateful past.

In the 1930s and 1940s, having discovered that male domination was fully as psychological as it was social, women became more openly aggressive, taking over the trousers as well as the causes once considered exclusively male and insisting that they were not only just like men but might even be superior to them. Indeed, one of Mary McCarthy's heroines, after a night of lovemaking with a businessman in a lower berth, could haughtily think of herself "as a citadel of socialist virginity, that could be taken and taken again, but never truly subdued. . . . She had come out of it untouched, while he had been reduced to a jelly." The women of those years wrote books that grimly attempted to prove that females were far more adaptable to the collectivized circumstances of modern life than males, and others that triumphantly stated that because the clitoris had measurably thicker nerve endings than the penis, female sexuality was immeasurably more rewarding than male.

All these feminist positions, however, had a single self-defeating characteristic in common; They defined femininity by comparison with, or in contradistinction to, masculinity. All were influenced by the viewpoint of the liberated slave, which seeks to first emulate, then compete with and finally destroy the exmaster. For at the bottom of it, the feminist was not seeking femininity at all but was still imprisoned by the idea that she could escape the demeaning role of "weaker sex" only by adopting yet another role: the masculinized woman.

Feminism was basically a movement of social reform, but though legislation and changing mores gradually emptied it of substance, it continued to have a more or less fugitive existence in the platforms of left-wing political parties, where it was known as "the woman question." No better indication of its final and complete demise can be found than the fact that the New Left (in whose ranks there are almost as many girls as boys) may be the first radical movement in modern history that does not concern itself with women's rights at all.

Doctrinaire feminism would strike the dedicated young women of Students for a Democratic Society as an anachronism about on a par with Prohibition, for they simply do not feel like an aggrieved minority that needs defending. Indeed, even the special status immemorially reserved for women who "worked for the cause" (manning the mimeograph rather than the barricades) seems silly to the New Girl of today, in light of that hunger for immediate, personal involvement that is her strongest motivation. It would never occur to her to stay behind, mailing out leaflets, when the bus leaves for the Pentagon; and the idea that there are certain confrontations from which she is excused on account of her sex is an idea as foreign to her as taking to her bed during menstruation. Confrontation, putting one's self on the line, walking down a Southern street side by side with a Negro youth (and thus risking the ugliest epithet—"Nigger lover"—that a bigot can think of to hurl at a woman, a sexual epithet specifically designed to insult her femininity); all this is precisely the *point* of her involvement; for by refusing to accept even a role that might exempt her from the consequences of her beliefs, she is affirming her conviction that *all* role playing is degrading to a human being. To help the Negro escape the necessity of playing Uncle Tom, she is willing to forgo the protection that is accorded Little Eva.

Feminism, then, is dead as a social movement; but is the New Girl really free of the psychic prejudices that succeeded it? Some raw comparisons may be illuminating.

In their day, Ingrid Bergman and Elizabeth Taylor flouted accepted social morality by changing marital partners without waiting to be divorced. Both risked, and suffered, the wrath of an outraged public, meanwhile portraying themselves as martyrs to a love so great it transcended custom. But both quickly married their lovers once they were free to do so. New Girl Julie Christie, on the contrary, lived openly and happily with her former mate, blandly announced that she had no plans to marry and averred that it was nobody's business but her own.

After Hedy Lamarr appeared nude in *Ecstasy* in the 1930s, she spent most of the rest of her career trying to live it down, confessing in interview after interview what a mistake it had been and refusing to pose for any but the most decorous pinup pictures. But when Vanessa Redgrave appeared nude in a movie in the 1960s, she did not feel that she had compromised herself or her craft, much less that the Academy Award nomination that she received for the role was a tribute to her figure rather than her talent.

Edna St. Vincent Millay's arrest in connection with the Sacco-Vanzetti case was the culmination of her revolt against the moral double standards of her time; for in her eyes, radical sexual attitudes assumed radical political ones. The young activists of a few years ago, however, who could (and did) boast of civil rights jail records as long as their arms, considered themselves morally superior to girls with none and would not have countenanced being treated like camp followers by anybody.

The difference is simple: The female rebels of the past defied the conventional roles of womanhood and then more or less meekly paid the price for that defiance, whereas today's New Girl thinks of herself as affirming her integrity as a person (a person who happens to be a woman) and fully expects to be rewarded for this affirmation by an increased sense of her individual worth.

All signs indicate that it is femininity itself that the New Girl seeks to experience and define afresh. She wants to know nothing less than what

it is like to be a female human being, no longer either a willing *or* a rebellious appendage to some man but her own unique self. In the process,
she has discovered that many of the assumed differences between men
and women are shabby myths and many of the denied ones have a stubborn reality. For instance, at one and the same time, she can assert that
her intelligence is as powerful as any man's and can also admit, with no
feeling of inferiority, that it tends to operate on a different current—A.C.
rather than D.C., as it were. But that she wants to accept and inhabit
herself as a woman (and not one or another version of Adam's rib) is
clear, no matter where you choose to look.

The most basic role that women were required to play in the past was
that of the mannequin, the clotheshorse, the *living* doll. Unlike men,
women were compelled to experience themselves as objects—vessels of
purity or seductiveness, fragile beauty or fleshly allure—things to be
adorned, posed, desired and possessed. In this sense, women's fashions
were so many costumes that identified the roles that women had chosen,
or were compelled to play. It was assumed that a girl's morals were reflected in her necklines.

The New Girl, however, is not interested in dressing up, or down, to
men's unexamined conceptions of women. Not for her to feel that her
body is shameful and thus, at the onset of puberty, to buy her cashmeres
three sizes too big and lower her skirts to disguise the fact that girls have
comely knees or risk being thought "fast and loose." Not for her (if she
is a few years older) to allow herself to be gotten up in a succession of
grotesque "new looks" by one or another Mr. Fruit, whose evident intention is to distort or humiliate her femininity.

Instead, she comes hurrying down the street in her white plastic boots
or plum-colored snubby flats, her figure *there* for all to see—in miniskirt or
minipants or miniseparates; her dress, more than not, designed to reveal
her lingerie and her lingerie, more than not, designed to reveal her body;
violets in wild clusters on her panties, bra more of a window than a gar-
ment; wearing her pajamas in the street and, like as not, little more than a
smile in her bed; arraying herself in a veritable peacock profusion of bold
colors and bolder prints, of wild fabrics and even wilder designs—all of
which add up to a style that is kinky, pert, daring, frivolous, flamboyant,
theatrical and unabashedly sexy; a style whose basic ingredients seem to
be flair and imagination, a style that is above all an *eccentric* style, resulting from *boutique* browsing, hours of experimentation before a mirror and
an eagerness to discover her own taste and her own chosen image.

The New Girl's fashions all emphasize femaleness (whether the model
be The Dragon Lady or Alice in Wonderland) and they are mostly created
by women, and young women at that. More than anything else, these
clothes express the conviction that the female body is superbly natural,
sensuous and efficient; that it was created to move (rather than stand still)
and to move men (rather than the envy of other women). When designer
Mary Quant was asked what was the *point* of the new fashion, she replied

unhesitatingly: "Sex." In short, it is clear that the New Girl, even in her manner of dress, is declaring a fresh awareness of herself and of men and, above all, of the relation between the two.

II

What most distinguishes the Postfeminist Girl from her mother is her attitude toward sex, and her own sex in particular. It is not so much a question of a wider moral latitude as it is a matter of deeper self-knowledge. I don't mean to imply that women are, in actual fact, exclusively sexual creatures (in thrall to their biology and its cycle) when I say that almost every aspect of the New Girl's personality reflects her final freedom from the sexual status that was the fate of women in the past. But nevertheless, a female's life, until recently, was defined by two all-but-irrevocable facts: the necessity of marrying young, which her subservient economic position made almost obligatory, and the constant possibility of pregnancy, which her gender made the essential condition of her existence. Like it or not, she was reduced to the level of a sexual object (as much by her body as by the male's), and if her emotional life often remained stunted, it was because she could never fully escape from the phantoms of marriage and motherhood that seemed to haunt her future. If most women dutifully played the roles of wife and momma (or felt guilty if they did not), it wasn't only because there were few other roles available but because they could not conceive of themselves *except* in terms of the mating and mothering to which their very bodies seemed to condemn them.

All this has changed now and it has changed forever, and the single most important factor in that change has been, quite simply, the advent of the contraceptive pill. At one stroke, it accomplished a triple liberation that centuries of *coitus interruptus,* calendar counting and precautionary technology had never been able to achieve. It freed women from their own biology, putting into their hands (rather than men's) an inexpensive, simple-to-use, foolproof method of preventing conception and even controlling menstruation, a method that involved neither temperature taking, humiliating diaphragm measurings well before the act nor mood-breaking diaphragm insertions just prior to it. No longer does a girl have to premeditate her desire by deciding whether to take her "equipment" along on a date or risk being overcome when unprepared. No longer does a girl have to excuse herself to "outwit" her anatomy at the very moment when she feels most like indulging it. And the degree to which the pill has made possible the preservation of feminine dignity and integrity is suggested by this reaction (on the part of a 22-year-old) to the famous diaphragm-fitting scene in Mary McCarthy's *The Group:* "My God, how could any girl feel that sex was going to be good, much less *fun,* after being so clinically groped and measured by a total stranger that way!" To the New Girl of today, the very mechanics of contraception before the pill tended to demean a woman in her own eyes.

But in freeing her *from* her body, the pill accomplished something considerably more important: It freed her *to* its desires. By allowing a woman to enjoy sex without either the fear of pregnancy or the embarrassment of premeditation, it encouraged her to discover sexuality itself—female sexuality. All nonerotic considerations having been removed, women can at last confront their sexual natures with the same libidinous directness that men have always exhibited, a directness (as Lenore Kandel says) that "devour[s] all my secrets and my alibis"—with the result that in the past ten years we have learned more about female sexual response than in the ten centuries that preceded them, and we have learned it from women themselves.

But the third liberation that the pill made possible may have the most far-reaching consequences of all, because, having freed women from biology, and thus sexual reticence, it freed them from men as well and from men's wishful images of them. No longer dependent on a man to marry her if she "gets caught," released from the secondary sexual role (and all its distractions) that this dependency imposed on her, the New Girl is finally free of role playing itself and has entered into an equality with men, psychic as well as legal, in which she can at last discover and develop a uniquely individual *and* a uniquely feminine personality.

Menstruation, marriage and motherhood: These were the central facts of female life heretofore. But this is no longer true and young women today exercise a degree of control over these facts that has made it possible for each of them to say and mean that she "enjoys being a girl." That unsettling moment, when the arrival of "the curse" and the budding of breasts were such a shame and an embarrassment to young girls, is no longer an ordeal. In this era of the training bra, 12-year-olds are envious of 13-year-olds *because* they have bosoms; and 14-year-olds, anticipating a beach party that is scheduled at an inopportune time, borrow Enovid, not to prepare for something sexual but to postpone anything biological that might curtail their fun. As the teenage heroine of Rosalyn Drexler's *I Am the Beautiful Stranger* puts it: "I'm so glad I got my period. I waited a long time. Now so much will change." It is this note of outright eagerness to be initiated into the mysteries of womanhood that is new.

College girls, 44 percent of whom (according to a recent survey) feel that premarital sex between engaged couples is perfectly all right, nevertheless insist that their moment of sexual decision be as free as possible of the dilemma once expressed by the paradoxical "If I do, he'll think I'm cheap. But if I don't, he'll think I'm prudish," just as they refuse to accept the male prejudices to which this age-old female watchword referred: "Don't act too bright, or he'll be intimidated. But don't act too dumb, either, or he won't be interested." Girls today simply do not regard themselves as being governed by masculine preconceptions such as these.

But it is the young single woman in the city, probably no longer a virgin and just as probably regarding this fact not as a troubling loss of innocence but as a valuable gain of experience, who best epitomizes the New Girl. Her life may be either a female facsimile of the hip bachelorhood of her male counterpart (her pad equipped with the same Herb Alpert LPs, wire wine rack, deep-enough-for-two divan and copper pot for that "special" casserole) or she may have taken to the lofts with her young man, living in the careless, tribal, improvised poverty of those who have dropped out. But whether her trip is to a dating bar for the purpose of meeting likely male swingers (a bar that she can enter, drink in and exit from alone, if no one strikes her fancy) or into inner space via LSD (a trip she makes equally on her own), the New Girl's venturesomeness implies, above everything else, an almost complete absence of all those tensions about "being single" that were etched in stress lines around the mouths of girls in their mid-20s heretofore.

The girl of today intends to marry, but she sees marriage as the *culmination* of a relationship that has survived intimacy, not as the beginning of one. She is looking for Mr. Cool, not Mr. Clean, and she will probably pass her 27th birthday with no nightmares of spinsterhood disturbing her dreams, much less those of the young man who may be sleeping beside her. Meanwhile, she is busy, inquisitive, excited, unsentimental (though not unromantic) and, above all, vividly alive. Probably she is more responsible than her boyfriend for making this the first dancing generation since the 1940s; and certainly male willingness to explore bolder sartorial, not to mention tonsorial, styles has been encouraged by her enthusiasm for the new—that enthusiasm for game playing itself that always emerges when one is no longer required to act a part.

Just as the assumption that all girls are feverish to get married has been proved obsolete, now that women are as free to experiment as men, so the notion that females are driven by some darkly visceral urge to have babies has not survived their ability to avoid them if they so choose. The matter is now firmly a question of voluntary decision, and soon there may be no reason the abortionist's curette cannot join the parental shotgun in the same oblivion. The New Girl probably wants babies—sometime. At least, she's no longer involved in the fierce denials of the so-called maternal instinct that made some of her older, "emancipated" sisters such a bore. But she's in no hurry. Or she's in the sort of hurry that Mary Quant expressed when she said, "Gestation is so slow, so out of date. I really don't see why it can't be speeded up." Which must stand as some ultimate in freedom from biology.

In any case, the New Girl refuses to act as though pots and pans, much less diapers and douches, add up to a satisfactory or fulfilling life. . . . This is at once an announcement that today's girl is free of her own sentimentalities and a warning that she can no longer be approached in terms of them. But if it sounds somehow antiromantic, it is also clearly prosexual. Done with roles herself, impatient with all the *routines* to which role playing leads, the New Girl fully expects her young man to act the same.

It could be argued, for example, that the very willingness on the part of the girls of the civil rights, free-speech, love or peace movements to dare fire hoses, cattle prods, tear gas and jail cells constituted the most decisive factor in spurring on their young men, for it was an unequivocal sign of the extent to which the Postfeminist Girl had severed herself from the clinging-vine, going-steady, bouncy-cheerleader roles of the past, and it served notice that she would no longer consider the football hero or big man on campus as her exclusive masculine ideal. In fact, it may well be that mutual commitment to the dangers and fulfillments of personal action has bound together the boys and girls of this generation in a compact that is actually *sexual* in nature, because each has passed the same rite of maturation in the other's presence. This similarity of male and female experience (sitting in together or tripping out—it doesn't matter which) is the most distinguishing characteristic of the New Youth, all of whom have more in common with one another than they do with any of their elders, regardless of sex.

But certainly today's girl feels that "words of love" are somehow empty unless they are grounded in the facts of life and, aside from being respected as a woman, she wants to be encountered as a human being. In return, she no longer expects such outworn gallantries as having her arm taken when crossing a street (her hand is much more to the point), nor does she get offended if the conversation strays from the demure, the lily-white or the trivial; and, as a consequence, the old-fashioned concept of the lady has little more meaning for her than the old-fashioned concept of the whore, neither being descriptive of the wide range of feminine experience that she is discovering.

Postfeminism has freed the girls of today to a candor and an articulateness about themselves that has infused all the arts; and never before have there been so many first-rate writers, painters and musicians among women, some of whom are so good that the age-old put-down, "It isn't *what* she does, it's the fact that she can *do* it at all," is now hopelessly moribund. Talents as sizable as Doris Lessing, Marisol and Buffy Sainte-Marie do not need to be apologized for with qualifiers such as *woman* writer, *lady* sculptor or *girl* composer. They are so accomplished that their gender has no bearing on the level of their achievement, though it has a great deal to do with the nature of the work itself, which is intensely, unapologetically feminine and makes no attempt to cultivate, much less ape, the masculine preconceptions that have dominated the arts for centuries —preconceptions that older artists such as Mary McCarthy and even Simone de Beauvoir tried so stubbornly to anticipate, and disarm, on their own terms.

What is different in the works of these New Girls is not the subject matter (both McCarthy and Lessing, for instance, write about similar types of women) but their attitude toward that subject matter—an attitude that makes use of, rather than trying to overcome or disguise, such distinctively female traits as subjectivity, compassion, sensuality, a taste for decoration and an involvement in the shifting immediacies of reality. If novelist Doris Lessing relies on these traits to creatively describe, for the first time, the elusive experience of female orgasm, critic Susan Sontag calls on them no less when she attempts to confront a work of art as nakedly and openly as she would a lover.

In such works, it is possible at last for men to glimpse the world of femininity from the inside: a world that is not exclusively made up of chintz curtains, baking dishes and billets-doux; a world in which *they* appear like slightly boyish Humphrey Bogarts as seen through the eyes of tolerant and affectionate Lauren Bacalls; a contemporaneously discordant world that is nevertheless keyed to the realities of the body and its un-panicked rhythms; the world you hear in the voice of Mama Cass Elliott, a voice that is as darkly oboe, as richly brocade, as *fat* (in the jazz sense) as the voice of a switched-on Lilith; that world of stockings to be rinsed out and emotional post-mortems to be made, of sagacious hopes and shopping lists, which men leave behind when they put on their shoes and go away with a kiss and a promise to call; a world with an indescribable aroma of scent and sensibility to it. And the books and paintings and songs that describe this world are (as anthologist Barbara Alson has said): "tougher, less sentimental, less euphemistic . . . more often per-sonal, much less often precious. And while not less feminine, certainly less ladylike." To which anyone, after all the Pearl Bucks and the Elizabeth Barrett Brownings of the past, will utter a profound "Amen!"

III

If the passage of time since enfranchisement, plus the pill, plus today's saner moral climate, have worked together to make the Postfeminist Girl possible, it may be the so-called generation gap that has made her a fact. For young Americans now are more passionately than ever before en-gaged in posing questions, and most of their questions have to do with the stereotyped life roles their elders expect them to take for granted. "The time it takes to hypnotize the young into standardization is called growing up" (as one of them has said), and they want no part of it. But never has a generation been less supine as regards its wars nor more committed as regards its causes. Never has a generation denied society so recklessly nor affirmed the individual so idealistically. And rarely has any generation felt so strongly, or with such sound reasons, that it con-stituted a community in itself that existed, separate and besieged, right in the middle of an uncomprehending environment, to which its very pro-cesses of awareness were alien and antithetical.

If the search for a new, more direct experience of the self is the over-riding quest of this time, and if this means getting down to what Negroes call the nitty-gritty and existentialists call the essential reality, women may be better equipped than men for the arduous journey inward. Having been forced into masks and made to act as if the masks were real, having had no choice but to somehow survive as themselves *within* a role, and having at last gained that psychic freedom without which all social freedom is a sham, young women today are singularly prepared to function on the personal, subjective, nonabstract, *now* level where this generation (boys as well as girls) believes its truths will be found. In one sense, women have been in this territory from the beginning. They intimately know the disparity between the actor and the part he plays, between social codes and human nature; and it is this very disparity that has come to obsess young people today, revealing, as it does, the layer on layer of hypocrisy, deceit and complacency under which most older citizens of modern society bury their bad consciences, while the world worsens for lack of simple love and honesty. The antidote to this obsession is to tell it like it is, as the New Girl is intent on doing; and it may not be too farfetched to prophesy that the girls of this generation will affect its future as decisively as the boys.

Indeed, there are even signs of a temporary imbalance between the sexes, for which the New Girl is partially responsible. Some young men find it difficult to adjust to her expectation of full sexual pleasure, as well as moral equality; or her insistence that, insofar as she has come out from behind her masks, he must do no less and meet her as nakedly as she wants to meet him; or her eager involvement in all the things that, up until now, he may have considered *his* province. Ironically, the New Girl's rediscovery of femininity may compel men into a re-evaluation of some of the more "he-mannish" aspects of masculinity, for she knows that having to prove one's manliness is as false as having to act womanly and, though she understands the dilemma, she has less and less patience with it, and this is bound to put a certain degree of pressure on men. Nevertheless, there are an equal number of signs that women have now evolved to a point where they can admit that today's men, far from being only protectors or breadwinners or Casanovas, sometimes suffer from the same anxieties, insecurities and identity crises that were thought of in the past as peculiarly female problems. Certainly the New Girl is better equipped than her older sister to offer that human understanding (as against simple mothering) that such problems deserve, and this feeling of likeness, this similarity of emotional experience, this sense of being in the same capsizable boat (in terms of the society) is a powerful asset.

There are even reasons to suspect that the eventual righting of these old sexual imbalances and the new, less antagonistic male-female polarity that could result may do away at last with the centuries-old notion that men and women are somehow unalterably locked in an oblique opposition to each other, like sumo wrestlers poised in an embrace at once violent and erotic—a notion that is at the bottom of what older generations have always called the battle of the sexes. There have been periods of armistice in this battle and there have been periods of armed truce, but the urge to dominate or undermine (from one side or the other) has gone on and on relentlessly.

What the emergence of the New Girl suggests is that at last there may be some hope for a real and lasting peace, in which the truly feminine and the truly masculine can exist side by side, acknowledging the similarity of desire that drives them to merge and the differences of consciousness that keep them happily distinct; neither any longer seeking to subject or subvert the other, but both united in the effort to cultivate those areas where polarities can converge.

In this light, the Postfeminist Girl is pioneering in what may be the emotional landscape of tomorrow, a new Garden of Eden from which only the sense of sin and dissemblance will be expelled, and clearly men will profit fully as much as she from her explorations into a more candid and authentic femininity. And meanwhile, they have the mingled pleasure and astonishment of her company.

Open Land: Getting Back to the Communal Garden

SARA DAVIDSON

Wheeler Ranch: free land—live-in, drop-in.
Commune Directory

The front wheels drop and the car thuds down a wet, muddy ravine. Thick night fog, raining hard. The car squishes to a stop, front end buried in clay and the right rear wheel spinning. I get out and sink to my ankles. No flashlight. No waterproof gear. Utter blackness, except for the car's dulled lights under the dirt. I climb back in, but because of the 45-degree angle, I'm pitched forward against the dashboard. Turn on the radio. Only eight o'clock—a long wait until daylight. Am I anywhere near Wheeler Ranch? Haven't seen another car or a light anywhere on this road. I start honking the horn. Cows bellow back from what seems very close range. I imagine angry ranchers with shotguns. Tomorrow is Sunday—eight miles back to the nearest town, and nothing will be open. Is there an AAA out here? Good God, I'll pay anybody anything! If they'll just get me out of this.

I had started north from San Francisco in late afternoon, having heard vague descriptions of a commune called Wheeler's that was much beloved by those who had passed through it. The commune had had trouble with local police, and no one was sure whether the buildings were still standing or who was there. At sunset, a storm came up, and rather than turn back, I continued slowly along narrow, unlit country roads, my headlights occasionally picking up messages like "Stop War," painted on the side of a barn, and "Drive slowly, no M.D. Around," on a fence post. When I reached the woodsy, frontier town I knew to be near Wheeler's, I stopped in a bar to ask directions. Heads turned. People froze, glasses in hand. A woman with an expressionless, milky face said, "Honey, there isn't any sign. You just go up the road six miles and there's a gate on the left. Then you have to drive a ways to git to it. From where I live, you can see their shacks and what have you. But you can't see anything from the road."

After six miles, there was a gate and a sign, "Beware of cattle." I opened it and drove down to a fork, picked the left road, went around in a circle and came back to the fork, took the right and bumped against two logs in the road. I got out and moved them. Nothing could stop me now. Another fork. To the left the road was impassable—deep ruts and rocks; to the right, a barbed-wire fence. Raining harder, darker. This is enough. Get out of here fast. Try to turn the car around, struggling to see . . . then the sickening dip.

I got into my sleeping bag and tried to find a comfortable position in the crazily tilted car. My mood swung between panic and forced calm. At about 5:00 A.M., I heard rustling noises, and could make out the silhouettes of six horses which walked around the car, snorting. An hour later, the rain let up, and a few feet from the car I found a crude sign with an arrow, "Wheeler's." I walked a mile, then another mile, through rolling green hills, thinking, "If I can just get out of here." At last, around a bend were two tents and a sign, "Welcome, God, love." The first tent had a light burning inside, and turned out to be a greenhouse filled with boxes of seedlings. At the second tent, I pushed open the door and bells tinkled. Someone with streaked brown hair was curled in a real bed on two mattresses. There was linoleum on the floor, a small stove, a table, and books and clothes neatly arranged on shelves. The young man lifted his head and smiled. "Come in."

I was covered with mud, my hair was wild and my eyes red and twitching. "I tried to drive in last night, my car went down a ravine and got stuck in the mud, and I've been sleeping in it all night."

"Far out," he said.

"I was terrified."

The young man, who had gray eyes set close together and one gold earring, said, "Of what?"

"There were horses."

He laughed. "Far out. One of the horses walked into Nancy's house and made a hole in the floor. Now she just sweeps her dirt and garbage down the hole."

My throat was burning. "Could we make some coffee?"

He looked at me sideways. "I don't have any." He handed me a clump of green weeds. "Here's some yerba buena. You can make tea." I stared at the weeds.

"What's your name?" I asked.

"Shoshone."

"Mine's Sara."

"Far out."

He got dressed, watered the plants in the greenhouse, and started down a path into the bushes, motioning for me to follow. Every few feet, he would stop to pick yerba buena, listen to birds, watch a trio of pheasants take off, and admire trees that were recently planted—almond, Elberta peach, cherry, plum. They were all in blossom, but I was in no mood to appreciate them. After every ten minutes of walking, we would come to a clearing with a tent or wooden shack, wake up the people in their soggy sleeping bags and ask them to help push the car out. The dwellings at Wheeler's are straight out of Dogpatch—old boards nailed unevenly together, odd pieces of plastic strung across poles to make wobbly igloos, with round stovepipes poking out the side. Most have dirt floors, though the better ones have wood. In one tent, we found a young man who had shaved his head except for one stripe of hair down the center, like a Mohican. He grinned with his eyes closed. "In an hour or so, I might feel like helping you." We came to a crooked green shack with a peace sign on the door and the inside papered with paintings of Krishna. Nancy, a blond former social worker, was sleeping on the floor with her children, Gregory, eight, and Michelle, nine. Both have blond hair of the same length and it is impossible to tell at first which is the girl and which the boy. At communities like this, it is common for children to ask each other when they meet, "What are you?" Nancy said, "Don't waste your energy trying to push the car. Get Bill Wheeler to pull you out with his jeep. What's your hurry now? Sunday's the best day here. You've got to stay for the steam bath and the feast. There'll be lots of visitors." She yawned. "Lots of food, lots of dope. It never rains for the feast."

Shoshone and I walked back to the main road that cuts across the 320-acre ranch. The sun had burned through the fog, highlighting streaks of yellow wild flowers in the fields. Black Angus cows were grazing by the road. People in hillbilly clothes, with funny hats and sashes, were coming out of the bushes carrying musical instruments and sacks of rice and beans. About a mile from the front gate we came to the community garden, with a scarecrow made of rusty metal in the shape of a nude girl. Two children were chasing each other from row to row, shrieking with laughter, as their mother picked cabbage. A sign read, "Permit not required to settle here."

Bill Wheeler was working in his studio, an airy, wood-and-glass building with large skylights, set on a hill. When Bill bought the ranch in 1963, looking for a place to paint and live quietly, he built the studio for his family. Four years later, when he opened the land to anyone who wanted to settle there, the county condemned his studio as living quarters because it lacked the required amount of concrete under one side. Bill moved into a tent and used the studio for his painting and for community meetings.

Bill is a tall, lean man of thirty with an aristocratic forehead, straight nose, deep-set blue eyes, and a full beard and flowing hair streaked yellow by the sun. His voice is gentle with a constant hint of mirth, yet it projects, like his clear gaze, a strength, which is understood in this community as divine grace. Quiet, unhurried, he progresses with steady confidence toward a goal or solution of a problem. He is also a voluptuary who takes Rabelaisian delight in the community's lack of sexual inhibitions and in the sight of young girls walking nude through the grass. He lives at the center of the ranch with his third wife, Gay, twenty-two, and their infant daughter, Raspberry. His humor and self-assurance make it easy for those around him to submit to the hippie credo that "God will provide," because they know that what God does not, Bill Wheeler will.

Bill promises to rescue my car after he has chopped wood and started a fire for the steam bath. "Don't worry," a friend says, patting me on the back. "Bill's saved people who've given up hope, lost all confidence." A grizzly blond called Damian says, "Why don't you let me pull her out?" Bill says, "Damian, I love you, but I wouldn't trust you with any of my vehicles." Later, we pass Damian on the road, into which he is blissfully urinating. "Ha," Bill says, "the first time I met Damian he was peeing."

With the jeep and a chain, Bill pulls out the car in less than two minutes, and as it slides back onto secure road, I feel my tension drain away. Maybe I should stay for the feast. Maybe it really is beautiful here. I park the car at the county road, outside the first gate, and walk the three miles back to Wheeler's. The access road cuts across property owned by James G. Kelly, a breeder of show cattle and horses, who is enraged at the presence of up to a hundred itinerant hippies on the ranch adjacent to his. He has started court action to block Wheeler from using the access road, and his hired hands walk around with guns slung over their shoulders and their faces pinched with bilious hate.

On a bluff behind Wheeler's garden, the steam bath is set to go. Red-hot rocks are taken from the fire into a plastic tent that can be sealed on all sides. Shifts of eight or nine people undress and sit on the mud floor, letting out whoops, chanting and singing. Gallon wine jugs filled with water are poured on the rocks, and the tent fills up with steam so hot and thick that the children start coughing and no one can see anyone else. After a few minutes, they step out, covered with sweat, and wash off in a cold shower. The women shampoo their hair and soap up the children. The men dig out ticks from under the skin. Much gaiety and good-natured ogling, and then, as the last shift is coming out, a teen-age visitor carrying the underground *Berkeley Tribe* wanders in and stops, dumbfounded, staring with holy-fool eyes, his mouth open and drooling, at all that flesh and hair and sweat.

The garden, like a jigsaw puzzle whose pieces have floated together, presents the image of a nineteenth century tableau: women in long skirts and shawls, men in lace-up boots, coveralls, and patched jeans tied with pieces of rope, sitting on the grass playing banjos, guitars, lyres, wood flutes, dulcimers, and an accordian. In a field to the right are the community animals—chickens, cows, goats, donkeys, and horses. As far as the eye can see, there are no houses, no traffic, nothing but verdant hills, a stream, and the ocean with whitecaps rising in the distance. Nine-year-old Michelle is prancing about in a pink shawl and a floppy hat warbling, "It's time for the feast!" Nancy says, "The pickin's are sort of spare, because tomorrow is welfare day and everybody's broke." She carries from the outdoor wood stove pots of brown rice—plain, she says, "for the purists who are on Georges Ohsawa's ten-day brown-rice diet"—and rice with fruit and nuts for everyone else; beans, red and white; oranges and apples; yogurt; hash; pot; acid; mescaline. A girl says there are worms in the green apples. Another, with a studious voice and glasses, says, "That's cool, it means they were organically grown. I'd rather eat a worm than a chemical any day." They eat with their fingers from paper plates, and when the plates are gone, directly from the pot. A man in his forties with red-spotted cheeks asks me if I have any pills. "I'll take anything. I'm on acid now." I offer him aspirin. He swallows eight.

Everyone who lives at Wheeler's ranch is a vegetarian. By some strange inversion, they feel that by eating meat they are hastening their own death. Vegetarianism is, ironically, the aspect of their lifestyle that aggravates even the most liberal parents. ("What? You won't eat meat? That's ridiculous!") Bill Wheeler says that diet is "very very central to the revolution. It's a freeing process which people go through, from living on processed foods and eating gluttonous portions of meat and potatoes, to natural foods and a simple diet that is kinder to your body. A lot has to do with economics. It's much cheaper to live on grains and vegetables you can grow in your garden. When Gay and I moved here, we had to decide whether to raise animals to slaughter. Gay said she couldn't do it. Every Thanksgiving, there's a movement to raise money to buy turkeys, because some people think the holiday isn't complete without them. But an amazing thing happens when carrion is consumed. People are really greedy, and it's messy. The stench and the grease stay with us for days."

Gravy, roast beef, mashed potatoes, Parker House rolls, buttered peas —the weekly fare when Bill was growing up in Bridgeport, Connecticut. His father, a lawyer who speculated famously in real estate, told Bill he could do anything with his life as long as he got an education. So Bill, self-reliant, introspective, who loved the outdoors, went to Yale and studied painting. After graduating, he came to San Francisco to find a farmhouse where he could work. When he saw the 320-acre ranch which was then a sheep and Christmas tree farm, he felt, "I've got to have it. This is my land." He bought it with his inheritance, and still has enough money to live comfortably the rest of his life. "My parents would be shocked out of their gourds if they saw the land now," Bill says. "They died before I opened it."

The idea of open land, or free land, was introduced to Bill by Lou Gottlieb, a singer with the pop folk group, "The Limelighters," who, in 1962, bought a 32-acre piece of land called Morning Star about ten miles from Wheeler's Ranch. Gottlieb visits Wheeler's every Sunday for the feast; when I met him, he was walking barefoot with a pink blanket wrapped around him like a poncho and fastened with a giant safety pin.

A man of soaring height with crow eyes and a dark, silky beard, he talks in sermonettes, rising on his toes with enthusiasm. Gottlieb and a friend, Ramon Sender, decided in 1966 to start a community at Morning Star with one governing precept: access to the land would be denied to no one. With no rules, no organization, they felt, hostilities would not arise, and people could be reborn by living in harmony with the earth. Gottlieb deeded the land to God, and, shortly, a woman sued God because her home had been struck by lightning. "Now that God owns property," her lawyer argued, "He can be sued for natural disasters." It was not until 1967, Gottlieb says, that hippies began to patronize open land.

"From the first, the land selected the people. Those who couldn't work hard didn't survive. When the land got crowded, people split. The vibrations of the land will always protect the community." Gottlieb points to the sky. "With open land, *He* is the casting director." What happens, I ask, if someone behaves violently or destructively? Gottlieb frowns. "There have been a few cases where we've had to ask people to go, but it's at terrible, terrible cost to everyone's soul that this is done. When the land begins to throw off people, everyone suffers." He shakes his body, as if he were the land, rejecting a germ. "Open land has no historical precedent. When you give free land, not free food or money, you pull the carpet out from under the capitalist system. Once a piece of land is freed, 'no trespassing' signs pop up all along the adjoining roads."

Bill Wheeler refers to his ranch as "the land," and talks about people who live on the land, babies that are born on the land, music played on the land. He "opened the land," as he phrases it, in the winter of 1967, after Sonoma County officials tried to close Morning Star by bulldozing trees and all the buildings except Gottlieb's house. Some Morning Star people moved to Wheeler's, but others traveled to New Mexico, where they founded Morning Star East on a mesa near Taos owned by another wealthy hippie. The Southwest, particularly northern New Mexico and Colorado, has more communes on open land than any other region. The communes there are all crowded, and Taos is becoming a Haight-Ashbury in the desert. More land continues to be opened in New Mexico, as well as in California, Oregon, and Washington. Gottlieb plans to buy land and deed it to God in Holland, Sweden, Mexico, and Spain. "We're fighting against the territorial imperative," he says. "The hippies should get the Nobel Prize for creating this simple idea. Why did no one think of it before the hippies? Because hippies don't work, so they have time to dream up truly creative ideas."

It was surprising to hear people refer to themselves as "hippies"; I thought the term had been rendered meaningless by overuse. Our culture has absorbed so much of the style of hip—clothes, hair, language, drugs, music—that it has obscured the substance of the movement with which people at Morning Star and Wheeler's still strongly identify. Being a hippie, to them, means dropping out completely, and finding another way to live, to support oneself physically and spiritually. It does not mean being a company freak, working nine to five in a straight job and roaming the East Village on weekends. It means saying no to competition, no to the work ethic, no to consumption of technology's products, no to political systems and games. Lou Gottlieb, who was once a Communist party member, says, "The entire Left is a dead end." The hippie alternative is to turn inward and reach backward for roots, simplicity, and the tribal experience. In the first bloom of the movement, people flowed into slums where housing would be cheap and many things could be obtained free— food scraps from restaurants, second-hand clothes, free clinics and services. But the slums proved inhospitable. The hippies did nothing to improve the dilapidated neighborhoods, and they were preyed upon by criminals, pushers, and the desperate. In late 1967, they began trekking to rural land where there would be few people and life would be hard. They took up what Ramon Sender calls "voluntary primivitism," building houses out of mud and trees, planting and harvesting crops by hand, rolling loose tobacco into cigarettes, grinding their own wheat, baking bread, canning vegetables, delivering their own babies, and educating their own children. They gave up electricity, the telephone, running water, gas stoves, even rock music, which, of all things, is supposed to be the cornerstone of hip culture. They started to sing and play their own music —folky and quiet.

Getting close to the earth meant conditioning their bodies to cold, discomfort, and strenuous exercise. At Wheeler's, people walk twenty miles a day, carrying water and wood, gardening, and visiting each other. Only four-wheel-drive vehicles can cross the ranch, and ultimately Bill wants all cars banned. "We would rather live without machines. And the fact that we have no good roads protects us from tourists. People are car-bound, even police. They would never come in here without their vehicles." Although it rains a good part of the year, most of the huts do not have stoves and are not waterproof. "Houses shouldn't be designed to keep out the weather," Bill says. "We want to get in touch with it." He installed six chemical toilets on the ranch to comply with county sanitation requirements, but, he says, "I wouldn't go in one of those toilets if you paid me. It's very important for us to be able to use the ground, because we are completing a cycle, returning to Mother Earth what she's given us." Garbage is also returned to the ground. Food scraps are buried in a compost pile of sawdust and hay until they decompose and mix with the soil. Paper is burned, and metal buried. But not everyone is conscientious; there are piles of trash on various parts of the ranch.

Because of the haphazard sanitation system, the water at Wheeler's is contaminated, and until people adjust to it, they suffer dysentery, just as tourists do who drink the water in Mexico. There are periodic waves of hepatitis, clap, crabs, scabies, and streptococcic throat infections. No one brushes his teeth more than once a week, and then they often use "organic toothpaste," made from eggplant cooked in tinfoil. They are experimenting with herbs and Indian healing remedies to become free of manufactured medicinal drugs, but see no contradiction in continuing to swallow any mind-altering chemical they are offered. The delivery of babies on the land has become an important ritual. With friends, children, and animals keeping watch, chanting, and getting collectively stoned, women have given birth to babies they have named Morning Star, Psyche Joy, Covelo, Vishnu God, Rainbow Canyon King, and Raspberry Sundown Hummingbird Wheeler.

The childbirth ritual and the weekly feasts are conscious attempts at what is called "retribalization." But Wheeler's Ranch, like many hippie settlements, has rejected communal living in favor of a loose community of individuals. People live alone or in monogamous units, cook for themselves, and build their own houses and sometimes gardens. "There should not be a main lodge, because you get too many people trying to live under one roof and it doesn't work," Bill says. As a result, there are cliques who eat together, share resources, and rarely mix with others on the ranch. There was one group marriage between two teen-age girls, a forty-year-old man, and two married couples, which ended when one of the husbands saw his wife with another man in the group, pulled a knife, and dragged her off, yelling, "Forget this shit. She belongs to me."

With couples, the double standard is an unwritten rule: the men can roam but the women must be faithful. There are many more men than women, and when a new girl arrives, she is pounced upon, claimed, and made the subject of wide gossip. Mary Cordelia Stevens, or Corky, a handsome eighteen-year-old from a Chicago suburb, hiked into the ranch one afternoon last October and sat down by the front gate to eat a can of Spam. The first young man who came by invited her to a party where everyone took TCP, a tranquilizer for horses. It was a strange trip—people rolling around the floor of the tipi, moaning, retching, laughing, hallucinating. Corky went home with one guy and stayed with him for three weeks, during which time she was almost constantly stoned. "You sort of have to be stoned to get through the first days here," she says. "Then you know the trip." Corky is a strapping, well-proportioned, large-boned girl with a milkmaid's face and long blond hair. She talks softly, with many giggles: "I love to go around naked. There's so much sexual energy here, it's great. Everybody's turned on to each other's bodies." Corky left the ranch to go home for Christmas and to officially drop out of Antioch College; she hitchhiked back, built her own house and chicken coop, learned to plant, do laundry in a tin tub with a washboard, and milk the cows. "I love dealing with things that are simple and direct."

Bill Wheeler admires Corky for making it on her own, which few of the women do. Bill is torn between his desire to be the benefactor-protector and his intolerance of people who aren't self-reliant. "I'm contemptuous of people who can't pull their own weight," he says. Yet he constantly worries about the welfare of others. He also feels conflict between wanting a tribe, indeed wanting to be chieftain, and wanting privacy. "Open land requires a leap of faith," he says, "but it's worth it, because it guarantees there will always be change, and stagnation is death." Because of the fluidity of the community, it is almost impossible for it to become economically self-sufficient. None of the communes have been able to live entirely off the land. Most are unwilling to go into cash crops or light industry because in an open community with no rules, there are not enough people who can be counted on to work regularly. The women with children receive welfare, some of the men collect unemployment and food stamps, and others get money from home. They spend very little— perhaps $600 a year per person. "We're not up here to make money," Bill says, "or to live like country squires."

When darkness falls, the ranch becomes eerily quiet and mobility stops. No one uses flashlights. Those who have lived there some time can feel their way along the paths by memory. Others stay in their huts, have dinner, go to sleep, and get up with the sun. Around 7:00 P.M., people gather at the barn with bottles for the late milking. During the week, the night milking is the main social event. Corky says, "It's the only time you know you're going to see people. Otherwise you could wander around for days and not see anyone." A girl from Holland and two boys have gathered mussels at a nearby beach during the day, and invite everyone to the tipi to eat with them. We sit for some time in silence, watching the mussels steam open in a pot over the grate. A boy with glassy blue eyes whose lids seem weighted down starts to pick out the orange flesh with his dirt-caked hands and drops them in a pan greased with Spry. A mangy cat snaps every third mussel out of the pan. No one stops it. . . .

Nancy, in her shack about a mile from the tipi, is fixing a green stew of onions, cabbage, kale, leeks, and potatoes; she calls to three people who live nearby to come share it. Nancy has a seventeen-year-old, all-American-girl face—straight blond hair and pink cheeks—on a plump, saggy-stomached mother's body. She has been married twice, gone to graduate school, worked as a social worker and a prostitute, joined the Sexual Freedom League, and taken many overdoses of drugs. Her children have been on more acid trips than most adults at the ranch. "They get very quiet on acid," she says. "The experience is less staggering for kids than for adults, because acid returns you to the consciousness of childhood." Nancy says the children have not been sick since they moved to Wheeler's two years ago. "I can see divine guidance leading us here. This place has been touched by God." She had a vision of planting trees on the land, and ordered fifty of exotic variety, like strawberry guava, camelia, and loquat. Stirring the green stew, she smiles vacuously. "I feel anticipant of a very happy future."

With morning comes a hailstorm, and Bill Wheeler must go to court in Santa Rosa for trial on charges of assaulting a policeman when a squad came to the ranch looking for juvenile runaways and Army deserters. Bill, Gay, Gay's brother Peter, Nancy, Shoshone, and Corky spread out through the courthouse, peeling off mildewed clothes and piling them on benches. Peter, a gigantic, muscular fellow of twenty-three, rips his pants all the way up the back, and, like most people at Wheeler's, he is not wearing underwear. Gay changes Raspberry's diapers on the floor of the ladies' room. Nancy takes off her rain-soaked long johns and leaves them in one of the stalls.

It is a tedious day. Witnesses give conflicting testimony, but all corroborate that one of the officers struck Wheeler first, leading to a shoving, running, tackling, pot-throwing skirmish which also involved Peter. The defendants spend the night in a motel, going over testimony with their lawyer. Bill and Corky go to a supermarket to buy dinner, and wheel down the aisle checking labels for chemicals, opening jars to take a taste with the finger, uhmmm, laughing at the "obsolete consciousness" of the place. They buy greens, Roquefort dressing, peanut butter, organic honey, and two Sara Lee cakes. The next morning, Nancy says she couldn't sleep with the radiator and all the trucks. Gay says, "I had a dream in which I saw death. It was a blond man with no facial hair, and he looked at me with this all-concealing expression." Bill, outside, staring at the Kodak blue swimming pool: "I dreamed last night that Gay and I got separated somehow and I was stuck with Raspberry." He shudders. "You know, I feel love for other people, but Gay is the only one I want to spend my life with."

The jury goes out at 3:00 P.M. and deliberates until 9:00. In the courtroom, a mottled group in pioneer clothes, mud-spattered and frizzy-wet, are chanting, "Om." The jury cannot agree on four counts, and finds Bill and Peter not guilty on three counts. The judge declares a mistrial. The county fathers are not finished, though. They are still attempting to close the access road to Wheeler's and to get an injunction to raze all buildings on the ranch as health hazards. Bill Wheeler is not worried, nor are his charges, climbing in the jeep and singing, "Any day now . . ." God will provide.

> *We must do away with the absolutely specious notion*
> *that everybody has to earn a living. . . . We keep*
> *inventing jobs because of this false idea that everybody*
> *has to be employed at some kind of drudgery because,*
> *according to Malthusian-Darwinian theory, he must justify*
> *his right to exist. . . . The true business of people should*
> *be to . . . think about whatever it was they were thinking*
> *about before somebody came along and told them they*
> *had to earn a living.*
>
> R. Buckminster Fuller

Highway 101 ribboning down the coast: narcotic pastels, the smell of charbroiled hamburgers cooking, motels with artificial gas-flame fireplaces. Total sensory Muzak. California banks now print their checks in salmon and mauve colors with reproductions of the Golden Gate Bridge, the High Sierras, the Mojave Desert, and other panoramas. "Beautiful money," they call it. As I cross the San Rafael Bridge, which, because the clouds are low, seems to shoot straight into the sky and disappear, Radio KABL in San Francisco is playing "Shangri-la."

South of the city in Menlo Park, one of a chain of gracious suburbs languishing in industrial smoke, Stewart Brand created the *Whole Earth Catalog,* and now presides over the Whole Earth Truck Store and mystique. Brand, a thirty-year-old biologist who was a fringe member of Ken Kesey's Merry Pranksters, put out the first catalog in 1968 as a mail-order source book for people starting communes or alternate life-styles. The success of the catalog—it is selling a thousand copies a day—indicates it is answering needs that cut across age and philosophical gaps. One of these is the need to regain control over the environment, so that when the refrigerator breaks, or the electric power goes out, you don't have to stand around helplessly waiting for repairmen, middlemen, and technical "experts" to fix things at your expense. The *Whole Earth Catalog* lists books and tools that enable one to build furniture, fix cars, learn real-estate law, raise bees for honey, publish your own books, build houses out of foam, auto tops, or mud, and even bury your own dead so that the rites of passage are simple and meaningful. The *Catalog* also speaks to the need to break out of the inflationary cycle of higher earning and higher spending. It offers books such as *How to Get Out of the Rat Race and Live on $10 a Month* and *How to Live on Nothing,* and suggests *The Moonlighters' Manual* for people who want to earn subsistence money with minimum commitment of psyche.

Brand says, "I admit we encourage starting from scratch. We don't say it will be easy, but education comes from making mistakes. Take delivering babies at home. That's hazardous! We carry books that tell how hazardous it is. People have lost babies that way, but it won't hit the fan until we lose a few mothers. When it works, though, it's glorious." Brand, with oversized blue eyes and gaunt cheeks, breaks into infectious laughter as he describes his fantasies. "The city-country pull is behind everything going on now. An anthropologist Cherokee we know feels the cycle goes like this: a kid grows up, has talent, goes to the city to fulfill himself, becomes an ideologue, his personality deteriorates, and to recuperate, he goes back to the land. The impulse to return to the land and to form "intentional communities," or communes, is being felt in the sudden demand for publications like *The Green Revolution,* founded in the 1940s to promote rural revival, and *The Modern Utopian,* produced by "Alternatives! Foundation" in Sebastopol, California, which also runs a commune matching service.

Brand says there are few real alternative life-styles right now: "There's black pride, and the long haired run for the hills. That's it. What we want are alternative economies and alternative political systems. Maybe alternative ecologies. You can't do this with six people." Brand points out that new social programs "are always parasitic, like newborn babies. They feed off the parent culture until they're strong enough to be self-sustaining." The communes in New Mexico, he says, can eventually develop their own economy by trading goods and services and paying in tokens, "like the casinos in Las Vegas. The climate is great for experiments now. There's no end of resources for promising ideas. But people had better hurry, because the avenues will start being closed off." He laughs, thrusting his chin up. "Things are getting weirder and weirder."

No society racing through the turbulence of the next
several decades will be able to do without [some] form
of future-shock absorber: specialized centers in which the
rate of change is artificially depressed. . . . In such
slow-paced communities, individuals who needed or
wanted a more relaxed, less stimulating existence could
find it.
                    Alvin Toffler, *"Coping with Future Shock"*

Roads across the upper northwest are flat and ruler-straight, snow-bound for long months, turning arid and dusty in the summer. At an empty crossing in a poor, wheat-growing county, the road suddenly dips and winds down to a valley filled with tall pines and primitive log cabins. The community hidden in this natural canyon is Freedom Farm, founded in 1963. It is one of the oldest communes to be started on open land. The residents—about twenty-four adults and almost as many children—are serious, straightforward people who, with calculated bluntness, say they are dropouts, social misfits, unable or unwilling to cope with the world "outside." The community has no rules, except that no one can be asked to leave. Because it predates the hippie movement, there is an absence of mystical claptrap and jargon like "far out." Only a few are vegetarians. Members do not want the location of the farm published for fear of being inundated with "psychedelic beggars."

I drove to the canyon in the morning and, having learned my lesson, left the car at the top and walked down the steep, icy road. The farm is divided into two parts—80 acres at the north end of the canyon and 120 acres at the south. The families live separately, as they do at Wheeler's but their homes are more elaborate and solidly built. The first house in the north end is a hexagonal log cabin built by Huw Williams, who started the farm when he was nineteen. Huw is slight, soft-spoken, with a wispy blond beard. His face and voice are expressionless, but when he speaks, he is likely to say something startling, humorous, or indicative of deep feeling. When I arrived, he was cutting out pieces of leather, wearing a green-and-brown lumberman's shirt and a knife strapped to his waist. His wife, Sylvia, was nursing their youngest son, while their two-year-old, Sennett, wearing nothing but a T-shirt, was playing on the floor with a half-breed Norwegian elkhound. The cabin was snugly warm, but smelled faintly of urine from Sennett peeing repeatedly on the rug. There was a cast-iron stove, tables and benches built from logs, a crib, an old-fashioned cradle, and a large bed raised off the floor for warmth and storage space. On the wall there was a calendar opened to January, although it was March.

I asked Huw how the community had stayed together for seven years.

He said, deadpan, "The secret is not to try. We've got a lot of rugged individualists here, and everyone is into a different thing. In reflection, it feels good that we survived. A lot of us were from wealthy backgrounds, and the idea of giving it all up and living off the land was a challenge." Huw grew up on a ranch 40 miles from the canyon. "I had everything. When I was fourteen, I had my own car, a half-dozen cows, and $600 in the bank." When he was fifteen, his house burned down and he saw his elaborate collections—stamps, models, books—disappear. He vowed not to become attached to possessions after that, and took to sleeping outdoors. He remembers being terrified of violence, and idolized Gandhi, Christ, and Tolstoy. At seventeen, he became a conscientious objector and began to work in draft resistance. While on a peace walk from New Hampshire to Washington, D.C., he decided to drop out of the University of Washington and start a nonviolent training center, a community where people could live by sharing rather than competing. He persuaded his mother to give him 80 acres in the canyon for the project, rented a house, called the Hart House, and advertised in peace papers for people to come and share it with him.

The first summer, more than fifty came and went and they all lived in the Hart House. One of the visitors was Sylvia, a fair-skinned girl with long chestnut hair and warm wistful eyes that hint of sadness. They were married, and Huw stopped talking about a peace center and started studying intentional communities. He decided he wanted a community that would be open to anyone, flexible, with no prescribed rules to live by. Work would get done, Huw felt, because people would want to do it to achieve certain ends. "It's a Western idea. You inspire people by giving them a goal, making it seem important: then they'll do anything to get there." If people did not want to work, Huw felt, forcing them would not be the answer.

The results were chaotic. "Emotional crises, fights over everything. A constant battle to get things done. A typical scene would be for one guy to spend two hours fixing a meal. He had to make three separate dishes —one for vegetarians, one for nonvegetarians, and one for people who wouldn't eat government-surplus food. He would put them on the table, everybody would grab, and if you stood back you got nothing. When people live that close together, they become less sensitive, and manners go right out the window. It was educational, but we knew it wasn't suitable for raising children." The group pooled resources and bought another 120 acres two miles away. Huw and Sylvia built their own cabin and moved out of the Hart House; another couple followed. Then around 1966, the drug scene exploded and the farm was swamped with speed freaks, runaways, addicts, and crazies. A schism grew between the permanent people and the transients. The transients thought the permanents were uptight and stingy. The permanents said the transients were abusing the land. When most of the permanents had built their own cabins, they began talking about burning down the Hart House. I heard many versions of the incident. Some say a man, whom I shall call George, burned it. Some say everyone did it. Some said they watched and were against it but felt they should not stop it. Afterwards, most of the transients left, and the farm settled into its present pattern of individual families tending their own gardens, buying their own supplies, and raising their own animals. Each family has at least two vehicles—a car and a tractor, or a motorcycle or truck. Huw says, "We do our share of polluting."

The majority at Freedom live on welfare, unemployment compensation, and food stamps. A few take part-time jobs picking apples or wheat, one does free-lance writing, and some do crafts. Huw makes about $50 a month on his leather work, Ken Meister makes wall hangings, Rico and Pat sell jewelry to psychedelic shops, and Steve raises rabbits. Huw believes the farm could support itself by growing organic grains and selling them by mail order, but he hasn't been able to get enough co-operation to do this. "It's impossible to have both a commune, where everyone lives and works collectively, and free land, where anyone can settle," he says. "Some day we might have a commune on the land, but not everyone who lived on the land would have to join it."

The only communal rituals are Thanksgiving at the schoolhouse and the corn dance, held on the first full moon of May. Huw devised the corn dance from a Hopi Indian ceremony, and each year it gets wilder. Huw builds a drum, and at sundown everyone gathers on a hillside with food, wine, the children in costumes, animals, and musical instruments. They take turns beating the drum but must keep it beating until dawn. They roast potatoes, and sometimes a kid, a pig, or a turkey, get stoned, dance, howl, and drop to sleep. "But that's only once a year," one of the men says. "We could have one every month, and it would hold the community together." Not everyone wants this solidarity, however. Some are like hermits and have staked out corners of the canyon where they want to be left alone. The families who live nearby get together for dinners, chores, and baby-sitting. At the north end, the Williamses, the Swansons, and the Goldens pop in and out constantly. On the day I arrive, they are having a garden meeting at the Swansons' to decide what to order for spring planting.

The Swansons, who have three young children, moved into the canyon this year after buying, for $1000, the two-story house a man called Steve had built for his own family. Steve had had a falling out with Huw and wanted to move to the south acres. The Swansons needed a place they could move into right away. The house has the best equipment at the farm, with a flush toilet (sectioned off by a blanket hung from the ceiling), running water, and electricity that drives a stove, refrigerator, and freezer. Jack Swanson, an outgoing, ruddy-faced man of thirty-five, with short hair and a moustache, works on a newspaper 150 miles away and commutes to the farm for weekends. His wife, Barbara, twenty-four, is the image of a Midwestern college girl: jeans cut off to Bermuda length, blouses with Peter Pan collars, and a daisy-printed scarf around her short brown hair. But it is quickly apparent that she is a strong-willed nonconformist. "I've always been a black sheep," she says. "I hate supermarkets—everything's been chemically preserved. You might as well be in a morgue." Barbara is gifted at baking, pickling, and canning, and wants to raise sheep to weave and dye the wool herself. She and Jack tried living in various cities, then a suburb, then a farm in Idaho, where they found they lacked the skills to make it work. "We were so ill-equipped by society to live off the earth," Jack says. "We thought about moving to Freedom Farm for three or four years, but when times were good, we put it off." Last year their third child was born with a lung disease which required months of hospitalization and left them deep in debt. Moving to the farm seemed a way out. "If we had stayed in the suburbs, we found we were spending everything we made, with rent and car payments, and could never pay off the debts. I had to make more and more just to stay even. The price was too high for what we wanted in life," Jack says. "Here, because I don't pay rent and because we can raise food ourselves, I don't have to make as much money. We get help in farming, and have good company. In two or three months, this house is all mine—no interest, no taxes. Outside it would cost me $20,000 and 8 per cent interest."

A rainstorm hits at midnight and by morning the snow has washed off the canyon walls, the stream has flooded over, and the roads are slushy mud ruts. Sylvia saddles two horses and we ride down to the south 120. There are seven cabins on the valley floor, and three hidden by trees on the cliff. Outside one of the houses, Steve is feeding his rabbits; the mute, wiggling animals are clustering around the cage doors. Steve breeds the rabbits to sell to a processor and hopes to earn $100 a month from the business. He also kills them to eat. "It's tough to do," he says, "but if people are going to eat meat, they should be willing to kill the animal." While Steve is building his new house, he has moved with his wife and four children into the cabin of a couple I shall call George and Liz Snow. George is a hefty, porcine man of thirty-nine, a drifter who earned a doctorate in statistics, headed an advertising agency, ran guns to Cuba, worked as a civil servant, a mason, a dishwasher, and rode the freights. He can calculate the angles of a geodesis dome and quote Boccaccio and Shakespeare. He has had three wives, and does not want his name known because "there are a lot of people I don't want to find me."

Steve, a hard-lived thirty-four, has a past that rivals George's for tumult: nine years as an Army engineer, AWOL, running a coffee house in El Paso, six months in a Mexican jail on a marijuana charge, working nine-to-five as chief engineer in a fire-alarm factory in New Haven, Connecticut, then cross-country to Spokane. Steve has great dynamism and charm that are both appealing and abrasive. His assertiveness inevitably led to friction in every situation, until, tired of bucking the system, he moved to the farm. "I liked the structure of this community," he says. "Up there, I can't get along with one out of a thousand people. Here I make it with one out of two." He adds, "We're in the business of survival while the world goes crazy. It's good to know how to build a fire, or a waterwheel, because if the world ends, you're there now."

Everyone at Freedom seems to share this sense of imminent doomsday.

Huw says, "When the country is wiped out, electricity will stop coming through the wires, so you might as well do without it now. I don't believe you should use any machine you can't fix yourself." Steve says, "Technology can't feed all the world's people." Stash, a young man who lives alone at the farm, asks, "Am I going to start starving in twenty years?"

Steve: "Not if you have a plot to garden."

Stash: "What if the ravaging hordes come through?"

Steve: "Be prepared for the end, or get yourself a gun."

There is an impulse to dismiss this talk as a projection of people's sense of their own private doom, except for the fact that the fear is widespread. Stewart Brand writes in the *Whole Earth Catalog*: "One barometer of people's social-confidence level is the sales of books on survival. I can report that sales on *The Survival Book* are booming; it's one of our fastest moving items."

Several times a week, Steve, Stash, and Steve's daughter Laura, fourteen, drive to the small town nearby to buy groceries, visit a friend, and, if the hot water holds out, take showers. They stop at Joe's Bar for beer and hamburgers—40 cents "with all the trimmings." Laura, a graceful, quiet girl, walks across the deserted street to buy *Mad* magazine and look at rock record albums. There are three teenagers at the farm—all girls—and all have tried running away to the city. One was arrested for shoplifting, another was picked up in a crash pad with seven men. Steve says, "We have just as much trouble with our kids as straight, middle-class parents do. I'd like to talk to people in other communities and find out how they handle their teenagers. Maybe we could send ours there." Stash says, "Or bring teen-age boys here." The women at the farm have started to joke uneasily that their sons will become uptight businessmen and their daughters will be suburban housewives. The history of utopian communities in this country has been that the second generation leaves. It is easy to imagine commune-raised children having their first haute-cuisine meal, or sleeping in silk pajamas in a luxury hotel, or taking a jet plane. Are they not bound to be dazzled? Sylvia says, "Our way of life is an overreaction to something, and our kids will probably overreact to us. It's absurd. Kids run away from this, and all the runaways from the city come here."

In theory, the farm is an expanded family, and children can move around and live with different people or build houses of their own. In the summer, they take blankets and sleeping bags up in the cliffs to sleep in a noisy, laughing bunch. When I visited, all the children except one were staying in their parents' houses. Low-key tension seemed to be running through the community, with Steve and Huw Williams at opposite poles. Steve's wife, Ann, told me, "We don't go along with Huw's philosophy of anarchy. We don't think it works. You need some authority and discipline in any social situation." Huw says, "The thing about anarchy is that I'm willing to do a job myself, if I have to, rather than start imposing rules on others. Steve and George want things to be done efficiently with someone giving orders, like the Army."

At dinner when the sun goes down, Steve's and George's house throbs with good will and festivity. The cabin, like most at the farm, is not divided into separate rooms. All nine people—Steve, Ann, and their four children, the Snows and their baby—sleep on the upstairs level, while the downstairs serves as kitchen, dining and living room. "The teen-agers wish there were more privacy," Steve says, "but for us and the younger children, it feels really close." Most couples at the farm are untroubled about making love in front of the children. "We don't make a point of it," one man says, "but if they happen to see it, and it's done in love and with good vibrations, they won't be afraid or embarrassed."

While Ann and Liz cook hasenpfeffer, Steve's daughters, Laura and Karen, ten, improvise making gingerbread with vinegar and brown sugar as a substitute for molasses. A blue jay chatters in a cage hung from the ceiling. Geese honk outside, and five dogs chase each other around the room. Steve plays the guitar and sings. The hasenpfeffer is superb. The rabbits have been pickled for two days, cooked in red wine, herbs, and sour cream. There are large bowls of beets, potatoes, jello, and the gingerbread, which tastes perfect, with homemade apple sauce. Afterwards, we all get toothpicks. Liz, an uninhibited, roly poly girl of twenty-three, is describing how she hitchhiked to the farm, met George, stayed, and got married. "I like it here," she says, pursing her lips, "because I can stand nude on my front porch and yell, fuck! Also, I think I like it here because I'm fat, and there aren't many mirrors around. Clothes don't matter, and people don't judge you by your appearance like they do out there." She adds, "I've always been different from others. I think most of the people here are misfits—they have problems in communicating, relating to one another." Ann says, "Communication is ridiculous. We've begun to feel gossip is much better. It gradually gets around to the person it's about, and that's okay. Most people here can't say things to each other's face."

I walk home—I'm staying in a vacant cabin—across a field, with the stars standing out in brilliant relief from the black sky. Lights flicker in the cabins sprinkled through the valley. Ken Meister is milking late in the barn. The fire is still going in my cabin; I add two logs, light the kerosene lamps, and climb under the blankets on the high bed. Stream water sweeps by the cabin in low whooshes, the fire sputters. The rhythm of the canyon, after a few days, seems to have entered my body. I fall asleep around ten, wake up at six, and can feel the time even though there are no clocks around. In the morning light, though, I find two dead mice on the floor, and must walk a mile to get water, then build a fire to heat it. It becomes clear why, in a community like this, the sex roles are so well-defined and satisfying. When men actually do heavy physical labor like chopping trees, baling hay, and digging irrigation ditches, it feels very fulfilling for the woman to tend the cabin, grind wheat, put up fruit, and sew or knit. Each depends on the other for basic needs—shelter, warmth, food. With no intermediaries, such as supermarkets and banks, there is a direct relationship between work and survival. It is thus possible, according to Huw, for even the most repetitive jobs such as washing dishes or sawing wood to be spiritually rewarding. "Sawing puts my head in a good place," he says. "It's like a yogic exercise."

In addition to his farming and leather work, Huw has assumed the job of teacher for the four children of school age. Huw believes school should be a free, anarchic experience, and that the students should set their own learning programs. Suddenly given this freedom, the children, who were accustomed to public school, said they wanted to play and ride the horses. Huw finally told them they must be at the school house every day for at least one hour. They float in and out, and Huw stays half the day. He walks home for lunch and passes Karen and another girl on the road. Karen taunts him, "Did you see the mess we made at the school?"

"Yes," Huw says.

"Did you see our note?"

Huw walks on, staring at the ground. "It makes me feel you don't have much respect for the tools or the school."

She laughs. "Course we don't have any respect!"

"Well, it's your school," Huw says softly.

Karen shouts, "You said it was your school the other day. You're an Indian giver."

Huw: "I never said it was my school. Your parents said that." Aside to me, he says, "They're getting better at arguing every day. Still not very good, though." I tell Huw they seem to enjoy tormenting him. "I know. I'm the only adult around here they can do that to without getting clobbered. It gives them a sense of power. It's ironic, because I keep saying they're mature and responsible, and their parents say they need strict authority and discipline. So who do they rebel against? Me. I'm going to call a school meeting tonight. Maybe we can talk some of this out."

In the afternoon I visit Rico and Pat, whose A-frame house is the most beautiful and imaginative at the farm. It has three levels—a basement, where they work on jewelry and have stored a year's supply of food; a kitchen-living-room floor; and a high sleeping porch reached by a ladder. The second story is carpeted, with harem-like cushions, furs, and wall hangings. There are low tables, one of which lifts to reveal a sunken white porcelain bathtub with running water heated by the wood stove. Rico, twenty-five, designed the house so efficiently that even in winter, when the temperature drops to 20 below zero, it is warm enough for him to lounge about wearing nothing but a black cape. Pat and Rico have talked about living with six adults in some form of group marriage, but, Pat says, "there's no one here we could really do it with. The sexual experiments that have gone on have been rather compulsive and desperate. Some of us think jealousy is innate." Rico says, "I think it's cultural." Pat says, "Hopefully our kids will be able to grow up without it. I think the children who are born here will really have a chance to develop freely. The older children who've come here recently are too far gone to appreciate the environment."

In the evening, ten parents and five children show up at the school, a one-room house built with eighteen sides, so that a geodesic dome can be constructed on top. The room has a furnace, bookshelves and work tables, rugs and cushions on the floor. Sylvia is sitting on a stool in the center nursing her son. Two boys in yellow pajamas are running in circles, squealing, "Ba-ba-ba!" Karen is drawing on the blackboard—of all things, a city skyscape. Rico is doing a yoga headstand. Steve and Huw begin arguing about whether the children should have to come to the school every day. Steve says, in a booming voice, "I think the whole canyon should be a learning community, a total educational environment. The kids can learn something from everyone. If you want to teach them, why don't you come to our house?" Huw, standing with a clipboard against his hip, says, "They have to come here to satisfy the county school superintendent. But it seems futile when they come in and say I'm not qualified to teach them. Where do they get that?"

Steve says, "From me. I don't think you're qualified." Huw: "Well I'm prepared to quit and give you the option of doing something else, or sending them to public school."

Steve says, "Don't quit. I know your motives are pure as the driven snow. . . ."

Huw says, "I'm doing it for myself as well, to prove I can do it. But it all fits together."

They reach an understanding without speaking further.

Steve then says, "I'd like to propose that we go door-to-door in this community and get everyone enthused about the school as a center for adult learning and cultural activity first, and for the kiddies second. Because when you turn on the adults, the kids will follow. The school building needs finishing—the dome should be built this summer. Unless there's more enthusiasm in this community, I'm not going to contribute a thing. But if we get everybody to boost this, by God I'll be the first one out to dig."

Huw says, "You don't think the people who took the time to come tonight is enough interest? I may be cynical, but I think the only way to get some of the others here would be to have pot and dope."

Steve: "Get them interested in the idea of guest speakers, musicians, from India, all over. We can build bunk dorms to accommodate them."

Huw: "Okay. I think we should get together every Sunday night to discuss ideas, hash things over. In the meantime, why don't we buy materials to finish the building?"

On the morning I leave, sunlight washes down the valley from a cloudless sky. Huw, in his green lumberman's shirt, rides with me to the top road. "My dream is to see this canyon filled with families who live here all the time, with lots of children." He continues in a lulling rhythm: "We could export some kind of food or product. The school is very important—it should be integrated in the whole community. Children from all over could come to work, learn, and live with different families. I'd like to have doctors here and a clinic where people could be healed naturally. Eventually there should be a ham radio system set up between all the communities in the country, and a blimp, so we could make field trips back and forth. I don't think one community is enough to meet our needs. We need a world culture."

Huw stands, with hands on hips, the weight set back on his heels—a small figure against the umber field. "Some day I'm going to inherit six hundred more acres down there, and it'll all be free. Land should be available for anybody to use like it was with the Indians." He smiles with the right corner of his mouth. "The Indians could no more understand owning land than they could owning the sky."

We've got to get ourselves back to the garden.
                    Joni Mitchell, from the song, *"Woodstock"*

Last Halloween in Jemez, New Mexico, the squidlike "rock-drug-alternate-culture" underground gathered itself together to discuss what to do with the energy manifested at Woodstock. How can we use that power, they asked, and prevent it from being sickened and turned as it was at the Rolling Stones Free Concert in Altamont? The answer seemed to generate itself: buy land, throw away the deed, open it to anyone and call it Earth People's Park. Hold an earth-warming festival and ecological world's fair—all free. A nonprofit corporation was formed to collect money and handle legal problems. But there would be no authorities and no rules in Earth People's Park. Paul Krassner, Tow Law, Milan Melvin, Ken Kesey, Mama Cass Elliot, and the Hog Farm traveling communal circus led by Hugh Romney fanned out to sell the idea. They asked everyone who had been at Woodstock in body or spirit to contribute a dollar. At first, they talked of buying 20,000 acres in New Mexico or Colorado. In a few months, they were talking about 400,000 acres in many small pieces, all over the country. They flooded the media with promises of "a way out of the disaster of the cities, a viable alternative." Hugh Romney, calling himself Wavy Gravy, in an aviator suit, sheepskin vest, and a Donald Duck hat, spoke on television about simplicity, community, and harmony with the land. The cards, letters, and money poured in. Some were hand-printed, with bits of leaves and stardust in the creases, some were typed on business stationery. One, from a young man in La Grange, Illinois, seemed to touch all the chords:

Hello. Maybe we're not as alone as I thought. I am 24, my developed skills are as an advertising writer-producer-director. It seems such a waste. I have energy. I can simplify my life and I want to help. I am convinced that a new life-style, one which holds something spiritual as sacred, is necessary in this land. People can return to the slow and happy pace of life that they abandoned along with their understanding of brotherhood. Thank you for opening doors.

P.S.—Please let me know what site you purchase so I can leave as soon as possible for it.

Suggested Readings, Viewings, and Listenings

BOOKS AND ARTICLES

Altizer, Thomas J. J. and William Hamilton, *Radical Theology and the Death of God.*

Altizer, Thomas, William A. Beardslee, *et al, Truth, Myth and Symbol* (especially Gregor Sebba's essay "Symbol and Myth in Modern Rationalistic Societies").

Ardrey, Robert, *African Genesis.*

——, *The Social Contract.*

Aristophanes, *Lysistrata.*

"Astrology: Fad and Phenomenon," *Time,* March 21, 1969.

Baldwin, James (interview), "How Can We Get the Black People to Cool It?" *Esquire,* July 1968, p. 49.

Battcock, Gregory, *The New Art.*

Beagle, Peter S.. *The Last Unicorn.*

Bender, Marylin, *The Beautiful People.*

Berne, Eric, *Games People Play.*

Birmingham, Stephen, *The Right People.*

Boorstin, Daniel, *The Image.*

Borden, William, *Superstoe.*

Brackman, Jacob, Review of "The Graduate," *New Yorker,* July 27, 1968, p. 34.

Bradbury, Ray, *Fahrenheit 451.*

Braun, Saul, "Life-Styles: the Micro-Boppers," *Esquire,* March 1968, p. 102.

Brautigan, Richard, *Trout Fishing in America.*

Brown, Claude, *Manchild in the Promised Land.*

Brown, Norman O., *Life Against Death.*

Burke, Tom, "Princess Leda's Castle in the Air," *Esquire,* March 1970, p. 104.

Calloway, Al and Claude Brown, "An Introduction to Soul," *Esquire,* April 1968, p. 79.

Castaneda, Carlos, *Further Conversations with Don Juan.*

Chapman, Abraham, ed., *Black Voices.*

Clarke, Arthur C., *Childhood's End.*

——, *2001.*

Cleaver, Eldridge, *Soul on Ice.*
Cowley, Malcolm, *Exile's Return.*
Cox Commission Report, *Crisis at Columbia.*
Cox, Harvey, *The Feast of Fools.*
————, "God and the Hippies," *Playboy,* January 1968.
————, *The Secular City.*
Crichton, Michael, *The Andromeda Strain.*
Cristgau, Robert, "Review of *Sergeant Pepper,*" *Esquire,* December 1967,
    p. 283.
Crumb, Robert, *The Adventures of Fritz the Cat.*
Darwin, Charles, *The Origin of Species.*
Davies, Hunter, *The Beatles.*
Debray, Regis, *Revolution in the Revolution?*
Decter, Midge, "Anti-Intellectualism in America," *Harper's,* April, 1968.
de Rougemont, Denis, *Love in the Western World.*
Dewey, John, *Democracy and Education.*
————, *Reconstruction in Philosophy.*
Dollard, John, *Caste and Class in a Southern Town.*
Dunlop, Bryan, "To Mr. Kazin," *Harper's,* Oct. 1967, p. 55.
Duberman, Martin, "On Becoming an Historian," *Evergreen,* April 1969,
    p. 57.
Ellison, Ralph, *Invisible Man.*
Erlich, Paul, *The Population Bomb.*
Euripides, *The Bacchae.*
Fairchild, John, *The Beautiful Savages.*
Fanon, Franz, *Black Skin, White Masks.*
————, *The Wretched of the Earth.*
Farina, Richard, *Been Down So Long It Looks Like Up to Me.*
Fast, Julius, *Body Language.*
Ferlinghetti, Lawrence, *Coney Island of the Mind.*
————, *Unfair Arguments with Existence.*
Fiedler, Leslie, "Academic Irresponsibility," *Playboy,* Dec. 1968, p. 225.
Fitzgerald, F. S. K. *et al,* "My Generation," *Esquire,* Oct. 1968 (4 essays).
Freud, Sigmund, *The Future of an Illusion.*
————, *The Interpretation of Dreams.*
Gibran, Kahlil, *The Prophet.*
Ginsberg, Allen, *Howl and Other Poems.*
Gold, Herbert, "The New Wave Makers," *Playboy,* Oct. 1967, p. 124.
Golding, William, *Lord of the Flies.*
Goodman, Paul, *Growing Up Absurd.*
Greenfeld, Josh, "The Marshmallow Literature," *Mademoiselle,* March,
    1969, p. 206.
Haley, Alex, *The Autobiography of Malcolm X.*
Hamilton, Kenneth, *God is Dead.*
Harmon, Jim, *The Great Radio Heroes.*
Hartshorne, Charles, *Reality as Social Process.*
Hayes, Harold, ed., *Smiling through the Apocalypse.*

Heinlein, Robert, *Stranger in a Strange Land.*
Heinsheimer, Hans W., "Music from the Conglomerates," *Saturday Review,* Feb. 22, 1969, p. 61.
Heller, Joseph, *Catch-22.*
Hentoff, Nat, "The War on Dissent," *Playboy,* Sept. 1968, p. 155.
———, "Youth: the Oppressed Majority," *Playboy,* Sept. 1967, p. 139.
Hesse, Hermann, *Siddhartha.*
———, *Steppenwolf.*
Hobbes, Thomas, *Leviathan.*
Hoffman, Abbie, *Revolution for the Hell of It.*
———, *Woodstock Nation.*
Hofstadter, Richard, *Anti-Intellectualism in American Life.*
Holloway, Mark, *Heavens on Earth.*
Huxley, Aldous, *Island.*
———, *Brave New World.*
Huysmans, Joris-Karl, *La-Bas.*
I Ching.
Jung, C. G., *Psyche and Symbol.*
Kahn, Roger, "The Collapse of the SDS," *Esquire,* Oct. 1969, p. 140.
Kaufman, Stanley, *A World on Film.*
Kerouac, Jack, "After Me, the Deluge," *Chicago Tribune Magazine,* Sept. 28, 1969, p. 20.
———, *The Dharma Bums.*
———, *On the Road.*
Kesey, Ken, *One Flew Over the Cuckoo's Nest.*
———, *Sometimes a Great Notion.*
Klapp, Orin, *Heroes, Villains and Fools.*
Krim, Seymour, *et al, The Beats.*
Leary, Timothy, "In the Beginning Leary Turned on Ginsberg and Saw that It Was Good, and then Leary and Ginsberg Decided to Turn on the World," *Esquire,* July 1968, p. 83.
———, "The Politics and Ethics of Ecstasy," *Cavalier,* July 1966, p. 35.
Lester, Eleanore, "The Final Decline and Total Collapse of The American Avant-Garde," *Esquire,* May 1969, p. 142.
Levine, Mark L., McNamee and Greenberg, eds., *The Tales of Hoffman: from the Trial of the Chicago 7.*
Lewis, Oscar, *Five Families.*
Lewis, R. W. B., *The American Adam.*
Lipton, Lawrence, "The Hip Sell," *Cavalier,* June 1967, p. 61.
Luce, John, "Haight-Ashbury Today: a Case of Terminal Euphoria," July 1969, p. 65.
Lundberg, Ferdinand, *The Rich and the Super-Rich.*
Machiavelli, *The Prince.*
———, *The Discourses.*
McGinniss, Joe, *The Selling of the President 1968.*
McKuen, Rod, *Lonesome Cities.*
McLuhan, Marshall, Interview with *Playboy, Playboy,* March 1969, p. 53.

———, *The Mechanical Bride.*

———, *Understanding Media.*

———, *War and Peace in the Global Village.*

Mailer, Norman, *Miami and the Siege of Chicago.*

Marcuse, Herbert, *Reason and Revolution.*

Margolis, John, "Our Country 'Tis of Thee Land of Ecology," *Esquire,* March 1970, p. 124.

Marx, Karl, *The Communist Manifesto.*

——— and Engels, *Das Kapital.*

Marx, Leo, *The Machine in the Garden.*

Masters, R. E. L., "Sex, Ecstasy and the Psychedelic Drugs," *Playboy,* Nov. 1967, p. 94.

——— and Jean Houston, *The Varieties of Psychedelic Experience.*

Mathewson, Joseph, "The Hobbit Habit," *Esquire,* Sept. 1966, p. 130.

May, Henry, *The End of American Innocence.*

May, Rollo, *Love and Will.*

Michelet, Jules, *Satanism and Witchcraft.*

Mill, John Stuart, *On Liberty.*

Miller, Michael, "Letter from the Berkeley Underground," *Esquire,* Sept. 1965, p. 85.

——— and Susan Gilmore, *Revolution at Berkeley.*

Milton, John, *Areopagitica.*

———, *Paradise Lost,* Books I, II, IX, XII.

More, Thomas, *Utopia.*

Morris, Desmond, *The Human Zoo.*

———, *The Naked Ape.*

Nietzsche, Friedrich, in Walter Kaufman, ed., *Friedrich Nietzsche: the Will to Power.*

Ogletree, Thomas W., *The Death of God Controversy.*

Orwell, George, *Nineteen Eighty-Four.*

Packard, Vance, *The Status Seekers.*

Plato, *Republic,* Book VIII (Cornford translation).

Podhoretz, Norman, "Making It," *Harper's,* Dec. 1967, p. 59.

Pritchard, Stan, "The Police: a Postscript," *Cavalier,* March 1969, p. 53.

Quant, Mary, *Quant by Quant.*

Quotations from Chairman Mao Tse-tung.

Rainwater, Lee and William Yancey, *The Moynihan Report and the Politics of Controversy.*

Reed, Rex, *Do You Sleep in the Nude?*

Reich, Charles, *The Greening of America.*

Ridgeway, James, "The Cops and the Kids," *The New Republic,* Sept. 1968, p. 11.

———, "The *Ramparts* story: Very, very Interesting," *The New York Times* Magazine, April 20, 1969, p. 34.

Robbe-Grillet, Alain, *For a New Novel.*

Rogers, Carl, *On Becoming a Person.*

Rose, Arnold, *The Negro in America.*

Roszak, Theodore, *The Making of a Counter-Culture.*

Ruark, Robert, "Nothing Works and Nobody Cares," *Playboy,* Dec. 1965, p. 134.

Rubin, Jerry, *Do It!*

Russell, Bertrand, in Robert F. Egner and Lester Dennon, eds., *The Basic Writings of Bertrand Russell.*

Salinger, J. D., *Catcher in the Rye.*

Scheer, Robert, ed., *The Diary of Che Guevara.*

Schneir, Walter, ed., *Telling It Like It Was: the Chicago Riots.*

Schultz, William C., *Joy.*

Schulz, John, "Pigs, Prague, Chicago, Democrats, and the Sleeper in the Park," *Evergreen,* Nov., 1968, p. 27.

Segal, Erich, *Love Story.*

Shakespeare, William, *The Tempest.*

Shaw, Arnold, "The Beautification of the Beatles," *Cavalier,* July 1968, p. 93.

Sjoman, Vilgot, *I Was Curious.*

Skinner, B. F., *Walden Two.*

Slavitt, David, "The Conscience of an Exhibitionist," *Esquire,* May 1968, p. 122.

Smith, Henry Nash, *Virgin Land.*

Soloman, Alan, "The *New* New York Art Scene: Who Makes It?" *Vogue,* August 1, 1967, p. 103.

Sontag, Susan, *Against Interpretation.*

Spengler, Oswald, *The Decline of the West.*

Steiner, Shari, "Europe and America: a Question of Self-Image," *Saturday Review,* Dec. 27, 1969, p. 18.

Sterba, James, "The Politics of Pot," *Esquire,* August 1968, p. 58.

Styron, William, *The Confessions of Nat Turner.*

Thoreau, Henry David, *Walden.*

Thucydides, *Peloponnesian War.*

Tolkien, J. R. R., *Lord of the Rings* trilogy.

———, *The Hobbit.*

Vahanian, Gabriel, *The Death of God.*

Van Vogt, A. E., *Slan.*

Veblen, Thorstein, *The Theory of the Leisure Class.*

Vidal, Gore, *Sex, Death and Money.*

von Hoffman, Nicholas, *We Are the People Our Parents Warned Us Against.*

Vonnegut, Kurt, *Cat's Cradle.*

Walker, Daniel, *Rights in Conflict: The Official Report to the National Commission on the Causes and Prevention of Violence.*

Wedeck, Harry, *A Treasury of Witchcraft.*

Weintraub, Bernard, "The Brilliancy of Black," *Esquire,* Jan. 1967, p. 130.

Whitehead, Alfred North, *The Aims of Education.*

Whitfield, Stephen E. and Gene Roddenberry, *The Making of Star Trek.*

Whyte, William H., Jr., *The Organization Man.*

Wicker, Tom, introduction, *U.S. Riot Commission Report: Report of the National Advisory Commission on Civil Disorders.*
Wills, Gary, "The Making of the Yippie Culture," *Esquire,* Nov. 1969, p. 135.
————, *The Second Civil War.*
Wolfe, Burton, "Attempts at Group Marriage," *Cavalier,* June 1969, p. 31.
Wolfe, Tom, *The Electric Kool-Aid Acid Test.*
————, *The Kandy-Kolored Tangerine-Flake Streamline Baby.*
————, *The Pump House Gang* (especially "What If He Is Right?")
————, *Radical Chic and Mau-mauing the Flak Catchers.*

MAGAZINES

The Atlantic
Cavalier
Cosmopolitan
Earth
Esquire
Essence
Evergreen
Glamour
Harper's Bazaar
Harper's magazine
Ingenue
Interplay
Mademoiselle
Marvel and underground comics
New Republic
Newsweek
New York Review of Books
Penthouse
Playboy
Psychology Today
Ramparts
The Realist
Rock and record magazines
Saturday Review
Time
Underground papers (especially the *Village Voice,* Chicago *Seed,* Berkeley *Barb,* and *East Village Other*)
Vogue (British and American versions)
Whole Earth Catalogue

FILMS

"Alice's Restaurant"
"Black Orpheus"
"Blowjob"
"Blow-Up"

"Blue Movie"
"Bonnie and Clyde"
"Carnal Knowledge"
"Catch-22"
"Chelsea Girls"
"The Damned"
"Easy Rider"
"8½"
"Elvira Madigan"
"Fahrenheit 451"
"Fellini's Satyricon"
"Five Easy Pieces"
"Gimmie Shelter"
"The Graduate"
"The Green Berets"
"A Hard Day's Night"
"Help!"
"How I Won the War"
"I A Woman"
"I Am Curious (Blue)"
"I Am Curious (Yellow)"
"If"
"Joe"
"Jules et Jim"
"Juliet of the Spirits"
"La Dolce Vita"
"Love Story"
"The Magician"
"Medium Cool"
"Midnight Cowboy"
"My Night at Maud's"
"O What a Lovely War!"
"Persona"
"The Seventh Seal"
"Shoot the Piano Player"
"Thunderball"
"Trash"
"2001"
"Vixen"
"Weekend"
"Without a Stitch"
"Woodstock"
"Zabriskie Point"

RECORDS

Note: To attempt a "definitive" listing of all the popular albums which have been made since, say, 1960 is an impossible task, particularly since

any such listing becomes obsolete long before its publication date. Therefore we have listed recordings in the three categories of folk (and folk-
rock), pure or "hard" rock and "soul" and blues which proved to be of
importance in the "classical" period of folk and rock (approximately
1962–8). Singing groups and artists rather than single recordings are
listed; the reader or listener can select from any of a number of recordings by each group. Much of the list was compiled by Mr. Thaddeus
Jochim, a student in the University of North Dakota Honors Program, as
part of a seminar project; we owe him a debt of gratitude for the thor-
oughness of the listings.

FOLK AND FOLK-ROCK

Recordings by:

Bob Dylan
Peter, Paul and Mary
Pete Seegar
Judy Collins
Tim Buckley
Janis Ian
Jake Holmes
Phil Ochs
Joan Baez
The Youngbloods
Buffy St.-Marie
Gordon Lightfoot
Arlo Guthrie
The Byrds
Tim Rose
Tim Hardin
Noel Harrison
Jim Kweskin Jug Band
Nitty Gritty Dirt Band
The Band
Bobbie Gentry
Roy Orbison
Tom Jones
Billy Joe Royal
Sandy Posey
Gene Pitney
Johnny Cash
Mimi and Richard Farina
Elton John
Ian and Sylvia

ROCK (AND SUB-CATEGORIES OF ROCK)

Recordings by:

The Rolling Stones
The Beatles
The Who
The Spencer Davis Group
Big Brother and the Holding Company
Janis Joplin
The Grateful Dead
The Doors
Moby Grape
Sonny and Cher
Donovan
Simon and Garfunkel
Jefferson Airplane
Jimi Hendrix
The Mothers of Invention
The Velvet Underground
Procol Harum
The Cream
Blood, Sweat and Tears
Country Joe and the Fish
Captain Beefheart
The Yardbirds
Van Morrison
The Animals
Frank Sinatra
Lesley Gore
Lou Rawls
Petula Clark
Dionne Warwick
The Motown Acts
Eric Burdon
Sonny
The Kinks
The Candymen
The Paupers
The Bee Gees
The Monkees
The 4 Seasons
Paul Revere and the Raiders

The Turtles
Herman's Hermits
Nancy Sinatra
The Dave Clark 5
The Buckinghams
Johnny Rivers
The Cowsills
The Shangri-Las
Peter and Gordon
Chad and Jeremy
The 5 Americans
The Tremloes
Gary Lewis and the Playboys
The Mamas and the Papas
The Beach Boys
The Lovin' Spoonful
The Left Banke
Buffalo Springfield
The Young Rascals
The Grassroots
Neil Diamond
The Hollies
Spanky and Our Gang
Harpers Bizarre
5th Dimension
Sopwith Camel
Clear Light
Van Dyke Parks
Traffic
Vanilla Fudge
Butterfield Blues Band
The Electric Flag
The Chambers Brothers
Steve Miller Blues Band
Siegel-Schwall Blue Band
The Free Spirits
Gary Burton Quartet
Hugh Maskela
The Godz
Pearls Before Swine
The Mystery Trend
The Charlatans
Mad River
Quicksilver Messenger Service
The Group Image
The Third World Raspberry
The Beorn Express

The Druids of Stonehenge
The Fugs
The Balling Jacks
Heavy Organ

SOUL AND BLUES

Recordings by:

Louis Armstrong
James Brown
Aretha Franklin
Otis Redding
The Supremes
Ramsey Lewis Trio
Cannonball Adderly
The Righteous Brothers
Sam and Dave
Joe Tex
Wilson Pickett
Jackie Wilson
Percy Sledge
James and Bobby Purify
Deon Jackson
Carla Thomas
Eddie Floyd
The Impressions
Ike and Tina Turner
Gladys Knight
The Four Tops
Smokey and the Miracles
Stevie Wonder
The Temptations
The Isley Brothers
Martha and the Vandellas
Marvin Gaye
The Marvellettes
Junior Walker
Young-Holt Trio
Jimmy Smith
Mitch Ryder
The Soul Survivors
The Young Rascals
Tom Jones
The Magnificent Men
The Cake
Jelly Roll Morton